Al[illegible] Western Esotericism

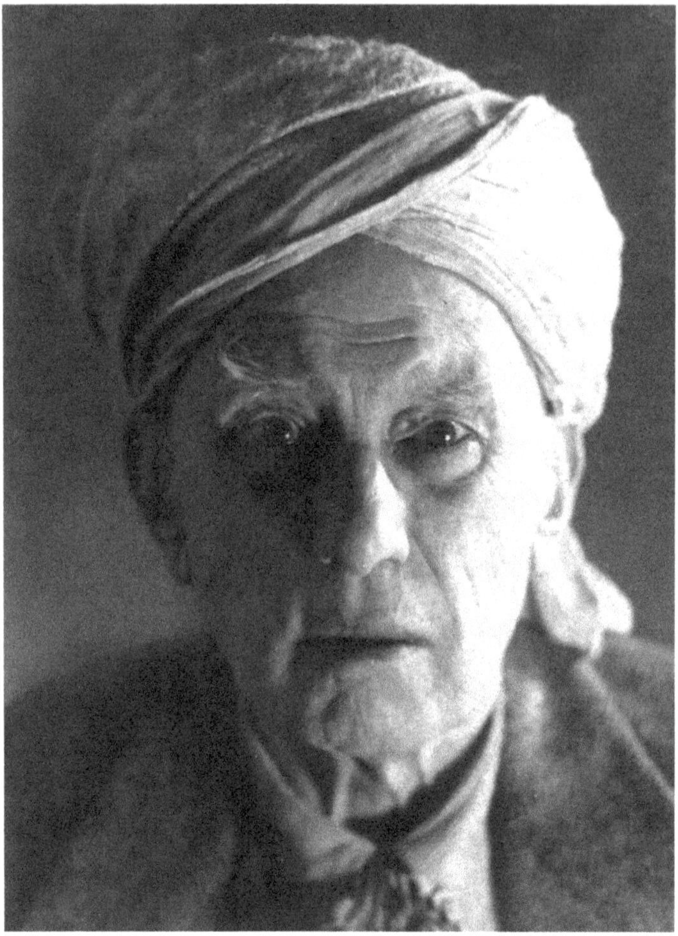

Aleister Crowley (1875–1947).

Aleister Crowley and Western Esotericism

Edited and introduced by

HENRIK BOGDAN AND

MARTIN P. STARR

Foreword by

WOUTER J. HANEGRAAFF

OXFORD
UNIVERSITY PRESS

OXFORD
UNIVERSITY PRESS

Oxford University Press is a department of the University of Oxford.
It furthers the University's objective of excellence in research,
scholarship, and education by publishing worldwide.

Oxford New York
Auckland Cape Town Dar es Salaam Hong Kong Karachi
Kuala Lumpur Madrid Melbourne Mexico City Nairobi
New Delhi Shanghai Taipei Toronto

With offices in
Argentina Austria Brazil Chile Czech Republic France Greece
Guatemala Hungary Italy Japan Poland Portugal Singapore
South Korea Switzerland Thailand Turkey Ukraine Vietnam

Published in the United States of America by Oxford University Press
198 Madison Avenue, New York, NY 10016

Library of Congress Cataloging-in-Publication Data
Aleister Crowley and Western Esotericism / edited and introduced
by Henrik Bogdan and Martin P. Starr; foreword by Wouter J. Hanegraaff.
pages cm
Includes index.
ISBN 978-0-19-986309-9 (pbk.: alk. paper)—ISBN 978-0-19-986307-5 (hardcover: alk. paper)
1. Crowley, Aleister, 1875–1947. 2. Occultism—History—20th century.
3. Hermetism—History—20th century. I. Bogdan, Henrik. II. Starr, Martin P., 1959–
BF1598.C7A65 2012
130.92—dc23 2011050288

1 3 5 7 9 8 6 4 2

Printed in the United States of America
on acid-free paper

Contents

Foreword

BRINGING LIGHT TO THE UNDERGROUND

Wouter J. Hanegraaff

STUDYING WESTERN ESOTERICISM is much like applying psychotherapy to the history of thought. Its first requirement is not to be satisfied with surface appearances and not to take for granted what the official narratives tell us, but to be curious about what they prefer *not* to talk about: the presence of subterranean archives, or memory vaults, where we store away everything we do not want to accept because it differs too much from our ideal image of ourselves and our cherished values. The German language has found a beautiful expression for this, in speaking of the occult as the *Untergrund des Abendlandes*.[1] These archives of suppressed memories do not exist just metaphorically but quite literally as well. Scholars of Western esotericism spend much of their time—or so one hopes!—reading and analyzing the primary sources of rejected knowledge: volumes that have been gathering dust on library shelves because nobody reads them anymore, books and manuscripts of authors who never made it into the canon of acceptable and respectable academic literature, or dropped out of it at some point in time, and so on. Such research may resemble a hunt for forgotten treasure, and it is true that, buried underneath lots of stuff that has not withstood the test of time, genuine gems wait to be found; with luck, one will come across profound thinkers and texts of high quality that should never have been forgotten and deserve to be recovered for their intrinsic merits alone. This hope for exciting discoveries is familiar to all working historians, but in the case of Western esotericism, more is at stake. There is a structural logic to the *Untergrund des Abendlandes*: far from being just a random collection of things that have happened to fall by the wayside, it is a reservoir that represents the shadow side of our own official identity, and we need to learn more about it if we wish to understand ourselves.

The basic identity of modern Western culture rests upon two pillars: a religious tradition of monotheism that defines itself with reference to Jewish and Christian scripture, and a tradition of rationality and science that sees itself as hailing back to the Greeks and culminating in modern science and Enlightenment. Summarized very briefly, the former is defined as standing against "paganism," the latter as standing against unreason and superstition. But if one tries to look beyond this official image, one discovers a historical reality that is much more complex and messy. Christianity did not simply triumph over paganism during the first centuries of the Common Era; on the contrary, ever since Platonism was accepted into Christian theology by a range of early church fathers, theologians and philosophers had to deal with a continuous presence of paganism *inside* Christianity, not as some kind of alien entity but as an integral part of its intellectual fabric. Only the more radical representatives of the Reformation were more or less successful in exorcizing pagan speculation from Christianity, but at the high price of setting in motion a process of rationalization that ultimately caused Enlightenment thinkers to throw out the Christian baby along with the pagan bathwater. The so-called Age of Reason was also an age of illuminism, theosophy, and other forms of esotericism, and the new scientists and rationalist philosophers were perfectly aware of the fact. The Enlightenment defined its very identity against this contemporary esoteric culture, by means of rejecting what now came to be known by generic labels such as *magic* and *the occult*: terms referring to a wastebasket category that contained everything associated with pagan superstitions and now successfully demonized or ridiculed as "irrational" nonsense. In this process of identity formation by means of polemical exclusion, "pagan" traditions were tacitly divested of their traditional status as players in the field of history and transformed into nonhistorical universals of human thinking and behavior: instead of discussing intellectual or religious traditions such as "Platonism" or "Hermeticism," one could now simply speak of "irrationality," "prejudice," or "stupidity."[2]

As the outcome of these developments, Western esotericism still functions in the academic imagination as the structural "other" of our collective modern identity, with its Christian roots and its commitment to rationality and science. It is like a dark canvas that allows us to draw the contours of our own identity in shining colors of light and truth. It is for this reason we have a vested interest in keeping it dark: if esoteric or occult currents and ideas are seen as integral parts of Christian culture, if their representatives appear to be capable of rational thinking, if they have contributed to genuine science, or their worldviews are reflective of modern and progressive tendencies—and all these things are in fact abundantly demonstrated by modern research—then the canvas begins to brighten up and it becomes more difficult to decipher what "we" are supposed to be all about. To preserve our identity, we would prefer "the occult" to stay in its own place: dark must be dark, light must be light, and never the twain should meet.

Few personalities seem to represent the dark side of the occult more extremely than the English magus and enfant terrible Aleister Crowley. There is no doubt that during his life, he did everything he could to set himself up as the perfect opposite of mainstream Western society and all its traditional values. Crowley was the self-proclaimed Beast from the Abyss who preached an anti-Christian religion revealed by a pagan deity or demon; he was the paragon of sexual perversion who experimented with every conceivable form of immorality; and, in an age of science and rational progress, he was the prophet of "magick" who was apparently bent on reviving all the "superstitions" of the past. It might seem hard to find clearer evidence for the allegedly anti-Christian, antirational, and antimodern nature of the occult: if mainstream society and its representatives have a vested interest in keeping the occult as dark as possible, one might say that Crowley was more than willing to oblige.

By playing the role of the demonic "other" to perfection, then, Crowley confirmed and strengthened the established canon and gave Christians and rationalists every argument they needed to keep seeing themselves as good and the occult as evil. Ironically, the present collection of scholarly essays might be much more profoundly subversive in its implications than Crowley's own strategies of provocation, because it does not accept the black-and-white stereotypes at face value but brings color and depth to the dark canvas by going into intricate detail, exploring a whole range of historical contexts, and asking uncomfortable questions. In his very criticism of modernity and his deliberate return to archaic traditions, Crowley turns out to have been a modernist. In his explorations of "magick" and altered states of consciousness, he turns out to have been a rationalist. And it could even be claimed—consider, for example, the profoundly biblical language of his experiential narratives in *The Vision and the Voice*—that in his very rejection of established Christianity he was a heretical Christian. In short: rather than representing their radical opposite, the Crowley phenomenon—including not only the Beast himself but also a vibrant contemporary subculture of Crowleyites, with multiple ramifications in literature, art, music, and film—provides us with a window on the complex *dialectics* of Christianity, rationalism, and modernity. As such, it is among the most extreme illustrations of a point that can be made about the domain of Western esotericism in its entirety. There is a world of difference between how this field, its representatives, and their ideas exist in the academic and the popular *imagination* and how they exist in the much more complex fabric of historical and social *reality*. If we do not make that distinction, not only will we misunderstand the occult on a very basic level, but we will also remain blind to crucial dimensions of modern culture and society.

Let the reader be warned, then: this collection of critical studies has much to teach him, but it is not for the fainthearted or the frivolous. It will introduce him to a strange, often grotesque, and profoundly disturbing world in which travelers are invited to question some of their most familiar assumptions, a world where nothing is quite what it might seem to be at first sight, and where established boundaries and distinctions seem to exist only in order to be transgressed. This field trip into the underground is supposed to affect the traveler and change his perspective: if his familiar world still looks the same at his return home, then he has been no more than a tourist watching "the primitives" from the air-conditioned safety of his touring bus. The intelligent reader will know better: he will realize that in looking at the shadow side of Western culture, we are ultimately looking at ourselves.

Wouter J. Hanegraaff
University of Amsterdam

Notes

1. Helmut Möller and Ellic Howe, *Merlin Peregrinus: Vom Untergrund des Abendlandes* (Würzburg: Königshausen & Neumann, 1986). The formulation hints at the title of Oswald Spengler's famous *Untergang des Abendlandes*. The expression *Abendland* (literally, evening-land—that is, the land of the setting sun) has no direct equivalent in English.
2. For a detailed analysis of the process summarized here in a few lines, see Wouter J. Hanegraaff, *Esotericism and the Academy: Rejected Knowledge in Western Culture* (Cambridge: Cambridge University Press, 2012).

Contributors

Henrik Bogdan is associate professor in history of religions at the University of Gothenburg. His main areas of research are Western esotericism, new religious movements, and Freemasonry. In addition to numerous articles, he is the author of *Western Esotericism and Rituals of Initiation* (2007) and editor of *Brother Curwen, Brother Crowley: A Correspondence*, by Aleister Crowley and David Curwen (2010). He is coeditor of the Approaches to New Religions Book Series.

Tobias Churton is an honorary fellow of Exeter University and faculty lecturer in Freemasonry and Rosicrucianism at Exeter University's Centre for the Study of Western Esotericism. His works include *Aleister Crowley: The Biography* (2011), *The Invisible History of the Rosicrucians* (2009), *Freemasonry: The Reality* (2007), *The Magus of Freemasonry: The Mysterious Life of Elias Ashmole* (2006), and *Gnostic Philosophy* (2005). He is also a novelist, filmmaker, and composer. His musical *You, Me and Yesterday*, cowritten with John Myatt, concerning the love affair between Nancy Cunard and Henry Crowder, was premiered at the Lichfield Garrick Theatre in 2011.

Gordan Djurdjevic, is a sessional instructor in the Department of Humanities at the Simon Fraser University in Burnaby, British Columbia. He is the author of *Masters of Magical Powers: The Nāth Yogis in the Light of Esoteric Notions* (2008) and *The Influence of South Asian Asian Spirituality on 20th Century British Occultism* (forthcoming).

Asbjørn Dyrendal is professor in history of religion at the Norwegian University of Science and Technology in Trondheim. His main areas of research are contemporary Western religions and conspiracy culture. He is the author of a book on demonology past and present, *Demoner* (2006), and editor of books on apocalyptic movements, fundamentalisms, and critical thinking.

Robert A. Gilbert is a writer and retired antiquarian bookseller who currently edits the journal *The Christian Parapsychologist*. He is the author of, among other volumes, *A. E. Waite: Magician of Many Parts* (1987) and editor of *The House of the Hidden Light*, by A. E. Waite and Arthur Machen (2003). His current research is in the field of the writing and publishing of esoteric literature in the nineteenth century, which formed the subject matter of his doctoral dissertation, "The Great Chain of Unreason" (2009, University of London).

Wouter J. Hanegraaff is professor of history of Hermetic philosophy and related currents at the University of Amsterdam, president of the European Society for the Study of Western Esotericism, and a member of the Royal Dutch Academy of Arts and Sciences. He has published numerous articles, and his books include *New Age Religion and Western Culture: Esotericism in the Mirror of Secular Thought* (1996), *Lodovico Lazzarelli (1447–1500): The Hermetic Writings and Related Documents* (2005; with Ruud M. Bouthoorn), *Swedenborg, Oetinger, Kant: Three Perspectives on the Secrets of Heaven* (2007), and *Esotericism and the Academy: Rejected Knowledge in Western Culture* (2012). He has also (co)edited seven collective volumes, including the *Dictionary of Gnosis and Western Esotericism* (2005).

Ronald Hutton is professor of history at the University of Bristol in Bristol, England. His main areas of research are the history of paganism and witchcraft, with a wider brief for early modern British history. He has published fourteen books, of which the most recent is *Blood and Mistletoe: The History of the Druids in Britain* (2009).

Massimo Introvigne is managing director of the Center for Studies on New Religions (CESNUR) in Turin, Italy. He is the author of sixty books—including the award-winning *Encyclopedia of Religions in Italy* (2001; 2nd ed., 2006)—and of more than one hundred articles in international journals in the area of the sociology of religion.

Richard Kaczynski is a research scientist and biostatistician whose affiliations include Yale University, the University of Detroit, and the US Veterans Health Administration. Since writing his doctoral dissertation, *The Structure and Correlates of Metaphysical Beliefs* (1993), he has maintained an active interest in Western esotericism, particularly in Aleister Crowley and his milieu. His publications in this area include *Perdurabo: The Life of Aleister Crowley* (rev. exp. ed., 2010), "The Crowley-Harris Thoth Tarot: Collaboration and Innovation" (2011), "Projective Geometry in Early Twentieth

Century Esotericism: From the Anthroposophical Society to the Thoth Tarot" (2011), and the forthcoming historical study *Forgotten Templars: The Untold Origins of Ordo Templi Orientis.*

Alex Owen is professor of history and gender studies at Northwestern University. She is the author of *The Darkened Room: Women, Power, and Spiritualism in Late Victorian England* (1989, 1990, 2004) and *The Place of Enchantment: British Occultism and the Culture of the Modern* (2004, 2007). She is currently working on a book titled *Culture, Psyche, and the Soul in Twentieth-Century Britain,* which investigates the post–World War I attempt to reconcile different forms of spirituality with a new (often Freudian) dynamic model of the mind.

Marco Pasi is assistant professor in history of Hermetic philosophy and related currents at the University of Amsterdam. He has written extensively on the history of occultism, on the concept of magic, and on methodological issues concerning the study of Western esotericism. He is the author of *Aleister Crowley e la tentazione della politica* (1999), translated into several languages. He has edited *Peintures inconnues d'Aleister Crowley: La collection de Palerme* (2008) and coedited *Kabbalah and Modernity: Interpretations, Transformations, Adaptations* (2010). He is the chief editor of the Aries Book Series.

Keith Richmond is an independent scholar with a graduate diploma in history from Monash University in Melbourne, Australia. He has a long-term interest in the history of Western occultism, in particular the lives and works of Aleister Crowley, Frank Bennett, and Rosaleen Norton. He is the author of *Progradior and the Beast* (2004) and *The Occult Visions of Rosaleen Norton* (2000) and has contributed to numerous other books and journals. He is co-owner of Weiser Antiquarian Books in Maine and publisher for the Teitan Press.

Matthew D. Rogers is an independent scholar holding graduate degrees in religious studies from the University of Amsterdam and Northwestern University. He has had articles published in the journal *Aries* and in *The Brill Dictionary of Religion.* His research on Crowley's *furores* was originally presented in a session on contemporary Neoplatonist survivals at the meeting of the American Academy of Religion in 2005.

Martin P. Starr is an independent scholar with research interests in Western esotericism and new religious movements. He is the editor of the Teitan Press series of the works of Aleister Crowley and is the author of *The Unknown God: W. T. Smith and the Thelemites* (2003).

Hugh B. Urban is professor of religious studies in the Department of Comparative Studies at Ohio State University. He is the author of seven books, including *Tantra: Sex, Secrecy, Politics, and Power in the Study of Religion* (2003), *Magia Sexualis: Sex, Magic, and Liberation in Modern Western Esotericism* (2006), and *The Church of Scientology: A History of a New Religion* (2011).

Aleister Crowley and Western Esotericism

1

Introduction

Henrik Bogdan and Martin P. Starr

THE FIRST COLLECTION devoted to critical studies of Aleister Crowley (1875–1947) requires some justification for its publication. The image of Crowley, so far as one exists in the dominant culture, is one of a stock figure of transgression and evil, the godfather of contemporary Satanism and the advocate of every kind of excess, from sex to drugs and, with some posthumous assistance from pop musicians, rock and roll. What claim does a countercultural life more fit for tabloid coverage possess for contemporary academic attention?

These collected essays reveal a developing notion of Crowley's legacy and influence. He was an influential twentieth-century religious synthesist. His esotericism was not a reversion to a medieval worldview; instead, in its questing for a vision of the self, it was a harbinger of modernity. Crowley acknowledged that his negative reputation served as a useful filter for the credulous and a near-complete bar to acceptance of his philosophy by his peers. He stood apart and claimed for his intellectual isolation a cosmic purpose. His mission was that of a charismatic prophet of a new dispensation for humankind that proclaimed the absolute liberty of the individual to self-actualize without regard for the moral codes and religious strictures of prior ages. The individual means to this end was through the practices of his occult bricolage, which he termed "magick," a thoroughly eclectic and highly personal combination of spiritual exercises drawn from Western European magical traditions and primarily Indic sources for meditation and Yoga disciplines. To this journey of self-liberation Crowley added the power of sexuality as a magical discipline. Crowley saw sexual magic as a simple and direct method of achieving the talismanic ends of the operator without the material trappings of ceremonial magic; the power is in the mind of the practitioner.

Yet Crowley as a proponent of a new religious movement does not fit neatly into a generalized construct of a charismatic revelator. Rather, it was a position into which he grew without seemingly abandoning his prior worldview. Before he assumed the role of prophet of a new age and promulgator of a scripture, *The Book of the Law* (1904), that could not be changed "so much as the style of a letter," as a university student he sought to understand philosophy and empirical science. His reaction against the fundamentalist faith of his childhood predicated on biblical inerrancy led him to seek for religious truths that could be justified in terms of the science and philosophy to which he was first exposed while at Cambridge. Crowley's signal contribution to Western esotericism was his attempt to legitimate his essentially religious approach to reality through appeals to elements of philosophical and empirical skepticism.[1] His first critical interpreter, J. F. C. Fuller, described Crowley's philosophical position as "Crowleyanity: or in other words, according to the mind of the reader;—Pyrrhonic-Zoroastrianism, Pyrrhonic-Mysticism, Sceptical Transcendentalism, Sceptical-Theurgy, Sceptical-Energy, Scientific-Illuminism, or what you will; for in short it is the conscious communion with God on the part of an Atheist, a transcending of reason by scepticism of the instrument, and the limitation of scepticism by direct consciousness of the Absolute."[2] In Crowley's view, contemporary science and revealed religion had failed to answer their own questions because of their inherent methodological limitations; the ultimate truths were to be found only in a union of their epistemological strengths. Crowley chose as the motto of his occult journal, *The Equinox*, "The Method of Science; the Aim of Religion." Magick was the third way.

Crowley's individualist personality is tightly bound with the development of his theory and praxis. Although he has been the subject of several full-length biographies,[3] the abundant details of his chronicled life tend to obscure the dominant trends in the development of his intellectual and spiritual topoi. Crowley was born in 1875 into a normative British upper-middle-class Victorian family. What set them apart from the mainstream of society was their commitment to the totalizing religious culture of the Exclusive Brethren sect of the Plymouth Brethren, an evangelical Christian restorationist movement. The high-demand religious practices combined with the rigid moralism (and apparent hypocrisy) of the Plymouth Brethren nurtured in the adolescent Crowley a sense of anomie. He rebelled, and in the process of the separation from his family he defined himself oppositionally to their God, taking as his model the "Great Beast" of Revelation, a primary text in the Plymouth Brethren's historical-grammatical method of scriptural interpretation. John Nelson

Darby, a central figure in the movement, developed a premillennial dispensational theology whose constructs shaped Crowley's worldview. Dispensationalism understood biblical history as a series of ages marked by covenants between God and his people. Premillennialism points to a blissful future in which God's rule will be established on earth by the return of Jesus. For Crowley there was little doubt that the comfortable world into which he was born was destined to be overthrown by a messiah.

Crowley attended Cambridge but did not receive a degree, having had a revelation that he should devote his life to religion. The form his devotion took was twofold from the start: sex and esotericism. He needed no schooling in the former, but by 1898 he found the Hermetic Order of the Golden Dawn (GD), which appeared to offer authentic instruction in Western esotericism and an initiatic gateway to the true invisible Rosicrucian order. His involvement with the GD was short-lived, as the London body broke apart over disputes regarding the legitimacy of its historical claims and the derived authority of one of its founders, S. L. Mathers. The lasting influences on Crowley were the GD's hierarchical structure of initiation based on the structure of the kabbalistic Tree of Life and its synthesis of Western esotericism.

With the seeming failure to find the "Hidden Church of the Holy Grail" incarnate in the GD, Crowley turned to the East and explored Yoga and Buddhism in India and Burma. Mysticism as such had not been a part of the curriculum of the GD. Crowley found that the training of concentration through yogic exercises formed a useful adjutant to the ceremonial methods of Western esotericism.

What Crowley described as a break from his past took place in Cairo in April of 1904. He was practicing ceremonial magical invocations with his wife, who (as Crowley relates the story) suddenly began to state that the Egyptian god Horus was waiting for him. Following her ritual instructions, Crowley claims to have received a text via direct voice, *The Book of the Law*, a revelation of a new age of which Crowley, in his persona of the "Great Beast," was the prophet. The past Aeon of Osiris, manifested as patriarchal religion and society, was to be replaced by the coming Aeon of Horus, the divine child, an eidolon of individual freedom. The Greek word *thelema* (will) was the "word" of the "law" of the Aeon of Horus, encapsulated in its seemingly antinomian dictum "Do what thou wilt."

Crowley was not quick to accept in its totality the charismatic authority granted him by *The Book of the Law*. His sense that its revelation put him at the head of the spiritual hierarchy vacated by S. L. Mathers first led him to form the A.'.A.'. in 1909; this order combined the ceremonial magic of the

GD with the Eastern practices he had learned, structured as a teacher–student chain of authority. He published the teachings of the order in a semiannual journal, *The Equinox* (1909–1913). Mathers sued Crowley over his publication in *The Equinox* of the "Rosicrucian" inner-order ritual of the GD; the publicity led to Crowley's taking a leadership role in another neo-Rosicrucian group, the Ordo Templi Orientis (OTO), a mixed masonic group that had at its center a closely guarded secret: the theory and practice of sexual magic. By the close of 1913 and Crowley's departure for the United States, he had two interconnected esoteric movements under his direction that he turned gradually into vehicles for the promotion of his revelation of Thelema and the Aeon of Horus. Like the GD, both groups had small memberships. Unlike Mathers, who could count W. B. Yeats among his colleagues, Crowley attracted mainly followers of marginal cultural or social influence.

World War I kept Crowley in the United States, from which he led the small groups of his followers in Canada, Britain, South Africa, and Australia. The movements did not flourish, and Crowley, unable to find a market for his books, wandered Europe and North Africa in an obscurity only briefly broken by the furor over the publication of his roman à clef *The Diary of a Drug Fiend* (1922). His textbook *Magick in Theory and Practice* (1930) had little distribution; he published other occult texts privately in small editions principally for his disciples. His last major work, *The Book of Thoth* (1944), was his exposition of the tarot, with the cards designed under his direction. When Crowley died in Hastings, England, in 1947, his life was framed by accounts in American newsmagazines such as *Time* and *Newsweek* as that of a fringe religious eccentric; this view was to dominate for several decades.

The late 1960s and early 1970s witnessed a revival of interest in Crowley, and many works by Crowley that had been out of print for decades were reissued. Instrumental in these publishing ventures were two of Crowley's former secretaries, Israel Regardie in the United States and Kenneth Grant in England. Regardie, who had been Crowley's secretary from 1928 to 1932, was a prolific author and central to the reemergence of the GD. Apart from his biography of Crowley, *The Eye in the Triangle* (1970), Regardie edited and introduced Crowley's *AHA* (1969), *The Vision and the Voice* (1972), *The Holy Books of Thelema* (1972), *Book Four* (1972), *Magick without Tears* (1973), *The Qabalah of Aleister Crowley* (1973), *The Law Is for All* (1975), and *Gems from "The Equinox"* (1974), a massive volume that included the bulk of the magical and mystical writings from the first volume of *The Equinox*. Grant, who had acted as Crowley's secretary for a period in 1944, collaborated with Crowley's literary executor, John Symonds, in introducing and editing a number of

Crowley's books, including *The Confessions of Aleister Crowley* (1969), *The Magical Record of the Beast 666* (1972), *The Diary of a Drug Fiend* (1972), *Moonchild* (1972), *Magick* (1973), *Magical and Philosophical Commentaries on "The Book of the Law"* (1974), and *The Complete Astrological Writings* (1974), and by writing an introduction to *The Heart of the Master* (1973). It was also during this period that Grant began to publish his three so-called Typhonian Trilogies, commencing with *The Magical Revival* in 1972, which were completed thirty years later with *The Ninth Arch* (2002).

Crowley's writings on magick, mysticism, sexuality, and drugs appealed to tastes of the time, and Crowley quickly became something of an antinomian icon for the counterculture movement and the flower-power generation. In fact, the Beatles included his image on the cover of their album *Sgt. Pepper's Lonely Hearts Club Band* (1967), where he is the second person from the left in the back row, and Led Zeppelin inscribed the vinyl of their album *Led Zeppelin III* (1970) with Crowley's central motto, "Do what thou wilt," while David Bowie sang, "I'm closer to the Golden Dawn / Immersed in Crowley's uniform / Of imagery" in the song "Quicksand," included on his album *Hunky Dory* (1971). The increasing number of books in print by Crowley coincided with a resurgence of activity within Thelemic organizations. Some of these groups were quite small and were active for only a few years, such as the Solar Lodge, which was active in the United States during the late 1960s, while others established themselves quite firmly on the esoteric scene. The largest of these latter groups is the Ordo Templi Orientis, which was reactivated around 1969 in California by a number of old-time members of the OTO under the leadership of Grady Louis McMurtry, who assumed the title of caliph. McMurtry's authority was challenged, however, by the Brazilian Thelemite Marcelo Motta and his Society Ordo Templi Orientis. In 1985 a court in California ruled in favor of McMurtry, and the OTO has since established itself as an international organization with a few thousand members worldwide. The early 1970s also saw the commencement of what is usually referred to as the Typhonian OTO (now called the Typhonian Order) under the leadership of Kenneth Grant, with its first official announcement published around 1973.

However, the importance of Crowley as a field of study lies not so much in his reception by the counterculture movement and popular culture, or in the various Thelemic new religious movements, as in the fact that Crowley can be used as an example of religious change in Western culture. Not only can Crowley's esoteric writings be seen as a prime example of what Wouter Hanegraaff has described as "secularized esotericism," but also, and perhaps more important, the study of Crowley reveals that he in many ways encapsulates central discourses of modernity and contemporary spirituality. In fact, Crowley is a harbinger of what Paul Heelas has termed the "sacralization of the self." This theme is discussed by Alex Owen in chapter 2, "The Sorcerer and His Apprentice: Aleister Crowley and the Magical Exploration of Edwardian Subjectivity," in which she places Crowley's magical work in the context of fin de siècle occultism with the argument that Crowley's magic articulates a modern sense of the self. Owen interprets the magical exploration of John Dee's "Aethyrs" that Crowley conducted together with his disciple Victor Neuburg in 1909 in Algiers as an attempt to understand the full implications of subjectivity. Although Crowley can be seen as a renovator of magical practice, his ideas on magic did not develop in a hermetically sealed environment; rather, they are reflective of the context in which he lived. Crowley was to all intents and purposes a *bricoleur*, a synthesist of diverse magical, mystical, spiritual, and philosophical ideas and practices. Marco Pasi focuses on two aspects in Crowley's esoteric work—magic and Yoga—in chapter 3, "Varieties of Magical Experience: Aleister Crowley's Views on Occult Practice," and discusses how Crowley transformed the understanding and the epistemological interpretation of occult practice. Pasi argues that there is an inherent paradox in Crowley's views on magic on one hand and on Thelema on the other. In his attempt to modernize magic by psychologizing and naturalizing it, he came to understand gods, demons, and other entities as part of the psyche (often implying the unconscious). Crowley interpreted the idea of "Knowledge of and Conversation with the Holy Guardian Angel," which was a central mystical experience for both the Hermetic Order of the Golden Dawn and Crowley's A∴A∴, as a union with the unconscious part of the mind. The problem for Crowley was that he claimed to be the prophet of a new religion, Thelema, as revealed by a "praeter-human intelligence" called Aiwass in 1904—later identified as his own Holy Guardian Angel. As a revealer of a new religion and dispensation for humankind, Aiwass belongs to the realm of spiritual reality, as opposed to being merely an aspect of Crowley's unconscious.

In chapter 4, "Envisioning the Birth of a New Aeon: Dispensationalism and Millenarianism in the Thelemic Tradition," Henrik Bogdan discusses the apocalyptic and millenarian understanding of history in the Thelemic tradition, as described in the writings of Crowley, primarily in his own commentaries on *The Book of the Law*. Bogdan argues that despite the fierce anti-Christian nature of Thelema, the Thelemic millenarian view of history is in fact deeply rooted in a Western esoteric understanding of biblical apocalypticism, as well as in the dispensationalism of John Nelson Darby (1800–1882).

The role of Yoga—and Tantra—is explored by Gordan Djurdjevic in chapter 5, "The Great Beast as a Tantric Hero." Djurdjevic argues that Crowley's practice of magick becomes clearer if one understands aspects of it against the background of Yoga and Tantra, especially the hidden aspects and powers of the human body as understood in tantric theory (i.e., *cakras* and the *kuṇḍalinī*) and the tantric spiritual techniques of "decadence" and "transgression." One can use the latter techniques to understand the spiritual crisis—or initiation, depending on one's point of view—that Crowley underwent at the Abbey of Thelema in Cefalù in the period 1920–1923.

Crowley's understanding of sex as a means to spiritual liberation and enlightenment was not restricted, however, to tantric theories and practices. In chapter 6, "Continuing Knowledge from Generation unto Generation: The Social and Literary Background of Aleister Crowley's Magick," Richard Kaczynski traces the various Western sources out of which Crowley synthesized his magical system. Chief among these sources was the vast contemporary literature on sex worship, phallicism, and the worship of the sun. Authors such as Richard Payne Knight and Hargrave Jennings saw solar-phallicism as the true origin of all world religions, and, according to Kaczynski, Crowley picked up these ideas and infused them in his magical and religious worldview, as exemplified by certain passages in the Gnostic Mass he wrote in 1913. Crowley acknowledged freely that he was influenced by various religious traditions, and he often drew on his considerable knowledge of comparative religion in order to elucidate and explain practices and ideas from his magical and religious worldview. One such curious example is his statement that Thelema is related to the Sumerian tradition and that the "author" of *The Book of the Law*, Aiwass, bore the most ancient name of the Yezidis. These statements form the basis for Tobias Churton's discussion in chapter 7, "Aleister Crowley and the Yezidis," which compares *The Book of the Law* with Yezidism and, further, assesses the relationship between Aiwass and the God of the Yezidis. Crowley's apparent fascination with pagan pre-Christian religious traditions was not restricted to the literature on phallicism; it also spanned a wide range of classical authors to whom he made references throughout his writings. Matthew D. Rogers focuses on a particular case of classical literature in chapter 8, "Frenzies of the Beast: The Phaedran *Furores* in the Rites and Writings of Aleister Crowley." According to Rogers, the classification of the *furores*, or "frenzies," from Plato's *Phaedrus*, along with its elaborations by later Platonists and Neoplatonists such as Marsilio Ficino, can be traced in Crowley's work—especially in his article "Energized Enthusiasm," which is an important source for our understanding of Crowley's notion of sexual magic.

Crowley's formal initiation into the mysteries of sexual magic occurred in 1912 when he joined the German mixed masonic organization Ordo Templi Orientis. The early history of the OTO still lacks a thorough study, but the bare facts point to the order's being an invention of the German mason, occultist, and former Theosophist Theodor Reuss. Although Reuss claimed that the OTO was founded in 1905 by Karl Kellner, it seems more likely that the order came into existence gradually, perhaps as late as 1912, out of a charter issued by John Yarker to Reuss in 1902 for the Antient and Primitive Rite of Freemasonry. This rite, a short-lived competitor to the English Ancient and Accepted Rite, was promoted by Yarker and his colleagues in the last quarter of the nineteenth century. Crowley, who affiliated to the Antient and Primitive Rite in 1910, was clearly ambivalent toward Freemasonry: while continually criticizing and ridiculing conservative (or "regular") Freemasonry, he sought to be admitted into conservative Freemasonry. In fact, while living for a number of years in the United States during World War I, he even tried to assume control over Freemasonry. In chapter 9, "Aleister Crowley—Freemason?!," Martin P. Starr examines Crowley's masonic contacts, separating the many myths surrounding Crowley and Freemasonry from the facts. To a certain extent, Crowley's ambivalent relationship with Freemasonry parallels his conflicting views of himself as the great magician and prophet, the Great Wild Beast 666, on one hand and a respectable British gentleman on the other.

The elusiveness of respectability was something that haunted Crowley throughout his adult life, and it appears that one of the reasons he sought to be admitted by "regular" Freemasonry was that it would allow him to become part of the respected establishment of British society. The combination of occultism, secret societies, Freemasonry, and respectability was not so far-fetched at the beginning of the twentieth century as it might seem. In fact, one of Crowley's contemporaries, the prolific author Arthur Edward Waite, seemingly managed to achieve just such a combination, and perhaps this was one of the reasons that Crowley took such a dislike to him. In chapter 10, "'The One Thought That Was Not Untrue': Aleister Crowley and A. E. Waite," Robert A. Gilbert discusses how Crowley wrote to Waite in 1898, requesting information about an existing "Hidden Church" that Waite had mentioned in his *The Book of Black Magic and of Pacts* (1898)—but for some reason Crowley later turned hostile toward Waite and published numerous attacks on him, often ridiculing the "pompous" style and arcane grammar of Waite's writings. The perhaps most humorous attack on Waite is to be found in Crowley's novel *Moonchild* (1929), in which Waite appears thinly disguised as a villain called Arthwaite. *Moonchild* was originally written in 1917 and contains references not only to a number of contemporary occultists and acquaintances but also—as Massimo Introvigne points out in chapter 11, "The Beast and the Prophet"—to such surprising persons as Joseph Smith, the founder of Mormonism. The reference to Joseph Smith was, however, not a mere accident; it actually reveals Crowley's deep-seated fascination with Smith, which stemmed from Crowley's reading of Sir Richard Francis Burton, in particular his book *The City of the Saints, and across the Rocky Mountains to California* (1896). Introvigne attempts to explain this fascination and discusses several extrinsic similarities between Crowley and Smith; furthermore, he analyzes how his findings are confirmed by the attitude of contemporary new magical movements toward Joseph Smith.

As a leading figure in twentieth-century magic and occultism, Crowley has influenced—directly or indirectly—the majority of all contemporary "new magical movements" (to borrow a label from Introvigne's chapter). While the Thelemic movement—and the various Thelemic organizations—today might count a total of a few thousand members, Crowley's influence on contemporary esotericism far outreaches the Thelemic organizations. The largest of these, perhaps, is modern pagan witchcraft, or Wicca, which Ronald Hutton addresses in chapter 12, "Crowley and Wicca." Although it is frequently stated that Gerald Gardner, generally credited as the founder of modern witchcraft, knew Crowley personally and was an initiated member of the OTO, the precise part that Crowley played in the origins of Wicca remains, according to Hutton, both uncertain and deeply controversial. Hutton goes to the heart of the matter and critically examines the relationship of Crowley and Gardner and the early history of the Wicca movement; he shows how Wicca at first drew heavily on Crowley's writings but how this influence was later downplayed. Furthermore, Hutton argues that Crowley was the "most important single identifiable influence" on the witchcraft movement in the early 1950s, next to Gardner himself. The influence of Crowley on Wicca can be seen as direct in the sense that Gardner knew Crowley personally and was involved with the small Thelemic movement in England for a short period after Crowley's death. The influence of Crowley can also be found, however, indirectly in the witchcraft of the Australian artist Rosaleen Norton. Norton not only stands out as Australia's most persecuted and prosecuted female artist, but, as Keith Richmond presents in chapter 13, "Through the Witch's Looking Glass: The Magick of Aleister Crowley and the Witchcraft of Rosaleen Norton," she was also the founder of a peculiar esoteric system that she herself described as witchcraft. Although Norton corresponded with Gardner, she came to create an idiosyncratic form of witchcraft into which she initiated only a very small group of persons. Norton never was a Thelemite or follower of Crowley, but Richmond shows that the references to Crowley in Norton's writings far outnumber those to any other individual occultist and that Crowley was a major influence on her.

In chapter 14, "The Occult Roots of Scientology?," Hugh B. Urban examines to what extent one of the most controversial of all contemporary new religious movements is influenced by the works of Aleister Crowley. The link between Crowley and the founder of Scientology, L. Ron Hubbard, is John W. Parsons, the lodge master of the only functioning OTO lodge during World War II. Parsons and Hubbard cooperated in a series of magical rites called the Babalon Working in 1946, but the magical partnership ended later in the same year when Parsons accused Hubbard of having stolen his money and his girlfriend. Despite the relatively short period that Hubbard was involved with Parsons, Urban argues, the links to Crowley shed important light not only on the origins of Scientology but also on the American spirituality of the 1950s, which was characterized by a "complex mélange of occultism, magic, science fiction, and the yearning for something radically new." Perhaps not as surprising as the case with Scientology, Crowley's influence is also to be found in modern Satanism. Even though Crowley identified himself as the Great Beast 666, and he was branded as a Satanist in his lifetime, there is actually little in his writings that can be considered as "satanic," much less as "Satanism," as Asbjørn Dyrendal points out in chapter 15, "Satan and the Beast: The Influence of Aleister Crowley on Modern Satanism." Focusing on Anton LaVey and Michael A. Aquino, Dyrendal discusses how modern Satanism has adopted aspects of Crowley's esotericism, albeit in a critical way. In short, the examples of modern witchcraft, Scientology, and Satanism show that Crowley has continued to have an influence on Western spirituality, perhaps accounting for the fact that he appears to be more popular than ever as we have entered the twenty-first century. The importance of Crowley in Western culture was made evident in the BBC's 2002 "100 Greatest Britons" poll, in which, with more than 300,000 votes, Crowley ranked at number seventy-three, before authors such as Geoffrey Chaucer (eighty-one) and J. R. R. Tolkien (ninety-two).

Notes

1. Discussions concerning the definition of Western esotericism are ongoing. For the most significant recent works on the subject, see Wouter J. Hanegraaff, *Esotericism and the Academy: Rejected Knowledge in Western Culture* (Cambridge: Cambridge University Press, 2012); and Kocku von Stuckrad, *Locations of Knowledge in Medieval and Early Modern Europe: Esoteric Discourse and Western Identities* (Leiden: Brill, 2010). The use of the term *Western esotericism* throughout this anthology is grounded in the field of research to which these two works are related.
2. J. F. C. Fuller, *The Star in the West: A Critical Essay upon the Works of Aleister Crowley* (London: Walter Scott Publishing, 1907), 212.
3. Several biographies have been published on Aleister Crowley, including the following: John Symonds, *The Great Beast* (London: Rider, 1951); Charles Richard Cammell, *Aleister Crowley: The Man, the Mage, the Poet* (London: Richards Press, 1951); John Symonds, *The Magic of Aleister Crowley* (London: Frederick Muller, 1958); Daniel P. Mannix, *The Beast* (New York: Ballantine Books, 1959); Israel Regardie, *The Eye in the Triangle: An Interpretation of Aleister Crowley* (St. Paul, Minn.: Llewellyn, 1970); John Symonds, *The Great Beast: The Life and Magic of Aleister Crowley* (London: Macdonald, 1971); Francis X. King, *The Magical World of Aleister Crowley* (London: Weidenfeld & Nicolson, 1977); Susan Roberts, *The Magician of the Golden Dawn: The Story of Aleister Crowley* (Chicago: Contemporary Books, 1978); Colin Wilson, *The Nature of the Beast* (London: Aquarian Press, 1987); Gerald Suster, *The Legacy of the Beast: The Life, Work, and Influence of Aleister Crowley* (London: W. H. Allen, 1988); John Symonds, *The King of the Shadow Realm: Aleister Crowley, His Life and Magic* (London: Duckworth, 1989); John Symonds, *The Beast 666* (London: Pindar Press, 1997); Roger Hutchinson, *Aleister Crowley: The Beast Demystified* (Edinburgh: Mainstream, 1998); Martin Booth, *A Magick Life: The Biography of Aleister Crowley* (London: Hodder & Stoughton, 2000); Lawrence Sutin, *Do What Thou Wilt: A Life of Aleister Crowley* (New York: St. Martin's Press, 2000); Richard Kaczynski, *Perdurabo: The Life of Aleister Crowley*, rev. ed. (Berkeley, Calif.: North Atlantic Books, 2010); Tobias Churton, *Aleister Crowley: The Biography* (London: Watkins, 2011). For specific studies, see Richard B. Spence, *Secret Agent 666: Aleister Crowley, British Intelligence, and the Occult* (Port Townsend, Wash.: Feral House, 2008); and Marco Pasi, *Aleister Crowley and the Temptation of Politics* (London: Equinox Publishing, 2013). See also Marco Pasi's critical discussion of a few Crowley biographies, "The Neverendingly Told Story: Recent Biographies of Aleister Crowley," *Aries* 3, no. 2: 224–45.

2

The Sorcerer and His Apprentice

ALEISTER CROWLEY AND THE MAGICAL EXPLORATION OF EDWARDIAN SUBJECTIVITY

Alex Owen

IN LATE 1909, two Englishmen, scions of the comfortable middle classes, undertook a journey to Algiers. Aleister Crowley, later to be dubbed "the wickedest man in the world," was in his early thirties; his companion, Victor Neuburg, had only recently graduated from Cambridge. The stated purpose of the trip was pleasure. Crowley, widely traveled and an experienced mountaineer and big-game hunter, loved North Africa and had personal reasons for wanting to be out of England. Neuburg probably had little say in the matter. Junior in years, dreamy and mystical by nature, and in awe of a man whom he both loved and admired, Neuburg was inclined to acquiesce without demur in Crowley's various projects. There was, however, another highly significant factor in Neuburg's quiescence. He was Crowley's chela, a novice initiate of the magical Order of the Silver Star, which Crowley had founded two years earlier. As such, Neuburg had taken a vow of obedience to Crowley as his Master and affectionately dubbed "holy guru," and he had already learned that in much that related to his life Crowley's word was now law. It was at Crowley's instigation that the two men began to make their way, first by tram and then by foot, into the North African desert to the southwest of Algiers, and it was Crowley's decision to perform there a series of magical ceremonies that prefigured his elaboration of the techniques of sex magic. In this case, the ceremonies combined the performance of advanced ritual magic with homosexual acts. It is this episode—sublime and terrifying as an experience, profound in its effects, and critical to the argument I seek to make for magical practice as a self-conscious exploration of subjectivity—that constitutes the focus of this chapter.

Magic, or, more specifically, ritual or ceremonial magic, has a long and august history in Western Europe. Associated strongly with the medieval and early modern periods, ritual magic has traditionally been associated with learned elites. Loosely understood to be the theory and practice of accessing and communicating with powerful but unseen natural or universal forces, ritual magic was invariably an occult or secret undertaking. Its procedures were confided in grimoires, textbooks of ritual magic, and these became the jealously guarded jewels of the magical tradition. This tradition, often assumed to be an archaic vestige with little purchase or relevance for the modern period, survived intact into the nineteenth century, when it began to emerge as a more accessible subject of study with the publication of classical grimoires in English translation. Francis Barrett's *The Magus* (London, 1801) was a landmark text, and by midcentury several formal groups had been established with the express purpose of studying the magical arts. Far from disappearing in the modern period, ritual magic became a central but hidden component of the nineteenth-century occult revival.[1]

A general fascination with the occult was a marked, if until relatively recently little understood, aspect of Victorian society and culture.[2] The middle to late decades of the nineteenth century witnessed the appearance of Spiritualism and Theosophy, which together accounted for many thousands of adherents, and the emergence of various small groups dedicated to different forms of Western and Eastern arcane teachings. The occult exerted a broad appeal, perhaps best exemplified by the huge success of "occult" fiction such as Rider Haggard's *She* (London, 1887) and Bram Stoker's *Dracula* (Westminster, 1897), that operated in tandem with the Victorian craze for orientalism and "the mysterious East." Serious students of the occult, however, were drawn less by the glamour of exoticism than by the promise of privileged access to secret knowledge and a hidden realm of alternative spiritual wisdom. In suggesting the possibility of spiritual revelation, the occult played upon a Victorian triumphalist notion of progress while allaying fears that advances in knowledge and understanding might result in the desecration of a mysterious and wonderful universe. Occultism's founding impulse, the elaboration of human destiny as a quest for the key that would unlock the secrets of creation, promised revelation as a prelude to spiritual growth and enlightenment.

Ritual magic was certainly suggestive of this promise. It emerged most strongly in the nineteenth century in its Rosicrucian form—that is, as a particular configuration of seventeenth-century occult learning.[3] The Rosicrucian tradition, with its roots in Jewish mysticism, Hebrew-Christian sources of ancient wisdom, and the powerful "Egyptian" writings of Hermes

Trismegistus, was marked by the elaborate interplay of the philosophical or spiritual with the practical and magical.[4] This combination of the philosophical and the magical found its way directly into the foremost Victorian magical order, the Hermetic Order of the Golden Dawn, and constituted one of its main attractions. The Hermetic Order of the Golden Dawn, established in the late 1880s, represented itself, in some respects correctly, as a direct link with the arcane traditions of the past. Although its founding documents were probably spurious, and its major rituals undoubtedly the work of Victorian scholars and magicians, its teachings were based upon an imaginative reworking of Hermetic writings further informed by nineteenth-century scholarship in Egyptology and anthropology. The order's name spoke to the realization of a Rosicrucian rebirth, the regeneration of the old, corrupt world and the dawning of a new spiritually enlightened age—timely notions for many at the fin de siècle.

The Golden Dawn is now chiefly remembered as a formative influence on the literary imagination of the poet and playwright W. B. Yeats, but its largely middle-class adherents numbered in the hundreds and included gifted men and women from the world of arts and letters. In contrast to Freemasonry, with which the Golden Dawn had certain links, women were welcomed as members and rose to positions of prominence. The order was structured around the symbolism of the kabbalah and organized into temples that were run on strictly hierarchical lines.[5] Authority was vested in leading individuals, and initiates were given a rigorous and systematic training in the "rejected" knowledge of Western esotericism. They studied the symbolism of astrology, alchemy, and kabbalah; were instructed in geomantic and tarot divination; and learned the underpinnings of basic magical techniques. A student progressed through the grades of the order by means of a series of examinations, but admission to the advanced Second (or Inner) Order was selective, a privilege rather than a right.[6] It was in the Second Order that adherents began to access the secrets of practical or operational magic, that is, magic as a unique undertaking through which invisible forces could be influenced and controlled in order to bring about specific change. The order's leaders took this practical magical Work extremely seriously, and senior adepts carefully assessed each student's suitability for such an undertaking. Unlike its French occult counterparts, British Rosicrucianism, at least at the organizational level, was ever concerned with standards and respectability.[7]

When Aleister Crowley was initiated into the Hermetic Order of the Golden Dawn in 1898 as Frater Perdurabo ("I will endure"), he assumed, along with the other adherents, that he was entering a magical society with an unbroken magical pedigree. Convinced that he had found the secret mystical brotherhood referred to in Councillor Karl von Eckartshausen's occult classic *The Cloud upon the Sanctuary* (London, 1896), he threw himself into his magical studies with enthusiasm. Crowley, Cambridge educated, highly intelligent, and capable of great powers of concentration, advanced quickly through the grades of the Outer Order of the Golden Dawn. He was contemptuous of the bourgeois mundanity of many of his fellow initiates, impatient with the slow, pedantic methods of the order, and eager to access the secrets of the cherished Second Order. His advancement, however, was blocked by senior officers, W. B. Yeats foremost among them, who were scandalized by Crowley's wild, unpredictable behavior and questionable morals. Crowley subsequently became involved in a bitter power struggle within the Golden Dawn, abandoned it in 1900, went on to study with other teachers, and finally established his own Order of the Silver Star. By 1909 he considered himself to be a master magician: wise in the ways of the ancient wisdom and skilled in the advanced techniques of operational magic. It was as a self-styled "Master" that he recruited Victor Neuburg and began to experiment with the sex magic that was later to help make him notorious.

The experiment in the desert in 1909, however, was not straightforwardly self-serving, as much of Crowley's magical Work was to become. Nor did it represent simply the indulgence of an exoticized and outlawed sexuality. What happened in the desert was the result of a serious, if misguided, attempt to access and explore a centuries-old magical system, and it represented an intense personal investment in the pursuit of magical knowledge. This chapter will seek to examine the meaning and significance of this magical Work both in its own terms and in terms of the wider cultural context. In particular, it will locate a revitalized magical tradition in relation to the fin de siècle formulation of new sexual identities and a contemporary preoccupation with the riddle of human identity and consciousness as manifested in competing ideas of the self. In situating the discussion within the conceptual framework implied by the term *subjectivity*, I am relying in my analysis on a particular theoretical formulation of selfhood that underscores its contingency. The poststructuralist concept of subjectivity is suggestive of a self that is both stable and unstable, knowable and unknowable, constructed and unique. My central argument in this chapter, however, is directed toward understanding fin de siècle advanced magical practice as a particular and self-conscious engagement with selfhood, an engagement that exposed the limitations of a unified sense of self upon which experiential gendered identity depends.

North Africa

When Aleister Crowley arrived in Algiers with Victor Neuburg in November 1909, he undoubtedly evinced the unmistakable, subtly superior, air of the English gentleman abroad. His attitude toward resident French officialdom was one of polite disdain, and he chose to ignore warnings that an unaccompanied trip through the desert could be dangerous. Crowley, confident and at ease, immediately set about buying the necessary provisions for the journey. He had a basic grasp of Arabic and understood a fair amount about Muslim culture, but was concerned that Neuburg, with his "hangdog look" and "lunatic laugh," threatened to undermine his credibility. According to Crowley, therefore, Neuburg's head was shaved, leaving only two tufts at the temples, which were "twisted up into horns." Crowley laughingly, but tellingly, comments that his chela was thus transformed into "a demon that I had tamed and trained to serve me as a familiar spirit. This greatly enhanced my eminence."[8] A concern with eminence was ever uppermost in Crowley's mind, and he would justify it here as giving him the necessary status to travel unmolested through isolated desert terrain. The reference to demons and spirits, however, although joking, is an indication of how intimately Crowley lived with the magical realities that were his concern in his capacity as the magician Perdurabo.

It was after spending only two nights sleeping under the desert stars that Crowley had the sudden insight that he must renew a magical undertaking begun in Mexico nine years earlier. This involved using a complex magical system developed by John Dee, the eminent Elizabethan mathematician and astrologer, and his clairvoyant, Edward Kelley. Dee and Kelley were well versed in practical kabbalah and experimented with the angel magic of the Renaissance magician Henry Cornelius Agrippa. Agrippa had elaborated a system of numerical and alphabetical tables for the summoning of angels, and it was within this framework that the two Elizabethans worked. John Dee used Kelley's gifts as an expert scryer, one who could "travel" in the many realms of spirit existence, to enter vicariously into conversation with the angels in order to tempt from them the secrets of the universe. During their lengthy séances, Kelley would "scry in the spirit vision" using a "shew-stone" in much the same way as a seer might use a crystal ball. Dee asked his questions through Kelley and duly recorded the results. In this way, Dee slowly built up an entire cosmology of angels and demons, and sketched out thirty Aethyrs (or Aires)—realms of otherworldly existence.[9]

Crowley was familiar with Dee's researches because they had been integrated into the teachings of the Order of the Golden Dawn. Although he had been denied entry to the Second Order, Crowley had studied with other Golden Dawn adepts—most notably Allan Bennett, considered second only to the highest-ranking member of the order. But whereas Golden Dawn initiates were set to study Dee's so-called Enochian system as a scholarly exercise, Crowley was prepared to test its efficacy. He was already skilled in exploring what the Golden Dawn referred to as the Astral Light, understood to be separate planes or orders of existence that interpenetrate the world of earthly perceptions.[10] He considered himself a master of astral travel and was in the process of teaching its necessary techniques and procedures to Neuburg. These included total familiarity with the language of occult symbolism so vital to safe travel in astral realms. Indeed, although at one level an interior journey made from within the confines of the stationary physical body, astral travel was acknowledged by magicians to be potentially dangerous. Novices such as Victor Neuburg returned exhausted from their forays, but Crowley was no novice. Knowledgeable and expert in astral travel, familiar with the means of astral defense and attack, and cognizant of the spirit world, Crowley considered that he was ready to undertake a journey through John Dee's Aethyrs.

Crowley's technique was simple. He would select a secluded spot and recite the appropriate Call—the ritual incantation that would give him access to the relevant Aethyr. After satisfying himself that the invoked forces were present, Crowley would take up his magical shew-stone, a large golden topaz, and "scry in the spirit vision" much as Kelley had done centuries before. He made "the topaz play a part not unlike that of the looking-glass in the case of *Alice*."[11] By making the relevant Call and concentrating on the topaz, Crowley could enter the Aethyr. He was clear about what this meant: "When I say I was in any Aethyr, I simply mean in the state characteristic of, and peculiar to, its nature."[12] In other words, Crowley recognized that this was an experience similar to that of astral travel: it was conducted within his own mind. Having accessed the Aethyr, he would describe his experiences to Neuburg, who would write them down. It is noteworthy that, typically, Crowley adapted the procedure to suit himself. Unlike Dee, he, the master magician, would be his own scryer. Neuburg, whom Crowley recognized to be a gifted clairvoyant, was the scribe.

As the two men made their way through the desert, Crowley increasingly fell under the spell of his experiences in John Dee's Aethyrs. He encountered celestial beings, both terrible and beautiful, who divulged in richly symbolic language something of the realms in which they dwelt. Crowley understood much of the symbolism and began to realize that the Calls did indeed give the scryer access to an intricate but cogent and coherent universal system of other worlds and beings. But as the Calls proceeded, Crowley began increasingly to feel something very akin to fear. It was as though, he says, a hand was holding his heart while a whispering breath enveloped him in words both awful and enchanting. In a gender reversal that was to typify much of this magical experience, Crowley reveals that he "began to feel—well, not exactly frightened; it was the subtle trembling of a maiden before the bridegroom."[13] In order to fortify himself against growing feelings of awe and dread, he began to recite the Koran as he marched across the desert. The great stretches of empty landscape, hot by day and icy at night, and continuous intoning of magical and religious formulas combined to effect a state of almost overwhelming spiritual intensity.

A little more than two weeks after they had arrived in Algiers, Crowley and Neuburg reached Bou Saada. This isolated haven in the desert, with its palm trees, gardens, and orchards, was where the desert road ran out. Bou Saada gave the impression of a last link with civilization. Some distance from the town was a mountain, Mount Da'leh Addin. It was here that Crowley, acting on instructions from previous angelic interlocutors, made Dee's Call and attempted to enter the fourteenth Aethyr. His attempt, however, was thwarted. He was met by "an all-glorious Angel," surrounded with blackness "and the crying of beasts." The angel issued a warning and instructed the magician to withdraw. Shaken, Crowley prepared to return to Bou Saada. As he did so, "suddenly came the command to perform a magical ceremony on the summit" of the mountain. Whatever form the "command" took, Crowley experienced it as absolute. He and Neuburg responded by building a great circle with loose rocks. They inscribed the circle with magical words of power, "erected an alter" in its midst, and there, in Crowley's words: "I sacrificed myself. The fire of the all-seeing sun smote down upon the alter, consuming every particle of my personality."[14]

What happened in prosaic terms was that Crowley was sodomized by Neuburg in a homosexual rite offered to the god Pan. Pan, the man-goat, had a particular significance for the two men. Crowley revered him as the diabolic god of lust and magic, and Neuburg literally had what acquaintances described as an elfin and "faun-like" appearance.[15] It is likely that what happened on Mount Da'leh Addin was a classic invocation; the young chela, in accordance with accepted magical technique, probably "called down" or invoked the god Pan. A successful invocation would result in the neophyte becoming "inflamed" by the power of the god. If this is what happened during the ceremony on the mountain, Neuburg, in his magical capacity, would momentarily identify with all that the man-goat god represented. Put simply, Neuburg with his tufted "horns" would become Pan—the "faun-like" yet savage lover of Crowley's psychosexual world. Although Crowley and Neuburg were involved in a homosexual relationship, this may well have been the first time that the two men performed a magical homosexual act. Crowley quickly came to believe that sex magic was an unrivaled means to great magical power, and he became one of its most innovative practitioners. The image of Pan was to haunt Neuburg for the rest of his life. It inspired some of his best early poetry but later filled him with dread. The experience was overwhelming for both men, but it temporarily devastated Crowley. His summation is brief: "There was an animal in the wilderness," he writes, "but it was not I."[16]

Crowley remembered nothing of his return to Bou Saada. As he slowly came to himself, however, he knew that he was changed.

> I knew who I was and all the events of my life; but I no longer made myself the centre of their sphere. . . . I did not exist. . . . All things were alike as shadows sweeping across the still surface of a lake—their images had no meaning for the water, no power to stir its silence.[17]

Crowley felt that he had ceremonially crossed the Abyss—a term reminiscent of Nietzsche (whom Crowley greatly admired) but denoting the last terrible journey that a magician must make before he could justifiably lay claim to the highest levels of adeptship. Master of the Temple, a grade of enlightened initiation achieved in Crowley's own magical order only by those who had crossed the Abyss, meant renunciation of all that life meant. The Order of the Golden Dawn taught that such awareness could not be accessed this side of death, and Crowley affirmed this in his own way. He taught that becoming a Master of the Temple implied not simply symbolic death and rebirth, a concept familiar to all magical initiates, but the annihilation of the personal self. The Abyss, then, was closely associated with the death of the individual—although not necessarily on the physical level.

A few days later, Crowley, who in the aftermath of the "sacrifice" on Mount Da'leh Addin had already acknowledged that at one level "I did not exist," prepared formally to undergo the Abyss ordeal. He understood that he would do so when he entered John Dee's tenth Aethyr. He knew that in the tenth Aethyr he must meet and defeat the terrible "Choronzon, the mighty devil that inhabiteth the outermost Abyss."[18] He also knew that he could do so only as Perdurabo, a magical adept, and that his success depended on his ability to master Choronzon through the dominating power of the magical Will. The complex techniques, rituals, and paraphernalia of magical practice are the means by which a magician develops and "inflames" his Will, the single most important attribute of a magician. Crowley understood that Choronzon's power could be bound and brought under control only through the silent but relentless application of the magical Will, and that this was critical for a successful crossing of the Abyss. Failure to force Choronzon into submission would enslave the magician to him, bringing disaster in its wake. Given this, and the warnings he had received in the previous Aethyrs, Crowley changed his magical procedure.

On December 6, 1909, Crowley and Neuburg left Bou Saada and went far out into the desert until they found a suitable valley in the dunes. There they traced a circle in the sand, inscribing it with the various sacred names of God. They then traced a triangle in close proximity, its perimeters likewise inscribed with divine names and also with that of Choronzon. This was correct magical practice. The magic circle provided protection for the magician; the Triangle of Art was intended to contain any visible manifestation of the forces "called up" or evoked by Perdurabo. The process of evocation was designed to produce a physical materialization of, in this case, the demonic inhabitant of the Abyss. Three pigeons were sacrificed and their blood placed at the three corners, Crowley taking particular care that it remained within the confines of the figure. The blood was to facilitate and help sustain any physical manifestation, and it was essential that this remain within the triangle. At this point Neuburg entered the circle. He was armed with a magic dagger and had strict instructions to use it if anything—even anything that looked like Crowley—attempted to break into the circle. At Crowley's instigation, Neuburg swore an oath to defend the circle's inviolability with his life. Crowley, dressed in his ceremonial black robe, then made an astonishing departure from accepted ritual practice. Instead of joining his chela in the relative safety of the circle, he entered the Triangle of Art. While Neuburg performed the Banishing Rituals of the Pentagram and Hexagram, a procedure designed to protect him, Crowley made the Call of the tenth Aethyr.[19]

The mighty Choronzon announced himself from within the shew-stone with a great cry, "Zazas, Zazas, Nasatanada Zazas":

> I am I. . . . From me come leprosy and pox and plague and cancer and cholera and the falling sickness. Ah! I will reach up to the knees of the Most High, and tear his phallus with my teeth, and I will bray his testicles in a mortar, and make poison thereof, to slay the sons of men.[20]

Crowley probably uttered these words. Thereafter, however, as far as Neuburg could tell, Crowley fell silent; he remained seated in the triangle in the sand, robed and hooded, deeply withdrawn, and "did not move or speak during the ceremony."[21] It was Neuburg who both heard and saw. Unlike the previous Calls, when he had acted merely as scribe, Neuburg now beheld—not Crowley seated within the triangle but all that Crowley conjured. Before him appeared Choronzon in the guise of a beautiful woman whom he had known and loved in Paris, and she tried to lure him from the circle. She was followed by a holy man and a serpent.

Slowly the demon in his various manifestations managed to engage the inexperienced Neuburg in discussion and then proceeded to mock him. Had he not, "O talkative One," been instructed to hold no converse with the mighty Choronzon? Undoubtedly Neuburg had been so instructed by Crowley, but in the heat of the moment he forgot himself. During the intense debate that ensued, with Neuburg scribbling furiously so as to record every detail, Choronzon began stealthily to erase the protective edges of the circle in the sand. Suddenly, Choronzon sprang from the triangle into the circle and wrestled Neuburg to the ground. The scribe found himself struggling with a demon in the shape of "a naked savage," a strong man who tried to tear out his throat with "froth-covered fangs." Neuburg, invoking the magical names of God, struck out with his dagger and finally forced the writhing figure back into the triangle. The chela repaired the circle, and Choronzon resumed his different manifestations and ravings. Cajoling, tempting, decrying, pleading, he continued to debate and attempt to undermine the scribe. Finally, the manifestations began to fade. The triangle emptied.[22]

Neuburg now became aware of Crowley, who was sitting alone in the triangle. He watched as Crowley wrote the name BABALON, signifying the defeat of Choronzon, in the sand with his Holy Ring.[23] The ceremony was concluded. It had lasted more than two hours. The two men lit a great fire of purification and obliterated the circle and the triangle. They had undergone a terrible ordeal. Crowley states that he had "astrally identified" himself with Choronzon throughout and had "experienced each anguish, each rage, each despair, each insane outburst."[24] Neuburg, however, had held forbidden converse with the Dweller of the Abyss. Both men now felt that they understood the nature of the Abyss. It represented Dispersion: a terrifying chaos in which there was no center and no controlling consciousness. Its fearsome Dweller was not an individual but the personification of a magnitude of malignant forces made manifest through the massed energy of the evoking magician. To experience these forces at the most immediate and profoundly personal level, and to believe, as Victor did, that he been involved in a fight to the death with them, was shattering. As Crowley says, "I hardly know how we ever got back to Bou Saada."[25]

Over the next two weeks Crowley and Neuburg continued the Calls as they made their way toward Biskra, a desert journey of more than one hundred miles. Some of Crowley's experiences in the Aethyrs were lyrical hymns of beauty and ecstasy, but others seemed full of foreboding—suggesting that he had stumbled into a world for which he was not yet prepared. By the time they reached Biskra on December 16, Crowley knew that he was perilously close to the absolute limit of his powers. Four days later he concluded the final Call. The magical Work was finished. The two men were utterly exhausted, but not by the hardships of the physical journey, which Crowley, at least, found delightful. It was the magical experience that had taken its toll. Those who knew them said that Neuburg "bore the marks of this magical adventure to the grave" and that Crowley, shattered psychologically, never recovered from the ordeal.[26] The two men recuperated in Biskra before returning to Algiers. They sailed for England on the last day of December 1909.

"I, Too, Am the Soul of the Desert"

Although Crowley was casual about the mise-en-scène of the Calls, it is unlikely that the setting for this magical undertaking was mere accident.[27] "Arabia" and the desert held a special significance for him. Crowley reveled in Arab, or, more specifically, Bedouin, culture. After a long day's tramp, he claimed to enjoy nothing more than to join the men of a remote village to while away the night drinking coffee and smoking tobacco or "kif" (hashish). He was already familiar with the effects of a "huqqa . . . laden with maddening cannabis" and felt emancipated by the desert and its society.[28] Crowley acknowledged that, while his spiritual self was at home in China, his "heart and hand are pledged to the Arab."[29] When he spoke of "the Arab," however, his abiding identification was with what he took to be the spirit of desert culture—the strong ties that bound man to man and an existence pared down to the aestheticized essentials. A romanticized ethos of masculinity was one of the aspects of "Arabia" that had particular resonance for him.

A great deal has been written about the European fascination with the desert, the romanticization of the Bedouin, and the creation in travel literature and elsewhere of a particular mythic "Orient."[30] Crowley was not immune to these fictions. Although his firsthand experience of the desert was powerful and direct, his affinity with "the Arab" had a different basis. When he assumed that he had intuitively penetrated the heart of the desert Arab, that he understood at an unspoken level the profound effect on the human spirit of living in unmediated dialogue with what he called the eight genii of the desert, it was because he had read so avidly in the "Arabia Deserta" literature.[31] And if there is a subtext for Crowley's North African adventure—indeed, for all his travels—it is found in the life and work of the Victorian adventurer and explorer Richard Burton.

Burton represented the kind of man Crowley most wished to be—strong, courageous, intrepid, but also a learned scholar-poet and a man who chafed against conventional restraints. His dark, scarred face and satanic aura seemed to suggest knowledge and powers beyond the accepted and acceptable, his exploits in Africa and the Near East were legendary, and his translations of Italian, Latin, Arabic, and Sanskrit texts had introduced a Victorian readership to European and "oriental" folklore and erotica.[32] A man of astonishing breadth and capabilities, Burton was without doubt a model for Crowley. When he undertook his lengthy travels in remote places, Crowley felt that he was "treading, though reverently and afar off, in the footsteps of my boyhood's hero, Richard Francis Burton."[33] He was one of three men to whom Crowley dedicated his *Confessions*: "the perfect pioneer of spiritual and physical adventure."

Crowley aspired to the kind of cultural mastery exhibited in Burton's famous 1853 "pilgrimage" to Mecca, when the explorer, perfectly disguised as a Muslim, had penetrated to the heart of a holy city denied to Europeans. Crowley's flamboyant use of a star sapphire ring during his North African travels with Neuburg was based on Burton's information that the stone was venerated by Muslims. According to Crowley, he put a stop to a coffee-shop brawl by calmly walking into the scrimmage and inscribing magical figures in the air with the ring while intoning a chapter from the Koran: "The fuss stopped instantly, and a few minutes later the original parties to the dispute came to me and begged me to decide between them, for they saw that I was a saint."[34] Although Crowley's account is self-parodying, he was, like Burton, implicated in the imperialist project. Both men rejected the stifling restrictions of Victorian society and, in different ways, sought to dissociate themselves from bourgeois notions of sober, restrained, industrious manhood. Nevertheless, while genuinely revering Arab culture and its peoples, they equally epitomized that unreflective assumption of superiority and desire for mastery that was integral to imperialist endeavors.[35] These issues, however, are complex. In the case of Burton and Crowley, neither a sense of superiority nor the drive for mastery was necessarily equated with the ruthless repression of the feminine that (following Freud) is often associated with accounts of modern masculine subjectivity. If the two men conformed in certain respects to the classic profile of the imperialist, they were also drawn to a culture that could apparently accommodate the expression of the feminine as an intrinsic part of virile masculinity. Imperialism invariably implies a degree of feminization, but Crowley, influenced by Burton, viewed Arab culture as a positive and irresistible blend of the masculine and the feminine.

"El Islam," Richard Burton had noted, "seems purposely to have loosened the ties between the sexes in order to strengthen the bonds which connect man and man."[36] This is suggestive of both the profoundly masculinist society of Crowley's imagination and its mirror image, and Burton was in part responsible for this particular characterization of the East. He had long been fascinated by "oriental" erotica when, late in life, he committed his considerable erudition to paper with the publication of his studies of Eastern pederasty. Through these and other writings, "Arabia" had become synonymous in the European imagination with homosexuality.[37] It is not insignificant that in the year in which Crowley and Neuburg tramped across the desert, T. E. Lawrence—later to be immortalized as Lawrence of Arabia—was undertaking a walking tour in the Middle East, and that rumors concerning Lawrence's homosexuality were linked with his early close relationship with an Arab assistant. It is also relevant that Oscar Wilde and Lord Alfred Douglas had anticipated Crowley's discovery of Algeria and enjoyed all that Algiers had to offer. Indeed, Wilde had arranged for a tremulous André Gide to spend the night with a young male Arab in that city, so confirming for Gide his own sexual identity.[38] For these European men, an apparent acceptance of *le vice contra nature* was part of the lure of the Arab world. Although it went far deeper than that for Crowley, as for Lawrence, the desert signified the expression—often the honorable expression—of a heterodox male sexuality.

Crowley's love of the desert, however, and its relationship to expressive sexuality, was more complex than this. In "The Soul of the Desert," published in 1914, Crowley writes a lyrical paean to the mystical power of this "wilderness of sand."[39] The desert, he says, has the power to strip a man of everything that he has and is, until he must finally stand naked in the face of the elements. So, he writes, "at last the Ego is found alone, unmasked, conscious of itself and of no other thing."[40] There is simply the unreflective consciousness of one who tramps through the dunes. It is this, an uncomplicated acknowledgment of what *is*, that makes it possible to love in the desert "as it is utterly impossible to do in any other conditions."[41] Here, a shared glance, a chosen place in the sand, and "life thrills in sleepy unison; all, all in silence, not names or vows exchanged, but with clean will an act accomplished." "Love itself becomes simple as the rest of life."[42]

This simple love, an effect of the crystallized intensity of desert existence, is a prelude to

> the bodily ecstasy of dissolution, the pang of bodily death, wherein the Ego for a moment that is an aeon loses the fatal consciousness of itself, and becoming one with that of another, foreshadows to itself that greater sacrament of death, when "the spirit returns to God that gave it."[43]

But Crowley goes further. In "The Soul of the Desert," "the wilderness of sand" becomes the figurative realization of an eroticized spirituality. It is equated with an ecstatic experience that far outstrips an orgasmic loss of sense of self—the "little death" of sexual climax. The desert, with its wastes of endless sand, inescapable solitude, and implacable indifference to the miserable struggles of humanity, is parent to the quintessential mystical experience: the dissolution of "the soul . . . into the abounding bliss of God." And, for Crowley, this "dissolution" is synonymous with what he calls here "the annihilation of the Self in Pan." The coded reference to Crowley's relationship with Neuburg, and the sacrificial ceremony undertaken with him on the summit of Da'leh Addin in 1909, is clear. In a marked eroticization of the supremely spiritual, Crowley writes: "Such must be the climax of any [magical] retirement to the desert."[44]

"It Was Like Jekyll and Hyde . . ."

Crowley used *self*, *ego*, and *soul* as interrelated, if not synonymous, terms. Speaking of the "sacrifice" on Mount Da'leh Addin, he could say that every particle of his "personality" was consumed; elsewhere, he talks of "the annihilation of the Self in Pan." Similarly, he writes of that moment of crisis in the desert "when it becomes necessary to penetrate beneath the shadow-show to the secret sanctuary of the soul" and, of that same moment, that "at last the Ego is found alone, unmasked, conscious of itself and of no other thing."[45] It was never Crowley's concern to provide a precise ontology of human identity, and he drew on an eclectic metaphysics when he alluded to the nature of being. Crowley's commentaries, however, suggest that he predicated his experiential sense of self on both an esoteric and a liberal-humanist understanding of a unique individual essence. He understood a good deal about the "shadow-show" of personality pyrotechnics that exemplified the man Aleister Crowley, but he adhered to the notion of a "secret sanctuary of the soul" as a kind of occult shrine of the ultimate "Self." The "moment of crisis in the desert" signifies a stripping away of the layers of the "personality"—a crucial unmasking in preparation for the unveiling of this final "Self."

Crowley was a man who knew all about masks. He delighted in playing with identity. At Cambridge he had become an ardent Jacobite, changing his name from Alexander to Aleister (a misspelling of its Gaelic equivalent), and afterward adopted the spurious persona of Lord Boleskine, a Highland laird. Shortly after his initiation into the Golden Dawn, he had taken a flat in London under the name of Count Vladimir Svareff and enjoyed posing as a young Russian nobleman. In Cairo in 1904 Crowley decided to pass himself off as a Persian prince and became Prince Chioa Khan. While Crowley undertook these experiments in a spirit of fun and adventure, they were also undoubtedly the results of a certain restiveness on Crowley's part over his given position in life. Crowley's wealth and education ensured his social acceptability, but his strict puritanical background and family ties to trade were far removed from his romantic fantasies of aristocratic lineage and lifestyle. Crowley longed to be other than a brewer's son.[46]

These adopted identities, however, were never anything more than a rich man's indulgent fictions. There is no sense, for example, that Crowley lived as Chioa Khan in the same way that both Richard Burton and T. E. Lawrence lived as Arabs. Indeed, this was never his intention. Crowley's impersonation of a Persian prince was simply the occasion for a piece of exotic showmanship, an opportunity to dress up in a series of gorgeous silk robes and swagger about the streets of Cairo. There is no sense in which Crowley experienced himself as traumatically "divided." He did not have Burton's abiding conviction that he was two men, or Lawrence's painful awareness of psychic dissonance in which he literally embodied the dislocation identified in theoretical discussions of masquerade.[47] Crowley's assumption of different identities, was, as he readily acknowledged, mere playacting. He did not experience his various dramatis personae as "selves."

This was not the case with his magical identity. Crowley *was* Perdurabo, and it was as a master magician that he traveled through the timeless Aethyrs of a sixteenth-century magus. The magical self was part of Crowley's concept of selfhood, but in a specific sense. From the time of his initiation into the Golden Dawn, Crowley, like other initiates, gained an understanding of magic as bound up in complex and interrelated ways with the person of the magician and the operation of the magical Will. By 1900 he was experimenting with the conscious movement between two separate selves and had perfected a practice that owed much to Robert Louis Stevenson:

> As a member of the Second Order [of the Golden Dawn], I wore a certain jewelled ornament of gold upon my heart. I arranged that when I had it on, I was to permit no thought, word or action, save such as pertained directly to my magical aspirations. When I took it off I was, on the contrary, to permit no such things; I was to be utterly uninitiate. It was like Jekyll and Hyde, but with the two personalities balanced and complete in themselves.[48]

Crowley's reference to Stevenson's *Strange Case of Dr. Jekyll and Mr. Hyde* is instructive. This highly popular novella, published in 1886, features a respectable doctor who uses his specialized knowledge to create a second self that manifests in his body through a process of startling transformation. The loathsome Mr. Hyde—"the beast Hyde"—is the literal embodiment of everything his creator is not; he is the shadow side of the late-Victorian bourgeois male. Hyde understands nothing of sober self-restraint and freely indulges his craving for unspecified "secret pleasures." The implication that Hyde's nocturnal escapades are sexual as well as violent was clear in the sensational London stage adaptation that opened in August 1888, and W. T. Stead's *Pall Mall Gazette* was quick to link the play with the gruesome Jack the Ripper murders of five prostitutes in London's East End that autumn. In the furor that followed, the play closed.[49]

Dr. Jekyll and Mr. Hyde articulates specific anxieties about bourgeois masculinity. By the 1880s significant cracks had appeared in the conventional formulation of the decent, disciplined, God-fearing gentleman as the epitome of middle-class male respectability. Late-Victorian concerns over prostitution, pornography, venereal disease, the moral welfare of children, and the safety of respectable women on city streets centered on a series of public campaigns that promoted the representation of male sexuality as predatory and dangerous.[50] In the rhetoric of these campaigns, married and single men were equal sources of concern. Indeed, although the marriage bed and supposedly redemptive qualities of pure Victorian womanhood had traditionally been seen as a bulwark against male profligacy, there was a growing sense that marriage merely exposed women to licensed sexual exploitation. An undifferentiated "male lust" accounted for the seemingly endemic spread of "vice," and social purity groups and vigilance committees mobilized throughout the country to combat its influence. Although Stevenson sought to deny any implicit reference to sexuality in his novella, the masculine world it depicts was widely regarded as the setting for a graphic representation of the debased Hyde in Everyman—the vile and murderous debaucher lurking beneath the surface of urbane gentility. The 1888 play made explicit the target of the villain's lusts.

Dr. Jekyll and Mr. Hyde is also centrally concerned, however, with the idea of the divided self and is equally a refiguring of the concept of dual personality that played upon the fin de siècle fascination with duality, fragmentation, and disintegration. In the novella, Dr. Jekyll can speak of his other self, his "devil," only through the disclaimer "he" ("He, I say—I cannot say, I"), while the potion with the power to turn a Jekyll into a Hyde is represented as an assault on "the very fortress of identity."[51] The novella's implied challenge to the notion of a unified self as the single source of identity was echoed elsewhere as the century drew to a close, and this was perhaps particularly marked in contemporary discussion of the human mind. Indeed, there is some indication that Stevenson was familiar with developments in European psychology and that he had been "deeply impressed" by a "scientific" paper he had read in French on "sub-consciousness."[52] The late-Victorian period witnessed an explosion of interest in the uncharted territory of mind and consciousness, and the relationships among mind, body, and sexual pathology. It was exemplified by new approaches in the relatively new field of medical psychology, the pioneering work of sexologists, and the establishment in London of the Society for Psychical Research.[53] In France, the renowned Jean-Martin Charcot was making bold interpretations of the bodily manifestations of psychological states, while Sigmund Freud, who worked with Charcot in the 1880s, was seeking to sever a necessary connection between physical cause and psychological effect. The Society for Psychical Research, which boasted as corresponding members many of the foremost international medical psychologists of the day, followed and participated in these debates in an effort to comprehend more fully the nature of noumenal experience and psychic (in the sense of supernatural or paranormal) phenomena.[54] What these different approaches and agendas had in common was a mutual commitment to understanding the complexities of emotional and psychological experience.

Increasingly, attention was focused on the conundrum of inexplicable bodily symptoms, hysteria, split and multiple personalities, and altered states of consciousness. At the same time, explanatory models that relied for their efficacy on the concept of a single, stable consciousness as the authorial root of behavior and meaning were seen to be outmoded and inadequate.

The mansion of the mind, it seemed, contained many rooms—some of them dark, subterranean, and not easy of access. The mind was revealed to be a labyrinth only parts of which were available to conscious self-scrutiny. This interpretation suggested that the psyche might best be understood in terms of division and fragmentation rather than unitary wholeness. At its most extreme, it proposed that the mind—the seat of conscious identity—exists as a state of perpetual anomie. Whether intended or not, these new areas of research constituted an implied assault on the integrity of the rational autonomous individual.

The founding of the Order of the Golden Dawn coincided with and, I would argue, directly addressed these contemporary concerns. It is surely no accident that the final flowering of the occult revival centrally involved practices such as astral travel, or that advanced magical practice taught adepts how to develop a second magical self that could conduct lengthy forays into worlds that were conceived as simultaneously inner and outer. But while these exercises can be interpreted as remarkable and sustained explorations of the psyche, late nineteenth- and early twentieth-century magicians were not concerned with theorizing the mind. They were absorbed in the magical enterprise, and their conceptual grasp of the endeavor was expressed in these terms. Magicians certainly understood that in pursuing magical knowledge and power they were also undertaking a journey within, but they spoke not of psyche but of Planes and Aethyrs. Magical practice was dedicated to understanding and gaining control of these planes, and adepts were not overly concerned with whether or not such realms had an objective or subjective existence. What mattered was that the magical enterprise could be shared with and verified by other magicians, and its authenticity was judged by the success of the desired outcome. The absolute reality of the experience was accepted without question.

Magical practice sought to develop a powerful and effective second self that would explore the spheres beyond conscious awareness. This second self, however, was not the dissociated personality of Spiritualist mediumship or psychological disorder. When he suggested that the existence of his two selves, the initiate and "uninitiate" personalities, was somehow similar to the divided self of Dr. Jekyll, Crowley was simply acknowledging the relevance of the novella's central theme to magical practice. The key difference for Crowley between himself and Dr. Jekyll lay in the fact that Crowley's "two personalities [were] balanced and complete in themselves." Crowley would also have wished to argue that Perdurabo was no monster. He was an initiated magical self and in no sense represented a personal crisis of identity. The point here is that an experienced magician is in control, through a ritualized series of practices, of the initiated personality; he (or she) can access it at will and hold it in perfect balance with the mundane self. In the true adept, there is no blurring of the line. It is in a magical sense, then, that Crowley acknowledged not one self but (over time) many. And because of his magical training, he did not experience this as a problematic splitting: "It was like Jekyll and Hyde, but with the two personalities balanced and complete in themselves."

As the new century unfolded, Crowley began to combine the conceptual lexicon of magic with insights gleaned from developments in the study of the mind. It seems likely that Crowley had discovered Freud by the time he wrote "The Soul of the Desert" in 1914, in which he refers, as we have seen, to the unmasking of the "Ego." Although this is not conclusive evidence that he understood "Ego" in the strictly Freudian sense—the term was adopted in translations of Freud but had been in use for almost a century to connote the conscious subject and was common currency among occultists—it is the case that by 1914 Freud's ideas had been circulating in England for several years. At all events, in "The Soul of the Desert," Crowley clearly conceptualizes the "Ego" as the "I" (Freud's original "das Ich") that speaks in the name of Aleister Crowley and suggests that this "I" is the tip of the iceberg. By the 1920s, Crowley was using key psychoanalytic concepts and acknowledging that Freudian theory offers confirmation of some of the critical insights of magical practice. Psychoanalysis in no way undermined the credibility of magical practice for Crowley or other like-minded magicians. It merely presents a different narrative of the heroic voyager and the landscape through which he or she travels.[55] Crowley made it plain that he approved of Freud's theorizing of the relationship between the conscious and unconscious, but he emphasized that Freud had arrived at his conclusions somewhat late in the day. According to Crowley, the father of psychoanalysis was simply articulating what magicians had known for centuries.[56]

Erasing the Line in the Sand

It was magical practice rather than psychoanalytic theory that taught Crowley that the apparent coherence of human selfhood is illusory. Although Crowley held to the idea of a hidden essential "Self," a unique core at the heart of the man, magic taught him that the "I" of Aleister Crowley was only one possible self among many. The most terrible lesson that Crowley had to learn, however, and he learned it in the desert, was that it is precisely this "I"—that which apparently secures one's place in the worldly order of things—that must undergo dissolution in the ordeal of the Abyss. Crowley understood the Abyss to be a great gulf fixed between "intelligible intuition" and "the intellect." Other commentators have seen it as "an imaginary gulf" between the real and ideal, or "the gulf existing between individual and cosmic consciousness."[57] As in all magical practice, however, the Abyss can manifest in physical form, the plastic representation of its assumed qualities. But whether understood in symbolic or literal terms, crossing the Abyss involves the final and irrevocable abandonment of the "I" along with its accompanying claim to sole rational authority.

The preamble to confronting the Abyss, and its demonic guardian, Choronzon, is a mental crisis, a "terrible pinnacle of the mind"; to cross the Abyss, "one must abandon utterly and for ever all that one has and is." As Crowley recognized, this is represented in the language of mysticism "as the complete surrender of the self to God"—mystical death as the prerequisite of mystical union; in secular terms, it is "the silencing of the human intellect."[58] Crowley, schooled in the magical tradition, conceptualized both Choronzon and the Abyss as having an external reality, and he made no subsequent attempt to amend this view. In psychoanalytic terms, however, terms that Crowley was later to embrace, it can be said that Choronzon is equally a manifestation of the dark, repressed components of the psyche. In this reading, Choronzon's great resistant cry, "I am I," is simultaneously the magician's last cry of horror and terror as he plunges headlong into the Abyss and the emergent voice of the unknown and unpatrolled unconscious. Characterized by Disintegration, Dispersion, and Chaos, qualities suggestive of the fracturing experience of modernity, the Abyss is both symbolic and real. It is emblematic of breakdown—the breakdown of the personal sense of self as manifested by the ego, the uncoupling of the body from the "I," and the dissolution of everyday consciousness. It marks the formal erasure of the boundary between the conscious and unconscious, an erasure that the future magus must invoke at will. Successful negotiation of the Abyss represents the ultimate test of high adeptship. The magus is one who can establish a harmonious relationship with the unconscious, working with it to achieve "change in conformity with the Will."[59]

The magician who makes a successful crossing of the Abyss is an initiate whose control is so complete that he can embrace personal disintegration, abandoning all knowledge or awareness of the "I," while retaining and asserting the power and authority of the magical self and the magical Will. The adept who emerges from the experience unscathed has confronted and contained the unleashed furies of the unconscious, not via the patrolling maneuvers of the myopic ego but by dint of a second operation—the exercise of an infinitely clear-sighted and all-powerful magical personality unconnected with the personal self. In this telling, the magus is a magical adept who has glimpsed the full implications of his subjectivity. Gone forever is the limiting and limited understanding of the "I" as the finite center of his universe. He has entered the unconscious and acknowledges the permeability of its boundaries. In Crowley's case, he had experienced for himself Choronzon's ability to erase the line in the sand.

The narrative that Crowley presents of the events in the desert is written in the direct language of realism. He does not make a psychoanalytic interpretation of his experience. Crowley deals with the episode as a magical undertaking and represents it as clear evidence that he has achieved enlightened consciousness. He felt that he had first experienced something akin to exalted awareness after the sacrifice at Da'leh Addin: "I knew who I was . . . [but] I did not exist." Crowley understood, in other words, that the "I" is simply a convenient fiction for negotiating one aspect of reality. After his confrontation with Choronzon, Crowley assumed that he had achieved the insights of the true magus, the Master of the Temple:

> I understood that sorrow had no substance; that only my ignorance and lack of intelligence had made me imagine the existence of evil. As soon as I had destroyed my personality, as soon as I had expelled my ego, the universe which to it was indeed a frightful and fatal force, fraught with every form of fear was so only in relation to this idea "I"; so long as "I am I," all else must seem hostile.[60]

As one who had "expelled" his ego and could never again experience anything in the universe as "a frightful and fatal force," Crowley now welcomed each and every new experience with a catholic embrace that refused discrimination. The reckless irresponsibility and amorality of his later behavior is legendary. Crowley increasingly incorporated what he called "repulsive rituals" into his magical practice, and by the 1920s he had secured his reputation as "the king of depravity" and "the wickedest man in the world"—a reputation that included (quite wrongly) a propensity for ritual murder.[61]

Unsympathetic observers take 1909 to be the point at which Crowley finally achieved his true potential and went mad. In magical terms it would be understood as failing to subdue the demon Choronzon and succumbing to his curse. Certainly, Crowley acknowledged that in the aftermath of his 1909 experiences he felt utterly lost and alone; in material terms, too, "it has become constantly more difficult to keep afloat."[62] Increasingly, Crowley seems to have lost a clear sense of the distinction between the enlightened magical self, which can access the unconscious at will and acknowledges no limits, and the man Aleister Crowley, who must still function in the world. Functioning in the world requires a stable sense of personal identity, a well-defined ego, even if that ego is understood to be only part of an infinitely complex story. The magus can move with ease between an initiate and "uninitiate" consciousness, but Crowley's encounter with Choronzon precipitated the blurring of that critical line between the magical self and the temporal "I." Crowley's subsequent behavior suggests, indeed, that he had not made a successful crossing of the Abyss—that he was caught in the grip of unconscious forces that he was unable to filter, monitor, or control. Far from establishing an all-seeing, harmonious relationship with the unconscious, working with it to achieve magical ends, he was now controlled and dominated by the unconscious.[63]

As a self-professed Master of the Temple, Crowley went on to devise a technique for the systematic destruction of the ego, which he regarded as a barrier to magical progress. During the 1920s, followers at his infamous Abbey of Thelema at Cefalù, Sicily, were punished severely if they used the word "I."[64] Crowley's insight was sound, but the technique was flawed. He was seeking to undermine the structural operation by which all meaning, including the sense of a unique, individuated, and gendered self, is produced. There can be no "I" without a clear understanding of that which is not "I," and, as Crowley put it, "so long as 'I am I,' all else must seem hostile." He was pursuing what we might think of as the erasure of difference, and such erasure is a traditional goal of occultism, conceived as moving beyond the conceptual grip of oppositional dualities—I/thou, self/other, male/female. Crowley was attempting to find a shortcut to one of the highest goals of occultism: a return to a lost Eden of wholeness and completion.

The notion of human beings as originally whole and androgynous is a persistent motif of occult and magical traditions. Esoteric teachings refer to a race of such beings who, like the biblical Adam and Eve, existed in the world prior to a tragic Fall. Modern magical practice recognized the occult significance of masculine/feminine complementarity, and the quest for psychic androgyny is one reading of the alchemist's project that advanced members of the Golden Dawn would have understood. Crowley was certainly aware that androgyny had an occult pedigree, and it came to have a particular magical significance for him. In 1904 Crowley had received, at the dictates of an incarnate being whom he referred to as his Holy Guardian Angel, a series of teachings that culminated in what he called *Liber Legis—The Book of the Law*. According to these communications, the world stood on the threshold of a new age—the New Aeon of Horus—the ruling characteristic of which is the unification of the male and female as represented in the androgynous figure of Horus. Although Crowley rejected these teachings at the time, they were to become fundamental to his subsequent development as a magician. Moreover, the image of Horus had a broader cultural significance—one with which Crowley had considerable sympathy.

The androgynous figure, so important in occult teachings, was also an icon of the fin de siècle. The work of Aubrey Beardsley during the 1890s captured the period's fascination with, and fear of, gender ambiguity. His unsettling illustrations for *The Yellow Book* and *The Savoy* quickly became symbols of a perverse sensibility that characterized "the decadence."[65] As discussion of the "woman question" was superseded by talk of the "new woman," and the nation was treated to the spectacle of Oscar Wilde's trial, the 1890s ushered in a range of social and sexual identities that many found deeply disturbing. The "manly woman" and apparently feminized man seemed to critics to be representative of a modern sexual economy marked by the descent into anarchy, androgynous creatures who were symptomatic of a brave new world characterized by perversity and decline.[66] These were fears that an emerging literature that opened up discussion of sexual typologies did nothing to allay. For Crowley, however, the decadent "yellow nineties," typified by the figures of Beardsley and Wilde, were the liberating years of his youth. At twenty-three he had fallen in love with another Cambridge man, Jerome Pollitt, a close friend of Aubrey Beardsley and a talented female impersonator, and in key respects Crowley remained wedded throughout his life to the outlook and modus operandi of the decadent movement.[67] A poseur extraordinaire in the style of Wilde, and a man who set out to replicate in life the dark, wicked, luxurious world of the fictional Dorian Gray, Crowley consistently experimented with the inversion of dominant categories. This was as much the case with his magic as with his own sexuality and gender identity; in each case, and in different but related ways, he played on the "yellow" theme of perverse delinquency. When the New Aeon of Horus beckoned in 1904, Crowley cannot have been altogether unresponsive, for *The Book of the Law* can be read as a hymn to decadence, while androgyny—possibly the ultimate heterodox masculinity—was an attribute that Crowley wished to claim for himself.

Writing in the 1920s, Crowley maintained that he had long held the conviction that he was in certain respects both male and female. Speaking of himself in the third person, a distancing technique reminiscent of Dr. Jekyll's disclaimer,[68] Crowley notes that, while "his masculinity is above the normal," he possesses female characteristics such as slight, graceful limbs and well-developed breasts:

> There is thus a sort of hermaphroditism in his physical structure; and this is naturally expressed in his mind. But whereas, in most similar cases, the feminine qualities appear at the expense of manhood, in him they are added to a perfectly normal masculine type. The principle effect has been to enable him to understand the psychology of women, to look at any theory with comprehensive and impartial eyes, and to endow him with maternal instincts on spiritual planes. . . . He has been able to philosophize about nature from the standpoint of a complete human being; certain phenomena will always be unintelligible to men as such, others, to women as such. He, by being both at once, has been able to formulate a view of existence which combines the positive and the negative, the active and the passive, in a single identical equation. . . . Again and again . . . we shall find his actions determined by this dual structure.[69]

While Crowley is here articulating the gendered categories of masculinity and femininity in essentialist terms, also an aspect of traditional occult philosophy, he conceives of himself as embodying a beneficial "dual structure": he is "both at once." Physical "hermaphroditism" is therefore replicated in terms of gender and represented as giving him the privileged insight of "a complete human being." Crowley maintained that his "dual structure" enabled him to act in the world and "philosophize" about it with an unusual degree of acuity and success. Furthermore, this "dual structure" extended to Crowley's sexual identity. He was flagrantly bisexual. There was no shortage of women in Crowley's life, and the Crowley mythology paints him as a tender and inventive lover. He was, in fact, prey to powerful and contradictory attitudes toward women, but these remained largely unacknowledged. Crowley believed that he was irresistible and that his success as a heterosexual lover was due to his unique ability to express (an again essentialized) "savage male passion to create" modified by a "feminine" gentleness.[70] Bisexuality is not the same as "hermaphroditism" or androgyny, but in Crowley's mind his sexuality was yet another expression of the wholeness implied by his "being both at once."

There is every indication that Victor Neuburg shared this view and that he applied it to himself. In a long poem in the *Triumph of Pan*, a collection published in 1910 that incorporates a complex amalgam of personal and magical references, Neuburg writes: "O thou hast sucked my soul, lord of my nights and days, / My body, pure and whole, is merged within the ways / That lead to thee, my queen, who gav'st life to me / When all my heart was green."[71] These lines, addressed to Pan, contain an element of Crowley's relationship to Neuburg—he is both "lord" and "queen"—that must form at least a subtext for the poem if not the collection. Similarly, there can be little doubt about Neuburg's meaning in the title poem: "there is a Great One, cold and burning, / Crafty and hot in lust, / Who would make me a Sapphist and an Urning, / A Lesbian of the dust."[72] Whether or not the "Great One" is Crowley, it is clear that Neuburg experienced his spirituality as a sexualized (or bisexualized) "Sapphist" and "Urning." The use of the term *Urning* gives a specific clue to Neuburg's thinking. The term, familiar from Plato's *Symposium*, had been adopted by Karl Heinrich Ulrichs half a century earlier in his discussion of homosexuality, and it reappeared in a book that greatly influenced Neuburg, Edward Carpenter's *The Intermediate Sex* (London, 1908). A great admirer of Carpenter, who had himself been influenced by Eastern religion and philosophy, and perhaps particularly taken with the suggestion that homosexuality might represent a new evolutionary form, Neuburg apparently absorbed the discussion of what Carpenter calls the "doubleness of nature"—the feminine soul trapped within the male body, and vice versa. In *The Triumph of Pan*, however, Neuburg reworks it, combining contemporary discussions of homosexuality with the enduring motif of the hermaphrodite. When he positions himself in his poem as both woman-desiring woman and man-desiring man, Neuburg is claiming a radically different "hermaphroditism": two "inversions" "at once."

Crowley, on the other hand, experienced his bisexuality in classic psychoanalytic terms as "the coincidence of two heterosexual desires within a single psyche."[73] This meant that, as a desiring man, Crowley gave vent to what he took to be the ultimate expression of masculinity—the (albeit modified) "savage male passion to create"; as a desiring woman, he sought to become the beautiful object of that "savage male passion." He often used the name Alys (a feminized form of Aleister) to signify his femininity and, as Alys, adopted what he thought of as the feminine sexual role. In his relationship with Victor Neuburg, Crowley assumed the subject position of a desiring woman. In doing so, however, he was caught up in a fantasy that went far beyond the receptive "feminine." As the object of male desire, Crowley was in thrall to a scenario marked by orgiastic violation. This was exemplified in his relationship with Neuburg by the central importance assumed by the god Pan—"'All devourer, all begetter'"; to know "Panic" is to experience both ecstasy and terror at the hand of the god.[74] Pan, representative of a pagan Greece that had special significance for Victorian homosexual men, and long associated in the Christian imagination with the devil, was a powerful signifier of the sexualized magic initiated by the two men.[75] When Crowley and Neuburg speak of Pan, the imagery is redolent with heat and violence: a god, half man, half beast, who rapes and ravishes men and women alike. Crowley, who in his younger years had feared and sought to avoid pain, actively recruited it as a woman. And as a desiring woman, Crowley acted out a fantasy in which he became the recipient of his own unrecognized hostility toward women. If his "dual structure" consistently modified the sadistic impulses of his masculine sexuality, it also facilitated—like the great circle of loose rocks at Da'leh Addin—a kind of closure. In a dual identification, he became the sacrificial object of his own desires.

The "sacrifice" at Da'leh Addin, during which Crowley experienced "the annihilation of the Self in Pan" and consummation with "that primal and final breath . . . of God," in fact represents a primal scene of considerable significance. It is one in which an erotic investment in pain and desecration, an investment that increasingly figured in the "repulsive rituals" of his magical practice, was played out in vivid tandem with fantasies of bestiality and male rape. The strong masochistic element that ran through his various sexual identifications, and that Crowley recognized as a constituent element of both his masculinity and his femininity, reached its apotheosis in the sacrificial moment.[76] But the "sacrifice" equally marks that elision of identifications, magical and mundane, upon which the Crowley–Neuburg relationship endlessly turned. For just as Crowley could insist that Neuburg, in one incarnation the savage god, was equally a "masochist" and a "pederast," so, too, Neuburg experienced Crowley, his seemingly feminized lover, as a "homo-sexual sadist." It is likely that Crowley's expressive femininity had little to do with the apparent powerlessness it celebrated. A sexual scene dominated by the elaboration of a rape fantasy was probably directed and controlled, like everything else in their relationship, by Crowley himself. Crowley glosses the ritual on the mountain with the simple comment: "There I sacrificed myself." Both active and passive, avowal and disavowal, he who sacrifices and he who is sacrificed, Crowley acknowledges the ambiguity of the covenant. And in a final significant move of disavowal and displacement, he closes the account with: "There was an animal in the wilderness, but it was not I."[77]

Crowley's is a Manichaean vision in which the principles of light and darkness do eternal battle, and in which supreme magical attainments are inextricably bound up with a "savage" bestiality. He is the enlightened magus and the "animal in the wilderness," "both at once . . . in a single identical equation." After crossing the Abyss in 1909, Crowley finally accepted *The Book of the Law*, and with it his destiny as the prophet of Horus. As such, Crowley took the title of the Beast 666, "the beast" of the book of Revelation with whom he had identified since childhood. His acceptance of this designation, celebrated in Neuburg's *Triumph of Pan*, and which in occult circles is synonymous with Crowley's name, marked a new phase in his magical Work.[78] Pain, blood, and excrement became the trademarks of Crowley's "repulsive rituals," and his followers were obliged to wear upon their bodies "the Mark of the Beast."[79] As lurid tales of his exploits at the Abbey of Thelema began to emerge in the 1920s, the popular press denounced Crowley as a devil-worshipping "human beast."[80] In an ironic reversal of his own earlier conception of his "two personalities," Crowley came to personify in the public imagination a kind of slavering, animalistic Mr. Hyde. He was transformed into the monstrous creature of Crowley legend, a black magician of mythic status whose demonic persona was reminiscent of W. T. Stead's Jack the Ripper—the sadistic murderer with an eroticized and "uncontrollable taste for blood."[81] Crowley had become the modern representative of a fin de siècle "cult of the beast," the monster howling at the dark side of the moon.[82]

In this chapter, I have presented one aspect of my broader discussion of the multidimensional relationship between fin de siècle ritual magic and key contemporary concerns. The analysis of Aleister Crowley's magical Work in the desert is part of the argument I make for magical practice as an important if unorthodox articulation of what we have come to understand as a modern sense of self. Certainly, one reading of Crowley's North African experience is that advanced ritual magic invited a radical "modernist" decentering of the subject, even as it pursued the occult goal of repairing a split and divided self.[83] Crowley's experiment equally indicates, however, that magical practice, with its supposedly timeless procedures and "truths," was both an intensely personal and a culturally specific enterprise. Crowley might have been Perdurabo, a master magician who explored the conceptual universe of a sixteenth-century magus, but he clearly brought *himself* to that endeavor. Perdurabo was the magical personality of an early twentieth-century middle-class man with very specific proclivities whose reworking of past magical practice was in constant dialogue with the concerns of the present. In magical terms, Crowley's Work was fatally flawed precisely because he was finally unable to distinguish between the magical self and the temporal "I." Nevertheless, whatever we might make of the magical episteme, it would be difficult to deny that the "two personalities" are in some way constitutive of the particular historical actor. The magus was the man.

I have sought to argue here that Crowley's magical Work, flawed or otherwise, represented a self-conscious engagement with the self in all of its complexity, recognized and unrecognizable, known and unknown. And as such, it has important implications for those of us who are concerned with historicizing the theoretical concept of subjectivity. The episode in the desert suggests that the magical self—created through the erasure of psychic boundaries and the unraveling of the processes through which the "I" is constituted—might represent the expression of a *fully realized*, historically contingent subjectivity. It is certainly clear that Crowley's magical exploration of the Aethyrs undertaken in the name of Perdurabo was simultaneously a direct interrogation of the undisclosed phenomena of the personal self. The displaced "I" of the magus was nevertheless expressive of a historicized self, and Crowley's experiences in the desert involved the display of unconscious elements as specific and theatrical as anything created by Robert Louis Stevenson. His magical Work was intrinsically bound up with the enactment of fears, hostilities, and desires that circulated around the expression of a rogue bourgeois masculinity. Certainly, the subtext of Crowley's account of events in the desert is a narrative of self that exceeds the exoteric revelations of his *Confessions*. Whatever the merits and demerits of Crowley's magical Work, his struggles in the desert—symbolized by the "sacrifice" at Da'leh Addin, the encounter with Choronzon, and that final despairing cry, "I am I"—signified an extraordinary attempt on the part of this Edwardian bourgeois to understand the full implications of his own subjectivity. This also suggests that the "magical tradition" and its teachings might indeed be characterized, as Crowley maintained, as the "table from which Freud . . . ate of a few crumbs that fell."[84]

Notes

This essay first appeared in the *Journal of British Studies* 36 (January 1997), pp. 99–133, and constitutes the basis for a chapter in Alex Owen, *The Place of Enchantment: British Occultism and the Culture of the Modern* (Chicago: University of Chicago Press, 2004).

1. There has been little scholarly historical treatment of modern European ritual magic, its place within nineteenth-century occultism, or its relationship to broader social and cultural themes. This is undoubtedly due in part to the arcane nature of much magical material, the traditional secrecy surrounding magical orders, and the difficulties involved in accessing reliable sources. The situation, however, is changing. The publication of some revered and secret Victorian material (see, for example, Israel Regardie, *The Complete Golden Dawn System of Magic* [Phoenix,

Ariz.: Falcon Press, 1984]) and the acquisition of private collections by research institutes and libraries are making the study of modern magic more manageable. Following the second occult revival of the 1960s, a number of general books appeared on magic. These were often the work of informed occultists. See, for example, Francis King, *Modern Ritual Magic: The Rise of Western Occultism* (1970; Bridport, England: Prism Press, 1989). More recently, new scholarly work on Western esotericism considers the spiritual and hermetic traditions of which ritual magic is a part. See, for example, Antoine Faivre, "Ancient and Medieval Sources of Modern Esoteric Movements," in *Modern Esoteric Spirituality*, ed. Antoine Faivre and Jacob Needleman (New York: Crossroad, 1992); Antoine Faivre, *Access to Western Esotericism* (Albany: State University of New York Press, 1994); and Roelof van den Broek and Wouter J. Hanegraaff, eds., *Gnosis and Hermeticism from Antiquity to Modern Times* (Albany: State University of New York Press, 1998). In *The Place of Enchantment: British Occultism and the Culture of the Modern* (Chicago: University of Chicago Press, 2004), I consider ritual magic centrally as intrinsic to elite British occultism at the end of the nineteenth century.

2. Long neglected as an area of scholarly study, modern occultism has received relatively scant treatment at the hands of historians. Again, recent studies have begun to rectify the situation, and there is growing interest in British, European (including Russian), and American movements. British studies include Ruth Brandon, *The Spiritualists: The Passion for the Occult in the Nineteenth and Twentieth Centuries* (New York: Prometheus Books, 1983); Diana Burfield, "Theosophy and Feminism: Some Explorations in Nineteenth Century Biography," in *Women's Religious Experience*, ed. Pat Holden (London: Barnes & Noble, 1983); Janet Oppenheim, *The Other World: Spiritualism and Psychical Research in England, 1850–1914* (Cambridge: Cambridge University Press, 1985); Logie Barrow, *Independent Spirits: Spiritualism and English Plebeians, 1850–1910* (London: Routledge & Kegan Paul, 1986); Alex Owen, *The Darkened Room: Women, Power, and Spiritualism in Late Victorian England* (London: Virago Press, 1989; Chicago: University of Chicago Press, 2004); Jenny Hazelgrove, *Spiritualism and British Society between the Wars* (Manchester: Manchester University Press, 2000); Joy Dixon, *Divine Feminine: Theosophy and Feminism in England* (Baltimore: Johns Hopkins University Press, 2001); and Owen, *The Place of Enchantment*.

3. The history of the Rosicrucian tradition is a vexed one, but we know that a Rosicrucian masonic order, the Societas Rosicruciana in Anglia, was founded in England in 1865. Its membership was involved in the formation of the Hermetic Order of the Golden Dawn, to which this chapter subsequently refers. The term *Rosicrucian* derives from the name "Rosencreutz" or "Rose Cross." "Christian Rosencreutz" first makes his appearance in the so-called Rosicrucian manifestos, two short pamphlets the titles of which are usually abbreviated as the *Fama* and the *Confessio*, which were published at Cassel in 1614 and 1615. A third pamphlet, translated from the German as *The Chemical Wedding of Christian Rosencreutz*,

was published in 1616. Frances A. Yates, *The Rosicrucian Enlightenment* (London: Routledge & Kegan Paul, 1972), suggests that the seventeenth-century Rosicrucian movement was in part an allegory for a renewed "general reformation" based on a strengthened Protestant alliance with Frederick V, Elector Palatine of the Rhine, at its center. I am indebted to her account, and to her explication of the Renaissance Hermetic tradition in *Giordano Bruno and the Hermetic Tradition* (Chicago: University of Chicago Press, 1964). For an account of Rosicrucianism written by an occultist scholar and early member of the Hermetic Order of the Golden Dawn, see Arthur E. Waite, *Brotherhood of the Rosy Cross* (London: William Rider and Son, 1924). For more recent studies, see Roland Edighoffer, *Les Rose-Croix* (Paris: Presses universitaires de France, 1982; 5th ed., 2005); Roland Edighoffer, *Les Rose-Croix et la crise de conscience européenne au XVIIe siècle* (Paris: Dervy, 1998); Christopher McIntosh, *The Rose Cross and the Age of Reason: Eighteenth-Century Rosicrucianism in Central Europe and Its Relationship to the Enlightenment* (Leiden: E. J. Brill, 1992); Tobias Churton, *The Golden Builders: Alchemists, Rosicrucians, and the First Free Masons* (Lichfield, England: Signal, 2002).

4. The vast body of literature ascribed to Hermes Trismegistus, thought by the Renaissance magi to be an ancient Egyptian priest, was probably the work of various unknown Greek authors. Isaac Casaubon (1559–1614) revealed the Hermetic writings to be more modern in origin, and scholars currently assume dates ranging from 100 to 300 C.E. See Garth Fowden, *The Egyptian Hermes* (Cambridge: Cambridge University Press, 1986); Yates, *Giordano Bruno*, 2–3; Anthony Grafton, *Defenders of the Text* (Cambridge, Mass.: Harvard University Press, 1991), 163.
5. Several reliable and relatively recent studies of the Hermetic Order of the Golden Dawn have helped to throw light on its organizational structure and membership. Particularly valuable, because they include or draw upon privately printed and unpublished sources and are written by scholarly enthusiasts (rather than enthusiastic occultists), are Ellic Howe, *The Magicians of the Golden Dawn: A Documentary History of a Magical Order, 1887–1923* (London: Routledge & Kegan Paul, 1972); R. A. Gilbert, *The Golden Dawn: Twilight of the Magicians* (Wellingborough, England: Aquarian Press, 1983); R. A. Gilbert, *The Golden Dawn Companion: A Guide to the History, Structure, and Workings of the Hermetic Order of the Golden Dawn* (Wellingborough, England: Aquarian Press, 1986). Scholarship on W. B. Yeats has been enormously helpful in unraveling the complexities of the Golden Dawn and contextualizing it in literary and intellectual terms; see, for an early influential example, George Mills Harper, *Yeats's Golden Dawn* (London: Macmillan, 1974).
6. The Second Order was established in 1892 and had a different name: Ordo Roseae Rubeae at Aureae Crucis (the Red Rose and the Cross of Gold). For the sake of clarity, however, I will follow the usual practice of referring to both orders as the Order of the Golden Dawn.

7. For discussion of fin de siècle French magic/occultism, which was much less "respectable" in tone, see Christopher McIntosh, *Eliphas Lévi and the French Occult Revival* (New York: Samuel Weiser, 1972); Robert Pincus-Witten, *Occult Symbolism in France: Joséphin Péladan and the Salons de la Rose-Croix* (New York: Garland, 1976).
8. Aleister Crowley, *The Confessions of Aleister Crowley*, ed. John Symonds and Kenneth Grant (London: Arkana, 1989), 626. Crowley wrote or dictated what he called his "autohagiography" during the 1920s, and it first appeared in edited form in the late 1960s. Crowley's reference to horns is, as we shall see, significant. His statement here is typical. Although he was writing tongue in cheek, he enjoyed a joke at Neuburg's expense, and probably did order the younger man to shave his head.
9. John Dee (1527–1608) recorded these experiences in his spiritual diary, published by Meric Casaubon in 1659 as *A True and Faithful Relation of what passed for many years between Dr. John Dee . . . and some spirits . . .* (London, 1659). Dee's system, often referred to as the Book of Enoch, exists in manuscript form in the British Museum, Sloane MSS. 3189. It was, as we shall see, understood and taught by senior adepts of the Golden Dawn. Agrippa's "Ziruph Tables" appear in his *De occulta philosophia*, III, 24, first published in 1533. See Yates, *Giordano Bruno*, 130–56. For a recent study, see Deborah E. Harkness, *John Dee's Conversations with Angels: Cabala, Alchemy, and the End of Nature* (Cambridge: Cambridge University Press, 1999).
10. The Golden Dawn followed Eliphas Lévi, the French occultist, in referring to planes other than the physical as the Astral Light. The term has a somewhat different meaning from the "astral plane" of the Theosophists. See King, *Modern Ritual Magic*, 56.
11. Crowley, *The Confessions*, 616.
12. Ibid. Crowley provides an early description of the Aethyrs (presumably based upon Neuburg's notes and his own memory) in "The Vision and the Voice," *The Equinox* I (5), special supplement (March 1911), 1–176. He asked Israel Regardie to prepare a full manuscript version in 1929, and the subsequent published edition is based on this manuscript together with Regardie's introduction. See Aleister Crowley, *The Vision and the Voice* (Dallas, Tex.: Sangreal Foundation, 1972). *The Vision and the Voice* is precisely that: a record of Crowley's visions in the Aethyrs, and of the voices he heard there.
13. Crowley, *The Confessions*, 619.
14. Ibid., 621.
15. See Ethel Archer, *The Hieroglyph* (London: Denis Archer, 1932). This loosely autobiographical novel provides compelling portraits of Crowley and Neuburg during the pre-1914 period. Archer's descriptions of Newton in the novel reflect the general observations about Neuburg. They emphasize his infectious "irresponsible" laughter, youthful features, and "faunlike" appearance. Neuburg retained a fay, elfin quality throughout his life.

16. Crowley, *The Confessions*, 621. *The Vision and the Voice*, 134, n. 9, gives scant details of the "sacrifice." See also Jean Overton Fuller, *The Magical Dilemma of Victor Neuburg* (London: W. H. Allen, 1965), 154–55. Fuller knew Neuburg during the 1930s, and her book (while not always accurate about the occult) is an invaluable source of biographical information. Crowley and Neuburg went on to perfect a form of homosexual magical Working before their final bitter separation in 1914. See also note 75 below.
17. Crowley, *The Confessions*, 621.
18. Crowley, *The Vision and the Voice*, 153.
19. John Symonds, *The King of the Shadow Realm: Aleister Crowley, His Life and Magic* (London: Duckworth, 1989), 118, notes that this is the only recorded instance of a magician seating himself within the triangle during an evocation. If Crowley really knew what he was doing, he must also have known that in magical terms he was taking a tremendous risk. He was inviting obsession by the demon. Crowley is cautious about revealing his exact position, perhaps not wanting others to emulate him, but it is clear from *The Vision and the Voice* that he was indeed inside the triangle.
20. Crowley, *The Vision and the Voice*, 161. The phrase "I am I" has a biblical resonance, but it was also used in Madame Blavatsky's *The Key to Theosophy* to connote "the true individuality" (as opposed to the temporal personality) of a human being. Although Crowley did not adhere consistently to a Theosophical understanding of the self, he would certainly have been familiar with Blavatsky's work. See H. P. Blavatsky *The Key to Theosophy* (1889; London: Theosophical Publishing House, 1968), 33–34.
21. Crowley, *The Vision and the Voice*, 162.
22. Crowley, *The Confessions*, 623.
23. This name had tremendous significance for Crowley. Its symbolism is complex, but the spelling is an adaptation of the name of the Babylon of the Apocalypse as given to him in *The Book of the Law* (London, 1938). Crowley later recognized BABALON as the feminine or androgynous equivalent of Pan. The name was synonymous for him with the biblical Scarlet Woman, the title later bestowed upon his most important female lovers and magical consorts.
24. Crowley, *The Confessions*, 623.
25. Ibid., 624.
26. Israel Regardie, *The Eye in the Triangle: An Interpretation of Aleister Crowley* (Las Vegas: Falcon, 1989), 409–10.
27. The quotation used as the heading for this section comes from Aleister Crowley, "The Soul of the Desert," *Occult Review* 20 (July–December 1914), 18. The full citation reads: "'I, too, am the Soul of the Desert; thou shall seek me yet again in the wilderness of sand.'—*Liber LXV*. v. 61." This is a reference to Crowley's *Liber LXV, The Book of the Heart girt with the Serpent* (London, 1909–10).
28. Aleister Crowley, *The Scented Garden of Abdullah the Satirist of Shiraz* (1910; Chicago: Teitan Press, 1991), 117. Crowley had experimented with hashish since

1906 and had discovered that controlled use could "push introspection to the limit." He wrote and later published "The Herb Dangerous—(Part 2): The Psychology of Hashish," *The Equinox* I (2) (September 1909), 31–89, in which he records his views. See also Crowley, *The Confessions*, 586.

29. Crowley, *The Confessions*, 587.
30. The milestone text in this fast-developing genre is Edward Said's *Orientalism* (New York: Vintage Books, 1978), but earlier commentators were not slow to recognize the construction of a particular "Arabia" in the writings of explorers and travelers. See, for example, Ahmad 'Abd Allah and T. Compton Pakenham, *Dreamers of Empire* (London: Harrap, 1930); R. H. Kiernan, *The Unveiling of Arabia* (London: Harrap, 1937); Thomas J. Assad, *Three Victorian Travellers: Burton, Blount, Doughty* (London: Routledge & Kegan Paul, 1964); Michael Foss, "Dangerous Guides: English Writers and the Desert," *New Middle East* 9 (June 1969), 38–42; Peter Brent, *Far Arabia: Explorers of the Myth* (London: Weidenfeld & Nicolson, 1977).
31. The phrase is taken from Charles M Doughty, *Travels in Arabia Deserta* (Cambridge, 1888). The eight genii, according to Crowley, were Sun, Space, Wind, Water, Earth, Fire, Wood, and Moon. See Crowley, "The Soul of the Desert," 21.
32. Richard Burton (1821–1890) was the author of numerous books, and toward the end of his life he concentrated increasingly on the translation and publication for private circulation of erotica. His works include *Personal Narrative of a Pilgrimage to El-Medinah and Meccah*, 3 vols. (London, 1855–56); *Wanderings in West Africa*, 2 vols. (London, 1863); *Unexplored Syria* (with Charles F. Tyrwhitt-Drake), 2 vols. (London, 1872); *The Kama Sutra of Vatsyayana*, trans. with F. F. Arbuthnot (Cosmopoli [London?], 1883); *A Plain and Literal Translation of the Arabian Nights' Entertainments*, 10 vols. (Benares, 1885–88); and *The Perfumed Garden of the Cheikh Nefzaoui*, trans. from the French (Cosmopoli [London?], 1886).
33. Crowley, *The Confessions*, 461.
34. Ibid., 626.
35. Edward Said's reading of Burton as a man who preferred Eastern life and culture while retaining an abiding commitment to the concept of empire is applicable to Crowley. See Said, *Orientalism*, 196–97.
36. Richard Burton, *First Footsteps in East Africa* (London, 1856), 38; quoted in Fawn M. Brodie, *The Devil Rides: A Life of Sir Richard Burton* (New York: W. W. Norton, 1967), 105.
37. See Burton's "Terminal Essay" in the *Arabian Nights' Entertainments* (1885). The manuscript on which he was working at the time of his death, *The Scented Garden*, was a new translation (this time from the original Arabic) of *The Perfumed Garden*. The projected publication was to include a previously omitted chapter on homosexuality. The themes of homosexuality and castration with which Burton was dealing greatly upset his wife, and she destroyed the manuscript after his death.
38. See Jonathan Dollimore, *Sexual Dissidence: Augustine to Wilde, Freud to Foucault* (Oxford: Oxford University Press, 1991), 3–6.

39. Crowley, "The Soul of the Desert," 18.
40. Ibid., 23.
41. Crowley, *The Confessions*, 655.
42. Crowley, "The Soul of the Desert," 22–23.
43. Ibid., 23.
44. Ibid., 23–24. By "magical retirement," Crowley means a magical retreat—a period devoted to magical practice and spiritual introspection. This was how he viewed the 1909 experiences.
45. Crowley, *The Confessions*, 627–28; and "The Soul of the Desert," 23.
46. Alexander, later Aleister, Crowley (1875–1947) was born to Edward and Emily Crowley, Plymouth Brethren of the strictest kind. The family fortune had been made in the brewery trade, but Edward Crowley had long since removed himself from direct involvement with the business. The Crowley family lived a retired, respectable life, and, until his death in 1887, Edward Crowley devoted himself to preaching.
47. See Mary Ann Doane, "Film and Masquerade: Theorising the Female Spectator," *Screen* 23, nos. 3/4 (1982), 74–87. Doane draws on Joan Riviere, "Womanliness as a Masquerade," in *Formations of Fantasy*, ed. Victor Burgin, James Donald, and Cora Kaplan (London: Routledge Kegan & Paul, 1986), 35–44. See, with particular reference to T. E. Lawrence, Kaja Silverman, "White Skin, Brown Masks: The Double Mimesis, or With Lawrence in Arabia," *Differences* 1, no. 5 (1989), 3–54. It is interesting to note that, while the relationships of Crowley, Burton, and Lawrence to imposture and disguise are different, all three men had vested interests in masking their origins and their uncertain social positions.
48. Crowley, *The Confessions*, 204. Denied entry to the Second Order by the London adepts, Crowley had been initiated in Paris by the Golden Dawn's "Chief," S. L. MacGregor Mathers, who was at odds with the London leadership.
49. Judith R. Walkowitz, *City of Dreadful Delight: Narratives of Sexual Danger in Late-Victorian London* (Chicago: University of Chicago Press, 1992), 206–8, discusses W. T. Stead's journalistic approach to the Ripper crimes and his use of Jekyll and Hyde "as a psychological model of the murderer."
50. For a discussion of these issues, see Edward J. Bristow, *Vice and Vigilance: Purity Movements in Britain since 1700* (Dublin: Rowman & Littlefield, 1977); Judith R. Walkowitz, *Prostitution and Victorian Society: Women, Class, and the State* (New York: Cambridge University Press, 1980); Frank Mort, *Dangerous Sexualities: Medico-Moral Politics in England since 1830* (London: Routledge & Kegan Paul, 1987). Walkowitz, in *City of Dreadful Delight*, is concerned with the narrative expression of the concept of sexual danger and engages in a detailed discussion of the contradictory implications of Stead's crusade against child prostitution.
51. Robert Louis Stevenson, *The Strange Case of Dr. Jekyll and Mr. Hyde, and Other Stories*, ed. Jenni Calder (Harmondsworth: Penguin Books, 1979), 94, 83; cited in a helpful discussion to which I am indebted: Stephen Heath, "Psychopathia Sexualis:

Stevenson's *Strange Case*," in *Futures for English*, ed. Colin MacCabe (Manchester: Palgrave Macmillan, 1988), 96, 97. Heath notes that the initial definite article was absent from the title of the novella in its first edition.

52. Stevenson's wife made this observation in connection with *Dr. Jekyll and Mr. Hyde*. See Heath, "Psychopathia Sexualis," 106, n. 8.

53. Sexology was introduced in Britain by Havelock Ellis's seven-volume work *Studies in the Psychology of Sex* (vol. 1, London, 1897; published as a set, Philadelphia, 1910) and by Dr. Richard von Krafft-Ebing's *Psychopathia Sexualis: With Especial Reference to Contrary Sexual Instinct; A Medico-Legal Study* (Stuttgart, 1886; trans. Philadelphia and London, 1892), which was published in the same year as *Dr. Jekyll and Mr. Hyde*. The Society for Psychical Research was founded in 1882 and led by a group of highly educated individuals, most of whom were Oxbridge men. Its goal was the scrupulous and impartial investigation of paranormal phenomena. The society was extremely interested in Spiritualist mediumship as a possible guide to the unknown power of the mind. One of its leaders, Frederic Myers, postulated a "subliminal consciousness" and "subliminal self" as the key to understanding so-called spirit communications and manifestations. See Alan Gauld, *The Founders of Psychical Research* (London: Schocken Books, 1968), 275–312; Oppenheim, *The Other World*, 249–66. For discussion of the relationship between Myers's ideas and those of occultists, see Owen, *The Place of Enchantment*, 174–82.

54. See J.-M. Charcot, *Leçons du Mardi à la Salpêtrière, Policlinique du Mars, 1889* (Paris: 1889), and *Lectures on the Diseases of the Nervous System*, trans. George Sigerson (London, 1887). Charcot drew attention to the sexual nature of hysterical body language with his infamous "arc en cercle"—the orgasmic paroxysm of a major hysterical convulsion. Freud further developed the connection between hysteria and the sexual, drawing attention to the manifestation of physical symptoms as a language of sexuality. Havelock Ellis and Frederic Myers (of the Society for Psychical Research) were among the first to introduce Freud's work to Britain during the 1890s.

55. Joy Dixon, "Sexology and the Occult: Sexuality and Subjectivity in Theosophy's New Age," *Journal of the History of Sexuality* 7, no. 3 (1997), 426, makes the point that members of the Theosophical Society also claimed that Freud merely presented in modern and materialistic terms centuries-old occult insights. One of the leading magically trained exponents of the psychoanalytic perspective was Dr. Francis Israel Regardie (1907–1985), who studied with Crowley as a young man. Regardie was expert in both Freudian and Jungian approaches and became a lay analyst. He applied the insights of psychoanalysis to magical practice but adhered to a belief in the efficacy of magic. Regardie's book *The Eye in the Triangle* offers a Freudian (oedipal) interpretation of Crowley's visions in the desert.

56. Crowley's *Confessions*, written during the early 1920s, is full of references to psychoanalysis, but, in typical fashion, Crowley thought that he understood "the Freudian position" better than Freud (72). Freud, who was a corresponding member of the

Society for Psychical Research, was interested in the occult and once remarked in a letter to Hereward Carrington that had he been able to live his life again he would have devoted it to psychical research. See Ernest Jones, *Sigmund Freud: Life and Work* (London: Hogarth Press, 1957), 3:419–20. The Freud-Ferenczi correspondence makes it clear that both men were thinking about the possible significance of occult phenomena during the early twentieth century, somewhat earlier than previously had been thought to be the case. See *The Correspondence of Sigmund Freud and Sandor Firenczi*, vol. 1, 1908–14, trans. Peter D. Hoffer, ed. Eva Brabant, Ernst Falzeder, and Patrizia Giampieri-Deutsch (Cambridge. Mass.: Belknap Press of Harvard University Press, 1994).

57. Crowley, *The Confessions*, 590; Regardie, *The Eye in the Triangle*, 329; John Symonds and Kenneth Grant, in Crowley, *The Confessions*, 929, n. 1.
58. Crowley, *The Confessions*, 515, 510.
59. [Aleister Crowley], *Magick in Theory and Practice* (Paris, 1929), xvi.
60. Aleister Crowley, *The Confessions*, 624.
61. *John Bull*, March 10, 1923, and March 24, 1923; cited in Gerald Suster, *The Legacy of the Beast: The Life, Work, and Influence of Aleister Crowley* (London: W. H. Allen, 1988), 84–85. Sensationalized accounts of Crowley's Abbey of Thelema in Sicily were appearing in the popular press during this period. The Abbey of Thelema, established in 1920, operated until 1923, when Crowley was expelled from Italy by Mussolini. Its byword, painted above the door, was the Rabelaisian "Do What Thou Wilt." This was taken from Crowley's *The Book of the Law*: "There is no law beyond Do what thou wilt."
62. Crowley, *The Confessions*, 921; see also 628, 661. Crowley had burned through his considerable fortune by his mid-thirties and thereafter was forced to rely on his wits and the support of admirers.
63. Symonds, *The King of the Shadow Realm*, x, states that if he had to write Crowley's epitaph, it would be "Aleister Crowley, 1875–1947. He delivered the psychotic goods." Symonds, well versed in the ways of magic and encyclopedic on the subject of Crowley, does not accept Crowley's estimate of his own magical attainments.
64. See ibid., 287–88.
65. The classic exposition of "the decadence" is presented in Holbrook Jackson, *The Eighteen Nineties: A Review of Art and Ideas at the Close of the Nineteenth Century* (1913; Atlantic Highlands, N.J.: Humanities Press, 1976). For Jackson, *The Yellow Book* and *The Savoy*, both new periodicals of the mid-1890s, encapsulated the spirit of fin de siècle decadence. Beardsley was art editor for *The Yellow Book* before moving on to *The Savoy*.
66. See Elaine Showalter, *Sexual Anarchy: Gender and Culture at the Fin de Siècle* (New York: Viking Press, 1990).
67. Pollitt, whom Crowley met at Cambridge, performed as Diane de Rougy, a character based on the actress Liane de Pougy. It is noteworthy that Crowley, mindful of the Wilde trial, was keen to defend Pollitt against accusations of "a tendency to

androgynity." See Crowley, *The Confessions*, 144. Crowley later immortalized Pollitt in his tribute to homosexual love (also a tribute of sorts to Richard Burton's *Perfumed Garden*), *The Scented Garden of Abdullah the Satirist of Shiraz.*

68. See the earlier reference to Dr. Jekyll's inability to speak of Hyde as "I." In his *Confessions*, Crowley consistently refers to himself during his childhood years as "he," stating that it feels as though he is writing about "the behaviour of somebody else" (53). Lengthy discussion of narrative voice is beyond the scope of this chapter, but it is worth noting that in *The Confessions* there is slippage between a child and adult "he." Equally, much could be made of the fact that Crowley dates his conception of himself as "I" from the moment of his father's death in 1887.
69. Ibid., 45.
70. Ibid. Crowley had earlier been deeply in love with his wife, Rose, who was in the process of divorcing him during his 1909 trip to Algiers with Victor Neuburg. The divorce was the major reason for Crowley's decision to leave England at that time. Women were always important in his magical life, and there was a succession of magical consorts, chief among them Leah Hirsig—the "Scarlet Woman" at the Abbey of Thelema.
71. Victor B. Neuburg, "The Romance of Olivia Vane," in *The Triumph of Pan* (1910; London: Skoob, 1989), 145. The introduction to the 1989 facsimile edition of *The Triumph of Pan* is written by Neuburg's granddaughter Caroline Robertson, who argues that Neuburg's work cannot be read as straightforwardly "homosexual" poetry. Neuburg certainly had sexual relationships with women, and he married in 1921. A son was born in 1924, but the marriage was unhappy, and by the early 1930s Neuburg and his wife were living separate lives. Robertson is anxious to refute the suggestion by Jean Overton Fuller and others that Neuburg's poems are simply "about" Crowley, and she bases her claim on the significance of male/female polarity within the occult tradition and the fact that Neuburg is often talking about spiritual (rather than physical) possession by the god Pan. Nevertheless, it seems clear that the poems operate simultaneously at several levels, and that both Crowley and the Crowley–Neuburg relationship, magical and mundane, are ever present. It seems impossible, for example, to misunderstand lines such as "Sweet wizard, in whose footsteps I have trod / Unto the shrine of the obscene god" (144), or to misinterpret the desert imagery (12). Victor Neuburg published his first book of poetry, *A Green Garland*, in London in 1908. *The Triumph of Pan* was widely reviewed, and Katherine Mansfield made it the book of the month in *Rhythm*.
72. Victor B. Neuburg, "The Triumph of Pan" in *The Triumph of Pan*, 6.
73. Judith Butler, *Gender Trouble: Feminism and the Subversion of Identity* (London: Routledge, 1990), 61. Theoretically, at least, hermaphroditism and androgyny would imply a self-referential desiring subject.
74. Crowley, *The Confessions*, 603. See also "The Lost Shepherd" and references to "Panic" in Neuburg, "The Triumph of Pan."

75. Neuburg (like Norman Mudd, also a follower of Crowley) had been a member of the Pan Society at Cambridge, and the god Pan had cultural importance in the revivalist classical drama and arts of the period. Pan meant much more than this to Crowley and Neuburg, however, and when the two men finally parted in 1914 Crowley apparently ritually cursed Neuburg in a formula said to be linked with the god Pan. Neuburg suffered a nervous collapse and lived thereafter in fear of Crowley's return. Jean Overton Fuller reports a conversation that took place between Neuburg and a friend in the 1920s during which Neuburg was shaken to be told that he was "'awfully goat-like.'" He replied: "'I *was* one. A goat was my curse.'" Fuller, *Magical Dilemma*, 239.
76. Crowley recognized that masochism played an important part in his relationships with women but sought to deflect it through gestures of misogynistic contempt: "Masochism, too, is normal to man; for the sex-act is the Descent into Hell of the Saviour." Recorded in Crowley's diary, 1919–1920. See Aleister Crowley, *The Magical Record of the Beast 666: The Diaries of Aleister Crowley, 1914–1920*, ed. John Symonds and Kenneth Grant (London: Duckworth, 1972), 257. Kaja Silverman, "Masochism and Male Subjectivity," *Camera Obscura* 17 (May 1988), 36, notes that masochism, traditionally characterized in psychoanalytic theory as "feminine," is equally a constituent of male and female subjectivity.
77. Crowley, *The Confessions*, 621.
78. See Neuburg, "The Triumph of Pan," 19.
79. The Mark of the Beast is a circle containing the seven-pointed star of Babalon. It symbolizes the conjoining of Babalon and the Beast. See Crowley, *The Confessions*, 789.
80. See "A Human Beast Returns," *John Bull*, August 30, 1924; cited in Suster, *The Legacy of the Beast*, 85.
81. "Occasional Notes," *Pall Mall Gazette*, September 10, 1888; cited in Walkowitz, *City of Dreadful Delight*, 207.
82. Nina Auerbach, *Private Theatricals: The Lives of the Victorians* (Cambridge, Mass.: Harvard University Press, 1990), 76–77, identifies a late-Victorian "obsession" with "hybrids"—fairies, wolfmen, vampires, and so on—which becomes "something like the cult of the beast." Interestingly, she notes that the "noble Victorian enterprise of mighty self-making always threatens to produce, not superior mutations, but monsters."
83. I am indebted to Jann Matlock for this insight.
84. Crowley, *The Confessions*, 45.

3

Varieties of Magical Experience

ALEISTER CROWLEY'S VIEWS ON OCCULT PRACTICE[1]

Marco Pasi

IT IS UNDISPUTABLE that Aleister Crowley has a special place in the history of occultism.[2] This is the case not only because of the enormous influence that he and his works have had on the development of esoteric and new religious movements in the twentieth century;[3] Crowley is important also because of the originality and creativity of his thought, which positively tries to renew and reinterpret the meaning of occult practices in a modern framework. He represents and encapsulates, almost paradigmatically, the attempts made by esotericism as a whole to come to terms with traditional esoteric concepts in a world that has been deeply transformed culturally and socially by the impact of secularization and modernity.[4]

This historical phenomenon has taken on different forms. One of the most significant can be described as the psychologization and naturalization of esotericism, which is particularly visible from the second half of the nineteenth century through the first half of the twentieth. This phenomenon has attracted increasing interest from scholars in recent years, and some of them, such as Alex Owen, Wouter Hanegraaff, and Egil Asprem, have focused particularly on the role played in it either by occultist magic in general or by Aleister Crowley in particular.[5]

In this chapter I will first discuss Crowley's attitudes toward paranormal phenomena in general, particularly in relation to psychical research and to Spiritualism. Then I will focus on two particular aspects of Crowley's attempts at elaborating new interpretations of occult practices, namely, his attitudes toward Yoga and toward magic. Both subjects, if investigated in all their nuances and implications, would require an extensive discussion that would far exceed the scope of this chapter. My aim here is more modestly to focus especially on the ways in which Crowley tried to naturalize and psychologize traditional interpretations of spiritual practices, and therefore to show to what extent his thought can be considered as a significant moment in the more general trend of transformation of esotericism to which I have referred above. This will also allow me to address some related questions that may be particularly interesting. For instance, how radical could Crowley be in his psychological, naturalistic interpretations of occult experiences? Did he invariably consider such experiences to be the result of an alteration of consciousness, as he in some places seems to imply, or was there a protected core where a "disenchanted" vision of occult experience would not be allowed? We will see that Crowley's call as prophet of a new religion probably produced a cognitive obstacle that prevented him from taking the process of psychologization to its logical extreme.

Crowley's Attitudes toward Psychic and Spiritualist Phenomena

When occultists offered new interpretations of occult practices, for the most part they were trying to make these practices understandable and acceptable to modern audiences.[6] The conflict between religion and science was perceived during the second half of the nineteenth century as of supreme importance for the destiny of human culture. For those who shared the ideals of positivism and of scientific naturalism, descending directly from those of the Enlightenment, the grip of traditional dogmatic religion on society was based on a series of superstitions and misconceptions that scientific progress would sooner or later dispel. This implied an ideology of emancipation from the naïveté of the past that had implications on various social, cultural, and even political levels (for instance, in European colonial enterprises, which reached their peak in the same period). Occultists were of course not alien to the influence of these all-pervading ideologies, and it is not surprising to find the latter absorbed and expressed particularly by persons who were at one point or another part of the establishment that produced them. This is clearly the case with Aleister Crowley, in whose formative years the experience of an education at Cambridge University played a crucial role.[7] The direction that Crowley and other occultists took in order to make sense of their occult endeavors was predictably in line with the developments of late nineteenth-century science, as far as the interpretations of religious and paranormal phenomena were concerned. It is in fact possible to observe occultists such as Crowley, around the beginning of the twentieth century, starting to be influenced by, or sometimes even anticipating, new discourses then emerging in the field of psychology, of which the most important were psychical research on one hand and psychoanalysis on the other.

In Crowley's case, this interest in new psychological theories was, to be sure, also related to his intense use of psychoactive substances during all his life, often in a ritualized, magical context.[8] In this field he was an experimenter, and it could well be said that some of his experiments have a certain historical value. He was one of the first Westerners, for instance, to experiment systematically with peyote (then known as *Anhalonium lewinii*) in the context of spiritual practices.[9] There is also reason to believe that he introduced Aldous Huxley to the use of mescaline in Berlin in the early 1930s.[10] This episode, and more generally Crowley's approach to the use of drugs, partly explains why he became a sort of countercultural icon during the psychedelic era of the 1960s, influencing such important figures as Timothy Leary and, more prosaically, ending up with his face (in the company of Aldous Huxley himself) on the sleeve of the Beatles album *Sgt. Pepper's Lonely Hearts Club Band*.

It is clear that Crowley used these substances consistently in order to alter his consciousness and that he perceived this alteration to offer meaningful spiritual insights. The correlation made between this kind of alteration and the one produced through certain "occult" practices was particular important for him and was the result of personal reflection and experimentation that went on during most of his life.[11] Of course, in order to relate all these forms of alteration of consciousness to each other, and to attribute to them a spiritual/magical meaning, Crowley needed some pertinent theories concerning the human mind and/or the human brain. The rest of this chapter provides a closer look at these theories.

As Wouter Hanegraaff has remarked, the psychologization of esotericism is a development that begins with F. A. Mesmer's discovery of animal magnetism and runs through the whole of the nineteenth century.[12] On the other hand, Ann Taves has shown how, during the same period, those who "offered naturalistic or secularizing explanations" of religious experiences were not necessarily "critics" or outsiders to religion.[13] In some cases, in fact, such as in Spiritualism, the "dominant tendency to dichotomize religious experience and naturalistic explanation" was actually challenged.[14] Therefore, naturalistic explanations of religious experiences were not necessarily understood as incompatible with their religious meaning. The occultist movement of the late nineteenth century took a similar approach. In this case, as with Spiritualism, the underlying rationale was the necessity of a reconciliation between science and religion. The attempt at a reconciliation between these two fields, perceived as increasingly distant, if not radically opposed to each other, has in fact been named as one of the fundamental characteristics of occultism.[15] There was something more specific, however, in what took place at the beginning of the twentieth century, when new dynamic psychological theories were being developed and popularized. The interest of Crowley's approach lies in the fact that, being acquainted with these developments, he tried to apply them to his own understanding of magical and spiritual practices. With him the psychologization of esotericism, and more specifically of magic and other related practices, took some new directions.[16]

One of the interesting aspects of Crowley's psychological interpretations is the possible influence of William James's famous classic *The Varieties of Religious Experience*, originally published in 1902. This book seems to have played a significant role in the way Crowley's perception of magical experiences took shape. In several of his works Crowley refers to James's book.[17] He seems to have been particularly interested in the distinction made by James between "once-born" and "twice-born" religions.[18] But he was also interested in what James had to say about Yoga on one hand and about the experiences of religious "geniuses"—that is to say, founders of religion—on the other. I will return to this aspect.

Another point of interest is that Crowley was also acquainted with the activities of the Society for Psychical Research (SPR) and with some of its members. In this respect there is an interesting detail in Crowley's biography that should be taken into account. In 1895 Crowley was admitted as an undergraduate student to Trinity College in Cambridge, where he would spend the next three years. Although he did not complete his degree, the period he spent in Cambridge was extremely important for him and left an indelible mark on his intellectual development, as I have argued elsewhere.[19] Trinity College was not only one of the oldest and most prestigious colleges of the University of Cambridge but also the place where the Society for Psychical Research had originated in 1882. Three of its most distinguished founders—Henry Sidgwick, Frederic Myers, and Edmund Gurney—were in fact fellows of that college.[20] Sidgwick and Myers died in 1900 and 1901, respectively (Gurney had died even earlier, in 1888), and we do not know if Crowley ever met them personally. He was acquainted at least with other younger members of the SPR, however, such as Everard Feilding (1867–1936), who served as secretary of the society between 1903 and 1920, and Hereward Carrington (1880–1958), author of a popular book on the projection of the astral body.[21] According to Crowley's biographer Richard Kaczynski, Feilding was so close to Crowley that he even signed the oath of the probationer of his occult order, the A∴A∴.[22] Furthermore, Crowley depicted Feilding with the pseudonym of Lord Anthony Bowling in his novel *Moonchild*.

In 1908 Feilding and Carrington were sent on behalf of the SPR to investigate the famous Italian medium Eusapia Palladino (1854–1918). The report of this investigation was published one year later, and it was positive toward the medium's claims.[23] In his autobiography, Crowley tells how he studied the book carefully and took the first occasion, during a stay in Italy in 1911/1912, to pay a visit to Palladino and test her during a séance.[24] It is interesting to note that Crowley seems to be much more skeptical about the phenomena produced by Palladino than were the two professional psychical researchers. In the end he comes to the conclusion that all the extraordinary phenomena he witnessed during the séance were very probably the results of tricks and sleight of hand. In the same pages Crowley also describes a few experiences he had with other mediums and makes some observations about psychical research.[25] His attitude is on the whole negative. Not only has he failed to be convinced of the authenticity of the presumed paranormal phenomena by any report he has read or any séance he has witnessed, but he also elaborates a theory in order to explain why so many men of science, often with impeccable reputations of skepticism, "convert" themselves at some point in their lives to a belief in Spiritualistic phenomena. According to Crowley, there is a pattern in the fact that this conversion often takes place at a certain age, when the "sexual power begins to decline."[26] In other words, psychical researchers are subject to credulity because their declining vital energies impair their judgment.

It is evident that Crowley's skepticism regarding the paranormal phenomena investigated by the SPR was somehow connected to the polemics that had divided occultists and Spiritualists since the two movements had come into existence.[27] The common polemical argument of the occultists had consisted in contesting the interpretation of Spiritualist phenomena—particularly concerning the identity of the entities supposedly involved in the séances—but not their preternatural status. Crowley, however, took a step further and decided to be even more radical in that he denied the very authenticity of the phenomena.

Crowley's Interpretation of Yoga

Crowley's naturalistic interpretation of preternatural phenomena was not limited to Spiritualism or to psychical research. As I have already remarked, he applied psychological and naturalistic interpretations also to his own spiritual practices. In order to assess this aspect of Crowley's ideas, I focus in the following pages on his approaches to Yoga on one hand and magic on the other.

Crowley "discovered" Yoga "on the spot"—that is to say, in India, or more precisely in Ceylon (now Sri Lanka) in 1901. This was still an uncommon thing for a European to do in those times.[28] All his subsequent work was later influenced by these experiences, and Yoga became an important aspect of Crowley's practical teachings.[29]

Crowley was only twenty-six years old when he went to India for the first time. In early August 1901, he was in Ceylon.[30] By then, he had been traveling for some months. In the spring of 1900 there had been the famous conflict in the Order of the Golden Dawn in which the chief of the order, MacGregor Mathers, had been contested by a group of prominent members. Crowley had been involved in this conflict, siding with Mathers, and had been one of the protagonists in the dramatic events that had brought about chaos and dissension in this occultist association.[31] In the aftermath, disappointed and disoriented, he decided to leave England for a long trip, one that would last more than a year.

His first destination was Mexico, which he reached in July 1900. He remained there for several months, and during his stay he was joined by his friend Oscar Eckenstein (1859–1921). Eckenstein was a railway engineer with a passion for mountaineering.[32] He and Crowley had already climbed several peaks of the Alps together, and in Mexico they climbed some of the country's highest mountains. These climbs were also meant to be training for an expedition the two were planning to the mountains of Himalaya. From Crowley's autobiography we learn that he admired Eckenstein greatly and that he considered him as his mentor in serious mountaineering. It is interesting, however, that climbing was not the only field in which Crowley learned something from Eckenstein. In his autobiography, Crowley writes that his friend, during their stay in Mexico, taught him a basic technique of concentration, which consisted in visualizing an object and trying to keep the image as steady as possible in his mind.[33] The purpose was, of course, to achieve a certain control over the thought processes. Unfortunately, Crowley does not say where Eckenstein learned this technique, although he makes it clear that his mentor had nothing to do with magic, and that he even made fun of his younger friend for his occult interests.[34] But it is interesting to note that, according to a source independent from Crowley, Eckenstein was particularly interested in telepathy.[35] Crowley started following the training suggested by his older friend.[36] It is evident that these early experiments prepared the ground for his encounter with Yoga a few months later.

After having parted from Eckenstein and having left Mexico, Crowley crossed the Pacific with the intention of reaching another friend, Allan Bennett (1872–1923), who had been a fellow member of the Golden Dawn and had shared a flat with him in London for some time.[37] Bennett had also played the role of mentor for Crowley, but this time more specifically in magical matters, and it is with him that Crowley had begun experimenting with drugs in relation to ceremonial magic. Bennett had left England a year before on account of his bad health and had retired to Ceylon, where he had converted to Buddhism and had begun studying Yoga with a native master. After his move to Ceylon, Bennett had lost any interest in the practice of Western ritual magic as he had learned it in the Order of the Golden Dawn. Crowley's disappointment with the recent dramatic events in the order had also made him lose his enthusiasm for magic and prepared him for new spiritual adventures.

Bennett's instructor of Yoga was the Shaivite Sri Parananda Ramanathan (1851–1930), a highly respected figure in the island who had been appointed solicitor general of Ceylon under British rule.[38] Upon his arrival, Crowley immediately joined Bennett in his Yogic exercises and experiments. Both men were determined, to use Crowley's words, to "work out the Eastern systems under an Eastern sky and by Eastern methods alone."[39] Crowley convinced Bennett to rent a bungalow in Kandy, in the inner part of the island, and to continue their practices on their own. The techniques that Crowley was practicing in that period were mostly taken from "classical" Yoga, fixed in Patañjali's principles. His daily exercises included *âsana* (holding a particular position with the body until perfect immobility is achieved), *prânâyâma* (techniques of breathing control), and *dhâranâ* (techniques of thought control that allow one to arrest the flow of thinking at will). Crowley claimed that in early October, after two full months of continuous training, he achieved one of the highest stages of Yogic realization, *dhyâna*. According to Patañjali, only *samâdhi* is higher than *dhyâna* and can be considered as the ultimate goal of Yoga, leading to liberation from the human condition. What Crowley perceived as the experience of *dhyâna* was extremely important for him. According to Israel Regardie, it was "the most important spiritual result that he had achieved thus far."[40] However, after this early success Crowley discontinued his training, and toward the end of November he left Ceylon. He wanted to travel up north in India, where he had an appointment with Eckenstein for organizing a new expedition to K2.

An interesting aspect of Crowley's direct experience of Yoga is the fact that, during his apprenticeship, he kept a diary that for him had the use of a scientific record. During the months he spent in Ceylon, he carefully recorded all his exercises, including his physical and mental condition when he performed them and the results obtained. This was a practice he had learned during his membership in the Golden Dawn and that he continued using for the rest of his life. For him, his spiritual and magical work always had an "experimental" aspect that was, ideally, not far removed from that of the members of the SPR.

It does not appear that Crowley, in the following years, took up again the systematic practice of Yoga, at least not with the same intensity as during the "retreat" in Ceylon, although it is evident that his experiences during that period had a profound influence on him. Later on, he claimed to have achieved *samâdhi* as well, and therefore to have completed the path of realization according to the canon of classical Yoga, even if this achievement was apparently not related to the practice of Yoga but rather to the use of ceremonial magic.

One thing should be kept in mind in any discussion of the relationship between Yoga and magic according to Crowley.[41] He interpreted his experience of *dhyâna*, and later of *samâdhi*, as belonging to the same spiritual path as his initiation in the Golden Dawn and his practice of magic.[42] This means that he continued to apply the same basic initiatic structure he had found in the Golden Dawn to all his spiritual experiences. Everything fit into this paradigm and was interpreted thereby. Being unable to progress further on that initiatic structure through formal rituals of initiation, because he had distanced himself from the order, he claimed for himself the subsequent degrees on the basis of the experiences he was making. Crowley believed that there was continuity and consistency throughout his spiritual career; the importance and meaning that these experiences had from his own personal perspective cannot be well understood apart from this.

On the other hand, this particular vision of his spiritual career did not prevent him from interpreting these experiences not only on the basis of traditional spiritual premises but also from a perspective based on psychology. In his autobiography, he writes that in the early months of 1904 he was with his wife Rose, whom he had married a few months before, on a ship that was taking them from Colombo to Egypt during their honeymoon. This was shortly before the events that took place in Cairo in the spring of the same year and that led him to the revelation of *The Book of the Law*. On the ship, he met the English psychiatrist Henry Maudsley (1835–1918), who had published a series of books on the relation between body and mind from a strictly materialist perspective.[43] Interestingly, Maudsley had also studied phenomena related to mysticism and had published an article on Swedenborg in which he concluded that the Swedish visionary had suffered from "messianic psychosis," which he considered to be a "monomania," possibly caused by epilepsy.[44] According to John Johnson, the article was severely criticized by the Swedenborgian community, which perhaps led Maudsley to abstain from further reference to Swedenborg in his later works.[45] The episode is interesting because it shows the kind of understanding that Maudsley could have had of mystical and spiritual phenomena in general, obviously based on their reduction to psychopathology. Apparently, Crowley was less than disturbed by Maudsley's ideas on mysticism. In fact, he jumped on the opportunity offered by this casual encounter and approached Maudsley with the intention of discussing with him the subject of Yoga. Crowley's account in *The Confessions* deserves to be quoted in full:

> We talked about Dhyana. I was quite sure that the attainment of this state, and a fortiori of Samadhi, meant that they remove the inhibitions which repress the manifestations of genius, or (practically the same thing in other words) enable to tap the energy of the universe. Now, Samadhi, whatever it is, is at least a state of mind exactly as are deep thought, anger, sleep, intoxication and melancholia. Very good. Any state of mind is accompanied by corresponding states of the body. Lesions of the substance of the brain, disturbances of the blood supply, and so on, are observed in apparently necessary relation to these spiritual states. Furthermore, we already know that certain spiritual or mental conditions may be induced by acting on physico- and chemico-physiological conditions. For instance, we can make a man hilarious, angry or what not by giving him whisky. We can induce sleep by administering such drugs as veronal. We can even give him the courage of anaesthesia (if we want him to go over the top) by means of ether, cocaine and so on. We can produce fantastic dreams by hashish, hallucinations of colour by anhalonium Lewinii; we can even make him "see stars" by the use of a sandbag. Why then should we not be able to devise some pharmaceutical, electrical or surgical method of inducing Samadhi; create genius as simply as we do other kinds of specific excitement? Morphine makes men holy and happy in a negative way; why should there not be some drug which will produce the positive equivalent? The mystic gasps with horror, but we really can't worry about him. It is he that is blaspheming nature by postulating discontinuity in her processes. Admit that Samadhi is *sui generis* and back comes the whole discarded humbug of the supernatural.[46]

This is perhaps one of the most fascinating passages of Crowley's autobiography, because, with its ostentation of psychological jargon ("inhibitions which repress"), it introduces us directly to the complexity of his attitude toward spiritual practices. We can clearly see the kind of discourse that he is trying to develop in order to make these practices acceptable to the science-minded modern man, even in his most radically reductionist tendencies, which were represented by a figure such as Maudsley. Crowley claims that the famous psychiatrist reacted positively to the arguments of his fellow traveler: "Maudsley—rather to my surprise—agreed with all these propositions, but could not suggest any plausible line of research."[47] It is a pity that we do not have Maudsley's version of the episode and that we will never know what he really thought of this casual conversation. However, considering his rather unsympathetic attitude toward mysticism in general, it is not too surprising that in the end he would not offer advice for a "plausible line of research."

What is also interesting here is that in the lines quoted above one can possibly trace the influence of William James and his discussion of "religious geniuses" at the beginning of his *Varieties of Religious Experience*.[48] This reminds us of the fact that, even if in the above passage Crowley is at pains to show how acceptable his ideas were for a hard-core materialist such as Maudsley, it is rather with James that he should have felt an affinity. In fact, it is important to note that James, together with the main figures involved in psychical research in England and in the United States, represented a much less radical position than Maudsley with respect to the ultimate spiritual value of religious experiences.[49] The idea of "genius" associated with the founders of religions is a theme that returns in Crowley's works. In another passage in *The Confessions* Crowley mentions James explicitly, precisely in relation to the problem of genius:

> The general idea of Eastern religions . . . is liberation from the illusion of existence. The effect of Samadhi is firstly to produce the bliss which comes from the relief from pain. Later, this bliss disappears and one attains perfect indifference. But we need not go so far into their philosophy or accept it. Thanks partly to William James's *Varieties of Religious Experience*, I got the idea of employing the methods of Yoga to produce genius at will. James points out that various religious teachers attained their power to influence mankind in what is essentially the same way; that is, by getting into Samadhi. The trance gives supreme spiritual energy and absolute self-confidence; it removes the normal inhibitions to action. I propose then that any man should use this

> power to develop his faculties and inspire his ambitions by directing the effects of the trance into the channel of his career. This idea at once connects mysticism with Magick; for one of the principal operations of Magick is to invoke the God appropriate to the thing you want, identify yourself with Him and flood your work with his immaculate impulse. This is, in fact, to make Samadhi with that God.[50]

Crowley here is surely thinking of the section on Yoga in James's *Varieties of Religious Experience*.[51] In reality in that section James is less than explicit about the role of *samâdhi*—or of analogous mystical experiences—in the life of religious leaders, but this is indeed a theme that recurs in other parts of the book, although not necessarily in the way Crowley renders it. Crowley had already presented the theme at greater length at the beginning of *Book Four*, in the part devoted to Yoga, first published in 1912.[52] It is important to understand that in those pages Crowley not only develops his own peculiar magical doctrine but also offers his interpretation of the mystical experience as the basis for a comparative understanding of religious phenomena. In doing so, he is clearly building upon his reading of James.

According to Crowley, all founders of religions disappear or hide in a retreat at some time in their lives. When they reappear, they possess the spiritual energy necessary to found a new religion. What happens during this retreat? According to Crowley, what happened to Moses, Jesus, Muhammad, Buddha, and all other founders of religions is a mystical experience that is analogous to what is defined as *samâdhi* in the tradition of Yoga. In other traditions, such as Christian mysticism, it is referred to as the "union with God."[53] If these religious leaders have described their experiences in different ways it is because of their different cultural backgrounds, but the phenomenon itself has been always and everywhere the same. Therefore, for instance, Muhammad conversed with the archangel Gabriel, Buddha reached illumination, and Moses met with God on Mount Sinai.

The implications of Crowley's reasoning are not difficult to see. If the experiences of these religious leaders are all the same phenomenon and can be equated with *samâdhi*, then Yoga (or a similar method, such as ceremonial magic) potentially offers a technique validated experimentally to obtain genius "at will" and, consequently, the capacity of founding a new religion. Crowley does not make this conclusion explicit, but I think it is transparent enough. Crowley himself, according to his own testimony, had achieved the *samâdhi*, and this had entitled him to found a new religion. This is exactly what Crowley claimed he had done after he received the text of *The Book of the Law* from what he thought to be a preterhuman entity, only a few months after his meeting with Maudsley on his way to Egypt. In *Book Four* as well Crowley seems to deny the necessity of a supernatural explanation for the occurrence of this experience and what follows from it:

> *To sum up*, we assert a secret source of energy which explains the phenomenon of Genius. We do not believe in any supernatural explanations, but insist that this source may be reached by the following out of definite rules, the degree of success depending upon the capacity of the seeker, and not upon the favour of any Divine Being. We assert that the critical phenomenon which determines success is an occurrence in the brain characterized essentially by the uniting of subject and object.[54]

Crowley's Interpretation of Magic in Relation to Spiritual Entities

With the creation of genius at will, and the consequent power to impose a new religion on humanity, we find ourselves at the crossroads of Yoga and magic, because, in Crowley's view, both pathways can potentially lead to this extraordinary result. I will therefore focus now on Crowley's attitudes toward magic, especially concerning the status of the entities with which the magician is supposed to communicate by ways of magical rituals.

As I have already pointed out, a thorough discussion of all the complex aspects of Crowley's relationship with magic, from both a theoretical and a practical point of view, goes beyond the scope of this essay. It will, however, be useful to mention at least certain fundamental points. Aleister Crowley's entire life centers on this relationship, which is therefore essential for understanding the man and his ideas. It could be argued that before Crowley magic had been, in the specific context of occultism, mostly an intellectual pursuit, and not the focus of a person's entire life in all its aspects. For many persons involved in occultism it was hardly more than an eccentric hobby, as seems to have been the case with many members of the Hermetic Order of the Golden Dawn.[55] For Crowley, magic becomes an all-consuming activity, the focus of all aspirations and ambitions a man may have in his life. It is a path of spiritual search that not only encompasses the whole course of one's existence but also demands an integral, absolute commitment. As a consequence, success in daily matters cannot serve as a measurement of the achievements on the spiritual path.[56] In principle, one should be prepared to give up all one's affections and earthly interests in order to reach the highest steps of the initiatic ladder.[57] Crowley claimed on several occasions that this was precisely what he had done in his life, and that this was the main reason for his loss of the fortune inherited from his family and for his other personal misadventures.[58] This, unexpectedly perhaps, introduces a form of asceticism into Crowley's magical system that seems to be at odds not only with the exuberant hedonism of Thelema, as expressed clearly in *The Book of the Law*, but also with Crowley's proclaimed intention of making magic accessible to the masses.[59]

Unlike some of his predecessors, such as Eliphas Lévi or H. P. Blavatsky, who had used a similar rhetoric in describing magic but without necessarily going to its practical consequences, Crowley saw in magic not only a theoretical concern but also one that is existentially experienced in all its aspects, up to its most extreme consequences. Moreover—once again unlike his predecessors—he demanded from his disciples and followers the same kind of absolute commitment to magic he was prepared to make for himself. As is well-known, this radicalization of the idea of magic had as one of its logical consequences the foundation of a "magical" commune: the famous Abbey of Thelema in Cefalù, Sicily, in 1920, where Crowley thought he could bring his vision of a new society, based on magic and Thelema, to life.[60] Here, the idea of a personal magical realization was linked to a form of retreat from the world, which was something relatively new in the context of occultism.

On the other hand, Crowley is the author who tries the most, among English occultists, to elaborate an accomplished "philosophy" of magic, focusing especially on its epistemological and psychological aspects. I have already mentioned the importance of the years spent in Cambridge for Crowley's intellectual development. This experience made him also one of the very few occultists to have received a formal higher education, even if in the end he did not care to get a degree. Many authors have emphasized the inaccuracies and superficiality that occultists often show in their works—for instance, with respect to history or philology—whereas ironically they claim to possess ultimate knowledge in all fields of human learning.[61] There are no doubt social reasons why this was so, including the fact that most of them, unlike Renaissance authors such as Marsilio Ficino and Pico della Mirandola, could devote only their spare time to magic and occultism and did not have the leisure or the means to achieve well-rounded educations in the humanities or in the natural sciences. It is also for this reason that Crowley represents, both for his intellectual gifts and for the amount of his work explicitly devoted to magic, a particularly significant moment in the history of occultism. During all his life his cultural interests remained extremely wide and eclectic. He drew ideas and inspiration from many disparate sources, both Western and Eastern, and blended them into his own peculiar system.

In a general sense, Crowley saw *magic* as a convenient term to define his doctrine as a whole, including the religion he had founded, Thelema. More specifically, Crowley understood magic mainly in two ways, both of which are far from uncommon in the context of occultist literature. The first one is mostly pragmatic in nature and considers magic as a technique for achieving specific goals by means that cannot as yet be explained scientifically but the results of which can (in theory at least) be tested in an empirical way. Gaining considerable sums of money or the effortless acquisition of extensive knowledge in a particular field could be mentioned in this respect as classic examples. In *Magick in Theory and Practice*, which is the summa of his mature thought on magic, Crowley presents his most famous definition of magic, which has been subsequently adopted (and adapted) by a plethora of authors: "Magick is the Science and Art of causing Change to occur in conformity with Will."[62] According to this definition any intentional act could be defined as magical, and this would of course seem to reduce the specificity of magic as a particular field of action. In reality, in referring to magic in this context Crowley usually had in mind a rather precise set of practices and ideas, based mostly on traditional ceremonial magic. He had learned their fundamentals during his membership in the Golden Dawn and had developed them considerably on the basis of his subsequent experiences.

In later years, Crowley's discovery of sexual magic led him to change his understanding and practice of magic significantly; in fact, sexual magic made most of the material apparatus of ceremonial magic superfluous. Sexual magical workings, based on notions of subtle physiology mostly borrowed from Eastern doctrines (in particular Hatha Yoga), may use the body of the magician as the only magical tool, eliminating the need for external implements such as a "temple" (the sacred space where the magician operates) or the traditional "weapons" of ceremonial magic. The aim of magic in this sense is not necessarily material in nature: magic can also be used to obtain communications from spiritual entities or to explore the "astral plane" by means of the techniques of astral travel that Crowley had learned in the Golden Dawn. The messages that he received through these magical practices often had meanings that were specific to his own spiritual evolution (but they could also be set on a grander scale and concern the evolution of humankind, as in the case of *The Book of the Law*). By the same token, through these practices Crowley thought he could improve his knowledge of the symbolic network of correspondences, which are supposed to create a unifying link among all the parts of the universe. It is worth noting that, especially in relation to this first, pragmatic sense of magic, Crowley claimed to have a scientific, rational approach—again, something far from uncommon in the context of occultist literature.

The other sense in which Crowley understood magic was certainly seen by him as the most important, although it can be considered as complementary to the first one. According to this second perspective, magic is not so much oriented toward immediate ends as it is a way to achieve what Crowley considered to be the supreme goal of one's life: spiritual attainment. Magic then loses its instrumental character and becomes instead a practice and a worldview that encompass all aspects of a person's life. On the whole, the difference lies less in the kind of techniques that are being used than in the interpretation that is being given of them. Traditional ceremonial and sexual magic could be used, in Crowley's vision, both for immediate purposes and as a means to achieve the ultimate goal of spiritual realization. In the latter case, as noted above, the individual should ideally devote him- or herself to this pursuit fully and be ready to sacrifice all earthly possessions and affections for its sake. Crowley uses various expressions to define the aim of magic in this spiritual sense. In some passages he describes it as comparable to the mystical "union with God." In *Magick in Theory and Practice* he describes what he considers to be the ultimate goal of magical practice:

> There is a single main definition of the object of all magical Ritual. It is the uniting of the Microcosm with the Macrocosm. The Supreme and Complete Ritual is therefore the Invocation of the Holy Guardian Angel; or, in the language of Mysticism, union with God.[63]

We have seen that Crowley also equated this concept with *samâdhi*. In the context of the Golden Dawn, this same notion had been expressed as the "Union with the Higher Self."[64] But perhaps his most famous definition describes it as the attainment of the "Knowledge and Conversation of the Holy Guardian Angel," a notion taken from the famous *Book of the Sacred Magic of Abra-Melin*, a magical text that had been discovered by S. L. MacGregor Mathers in the Bibliothèque de l'Arsenal in Paris and that Mathers had edited in 1898, the same year in which Crowley joined the Golden Dawn.[65] This book, whose origins date back to the sixteenth or seventeenth century, describes a system of ritual practices aimed at establishing contact with an individual's guardian angel—that is, the angelic entity traditionally seen as attached to a person with the special task of advising and protecting him or her in moments of trouble. The goal of this magical system is therefore the "knowledge and conversation with one's Guardian Angel."[66] Among the members of the original (pre-1900) Golden Dawn, Crowley was certainly the one who was most influenced by this book (which, as should be remembered, was never a part of the official curriculum of the order). He is probably also the only one, among the members of the original order, who actually tried to put its instructions into practice.[67] Crowley claimed to have attained in 1906 the goal described in the book, and this was certainly a very important step in his spiritual career.

But who was this Guardian Angel? The importance given to this entity in the context of magical practices should not come as a surprise. After all, traditional ceremonial magic, as described and taught in a plethora of grimoires, almost invariably insists on the necessity for the practicing magician of contact with nonhuman or superhuman entities, which are supposed to help the magician or be at his service. This would mean of course mainly demons and angels, but sometimes also other kinds of entities, such as the spirits of the dead (for instance in necromancy) or elementals. The Guardian Angel, however, seems to have a particular role in this army of invisible creatures, because it is supposed to have a special, unique relationship with the magician.[68]

Crowley interpreted this relationship as akin to the mystical experience that for him was one of the essential—if not *the* essential—goals of magic. However, before we take a closer look at Crowley's understanding of this notion, it may be interesting to examine his general attitude toward the entities with whom the magician is supposed to get in contact during magical operations. This is especially relevant in relation to Crowley's rationalizing approach to spiritual matters, which I have discussed so far.

In 1904 Crowley published a version of the *Goetia*, a section of a famous grimoire, *The Lesser Key of King Solomon* (or *Lemegeton*).[69] The adaptation (not really a translation) into modern English had been done by Mathers, with whom Crowley had by then fallen out. The editing and the publication of these old magical texts by Mathers is to be understood as part of that magical synthesis that had been one of the main features of the Golden Dawn since its inception.[70] The Abramelin book previously mentioned was also an expression of this attempt at a synthesis. This explains why different notions derived from these texts could be put together to form a coherent theoretical framework for the magical activities of the Golden Dawn members. One could mention as an example of this magical syncretism the use of a ritual found in a Greco-Egyptian papyrus of the Hellenistic period, usually referred to as "the Bornless Ritual."[71] In Crowley's interpretation the ritual contained in this text was believed to provide access to the "Higher Genius" or "Higher

Self," a notion that had primordial importance in the teachings of the Golden Dawn and to which I will return.

When Crowley published Mathers's adaptation of the *Goetia* he added a small introductory essay titled "The Initiated Interpretation of Ceremonial Magic," in which he addressed the problem of the reality of the entities described by the grimoire and the efficacy of magic.[72] In this text, he expressed the view that it is not necessary to consider these spirits and demons as "really" existing—that is to say, as existing independently from the magician's self. They can be seen, on the contrary, as "portions of the human brain."[73] As a result of the invocation of one of these spirits a specific part of the magician's brain is stimulated that corresponds to that particular spirit. Here is how Crowley presents this idea:

> If, then, I say, with Solomon: "The Spirit Cimieries teaches logic," what I mean is: "Those portions of my brain which subserve the logical faculty may be stimulated and developed by following out the processes called 'The Invocation of Cimieries.'" And this a purely materialistic rational statement.[74]

From this quotation it seems clear that Crowley was willing, at least in certain contexts, to interpret the effects of ceremonial magic, and the entities traditionally involved with them, purely in physiological (not even psychological) terms. Magical phenomena are explained from a strictly materialistic point of view: it is just in the brain that they are taking place and this creates, as a secondary effect, the illusionary perception of spiritual entities. This is of course a kind of reductionist explanation of magic, one in fact that even someone like Maudsley may have found worth considering together with Crowley's interpretation of Yoga. And again, as with Yoga, it seems fairly evident that this approach is motivated by the desire to make sense of traditional spiritual practices in a modern, secular context, in order to make them compatible with a positivist and naturalistic way of thinking.

Crowley presented this naturalistic interpretation of magic in the early years of his spiritual career (by an interesting coincidence, it was published in 1904, the same year in which Crowley received from Aiwass the text of *The Book of the Law*). It appears however that, while being certainly significant for him from an intellectual point of view, he did not adopt it consistently or remain faithful to it in the following years. We have in fact plenty of examples in Crowley's magical curriculum in which he makes contact with entities that he is far from considering as mere "portions of his brain" or as parts of his unconscious psyche (as his discovery of psychoanalysis may have led him to believe). It is interesting to note that Crowley established initial contact with most of these entities through the aid of a visionary partner, very often a woman. This is in fact the case for the most spectacular example among them, namely, the apparition of Aiwass through his wife Rose and the consequent revelation of *The Book of the Law*. But it is also true for such "minor" entities as Amalantrah and Ab-ul-Diz.[75] It appears that Crowley generally did not consider these entities as products of his (or his partner's) unconscious mind or brain. They were not figments, albeit spiritually significant ones; they were independent, praeterhuman beings, with their own autonomous personalities and existences. The fact that all these entities were subjected to very careful testing is a clear indicator of this.[76] The point of the testing was precisely to prove not only the identity of the entities (so that the possibility of an evil creature in disguise would be ruled out) *but also* their autonomy from the personality of the magician and/or of his skryer. In that sense Aiwass and his kin rather resembled the mysterious "Secret Chiefs" of the Golden Dawn or the elusive "Mahatmas" of the Theosophical Society, who were understood as enlightened masters who had reached a very high level of initiation but were still living on this planet.[77]

On the other hand, in Crowley's interpretation, the concept of the "Holy Guardian Angel" was the same as that of the "Higher Self" (or "Higher Genius").[78] Crowley clearly got the idea that magic offered the magician a technique to discover his (or her) "Higher Self" in the Golden Dawn, and this influenced him considerably. The immediate origin of this idea was to be found in the writings of Madame Blavatsky and of the Theosophical Society.[79] Spiritual realization was understood as the reintegration of a divine or superior part of the self that remains, in normal conditions, unknown and inaccessible.

The presence of the guardian angel in Western esoteric, and more specifically magical, literature certainly deserves closer attention, as it has rarely been the object of scientific research. One of the reasons surely is that the traditional concept of the guardian angel has not been as prominent in the context of modern Western esotericism, even in its more magically oriented currents, as that of other entities. One can surely find in the modern period many examples of magical or theurgical practices in which angels are very much present, sometimes even hundreds of them. One need only think of the Enochian evocations of John Dee, the theurgical operations of Martinez de Pasqually's Elus Coëns, or Cagliostro's Egyptian masonic rites.[80] But in none of these examples does the guardian angel seem to be present as a specific entity.

A possible exception could be the group of the Illuminés d'Avignon, which was led during the 1780s by Dom Antoine-Joseph Pernety.[81] In the teachings of this group we find a series of spiritual practices (which, interestingly, are not referred to as "magic") whose final goal is the apparition of a person's guardian angel.[82] Apparently, the necessary instructions were transmitted by the "Sainte Parole," a mysterious oracle whose responses determined the activities and the policies of the group.[83] It would appear that the messages of the Sainte Parole were in fact coming from Johann Daniel Müller (1716–after 1785), an esotericist who was known in the milieus of German illuminism under the pseudonym of "Elias Artiste." One might wonder what were Müller's sources for the teachings related to the Guardian Angel, and whether he knew the text of the Abramelin book, which—as noted previously—had its probable origins in Germany and was first published in that country toward the end of the eighteenth century. More research would be needed in order to clarify this point.

However that may be, it is important to consider that, well before Pernety's group, a specific tradition of manuscripts existed in which guardian angels played a very important role in the context of magical practices. This tradition seems to have taken shape toward the end of the Middle Ages and was close to the Ars Notoria. The writings of Pelagius, the Hermit of Majorca, which have been studied by Jean Dupèbe and Julien Véronèse, clearly belong to this tradition, and so does *The Book of the Sacred Magic of Abra-Melin*.[84] If we exclude the exceptional case of the Illuminés d'Avignon, we can conclude that Mathers's publication was largely responsible for the revitalization in the nineteenth century of a magical tradition that had long fallen into oblivion.

The book of Abramelin prescribed a solitary retreat of six months, which included a regime of prayers and fasting. It is obvious that this system of practices was not easy to perform for persons who had a normal social life, as was the case for many members of the Golden Dawn. The interesting aspect of the interpretation of the Abramelin book that emerged in this context, first suggested by Mathers and then further developed by Crowley, is the identification of the Guardian Angel described therein with the concept of the "Higher Self" or "Higher Genius," which could be found in the literature of the Theosophical Society and in the teachings of the Golden Dawn.[85] It is also clear that Crowley made this identification quite early, because we find it in the text of a magical oath he took in 1900, when he first attempted to perform the Abramelin operation shortly before the end of his experience as a member of the Golden Dawn.[86] Another aspect of this identification was his interpretation of the ancient Bornless Ritual, which for him became the main ritual to be used in order to achieve contact with the Higher Self.

In 1904 Crowley claimed to have received from Aiwass *The Book of the Law*, which would play a fundamental role in his life.[87] The book eventually became the basis of Crowley's new religion, Thelema. Obviously, he saw himself as the prophet of this new religious revelation, which would supersede all existing religions. I will not enter into details here concerning the philosophical and ethical principles of this system, because this would take us far from our topic,[88] but the Cairo revelation is important if we want to consider the nature of Aiwass himself. Did Crowley perceive Aiwass as being his Holy Guardian Angel, as described in the Abramelin book? It is difficult to give a clear-cut answer, because Crowley's ideas in this respect seem to have changed with time. When Crowley received the book, and then in the years immediately following the event, there seemed to be no identification at all between Aiwass and his own Guardian Angel. As we have seen, Crowley consistently perceived Aiwass as a distinct personality who existed completely autonomously. It is easy enough to understand, from a psychological point of view, why Crowley always remained adamant on this point. It seems likely that Crowley could not understand Aiwass as being simply a manifestation of his psyche, be it called "unconscious" (in psychoanalytic terms), "Higher Self" (in occultist terms), or otherwise. This, in fact, would have undermined the universality of his religious claims concerning Thelema. The source of the revelation had to be in a metaphysical (or at least praeterhuman) dimension that was completely distinct from Crowley's individual personality. How could he have claimed that his message was going to change the destiny of millions of people for centuries to come if its ultimate source was just his unconscious (or even higher) mind? For Crowley, Thelema was a message from the gods, carried to him by Aiwass, their chosen messenger. This is why Aiwass, as noted above, belonged to same class of entities as Ab-ul-Diz and Amalantrah, and as the Mahatmas of the Theosophical Society.[89]

On the other hand, if Crowley had perceived Aiwass as his Guardian Angel, then he might have interpreted the reception of *The Book of the Law* as the "Knowledge and Conversation of the Holy Guardian Angel" described in the Abramelin book. However, Crowley made no such claim. He always interpreted the Knowledge and Conversation as a mystical experience that had its frame of reference in the teachings of the Golden Dawn and in William James's psychological theories. This is made even more evident by the fact that Crowley claimed to have attained the Knowledge and Conversation (and the initiatic degree that he equated with this experience) only in 1906—that is, two years *after* the revelation of *The Book of the Law*. This means that in 1904, in his perception, he had not yet attained this result, because he did not interpret the contact with Aiwass as the Knowledge and Conversation of his Guardian Angel. It is interesting to note that he called the ritual by which he achieved the final goal of the magic of Abramelin in 1906 "Augoeides," an explicit reference to the constellation of concepts (Holy Guardian Angel, Higher Self/Genius, Augoeides, Adonai) he had been trying to synthesize from different sources since his days in the Golden Dawn.[90]

The ritual of the Augoeides is interesting because it took place almost exclusively in an imagined ritual space.[91] Since it was performed during a long trip in China, where a physical ritual space meeting the requirements described in Abramelin's book was not available, Crowley decided to use his imagination. Therefore he followed the instructions given in the book carefully, but only by visualizing the actions that were necessary for performing the ritual, as well as the particular ritual space in which they were supposed to take place. In his autobiography, Crowley claims that in the end he obtained the same final result—that is, the Knowledge and Conversation—as if he had performed the ritual physically. It was a mystical experience, and was perceived by him as one of the most important magical achievements of his entire life.

In 1929 Crowley published his *Magick in Theory and Practice*, which presents his views on magic in the most systematic fashion. What is of interest for this discussion is that in this book we can observe a radical innovation concerning the concept of the Holy Guardian Angel. Crowley now identifies this concept with Aiwass. In the context of a discussion on black magic and on the existence of the Christian "Devil," he adds, in a footnote:

> "The Devil" is, historically, the God of any people that one personally dislikes. This has led to so much confusion of thought that THE BEAST 666 has preferred to let names stand as they are, and to proclaim simply that AIWAZ—the solar-phallic-hermetic "Lucifer"—is His own Holy Guardian Angel, and "The Devil" SATAN or HADIT of our particular unit of the Starry Universe.[92]

The identification between Aiwass and Satan is interesting enough, and it has of course offered some arguments to those who perceive Crowley as a Satanist.[93] However, it is the change of perspective in relation to the Holy Guardian Angel that is particularly significant here. If Crowley's Guardian Angel is Aiwass, and if he considers Aiwass as an autonomous entity, then the Guardian Angel is not a higher aspect of the "self" that must be awakened and attained through certain magical techniques or through Yoga. It is not the "Higher Genius" of the Golden Dawn anymore. At first sight, the reason for this shift of perspective is not clear. I have already suggested why, in my opinion, Crowley was so deeply convinced that Aiwass could not be interpreted in the same way as the spirits of the *Lemegeton* or as the Higher Self. Crowley perceived the completely autonomous status of Aiwass as more compatible with the universal religious claims of Thelema. The Knowledge and Conversation of the Holy Guardian Angel, on the other hand, remained an individual experience that concerned mainly the spiritual advancement of a single person. But then why would Crowley at one point identify Aiwass with the Guardian Angel? One possible explanation lies in Crowley's personal evolution, and his increasing conviction, since the 1910s, that he was the prophet of a universal religious message.[94] *Magick in Theory and Practice* is full of references to *The Book of the Law* and of discussions of Thelemic principles. It is therefore likely that Crowley at one point felt it necessary to identify Aiwass with his Guardian Angel because he was now perceiving himself as fully invested in his role of prophet and messiah. Crowley the man was increasingly replaced by the Beast 666, the Logos of the Æon. Everything was then reinterpreted and subsumed within the framework of the new religion.

This new interpretation was not modified in Crowley's later years. In his last book, which was published posthumously, Crowley comes to a conclusion that was already implicit in the identification of Aiwass with the Guardian Angel and confirms thereby the validity of the suggestion I have made:

> We may readily concur that the Augoeides, the "Genius" of Socrates, and the "Holy Guardian Angel" of Abramelin the Mage, are identical. But we cannot include this "Higher Self"; for the Angel is an actual Individual with his own Universe, exactly as a man is; or for the matter of that, a bluebottle. He is not a mere abstraction, a selection from, and exaltation of, one's own favourite qualities, as the "Higher Self" seems to be.[95]

In the same context, Crowley rejects eventually any psychological explanation concerning the existence of praeterhuman entities: "They are objective, not subjective."[96] Obviously, he realized that this idea was incompatible with what he had written in the foreword to the *Lemegeton* or in the first part of *Book Four*. In both cases Crowley had suggested a rationalizing, psychological interpretation of the entities involved in magical practices. But as soon as the "Guardian Angel," or "Higher Genius," becomes an autonomous entity, things are not the same anymore. The contact that a magician may have with the Guardian Angel is no longer necessarily related to spiritual realization.

This relationship is now rather "of friendship, of community, of brotherhood, or Fatherhood [*sic*]."[97] Then, from the psychologizing interpretation that Crowley seemed to have adopted, we find ourselves back to a traditional one: the magician evokes the spirits in order to ask for their help, as someone might call for a doctor or a plumber in case of need. In this respect, it is interesting to note that in *Magick without Tears* Crowley makes an explicit, sharp distinction between magic on one hand and mysticism and Yoga on the other, and expresses his preference for the former.[98] This distinction would not have made sense in the earlier period, when he wrote *Book Four* or even *Magick in Theory and Practice.*

Conclusion

The influence of authors such as James and Maudsley on an occultist such as Crowley can be understood only in the context of the more general attempt made by nineteenth-century occultism to come to terms with modernity. This influence shaped not only Crowley's understanding of magic but also his understanding of Yoga, and made it possible for him to apply a comparative perspective to spiritual practice, which allowed him to equate Western ritual magic with Yoga. The desire to find commonalities between different spiritual traditions was certainly not new in esotericism. What was perhaps new was the idea of doing it by using new psychological and scientific theories, rather than mystical insight or traditional wisdom.

Crowley was influenced considerably by the scientific naturalistic ideas that were widespread in England in the last quarter of the nineteenth century and that were also expressed in new psychological theories applied to religion. However, this attempt at modernizing magic, by psychologizing and naturalizing it, found an unexpected and unavoidable obstacle in the religious revelation of Thelema. From the moment in which Crowley became convinced that his personal mission on this planet was to spread the new religious truth he had found, the tension with his naturalizing interpretations of magic was destined to surface sooner or later. This tension is precisely what led Crowley increasingly to identify his own Guardian Angel with Aiwass, and consequently to deny implicitly the purely mystical value of the experience described in Abramelin's book. Aiwass had to exist not in his mind, but in the realms of a spiritual reality that was as objective as the material one, if not more. This is why, although the psychologization of magic and of related spiritual practices attained a degree of boldness that was probably unprecedented in esotericism, it still was not—nor could be—complete.

A comparison of Crowley's ideas with the ideas of one of his most interesting disciples, Israel Regardie, would be useful here.[99] It is impossible to enter into details, but a quotation from Regardie can give an idea of his understanding of magic, especially in relation to (analytical) psychology:

> Analytical psychology and magic comprise in my estimation two halves or aspects of a single technical system. Just as the body and mind are not two separate units, but are simply the dual manifestations of an interior dynamic "something," so psychology and magic comprise similarly a single system whose goal is the integration of the human personality.[100]

For Regardie, there seems to be an almost perfect equation between psychology and magic, to the extent that they even share the same goal (the "integration of the human personality"). Metaphysical aspects related to the practice of magic seem to disappear from sight in an even more radical way than with Crowley. If Crowley could not go all the way down to a complete naturalization and psychologization of magic, because he needed to preserve the universal claims of his religion, Regardie did not have the same kind of limitations. Because he was not interested in creating a new religion or in adopting Crowley's, he was able to bring the process of psychologization of magic to its ultimate consequences, by using in particular psychoanalytic theories. For Regardie, magic and psychoanalysis were using similar means in order to achieve similar goals, and he had no need to maintain a belief in preternatural entities as Crowley did.

Notes

1. The present essay has been published in an expanded version in *Magic, Ritual, and Witchcraft*, 6:2 (2011). Reprinted with the permission of the University of Pennsylvania Press.
2. As I have explained elsewhere, by *occultism* I mean a specific current in the history of Western esotericism. See Marco Pasi, "Occultism," in Kocku von Stuckrad (ed.), *Dictionary of Religion* (Leiden: Brill, 2005), 3:1364–68. See also Antoine Faivre, "Occultism," in Lindsay Jones (ed.), *Encyclopedia of Religion*, 2nd ed. (Detroit: Macmillan Reference, 2005), 10:6780–83.
3. Credit should be given to Massimo Introvigne for having been one of the first scholars—if not the very first—to engage in a serious analysis of Crowley's work and ideas within the context of magical movements and modern Western esotericism. See his seminal work, *Il cappello del mago: I nuovi movimenti magici, dallo spiritismo al satanismo* (Milan: SugarCo, 1990), passim and esp. 268–79.

4. For a general analysis of the impact of secularization on modern Western esotericism see Wouter J. Hanegraaff, *New Age Religion and Western Culture: Esotericism in the Mirror of Secular Thought* (Leiden: Brill, 1996), esp. 411–513.
5. See Wouter J. Hanegraaff, "How Magic Survived the Disenchantment of the World," *Religion*, 33 (2003), 357–80; Alex Owen, *The Place of Enchantment: British Occultism and the Culture of the Modern* (Chicago: University of Chicago Press, 2004), esp. chap. 6, "Aleister Crowley in the Desert," 186–220; and Egil Asprem, "Magic Naturalized? Negotiating Science and Occult Experience in Aleister Crowley's Scientific Illuminism," *Aries: Journal for the Study of Western Esotericism*, 8:2 (2008), 139–66. I should add that these aspects have also been one of the main foci of my own PhD dissertation, "La notion de magie dans le courant occultiste en Angleterre (1875–1947)," Ecole Pratique des Hautes Etudes, Paris (2004).
6. This process corresponds partly to what Olav Hammer has described in terms of "discursive strategies" within Western esotericism. See his *Claiming Knowledge: Strategies of Epistemology from Theosophy to the New Age* (Leiden: Brill, 2001), esp. 42–45.
7. I discuss this aspect in my "L'anticristianesimo in Aleister Crowley," in PierLuigi Zoccatelli (ed.), *Aleister Crowley: Un mago a Cefalù* (Rome: Edizioni Mediterranee, 1998), 47–51.
8. See Israel Regardie (ed.), *Roll Away the Stone* (North Hollywood, Calif.: Newcastle, 1994).
9. Mike Jay, *Emperors of Dreams: Drugs in the Nineteenth Century* (Sawtry, England: Dedalus, 2000), 216.
10. Marco Pasi, *Aleister Crowley und die Versuchung der Politik* (Graz: Ares Verlag, 2006), 52–53, n. 80.
11. It is well-known that for Crowley ceremonial magic and Yoga were the most important among them. With respect to Yoga, the techniques he learned were based on traditional forms of breathing, bodily postures, concentration, and meditation, as taught to him in Ceylon in the early years of the century. I will return to this below.
12. See Hanegraaff, *New Age Religion*, 482–84. Hanegraaff refers in particular to the works of Robert C. Fuller.
13. Ann Taves, *Fits, Trances, and Visions: Experiencing Religion and Explaining Experience from Wesley to James* (Princeton, N.J.: Princeton University Press, 1999), 3.
14. Ibid.
15. For an overview that addresses this issue, see Pasi, "Occultism."
16. In a number of previous works I have touched upon subjects related to these issues, and I have tried to offer some suggestions toward a better assessment of this important element in Crowley's work. See in particular my "Aleister Crowley e lo Yoga," *Arkete: Esoterismo Sacralità Gnosi*, 2:1 (2001), 77–87; and "La notion de magie," 341–79.

17. Perhaps the most glaring example of the influence of William James's work on Crowley and his circle of disciples can be found in the first part of "The Temple of Solomon the King." This serialized account of Crowley's spiritual career, compiled by his disciple J. F. C. Fuller (surely under close supervision by Crowley), was published in several issues of Crowley's periodical *The Equinox*. Significantly, the series opens with a long quotation from James's *Varieties of Religious Experience*, and the first pages of the very first installment are full of references to, and quotations from, James's book. See [John Frederick Charles Fuller and Aleister Crowley], "The Temple of Solomon the King (Book I)," *The Equinox* I (1) (1909), 141–57. On Crowley's relationship with Fuller, see my *Aleister Crowley und die Versuchung der Politik*, 139–51.
18. See for instance The Master Therion [Aleister Crowley], *Magick in Theory and Practice* ([London–Paris]: published for subscribers only, [1929–1930]), 30, and 50, n. 1; and the unabridged chapters from Crowley's autobiography, *The Confessions*, published as appendix IX of Aleister Crowley, *Magick: Liber ABA: Book Four: Parts I-IV* (York Beach, Maine: Samuel Weiser, 1997), 702.
19. See my "L'anticristianesimo in Aleister Crowley." In my *Aleister Crowley und die Versuchung der Politik*, 133, n. 214, I have noted that another fellow of Trinity College when Crowley was a student there was James G. Frazer, whose work also influenced Crowley significantly.
20. On the early history of the SPR and of its founders, see Alan Gauld, *The Founders of Psychical Research* (New York: Schocken Books, 1968); Janet Oppenheim, *The Other World: Spiritualism and Psychical Research in England 1850–1914* (Cambridge: Cambridge University Press, 1985); Frank Miller Turner, *Between Science and Religion: The Reaction to Scientific Naturalism in Late Victorian England* (New Haven, Conn.: Yale University Press, 1974); and Germana Pareti, *La tentazione dell'occulto: Scienza ed esoterismo nell'età vittoriana* (Turin: Bollati Boringhieri, 1990).
21. Hereward Carrington and Sylvan J. Muldoon, *The Projection of the Astral Body* (London: Rider, 1929). On Crowley's relationship with psychical research, and more particularly with Feilding and Carrington, see also Asprem, "Magic Naturalized?," 148–49.
22. Richard Kaczynski, *Perdurabo: The Life of Aleister Crowley* (Berkeley: North Atlantic Books, 2010), 185–88.
23. Hereward Carrington, *Eusapia Palladino and Her Phenomena* (New York: B. W. Dodge, 1909).
24. Aleister Crowley, *The Confessions of Aleister Crowley: An Autohagiography* (London: Arkana, 1989), 681–82.
25. Ibid., 681–86.
26. Ibid., 685.
27. On this issue, which still requires further investigation, see Oppenheim, *The Other World*, 158–97.

28. Concerning the history of the "discovery" of Yoga in the West and its relationship to Western esotericism, see Karl Baier, *Meditation und Moderne: Zur Genese eines Kernbereichs moderner Spiritualität in der Wechselwirkung zwischen Westeuropa, Nordamerika und Asien*, 2 vols. (Würzburg: Königshausen & Neumann, 2009); and Elizabeth De Michelis, *A History of Modern Yoga: Patañjali and Western Esotericism* (London: Continuum, 2004). On developments in France, see Silvia Ceccomori, *Cent ans de Yoga en France* (Paris: Edidit, 2001). On Yoga in Germany, see Walter Schmidt, *Yoga in Deutschland: Verbreitung, Motive, Hintegründe* (Stuttgart: Kreuz-Verlag, 1967); and Christian Fuchs, *Yoga in Deutschland: Rezeption—Organisation—Typologie* (Stuttgart: Kohlhammer Verlag, 1990).
29. Crowley published two main works on Yoga: Frater Perdurabo [Aleister Crowley] and Soror Virakam [Mary Desti], *Book Four, Part I* (London: Weiland, 1912); and Mahatma Guru Sri Paramahansa Shivaji [Aleister Crowley], *Eight Lessons on Yoga* (London: OTO, 1939).
30. On the period Crowley spent in Ceylon, see Crowley, *The Confessions*, 232–54; [J. F. C. Fuller and Aleister Crowley], "The Temple of Solomon the King. IV," *The Equinox* I (4) (1910), 150–96; Israel Regardie, *The Eye in the Triangle: An Interpretation of Aleister Crowley* (Phoenix, Ariz.: New Falcon, 1993), 229–65; Lawrence Sutin, *Do What Thou Wilt: A Life of Aleister Crowley* (New York: St. Martin's Press, 2000), 90–95; Kaczynski, *Perdurabo*, 93–96.
31. Ellic Howe, *The Magicians of the Golden Dawn: A Documentary History of a Magical Order, 1887–1923* (Wellingborough, England: Aquarian Press, 1985), chaps. 14 and 15.
32. On Eckenstein, see John Gill, *The Origins of Bouldering. An Informal Survey of the Sport from the Late 1800s to the 1960s and Beyond* (San Francisco: John Gill/Blurb, 2008), 9–28. See also the online version, John Gill, "Origins of Bouldering," http://www128.pair.com/r3d4k7/Bouldering_History1.01.html (June 5, 2011).
33. See Crowley, *The Confessions*, 213–14.
34. It should be noted that Eckenstein had spent a period in India; he had been a member of the Conway expedition that had made a first attempt at climbing K2 in 1892.
35. See Gill, *The Origins of Bouldering*, 12. See also Crowley, *The Confessions*, 159 and 213.
36. An account of these experiments can be found in [Fuller and Crowley], "The Temple of Solomon the King. IV," 107–24. Eckenstein is indicated there by the initials "D.A."
37. On Bennett, see John L. Crow, "The White Knight in the Yellow Robe: Allan Bennett's Search for Truth," research master's thesis, University of Amsterdam (2009).
38. It is interesting to note that Ramanathan belonged to a prominent family in Ceylon and that he was closely related to the family of the perennialist philosopher and art historian Ananda K. Coomaraswamy, whom Crowley befriended (and

later reviled) during his stay in the United States in the World War I period. Ramanathan was also closely associated with the president of the Theosophical Society, Colonel H. S. Olcott, during the latter's stay in Ceylon. See Kaczynski, *Perdurabo*, 93.

39. [Fuller and Crowley], "The Temple of Solomon the King. IV," 123.
40. Regardie, *The Eye in the Triangle*, 249.
41. See ibid., 253.
42. The first systematic attempt Crowley made to equate Eastern doctrines with Western magic can be found in *Berashith*, which dates to 1903. He expanded further on the topic in the first two parts of *Book Four*, published together with Mary Desti in 1912 and 1913, respectively. [Crowley and Desti], *Book Four, Part I*; and Frater Perdurabo [Aleister Crowley] and Soror Virakam [Mary d'Este Sturges], *Book Four, Part II—Magick* (London: Wieland, [1913]). See also Pasi, "La notion de magie," 348–49, 355–57.
43. The most famous among these was Henry Maudsley, *Body and Mind: An Inquiry into Their Connection and Mutual Influence* (London: Macmillan, 1870). On the explanation of alleged supernatural aspects in the body–mind relationship, see his *Natural Causes and Supernatural Seemings* (London: Kegan Paul, Trench, 1887). On Maudsley, see Aubrey Lewis, "The Twenty-Fifth Maudsley Lecture. Henry Maudsley: His Work and Influence," *Journal of Mental Science*, 97:407 (1951), 259–77; Michael Collie, *Henry Maudsley: Victorian Psychiatrist: A Bibliographical Study* (Winchester, England: St. Paul's Bibliographies, 1988); and Trevor Turner, "Henry Maudsley: Psychiatrist, Philosopher, and Entrepreneur," *Psychological Medicine*, 18:3 (August 1988), 551–74. On Maudsley and Crowley, see Justin Sausman, "Science, Drugs, and Occultism: Aleister Crowley, Henry Maudsley, and Late-Nineteenth Century Degeneration Theories," *Journal of Literature and Science*, 1:1 (2007), 40–54; and Asprem, "Magic Naturalized?," 147–48.
44. Henry Maudsley, "Emanuel Swedenborg," *Journal of Mental Science*, 15 (1869), 169–96. See also John Johnson, "Henry Maudsley on Swedenborg's Messianic Psychosis," *British Journal of Psychiatry*, 165 (1994), 690–91; and the critical response by Kurt Simons, "'Henry Maudsley on Swedenborg's Messianic Psychosis': Some Comments," *New Philosophy*, 101 (1998), 113–17. On Maudsley's views on Spiritualism as strictly related to forms of "lunacy," and his medical treatment of a Spiritualist medium along these lines, see Alex Owen, *The Darkened Room: Women, Power, and Spiritualism in Late Victorian England* (Philadelphia: University of Pennsylvania Press, 1990), 144–48 and 183–92.
45. Johnson, "Henry Maudsley," 690. Simons, however, contests this, pointing out that Johnson omits mentioning his sources for this episode. See Simons, "'Henry Maudsley,'" 113.
46. Crowley, *The Confessions*, 386.
47. Ibid.

48. William James, *The Varieties of Religious Experience: A Study in Human Nature* (New York: Longmans, Green, 1920), 6.
49. On the other hand, it is very significant that, in the first part of the "The Temple of Solomon the King," to which I have referred above, a passage from James's *Varieties of Religious Experience* is also quoted, in which James tries to reconcile his own position with that of Maudsley on the basis of a common "empiricist criterion" in testing religious beliefs. Crowley evidently agrees to that. See [Fuller and Crowley], "The Temple of Solomon the King (Book I)," 150.
50. Crowley, *The Confessions*, 244.
51. James, *The Varieties of Religious Experience*, 400–401. The fact that Crowley read carefully this section of James's work is also interesting for a different reason: it provides an indirect link to a figure, the German industrialist and occultist Karl Kellner (1850–1905), who plays a significant role in the history (or rather prehistory) of the Ordo Templi Orientis, the occultist group of which Crowley became the international leader around 1923. Kellner was one of the first Westerners to write a book on Yoga from a practical point of view: *Yoga: Eine Skizze über den psycho-physiologischen Teil der alten indischen Yogalehre* (Munich: Kastner & Lossen, 1896). James refers to this book in a footnote at p. 401, also quoting from it. As far as it is known, Crowley was never personally in contact with Kellner, and, although he must have known of his role in the history of the OTO, he does not make any comment about him in relation to James's quotation.
52. [Crowley and Desti], *Book Four, Part I*.
53. The equivalence between *samâdhi* and the "union with God," which has some importance (as we will see) also for Crowley's understanding of magic, is clearly founded on the idea of a comparative phenomenology of mystical experiences that is also at the core of William James's work. Crowley refers to this equivalence in several places in his works, but it is most clearly presented in the first part of *Book Four*. See [Crowley and Desti], *Book Four, Part I*, 79–80.
54. Ibid., 19–20.
55. Not for all, of course. MacGregor Mathers is an obvious case in point. It seems clear that he was a model for Crowley also in this respect. For other members, such as the aforementioned Allan Bennett, it could be argued that magic was also a very important pursuit that included both speculative and practical aspects and had a very deep existential meaning (in Bennett's case at least until he converted to Buddhism).
56. This, among other things, differentiates Crowley's system strongly from certain forms of contemporary Satanism, especially those that are inspired by Anton Szandor LaVey's ideas and his Church of Satan, despite the obvious influence of Crowley's ideas on them. For an analysis of the opposition between this-worldly and otherworldly ideologies in contemporary Satanism, see my "Dieu du désir, dieu de la raison (Le Diable en Californie dans les années soixante)," in *Le Diable* (Paris: Dervy, 1998), 87–98.

57. On crossing "the Abyss" one enters the last stage of initiation, according to Crowley's magical system. At that moment the individual is supposed to have "destroyed all that He is and all that He has." Aleister Crowley, "One Star in Sight," in [Crowley], *Magick in Theory and Practice*, 233–34. This stage can of course be attained only by the most advanced adepts.
58. See for instance Crowley, *The Confessions*, 795–97.
59. The hedonistic aspects of Thelema, in relation to sex, food, and drugs, are prominent in some of the most famous verses of *The Book of the Law*, such as I, 51: "Be goodly therefore: dress ye all in fine apparel; eat rich foods and drink sweet wines and wines that foam! Also, take your fill and will of love as ye will, when, where and with whom you will! But always unto me." As to the "popularization" of magic, this is particularly evident in the introduction to *Magick in Theory and Practice*, xi–xii. The aspect of asceticism in Crowley, and the implicit tension that it creates with other parts of his doctrinal system, has hardly been noted by commentators, who usually prefer to insist on the much more visible, and perhaps even glamorous (if sometimes misunderstood), "anarchistic" aspect of Thelema. This is of course also related to the political side of Crowley's ideas, which is the focus of my *Aleister Crowley und die Versuchung der Politik* (an English-language edition of which, titled *Aleister Crowley and the Temptation of Politics*, is now forthcoming from Equinox Publishing). In relation to these problems, see in particular the second chapter.
60. See Crowley, *The Confessions*, 848–55.
61. On French occultism, for instance, see François Secret, "Eliphas Lévi et la Kabbale," *Charis: Archives de l'Unicorne*, 1 (1988), 81–89.
62. [Crowley], *Magick in Theory and Practice*, xii. It should be noted that this book was a development of the *Book Four* project, which Crowley had begun in 1912 with the publication of the first two parts.
63. Ibid., 11.
64. See, for instance, Samuel Liddell MacGregor Mathers et al., *Astral Projection, Ritual Magic and Alchemy*, ed. Francis King (London: Neville Spearman, 1971), 115, 151, 156. See also Israel Regardie, *What You Should Know about the Golden Dawn* (Phoenix, Ariz.: New Falcon, 1993), 51.
65. Samuel Liddell MacGregor Mathers (ed.), *The Book of the Sacred Magic of Abra-Melin the Mage, as Delivered by Abraham the Jew unto his Son Lamech, A.D. 1458* (London: J. M. Watkins, 1898). Robert Ambelain has edited the text in its original French version: *La magie sacrée ou livre d'Abramelin le mage* (Paris: Niclaus, 1959). Authors writing on the Golden Dawn (even the most serious ones) have long believed that the French manuscript in the Bibliothèque de l'Arsenal was unique and that Mathers's translation was (as he himself thought) the first published version of the book. In reality, Gershom Scholem, in his *Bibliographia Kabbalistica* (Leipzig: Verlag von W. Drugulin, 1927), 2, had already drawn attention to several German manuscript versions of this text, one of which was

published probably around 1800 (but antedated to 1725): Abraham von Worms, *Die egyptischen grossen Offenbarungen, in sich begreifend die aufgefundenen Geheimnißbücher Mosis; oder des Juden Abraham von Worms. Buch der wahren Praktik* [etc.] (Cologne: Peter Hammer, 1725). Moreover, there is a Hebrew version, probably translated from one of the German manuscripts, at the Bodleian Library in Oxford, to which Rafael Patai devotes a whole chapter of his *The Jewish Alchemists: A History and a Source Book* (Princeton, N.J.: Princeton University Press, 1994), 271–88. See also the more recent contribution by Bernd Roling, "The Complete Nature of Christ: Sources and Structures of a Christological Theurgy in the Works of Johannes Reuchlin," in Jan N. Bremmer and Jan R. Veenstra (eds.), *The Metamorphosis of Magic from Late Antiquity to the Early Modern Period* (Leuven: Peeters, 2002), 244–49. An edition of the text based on the known German manuscripts has recently been produced by Georg Dehn, *Buch Abramelin, das ist Die egyptischen großen Offenbarungen oder das Abraham von Worms Buch der wahren Praktik in der uralten göttlichen Magie*, ed. G. Dehn (Saarbrücken: Verlag Neue Erde, 1995; 2nd ed., Leipzig: Edition Araki, 2001), and translated into English (with Dehn's collaboration) by Steven Guth as Abraham von Worms, *The Book of Abramelin. A New Translation* (Lake Worth, Fla.: Ibis Press, 2006). In Mathers's edition the name in the title of the book is spelled as "Abra-Melin," but "Abramelin" is a much more common spelling among authors referring to the book (including Crowley) and in other editions of the text. I use therefore the latter spelling throughout this chapter.

66. This is how Mathers describes the goal in his introduction to the book; see Mathers (ed.), *The Book of the Sacred Magic*, xxvi. On the same page, Mathers suggests that this operation is related, "in the language of the Theosophy of the present day, [to] the knowledge of the Higher Self."
67. Interesting material on Crowley's use of the book and also on later attempts made by other occultists to practice Abramelin's system can be found in Peter-R. König (ed.), *Abramelin & Co.* (Munich: Abeitsgemeinschaft für Religions- und Weltanschauungsfragen, 1995). See also Christopher McIntosh, *The Devil's Bookshelf: A History of the Written Word in Western Magic from Ancient Egypt to the Present Day* (Wellingborough, England: Aquarian Press, 1985), 113–22.
68. On this issue, see my "Anges gardiens et esprits familiers dans le spiritisme et dans l'occultisme," in Jean-Patrice Boudet (ed.), *De Socrate à Tintin: Anges gardiens et démons familiers de l'Antiquité à nos jours* (Rennes: Presses Universitaires de Rennes, 2011), 249–65. See also the discussion below.
69. See Aleister Crowley (ed.), *The Goetia: The Book of the Goetia of Solomon the King* (Foyers, Scotland: Society for the Propagation of Religious Truth, 1904). For a recent edition, see Aleister Crowley and Samuel Liddell MacGregor Mathers (eds.), *The Goetia: The Lesser Key of Solomon the King* (York Beach, Maine: Samuel Weiser, 1995). A recent PhD dissertation by Francisco Silva focusing on Mathers's edition of another grimoire, *The Key of Solomon the King* (London: George

Redway, 1889), discusses also at length his edition of the *Goetia*: "Mathers' Translation of the Clavicula Salomonis: The Relationship between Translator, Text and Transmission of a 'Religious Text,'" University of Manchester (2009), passim.

70. For general discussions of Mathers's editions of ancient magical texts, see Francis King, *Modern Ritual Magic: The Rise of Western Occultism* (Bridport, England: Prism Press, 1989), 194–97; and Silva, "Mathers' Translation," chaps. 4 and 5.
71. See Hymenaeus Beta [William Breeze], "Editor's Foreword," in Crowley and Mathers, *The Goetia*, xxi–xxii. It would appear that this particular text was not part of the curriculum of the Golden Dawn and was not generally practiced by its members but was adapted by Allan Bennett, on his own initiative, into a workable ritual. However, Bennett's idea was perfectly consonant with the general syncretistic enterprise of the Golden Dawn. The famous pioneer of English Egyptology Charles Wycliffe Goodwin had published the original Greek text in 1852; Charles Wycliffe Goodwin (ed.), *Fragment of a Graeco-Egyptian Work upon Magic from a Papyrus in the British Museum* (Cambridge: Macmillan, J. W. Parker, J. H. Parker, 1852). Crowley rewrote and transformed it into his Liber Samekh, a ritual that is supposed to offer a shortcut to the final goal of Abramelin's system (i.e., the Knowledge and Conversation of the Holy Guardian Angel); Aleister Crowley, "Liber Samekh," in [Crowley], *Magick in Theory and Practice*, 265–301.
72. Aleister Crowley, "The Initiated Interpretation of Ceremonial Magic," in Crowley and Mathers (eds.), *The Goetia*, 15–20.
73. Ibid., 17.
74. Ibid.
75. See Crowley, *The Confessions*, 676–78 (Ab-ul-Diz), and 832–35 (Amalantrah). See also John Symonds, *The King of the Shadow Realm: Aleister Crowley, His Life and Magic* (London: Duckworth, 1989), 135–51 (Ab-ul-Diz), and 222–32 (Amalantrah). Crowley's accounts of these experiences can be found in Aleister Crowley, with Victor B. Neuburg and Mary Desti, *The Vision and the Voice, with Commentary and Other Papers* (York Beach, Maine: Samuel Weiser, 1998). The communications received from Ab-ul-Diz were at the origin of the *Book Four* project.
76. It should be noted that the testing itself, usually based on a series of questions, resembled the procedures already in use for years in the circles of Spiritualism and of psychical research. On the role of testing in Crowley's magical practice, see Asprem, "Magic Naturalized?," 156–62.
77. On the Mahatmas of the Theosophical Society and their possible identification with living persons with whom Madame Blavatsky had been in contact, see K. Paul Johnson, *The Masters Revealed: Madame Blavatsky and the Myth of the Great White Lodge* (Albany: State University of New York Press, 1994) and *Initiates of the Theosophical Masters* (Albany: State University of New York Press, 1995).
78. We have seen that Mathers had already suggested the equation between the Holy Guardian Angel and the Higher Self. See note 66, above.

79. See, for instance, Helena Petrovna Blavatsky, *The Theosophical Glossary* (London: Theosophical Publishing Society, 1892), 141. See also my discussion in "La notion de magie," 307–8.
80. The literature concerning these examples is of course very abundant. For a general perspective concerning the different forms of theurgy involving angels in modern Western esoteric currents, see Massimo Introvigne, "Arcana Arcanorum: Cagliostro's Legacy in Contemporary Magical Movements," *Syzygy: Journal of Alternative Religion and Culture*, 1:2–3 (1992), 122.
81. For an overview of the history of this group, see Jan A. M. Snoek, "Illuminés d'Avignon," in Wouter J. Hanegraaff et al. (eds.), *Dictionary of Gnosis and Western Esotericism* (Leiden: Brill, 2005), 597–600, which also includes an exhaustive bibliography. The classical study on this group is Micheline Meillassoux-Le Cerf, *Dom Pernety et les Illuminés d'Avignon suivi de la transcription intégrale de la Sainte Parole* (Milan: Archè, Edidit, 1992).
82. On this point, see René Le Forestier, *La franc-maçonnerie templière et occultiste* (Paris: La Table d'Emeraude, 1987), 877–81; and Joanny Bricaud, *Les Illuminés d'Avignon: Etude sur Dom Pernety et son groupe* (Paris: Nourry, 1927), 45–52.
83. This has been discovered by Reinhard Breymayer; see his "'Elie Artiste': Johann Daniel Müller de Wissenbach/Nassau (1716 jusqu'après 1785); Un aventurier entre le piétisme radical et l'illuminisme," in Mario Matucci (ed.), *Actes du Colloque International Lumières et Illuminisme* (Pisa: Pacini, 1984), 65–84. See also Antoine Faivre, "Elie Artiste, ou le messie des Philosophes de la Nature (première partie)," *Aries: Journal for the Study of Western Esotericism*, 2:2 (2002), 145–49.
84. The analogies between Pelagius's works and *The Book of the Sacred Magic* are striking and can hardly be taken as mere coincidences. Dupèbe had first studied Pelagius in relation to Trithemius: Jean Dupèbe, "Curiosité et magie chez Johannes Trithemius," in Jean Céard (ed.), *La curiosité à la Renaissance* (Paris: Société d'Édition d'Enseignement Supérieur, 1986), 71–97. He went on with his research on Pelagius in "L'écriture chez l'ermite Pélagius: Un cas de théurgie chrétienne au xve siècle," in R. Laufer (ed.), *Le texte et son inscription* (Paris: Editions du Centre National de la Recherche Scientifique, 1989), 113–53; and "L'ermite Pélagius et les Rose-Croix," in *Rosenkreuz als europäisches Phänomen im 17. Jahrhundert* (Amsterdam: In de Pelikaan, 2002), 137–56. See also Julien Véronèse, "La notion d''auteur-magicien' à la fin du Moyen Âge: Le cas de l'ermite Pelagius de Majorque († v. 1480)," *Médiévales*, 51 (Autumn 2006), 119–38. Robert Amadou has published a facsimile of a relatively recent manuscript of *L'Anacrise*, one of Pelagius's most significant texts: Pélagius ermite de Majorque, *L'Anacrise*, ed. Robert Amadou (Paris: Cariscript, 1988).
85. This is made clear in a text quoted in the first installment of "The Temple of Solomon the King," which was probably a letter Crowley wrote to his disciple J. F. C. Fuller: "Lytton calls him Adonai in *Zanoni*. . . . Abramelin calls him Holy Guardian Angel. . . . Theosophists call him the Higher Self, Silent Watcher, or

Great Master. The Golden Dawn calls him the Genius. Egyptians say Asar Un-nefer" (159). In this text a complete synthesis is made among all these different concepts (and others I have omitted here). See also James A. Eshelman, *The Mystical and Magical System of the A.'.A.'.. The Spiritual System of Aleister Crowley and George Cecil Jones Step-by-Step* (Los Angeles: College of Thelema, 2000), 122. The Higher Self (or Genius) had already been identified in the Theosophical literature with Adon-Ai (or Adonai) and the Augoeides, both taken from Edward Bulwer-Lytton's Rosicrucian novel *Zanoni* and to which Crowley also refers in the above quotation. Asar Un-nefer refers on the other hand to the Bornless Ritual, which I have already mentioned.

86. "I, Perdurabo [Crowley's magical motto in the Order] . . . do this day spiritually bind myself anew: . . . That I will devote myself to the Great Work: the obtaining of Communion with my own Higher and Divine Genius (called the Guardian Angel) by means of the prescribed course; and that I will use my Power so obtained in the Redemption of the Universe. So help me the Lord of the Universe and my own Higher Soul!" Crowley, *The Confessions*, 190.
87. The text has been published many times and is widely available in several formats and editions. It can be found in Crowley, *Magick: Liber ABA*, 305–18.
88. An overview of the fundamental tenets of Thelema can be found in Marco Pasi, "Crowley, Aleister," in Hanegraaff et al., *Dictionary*, 281–87.
89. J. Symonds's comment on this subject seems to me particularly to the point: "In spite of his knowledge of symbolism, and his familiarity with the works of Freud, and with Jung's *Psychology of the Unconscious* . . . [Crowley] made no attempt to interpret this material in terms of consciousness. . . . He would not have been surprised to meet Ab-ul-Diz or Amalantrah strolling up Fifth Avenue." Symonds, *The King of the Shadow Realm*, 225.
90. The ritual of the Augoeides was based on Crowley's version of the Bornless Ritual.
91. See Crowley, *The Confessions*, 514–33. See also Regardie, *The Eye in the Triangle*, 303–37; and Pasi, "La notion de magie," 373–76.
92. [Crowley], *Magick in Theory and Practice*, 193, n. 1.
93. On Crowley and Satanism, see Massimo Introvigne, *Enquête sur le satanisme* (Paris: Dervy, 1997), 209–19; and Asbjørn Dyrendal, "Satan and the Beast: The Influence of Aleister Crowley on Modern Satanism," in the present volume. Introvigne, who refers to the quoted passage as well (216), discusses and rightly dismisses interpretations of Crowley as a Satanist. As will be clear however, his interpretation differs from mine. He does not seem to realize, in fact, that Aiwass, until *Magick in Theory and Practice*, had nothing to do with Crowley's Holy Guardian Angel, and that Crowley had always seen Aiwass as an autonomous personality. On the other hand, Introvigne quotes a passage (215) taken from one of the commentaries of *The Book of the Law*, written at around the same time as *Magick in Theory and Practice* (early 1920s, during the Cefalù period), where Crowley still claims that the Holy Guardian Angel "represents the Higher Self"

and that "he is almost the 'unconscious' of Freud." Aleister Crowley, *The Law Is for All* (Phoenix, Ariz.: New Falcon, 1993), 78, 80. It seems therefore likely that the footnote in *Magick in Theory and Practice* was written later than this passage, which still shows the usual interpretation of the Guardian Angel. The footnote to *Magick in Theory and Practice* could have been added at any time between the writing of the bulk of the book in the early 1920s and its actual printing in 1929.

94. On this point, see Pasi, *Aleister Crowley und die Versuchung der Politik*, 62–65.
95. Aleister Crowley, *Magick without Tears* (St. Paul, Minn.: Llewellyn, 1973), 276. See also ibid., 94, where Crowley wonders whether Aiwass is a man or an angel, but does not even mention the possibility of the "Higher Self."
96. Ibid., 282.
97. Ibid.
98. Ibid., 495–506.
99. I discuss at length Regardie's ideas on magic, also in relation to Crowley, in my "La notion de magie," 390–98. As I have mentioned, Regardie offers his interpretation of Crowley's magical system in *The Eye in the Triangle*. He presents his own ideas on the relationship between magic and psychoanalysis especially in *The Middle Pillar: A Co-relation of the Principles of Analytical Psychology and the Elementary Techniques of Magic* (St. Paul, Minn.: Llewellyn, 1970).
100. Regardie, *The Middle Pillar*, 16.

4

Envisioning the Birth of a New Aeon

DISPENSATIONALISM AND MILLENARIANISM IN THE THELEMIC TRADITION[1]

Henrik Bogdan

ACCORDING TO THE British occultist Aleister Crowley, the vernal equinox of 1904 and the "reception" of *Liber AL vel Legis* (*The Book of the Law*) two weeks later marked a fundamental shift in the history of humankind.[2] A channeled text that consists of 220 short verses divided into three chapters, *The Book of the Law* identified Crowley as "the Beast 666," the prophet of a new religion, "Thelema." The then-current Age or Aeon of Osiris was characterized by the figure of a suffering and dying God, which the book proclaimed would be swept away by a vigorous new Age, the Aeon of Horus, "the Crowned and Conquering Child."[3]

The core doctrines of this new creed of Thelema were expressed in three short dictums: "Do what thou wilt shall be the whole of the Law,"[4] "Love is the law, love under will,"[5] and "Every man and every woman is a star."[6] *The Book of the Law* further warned that the transition from the Aeon of Osiris to the Aeon of Horus would not be a peaceful one; rather, it was envisioned in almost biblical terms as a time of catastrophe and disruption, marked by war, destruction, and chaos.

This chapter will discuss the apocalyptic and millenarian understanding of history in the Thelemic tradition, as described in the writings of Aleister Crowley, primarily in his own commentaries on *The Book of the Law*. I will argue that despite the fierce anti-Christian nature of Thelema, the Thelemic millenarian view of history is in fact deeply rooted in a Western esoteric understanding of biblical apocalypticism, as well as in the dispensationalism of John Nelson Darby. I will also briefly mention some post-Crowley reinterpretations of Thelemic dispensationalism.

The Birth of a New Aeon

Based on the revelations of *The Book of the Law*, Crowley saw human history as divided into three ages or aeons, each of which lasts for approximately two thousand years. These aeons mark evolutionary leaps in the development of humankind, and each is ruled by certain magical formulas.[7] The new Aeon of Horus was preceded by the Aeons of Isis and Osiris, and it will in the future be superseded by a fourth aeon, that of Maat (Ma /Hrumachis), also termed the "Aeon of Justice." In the text known as the "Old Commentary" (to *The Book of the Law*), Crowley explained the four aeons thus:

> The Hierarchy of the Egyptians gives us this genealogy: Isis, Osiris, Horus.
>
> Now the "pagan" period is that of Isis; a pastoral, natural period of simple magic. Next with Buddha, Christ, and others there came in the Equinox of Osiris; when sorrow and death were the principal objects of man's thought, and his magical formula is that of sacrifice.
>
> Now, with Mohammed perhaps as its forerunner, comes in the Equinox of Horus, the young child who rises strong and conquering (with his twin Harpocrates) to avenge Osiris, and bring on the age of strength and splendour.
>
> His formula is not yet fully understood.
>
> Following him will arise the Equinox of Ma, the Goddess of Justice, it may be a hundred or ten thousand years from now; for the Computation of Time is not here as There.[8]

The concept that religion developed through a series of stages or evolutionary leaps was consistent with contemporary scholarly literature on the history of religions. Darwin's theory of evolution had been adopted by the leading scholars of the emerging disciplines of history of religions (or comparative religion) and anthropology, and religious thought was often believed to have evolved from matriarchy to patriarchy—the Aeons of Isis and Osiris in the terminology of *The Book of the Law*.

The Swiss antiquarian and anthropologist Johann J. Bachofen (1815–1887) further expounded the theory of a replacement of the "primitive" veneration of female generative power by a "rational" knowledge of male paternity and its subsequent shift from the worship of fertility goddesses (often envisioned as the Great Goddess) to the worship of male gods in his highly influential work *Das Mutterrecht* (the mother-right) in 1861. According to Bachofen, human culture has evolved in four stages. The first of these was a primitive, nomadic, and polyamorous "tellurian" stage in which an early version of the fertility goddess Aphrodite was the dominant deity. The second was the "mother-right" stage, described by Bachofen as a lunar phase centered on agriculture, law, and mystery cults. The dominant deity of this stage was the goddess Demeter, who was worshipped as the embodiment of fertility and femininity. Bachofen's description of the "mother-right" stage would become highly influential for later understandings of a supposed matriarchy that was believed to have existed prior to the emergence of patriarchal cultural and religious systems.

According to Bachofer, the transition from matriarchy to patriarchy was marked by an intermediate, third stage, which he labeled the Dionysian. Dionysus was the principal god of this stage, which was marked by a gradual masculinization of the earlier feminine traditions. The transitional process culminated in the fourth stage, the Apollonian. This was, according to Bachofer, the patriarchal "solar" stage, in which all traces of the matriarchal and Dionysian past were wiped out and modern civilization emerged.[9]

The theory that a widespread religious and cultural matriarchy once existed that then gave way to patriarchal religious systems, such as Christianity, was highly popular at the time of the reception of *The Book of the Law* in 1904.[10] This theory was widely criticized during the second half of the twentieth century, however, and it is now largely discredited, although surviving versions of it can still be found in certain pagan and esoteric schools of thought.

Crowley's understanding of the history of religious evolution was to a large extent influenced by the work of Sir James Frazer (1854–1941), the British anthropologist and historian of religion. Crowley adopted the unspoken but obvious postulate in Frazer's *The Golden Bough*—a work that Crowley described as "invaluable to all students"[11]—that Christianity is in fact based on a primitive form of thought that is incompatible with a modern scientific worldview.[12] The main argument of *The Golden Bough* is that the theme of violent death and resurrection was central to many ancient eastern Mediterranean myths and rites, such as those of Adonis, Attis, Dionysus, and Osiris. According to Frazer, the dying-and-reviving gods were the main protagonists of a recurrent vegetational drama, which in "primitive societies" was often identified with priest-kings who incarnated the well-being of the community. In his analysis of the dying-and-reviving gods Frazer argues that the myths and rites were based on the logic of the "primitive mind," which was less developed than the modern mind. The obvious target of Frazer's criticism is, however, not ancient myths but contemporary Christianity. In the words of the Frazer scholar Robert Ackerman:

> Frazer was interested in even bigger game than primitive-epistemology. For although in his survey of the dying-and-reviving gods of the eastern Mediterranean Frazer never mentions the name of Jesus, only the slowest of his readers could have failed to make the comparison between the pagan rites that result from an imperfect (because irrational) understanding of the universe and contemporary Christianity. Frazer employed the "objective," scientific comparative method as a weapon to finally dispatch Christianity as an outworn relic of misunderstanding, credulity, and superstition.[13]

The formula of the dying and resurrecting God was, according to Crowley, an ignorant belief that stood in sharp contrast to the more advanced form of thinking that characterized the new age. Furthermore, Crowley argued that from a magical point of view, the magic of the old age was no longer efficient, since it was based on irrational thinking. This is expressed in *The Book of the Law* as "Abrogate are all rituals, all ordeals, all words and signs."[14] Crowley elaborated upon this passage in the following comment:

> This verse declares that the old formula of Magick—the Osiris-Adonis-Jesus-Marsyas-Dionysus-Attis-et cetera formula of the Dying God—is no longer efficacious. It rested on the ignorant belief that the Sun died every day, and every year, and that its resurrection was a miracle.
>
> The Formula of the New Aeon recognizes Horus, the Child crowned and conquering, as God. We are all members of the Body of God, the Sun; and about our System is the Ocean of Space. This formula is then to be based upon these facts. Our "Evil," "Error," "Darkness," "Illusion," whatever one chooses to call it, is simply a phenomenon of accidental and temporary separateness. If you are "walking in darkness," do not try to make the sun rise by self-sacrifice, but wait in confidence for the dawn, and enjoy the pleasures of the night meanwhile.[15]

According to Crowley, the magic, or rather "magick" (to give it his preferred spelling), of the New Aeon differed from previous "old-aeonic" forms of magic in that it would be based upon a modern scientific worldview, whereas that of the Old Aeon was based on primitive and irrational thinking. Crowley described his spiritual system as "Scientific Illuminism," with the motto of his journal *The Equinox* reading, "The Method of Science, the Aim of Religion."[16]

Magic had become the subject of serious study toward the end of the nineteenth century, with the emergence of the disciplines of social anthropology and comparative religion. Crowley's criticism of old-aeonic forms of magic as something irrational was quite congruent with the contemporary academic viewpoints expressed in these disciplines. Writing in his influential study *Primitive Culture*, one of the leading scholars in the field, Edward Burnett Tylor (1832–1917), not only termed the belief in magic a "contemptible superstition" but also famously declared magic to be "one of the most pernicious delusions that ever vexed mankind."[17]

Tylor and, after him, Sir James Frazer are often referred to as the chief exponents of the "intellectualist school" in the study of magic—that is, they define magic as a specific form of thought based on an erroneous "pseudoscientific" belief in the potency of the association of ideas. Tylor views magic as nothing but a primitive form of thought that goes back to the earliest phases of human evolution. He dismisses modern occurrences of magical practices as surviving remnants of this archaic form of thought.

> Its place in history is briefly this. It belongs in its main principle to the lowest known stages of civilization, and the lower races, who have not partaken largely of the education of the world, still maintain it in vigour. From this level it may be traced upward, much of the savage art holding its place substantially unchanged, and many new practices being in course of time developed, while both the older and newer developments have lasted on more or less among modern cultured nations. But during the ages in which progressive races have been learning to submit their opinions to closer and closer experimental tests, occult science has been breaking down into condition of a survival, in which state we mostly find it among ourselves.[18]

The notion of magic as antithetical to modern Western culture was to a large extent based on the premise that magic is a form of "primitive" superstitious (or nonrational) thought.[19] This superstitious way of thinking was often described as associative thinking, in which similarity-based notions of causality constitute the modus operandi of magical practice. According to this pattern of belief, an act that resembles or imitates the desired object of the magician will cause the desired object to occur. The concept of mental causation—that is, the conviction that the mind can influence the physical world—is of course inextricably intertwined with that of associative thinking. To use a stereotypical example: inserting a needle in a doll will not alone suffice to cause harm to an enemy—the efficacy of magic thinking is believed to be dependent on the intention of the magician. Although it was Tylor who first identified magic with associative thinking, it is Frazer's elaboration on this that has made the deepest mark on the study of magic, with its well-known distinction of sympathetic magic into two categories, contagious and homeopathic. Furthermore, Frazer claimed that this type of thinking represents an archaic and primitive form of thought that preceded religious and scientific thinking, thus emphasizing the incompatibility of magic with a modern rational-positivistic worldview. Although Crowley shared Frazer's criticism of (old-aeonic) magic as based on primitive thought, he nevertheless held the view that old-aeonic magic had been efficacious during the age of Osiris. The important things to note in the present discussion are that Crowley believed that the premises of magic and initiation changed with each new age or dispensation and that he shared Frazer's belief that culture had evolved through three different stages: magic, religion, and science according to Frazer, and the Aeons of Isis, Osiris, and Horus according to *Liber AL*.

A Time of War

The notion of the coming of a New Age was by no means unique to Thelema and *The Book of the Law* but was in fact a common feature in the discourse of fin de siècle occult and religious movements.[20] However, the great majority of esoteric speculations concerning a New Age saw its emergence as a gradual and peaceful process. Scholars such as Wouter Hanegraaff have observed that the occultism (or secularized esotericism) of the late nineteenth and early twentieth centuries was characterized by, among other things, the impact of positivism and Darwinian evolutionism, which often took the form of a belief in personal transformation as well as societal change.[21] The progress of humankind was seen as a result of spiritual evolution, a natural process that would lead to a continuously improving and more advanced society. The conscious application of a broad range of esoteric practices would, however, help speed up the process. This belief, which assumed various forms and was expressed in different ways, became a firmly embedded discourse of twentieth-century occultism.

The New Age was commonly also defined in astrological terms, with the Age of Pisces said to be supplanted by the Age of Aquarius. The consequent evolutionary leap in the development of humankind was often portrayed as heralding a fundamental change in the understanding of the relationship between human beings and the universe. Such thought culminated in the blossoming of the New Age movement of the 1960s and early 1970s, with its characterization of the Age of Aquarius as the embodiment of holistic principles, in contrast to the dualism that it was suggested defined the Age of Pisces. The dualism of the preceding age was held to be responsible for the strife and conflict between patriarchal religious systems such as Christianity and Islam, whereas the New Age would be marked by peace and harmony.[22]

While exponents of the Aquarian New Age seem to have viewed the transition between ages as generally harmonious, with the conflict of duality slowly replaced by the peace of unity, the birth of the New Aeon of Horus was described in very different terms. *The Book of the Law* describes the transition from the Old Aeon to the New as being marked by war and destruction. Crowley outlines this in the following seemingly prophetic passage, which he is said to have written in 1911, three years prior to the outbreak of World War I:

> There is a Magical Operation of maximum importance: the Initiation of a New Aeon. When it becomes necessary to utter a Word, the whole Planet must be bathed in blood. Before man is ready to accept the Law of Thelema, the Great War must be fought. This Bloody Sacrifice is the critical point of the World-Ceremony of the Proclamation of Horus, the Crowned and Conquering Child, as Lord of the Aeon.
>
> This whole matter is prophesied in the Book of the Law itself; let the student take note, and enter the ranks of the Host of the Sun.[23]

According to Crowley, the reason for the destructive transition lay in the extreme divergence between the ethos of the Aeon of Osiris and that of Horus. Not only did the two aeons rely on fundamentally different magical formulas—that of sacrifice as opposed to that of the discovery of the True Will (Thelema)—but also, and perhaps most important, the blossoming of the Aeon of Horus necessitated freedom from the oppressive religious systems of the Old Aeon. To Crowley this meant in particular freedom from the restrictions of Christianity. By identifying his role of prophet of the New Aeon with the reviled Beast 666 of the book of Revelation, Crowley believed that he was seizing a cosmic task as the commander of the forces that would overthrow Christianity:

> It is proper to obey The Beast, because His Law is pure Freedom, and He will give no command which is other than a Right Interpretation of this Freedom. But it is necessary for the development of Freedom itself to have an organization; and every organization must have a highly-centralized control. This is especially necessary in time of war, as even the so-called "democratic" nations have been taught by Experience. . . . Now this age is pre-eminently a "time of war," most of all now, when it is our Work to overthrow the slave-gods.[24]

It is clear not only that Crowley paid close attention to the many references in *The Book of the Law* to war, violence, and destruction but also that his interpretation of the violent and apocalyptic passages changed over time. Crowley wrote two significant verse-by-verse commentaries on *The Book of the Law*, termed by him simply the "Old Comment" and the "New Comment"; he also wrote a third titled "The Comment called D" (often referred to as "The Djeridensis Working") and the "Short" or "Tunis Comment." It is striking to see in these how Crowley's interpretations of the most violent passages of the book changed over time.[25] The "Old Comment" was written before the outbreak of World War I and published in 1912 in his journal *The Equinox*, volume I, number 7. In the "Old Comment" Crowley tended to interpret the violent passages in a mystical way, as referring to spiritual exercises or qualities. In the "New Comment," written in the early 1920s, however, the interpretation is radically historical and apocalyptic.

The violent language and symbolism is particularly striking in the third chapter of *The Book of the Law*. Fittingly, this chapter is attributed to the god Ra-Hoor-Khuit, who is described as a god of "war and vengeance." Crowley acknowledged the difficulty of interpreting this chapter and admitted that many would find its more radical sentiments repugnant. In spite of this, when commenting upon the third chapter Crowley stressed the importance of interpreting it literally, although he would continue the search for more subtle, esoteric meanings.

> Comment seems hardly necessary. The Great War [i.e., World War I] is a mere illustration of this text. The only nations which have suffered are those whose religion was Osirian, or, as they called it, Christian.[26]

In the "Old Comment" Crowley remarked that "this whole book seems intended to be interpreted literally . . . yet a mystical meaning is easy to find." Crowley thus seemed to be open to both literal and metaphorical interpretations, but it is clear that prior to World War I he preferred the mystical approach to *The Book of the Law*. Three short passages from the third chapter serve as a good entrance point to Crowley's differing interpretations: "Choose ye an island!," "Fortify it!," "Dung it about with enginery of war!"[27]

In the "Old Comment" these passages were taken as referring to the importance of concentrating the mind upon the chakras, whereas in the "New Comment" Crowley observed, "This phrase is curiously suggestive of the 'mine-layer' to those who have seen one in action." Similarly in the "Old Comment" Crowley suggested that the part of verse 7 that states "I will give you a war-engine" should be taken as indicating that a new method of meditation would be imparted; in the "New Comment," he wrote: "This suggests the Tank, the Island chosen being England. But this is probably a forthshadowing of the real Great War, wherein Horus shall triumph utterly."[28]

According to Crowley, the cosmic role of Thelema was not restricted to the overthrow of the old religions and the promotion of the new law; it also had the potential to have a direct effect on the global political situation. Crowley had political aspirations for Thelema and firmly believed that the first government to adopt it would become invincible. One of Crowley's German followers, Martha Küntzel (1857–1941), translated *The Book of the Law* into German and allegedly sent a copy to Adolf Hitler in 1925. According to Crowley, the German dictator was sufficiently impressed with the book to correspond with Küntzel about it for several years, although it seems most unlikely that this really happened. Crowley supposedly also tried to get in contact with Hitler in the fall of 1930 through his former disciple J. F. C. Fuller (1878–1966), while at the same time trying to reach out to Stalin through the journalist Walter Duranty (1884–1957).[29] There can be no doubt that these approaches were entirely opportunistic and driven solely by Crowley's ambition to spread Thelema rather than being indicative of any basic sympathy with the respective ideologies.[30]

Reflecting on the previously cited passages of *The Book of the Law*, in his "New Comment" Crowley expressed his certainty that they affirmed the potential political potency of the creed of Thelema:

> This is a practical instruction; and, as a "military secret," is not in any way soever to be disclosed. I say only that the plans are complete, and that *the first nation to accept the Law of Thelema Shall, by My counsel, become sole Mistress of the World.*[31]

Table 4.1. Comparison of Crowley's "Old Comments" and "New Comments" on *Liber AL vel Legis*

Liber AL vel Legis	Old Comment	New Comment
AL III:4: "Choose ye an island!"	An Island = one of the Cakkrams or nerve-centres in the spine.	This is a practical instruction; and, as a "military secret," is not in any way soever to be disclosed. I say only that the plans are complete, and that the first nation to accept the Law of Thelema Shall, by My counsel, become sole Mistress of the World.
AL III:5: "Fortify it!"	Fortify it = concentrate the mind upon it.	Fortify it = concentrate the mind upon it.
AL III:6: "Dung it about with enginery of war!"	Prevent any impressions reaching it.	This phrase is curiously suggestive of the "mine-layer" to those who have seen one in action.
AL III:7: "I will give you a war-engine."	I will describe a new method of meditation by which [See Verse 8, Old Comment].	This suggests the Tank, the Island chosen being England. But this is probably a forthshadowing of the real Great War, wherein Horus shall triumph utterly.

In a strange affirmation of his apocalyptic interpretation of *The Book of the Law*, Crowley also claimed that the publication of book itself could be directly linked to the outbreaks of a number of wars. Thus he suggested that the first four publications of the book led, respectively, to the Balkan War, World War I, the Sino-Japanese War, and World War II.[32] Crowley saw these wars as necessary steps in the establishment of the New Aeon: humankind had to face a period of war, chaos, and destruction in order to free society from the shackles and restrictions of the old gods and to pave the way for a New Aeon of Light, Love, and Liberty. While this view of history stood in sharp contrast to other contemporary esoteric visions of the coming of a New Age, it was—and continues to be—a recurrent discourse in many Christian premillenarian groups that viewed an apocalyptic period of tribulation as prerequisite to the inauguration of Christ's millennial reign.

Christian Premillenarianism and Dispensationalism

Crowley was well acquainted with Christian premillenarianism as a result of the religious upbringing provided for him by his parents, who belonged to the fundamentalist evangelical sect known as the Plymouth Brethren.[33] This movement, founded by the Calvinist John Nelson Darby (1800–1882) during the first half of the nineteenth century, is characterized by a literal interpretation of the Bible and by a conservative theology centered on Darby's teachings of dispensationalism.[34]

According to Darby's theology, the history of the world can be divided into a series of seven ages or dispensations. God relates differently to humanity in each of these dispensations and sets different lessons for humankind to learn. The dispensations are termed those of "Innocence" (up until the Fall), "Conscience" (from Adam to Noah), "Government" (from Noah to Abraham), "Patriarchal Rule" (from Abraham to Moses), "Mosaic Law" (from Moses to Christ), "Grace" (from Christ to the present day), and the "Thousand-Year Rule," which will be ushered in at the end of the ages. Darby was deeply interested in eschatology, and his theology emphasizes the imminent end-time. He held the premillennial view that the physical return of Christ to the earth would occur prior to the inauguration of the millennial rule. In this his thought differed from other forms of Christian eschatology, notably that of postmillennialism, which foresaw the millennial rule as occurring before the Second Coming.

Darby preached a pretribulational return of Christ, in which Christ would return to take up Christians into heaven by means of "the Rapture" immediately before the worldwide Tribulation. The theologian Jan S. Markham explains that Darby believed that the Bible stipulates that the Second Coming of Christ will be divided into two distinctive phases. The first is "the Rapture," when those born again in Christ rise and meet him in the skies, and the second is the "Visible Return," which will usher in the Thousand-Year Rule on earth. In between these two stages, Darby taught, there will be a seven year-period of tribulation, during which the Antichrist will rise to prominence.[35]

Although Crowley rebelled against the religious views of his parents when still in his teens—and continued this revolt throughout his life—it is striking that two characteristic aspects of the religious worldview of the Plymouth Brethren, the importance placed on the study of the Holy Scripture and the notion of dispensationalism, are echoed in the religious system of Thelema. In Crowley's new religion the Holy Scripture of the Bible was replaced by *The Holy Books of Thelema*, the most important of which was *The Book of the Law*. The new dispensation was not that of the imminent period before the return of Christ, but rather the Aeon of Horus, formally inaugurated at the vernal equinox in 1904.

It seems likely that Crowley's animosity toward Christianity was in part a reaction to the traumas of his upbringing in the cultic milieu of the Exclusive Branch of the Plymouth Brethren. According to his autobiography, Crowley had been relatively happy up to the age of eleven, when his father died and, in her grief, his mother strengthened her embrace of religion. Commenting on this pivotal point in his life, Crowley notes:

> I accepted the theology of the Plymouth Brethren. In fact, I could hardly conceive of the existence of people who might doubt it. I simply went over to Satan's side; and to this hour I cannot tell why.[36]

Crowley's attitude toward Christianity is actually much more complex than might be expected from someone who identified himself with the Beast of Revelation. In common with H. P. Blavatsky and other occultists of the period, he seems to have maintained a profound respect for Christ as an individual who had attained enlightenment, although he remained skeptical as to the historical reality of the Christ figure as described in the Gospels. He also despised Christianity and its moral teachings, being particularly hostile to the Protestant and reformed churches. Although Crowley included discussion in his autobiography of his childhood experiences with the Plymouth Brethren and the various Brethren schools to which he was sent, he reserved his most outspoken and self-revealing exploration of this painful period of his life, which he called "a childhood in hell," for the introduction to his epic poem *The World's Tragedy* (1910):

> I therefore hold the legendary Jesus in no wise responsible for the trouble: it began with Luther, perhaps, and went on with Wesley; but no matter!—what I am trying to get at is the religion which makes England to-day a hell for any man who cares at all for freedom. That religion they call Christianity; the devil they honour they call God. I accept these definitions, as a poet must do, if he is to be at all intelligible to his age, and it is their God and their religion that I hate and will destroy.[37]

Concluding Remarks

Throughout his life Crowley revisited the violent passages of *The Book of the Law*, and increasingly he viewed them as prophesying the world events that were unfolding around him. This became most evident toward the end of his life with the advent of World War II, an event that he claimed was a direct consequence of the 1937 publication of *The Book of the Law*. Thus in 1945, with the unleashing of the atomic bomb, he revised his opinion of the "war-engine" of *The Book of the Law* from "tank" to "atomic bomb."[38] After Crowley's death in 1947, Thelemites such as Karl J. Germer (1885–1962) and Marcelo R. Motta (1931–1987) reinterpreted certain of the apocalyptic passages of *The Book of the Law* in the light of the Cold War and anticipated an imminent World War III in which much of humanity might be annihilated by nuclear weapons.[39] During the 1950s, Germer, who had taken over the Ordo Templi Orientis (OTO) after Crowley, collaborated with Gerald Yorke, a former Crowley disciple and collector of his works, to make typescript copies of all the surviving Crowley letters, diaries, and manuscripts. One set of copies would be kept in London, another in the United States, and another in Australia, with the aim that at least one relatively complete body of the Beast's writings might survive in the event of some global war or cataclysm.[40]

Kenneth Grant (1924–2011), who had acted as Crowley's personal secretary for a brief period near the end of the Beast's life, participated in this project in the late 1940s and early 1950s by transcribing materials for Yorke and Germer. Starting in the late 1960s, Grant went on to collaborate with Crowley's literary executor, John Symonds, in the publication of a number of significant works by the Beast. It was not long after this that Grant launched his own version of the OTO (later referred to as the Typhonian OTO and now called the Typhonian Order) and published the first volumes of his influential "Typhonian Trilogies." Grant's work is firmly rooted in the Thelemic tradition, although traditionalists within the movement perceive his work as unorthodox and idiosyncratic. Grant discusses *The Book of the Law* at length in various of his works, and it is clear that he shared Crowley's belief that the transition from the Old Aeon to the New would be marked by violent upheaval. His perspective was possibly more apocalyptic than Crowley's, for he predicted an imminent and global catastrophe. In his *Outside the Circles of Time* (1980) Grant suggests:

> The significance of Crowley's work . . . is only now becoming apparent as the values of the old world, the old aeon, crumble away or undergo radical change. Furthermore the entire mass of humanity—not a mere handful of nations, however large and powerful—is now threatened with destruction as, once before, when it succumb to almost annihilation in the days of Atlantis. There are those who believe that it is already too late to avert a repetition of that catastrophe, although it is

> considered possible for certain members of the human race to survive the holocaust and its effects.[41]

Grant's understanding of the mechanics of time also differed from Crowley's, for where Crowley had a relatively linear understanding of history as being divided by dispensations, Grant adopted a cyclical concept, apparently drawn from Hindu thought on the matter.[42] Looking at events from that perspective, Grant suggested that humankind is facing the final phases of *Kali Yuga*, or the Black Age, and that the violence around us and the imminent catastrophe are the birth pangs of the New Aeon, interpreted as the *Satya*, or Golden Yuga. In a short text titled "Looking Forward," which he wrote in 2004 to commemorate the one hundredth anniversary of the reception of *The Book of the Law*, Grant seems to have embraced contemporary apocalyptic speculation about the Mayan calendar and the "end of time," which posits that the destruction of the world will happen toward the end of 2012.[43]

The writings of Kenneth Grant are a good example of how the millenarian and dispensationalist themes of *The Book of the Law* are being reinterpreted by some post-Crowley Thelemites. A quick search of the Internet reveals a wide range of other contemporary interpretations, ranging from purely symbolic to literal and historical.

In summary, then, Crowley's understanding of history as a succession of aeons, or dispensations, can be seen as a reflection of the teachings of John Nelson Darby and the Plymouth Brethren that he encountered during his childhood. Darby's description of human history as divisible into a series of chronologically successive dispensations is paralleled by Crowley's succession of aeons. The Christian end-times theology of premillennialism, with its belief in the tribulation preceding the millennium, is reinterpreted as the birth pangs of the New Aeon of Horus. According to premillennial theology, the Christian faithful will be saved from the Tribulation by the Rapture. While there is arguably no direct Thelemic counterpart to this, certain passages in the first chapter of *The Book of the Law*—for instance, verse 58: "I give unimaginable joys on earth: certainty, not faith, while in life, upon death; peace unutterable, rest, ecstasy"—do appear to offer great reward to the true believers who accept the Law of Thelema. Finally, just as Christ will have a central role in the battle against Satan and the forces of evil according to Christian millennial and apocalyptic traditions, Crowley—as the Great Beast 666—claimed to be the commander of the forces that will overthrow the "slave-gods" of the Old Aeon. This (partly) inverted form of Christian premillennialism can thus be view as an interesting example of the ways in which

Christian doctrines may consciously or otherwise be reinterpreted and adopted by contemporary esoteric new religious movements, and therefore how important it can be for scholars of Western esotericism to take Christian beliefs and practices into account.

Notes

1. I wish to thank Keith Richmond for his valuable comments and suggestions for this chapter.
2. *The Book of the Law* was first published in the third volume of [Aleister Crowley], *ΘΕΛΗΜΑ* [*Thelema*], 3 vols. (London: privately printed, 1909), with the title "Liber L vel Legis sub figura CCXX as Delivered by LXXVIII unto DCLXVI." The facsimile of *Liber Legis* was first published in *The Equinox* I (7) (March 1912). *The Book of the Law* was published several times in Crowley's lifetime: 1913, 1926, 1936, 1937, and 1938. Numerous modern editions are in print.
3. For Crowley's own account of the reception of *The Book of the Law* in Cairo, 1904, see Aleister Crowley, *The Equinox of the Gods* (London: OTO, 1936). The Latin title of *The Book of the Law* was initially *Liber L vel Legis*, but this was later changed to *Liber AL vel Legis* after Crowley's "magical son" Charles Stansfeld Jones (1886–1950) discovered in 1918 that AL is the secret key to *The Book of the Law*, which Crowley accepted in September 1919. For further information on this, see Frater Achad [Charles Stansfeld Jones], *Liber 31, and Other Related Essays* (San Francisco: Level Press, 1974).
4. *Liber AL vel Legis* I:40.
5. Ibid., I:57.
6. Ibid., I:3.
7. "Abrahadabra is the Magick Formula of the Aeon, by which men may accomplish the Great Work. This Formula is then the 'reward' given by the God [Ra Hoor Khuit], the largesse granted by Him on His accession to the Lordship of the Aeon, just as INRI-IAO-LVX formula of attainment by way of Crucifixion was given by Osiris when he came to power in the last Aeon." Aleister Crowley, *Magical and Philosophical Commentaries on "The Book of the Law,"* ed. John Symonds and Kenneth Grant (Montreal: 93 Publishing, 1974), 257.
8. Aleister Crowley, "*Liber Legis*: The Comment," *The Equinox* I (7) (1912), 400. This comment to *The Book of the Law* is referred to as the "Old Comment."
9. Johann Jacob Bachofen, *Das Mutterrecht: Eine Untersuchung über die Gynaikokratie der alten Welt nach ihrer religiösen und rechtlichen Natur* (Stuttgart: Verlag von Krais und Hoffmann, 1861). For critical discussions of Bachofen's work, see Uwe Wesel, *Der Mythos vom Matriarchat: Über Bachofens Mutterrecht und die Stellung von Frauen in frühen Gesellschaften vor der Entstehung staatlicher Herrschaft* (Frankfurt: Suhrkamp, 1980); Josef Rattner and Gerhard Danzer, "Johann Jakob Bachofen

und die Mutterrechtstheorie," in *Europäische Kulturbeiträge im deutsch-schweizerischen Schrifttum von 1850–2000* (Würzburg: Königshausen & Neumann, 2003), 9–28.

10. Joan Bamberger, "The Myth of Matriarchy: Why Men Rule in Primitive Society," in *Woman, Culture, and Society*, ed. Michelle Zimbalist Rosaldo and Louise Lamphere (Stanford, Calif.: Stanford University Press, 1974), 263–80; Cynthia Eller, *The Myth of Matriarchal Prehistory: Why an Invented Past Will Not Give Women a Future* (Boston: Beacon Press, 2000).
11. Aleister Crowley, *Magick in Theory and Practice* (Paris: Lecram Press, 1930), 211. For a discussion of the influence of Frazer upon Crowley, see Martin P. Starr, editor's introduction, in Aleister Crowley, *Golden Twigs*, ed. Martin P. Starr (Chicago: Teitan Press, 1988), vii–xv.
12. On Frazer, see Robert Ackerman, *J. G. Frazer: His Life and Work* (Cambridge: Cambridge University Press, 1987); Robert Ackerman, *The Myth and Ritual School: J. G. Frazer and the Cambridge Ritualists* (New York: Garland, 1991); Jonathan Z. Smith, "The Glory, Jest and Riddle: James George Frazer and *The Golden Bough*," PhD diss., Yale University, 1969.
13. Robert Ackerman, "Frazer, James G.," in *Encyclopedia of Religion*, 2nd ed. (Detroit: Macmillan Reference, 2005), 3192.
14. *Liber AL vel Legis* I:49.
15. Crowley, *Magical and Philosophical Commentaries*, 137.
16. For a detailed discussion of Crowley's positivistic and scientific understanding of magic, see chapter 3 in this collection, Marco Pasi's "Varieties of Magical Experience: Aleister Crowley's Views on Occult Practice."
17. Edward Burnett Tylor, *Primitive Culture: Researches into the Development of Mythology, Philosophy, Religion, Language, Art, and Custom*, 6th ed. (London: John Murray, 1920), 1:112.
18. Ibid., 1:112–13.
19. As I have discussed elsewhere, the notion of magic as antithetical to Western society is based on four interlinked discourses: (1) magic is based on "primitive" superstitious (or nonrational) thought; (2) magic is something that originates from other parts of the world, and as such is a foreign element in Western culture; (3) magic is incompatible with the Christian faith; and (4) magic is inherently evil by nature. Henrik Bogdan, "Introduction: Modern Western Magic," *Aries: Journal for the Study of Western Esotericism* 12:1 (2012), 1–16.
20. Alex Owen, *The Place of the Enchantment: British Occultism and the Culture of the Modern* (Chicago: University of Chicago Press, 2004).
21. Wouter J. Hanegraaff, "The Study of Western Esotericism," in *New Approaches to the Study of Religion*, ed. Peter Antes, Armin W. Geertz, and Randi R. Warne (Berlin: Walter de Gruyter, 2004), 490–519.
22. On the New Age and Western esotericism, see Wouter J. Hanegraaff, *New Age Religion and Western Culture: Esotericism in the Mirror of Secular Thought*

(Albany: State University of New York Press, 1998); Olav Hammer, *Claiming Knowledge: Strategies of Epistemology from Theosophy to the New Age* (Leiden: Brill, 2004).

23. Crowley, *Magick in Theory and Practice*, 96–97.
24. Crowley, *Magical and Philosophical Commentaries*, 122.
25. The "Old Comment" to *The Book of the Law* was published as Aleister Crowley, "*Liber Legis*: The Comment," *The Equinox* I (7) (March 1912), 387–40[1]. The "New Comment," written in 1920, and the incomplete "Commentary Called D[jeridensis]," written at the Hotel du Djerid in the oasis of Nefta, Tunisia, in the autumn of 1923, remained unpublished during Crowley's lifetime. They were published for the first time, together with the "Old Comment," in Crowley, *Magical and Philosophical Commentaries*. The "Old" and "New" comments were also published as Aleister Crowley, *The Law Is for All: An Extended Commentary on "The Book of the Law,"* ed. Israel Regardie (St. Paul, Minn.: Llewellyn, 1975); and Aleister Crowley, *The Commentaries of AL: The Equinox* V(1), ed. Marcelo Motta (New York: Samuel Weiser, 1975). In 1945 Crowley contracted his friend Louis Wilkinson (1881–1966) to edit the lengthy commentary on *The Book of the Law* in popular form, which was published as Aleister Crowley, *The Law Is for All: The Authorized Popular Commentary to "The Book of the Law,"* ed. Louis Wilkinson and Hymenaeus Beta (Tempe, Ariz.: New Falcon, 1998). The "Short" or "Tunis Comment" was written in 1925 and published for the first time in [Aleister Crowley], *AL: The Book of the Law* (Tunis: privately printed, 1926), in a limited edition of eleven numbered copies. The text of this comment is included at the end of most later editions of *The Book of the Law*.
26. Crowley, *Magical and Philosophical Commentaries*, 258.
27. *Liber AL vel Legis* III:4–6.
28. Crowley, *Magical and Philosophical Commentaries*, 259.
29. See Crowley's letter to David Curwen dated December 5, 1945, in Aleister Crowley and David Curwen, *Brother Curwen, Brother Crowley: A Correspondence*, ed. Henrik Bogdan (York Beach, Maine: Teitan Press, 2010), 89. See also Richard B. Spence, *Secret Agent 666: Aleister Crowley, British Intelligence and the Occult* (Port Townsend, Wash.: Feral House, 2008), 212–13.
30. See Marco Pasi, *Aleister Crowley and the Temptation of Politics* (London: Equinox Publishing, 2013).
31. Crowley, *Magical and Philosophical Commentaries*, 259; emphasis added.
32. "THE FIRST PUBLICATION:
Nine months before the outbreak of the Balkan War, which broke up the Near East.
THE SECOND PUBLICATION:
Nine months before the outbreak of the World War, which broke up the West.
THE THIRD PUBLICATION
Nine months before the outbreak of the Sino-Japanese War, which is breaking up the Far East.

THE FOURTH PUBLICATION
6.22 a.m., December 22, 1937, e.v., nine months before the betrayal, which stripped Britain of the last rags of honour, prestige and security, and will break up civilization. To repeat: "the event will establish the kingdom of the Crowned and Conquering Child over the whole earth, and all men shall bow to the Law, which is love under will." Aleister Crowley, *Thumbs Up! A Pentagram—A Pantacle to Win the War* (London: OTO, 1941), n.p.

33. For Crowley's own account of his experiences with the Plymouth Brethren, see *The Confessions of Aleister Crowley: An Autohagiography*, ed. John Symonds and Kenneth Grant (London: Arkana, 1989), 35–81; Aleister Crowley, *The World's Tragedy* (1910; Scottsdale, Ariz.: New Falcon, 1991), xi–xxxiv. See also Aleister Crowley, *Crowley on Christ*, ed. Francis King (London: C. W. Daniel, 1974).
34. For information on the Plymouth Brethren, see James Patrick, *Primitivist Piety: The Ecclesiology of the Early Plymouth Brethren* (Lanham, Md.: Scarecrow Press, 1996); Roy F. Coad, *A History of the Brethren Movement* (Exeter: Paternoster Press, 1968); Harold Rowdon, *The Origins of the Brethren, 1825–1850* (London: Pickering & Inglis, 1967).
35. Jan S. Markham, *The Blackwell Companion to the Theologians*, vol. 2, *Enlightenment to the Twenty-First Century* (Chichester, West Sussex: Wiley-Blackwell, 2009), 43–44.
36. Crowley, *The Confessions*, 67.
37. Crowley, *The World's Tragedy*, xxxi.
38. Letter from Aleister Crowley to Louis Wilkinson, August 7, 1945. Warburg Institute, University of London.
39. Martin P. Starr, "A Hundred Years Hence: Visions of a Thelemic Future," *Starfire: A Journal of the New Aeon* 2:3 (2008), 151–54.
40. Yorke's collection is now deposited at the Warburg Institute, University of London.
41. Kenneth Grant, *Outside the Circles of Time* (London: Frederick Muller, 1980), 2.
42. Grant was also inspired by Charles Stansfeld Jones, who in the spring of 1948 began to receive a series of revelations that, according to Jones, inaugurated a new aeon, that of Ma-Ion or Maat. Within a year Jones had written approximately two hundred letters to his "witnesses" Gerald Yorke, Karl J. Germer, and Albert Handel, in which he discussed the revelations. See Frederick J. Kayser, *Son of the Magus: A Biographic Essay Composed from the Writings of Frater Achad* (unpublished, in the author's collection); Charles Stansfeld Jones, *The Incoming of the Aeon of Maat* (London: Starfire, forthcoming).
43. "It is the reception of the text which we know as 'the threefold book of Law' that the present gathering is set on re-membering. The freedoms and ecstasies offered by Nuit and Her Son, Hadit, in chapters one and two, now begin to merge with the Mysteries of 'a god of war and Vengeance'—Ra-Hoor-Khuit—and it is the latter Mysteries which we now confront in the final phases of the kali Yuga—the 'Black Age' of Goddess Kali, the Night-Dark Mother of Time; of Time which is coming to an end, as also is the universe *as we know it*." Kenneth Grant, "Looking Forward!," *Starfire: A Journal of the New Aeon* 2:3 (2008), 13.

5

The Great Beast as a Tantric Hero

THE ROLE OF YOGA AND TANTRA IN ALEISTER CROWLEY'S MAGICK

Gordan Djurdjevic

IN THE SUMMER of 1900, Aleister Crowley (1875–1947) found himself in Mexico pursuing his two great passions, mountaineering and magick.[1] Although only twenty-four years old, Crowley was already one of the highest initiates of the Hermetic Order of the Golden Dawn, the most important fin de siècle occult fraternity in the West. He considered himself an adept in magick, but the futility of his endeavors and a sense of dissatisfaction were now starting to assert themselves with increasing force. When a fellow mountaineer, Oscar Eckenstein (1859–1921), joined him in Mexico toward the end of the year, Crowley confided his concerns to his friend. Eckenstein, a railway engineer and an analytical chemist by profession who had no interest in the occult, gave a response that addressed the heart of the matter: Crowley's problems stemmed from his inability to concentrate. "Give up your Magick, with all its romantic fascinations and deceitful delights," Eckenstein advised him. "Promise to do this for a time and I will teach you how to master your mind."[2]

Crowley agreed to the proposal and before long immersed himself in a set of exercises devised by Eckenstein, the purpose of which was to enable him to focus his thoughts on a chosen mental image or sensory input. These exercises were in their essence the initial steps in the path of Yoga, undertaken by a person who was later to become one of the principal transmitters of Yogic and, to a lesser degree, Tantric teachings into the field of Western esotericism. Crowley's influence on the twentieth century and contemporary occultism has been enormous,[3] but his unusual lifestyle and teachings continue to be controversial and misunderstood. This chapter will focus on the place of Yoga and Tantra in Crowley's writings, within the structure of the magical orders of which he was the head, and in his own spiritual practice. My argument is simple: not only is Crowley important for the fusion of Eastern and Western esoteric traditions,[4] but also his own practice of magick becomes clearer if aspects of it are understood against the background of Yoga and Tantra.

India, Western Esotericism, and Crowley

The tendency toward syncretism is one of the defining characteristics of Western esotericism. By the end of the nineteenth century, this tendency was strongly manifest as openness toward Eastern, most notably Indian, religious traditions. These were otherwise becoming increasingly familiar through numerous translations of original texts and through popular accounts written by colonial officials and travelers. A landmark event in this regard, as far as Western esotericism is concerned, was the formation of the Theosophical Society in 1875.[5] This same year also gave birth to arguably the most important and influential occultist of the twentieth century, Edward Alexander, or Aleister, Crowley. In his numerous writings and in his own spiritual practice and teaching, Crowley engaged and incorporated significant elements of Indian Yoga and Tantra. It may be claimed that Yoga on one hand and the Western esoteric tradition in general (including magic, alchemy, astrology, and kabbalah) on the other form the twin aspects of what Crowley called magick.[6] In addition to this, he often asserted that Eastern and Western esoteric traditions share a fundamental resemblance, which he attempted to elucidate and which he regularly emphasized.

A clarification is appropriate at the outset. While Crowley's engagement with Indian Yoga is a straightforward affair that may be easily documented on the basis of his theoretical writings, practical instructions, and personal records of practice,[7] his involvement with Tantra is much more complex and controversial. To a significant extent, this involvement shares primarily *functional* parallels with the Tantric path. It is feasible to recognize in the whole project of Crowley's magick an *analogy* with the approach of Tantra, even if his formal knowledge of the latter was limited. I will, later on, anchor my arguments by focusing on three areas of convergence between Crowley's and Tantric methods: employment of sex (e.g., ingestion of sexual fluids) as a tool of achievement; harnessing of the occult aspects of the human (subtle) body (represented by *cakras* and the *kuṇḍalinī*); and the use of transgression as a spiritual technique.

Sketch of Crowley's Early Biography: Magick, Yoga, Thelema, and the Esoteric Orders

Aleister Crowley's spiritual career begun with his initiation into the Hermetic Order of the Golden Dawn, which he joined in 1898.[8] He rose rapidly within the order's hierarchy, having a superb tutor in the person of Allan Bennett (1872–1923). Bennett would in time leave England to join the Buddhist Saṅgha in Burma (now Myanmar), as one of the first Westerners to receive ordination in the Theravāda tradition.[9] In 1901, Crowley joined Bennett for several months in Ceylon (now Sri Lanka). They studied Yogic meditation together, taking advantage of the knowledge Bennett acquired from Ponnambalam Ramanathan, the solicitor general of Ceylon, who was also a Tamil Śaivite guru and the author of a book that interpreted the gospels of Matthew and John from the standpoint of Yoga.[10] After his initial exposure to the exercise of mental cultivation under the tutelage of Oscar Eckenstein, this was Crowley's first attempt in the formal practice of Yoga. He claimed that as the result of these meditations he successfully attained a deep stage of Yogic meditation, *dhyāna*, on October 2 of the same year.[11]

In addition to his engagement with Yogic practices proper, in this period Crowley also learned the essentials of Buddhist meditation.[12] He described a classical Buddhist form of meditation, the *mahāsatipaṭṭhāna*, in his essay "Science and Buddhism," written in India in 1901.[13] He also incorporated basic methodology of this practice into two of his instructional manuals for the Order of A∴A∴ (see below), "Liber Ru vel Spiritus"[14] and "Liber Yod."[15] The fundamental practices of classical Yoga, consisting of posture, breathing exercises, and concentration of the mind, are described concisely in "Liber E vel Exercitiorum," originally published in *The Equinox*, Crowley's "Review of Scientific Illuminism."[16] The general theory of Yoga is laid out in the text called "Mysticism," which is incorporated into Crowley's magnum opus, *Book Four* or *Magick.*[17]

In the spring of 1904, the most significant event in Crowley's career occurred. According to his account, while on his honeymoon in Cairo, Egypt, he received a short prophetic text, which came to be known as *Liber AL vel Legis* or *The Book of the Law.*[18] The book announces the doctrines of a new religion called Thelema, with Crowley—referred to in the book as "the prince-priest the Beast"[19]—as its prophet.[20] On the basis of this revelation and his continuous research into, and practice of, various mystical and magical traditions, Crowley felt that the time was ripe to start a new magical order, as he was convinced that the Golden Dawn has lost its charisma and authority. The new order, the structure of which Crowley developed in collaboration with his friend and mentor George Cecil Jones around 1907, is officially known only by its initials, the A∴A∴. Like the Golden Dawn, this order is modeled on the pattern of the Tree of Life, where every *sephira* on the Tree corresponds to a particular mystical or magical achievement.[21]

In its essence, the method of the A∴A∴ rests on the fusion of ceremonial magick and Yoga. One of the introductory grades of the order, the grade of Zelator, involves mastery of the posture or *āsana* and the control of breathing, *prāṇāyāma*. In the grade of Dominus Liminis, the practitioner is expected to master the methods of Yogic introspection (or withdrawal of senses from outside objects), *pratyāhāra*, and concentration, *dhāraṇā*. An initiate of the grade of Adeptus needs to attain mastery in deep meditation, *dhyāna*, while the Master of the Temple—a grade that involves the dissolution of the ego—has to achieve the final step in classical Yoga, *samādhi*. In this manner, the methods and stages of Indian Yoga are firmly implanted into an order that simultaneously embraces several branches of Western esoteric traditions.[22] This shows that Crowley, in reorganizing the Golden Dawn, relied on what may be called the principle of "occult cosmopolitanism," which is to say that the Thelemic path to spiritual perfection rested upon the amalgamation of Eastern and Western methods of achievement. This was a significant innovation, since the Eastern spiritual traditions had almost no role in the original Golden Dawn.

In 1912, Crowley met Theodor Reuss (1855–1923).[23] Reuss was at the time the head of a fringe Freemasonic order known as Ordo Templi Orientis (OTO).[24] An important impetus toward the establishment of the OTO came from the wealthy Austrian chemist Carl Kellner (1851–1905), who supposedly received secrets of sexual magic from three oriental adepts.[25] Both Kellner and Reuss wrote texts on the principles of Yoga and Tantra.[26] After his meeting with Reuss, Crowley was given a high initiation and made the head of the British section of the OTO. He eventually became the international head of the order, which he reorganized in order to infuse it with the teaching of Thelema. Discussion of the history and structure of the OTO is beyond the scope of this essay, but it may be important to emphasize that the central teaching of the order is often considered to have connections and parallels with some Tantric practices. Gerald Yorke, Crowley's friend and one-time disciple, and a major collector of his works, explains the essence of the OTO's teaching as handed down by Reuss:

> He explained to Crowley the theory behind that school of Alchemy which uses sexual fluids and the Elixir of Life. He enlarged on the

> Baphomet tradition of the Knights Templar and traced its alleged survival through the Hermetic Brotherhood of Light [a nineteen-century esoteric society]. He then showed the connection with *those Tantrics who follow the left hand path* [utilizing ritual sexual intercourse as a means of spiritual union with the godhead], and *the Hathayogins who practice sexual mudras* [sacred postures]. What however was more to the point[,] he offered Crowley leadership in the O.T.O.[27]

Accordingly, in addition to his writings on the subjects, Aleister Crowley was instrumental in incorporating and elucidating the theory and practice of Indian Yoga and Tantra within two major initiatory Western esoteric orders, the A.·.A.·. and the OTO. This fact is highly significant, keeping in mind Crowley's importance and influence on contemporary occultism. That his followers exhibit a continuing interest in Eastern esotericism is a mark of Crowley's legacy.[28]

Before venturing into the exploration of those of Crowley's own practices inspired by Yogic and Tantric ideas, it is appropriate to devote some space to his interpretations of the similarity between the Western and the Eastern esoteric traditions. Two elements of his interpretations stand out. On one hand, he was consistent in his conviction that the method of magick requires the training of the mind. In that sense, it may be argued that he was elucidating Western magical tradition as if it were a kind of Yoga. On the other hand, Crowley assimilated Yoga to the Western models by structuring it onto the design of the Tree of Life and by translating its principles into Western esoteric concepts. In either case, what remains as a constant is his persuasion that Yoga and magick represent two different aspects of the same phenomenon.[29]

Yoga in Theory and Practice and Its Correspondence with Western Esoteric Traditions According to Crowley

To elaborate on the ways in which Crowley amalgamated theories and practices of Indian Yoga and Tantra with Western esotericism, the following examples are illustrative. We shall set out with the assumed similarity between Yoga and magick, as proposed in the "Postcards for Probationers" of the A.·.A.·.. Following this, we will investigate a section of the *Eight Lectures on Yoga*, where the Yogic concept of *niyama* (discipline or "positive power" in Crowley's exposition) is brought into correlation with Western astrology and the kabbalistic Tree of Life. Finally, we will examine the ritual of Crowley's

Gnostic Mass, where the Tantric notions that relate to the awakening of the subtle energy within the body and the consummation of sexual fluids are translated into an ecclesiastical rite.

In an early short text from 1909 titled "Postcards for Probationers," Crowley set out to establish a parallelism between the methods of Indian Yoga and Western ceremonial magic. He defined each discipline as "the art of uniting the mind to a single idea."[30] Thus *jñāna* Yoga and the Holy Kabbalah represent "Union by Knowledge." *Rāja* Yoga and the Sacred Magic stand for "Union by Will." *Bhakti* Yoga and the Acts of Worship exemplify "Union by Love." Finally, *haṭha* Yoga and the Ordeals stand for the methods of "Union by Courage."[31] Here we have a clear exercise in the practice of concordance, which Antoine Faivre asserts is a major component of Western esotericism.[32] Throughout his career, Crowley consistently argued a deep similarity between the assumptions and methods of Eastern and Western esoteric traditions.[33] In doing so, he postulated the human mind as the *fons et origo* of mystical and magical phenomena,[34] and he saw its cultivation as the unifying element behind the multiplicity of various local traditions: "All phenomena of which we are aware take place in our own minds, and therefore the only thing we have to look at is the mind; which is a more constant quantity over all the species of humanity than is generally supposed."[35] Crowley thus interprets even the traditional magical paraphernalia from a mentalist perspective: the Temple is coterminous with the extent of one's consciousness, the magical circle protects one from hostile thoughts, the wand symbolizes the will, the cup is understanding, the sword refers to the analytical faculty.[36] Similarly, "To call forth the Spirits means to analyze the mind; to govern them means to recombine the elements of that mind according to one's will."[37] This is a significant reinterpretation of magical technique, which is otherwise habitually associated with ritual action. Crowley did not neglect ritual, but by placing emphasis on mental concentration as the key to success he was elucidating an aspect of magick that has a common denominator in the practice of Yoga.

Eight Lectures on Yoga comprises the texts of a series of talks that Crowley delivered to small audiences in the upper rooms of London restaurants starting in January 1937.[38] The third lecture deals with one of the preliminary stages of classical Yoga, the concept of discipline or *niyama*. Patañjali, the author of the foundational *Yoga Sūtras*, defines this practice as consisting of "Cleanliness, Contentment, Purificatory action, study and the making of the Lord the motive of all action."[39] In his elucidation of the concept, Crowley takes advantage of "a sort of Abacus," which he alleges to be "very useful in all kinds of thinking."[40] This Abacus is the kabbalistic Tree of Life. Simply put, the Tree of Life as used in Western occultism is a symbolic representation of the totality of existence, consisting of ten circles, or *sephiroth*, connected by twenty-two paths, arranged in a regular design. Each of these circles and paths is a focal point for a cluster of correspondences.[41] In accordance with a standard practice, the planets of the solar system in their astrological signification are also assigned their appropriate positions on the Tree.

Crowley explains the qualities of the planets as understood by Western astrology, and in the process stresses the "virtue" or "the positive power" of each of the planets as an aspect of its *niyama*. Thus Saturn—traditionally correlated with the human skeleton—represents the firm foundation of one's spiritual practice. In addition, melancholy associated with Saturn carries a virtue of "the Trance of Sorrow that has determined one to undertake the task of emancipation."[42] Jupiter is "the vital, creative, genial element of the cosmos."[43] Mars refers to energy and strength associated with the muscular system. Its *niyama* is "the virtue which enables one to contend with, and to conquer, the physical difficulties of the Work."[44] The sun is harmony and beauty, the heart of the system as of the human being. The *niyama* of Venus consists in ecstasy and graciousness. Mercury relates to intellectual powers.[45] Finally, the *niyama* of the moon is "that quality of aspiration, the positive purity which refuses union with anything less than the All."[46]

The originality of the above correlation between the principles of Yogic discipline and Western astrology in its connection to the Tree of Life lies in several factors. In addition to its manifest value as an exercise in comparative esotericism, the correlation serves the purpose of illustrating the point that "similar methods producing similar results are to be found in every country. The details vary, but the general structure is the same. Because all bodies, and so all minds, have identical Forms."[47] Crowley thus anticipates the cognitive view of religious systems, championed recently by the late Romanian scholar Ioan P. Couliano.[48] According to this view, various religions are fundamentally *systems* generated by the human mind. In Couliano's own words, "The fundamental unity of humankind does not reside in a unity of *views or solutions*, but in the unity of *operations* of the human mind."[49] From this perspective, Yoga is stripped of its otherness, its exoticism. Instead, it is shown to be a discipline embedded in the potentials and proprieties of the human body and mind. This anthropocentric approach is congenial to Crowley, whose characteristic claim is "There is no god but man."[50]

"Liber XV, Ecclesiæ Gnosticæ Catholicæ Canon Missæ," or simply the Gnostic Mass,[51] is the major OTO ritual that Crowley composed in 1913 while in Russia. This hieratic ceremony is one of the quintessential expressions of

Crowley's religious philosophy, and it combines influences and ideas from Western Gnosticism, Crowley's Thelema, and, arguably, Hindu Tantra. The principal officers of the Mass are the Priest and the Priestess, who are assisted by the Deacon and the two "Children." This is a synopsis of the ritual: The Priestess enters the Temple and "wakes up" the "dead" Priest from his tomb (an event symbolized by the lifting of the Priest's lance, with obvious sexual referent). Together they approach the high altar at the opposite end of the Temple, upon which the Priest installs the Priestess, who then hides behind the veil. The Priest invokes the Goddess Nuit, a major deity in the Thelemic pantheon, identified as the "Infinite Space, and the Infinite Stars thereof."[52] The Priestess answers, becoming at this point one with the Goddess, whose speech from *The Book of the Law* she now quotes. Now the veil is rendered apart and the Priestess is seen holding the cup with wine or "Holy Grail" in her hand. The so-called Cake of Light, an equivalent of the Eucharist, is consecrated and placed on the tip of the Priest's lance, whereupon the top of the lance is depressed into the cup, allowing a part of the Cake of Light to dip into the wine within. The Priest eats the rest of the Cake of Light and drinks the wine, after which he declares, "There is no part of me that is not of the Gods." This in effect represents the consummation of the ritual.

In composing this ritual, Crowley was clearly influenced by the formal ceremony of the Mass as practiced within both the Catholic and Eastern Orthodox Churches. However, although the form is Western and ecclesiastic, the underlying process that the Mass portrays in its ritual mode of enactment has its parallels in some fundamental Tantric notions. Hugh B. Urban explains the essentials of Tantric practice by stating that "the aim of *sādhanā* [practice] is therefore to reunite the divine male and female principles, to achieve the ideal union of semen and menstrual blood within the individual body. Through the use of both meditative imagination and physical rituals, *sādhanā* proceeds as *a kind of mystical marriage*, or, rather, an internalization and alchemical transformation of the ordinary process of marriage."[53]

Keeping in mind that the Gnostic Mass operates at several levels of meaning, a possible interpretation of the ritual is as follows: The Priestess represents divine feminine energy, or in Tantric vocabulary Śakti, while the Priest symbolizes her masculine divine counterpart or Śiva, who is often associated with a stylized phallus (*lingam*); the Cake of Light stands for semen (*bindu*), and the wine in the cup refers to either the menstrual blood (*rajas*) or vaginal sexual fluids (*yonitattva*). The Priestess inspires and brings back to life the inert Priest—who is at the beginning of the rite hidden in his "tomb"—in a manner that carries associations to the famous Tantric adage according to which "Without his Śakti, Śiva is just a corpse." The Temple where the Gnostic Mass takes place is arranged in accordance with the symbolic structure of the Tree of Life. In such a setting, the tomb corresponds to the lowest *sephira*, Malkuth, which in its turn corresponds to the *mūlādhāra cakra*.[54] According to Tantric theory, the semen, which in its original state (and situated at the top of the head) has ambrosial properties, turns into poison when it reaches lower parts of the body, specifically the genitals (i.e., the *mūlādhāra cakra*). For this situation to be remedied, the semen needs to be brought back to the top of the head. This return is represented in the Gnostic Mass by the progression of the officers from the tomb to the high altar. Once the Priestess is seated upon the throne, she becomes divine and as such delivers the speech of the Goddess Nuit. The immersion of the Cake of Light from the tip of the Priest's lance into the wine within the cup held by the Priestess corresponds to the mingling of the semen with the menstrual blood, which is one of the standard procedures in Tantric sex rituals.[55] The consummation of these consecrated substances—the Cake of Light and the wine—parallels the ingestion of the combined sexual fluids as done in Tantric ceremonies. The purpose of this is to confer divine status on the participants, clearly expressed by the concluding formula of the Mass, where the Priest declares that every part of his body has become one with the Gods.

Sexual Magick and Tantra

The Gnostic Mass is a public ritual, and as such it refers to the actual performance of sexual magick in a veiled form. It is clear from Crowley's writings that he associated some aspects of sexual magick with certain elements of Tantra. Hugh Urban has recently argued, too strongly and not quite correctly, in my view, that "Crowley's practice is the clearest example of Western sexual magic combined (and perhaps hopelessly confused) with Indian Tantra."[56] The methodological aspects of the practice of sexual magick are elaborated for the most part in Crowley's official instructions for the highest degrees of the OTO, while references to his actual performance of this form of magick are scattered throughout his diaries.[57] Succinctly stated, in Crowley's view the sex act is a sacrament and the consummation of sexual fluids a Eucharist. The key to success in sex-magick ritual lies in the ability to concentrate one's mind so that it remains focused on the goal of operation, especially during the orgasm. "For in the preparation of the Sacrament, and in its consummation also," writes Crowley, "the mind of the Initiate must be concerned absolutely in one rushing flame of will upon the determined object of his operation."[58]

He describes the essence of the practice by indicating the similarity between sexual and meditative ecstasy, which is otherwise a standard argument of a Tantric orientation: "The spiritual flower of this process is that at the moment of [sexual] discharge a physical ecstasy occurs, a spasm analogous to the mental spasm which meditation gives. And further, in the sacramental and ceremonial use of the sexual act, the divine consciousness may be attained."[59]

Although it is not entirely clear through which channels Crowley arrived at the technique of sexual magick—through intuition and books, through actual contacts with Hindu and Muslim practitioners of similar rites, through the OTO teachings[60]—there is no doubt that *similar* methods have a long history of use in some forms of Hindu and Buddhist Tantra. Belief in the potentially divine nature of the semen, so strongly present in Crowley's theories, is evidenced in Hinduism since earliest times. In his study of asceticism in Vedic India, Walter O. Kaelber explores at length the notions of the fertility of male seed—esoterically often associated with rain—and states: "Male seed, even without benefit of female contribution, is fertile and semen or seed retained increases in potency. It is capable of producing rain and fertilizing fields. Yet *it is also capable of generating spiritual rebirth and immortality*."[61] (It needs to be said that both Indian Tantra and Crowley display a tendency to overvalue the importance of the male seed.) Since retained semen brings about power, celibacy is in India often encouraged—not necessarily because there is something inherently immoral about the sexual act, but because the loss of semen is perceived to be conducive to disease, aging, and ultimately death. The connection between eros and spirituality was eventually to receive the highest emphasis in some theories and practices associated with Tantra.[62]

In the system of the Nāth Siddhas, a North Indian tantric tradition credited with the development of *haṭha* Yoga,[63] the semen or *bindu* was perceived as the carrier of immortality. It however continuously drips from its origin at the top of the head and either gets burned by the digestive fire in the stomach or is ejaculated through the sexual act. Crowley was familiar with important Yogic treatises composed from the Nāthist perspective, such as the *Gheranda Saṃhitā*, *Śiva Saṃhitā* and *Haṭha Yoga Pradīpikā*,[64] so it is quite possible that he adopted ideas about the divine potential of (male) sexual fluid(s) from these sources. However, there are differences: the Nāths are habitually celibate, and their main objective is to achieve the return of the semen to the top of the head through the manipulation of bodily postures, muscular contractions, breathing exercises, and meditation.[65] Alternatively, some forms of Tantric practice allow for the actual sexual congress to occur, but the male adept is not supposed to release his semen. As Wendy Doniger O'Flaherty explains,

"The upward motion of the seed . . . represents the channeling of the life forces, and in order for the ritual to be effective *it was essential for the yogi to restrain his seed.*"[66] If, on the other hand, the seed is ejaculated, it is necessary to reabsorb it, sometimes through urethral suction (*vajroli mudra*). In Crowley's practice, however, the semen is emitted, commingled with female sexual fluids, and orally consumed.[67]

The method favored by Crowley, nevertheless, also has its parallels in Tantra. In his erudite study of Indian esoteric Buddhism, for example, Ronald M. Davidson describes a practice of Tantric sexual ritual as follows: "The secret consecration involved the disciple bringing a female sexual partner (*prajñā/mudrā/vidyā*) to the master, who copulated with her; the combination of ejaculated fluids, termed the 'thought of awakening' (*bodhicitta*), was then ingested by the disciple as nectar."[68] Two elements of this account correspond with Crowley's practice: the actual ejaculation of the seed and the consummation of the mixed sexual fluids. On the theoretical level, there is a correspondence in viewing the sexual emissions as ambrosial. The necessity of mingling sexual fluids is also occasionally noted among the Nāth yogis. As George Weston Briggs explains, "Within the yonisthāna [vagina] there is union of bindu [semen] and rajas [menstrual blood]. . . . Adepts, it is claimed, are able to [effect the return of the semen] . . . even drawing up after the act of coition both rajas and bindu. This is essential to the highest bliss."[69] The sex act involving the emission of the male seed and its mingling with menstrual blood, followed by the ingestion of the resulting mixture, is also observed among the Kartābhajās[70] and the Bauls of Bengal.[71] Hugh Urban[72] and David Gordon White[73] have also suggested that the practice involving male ejaculation and the ingestion of sexual fluids represents a genuine and in fact older Tantric tradition, eventually replaced by the custom of seminal retention. These examples reinforce the similarity between Crowley's and Tantric methods.[74]

Arguably, the rationale behind the practice of the ingestion of sexual fluids for magico-religious reasons rests on a meaningful foundation. At the most obvious level, the semen and vaginal secretions form the basis of human life. The sense of their importance is observable in numerous taboos that surround methods of dealing with these substances in various cultural traditions. In Hindu Tantra, the semen is habitually homologized with the god Śiva and the menstrual blood with his divine spouse, Śakti. Thus we read in a Nāth Yogic text: "Semen is Śiva, menstrual blood is Śakti; semen is the Moon, menstrual blood the Sun. Highest station is obtained only by joining them together. Semen is associated with the Moon, and menstrual blood is associated with the Sun. The person who knows that they are of equal essence is the knower of yoga."[75] In Tantric Buddhism, the semen is often associated with the "thought of awakening" (*bodhicitta*). The Buddha describes his esoteric nature in the *Hevajra-Tantra* in strong language: "I dwell in the *Sukhāvatī* [Land of Bliss] of the woman's vagina in the name of semen."[76] The Bauls and the Kartābhajās of Bengal also teach similar doctrines.[77]

A recurrent motif of Indian spiritual traditions associates semen with the elixir of immortality, *amṛta*,[78] or with the divine liquor, the *soma*. Shashibhushan Dasgupta draws attention to the parallel between the Yogic practice of drinking the nectar and the Vedic *soma* sacrifice, which "rejuvenates and invigorates the body and gives the drinker, whether god or man, eternal life in heaven or earth."[79] Crowley also taught that "Vindu [i.e., *bindu*, semen] is identified with Amrita," which according to him "has a will of its own, which is more in accordance with the Cosmic Will, than that of the man who is its guardian and servant."[80] In a similar vein, he describes the effect of partaking of what he calls the Eucharist—which is a veiled term for the consummation of sexual fluids[81]—as consisting of deification of the practitioner:

> The Magician becomes filled with God, fed upon God, intoxicated with God. Little by little his body will become purified by the internal lustration of God; day by day his mortal frame, shedding its earthly elements, will become in very truth the Temple of the Holy Ghost. Day by day the matter is replaced by Spirit, the human by the divine; ultimately the change will be complete: God manifest in flesh will be his name.[82]

The Occult Aspects and Powers of the Human Body: Cakras *and the* Kuṇḍalinī

The theory and practice of Yoga and Tantra postulate the existence and spiritual importance of hidden aspects of the human body. Within the gross material body there is another, subtle body (*sūkṣma śarīra*), consisting of the centers of energy positioned along the axis that stretches from the genital organs through the spinal column to the top of the head. These subtle centers are customarily called "wheels" (*cakras*) or "lotuses" (*padmas*), and their numbers are habitually given as four in Buddhist and six or seven in Hindu Tantra. It is assumed that the *cakras* are latent or "asleep" in the case of an ordinary person. When awakened, however, they bring about occult powers (*siddhis*) and gnostic insights. The Tantric teachings conceptualize that the primary spiritual energy lies at the base of the spine in the form of the "coiled snake" *kuṇḍalinī*.[83] This "serpent power" (*kuṇḍalinī śakti*) is a microcosmic equivalent of the Great Goddess, whose divine spouse, Śiva, has his own esoteric dwelling place on the top of the human head. When the two appear as separate, the result is the illusory existence, suffused with pain, in which ordinary people live. If a yogi manages to bring these two inner divinities together, by making the *kuṇḍalinī* rise along the spinal column until she reaches the top of the head, "waking up" the *cakras* along the way, the result will be spiritual awakening. In this manner, the yogi gains immense powers and effectively becomes a "second Śiva."

There are numerous references to the *cakras* and *kuṇḍalinī* in Crowley's writings. The earliest mention and description of the *cakras* is given in the fourth installment of the serial "The Temple of Solomon the King" in *The Equinox* (1910). There is in this issue an illustration showing a yogi with the seven *cakras* along the central axis of his body. At a later date, Crowley added notes to his own copy of the book providing the correlation between the *cakras* and the introductory degrees of the OTO.[84] It is not entirely clear if the intention was to suggest that the OTO rituals actually "activate" the *cakras* during the initiation of the candidate. It is, however, important that the two esoteric traditions—represented by references to the Western magical fraternity and Indian Yoga—were brought into correlation on the basis of the perceived analogical convergence of their respective experiential character, their mutual conceptual and symbolic correspondence.

As far as the practical work with the *cakras* is concerned, of particular importance and interest is Crowley's short instructional manual titled the "Liber Yod."[85] The text is introduced as providing "three methods whereby the consciousness of the Many may be melted to that of the One."[86] The first method is anchored in the Western magical tradition and consists of a series of banishing rituals that refer to the planets, zodiacal signs, and finally the *sephiroth* on the Tree of Life. The rituals culminate in the banishment, we might say deconstruction, of the symbolic order represented by the highest *sephira*, *Kether*, or the "crown." In this final phase, the magician tramples his foot upon the light of the candle and falls outside the circle that is symbolic of his individual consciousness. This represents the return to the primordial condition prior to the manifestation of the phenomenal universe, before the emergence of the separate sense of identity and the discriminative mind.

The second and third methods are meditative in character.[87] The second method is a virtual parallel to the ritual described above, the difference being that the technique of reducing consciousness to the state of unity works by dissolution of the symbolic order associated with each particular *cakra*: "Let then the Hermit [i.e., the practitioner], seated in his *āsana*, meditate upon the *mūlādhāra cakra*[88] and its correspondence as a power of the mind, and destroy it in the same manner as aforesaid.... Let the other *cakras* in their turn be thus destroyed, each one with its mental and moral attitude. . . . Lastly, having drawn all his being into the highest *sahasrāra cakra*, let him remain eternally fixed in meditation thereupon."[89] The third method suggests the transfer of the seat of perception, volition, and sensation (of movement and other activities) into the *ājñā cakra.*[90] "Beware thinking of '*my ājñā*,'" warns Crowley. "In these meditations and practices, *ājñā* does not belong to you; *ājñā* is the master and worker, you are the wooden monkey."[91] Since this particular *cakra* is associated with impersonal divine wisdom, the implication is that the end result of the practice leads to the telescoping of consciousness into the unitive experience, beyond the sense of duality. What needs to be emphasized is Crowley's ability to incorporate into a meaningful whole what are usually thought of as distinct methods of esoteric practice. The magical ritual and Yogic meditation are thus brought together and employed as alternative means in the service of the shared goal.

Crowley has also provided descriptions of and instructions for the "waking up" of the *kuṇḍalinī śakti*. "The Book of the Heart Girt with the Serpent,"[92] one of the inspired or "holy books" of Thelema, is at its core a long poetic description of the intense spiritual experience of "the relations of the Aspirant with his Holy Guardian Angel."[93] The opening verses suggest in strong terms that the Serpent is, in at least one symbolic register, representative of the "snake" *kuṇḍalinī*: "I am the Heart; and the Snake is entwined / About the invisible core of the mind. / Rise, O my snake! It is now the hour / Of the hooded and holy ineffable flower."[94] Even more important in this regard is Crowley's comment on one of the verses from *The Book of the Law*, where he suggests that the love mentioned in the phrases "Love is the law, love under will"[95] and "Nor let the fools mistake love; for there are love and love. There is the dove, and there is the serpent,"[96] may refer to "the serpent love, the awakening of the *kuṇḍalinī*."[97]

The awakening of the *kuṇḍalinī* is also a subject of the essay "Energized Enthusiasm: A Note on Theurgy," which appeared in volume I, issue 9 of *The Equinox* (1913), although the Sanskrit term itself is not mentioned in the text. The essay describes a method of inducing the trance state with the use of "wine, woman and song," providing in addition some practical and interesting suggestions for the practice of mantra chanting. The most explicit technique of waking up the "serpent power" is, however, given in the third section of the short text titled "Liber HHH."[98] This text, and especially its third section, is a very good example of the syncretic tendency that is so characteristic of Crowley's teaching. Again, the term *kuṇḍalinī* is not employed (although other Sanskrit vocabulary that refers to the practice of Yoga is there);[99] there is no doubt, however, that the practice refers to it.[100] The brief description of the technique is as follows:

The practitioner is to sit in the Yogic posture and to imagine that the cavity of the brain is the *yoni* or vagina. Other images are also suggested: the womb of Isis or the body of Nuit. The spinal column is to be identified with the *lingam*, or "the phallus of Osiris, or the being of Hadit."[101] This aspect of the meditation merits a comment. It is typical for Tantra to project divine entities into the human microcosm, but the gender arrangement is usually reversed: the god Śiva is thought to be present in the head, while the goddess dwells at the base of the spine.[102] What is important in either case, however, is the presence of gender polarity within the subtle body. The practitioner now focuses on the yearning of these sexual centers for each other and attempts to prolong this feeling as long as possible. Next, an additional element is added: the practitioner is to imagine a current of light passing along the spine in as slow a manner as possible. Finally, the yogi is allowed to accelerate the passage of light between the genitals and the head so that the experience culminates in orgasmic ecstasy.

The above examples are intended as illustration of the importance Crowley attached to the experience and use of hidden powers within the (subtle) body. I would like to underscore the similarity of Crowley's and Tantric methods by making a reference to a recent definition, according to which "Tantra is that . . . body of beliefs and practices [that] . . . seeks to ritually appropriate and channel [the divine] energy, within the human organism, in creative and emancipatory ways."[103] I would in fact argue that the emphasis on *kuṇḍalinī* as "the magical power itself, the manifesting side of the Godhead of the Magician"[104] represents the strongest link between Crowley's magick and Tantra. As he wrote in a letter to his "magical son," Charles Stansfeld Jones: "All magical methods are merely methods of arousing kundalini."[105] In the next section I focus on the use of transgression as a tool of spiritual liberation, which is yet another element of resemblance between Crowley's modus operandi and that of Indian Tantra.

Cefalù: Decadence and Transgression as a Spiritual Technique

In order to assess Crowley's practices that contain Tantric characteristics, it is useful to focus on certain controversial episodes that took place at the "Abbey of Thelema."[106] The Abbey was established in the small Italian town of Cefalù in the period between 1920 and 1923. It consisted of one large house occupied by a small number of Crowley's disciples and mistress(es). Life at the Abbey was for the most part Crowley's attempt to translate his magical and Thelemic ideas into social reality. For the participants, the regime of life involved a great deal of occult and sex-magic activity as well as experiments with various mind- and mood-altering substances, such as hashish, cocaine, heroin, and opium.[107] Crowley wrote extensively and claimed to have attained the highest grade of the A.˙.A.˙. during this period,[108] but life at the Abbey was far from the ideal. In addition to internal turmoil and friction, he and his community became frequent targets of the yellow press, with Crowley being labeled "the wickedest man in the world" and "the man we'd like to hang."[109] He was eventually expelled from Italy by the order of Mussolini.[110]

In a certain sense, life at the Abbey of Thelema may be taken to paradigmatically represent Crowley's lifestyle and philosophy in their most intense aspects. He considered himself the prophet of the New Aeon, which was to replace the old patriarchal religions that are most typically exemplified by Christianity. He was thus in a very important sense asserting his self-identity and pursuing his orientation against the grain of what was accepted as normative by his contemporary society, religion, and culture. I would like to single out this element of intentional opposition to the normative societal values and to emphasize its consanguinity with the Tantric worldview in general. The ethics of Tantra is often characterized by its opposition to Brahmanic priestly orthodoxy, and its method of practice is often defined as the process of regression.[111] This regression or going against the current, *ulṭa* or *ujāna sādhana*, addresses an array of lifestyle choices as well as the actual methodology of Tantric Yoga. Crowley expresses the same orientation when he writes, "I recognize Magick as concerned to *reverse* any existing order."[112] This implies the transformation and transcendence of everyday profane reality by the method of going against its flow. From this perspective, the profane world is topsy-turvy and is set right only by being turned upside down. This is a difficult task, and for that reason the Tantric practitioner is often described as the "hero" (*vīra*).

A newcomer to the Abbey of Thelema was expected to spend a night in what Crowley designated as the "Chambre des Cauchemars," where Crowley himself had painted, in vivid colors and sinister imagery, murals representing hell, heaven, and earth. The intention was "to pass students of the Sacred Wisdom through the ordeal of contemplating every possible phantom which can assail the soul. Candidates for this initiation are prepared by a certain secret process before spending the night in this room; the effect is that the figures on the wall seem actually to become alive, to bewilder and obsess the spirit that has dared to confront their malignity."[113] The "secret process" probably involved the use of a psychedelic substance, possibly mescaline.[114] Crowley describes the outcome of the ordeal as follows:

> Those who have come successfully through the trial say that they have become immunized from all possible infection by those ideas of evil which interfere between the soul and its divine Self. Having been forced to fathom the Abysses of Horror, to confront the most ghastly possibilities of Hell, *they have attained permanent mastery over their minds*. The process is similar to that of "Psycho-analysis"; *it releases the subject from fear of Reality and the phantasms and neuroses thereby caused*, by externalizing and thus disarming the spectres that lie in ambush for the Soul of Man.[115]

Although Crowley compared the process of facing and conquering one's fears with the method of psychoanalysis, there is here also a functional parallel to a standard procedure in the practice of Tantra, which consists in spending the night and performing rituals in a cremation ground or in a similar fear-inspiring place. Mircea Eliade suggests that by meditating at the cemetery, the Tantric yogi "more directly achieves the combustion of egotistic experiences; at the same time, *he frees himself from fear, he evokes the terrible demons and obtains mastery over them*."[116] This is the philosophy of method that carries associations to the Nietzschean precept, according to which what does not kill one makes one stronger.

In his study of the Bengali saint Ramakrishna, Jeffrey J. Kripal argues against overly philosophical and whitewashed representations of Tantra. "Too often scholars have equated Tantra with a philosophical school enshrined in ancient Sanskrit texts," claims Kripal, "and have ignored the popular connotations of the term *Tāntrika*, almost all of which revolve around the notions of magical power, strangeness, seediness, and sex."[117] He suggests instead approaching Tantra "as a 'dirty path' to ontological truths that are as terrifying as they are profound," a path that "*consciously* uses decadence as a spiritual technique."[118] In a similar vein, Crowley's spiritual path may be conceptualized as an intentional use of "decadence, strangeness, seediness, and sex" as spiritual techniques with the aim of conquering inner limitations and psychological barriers. Crowley was possessed of an intuitive understanding of the transformational power of sexuality since his youth. For example, if we are to believe his *Confessions*, he asserted his sense of independence and rebellion against the religious fanaticism of his family by performing one of his first sexual acts with a servant maid on his mother's bed.[119] Kripal quotes Ramakrishna's saying "Shame, disgust, and fear—these three must not remain" as one of the definitions of Tantra.[120] This precept is equally applicable to Crowley and his own experiments in conquering shame, disgust, and fear. He argues:

> The Magician should devise for himself a definite technique for destroying "evil." The essence of such a practice will consist in training the mind and the body to confront things which cause fear, pain, disgust, shame and the like. He must learn to endure them, then to become indifferent to them, then to analyze them until they give pleasure and instruction, and finally to appreciate them for their own sake, as aspects of Truth. When this has been done, he should abandon them, if they are really harmful in relation to health and comfort.[121]

Several examples should provide substance to this thesis.

In July of 1920, a Hollywood silent film actress named Jane Wolfe (1875–1958) joined the community at Cefalù. Prior to that time she had been engaged in an intense correspondence with Crowley, and there was a strong mutual attraction between the two. When she finally met Crowley face-to-face, she was appalled by his unkempt looks and by the general state of affairs at the Abbey. Only later was she to learn from another of Crowley's disciples that he was at the time undergoing a phase of deliberate exposure to the "mystery of filth."[122] It appears that Crowley was guided in this practice by the verses from "The Book of the Heart Girt with a Serpent" that state: "Go thou unto the uttermost places and subdue all things. *Subdue thy fear and thy disgust.* Then—yield."[123]

Since the pioneering work of Mary Douglas, scholars have been alerted to the complexity of human behavior and emotions surrounding the issues of purity and dirt.[124] Alexis Sanderson has thus contrasted the Brahmanic fixation on the rules of purity with the Tantric deliberate disregard of the same: "The conscientiousness essential to the preservation of purity and social system was to be expelled from his identity by the Tantric Brahman as impurity itself, the only impurity he was to recognize, a state of ignorant self-bondage through the illusion that purity and impurity, prohibitedness and enjoinedness were objective qualities residing in things, persons and actions."[125] The functional parallel to this spiritual orientation is provided in Crowley's intentional exploration of the "mystery of filth." He writes in his magical diary about "a protest against . . . the thought that *anything is common or unclean*."[126] Even more intense in this respect were some forms of his practice of sexual magick, conducted with the same objective of transcending the sense of shame and disgust.

Crowley's principal partner during the Cefalù years was an American citizen of Swiss origin, Leah Hirsig (1883–1975). She was in this period his "Scarlet Woman," a role designated by *The Book of the Law*, a female counterpart to Crowley as the Beast. (It is significant, in the light of present considerations, that Crowley defines these two officers as follows: "The Beast and the Scarlet Woman are avatars of . . . Shiva and Shakti.")[127] In addition to being each other's principal partners, both Crowley and Hirsig had sexual relations with other persons. Crowley's ideas on sexuality were in agreement with the liberal injunctions expressed in *The Book of the Law*, which contains statements such as "Take your fill and will of love as ye will, when, where, and with whom ye will!"[128] and "The word of Sin is Restriction. O man! refuse not thy wife, if she will! O lover, if thou wilt, depart! There is no bond that can unite the divided but love: all else is a curse."[129] Commenting on the latter verse, Crowley writes: "The sexual act is a sacrament of Will. To profane it is the great offence. All true expression of it is lawful; all suppression or distortion is contrary to the Law of Liberty."[130] Crowley's sexual life was consequently uninhibited and rich and included both heterosexual and homosexual liaisons.[131]

With Hirsig, whom he met in New York City in 1918, Crowley explored some darker areas of sexuality from the very beginning of their affair. It might be safely said that Eros and Thanatos were intensely intertwined and frequently interpenetrating in their relationship. On her second visit to Crowley's studio, Leah posed naked for Crowley. "When she took the pose I had asked her, 'What shall I call the picture; what shall I paint you as?' She had said, 'Paint me as a dead soul.'"[132] On another occasion, Crowley wrote that making love to anorexic Leah was like having sex with a skeleton.[133] This blending of sexuality and death is also typical of Tantra. Its imagery is teeming both with representations of erotic coupling (the *maithuna*) between gods and goddesses and yogis and yoginīs and with the motifs of skulls, spilled blood, cremation grounds, and ferocious divinities such as the god Śiva in his destructive aspect as Bhairava and the goddess Kālī, who dances upon a corpse with a necklace made of severed heads. Crowley's relationship with Hirsig had in addition a strong self-destructive component, which occasionally manifested as a masochistic drive.[134] "I want to be Leah's slave, her abject," he wrote in his diary. "I want to abrogate the Godhead that melts soul in soul."[135] It is within this relational context that Leah imposed on Crowley a major ordeal.[136]

Some schools of Tantra, most notably the Aghorīs,[137] maintain that an adept may achieve a peculiar power: the ability to consume with equanimity any kind of food, be it even excrement or the flesh of the human corpse. "They justify these practices," writes Eliade, "by saying that all of man's natural inclination and tastes should be destroyed, that there is neither good nor evil, pleasant or unpleasant, etc. Even as human excrement fertilizes a sterile soil, so assimilating every kind of filth makes the mind capable of any and every meditation."[138] Similarly Crowley once boasted to Leah, while making love to her, of his ability to transmute even that which he loathed by the power of love and to "make it God's Body, or Blood, consume it, worship and delight in it, nourish and energize my soul thereon."[139] At that point Leah offered to Crowley her excrement and demanded of him to practice what he preached. Crowley was reluctant. "False Priest," Leah replied, "tear off thy robe: forsworn to Me, forth from my Temple!"[140] Finally he obeyed: "My mouth burned; my throat choked; my belly wretched; my blood fled wither who knows, and my skin sweated."[141] But he did it; he *ate* the "Eucharist" and passed the test: "I am indeed High Priest. I'll blush no more, nor in that matter nor another."[142] Despite the inner instinctual opposition to the experience, he had demonstrated in a physical way his adherence to the creed, which asserts that there should be no difference between things,[143] which claims that "All phenomena are Sacraments,"[144] and which sees every part of the human body as divine.[145]

This episode is best understood if read in the light of a pertinent remark by Gerald Yorke: "Crowley didn't *enjoy* his perversions! He performed them in order to overcome his horror of them."[146] Commenting on this statement, Crowley's biographer Richard Kaczynski suggests that by following these methods the Great Beast sought "to reprogram his mind of Victorian mores."[147] But the intentional pursuit of those experiences that one regards with "shame, fear, and disgust" is also a distinctive orientation in the method of Tantra, whether conceptualized as the "conscious use of decadence as a spiritual technique"[148] or as the path that seeks "power through impurity."[149] As Jeffrey Kripal suggests, it is a Tantric notion that "pollution and impurity can be used to induce mystical states."[150] In addition, Crowley's method of sexual magick bears a "family resemblance" to Indian Tantra through the paramount importance attached to the human body. In Tantra as in Crowley's magick, the human body is both the instrument and the locus of gnosis. One can generalize that in both Indian and Western esotericism there is a tendency to sublimate religious quest. Crowley is similar to those Tantric practitioners who maintain the necessity or even the supremacy of embodied spirituality and/or bodily gnosis. This attitude is also congenial to alchemy as the science of transformations (of "base metals" into "gold"), and it is interesting to note that in India there was a close connection between Tantric Yoga and the methods of alchemy. In Crowley's case, this orientation was yet another application of his fundamental precept, "There is no god but man."[151]

Conclusions

Aleister Crowley's connections with Indian Yoga and Tantra were both considerable and complex. Crowley had direct exposure to some forms of these practices and was familiar with the contemporary literature on the subjects, wrote extensively about them, and—what is perhaps most important—he *practiced* them. In his assessment of the value of Tantra, he was ahead of his time, which habitually considered Tantra a degenerate form of Hinduism. Instead, he claimed that, "paradoxical as it may sound the Tantrics are in reality the most advanced of the Hindus."[152] Crowley's influence in bringing Eastern, primarily Indian, esoteric traditions to the West extends also to his incorporation of the elements of Yoga and Tantra into the structure and program of two influential magical orders, the A.'.A.'. and the OTO. In addition, in his theoretical writings, Crowley is notable for his practice of concordance, where he consistently attempted to emphasize the similarity of principles involved in Yoga and magick. "The two seem, at first glance, to be opposed," he wrote in one of his late works, a collection of letters to a disciple, published posthumously, "but when you have advanced a little in both, you find that concentration learnt in Yoga is of immense use in attaining the mental powers necessary in Magick; on the other hand, the discipline of Magick is of the greatest service in Yoga."[153] He came to consider these two traditions as two orientations along the same path, one consisting in "Will to Death" or introversion (Yoga), another being "Will to Life" or extroversion (magick).[154] Given the enormous influence that Crowley continues to exert on Western esotericism, there is no doubt that his interpretations of Yoga and Tantra will also loom large.

It has been observed, most recently by Hugh Urban, that Crowley did not actually know that much of the real Tantra on one hand and that he misinterpreted it as a solely sexual practice on the other.[155] This view has its merit, but it may be challenged, in particular the suggestion that Crowley conflated Tantra with sexuality. There is no doubt that there are differences between Crowley's understanding of Tantra and what is implied by that appellation in India. However, this is a regular occurrence whenever cultural appropriation of some foreign ideas and practices takes place.[156] As Urban himself wrote on another occasion, it is "the very nature of cross-cultural dialogue, [that] the mutual re- and misinterpretations . . . occur in every cross-cultural encounter."[157] The regional differences between various forms of Buddhism are a case in point. Are we to argue that Zen is not Buddhism, because it differs in discourse and methodology from Theravāda? Equally important, we should not assume that Tantra is a unified phenomenon.[158] There are, sometimes significant, differences between Japanese Shingon Buddhism, Tibetan Kālacakra system, Indian Vaiṣṇava Sahajiyās, Nāth yogis, Bengali Bauls, and the ideas and practices as observed among the devotees of the Goddess Kālī.[159] "Western Tantra," significantly influenced by Crowley, does differ from the above but not to the point of not being Tantric in character at all. Finally, and most significant, Crowley did not relate Tantra only to sexuality. The conflation between these two categories is in fact a legacy of Crowley's biographers and interpreters, while he himself is largely innocent of the charge. He was actually more impressed by Tantra's positive evaluation of the phenomenal universe and the human experience, and for these reasons he classified it as a White School of Magick, akin to his own Thelema.[160] As already argued, he was also similar to *tāntrikas* in his countercultural and antinomian practices and in his approach to the human body, particularly in its subtle aspects, as an instrument of liberation. For these reasons it is meaningful to talk about "Crowley's Tantra" as a *functional* parallel to, a variety of, Indian Tantra, to which it bears a family resemblance, a formal similarity.

Crowley's unconventional lifestyle was an occasion for numerous and gross misunderstandings. His opposition to the prevalent morality, religion, and culture of his time has given rise to the popular image of him as a "Satanist,"[161] which he emphatically was not, if for no other reason than simply because he did not identify himself as such. Like any other binary opposition, Christianity and Satanism are entangled in a web of mutual correlation and codependence. They inhabit a common universe of discourse, albeit with a differing set of values. Crowley was about something else. He was a Thelemite. He was also a person deeply steeped in the practice of what he designated as Magick, the considerable part of which involved a pursuit of Yoga and Tantra. Being a child of his time, he also shared some typical misconceptions about these traditions.[162] He was also, unfortunately, perfectly capable of displaying on occasion an attitude of colonial and gender supremacy. It is nevertheless crucial that Crowley's life and work be evaluated not against some abstract canon of truth and morality but in the light of the principles that are congenial to his methods. In addition, it needs to be remembered that, his erudition notwithstanding, he was not a scholar but primarily a practitioner of esotericism. In a certain sense, part of what he was attempting to do was to liberate himself from the constraint of Edwardian limits on self-identification. As Alex Owen has suggested, Crowley belonged to the group of people whose experience of modernity included the search for a new, flexible, magical self that is potentially divine.[163] In order to reach freedom from the "shame, disgust, and fear" that obscure the experience of this self, Crowley—like many other twentieth-century and present-day esotericists—engaged in practices of syncretic character. All the wisdom or folly of such an endeavor aside, as far as the academic study of Crowley's life and work is concerned, an interdisciplinary approach involving, inter alia, the comparative study of Eastern and Western esoteric traditions appears to be the most constructive methodology to adopt.

Notes

1. This is a revised version of a paper originally delivered at the Second International Conference of the Association for the Study of Esotericism (University of California, Davis, June 8–11, 2006). I have benefited from comments offered by William Breeze and an anonymous reviewer of this chapter; any remaining errors are my sole responsibility.
2. Aleister Crowley, *The Confessions of Aleister Crowley: An Autohagiography*, abridged ed., ed. John Symonds and Kenneth Grant (1969; London: Arkana, 1989), 213–14.
3. One indication of Crowley's influence is the number of biographies of which he is the subject. Richard Kaczynski lists sixteen of these in his own *Perdurabo: The Life of Aleister Crowley* (Tempe, Ariz.: New Falcon, 2002), 485.
4. I imply throughout this essay that there is at least a functional parallel between what I call rather vaguely "Eastern" and "Western" esoteric traditions. I am aware of the contested nature of my chosen conceptual vocabulary but continue to employ it for several reasons, elaboration of which is beyond the scope of this essay. Let it suffice to mention that I consider *esotericism* to be a second-order (etic) term that is applied by scholars to the subject under scrutiny much more consistently than it is used as a self-referential (emic) designation. (Crowley, for example, vary rarely uses

the term.) It is emphatically not my intention to conflate Eastern Tantra and Western magic, although I find it heuristically useful to refer to both of them as forms of esotericism.

5. This subject is explored in detail in Joscelyn Godwin, *The Theosophical Enlightenment* (Albany: State University of New York Press, 1994).
6. Crowley was also instrumental in popularizing Chinese esotericism. See, for example, his inspired "translation" of Lao Tzu, *Tao Te Ching: Liber CLVII*, trans. Ko Hsüan [Aleister Crowley], ed. Hymenaeus Beta (York Beach, Maine: Samuel Weiser, 1995).
7. See, inter alia, Crowley's diaries published in "John St. John," *The Equinox* I (1) (1909); and "The Temple of Solomon the King," *The Equinox* I (4) (1910).
8. The Golden Dawn material is collected in Israel Regardie, *The Golden Dawn: An Account of the Teachings, Rites and Ceremonies of the Order of the Golden Dawn* (1937–1940; St. Paul, Minn.: Llewellyn, 1978). For a more skeptical account, see Ellic Howe, *The Magicians of the Golden Dawn: A Documentary History of a Magical Order, 1887–1923* (London: Routledge & Kegan Paul, 1972).
9. On Bennett, see Godwin, *The Theosophical Enlightenment*, 369–77.
10. See Crowley, *The Confessions*, 237.
11. See ibid., 248–49.
12. The difference between the two methods of the training of the mind lies in the following: in Yoga, there is ordinarily an attempt to arrest the fluctuations of the mind by keeping it focused on a chosen object, whereas in Buddhist meditation the objective is usually to maintain awareness of bodily, emotional, or mental processes without attempting to arrest their modifications.
13. See Aleister Crowley, "Science and Buddhism," in *The Works of Aleister Crowley* (Foyers, Scotland: Society for the Propagation of Religious Truth, 1906), 2:244–61.
14. See "Liber Ru vel Spiritus sub figura CCVI," *The Equinox* I (7) (1912); reprinted in Aleister Crowley, *Magick: Liber ABA: Book Four: Parts I–IV*, 2nd ed., ed. Hymenaeus Beta (York Beach, Maine: Samuel Weiser, 1997), 638–42.
15. Originally published as "Liber Tau sub figura XCIII," *The Equinox* I (7) (1912); reprinted as "Liber Yod sub figura DCCCXXXI," in Crowley, *Magick*, 643–46.
16. Aleister Crowley, "Review of Scientific Illuminism," *The Equinox* I (1) (1909); reprinted in Crowley, *Magick*, 604–12.
17. Originally published as *Book 4*, Part I (London: Wieland, n.d. [1912]). Reprinted as "Part I: Mysticism," in Crowley, *Magick*, 1–44.
18. For the text of *The Book of the Law* (or *Liber AL vel Legis*, as it is technically called) see, inter alia, Aleister Crowley, *The Holy Books of Thelema*, ed. Hymenaeus Alpha (York Beach, Maine: Samuel Weiser, 1983), 105–28. Numerous reprints of this text are available. It is interesting in the present context that Kenneth Grant, one of Crowley's major disciples, refers to *The Book of the Law* as "the New Gnosis, *the latest Tantra*, the most complex Grimoire." Kenneth Grant, *The Magical Revival* (1972; London: Skoob Books, 1991), 7; emphasis added.

19. *Liber AL vel Legis* I:15.
20. Crowley's position vis-à-vis philosophical, religious, and scientific aspects of the message of *The Book of the Law* is summarized in the text "On the Reception of *The Book of the Law*," in Crowley, *Magick*, 693–708.
21. The structure of the A.·.A.·. is set out formally in "One Star in Sight," in Crowley, *Magick*, 486–98.
22. Western esoteric subjects studied and practiced within the A.·.A.·. include astral travel, divination (tarot, astrology, geomancy), kabbalah, fashioning of magical instruments, evocations, and invocations (one of the central objectives involves the invocation of one's Holy Guardian Angel). See, inter alia, ibid.; and "Liber XIII vel Graduum Montis Abiegni," *The Equinox* I (3) (1910), 3–8; reprinted in Aleister Crowley, *Gems from "The Equinox": Instructions by Aleister Crowley for His Own Magical Order*, ed. Israel Regardie (1974; Phoenix, Ariz.: Falcon Press, 1986), 43–50.
23. For Crowley's views on the Ordo Templi Orientis, a good place to start is the seventy-second chapter of his (abridged) *Confessions*. His meeting with Reuss is described at pp. 709–10. See also *The Equinox* III (1) (1919; York Beach, Maine: Samuel Weiser, 1992).
24. The literature on Freemasonry is vast, but for a survey from the perspective of esoteric studies, see Henrik Bogdan, *From Darkness to Light: Western Esoteric Rituals of Initiation* (Gothenburg: University of Gothenburg, 2003), recently republished as *Western Esotericism and Rituals of Initiation* (Albany: State University of New York Press, 2007). See also a comparative essay by Hugh B. Urban, "Elitism and Esotericism: Strategies of Secrecy and Power in South Indian Tantra and French Freemasonry," *Numen* 44, 1 (1997): 1–38.
25. "[Kellner] is believed to have studied Yoga with Bhima Sen Pratap and Śrī Mahātmā Agamya Guru Paramahansa." Hymenaues Beta, "Editorial Notes," in Aleister Crowley, *Eight Lectures on Yoga* (1939; Tempe, Ariz.: New Falcon, 1991), 121, n. 3.
26. See Carl Kellner, "Yoga, eine Skizze über den Psychophysiologischen Teil den Alten Indischen Yogalehre," III International Congress for Psychology (Munich, 1896); Theodor Reuss, "Mystic Anatomy," *Oriflamme: Amtliches Organ des Ordens der Orientalischen Templer* (1913): 4–7.
27. Gerald Yorke, "666, Sex, and the O.T.O."; quoted in Lawrence Sutin, *Do What Thou Wilt: A Life of Aleister Crowley* (New York: St. Martin's Press, 2000), 226; emphasis added. The explanatory notes within brackets are Sutin's. This essay is included in the recent anthology *Aleister Crowley, the Golden Dawn and Buddhism: Reminiscences and Writings of Gerald Yorke*, ed. Keith Richmond (York Beach, Maine: Teitan Press, 2011), 14–24.
28. See, for example, Nancy Wasserman, *Yoga for Magick*, ed. and intro. James Wasserman (San Francisco: Red Wheel/Weiser, 2007).
29. "It will now be apparent that there is no distinction between Magick and Meditation except of the most arbitrary and accidental kind." Crowley, *Magick*, 232.

30. Aleister Crowley, "Postcards for Probationers," *The Equinox* I (2) (1909), 199.
31. Ibid. In addition to these four major methods of achievement, Crowley adds *mantra* Yoga and the Invocations as examples of "Union through Speech," while *karma* Yoga and the Acts of Service represent "Union through Work." See ibid. *Bhakti* Yoga is also treated separately in an important manual of practice titled "Liber Asterté vel Berylli sub figura CLXXV," first published in *The Equinox* I (7) (1912); reprinted in Crowley, *Magick*, 627–37.
32. See, for example, Antoine Faivre, *Access to Western Esotericism* (Albany: State University of New York Press, 1994), 14.
33. In a later work, for example, Crowley draws a correlation between the major forms of Yoga and the so-called Hermetic virtues or "the powers of the Sphinx": "By Gñana Yoga cometh thy Man to Knowledge; by Karma Yoga thy Bull to Will; by Raja Yoga is thy Lion brought to his Light; and to make perfect thy Dragon, thou hast Bhakta Yoga for the Eagle therein, and Hatha Yoga for the Serpent." Aleister Crowley, *Liber Aleph vel CXI: The Book of Wisdom or Folly*, ed. Hymenaeus Beta (1962; York Beach, Maine: Samuel Weiser, 1991), 159.
34. This statement should not, however, be construed to mean that Crowley neglected the value of the human body in the pursuit of spiritual goals. See below.
35. Crowley, *Eight Lectures on Yoga*, 13–14.
36. See Crowley, *Magick*, 48. Keeping in mind that the Temple symbolizes the external universe, the following remark is equally pertinent: "When one realizes as an actual fact in experience that the starry universe is only a picture of one aspect of one's mind—no apodosis seems possible." Aleister Crowley, *The Magical Record of the Beast 666: The Diaries of Aleister Crowley, 1914–1920*, ed. John Symonds and Kenneth Grant (London: Duckworth, 1972), 113.
37. Crowley, *Magical Record*, 104.
38. See Hymenaeus Beta, "Foreword to the Second Edition," in ibid., 8–9.
39. *Yoga Sūtras*, 159.
40. Crowley, *Eight Lectures on Yoga*, 36.
41. See Aleister Crowley, *777 vel Prolegomena Symbolica ad Systemam Sceptico-Mysticae Viae Explicandae, Fundamentum Hieroglyphicum Sanctissimorum Scientiae Summae* (1955; New York: Samuel Weiser, 1970).
42. Crowley, *Eight Lectures on Yoga*, 36.
43. Ibid., 38.
44. Ibid.
45. According to Crowley, "In one sense Mercury is the great enemy; Mercury is mind, and it is the mind that we have set out to conquer." Ibid., 41.
46. Ibid., 42.
47. Ibid., 14.
48. See, for example, Ioan P. Couliano, "Introduction: Religion as a System," in Mircea Eliade and Ioan P. Couliano, with Hillary S. Wiesner, *The HarperCollins Concise Guide to World Religions* (1991; San Francisco: HarperCollins, 2000).

49. Ibid., 7.
50. See, for example, "Liber Oz sub figura LXXVII," in Crowley, *Magick*, 689.
51. See Crowley, *Magick*, 584–97.
52. *Liber AL vel Legis* I:22, in Crowley, *The Holy Books of Thelema*, 108.
53. Hugh B. Urban, *The Economics of Ecstasy: Tantra, Secrecy, and Power in Colonial Bengal* (Oxford: Oxford University Press, 2001), 145; emphasis added.
54. For these correspondences, see Crowley, *777*.
55. See, for example, Kamil Zvelebil, *The Siddha Quest for Immortality* (1996; Oxford: Mandrake, 2003), esp. 115–28.
56. Hugh B. Urban, "The Cult of Ecstasy: Meldings of East and West in a New Age of Tantra," in *Tantra: Sex, Politics, and Power in the Study of Religion* (Berkeley: University of California Press, 2003), 218–19. For similarly construed arguments, see also the following publications by Urban: "Unleashing the Beast: Aleister Crowley, Tantra, and Sex Magick in Late Victorian England," *Esoterica* 5 (2003), 138–92; "The Beast with Two Backs: Aleister Crowley, Sex Magick and the Exhaustion of Modernity," *Nova Religio* 7, 3 (2003), 7–25; "The Power of the Impure: Transgression, Violence and Secrecy in Bengali Śākta Tantra and Modern Western Magic," *Numen* 50, 3 (2003), 269–308; and *Magia Sexualis: Sex, Magic, and Liberation in Modern Western Esotericism* (Berkeley: University of California Press, 2006). I shall engage the question of the authenticity of Crowley's Tantric endeavors in the concluding part of this essay.
57. See, for example, "Rex de Arte Regia," in Crowley, *Magical Record*, 1–82.
58. Aleister Crowley, "De Arte Magica," in *Crowley on Christ*, ed. Francis King (London: C. W. Daniel, 1974), 216.
59. Aleister Crowley, "Energized Enthusiasm," *The Equinox* I (9) (1913), 17–46; reprinted in *Gems from "The Equinox,"* 615–41.
60. Henrik Bogdan suggests Paschal Beverly Randolph and his Hermetic Brotherhood of Light as important sources of the sexual magic associated with the OTO; see Bogdan, "Challenging the Morals of Western Society: The Use of Ritualized Sex in Contemporary Occultism," *The Pomegranate: The International Journal of Pagan Studies* 8, 2 (2006), 222 and 226–27. On Randolph, see John Patrick Deveney, *Paschal Beverly Randolph: A Nineteen-Century Black American Spiritualist, Rosicrucian, and Sex Magician* (Albany: State University of New York Press, 1997); and Joscelyn Godwin, Christian Chanel, and John Patrick Deveney, *The Hermetic Brotherhood of Luxor: Initiatic and Historical Documents of an Order of Practical Occultism* (York Beach, Maine: Samuel Weiser, 1995).
61. Walter O. Kaelber, *Tapta Mārga: Asceticism and Initiation in Vedic India* (Albany: State University of New York Press, 1989), 40; emphasis added.
62. "Sexuality is ritual; this fact is the key to the understanding of all tantric and Siddha sexuality, even of the seeming obscenities of the language of the texts in question. That is: the sexual plane is sanctified and homogenized with myth and ritual; and, vice versa, the ritual and the myth may be and often is explained in sexual terms."

Kamil Zvelebil, *The Poets of the Powers: Magic, Freedom, and Renewal* (1973; Lower Lake, Calif.: Integral Publishing, 1993), 47.

63. On the Nāth Siddhas, see Véronique Bouillier, *Ascètes et rois: Un monastère de Kanphata Yogis au Népal* (Paris: CNRS Éditions, 1997); George Weston Briggs, *Gorakhnāth and the Kānphaṭa Yogīs* (1938; Delhi: Motilal Banarsidass, 1998); Shashibhushan Dasgupta, *Obscure Religious Cults*, 3rd ed. (1946; Calcutta: K. L. Mukhopadhyay, 1995); Ann Grodzins Gold, *A Carnival of Parting: The Tales of King Bharthari and King Gopi Chand as Sung and Told by Madhu Natisar Nath of Ghatiyali, Rajasthan* (Berkeley: University of California Press, 1992); and David Gordon White, *The Alchemical Body: Siddha Traditions in Medieval India* (Chicago: University of Chicago Press, 1996). For an attempt to correlate the system of the Nāth Siddhas (and Indian Tantra in general) with the Western esoteric tradition, see Gordan Djurdjevic, *Masters of Magical Powers: The Nāth Yogis in the Light of Esoteric Notions* (Saarbrücken: Verlag Dr. Müller, 2008).

64. The *Gheranda Saṃhitā* is referenced several times in Crowley, "The Temple of Solomon the King." The other two texts are included in the A∴A∴ curriculum of books to be studied by a novice student. (In addition, the Indian spiritual tradition is represented in the curriculum by *The Upanishads*, *The Bhagavad-gītā*, *Rāja-Yoga* by Swami Vivekananda, *The Aphorisms of Patañjali*, *The Dhammapada*, and *The Questions of King Milinda.* See Crowley, *Magick*, 452.)

65. See White, *The Alchemical Body.*

66. Wendy Doniger O'Flaherty, *Asceticism and Eroticism in the Mythology of Śiva* (London: Oxford University Press, 1973), 262; emphasis added.

67. It is obvious from Crowley's writings that he was aware of the Tantric practice involving seminal retention (see, for example, "De Arte Magica," 228). He occasionally practiced it himself, as the following entry shows: "The Operation was most extraordinary. I figured [i.e., kept a mental image of] the God well on the whole, and experienced the complete orgasm *without the emission of even a single drop of semen.*" Crowley, *Magical Record*, 15; emphasis added.

68. Ronald M. Davidson, *Indian Esoteric Buddhism: A Social History of the Tantric Movement* (New York: Columbia University Press, 2002), 197.

69. Briggs, *Gorakhnāth*, 333.

70. On Kārtabhajās, see Hugh B. Urban, *Economics of Ecstasy*; and *Songs of Ecstasy: Tantric and Devotional Songs from Colonial Bengal* (Oxford: Oxford University Press, 2001).

71. See, for example, Jeanne Openshaw, *Seeking Bāuls of Bengal* (Cambridge: University Press, 2002), esp. 203–39 and passim.

72. See Urban, "Unleashing the Beast," 157.

73. See David Gordon White, *Kiss of the Yoginī: "Tantric Sex" in its South Asian Context* (Chicago: University of Chicago Press, 2003).

74. On this subject, see also Gordan Djurdjevic, "Solve et Coagula: Attitudes Towards the Ambrosial Aspects of Human Seed in Certain Yogic Traditions and in the

Sexual Magick of Aleister Crowley," *Aries: Journal for the Study of Western Esotericism* 10, 1 (2010), 85–106.

75. *Gorakṣa-Vacana-Saṃgrahaḥ*, v. 38–39, in *Collection of Gorakṣa's Sayings: Translation of Gorakṣa-Vacana-Saṃgrahaḥ*, trans. Narayana Mishra, ed. Gordan Djurdjevic (unpublished manuscript, Benares and Vancouver, 2003). The Sanskrit text may be found in Akshaya Kumar Banerjea, *Philosophy of Gorakhnath: With Goraksha-Vacana-Sangraha* (1962; Delhi: Motilal Banarsidass, 1999), 333–44.
76. Quoted in Shashi Bhushan Dasgupta, *An Introduction to Tantric Buddhism* (1958; Berkeley, Calif.: Shambhala, 1974), 142. I have slightly edited this translation from Dasgupta's "I dwell . . . in the vagina of the female."
77. "Kartābhajās' bodily cosmology and physical practice centers around the mystery of the sexual fluids, semen (*bīja, bindu, śukra*) and menstrual blood (*raja*). Identified with the supreme male and female principles of reality, Puruṣa and Prakṛti or Kṛṣṇa and Rādhā, the semen and uterine blood are the very particles of the absolute which lie hidden within each human body." Urban, *Economics of Ecstasy*, 143.
78. For Crowley's writings on this subject, see *Amrita: Essays in Magical Rejuvenation* (Kings Beach, Calif.: Thelema Publications, 1990). This matter is also treated in some of the epistolary exchange between aged Crowley and David Curwen, for which see Henrik Bogdan, ed., *Brother Curwen, Brother Crowley: A Correspondence* (York Beach, Maine: Teitan Press, 2010).
79. Dasgupta, *Obscure Religious Cults*, 250.
80. Aleister Crowley, *The Book of Lies Which Is Also Falsely Called Breaks: The Wanderings or Falsifications of the One Thought of Frater Perdurabo (Aleister Crowley) Which Thought Is Itself Untrue* (1913; York Beach, Maine: Samuel Weiser, 1981), 47.
81. The actual process is hinted at with these words: "Take a substance [which, as the note adds, may be of composite character] symbolic of the whole course of Nature, make it God, and consume it." Crowley, *Magick*, 267.
82. Ibid., 269.
83. On this subject, see Lilian Silburn, *Kuṇḍalinī: The Energy of the Depths*, trans. Jacques Gontier (Albany: State University of New York Press, 1988).
84. The illustration with Crowley's annotations is reproduced in *The Equinox* III (10) (1986), 193.
85. First published as "Liber Tau," *The Equinox* I (7) (1912). My references are to the edition in Crowley, *Magick*, 643–46.
86. Ibid., 643.
87. As the editor, Hymenaeus Beta, mentions in the notes, these two methods are rooted in the Buddhist practice of *mahāsatipaṭṭhana* and in the techniques described in the books of Yogic instruction *Haṭhayogapradīpikā* and *Śiva Saṃhitā*. See Crowley, *Magick*, 785–86, nn. 364–67.
88. The *mūlādhāra cakra* is the root *cakra* situated at the base of the spine.
89. Crowley, *Magick*, 644.
90. The *ājñā cakra* is popularly known and represented as the "third eye."

91. Crowley, *Magick*, 646.
92. "The Book of the Heart Girt with the Serpent," or "Liber Cordis Cincti Serpente sub figura LXV," was first published in *The Equinox* III (1) (1919). See also Crowley, *The Holy Books of Thelema*, 51–83. My references are to the annotated edition in Aleister Crowley et al., *Commentaries on the Holy Books and Other Papers: Being "The Equinox," Volume Four, Number One* (York Beach, Maine: Samuel Weiser, 1996), 85–219.
93. Ibid., 87.
94. Ibid., 89.
95. *Liber AL vel Legis* I:57.
96. Ibid.
97. Aleister Crowley, *The Law Is for All: The Authorized Popular Commentary on Liber AL vel Legis sub figura CCXX, The Book of the Law*, ed. Louis Wilkinson and Hymenaeus Beta (Tempe, Ariz.: New Falcon, 1996), 78, n. 2.
98. "Liber HHH," *The Equinox* I (5) (1911); reprinted in Crowley, *Magick*, 598–603.
99. I refer to the terms *āsana*, *yoni*, *linga*, *samādhi*, *prāṇāyāma*, and *kumbhaka*. See ibid.
100. "In the essay 'Energised Enthusiasm' is given a concise account of one of the classical methods of arousing *kuṇḍalinī*." Ibid., 233.
101. Ibid., 602. Hadit, complement of the goddess Nuit, is one of the central concepts in *The Book of the Law*. "Nuit is Matter, Hadit is Motion, in their full physical sense. They are the *tao* and *te* of Chinese Philosophy; or, to put it very simply, the Noun and Verb in grammar. Our central Truth—beyond other philosophies—is that these two infinities cannot exist apart." Crowley, *The Law Is for All*, 23.
102. Functionally, however, when the *kuṇḍalinī* makes her way up the spine, piercing the (female) lotuses of energy along the way, she does assume *phallic* attributes.
103. David Gordon White, "Mapping a Tradition," in *Tantra in Practice*, ed. David Gordon White (Princeton, N.J.: Princeton University Press, 2000), 9.
104. Crowley, *Magick*, 105.
105. Letter from Aleister Crowley to Charles Stansfeld Jones, April 14, 1916. Warburg Institute, University of London.
106. I focus on controversial events because they involve the breaking of societal norms, which is also typical of some forms of Tantra.
107. For informative accounts of life at the Abbey, see the following two books by Keith Richmond, both of which focus on Crowley's disciple Frank Bennett: *Progradior and the Beast: Frank Bennett and Aleister Crowley* (London: Neptune, 2004); and *The Magical Record of Frater Progradior* (London: Neptune, 2004).
108. "Discarding his clothes, he entered the temple with Leah [Hirsig] at his side. There, before his Scarlet Woman and all the powers of the universe as his witness, Crowley took the Oath of an Ipsissimus, (1° = 10°), the final grade in the A∴A∴ hierarchy. The oath began his final and greatest initiation, one which would not see its conclusion until 1924." Kaczynski, *Perdurabo*, 290.

109. See, for example, ibid., 309. Crowley and his community were especially the targets of the tabloids *Sunday Express* and *John Bull*. See ibid.
110. For discussion of Crowley's Cefalù period, see, inter alia, Sutin, *Do What Thou Wilt*, 278–309 and Kaczynski, *Perdurabo*, 276–312.
111. For example: "The school of the Nāthas and Siddhas employed a well-known yogico-tantric technique: *ulṭā sādhana* or *ujāna sādhana*, the process of 'regression' or 'going against the current'—that is, the complete reversal of human behavior." Mircea Eliade, *Yoga: Immortality and Freedom* (Princeton, N.J.: Princeton University Press, 1969), 318. "This union of Śiva and Śakti symbolizes in the wider sense the stoppage of ordinary process of becoming and the retrogression of the whole world-process for the attainment of the changeless state of the Immortal Being. . . . The process has also been explained under the imagery of proceeding against the current (*ujānasādhana*)." Dasgupta, *Obscure Religious Cults*, 231.
112. Crowley, *Magical Record*, 248.
113. Aleister Crowley, untitled brochure; quoted in Sutin, *Do What Thou Wilt*, 281. Richard Kaczynski suggests that Crowley's style of painting was influenced by the work of Paul Gaugin (1848–1903). See Kaczynski, *Perdurabo*, 280.
114. See Martin P. Starr, "Aleister Crowley: Virgin Painter or Old Master," in *An Old Master: The Art of Aleister Crowley*, ed. Hymenaeus Beta (London: OTO and October Gallery, 1998), 8.
115. Crowley, untitled brochure; quoted in Sutin, *Do What Thou Wilt*, 282; emphases added.
116. Eliade, *Yoga*, 296; emphasis added.
117. Jeffrey J. Kripal, *Kālī's Child: The Mystical and the Erotic in the Life and Teachings of Ramakrishna*, 2nd ed. (1995; Chicago: University of Chicago Press, 1998), 28.
118. Ibid., 29.
119. See Crowley, *The Confessions*, 80.
120. Kripal, *Kālī's Child*, 32.
121. Crowley, *Magick*, 579–80.
122. For descriptions of this episode, see Sutin, *Do What Thou Wilt*, 286–87; and Kaczynski, *Perdurabo*, 284.
123. Quoted in Sutin, *Do What Thou Wilt*, 287; emphasis added. See also "The Book of the Heart Girt with a Serpent," I:44–45.
124. See Mary Douglas, *Purity and Danger: An Analysis of Concepts of Pollution and Taboo* (1966; Harmondsworth: Penguin, 1970).
125. Alexis Sanderson, "Purity and Power among the Brahmans of Kashmir," in *The Category of the Person: Anthropology, Philosophy, History*, ed. Michael Carrithers et al. (Cambridge: Cambridge University Press, 1985), 198.
126. Crowley, *Magical Record*, 257.
127. Aleister Crowley, *Magical and Philosophical Commentaries on "The Book of the Law,"* ed. John Symonds and Kenneth Grant (Montreal: 93 Publishing, 1974), 103.
128. *Liber AL vel Legis* I:51, in Crowley, *The Holy Books of Thelema*, 111.

129. *Liber AL vel Legis* I:41, in Crowley, *The Holy Books of Thelema*, 110.
130. Crowley, *The Law Is for All*, 42.
131. For information on Crowley's approach to the mystical aspects of homosexuality, see Aleister Crowley, *The Scented Garden of Abdullah the Satirist of Shiraz*, ed. Martin P. Starr (1910; Chicago: Teitan Press, 1991).
132. Crowley, *The Confessions*, 793.
133. See Kenneth Grant, *Cults of the Shadow* (1975; London: Skoob Books, 1994), 145.
134. See, for example, Aleister Crowley, *Leah Sublime* (Quebec: 93 Publishing, 1976), a poem in 156 lines written around 1920.
135. Crowley, *Magical Record*, 257.
136. The larger context of the Cefalù period involves Crowley's self-initiation into the grade of Ipsissimus, the summit of the A∴A∴ order. The essence of the grade is that "the Ipsissimus is wholly free from all limitations soever, existing in the Nature of all things without discriminations of quantity and quality between them." Crowley, "One Star in Sight," 491.
137. On the Aghorīs, see Robert E. Svoboda, *Aghora: At the Left Hand of God* (Albuquerque: Brotherhood of Life, 1986).
138. Eliade, *Yoga*, 296–97. Briggs, in *Gorakhnāth*, 224, claims that "the practice of making no discrimination in food is an old Pāśupata one."
139. Crowley, *Magical Record*, 235.
140. Ibid.
141. Ibid. This episode and its transgressive aspects are also discussed in Urban, "Unleashing the Beast," 163.
142. Crowley, *Magical Record*, 235. Commenting on similar practices carried out by Ramakrishna, Kripal states: "Thus Ramakrishna, possessed by Kālī, extends an ecstatic tongue to commune with rotting human flesh, polluted rice, river-bank feces, and symbolic vaginas, that preeminent 'place of disgust.' Kālī's tongue here is not about shame but about the destruction of disgust." Kripal, *Kālī's Child*, 305.
143. See *Liber AL vel Legis* I:22: "Let there be no difference made among you between any one thing & any other thing; for thereby there cometh hurt." In Crowley, *The Holy Books of Thelema*, 108.
144. Crowley, *Magick*, 95.
145. See the Gnostic Mass: "There is no part of me that is not of the Gods." In Crowley, *Magick*, 597.
146. Quoted in Kaczynski, *Perdurabo*, 284. See also Jean Overton Fuller, *The Magical Dilemma of Victor Neuburg* (London: W. H. Allen, 1965), 244. There is an interesting entry in Crowley's magical diary in which he records a sex-magick operation conducted with the intention of acquiring "the Divine Knowledge—with the special idea of *sacrificing the divine ecstasy* for that Knowledge: *Ananda* for *Chit*." Crowley, *Magical Record*, 52; emphasis added.
147. Kaczynski, *Perdurabo*, 284.
148. See Kripal, *Kālī's Child*, 29.

149. See Sanderson, "Purity and Power," 200.
150. Kripal, *Kālī's Child,* 290.
151. See "Liber Oz," in Crowley, *Magick*, 689.
152. Aleister Crowley, *Magick without Tears*, ed. Israel Regardie (1973; Scottsdale, Ariz.: New Falcon, 1991), 74.
153. Ibid., 492.
154. Ibid. See also the footnote to Crowley, *Magick*, 232, where he says, "There is the general metaphysical antithesis that Magick is the Art of the Will-to-Live, Mysticism of the Will-to-Die; but 'Truth comes bubbling to my brim; Life and Death are one to Him.'" As the editor of *Magick*, Hymenaeus Beta, mentions in his notes, the quotation comes from Aleister Crowley, "Scorpion," *The Equinox* I (6) (1911), 67.
155. See Urban, "Unleashing the Beast."
156. Henrik Bogdan, arguing against the tendency of some scholars to dismiss the "New Age Tantra" as "a product of impostors," claims: "Throughout the history of religions the transmission of ideas, symbols and practices from one religious system to another has been a permanent factor of religious change. New interpretations of religious symbols do not make them less authentic than older interpretations. For the historian of religions, new interpretations and uses of religious symbols is part of the ongoing development of religious traditions." Bogdan, "Challenging the Morals," 214, n. 10.
157. Hugh B. Urban, "Introduction: Diagnosing the 'Disease' of Tantra," in *Tantra*, 3. Urban also writes: "Since at least the time of Agehananda Bharati, most Western scholars have been severely critical of these [Western] new forms of pop Tantra or neo-Tantra. . . . My own view, however, is that 'neo' or 'California' Tantra is not 'wrong' or 'false' any more than the Tantra of the *Mahānirvāṇa* or other traditions; it is simply a different interpretation for a specific historical situation. As such, the historian of religions must take it very seriously as an example of a new adaptation of a religious form to a new social and political context." Urban, "The Cult of Ecstasy," 205.
158. "In the face of this intense confusion and contradiction, many scholars have abandoned the very idea of asserting a singular, monothetic definition for Tantra." Urban, "Introduction," 6.
159. All of these, in addition to Kāpālikas, Siddhas, Śaivas, Śāktas, Isma˘ilis, Vaiṣṇava Sahajiyās, Jain yogis, Bhāgavatas (India), worshippers of the Goddess Taleju (Nepal), Chinese Esoteric Buddhists, followers of Japanese Soto Zen and Tachikawa-ryū, as well as Tibetan practitioners of Yoga, Gelugpa, Gcod, and Dzogchen traditions, are included in David Gordon White's anthology *Tantra in Practice* (Princeton, N.J.: Princeton University Press, 2000). It could be argued that "Western Tantra" differs from these traditions to a similar degree that they mutually differ from each other.
160. "We may define the doctrine of the White School in its purity in very simple terms. Existence is pure joy. Sorrow is caused by failure to perceive this fact; but

this is not a misfortune. . . . The Tantric is not obsessed by the will-to-die. It is a difficult business to get any fun out of existence; but at least it is not impossible." Aleister Crowley, "The Three Schools of Magick," in *Magick without Tears*, 77, 75.

161. See the pertinent comments on this issue by Hymenaeus Beta in Crowley, *Magick*, lxii–lxvi.

162. See, for example, Urban, "Unleashing the Beast," 139.

163. See Alex Owen, *The Place of Enchantment: British Occultism and the Culture of the Modern* (Chicago: University of Chicago Press, 2004).

6

Continuing Knowledge from Generation unto Generation

THE SOCIAL AND LITERARY BACKGROUND OF ALEISTER CROWLEY'S MAGICK

Richard Kaczynski

WHEN ALEISTER CROWLEY'S magnum opus, *Magick in Theory and Practice*, appeared in 1929, it was the first modern textbook on magic. "People generally do want a book on Magick," he remarked to one of his students. "There never has been an attempt at one, anyhow, since the Middle Ages. . . . The book is revolutionary."[1] Since then, Crowley's impact has been inescapable, and it has not been limited to occultism. Urban credits Crowley with Western society's appropriation of Hindu Tantra as a popular form of spiritual sexuality.[2] Likewise, his cultural influence spans genres, including the literature of his contemporaries (from Somerset Maugham to Ernest Hemingway), fantastic fiction (from Robert Heinlein to Marion Zimmer Bradley), and popular music (from the Beatles to Tool). In a 2002 BBC poll, Crowley ranked seventy-third among the "100 Greatest Britons" of all time, right after Henry V.[3]

"Magick," however, did not emerge fully formed from nothing but Crowley's head. It was a demonstrable outgrowth of social and literary currents prevailing during his lifetime, including Victorian fascination with Spiritualism, occultism, sexuality, and the phallic basis of religion. Crowley freely acknowledged his sources and influences, noting that even his trademark motto—"Do what thou wilt shall be the whole of the Law"—echoes previous writers such as Saint Augustine and François Rabelais.[4] Placing Crowley's numerous writings on magic in the context of the thought and literature of his day underscores his contribution as a synthesist of these ideas into an innovative and original system of spiritual praxis.[5]

Occultism

In the latter part of the nineteenth century, Spiritualism was all the rage in the United States, echoing England's earlier fascination with the subject. Occultists such as P. B. Randolph, H. P. Blavatsky, and Emma Hardinge Britten famously attached themselves to this movement in order to promote their own writings. Those interested in Spiritualism often encountered dynamic leaders who served as introductions to groups such as the Theosophical Society, Hermetic Society, and the Rosicrucians, as part of the new occultism that emerged on both sides of the Atlantic beginning around 1880.[6] Thus, popular interest in subjects falling under the broad term *Spiritualism* brought members into the world of occult organizations.[7] That Spiritualism formed in the popular mind a broad and inclusive umbrella for varied spiritual practices is demonstrated by Harry Kemp's description of one of Crowley's ceremonial magic rituals as a "séance" even though it had nothing to do with contacting spirits of the dead.[8] Indeed, Crowley revived the archaic and idiosyncratic spelling of *magick* to distinguish his teachings from sleight of hand and charlatanism. As he states in *Magick in Theory and Practice*:

> I found myself at a loss for a name to designate my work, just as H. P. Blavatsky some years earlier. "Theosophy," "Spiritualism," "Occultism," "Mysticism," all involved undesirable connotations. I chose therefore the name "Magick" as essentially the most sublime, and actually the most discredited, of all the available terms. I swore to rehabilitate magick, to identify it with my own career.[9]

Primary among those groups whose Spiritualism formed part of a larger organization was the Theosophical Society (TS), founded by Helena Petrovna Blavatsky (1831–1891) and Colonel Henry Steel Olcott (1832–1907) in 1875. Blavatsky's teaching—that the world's religions represent a universal esoteric doctrine that is compatible with science—was promulgated by her books *Isis Unveiled* (1877) and *The Secret Doctrine* (1888).[10] As will be shown, Blavatsky was but one of many writers at this time positing a universalist view of religion. The TS attracted many bright and prolific minds, including G. R. S. Mead, Isabel Cooper-Oakley, Emma Hardinge Britten, Anna Kingsford, and William Butler Yeats. Immense popularity allowed the TS to weather two major scandals: First, Richard Hodgson of the Society for Psychical Research declared Blavatsky's séances—in which her famous Mahatma letters were produced—to be fraudulent.[11] His 207-page report concluded:

> For our own part, we regard her neither as the mouthpiece of hidden seers, nor as a mere vulgar adventuress; we think that she has achieved a title to permanent remembrance as one of the most accomplished, ingenious, and interesting impostors in history.[12]

Second, it was revealed that large portions of Blavatsky's books quoted heavily, without attribution, from earlier works in the field, chief among them being Godfrey Higgins's *Anacalypsis* (1836).[13] Nevertheless, the faithful defended her by attributing any apparent plagiarism to her receiving her text "in the astral light."[14]

Crowley regarded Blavatsky highly, attributing great significance to the fact that she founded the TS in the same year he was born,[15] and "always held her in absolute reverence as a genuine messenger from the Masters."[16] He also met her successor, Annie Besant (1847–1933), while sailing from Cairo to England in 1904,[17] but ultimately he formed a less glowing opinion of her. The wisdom revealed through the agreement of spirituality and science, promoted by Blavatsky and others,[18] found expression in the motto of Crowley's publication *The Equinox* as "The method of science, the aim of religion." In addition, Blavatsky's Mahatmas—the "great souls" or mysterious adepts who steer the spiritual evolution of humankind—paralleled the "Secret Chiefs" of the Hermetic Order of the Golden Dawn and made their way into Crowley's own magical hierarchy. The magical motto of his Scarlet Woman Jeanne Robert Foster was, in fact, taken from one of Blavatsky's Mahatmas, Hilarion.

In 1919, Crowley sought the attention of the TS by republishing Blavatsky's *The Voice of the Silence* as a special supplement to *The Equinox*.[19] He believed that the text "offers indefeasible evidence of intimate initiated knowledge," and he proposed himself as the group's successor.[20] This effort—unsurprisingly—failed, and six years later he released a series of anonymous broadsheets critical of the TS leadership under Annie Besant and Charles W. Leadbeater.[21]

Whatever his misgivings about the TS's succession, many publications under the Theosophical Publishing Society imprint had significant impacts on the traditions that Crowley embraced. For instance, Cooper-Oakley's *Traces of a Hidden Tradition in Masonry and Mediæval Mysticism* (1900) argued that the Masons, Templars, Grail Knights, and similar groups were manifestations of a single spiritual tradition spanning eighteen hundred years: This work was cited by Crowley associates John Yarker (1909), Arthur Edward Waite (1909), and Theodor Reuss (1914).[22] Another member of the TS was Gnostic scholar George Robert Stow Mead (1863–1933). Crowley gravitated to Gnosticism, possibly because it was a faith about which so little was known that it encouraged unrestrained speculation, in much the same way that Egyptian hieroglyphics, prior to the discovery of the Rosetta Stone, prompted speculation by de Gebelin that tarot cards originated in ancient Egypt.[23] Mead's influence is visible in Crowley's first magical text, *The Sword of Song* (1904): there, he refers to the Gnostic *Codex Brucianus*, which consists of the Coptic-Gnostic *Books of Jeu* and another untitled work. In 1904, the only two translations of this codex were by Schmidt (in German) and Mead.[24] During his American period (1914–1919), Crowley sought out Mead's translation of the Gnostic *Pistis Sophia*;[25] he subsequently included the book in his syllabus for students of magic.[26]

One of the most important authors (for the present study) of the Theosophical Publishing imprint was William Wynn Westcott (1848–1925). Aside from being a member of the Theosophical Society's Esoteric Section, he was Supreme Magus of the Societas Rosicruciana in Anglia (SRIA), Worshipful Master of the prestigious masonic research lodge Quatuor Coronati, and a member of various other masonic rites, revivals, and spin-offs. He was also cofounder of the Hermetic Order of the Golden Dawn (GD), the secret society par excellence of the Victorian era. He was a prolific writer, and through the TS he published works on kabbalah, numerology, alchemy, and Rosicrucianism.[27] He also contributed to and edited an acclaimed series of nine monographs titled *Collectanea Hermetica* (1893–1902).[28] This series included a translation of perennial favorite *The Divine Pymander* of Hermes Trismegistus; other versions were edited by occultists including P. B. Randolph (1871), Hargrave Jennings (1884), and G. R. S. Mead (1906).[29] These publications occurred during a brief period of amity between the GD and the TS, the politics of which are discussed by Gilbert.[30] Westcott's translation of the *Chaldean Oracles* figured prominently in the Hermetic Order of the Golden Dawn and was frequently quoted by Crowley.[31] For instance, a favorite Golden Dawn purification by incense involved reciting the 199th oracle: "And, when after all the phantasms are vanished, thou shalt see that holy and Formless Fire, that Fire which darts and flashes though the hidden depths of the Universe, hear thou the Voice of the Fire."[32] References to this passage pepper Crowley's writings, including "Liber Samekh" in *Magick in Theory and Practice*, the 17th Aethyr of *The Vision and the Voice*, and "An Evocation of Bartzabel the Spirit of Mars."[33] For example, the first verse of chapter 7 of "Liber DCCCXIII vel Ararita" reads, "Then in the might of the Lion did I formulate unto myself that holy and formless fire, קדש, which darteth and flasheth through the depths of the Universe."[34] A similar paraphrase in verse 37 of "Liber Tzaddi vel Hamus Hermeticus sub figura XC"—"Many have arisen, being foolish. They have said, 'Stoop down unto the darkly splendid world, and be wedded to that Blind Creature of the Slime'"[35]—references verse 145 of the *Chaldean Oracles*:

> Stoop not down unto the Darkly-Splendid World; wherein continually lieth a faithless Depth, and Hades wrapped in clouds, delighting in unintelligible images, precipitous, winding, a black ever-rolling Abyss; ever espousing a Body unluminous, formless and void.[36]

In addition to Westcott's contributions, four of *Collectanea Hermetica*'s titles were written by Florence Farr (1860–1917), Praemonstrix of the GD's Isis-Urania Lodge in London.[37]

A comment from author Arthur Edward Waite (1857–1942) inadvertently led Crowley himself to the GD. Waite verified for Crowley that the "invisible college" of occultism mentioned in the introduction to *The Book of Black Magic and of Pacts* truly existed.[38] Crowley deplored Waite's scholarship and berated him often in the pages of *The Equinox* and elsewhere.[39] Nevertheless, he acknowledged his debt to Waite, writing:

> Waite certainly did start a revival of interest in Alchemy, Magic, Mysticism, and all the rest. That his scholarship was so contemptible, his style so over-loaded, and his egomania so outrageous does not kill to the point of extinction the worth of his contribution. If it had not been for Waite, I doubt if, humanly speaking, I should ever have got in touch with the Great Order. You may of course, if you like, go one step further, back to Anna Kingsford and Edward Maitland, but their work, superior as it is to him, lacked one great asset. They gave us no idea of the bulk of medieval literature. To go back further still, H.P.B., genius as she was, was far too "oriental" to produce the necessary effect. Waite occupies a position not unlike that of Samuel Johnson. There is an omnivalence about him, which did just what was necessary at the time.[40]

Crowley ultimately found the GD and took his Neophyte initiation in November 1898.[41]

Through 1898 and 1899, he advanced regularly through the ranks of the GD until he hit a glass ceiling, owing both to his controversial personal life and to political wrangling between the London lodge and the order's head, Samuel Liddell MacGregor Mathers (1854–1918), whom Crowley had befriended.[42] Mathers was the eccentric author of the majority of the GD's papers and rituals, and the leading light of the order. He wrote an impressive array of occult books as well, covering topics that included kabbalah, tarot, and ceremonial magic.[43] Like his GD cofounder Westcott, Mathers belonged to the Masons, the SRIA, and the TS. He also lectured on kabbalah to the Hermetic Society of Anna Kingsford (1846–1888) and Edward Maitland (1824–1897). Being greatly influenced by their feminist, vegetarian, and anti-vivisectionist philosophies, he dedicated his *Kabbalah Unveiled* (1887) to them. Mathers's influence over the GD's London lodge, however, eroded when he moved to France, became increasingly autocratic, called into question the authenticity of the GD's foundational "cipher manuscript," and demanded that all members sign an oath of allegiance to him.

By 1900, these internal politics doomed the London lodge, and Crowley moved on to independent study. He ultimately founded his own secret society, the Argenteum Astrum (A.·.A.·.), in 1907, with Golden Dawn alumnus George Cecil Jones and new recruit John Frederick Charles Fuller (1878–1966). The influence of the GD in this venture cannot be understated, and an appreciation of Crowley's magic truly requires an understanding of the GD system. Crowley's frequent references to the Abramelin Working—and subsequent utilization of the Preliminary Invocation from the *Goetia* for this working—derive from Mathers's translations of magical texts on these topics. In the following account of a ritual for invisibility that he performed in Mexico City in 1900, he was almost certainly referring to the Golden Dawn's Z2 document,[44] which adapts the structure of its Neophyte initiation ritual for numerous other workings, including invisibility.

> I reached a point when my physical reflection in a mirror became faint and flickering. It gave very much the effect of the interrupted images of the cinematograph in its early days. But the real secret of invisibility is not concerned with the laws of optics at all; the trick is to prevent people noticing you when they would normally do so. In this I was quite successful. For example, I was able to take a walk in the street in a golden crown and a scarlet robe without attracting attention.[45]

Similarly, Allan Bennett's (1872–1923) "Ritual for the Evocation unto Visible Appearance of the Great Spirit Taphthartharath" was published in *The Equinox* as an exemplar of this applied ritual formula.[46] Crowley himself utilized this model for a ritual to evoke Typhon-Seth to visible appearance, "in which, by raising the sigil of Typhon to the grade of 1° = 10□, he bewitched a certain refractory brother of the order, known as Fra. D.P.A.L., who at this time was worrying Fra. D.D.C.F. by legal proceedings."[47] These GD ideas also appear in the discussion of other formulas in *Magick in Theory and Practice*.

Crowley owed numerous other debts to the GD as well. In 1904, he published, through his own Society for the Propagation of Religious Truth imprint, Mathers's translation of *The Key of Solomon*, although his former mentor was credited only as "A Dead Hand."[48] The Lesser and Greater Banishing Rituals of both the Pentagram and Hexagram in "Liber O" are those of the GD.[49] His tables of correspondences, *777*,[50] are likewise based upon a GD manuscript given to him by its compiler, Allan Bennett, when Bennett moved from London to Kashmir.[51] Crowley's essay on the kabbalah draws heavily upon Mathers's introduction to *The Kabbalah Unveiled*. "Liber Librae" adapts without acknowledgment an older GD paper, which is also quoted in its Neophyte ritual: "Remember that unbalanced force is evil; that unbalanced severity is but cruelty and oppression; but that also unbalanced mercy is but weakness which would allow and abet Evil."[52] "Liber Israfel"—an invocation of the Egyptian god of magic, Thoth or Tahuti—is likewise drawn from a ritual by his GD mentor Allan Bennett, itself a paraphrase of the sixty-fourth chapter of *The Egyptian Book of the Dead* (which was also printed in volume 8 of the *Collectanea Hermetica*, titled *Egyptian Magic*, 1896).[53] And the Gnostic Mass (discussed later) quotes both the Neophyte and Adeptus Minor rituals.

Between 1909 and 1918, Crowley experimented with more flexible and spontaneous ritual structures, frequently uniting an episodic series of rites by a common theme or goal, the whole of which he referred to as a "working." Crowley's Rites of Eleusis constituted one of his earliest and most ambitious forays in this direction. They consisted of seven dramatic rituals, one for each of the planets in traditional astrology, performed for a paying audience on consecutive Wednesdays at London's Caxton Hall from October 19 to November 30, 1910. The Rites incorporated drama, music, and poetry into their structure, resulting in a mix of theater and religion whose innovativeness in terms of Symbolist drama and other theater traditions has only recently been appreciated.[54] Throughout the Rites, Crowley leaned on his poetic heroes for content, intermixing works by Charles Swinburne ("Ilicet," "The Garden of Proserpine," "Atalanta in Calydon," "Hertha") and Paul Verlaine ("Colloque Sentimental"), as well as the Bible (Psalm 91), alongside his own oeuvre.

Poetry featured prominently in Crowley's experimentation with ritual because he was just as much a poet as he was a magician. Several of his earliest works were issued under the byline "A Gentleman of the University of

Cambridge" as homage to Percy Bysshe Shelley, whose 1811 book *St. Irvyne; or, The Rosicrucian: A Romance*, was released by "a Gentleman of the University of Oxford."[55] Several years later, Crowley penned the *English Review*'s centenary essay on Shelley, signing it "Prometheus" after Shelley's *Prometheus Unbound*.[56] Crowley's future scripted rituals, both published and unpublished, would continue to incorporate music, poetry, and other readings.

Subsequent to the Rites of Eleusis, Crowley experimented with even less structured techniques. His Abuldiz, Paris, and Amalantrah workings employed sex, alcohol, and other intoxicants to induce a state of spiritual ecstasy through which participants identified with deific archetypes or achieved contact with beings from nonphysical realms.[57] In these workings, the method of achieving the trance state seemed almost secondary to the dialogue that would result.

Crowley's magical practice changed radically when he encountered the sexual occultism of Ordo Templi Orientis (OTO) in 1912.[58] Under the leadership of Theodor Reuss (1855–1923), OTO evolved out of an aspiring "Academia Masonica" following the death of its benefactor, Austrian industrialist Carl Kellner (1850–1905). Crowley became the order's National Grand Master for the United Kingdom in 1912 and would eventually become Outer Head of the Order. If the GD drew its grade system from eighteenth- and nineteenth-century Rosicrucians, then the OTO structured itself largely upon Freemasonry. So closely was the OTO allied with Masonry that, in his day, Crowley allowed initiates of the Scottish and Memphis-Misraim Rites to "affiliate" to the equivalent degrees in OTO. In fact, Crowley characterized his rituals as distillations of these other rites:

> John Yarker saw in 1911 and 1912 that his 33 degrees were themselves unworkable. He gave me a printed copy of the 30 rituals—4° to 33°—the first three, of course, the Craft degrees of Masonry. This devastating volume I took with me on one of my journeys across the Sahara desert, and from it extracted anything that seemed useful to preserve, and very little there was. The desert was left dry.
>
> All of it, such as it is, is incorporated in the rituals of the O.T.O.[59]

Yarker knew and approved of his revisions, Crowley contended, but died before he could review the results. Table 6.1—based on a sketch by Crowley[60]—indicates the strong parallels between the OTO degrees and those of the Scottish Rite, as well as those of Yarker's Rite of Memphis and Misraim. Many established or "regular" masonic groups regard the OTO as a form of fringe, irregular, or clandestine masonry.

Table 6.1. Crowley's Synopsis of the OTO Degrees

OTO		Blue Lodge Freemasonry		
0°	Minerval	—		
I°	Man and Brother	Entered Apprentice		
II°	Magician	Fellow-Craft		
III°	Master Magician	Master Mason		
		Scottish Rite (AASR)	**Rite of Memphis**	**Rite of Misraim**
IV°	Lodge of Perfection	Royal Arch Mason	4°—7°	4°—
	Perfect Magician	4°—14°: Perfect and Sublime Mason		
	Perfect Initiate	15°—16°: Prince of Jerusalem	8°—9°	
	Knight of the East and West	17°: Knight of the East and West	10°	
V°	Sovereign Prince of Rose Croix	18°: Sovereign Prince of Rose Croix	11°	44°
	Knight of the Red Eagle	19°—29°	12°—17°	
VI°	Knight Kadosch, Companion of the Holy Grail	30°: Grand Elect Knight Kadosh	18°	65°
	Grand Inquisitor Commander	31°: Grand Inspector Inquisitor Commander		66°
	Prince of the Royal Secret	32°: Sublime Prince of the Royal Secret	19°	
VII°	Sovereign Grand Inspector General	33°: Sovereign Grand Inspector General	20°	
VIII°	Epopt/Pontiff of the Illuminati	—		
IX°	Perfect Illuminate	—	33° (95°)	90°
X°	Grand Master	—	(96°)	—
XI°		—		—
XII°	Outer Head of the Order	—	(97°)	—

Although initiated into a French masonic lodge,[61] Crowley believed that his revisions to Yarker's rituals had restored the lost keys of Freemasonry. He later revised the OTO degrees up to III° to reduce their similarity to their Blue Lodge counterparts, in an unsuccessful effort to convert regular masons to his view. Crowley later distanced himself and the OTO from the Craft and criticized what he saw as its endemic problems. Nevertheless, the OTO's rituals beyond III° retain similarity to their masonic counterparts.[62]

The OTO's chief innovation is found in its upper-degree teachings on sexual magic. As shown below, these teachings emerged amid a culture awash with literature on the phallic nature or religion. Crowley devoted the years 1914–1919 to experimenting systematically with this technique, as recorded in his *Rex de Arte Regia* diaries.[63] Likewise, in the 1930s, he would also collect his systematic experiments on the medicinal properties of this technique under the title *Amrita*.[64]

These Victorian occult movements had a political agenda, and Crowley's was no exception. Harvey demonstrates how the Martinist movement in France was not merely an occult organization but exerted political influence as well.[65] In England and the United States, Spiritualism provided a mechanism for women to experience empowerment in a disempowering culture, thereby abetting the emerging suffrage and other feminist struggles of the time.[66] Dixon similarly connects Theosophy to popular feminist movements.[67] In the United States, meanwhile, sexual mystic Ida Craddock defended the belly dancing of Fahreda Mahzar (a.k.a. Little Egypt) at Chicago's 1893 World Columbian Exhibition against federal obscenity laws; this was part of her own crusade for open discourse on equal sexual standards for men and women.[68] To be fair, while feminism constituted a common theme in many Spiritualist and occult movements, opinions differed widely on its exact form. For instance, while Theosophist Annie Besant promoted contraceptive rights, Craddock opposed both contraception and abortion.

A significant feature of the TS, GD, and OTO is their break with the common tradition of occult fraternities admitting only men as members. Whereas Freemasons took oaths against admitting women to their ranks, these groups welcomed members of either sex. Indeed, Crowley entrusted to women several important jobs in the OTO, including Grand Secretary General (Leila Waddell), Grand Treasurer General (Vittoria Cremers), and Lodgemaster (Mary Davies)—a significant gesture in a traditionally male-dominated field. Crowley's esoteric thought, like that of other occultists, impinged on his view of social norms, and vice versa. Throughout his life, Crowley advocated social and sexual reform, crossing class, gender, and other traditional boundaries. He considered England's laws and mores regarding the conduct of consenting adults to be unenlightened, and he believed that every man and woman had the right to "take your fill and will of love as ye will, when, where, and with whom ye will" (*The Book of the Law* 1:51). Crowley was also familiar with the notion of an "intermediate sex" containing both masculine and feminine elements, as expressed in the writings of Ulrichs (1898), Leland (1904), and Carpenter (1908).[69] In *The Sword of Song* (1904) Crowley used Ulrichs's term "Urning" for people who belong physically to one gender but mentally and emotionally to another:

> Here's how I got a better learning.
> It's a long lane that has no turning!
> Lehrjahre. Wanderjahre. "The magician of Paris."
> Mad as a woman-hunted Urning,
> The lie-chased alethephilist . . .[70]

The bisexual outlook of his disciple and lover Victor Neuburg (1883–1940) was similarly influenced by Carter's *Intermediate Sex*. Crowley's *The World's Tragedy* (1910) contains a defense of sodomy, and in his *Confessions* he describes how sexual repression and ownership are responsible for "the shocking evils which we all deplore."[71]

Phallicism and Related Literature

Contrary to common misperceptions of the Victorian era as sexually repressive, critical historical studies reveal that it was actually an unprecedented period of open discourse on all matters sexual.[72] Foucault's summary of Victorian sexuality is especially pertinent to our discussion of sacred sexuality: "What is peculiar to modern societies, in fact, is not that they consigned sex to a shadow existence, but that they dedicated themselves to speaking of it ad infinitum, while exploiting it as *the* secret."[73]

Early on, Crowley encountered the Victorian fascination with sexuality in two literatures: that of the medical profession and that of the decadents. He was familiar with Krafft-Ebing's analysis of sexual pathologies, *Psychopathia Sexualis* (1886).[74] Disagreeing vehemently with its thesis, Crowley offered his rebuttal using the medium with which he was most familiar: poetry. The resulting book, *White Stains*[75]—often dismissed as pornographic—properly belongs to the fin de siècle decadent literature.[76]

Given Crowley's proclivity for both expensive books and sexual license, it was inevitable that he should discover the considerable contemporary literature on phallicism. It was part of a larger tendency to incorporate all religion under a single umbrella, to understand it scientifically as a unitary phenomenon.[77] As Verter notes incisively:

> Research by anthropologists, philologists, and folklorists was more subtly damaging to Christian hegemony than the work of evolutionary theorists and Biblical critics, as they inadvertently offered the public a panoply of intriguing alternatives to the Church whose monopoly they challenged.[78]

This literature began initially as an outgrowth of various British societies formed for the study of antiquities or anthropology. These were not professional societies;, they were open to any interested parties, and they typically attracted members of England's leisure class.

For example, the Society of Dilettanti was founded in 1732 by Sir Francis Dashwood to promote appreciation of ancient Greek art. In 1786, one of its members, British MP Richard Payne Knight (1750–1824)—best known for his theories of picturesque beauty—published *An Account of the Remains of the Worship of Priapus* for distribution to the society's members. The book documented ancient phallic worship by including numerous explicit plates of ancient relics and suggested that remnants of this worship had continued down to the present day. Knight naively offered the book as a scholarly essay and was mortified when recipients objected to its contents. He sought to recall and destroy all remaining copies.[79] This made the book exceedingly scarce, but its republication in 1865 stirred popular interest in the phallic nature of religious worship, with an extract republished in 1883, edited and introduced by Hargrave Jennings.[80] Godwin provides an excellent account of how changes in social, literary, and occult thinking of the late 1700s and early 1800s set the stage for this interest in phallicism.[81]

A higher-profile, and less apologetic, proponent of anthropological erotica was explorer and orientalist Sir Richard Francis Burton (1821–1890). After serving in the East India Company for a dozen years, he became famous for disguising himself in Arabic garb and making the hajj, or holy pilgrimage to Mecca, in 1853. His lifelong interest in sexual practices led him to publish several risqué Arabic and Hindu texts under the imprint of the Kama Shastra Society, including *The Kama Sutra of Vatsyayana* (1883), *Ananga-Ranga: (Stage of the Bodiless One); or, The Hindoo Art of Love* (1885), the ten-volume *Book of the Thousand Nights and a Night* (1885), with its seven-volume supplement (1886–1888), and *The Perfumed Garden of the Cheikh Nefzaoui: A Manual of Arabian Erotology* (1886).[82] He was also an acquaintance of the publisher Leonard Smithers, and together they produced *Priapeia or the Sporting Epigrams of Divers Poets on Priapus* (1890) and *The Carmina of Caius Valerius Catullus* (1894).[83]

In 1863, Burton and James Hunt cofounded the Anthropological Society of London "to supply travelers with an organ that would rescue their observations from the outer darkness of manuscript and print their curious information on social and sexual matters."[84] This was another British society for laypersons with an interest in other cultures to study and share. The proceedings of the society's annual meetings covered topics as diverse as skull shapes, hermaphroditism, and "the alleged sterility of the women of savage races with native males, after having had children by a white man."[85] Among its notable members were Edward Sellon (1818?-1866),[86] Charles Staniland Wake (1835–1910),[87] and Hodder Michael Westropp (1820–1885).[88]

Several writers on phallicism enjoyed a small and incestuous circle, both within and outside the societies promoting their discussion. Westropp and Wake shared the byline of *Ancient Symbol Worship* (1875). Wake also penned a review of Major General James George Roche Forlong's (1824–1904) *Rivers of Life* (1883), which traced the world's great religions back to solar-phallic worship.[89] Forlong reciprocated with a memorial introduction to Westropp's posthumous publication *Primitive Symbolism, as Illustrated in Phallic Worship* (1885). In this introduction, Forlong commented on how freely phallicism was discussed in the old days, recalling that Westropp "read a Paper, which justly attracted much attention, in 1870, before the Anthropological Society, London, in the days when such subjects were then possible, as they are not now, owing to admission of lady members."[90] Phallicism quickly developed into a substantial literature, the major works of which are summarized here in Table 6.2, which begins with Knight's *A Discourse on the Worship of Priapus* (1786) and (for our purposes) ends with Goodland's (1931) *A Bibliography of Sex Rites and Customs*.[91] Writers in both England and the United States contributed to the ongoing discussion of how all religions, including Christianity, had their basis in worship of the sex organs.

The influence of these personalities and ideas is as inescapable as the GD in Crowley's magic. He included works by Burton, Forlong, Jennings, and Knight on his list of recommended readings for students.[92] Burton's influence extended even farther, inspiring Crowley both to travel and to publish in a similar vein. He unabashedly said, "Burton was always my hero,"[93] and Burton's masquerade as a Muslim in order to complete the hajj occurred to Crowley when he visited the rock temples in Madura, India:

Table 6.2. Chronology of Major Works on Phallicism and Related Literature through 1931

Author	Year	Title
Knight	1786	*A Discourse on the Worship of Priapus*
Knight	1865	*A Discourse on the Worship of Priapus* (new edition)
Sellon	1865	*Annotations on the Sacred Writings of the Hindus*
Sellon	1866	*Memoirs Read before the Anthropological Society of London*
Inman	1868–1869	*Ancient Faiths Embodied in Ancient Names* *Ancient Pagan and Modern Christian Symbolism*
Davenport	1869	*Aphrodisiacs and Anti-Aphrodisiacs*
Jennings	1870	*The Rosicrucians: Their Rites and Mysteries*
Ward	1871	*History of the Cross: The Pagan Origin and Idolatrous Adoption and Worship of the Image*
Westropp and Wake	1875	*Ancient Symbol Worship*
Forlong	1883	*Rivers of Life*
Jennings	1884	*Phallicism, Celestial and Terrestrial, Heathen and Christian*
Westropp	1885	*Primitive Symbolism, as Illustrated in Phallic Worship*
Campbell	1887	*Phallic Worship*
Wake	1888	*Serpent Worship, and Other Essays*
[Jennings]	1889	*Phallism*
[Jennings]	1889	*Ophiolatreia*
[Jennings]	1889	*Phallic Objects, Monuments and Remains*
[Jennings]	1890	*Cultus Arborum*
Dulaure	1890	*Priapic Divinities and Phallic Rites*
Morgan	1890	*Light of Britannia*
[Jennings]	1890	*Fishes, Flowers and Fire*
[Jennings]	1891	*Archaic Rock Inscriptions*
[Jennings]	1891	*Nature-Worship*
[Jennings]	1891	*Phallic Miscellanies*
[Jennings]	1891	*Mysteries of the Rosie Cross*
Bourke	1891	*Scatalogical Rites of All Nations*
Wheeler	1892	*Bible Studies: Essays on Phallic Worship*

Table 6.2. (*continued*)

Author	Year	Title
Parsons	1895	*Our Sun-God, or, Christianity before Christ*
Parsons	1896	*The Non-Christian Cross*
Forlong	1897	*Short Studies on the Science of Comparative Religions*
Gamble	1897	*The God-Idea of the Ancients, or Sex in Religion*
Howard	1897	*Sex Worship: An Exposition of the Phallic Origin of Religion*
Adiramled	1901	*The Divine Symbols*
Crawley	1902	*The Mystic Rose*
Adiramled	1904	*The Art of Alchemy*
Swiney	1906	*The Cosmic Procession, or, The Feminine Principle in Evolution*
Member of the Royal Asiatic Society	1909	*Marriage Ceremonies and Priapic Rites in India and the East*
Hannay	1913	*Christianity: The Sources of Its Teaching and Symbolism*
Brown	1916	*The Sex Worship and Symbolism of Primitive Races*
Craddock	1918	*Heavenly Bridegrooms*
Wall	1919	*Sex and Sex Worship (Phallic Worship)*
Carpenter	1920	*Pagan and Christian Creeds: Their Origin and Meaning*
Hannay	1922	*Sex Symbolism in Religion*
Goldsmith	1924	*Life Symbols as Related to Sex Symbolism*
Howard	1925	*Sex and Religion*
McCabe	1926	*Phallic Ancient Civilizations and the Cult of Love*
Stone	1927	*The Story of Phallicism, with Other Essays on Related Subjects*
Olliver	1928	*An Analysis of Magic and Witchcraft*
Wake	1929	*Sacred Prostitution and Marriage by Capture*
Goldsmith	1929	*Ancient Pagan Symbols*
Cutner	1930	*Sex Worship*
Goldberg	1930	*The Sacred Fire: The Story of Sex in Religion*
Goodland	1931	*A Bibliography of Sex Rites and Customs*

> I knew, of course, that the average European would not be permitted to visit the most interesting parts of the temple, and I thought I would see what I could do to take a leaf out of Burton's book. So I disposed of my European belongings and took up my position outside a village near by, with a loincloth and a begging bowl. The villagers knew, of course, that I was an Englishman, and watched me suspiciously for some time from the edge of the jungle. But as soon as they found that I was really expert in Yoga, they lost no time in making friends.[94]

Crowley's *Snowdrops from a Curate's Garden* (1904) was printed with the false imprint of Cosmopoli, the same fictitious place used in Burton's *Kama Sutra* (1883), *Ananga Ranga* (1885), and *Perfumed Garden* (1886), as well as Smithers and Burton's *Priapeia* (1890).[95] That Burton's *Perfumed Garden* was the model for Crowley's *Scented Garden* (1910) is made clear in the latter text's fictional account of the discovery of the "Bagh-i-Muattar" manuscript: "Why! I exclaimed, this is the Scented Garden! the famous Arab treatise of the Sheik al Nefzawi, which Burton rendered into English and his silly wife destroyed. This is the Ars Amoris of the Bedawin!"[96] While Crowley's tongue-in-cheek humor seems lost on Colligan, she nevertheless offers a compelling analysis of how the book, its essay "On Pederasty," and even Crowley's *The Vision and the Voice* working are modeled on Burton.[97]

Crowley would encounter these ideas throughout his travels, including his stay in the United States during World War I while he was refining the practice of sex magic. From the time he arrived in New York in December 1914, he corresponded with lawyer Theodore Schroeder (1864–1953), who published on "the erotogenesis of religion." Crowley tried to entice Schroeder into purchasing a rare copy of his *Scented Garden*, while Schroeder introduced Crowley to his book on sexual mystic Ida Craddock (discussed below). Schroeder was also interested in the OTO's upper-degree papers, which Crowley was unwilling to release unless Schroeder affiliated to the VII° and took the appropriate oaths of secrecy. Similarly, when Crowley found an American publisher for *The Equinox* in Albert Winslow Ryerson (b. 1872), he also found an esoteric book dealer specializing in sacred sexuality in religion. This publishing arrangement therefore included Ryerson not only distributing Crowleyana to his clientele but also locating rare books on sex magick for Crowley.[98]

Of all the writers on phallicism discussed here in relation to Crowley, the most important is unquestionably Hargrave Jennings (1817–1890). While others examined phallicism manifested in ancient religions, Jennings's *The*

Rosicrucians: Their Rites and Mysteries (1870)[99] appeared early on the scene and distinguished itself by suggesting that not only religion but also Western mystery schools such as Rosicrucianism were based upon phallic worship. Blavatsky called it "the ablest book that was ever written on Symbols and Mystic Orders"[100] and wrote, "No one, truly in Christian countries before him has ever had the moral courage to speak so openly as he does of the phallic element with which the Christian Church (the Roman Catholic) is honey-combed, and this is the author's chief desert and credit."[101] The meaning of this association was driven home for Crowley in a 1912 meeting with OTO leader Theodor Reuss, who, in 1906, had translated and published Jennings's later work, *Phallicism: A Description of the Worship of Lingam-Yoni in Various Parts of the World* (1889).[102] When Reuss explained the secret to Crowley, "It instantly flashed upon me. The entire symbolism, not only of freemasonry but of many other traditions, blazed upon my spiritual vision."[103] Jennings's work brought everything together: Masonry, Templarism, other secret societies, magic, sex, and religion. Despite the fact that many of the illustrations in *The Rosicrucians* were taken without credit from Georg von Welling's *Opus Mago-Cabalisticum et Theologicum* (1719), and that the book received a brutal review by A. E. Waite (who was doubtless protecting his own *Real History of the Rosicrucians*, which was written as "a corrective to the lunacies of Hargrave Jennings"),[104] Jennings's book was nevertheless extremely popular and enjoyed several printings.

Sexual Magic Practitioners

Crowley, surprisingly, makes little reference to Tantra in his writings. He lived for a time in India, studying Buddhism and Hinduism with his Golden Dawn mentor Allan Bennett—who had become the Buddhist monk Bikkhu Ananda Metteya and a student of Shaivite guru Sri Parananda, better known as Ponnambalam Ramanathan (1851–1930), the solicitor general of Ceylon. While Crowley recommended the *Shiva Samhita* to students of magick, he also spoke ambivalently of Tantra in his *Confessions*, referring to "these follies of vamacharya."[105] Later, in *Magick without Tears*, he wrote more directly:

> To the *Vedas*, the *Upanishads*, and the *Tripitaka* of the Buddhists, we have only to add the *Tantras* of what are called the Vamacharya Schools. Paradoxical as it may sound the Tantrics are in reality the most advanced of the Hindus. Their theory is, in its philosophical ultimatum, a primitive stage of the White tradition, for the essence of the Tantric cults is that by the performance of certain rites of Magick, one

> does not only escape disaster, but obtains positive benediction. The Tantric is not obsessed by the will-to-die. It is a difficult business, no doubt, to get any fun out of existence; but at least it is not impossible. In other words, he implicitly denies the fundamental proposition that existence is sorrow, and he formulates the essential postulate of the White School of Magick, that means exist by which the universal sorrow (apparent indeed to all ordinary observation) may be unmasked, even as at the initiatory rite of Isis in the ancient days of Khem. There, a Neophyte presenting his mouth, under compulsion, to the pouting buttocks of the Goat of Mendez, found himself caressed by the chaste lips of a virginal priestess of that Goddess at the base of whose shrine is written that No man has lifted her veil.[106]

While this passage speaks of the Tantric philosophical outlook, it says nothing about actual practice. Indeed, references to England's popularizer of Tantra, Arthur Avalon (pen name of Sir John Woodroffe, 1865–1936), are conspicuous by their absence. Although criticized for sanitizing his subject matter for Western readers,[107] Avalon is one of the most important disseminators of Tantra, having translated roughly twenty texts and authored influential works such as *Principles of Tantra* (1914), *Shakti and Shâkta* (1918), *The Serpent Power* (1919) and *The Garland of Letters* (1922).[108] Despite the absence of any significant Tantric teachings in Crowley's sex magick,[109] Crowley encountered throughout his travels examples of people who integrated other forms of spiritual praxis, in one way or another, into their sexuality.

Thomas Lake Harris

Homeopathic physician Dr. Edward W. Berridge (c. 1843–1923) was a vocal advocate of American utopian Thomas Lake Harris (1823–1906), whose mystic Christian teachings included breath control, sexual technique, polyfidelity, and fairies. Harris founded the Brotherhood of the New Life in 1861 and traveled to the United Kingdom several times in search of followers. Among them was wealthy diplomat Laurence Oliphant (1829–1888), future author of *Scientific Religion* (1888).[110] With help from Oliphant's fortune, Harris established communes in Brockton, New York, and Santa Rosa, California.

In 1896, under the pen name of Respiro ("I breathe"), Berridge began publishing a series of works explicating the teachings of Harris, collectively titled

The Brotherhood of the New Life: An Epitome of the Works and Teachings of Thomas Lake Harris.[111] After he circulated copies among members of the GD, Annie Horniman (1860–1937) complained to the head of the order. Mathers counseled her that her own level of initiation was not advanced enough to allow her to understand or appreciate these works, and that she should disregard the matter.[112] When she continued her objections, Mathers responded by expelling her from the GD.

Given that Horniman was Mathers's benefactor—paying him a monthly stipend to do his occult work—this radical action spurred speculation among historians that the GD either incorporated or tacitly tolerated the mystic sexuality of Thomas Lake Harris in its advanced curriculum.[113] Crowley certainly implied as much in his recollection of the GD: *The Rosicrucian Scandal* (1910) offered a fictitious dialogue between a barrister (Scorpio) and the head of the GD:

SCORPIO, K.C. What complaints were made against Dr Berridge?
MATHERS That girls who came to him for examination in the Knowledge Lectures were subjected to insult.
SCORPIO, K.C. Did you investigate this charge?
MATHERS Astrally, yes.
SCORPIO, K.C. Was there any other charge?
MATHERS Yes.
SCORPIO, K.C. What was it?
MATHERS That he was disseminating objectionable literature.
SCORPIO, K.C. What?
MATHERS The works of Thomas Lake Harris.
SCORPIO, K.C. What is objected to?
MATHERS He recommends his pupils to invoke elemental spirits or "astral counterparts" for the purpose of carnal copulation.
SCORPIO, K.C. Was this charge denied?
MATHERS No.
SCORPIO, K.C. What did you do?
MATHERS I expelled his accuser.
SCORPIO, K.C. Name the accuser.
MATHERS Miss Horniman.[114]

Crowley's impression of Harris appears favorable, as evidenced by his review of Berridge's book, *Counterparts*, volume 16 of *The Brotherhood of the New Life: An Epitome of the Works and Teachings of Thomas Lake Harris*:

> We need not be surprised if the Unity of Subject and Object in Consciousness which is Samadhi, the uniting of the Bride and the Lamb which is Heaven, the uniting of the Magus and the god which is Evocation, the uniting of the Man and his Holy Guardian Angel which is the seal upon the work of the Adeptus Minor, is symbolized by the geometrical unity of the circle and the square, the arithmetical unity of the 5 and the 6, and (for more universality of comprehension) the uniting of the Lingam and the Yoni, the Cross and the Rose. For as in earth-life the sexual ecstasy is the loss of self in the Beloved, the creation of a third consciousness transcending its parents, which is again reflected into matter as a child; so, immeasurably higher, upon the Plane of Spirit, Subject and Object join to disappear, leaving a transcendent unity. This third is ecstasy and death; as below, so above.
>
> It is then with no uncleanness of mind that all races of men have adored an ithyphallic god; to those who can never lift their eyes above the basest plane the sacrament seems filth.
>
> Much, if not all, of the attacks upon Thomas Lake Harris and his worthy successor "Respiro" is due to this persistent misconception by prurient and degraded minds. . . .
>
> This is the Magic Mirror of the Soul; if you see God in everything, it is because you are God and have made the universe in your image; if you see Sex in everything, and think of Sex as something unclean, it is because you are a sexual maniac.
>
> True, it is, of course, that the soul must not unite herself to every symbol, but only to the God which every symbol veils.
>
> And Lake Harris is perfectly clear on the point. The "counterpart" is often impersonated, with the deadliest results. But if the Aspirant be wise and favoured, he will reject all but the true.
>
> And I really fail to see much difference between this doctrine and our own of attaining the Knowledge and Conversation of the Holy Guardian Angel, or the Hindu doctrine of becoming one with God. We may easily agree that Lake Harris made the error of thinking men pure-minded, and so used language which the gross might misinterpret; but sincere study of this book will make the truth apparent to all decent men.[115]

Here, Crowley places Harris in the context of phallicists such as Knight and Jennings, and identifies union with one's angel as another metaphor for the universal tradition.

Theodor Reuss

According to the jubilee edition of the OTO's newsletter, the *Oriflamme*:

> Our Order possesses the KEY which unlocks all Masonic and Hermetic secrets; it is the doctrine of *sexual magic*, and this doctrine explains without exception all the riddles of Nature, all Masonic symbolism and all religious systems.[116]

Crowley reports that after publishing his *Book of Lies* (1912),[117] he was taken to task by Theodor Reuss for openly printing the secret of sexual magic. Reuss subsequently admitted Crowley to the Sovereign Sanctuary of the Gnosis in order to swear him to secrecy.

Like many nineteenth-century occultists, Reuss belonged to numerous organizations, and his acquaintances included SRIA Supreme Magus Wynn Westcott, Martinism founder Gérard Encausse (1865–1916), German Theosophist Franz Hartmann (1838–1912), and masonic leader John Yarker (1833–1913). Aside from spearheading the German revival of the Bavarian Order of Illuminati, Reuss was also Magus of the High Council in Germania of the SRIA, Special Inspector for the Martinist Order, Sovereign Grand Inspector General of the Cerneau Scottish Rite, and Grand Master of the Swedenborgian Rite. He also held charters from Yarker to operate the Antient and Primitive Rite of Memphis, the Ancient Oriental Rite of Mizraim, and the Cerneau Ancient and Accepted Scottish Rite.

Because it was such a revelation, the OTO's central secret spurred Crowley to shift his personal praxis in its direction.[118] He opined that Reuss had applied the secret on but a couple of occasions in his lifetime:

> He fully understood the importance of the matter and he was a man of considerable scientific attainment in many respects; yet he had never made a systematic study of the subject and had not even applied his knowledge to his purposes, except in rare emergencies. As soon as I was assured by experience that the new force was in fact capable of accomplishing the theoretically predictable results, I devoted practically the whole of my spare time to a course of experiments.[119]

Crowley, by contrast, spent the rest of his life exploring the technique that the order was sworn to preserve and pass on.

An interesting question is how the OTO came to be in possession of this secret. The order's spiritual father, Carl Kellner, was an Austrian paper chemist who traveled widely. In his journeys, he met three adepts, the Sufi Soliman ben Aïssa and the Hindus Bheema Sena Pratapa and Sri Mahatma Agamya Paramahamsa; these three are often cited as the sources of the OTO's teachings on sex magic.[120] Others point to a passage in the *Oriflamme* that states, "During his many and extensive trips in Europe, America and Asia Minor, Brother∴ Kellner came in contact with an organization which bore the name 'The Hermetic Brotherhood of Light'" or Hermetic Brotherhood of Luxor (HBL). Thus, one popular hypothesis is that Kellner received the teachings from the HBL, who in turn received them from American Rosicrucian P. B. Randolph.[121]

Paschal Beverly Randolph (1825–1875) was a self-taught physician in upstate New York who specialized in curing sexual complaints. In 1853, he became a Spiritualist, receiving messages from various spirits through automatic writing and speaking. His reputation brought him to London and France in 1855 and 1856, where he channeled spirits for Emperor Napoleon III. He was also purportedly made the Rosicrucian Supreme Grand Master for the West at this time; whether this is true or not, the works on "affectional alchemy" that he began publishing in the 1860s identified him a Rosicrucian. Despite this pedigree, in *Eulis* (1874) he wrote:

> I studied Rosicrucianism, found it suggestive, and loved its mysticism. So I called myself The Rosicrucian, and gave my thought to the world as Rosicrucian thought; and lo! The world greeted with loud applause what it supposed had its origin and birth elsewhere than in the soul of P. B. Randolph.[122]

Much as *Spiritualism* in the popular mind became a catchall term for all manner of mysticism, so too was *Rosicrucian* so vague a term that any—be it Bulwer-Lytton, Randolph, Jennings, the SRIA, or the GD—could claim it without contest.

Randolph, however, acknowledged the influence of Hargrave Jennings, whom he quoted frequently in his own writings. Jennings apparently initiated Randolph into Rosicrucianism.[123] Randolph, in turn, called Jennings "the chief Rosicrucian of all England" and recognized him as Grand Master.[124] The feeling, however, was not mutual. To their common printer and bookseller Robert H. Fryar, Jennings complained of "Randolph, with his mischievous books, which ought not to have been published."[125]

Jennings also had a long friendship with Peter Davidson (1842–1916), chief of the HBL. When the HBL announced itself to the world through an edition of *The Divine Pymander*, Jennings contributed a supporting preface.[126]

With the formal appearance of the HBL, Jennings coincidentally began publishing a series of books on phallicism, beginning with *Phallicism, Celestial and Terrestrial, Heathen and Christian* (1884), followed by a series of ten anonymous volumes bearing his unmistakable style.[127] His influence is apparent throughout Davidson's writing, particularly *Wheel of Ezechiel*.[128] Likewise, Randolph's works were recommended to HBL students. Thus, Jennings's perspective—through Randolph and Davidson—was inculcated in the thinking of the HBL, the Brotherhood of Eulis, and the Fraternitas Rosae Crucis, and carried on by Randolph's Rosicrucian successor Freeman Dowd, as evidenced in books such as *The Temple of the Rosy Cross: The Soul, Its Powers, Migrations, and Transmigrations* (1901) and *Regeneration: Being Part II of the Temple of the Rosy Cross* (1900).[129] Further, Melton demonstrates that these ideas also disseminated into other American Rosicrucian traditions in the early twentieth century.[130] Likewise, the OTO claimed that "the Rosicrucian esoteric teachings of the *Hermetic Brotherhood of Light* were reserved for the few initiated into the Occult Inner Circle."[131]

Ida Craddock

As indicated earlier, Crowley became aware of Ida Craddock (1875–1902) through his friend New York lawyer Theodore Schroeder. A decade after Craddock committed suicide rather than go to prison for mailing literature judged obscene, Schroeder became interested in her court battle. Discovering her surviving papers, he published her book, *Heavenly Bridegrooms* (written in 1894),[132] in *Alienist and Neurologist*, a quarterly journal of scientific, clinical, and forensic psychiatry and neurology. In her book, Craddock wrote openly about sex, claiming that her experience in these matters stemmed from her marriage to an angel. Her unpublished works are even more interesting: In *Psychic Wedlock*, she outlined a tripartite system of sexual initiation—most curious, considering the parallels with other triple systems, including the OTO, the Tantrik Order, Masonry, Martinism, and that outlined by Randolph in his *Book of the Triplicate Order* (1875).[133] She also penned a pair of studies of sex in religion—*Lunar and Sex Worship* and *Sex Worship (Continued)*, only recently published—that examined the role of sexuality in religious worship as practiced by ancient cultures around the world.[134] Reviewing *Heavenly Bridegrooms* in *The Equinox* (1919), Crowley wrote:

> I may say that it is one of the most remarkable human documents ever produced, and it should certainly find a regular publisher in book form.

> The authoress of the MS. claims that she was the wife of an angel. She expounds at the greatest length the philosophy connected with this thesis. Her learning is enormous. She finds traces of similar beliefs in every country in the world, and (having a similar experience of her own) she can hardly be blamed for arguing that one thing confirms the other. Mr. Schroeder is quite logical in calling her paper An Unintentional Contribution to the Erotogenic Interpretation of Religion. . . .
>
> I am very far from agreeing with all that this most talented woman sets forth in her paper, but she certainly obtained initiated knowledge of extraordinary depth. She seems to have had access to certain most concealed sanctuaries. . . . She has put down statements in plain English which are positively staggering. This book is of incalculable value to every student of occult matters. No Magick library is complete without it.[135]

This review spawned one of Crowley's more memorable lines: "When you have proved that God is merely a name for the sex instinct, it appears to me not far to the perception that the sex instinct is God." Elaborating on this theme, he wrote to Schroeder:

> It may interest you that, a day or so ago, attempting to discuss your ideas with regard to sex and religion, my eccentric friend, fixing his eyes rather fiercely upon me, growled abruptly: "Semen is God."
>
> Unwilling to excite him further, I replied: Sir, though I understand perfectly what you mean by Semen, I am unacquainted with the connotation which you attach to the term "God."[136]

Crowley's heir apparent, Charles Stansfeld Jones (1886–1950), wrote to Schroeder in 1919, "I am much interested in the Erotogenetic Interpretation of Religion, and have heard of your book, *Heavenly Bridegrooms*, as being an excellent treatise on this subject."[137] In 1946, Crowley's designated successor, Karl Germer (1885–1962), also wrote to Schroeder, requesting a replacement copy of *Heavenly Bridegrooms*.[138] When Louis T. Culling (1894–1973) published his version of the curriculum of the Gnostic Body of God—a splinter group of estranged Crowley student Cecil Frederick Russell (1897–1987)—he wrote:

> Among other instructions received from Headquarters, the Primate was referred to a paper-bound booklet of some hundred pages, written

> by Ida C. Even back in the thirties this book was scarce and hard to come by, although it had been used by the psychiatrist Dr. Theodore Schroeder in his publication, *The Erotogenesis of Religion*. The title of the book published by Ida C. was *The Heavenly Bridegroom*[*s*].[139]

The three-degree grade structure proposed by Culling echoed that given in *Psychic Wedlock*.[140] In 1981, Marcelo Motta, a student of Germer's, published *Heavenly Bridegrooms* and *Psychic Wedlock* in his *Sex and Religion* volume.[141] Thus, both Schroeder and Craddock influenced Thelema throughout the twentieth century.

The Gnostic Mass

Penned in Russia in 1913 under the inspiration of the Liturgy of St. Basil, the Gnostic Mass is arguably the pinnacle of Crowley's work in ceremonial magic.[142] He had already been through the GD, started the A.·.A.·., and become British head of the OTO. Shortly after he wrote the ritual, his attention drifted toward sex magic, making the Gnostic Mass the last great ceremonial ritual that he wrote and shared with the general public. Subsequent rituals, such as his revisions of the OTO initiations, remain proprietary documents of the OTO. In its forty-five-minute span, the Gnostic Mass draws upon and synthesizes all the themes discussed in this essay.

Its form is based largely upon the Roman Missal, including Crowley's Latinization of the "Gnostic Catholic Church" as "Ecclesia Gnostica Catholica," as well as his rite's title, "Ecclesiæ Gnosticæ Catholicæ Canon Missæ." Various other elements of the ritual also echo the Roman rite, including the Collects, Trisagion, and Fraction. The major implements of the Gnostic Mass are those associated with the mysteries of John the Baptist (the sword and paten) and Jesus Christ (the cup and spear or lance).[143] However, acknowledging writers who insisted that Catholicism derived from ancient pagan traditions, Crowley happily mixes the names of ancient solar gods such as On, Mithras, and Abrasax alongside traditional Christian terms such as Αθανατος (immortal one) and Ισχυρος (strong one) in his Mass. In *Magick in Theory and Practice*, in his chapter on the Eucharist, Crowley writes:

> One of the simplest and most complete of Magick ceremonies is the Eucharist.
>
> It consists in taking common things, transmuting them into things divine, and consuming them. . . .

> The Eucharist of *two* elements has its matter of the passives. The wafer (pantacle) is of corn, typical of earth; the wine (cup) represents water. (There are certain other attributions. The Wafer is the Sun, for instance: and the wine is appropriate to Bacchus). . . .
>
> **The highest sacrament, that of One element, is universal in its operation; according to the declared purpose of the work so will the result be. It is a universal Key of all Magick. . . .**
>
> With regard to the preparations for such Sacraments, the Catholic Church has maintained well enough the traditions of the true Gnostic Church in whose keeping the secrets are.[144]

To this final sentence he appends a footnote: "Study, in the Roman Missal, the Canon of the Mass, and the chapter of 'defects.'" He makes a similar recommendation in "De Arte Magica."

The influence of various secret societies is also clear. When the furnishings of the temple are described as including a raised dais of three black-and-white-checked steps in the east, Crowley is describing a typical masonic hall. Indeed, in "The Crisis in Freemasonry," Crowley readily admits his perceived connection between the Mass and Masonry:

> As Freemasonry has been "exposed" every few minutes for the last century or so, and as any layman can walk into a Masonic shop and buy the complete Rituals for a few pence, the only omissions being of no importance to our present point, it would be imbecile to pretend that the nature of the ceremonies of Craft masonry is in any sense a "mystery."
>
> There is therefore no reason for refraining from the plain statement that, to anyone who understands the rudiments of Symbolism, the Master's Degree is identical with the Mass. This is in fact the real reason for the Papal Anathema; for Freemasonry asserts that every man is himself the living, slain, and re-risen Christ in his own person.[145]

Theodor Reuss was so impressed with the Gnostic Mass that when he attended the 1920 Congress of the World Federation of Universal Freemasonry in Zurich, he proposed (unsuccessfully) that the ritual be adopted as the official religion of the Scottish Rite's 18°, or Sovereign Prince of Rose Croix, initiates.[146]

When the seventh Collect of the Mass, titled "The Principles," refers to "mysterious energy, triform, mysterious Matter, in fourfold and sevenfold division," Crowley pays tribute to the TS. In *Isis Unveiled*, Blavatsky describes the seven parts of an incarnated human being as the physical body, life-force, astral body, body of desire, animal soul, spiritual soul, and pure spirit. The first three die with the physical body, the next two survive after death for only a short time, and the last two are eternal. In Theosophy, these seven parts are referred to as "The Principles." Later, Kingsford and Maitland simplified these into a fourfold division of principles: the material body, astral body, soul, and divine spirit.[147]

The influence of the GD appears when the Priest and congregation, communicating with Host and Wine, declare, "There is no part of me that is not of the gods." This line—apart from being a favorite of Mathers—comes from the GD Adeptus Minor (or Rose Cross) initiation ritual.[148] It is taken from plate 32 of the *Egyptian Book of the Dead*, more accurately translated as "there is no member of mine devoid of a god."[149] Likewise, when the Priest concludes the Mass with the benediction, "The LORD bring you to the accomplishment of your true Wills, the Great Work, the *Summum Bonum*, True Wisdom and Perfect Happiness," he is echoing the GD Neophyte initiation ritual: "May what we have partaken of sustain us in our search for the Quintessense; the Stone of the Philosophers and Perfect Happiness and the *Summum Bonum*."[150]

Most of all, in Crowley's hands, the Mass becomes a symbolic rite of *unio mystica*, with masculine elements such as the Lance associated with the Priest and feminine elements such as the Paten and Cup associated with the Priestess. While phrases spoken over the Host (*τουτο εστι το σομα μου*, "This is my body") and Cup (*τουτο εστι το ποτηριον του αιματος μου*, "This is the cup of my blood") would not be out of place in a traditional Christian service, the phrase spoken over the Fraction of the Host (*τουτο εστι το σπερμα μου*, "This is my seed") is more explicitly of sacred sexuality. Not that there can be any doubt of the symbolic subtext, as the ritual involves the Priestess ceremonially stroking and kissing the Lance and the Priest adoring the Cup. At the moment that the Fraction is dropped from the Priest's Lance into the Priestess's Cup, the pair say, "Hriliu," which Crowley defines in *The Vision and the Voice* as "the shrill scream of orgasm." However, any remaining skeptics need only look at the list of Gnostic saints to find the names of Richard Payne Knight, Richard Burton, Hargrave Jennings, J. G. R. Forlong, Carl Kellner, and Theodor Reuss. In incorporating sexual symbolism into a eucharistic ritual, Crowley was being neither prurient nor anti-Catholic; rather, he was being absolutely sincere in what he believed was the restoration of the true meaning of the Mass.

Conclusion

Aleister Crowley's interest in alternative spirituality, secret societies, and sacred sexuality emerged within a culture that embraced these topics as part of a contemporary occult renaissance. Popular interest in alternative forms of spirituality—from séances to Theosophy—prompted broad acceptance of the idea of universal religion, or of an underlying tradition common to all faiths. Researchers and scholars sought profound truths in ancient pagan traditions and ultimately proposed that all religions stem from phallicism, or sex worship. This theory was facilitated by a broader, open discourse on sexuality in areas ranging from religion to medicine that was part of the Victorian sexual and intellectual revolution. In this context, Crowley's practice of sex magick was not a dramatic departure from tradition but a product of the times in which he and his predecessors lived. Rather than merely echo these prevailing streams from the armchair, however, Crowley inventively fused the social milieus of his time into an innovative system of magical practice. This syncretism is best exemplified in the Gnostic Mass, with its allusions to solar gods, sacred sexuality, Thelema, Theosophy, and the Golden Dawn all enshrined in a religious ritual whose structure resembles the Tridentine Mass. Thus, Crowley placed his unique mark upon his synthesis and practice of the occultism that flourished around him.

Notes

1. Letter from Aleister Crowley to Gerald Yorke, November 20, 1928, Gerald Yorke Collection, Warburg Institute, University of London.
2. Hugh B. Urban, "Unleashing the Beast: Aleister Crowley, Tantra and Sex Magic in Late Victorian England," *Esoterica: The Journal of Esoteric Studies* 5 (2003), 138–92; "The Beast with Two Backs: Aleister Crowley, Sex Magic and the Exhaustion of Modernity," *Nova Religio: The Journal of Alternative and Emergent Religions* 7, no. 3 (2004), 7–25; "Magia Sexualis: Sex, Secrecy, and Liberation in Modern Western Esotericism," *Journal of the American Academy of Religion* 72, no. 3 (2004), 695–731; *Magia Sexualis: Sex, Magic, and Liberation in Modern Western Esotericism* (Berkeley: University of California Press, 2006).
3. Wikipedia, "100 Greatest Britons," http://en.wikipedia.org/wiki/100_Greatest_Britons.
4. Aleister Crowley, "Antecedents of Thelema," in *The Revival of Magick, and Other Essays*, ed. Hymenaeus Beta and Richard Kaczynski (Tempe, Ariz.: New Falcon, 1998).
5. Bradford J. M. Verter, "Dark Star Rising: The Emergence of Modern Occultism, 1800–1950" (PhD diss., Princeton University, 1998).

6. Alex Owen, *The Place of Enchantment: British Occultism and the Culture of the Modern* (Chicago: University of Chicago Press, 2004); Joscelyn Godwin, *The Theosophical Enlightenment* (Albany: State University of New York Press, 1994).
7. Richard Kaczynski, "Seances and Suffrage: The Victorian New Age and Equal Rites" (paper presented at the conference of the Mid-Atlantic Popular/American Culture Association, Baltimore, 2006).
8. See William Brevda, *Harry Kemp: The Last Bohemian* (Lewisburg, Pa.: Bucknell University Press, 1986), 94.
9. Aleister Crowley [The Master Therion], *Magick in Theory and Practice* (Paris: Lecram Press, 1929), xii.
10. Helena Petrovna Blavatsky, *Isis Unveiled: A Master-Key to the Mysteries of Ancient and Modern Science and Theology*, 2 vols. (New York: J. W. Bouton, 1877); *The Secret Doctrine: The Synthesis of Science, Religion, and Philosophy*, 2 vols. (London: Theosophical Publishing, 1888).
11. The Society for Psychical Research was founded in London in 1882; its mission was the impartial investigation and documentation of paranormal claims.
12. Society for Psychical Research, "Report of the Committee Appointed to Investigate Phenomena Connected with the Theosophical Society," *Proceedings of the Society for Psychical Research*, part 9 (December 1885), 1–207.
13. Godfrey Higgins, *Anacalypsis: An Attempt to Draw aside the Veil of the Saitic Isis; Or, An Inquiry into the Origin of Languages, Nations and Religions*, 2 vols. (London: Longman, Rees, Orme, Borwn, Green and Longman, 1836); William Emmette Coleman, "The Sources of Madame Blavatsky's Writings," in Vsevolod Sergeevich Solovyoff, *A Modern Priestess of Isis* (London: Longmans, Green, 1895), 353–66; G. R. S. Mead, "Facts about *The Secret Doctrine*," *Occult Review* 45 (April 1927), 247–52; Leslie Shepard, "The *Anacalypsis* of Godfrey Higgins: Precursor of H.P.B." *Theosophical History* 1, no. 3 (1985), 46–53.
14. Shepard, "The *Anacalypsis* of Godfrey Higgins," 46.
15. Aleister Crowley [Khaled Khan], *The Heart of the Master* (London: OTO, 1938).
16. Aleister Crowley, "Manifesto to the President of the Blavatsky Association," in Richard Kaczynski, *Panic in Detroit: The Magician and the Motor City*, Blue Equinox Journal 2 (Troy, Mich.: privately printed, 2006), 7.
17. Aleister Crowley, *The Confessions of Aleister Crowley*, ed. John Symonds and Kenneth Grant (London: Jonathan Cape, 1969), 403.
18. Owen, *The Place of Enchantment*, discusses British occultists' application of the language of science and rationalism to their intellectual pursuits, combining ancient wisdom with modern ideas about the inner life of the self.
19. Helena Petrovna Blavatsky, *The Voice of the Silence: Being Chosen Fragments from the "Book of the Golden Precepts"* (London: Theosophical Publishing, 1889); reprinted, with Crowley's additional commentary, in *The Equinox* III (1) (1919), supplement.
20. Crowley, "Manifesto to the President," 7.

21. Aleister Crowley [Anonymous], *To Man* (Tunis: privately printed, 1924); [Ankh-f-n-Khonsu], *The World Teacher to the Theosophical Society* (Tunis: privately printed, 1924); [Alastor], *The Avenger to the Theosophical Society* (Tunis: privately printed, 1925); [Fra. H. I. Edinburgh], *Madame Tussaud-Besant* (Tunis: privately printed, 1925).
22. Isabel Cooper-Oakley, *Traces of a Hidden Tradition in Masonry and Mediæval Mysticism* (London: Theosophical Publishing Society, 1900); John Yarker, *Arcane Schools: A Review of Their Origin and Antiquity; With a General History of Freemasonry and Its Relation to the Theosophic, Scientific, and Philosophic Mysteries* (Belfast: W. Tait, 1909); Arthur Edward Waite, *The Hidden Church of the Holy Graal: Its Legend and Symbolism; Considered in Their Affinity with Certain Mysteries of Initiation and Other Traces of a Secret Tradition in Christian Times* (London: Rebnar, 1909); Theodor Reuss, "Exkursion zu den 'Fundstätten der Bausteine zum O.T.O.-Tempel'" (1914), in Helmut Möller and Ellic Howe, *Merlin Peregrinus: Vom Untergrund des Abendlandes* (Würzburg: Königshausen & Neumann, 1986), 279–85.
23. Antoine Court de Gebelin, *Monde primitif: Analysé et comparé avec le monde moderne*, 9 vols. (Paris: Chez Boudet, 1773–1782).
24. "Codex Brucianus," MS Bruce 96, Bodleian Library, Oxford; Carl Schmidt, *Gnostische Schriften in koptischer Sprache aus dem Codex Brucianus* (Leipzig: J. C. Hinrichs, 1892); G. R. S. Mead, *Fragments of a Faith Forgotten: Some Short Sketches among the Gnostics, Mainly of the First Two Centuries; A Contribution to the Study of Christian Origins Based on the Most Recently Recovered Materials* (London: Theosophical Publishing Society, 1900).
25. G. R. S. Mead, *Pistis Sophia: A Gnostic Gospel (with Extracts from the Books of the Saviour Appended) Originally Tr. from Greek into Coptic and Now for the First Time Englished from Schwartze's Latin Version of the Only Known Coptic MS. and Checked by Amélineau's French Version with an Introduction by G. R. S. Mead* (London: Theosophical Publishing Society, 1896). On Crowley's seeking this book, see Kaczynski, *Panic in Detroit.*
26. *The Equinox* III (1) (1919), 21.
27. William Wynn Westcott, *The Sepher Yetzirah: The Book of Formation and the Thirty-Two Paths of Wisdom. Translated from the Hebrew* (Bath: Robert H. Fryar, 1887; 2nd rev. ed., London: Theosophical Publishing Society, 1893); *Numbers: Their Occult Power and Mystic Virtue: Being a Résumé of the Views of the Kabbalists, Pythagoreans, Adepts of India, Chaldean Magi, and Mediæval Magicians* (London: Theosophical Publishing Society, 1890); *The Science of Alchymy: Spiritual and Material* (London: Theosophical Publishing Society, 1893); *Christian Rosenkreuz and the Rosicurians [and] The Platonic Philosopher's Creed* (London: Theosophical Publishing Society, 1894).
28. The following nine volumes of *Collectanea Hermetica* were published by London's Theosophical Society under the editorship of William Wynn Westcott: *An English Translation of the Hermetic Arcanum of Penes Nos Unda Tagi, 1623* (1893); *The Pymander of Hermes* (1894); *A Short Enquiry Concerning the Hermetic Art, by a*

Lover of Philathes, London, 1714 (1894); *Æsch Mezareph, or Purifying Fire: A Chymico-Kabalistic Treatise Collected from the Kabala Denudata of Knorr von Rosenroth. Translated by a Lover of Philathes, 1714* (1894); *Somnium Scipionis: The Vision of Scipio* (1894); *The Chaldean Oracles of Zoroaster* (1895); *Euphrates, or the Waters of the East by Eugenius Philathes, 1655* (1896); *Egyptian Magic* (1896); and *Numbers: Their Occult Power and Mystic Virtues*, 2nd rev. ed. (1902).

29. Hermes Mercurius Trismegistus, *His Divine Pymander. Also the Asiatic Mystery, the Smaragdine Table and the Song of Brahm*, trans. Dr. Everard, ed. P. B. Randolph (Boston: Rosicrucian Publishing, 1871); *The Divine Pymander of Hermes Mercurius Trismegistus. Translated from the Arabic by Dr. Everard (1650)*, ed. Hargrave Jennings (Bath: Redway for R. H. Fryar, 1884); "The Divine Pymander of Hermes Trismegistus," in G. R. S. Mead, *Thrice Greatest Hermes: Studies in Hellenistic Theosophy and Gnosis*, vol. 2 (London: Theosophical Publishing Society, 1906).
30. Robert A. Gilbert, *The Golden Dawn and the Esoteric Section* (London: Theosophical History Centre, 1987).
31. Richard Kaczynski, *Shards of Light: The Chaldean Oracles in Aleister Crowley and the Golden Dawn* (Troy, Mich.: in preparation).
32. *The Equinox* I (3) (1910), 175.
33. Aleister Crowley, "Liber Samekh: Theurgia Goetia Summa Congressus Cum Daemone Sub Figura DCCC," in *Magick in Theory and Practice*, 265–301; "Liber XXX Aerum vel Saeculi sub figura CCCCXVIII: (Being of the Angels of the 30 Aethyrs): The Vision and the Voice," *The Equinox* I (5) (1911), special supplement. For the evocation of Bartzabel, see *The Equinox* I (9) (1913), 125.
34. Aleister Crowley, *ΘΕΛΗΜΑ: The Holy Books of Thelema*, ed. Hymenaeus Alpha and Hymenaeus Beta (York Beach, Maine: Samuel Weiser, 1983), 228.
35. *The Equinox* I (6) (1911), 17–22.
36. Sapere Aude [William Wynn Westcott], *The Chaldæn Oracles* (London: Theosophical Publishing Society, 1895).
37. The *Collectanea Hermetica* works authored or translated by Farr are *A Short Enquiry Concerning the Hermetic Art* (1894); *Æsch Mezareph, or Purifying Fire* (1894); *Euphrates, or the Waters of the East* (1896); and *Egyptian Magic* (1896).
38. Arthur Edward Waite, *The Book of Black Magic and of Pacts: Including the Rites and Mysteries of Goëtic Theurgy, Sorcery, and Infernal Necromancy* (London: George Redway, 1898).
39. Aleister Crowley, "Waite's Wet," *The Equinox* I (8) (1912), 233–42; "Dead Weight," *The Equinox* I (10) (1913), 211–23; "Arthur Back from Avalon," *The Equinox* III (1) (1919), reproduced in Kaczynski, *Panic in Detroit*, 21; [A Past Grand Master], "The Crisis in Freemasonry," *English Review* (August 1922), 127–34.
40. Letter from Aleister Crowley to Louis Wilkinson, December 30, 1944, Crowley Papers, Harry Ransom Humanities Research Center, University of Texas at Austin.
41. See chapter 10 in this volume, Robert A. Gilbert's "'The One Thought That Was Not Untrue': Aleister Crowley and A. E. Waite."

42. Ellic Howe, *The Magicians of the Golden Dawn: A Documentary History of a Magical Order, 1887–1923* (London: Routledge & Kegan Paul, 1972); Richard Kaczynski, *Perdurabo: The Life of Aleister Crowley*, rev. exp. 2nd ed. (Berkeley, Calif.: North Atlantic Books, 2010).
43. Samuel Liddell MacGregor Mathers, *The Kabbalah Unveiled [Kabbala Denudata]:* (London: George Redway, 1887); *The Tarot, Its Occult Signification, Use in Fortune Telling, and Method of Play* (London: George Redway, 1888); *The Key of Solomon the King (Clavicula Solomonis)* (London: Redway, 1889); *The Book of the Sacred Magic of Abra-Melin the Mage, as Delivered by Abraham the Jew unto His Son Lamech, A.D. 1458.* (London: J. M. Watkins, 1898).
44. *The Equinox* I (3) (1910), 151–69.
45. Crowley, *The Confessions*, 204.
46. Allan Bennett, "The Ritual for the Evocation unto Visible Appearance of the Great Spirit Taphthartharath," *The Equinox* I (3) (1910), 170–90.
47. *The Equinox* I (3) (1910), 170. D.P.A.L. (*De Profundis Ad Lucem*) was Frederick Leigh Gardner, who participated in the London lodge's rebellion against Mathers (D.D.C.F. or *Deo Duce Comite Ferro*).
48. Samuel Liddell MacGregor Mathers [A Dead Hand], *The Book of the Goetia of Solomon the King, Translated into the English Tongue by a Dead Hand and Adorned with Diverse Other Matters Germane, Delightful to the Wise, the Whole Edited, Verified, Introduced and Commented by Aleister Crowley* (Inverness: Society for the Propagation of Religious Truth, 1904).
49. Aleister Crowley, "Liber O vel Manus et Sagittae sub figura VI," *The Equinox* I (2) (1909), 11–30.
50. Aleister Crowley [Anonymous], *777 vel Prolegomena Symbolica ad Systemam Sceptico-Mysticae Viae Explicande, Fundamentum Hieroglyphicum Sanctissimorum Scientiae Summae* (London: Walter Scott, 1909).
51. F. L. Gardner's copy of *777* (private collection) contains the inscription "*Borrowed Plumes*. A valuable book written by a Renegade Frater, who passed off & posed as a Hierophant."
52. Aleister Crowley, "Liber Librae, the Book of the Balance," *The Equinox* I (1) (1909), 15–21. Compare verse 12, "Remember that unbalanced force is evil; that unbalanced severity is but cruelty and oppression; but that also unbalanced mercy is but weakness which would allow and abet Evil," to the GD Neophyte ritual: "Remember that Unbalanced Force is evil. Unbalanced Mercy is but weakness: Unbalanced Severity is but oppression." *The Equinox* I (2) (1909), 257. Crowley's text closely follows the GD Practicus grade paper "On the General Guidance and Purification of the Soul," printed in Israel Regardie, *The Complete Golden Dawn System of Magic* (Phoenix, Ariz.: Falcon Press, 1984), 3:19–21.
53. Aleister Crowley, "Liber Israfel sub figura LXIV," *The Equinox* I (7) (1912), 21–27. Note that the number of the book—64—corresponds to the chapter of *The Book of the Dead* from which it is adapted.

54. Aleister Crowley, "The Rites of Eleusis," *The Equinox* I (6) (1911), special supplement; J. F. Brown, "Aleister Crowley's *Rites of Eleusis*," *Drama Review* 22, no. 2 (1978), 3–26; Tracy W. Tupman, "Theatre Magick: Aleister Crowley and the *Rites of Eleusis*" (PhD diss., Ohio State University, 2003); Justin Scott van Kleeck, "The Art of the Law: Aleister Crowley's Use of Ritual and Drama," *Esoterica* 5 (2003), 193–218.
55. Aleister Crowley [A Gentleman of the University of Cambridge], *Aceldama: A Place to Bury Strangers In* (London: privately printed, 1898); *The Tale of Archais: A Romance in Verse* (London: Kegan, Paul, Trench, Trübner, 1898); *Jephthah: A Tragedy* (London: privately printed, 1898); Percy Bysshe Shelley [A Gentleman of the University of Oxford], *St. Irvyne; or, The Rosicrucian: A Romance* (London: printed for J. J. Stockdale, 1811).
56. Aleister Crowley [Prometheus], "Percy Bysshe Shelley," *English Review* (July 1922), 16–21; Percy Bysshe Shelley, *Prometheus Unbound: A Lyrical Drama in Four Acts with Other Poems* (London: C. & J. Ollier, 1820).
57. Aleister Crowley, Victor Neuburg, and Mary Desti, *The Vision and the Voice, with Commentary and Other Papers*, ed. Hymenaeus Beta (York Beach, Maine: Samuel Weiser, 1998).
58. Richard Kaczynski, "The Evolution of Magical Practice in the Career of Aleister Crowley" (paper presented at the national meetings of Ordo Templi Orientis, Portland, Ore., August 2003).
59. Letter from Aleister Crowley to R. C. Newman, August 16, 1944, Gerald Yorke Collection, Warburg Institute, University of London. For more on Crowley's likely sources for his rituals, see Martin P. Starr, *The Unknown God: W. T. Smith and the Thelemites* (Bolingbrook, Ill.: Teitan Press, 2003), 24–25.
60. Aleister Crowley, manuscript notebook 30, Gerald Yorke Collection, Warburg Institute, University of London.
61. Martin P. Starr, "Aleister Crowley: Freemason!," *Ars Quatuor Coronatorum* 108 (1995), 150–61.
62. Kaczynski, *Panic in Detroit*; Crowley, "The Crisis in Freemasonry"; Starr, *The Unknown God.*
63. Aleister Crowley, *The Magical Record of the Beast 666: The Diaries of Aleister Crowley, 1914–1920*, ed. John Symonds and Kenneth Grant (Montreal: Next Step, 1972).
64. Aleister Crowley, *Amrita: Essays in Magical Rejuvenation* (King's Beach, Calif.: Thelema Publications, 1990).
65. David Harvey, "Beyond Enlightenment: Occultism, Politics, and Culture in France from the Old Regime to the Fin-de-Siècle," *The Historian* (March 23, 2003); David Allen Harvey, *Beyond Enlightenment: Occultism and Politics in Modern France* (DeKalb, Ill.: Northern Illinois University Press, 2005).
66. Ann Braude, *Radical Spirits: Spiritualism and Women's Rights in Nineteenth-Century America* (Boston: Beacon Press, 1989); Alex Owen, *The Darkened Room: Women, Power, and Spiritualism in Late Victorian England* (Philadelphia: University of Pennsylvania Press, 1990).

67. Joy Dixon, *Divine Feminine: Theosophy and Feminism in England* (Baltimore: Johns Hopkins University Press, 2001).
68. Shirley J. Burton, "Obscene, Lewd and Lascivious: Ida Craddock and the Criminally Obscene Women of Chicago, 1873–1913," *Michigan Historical Review* 19, no. 1 (1993), 1–16.
69. Karl Heinrich Ulrichs, *Forschungen über das Rätsel der mannmännlichen Liebe* (Leipzig: Spohr, 1898); Charles Godfrey Leland, *The Alternate Sex; or The Female Intellect in Man, and the Masculine in Woman* (London: Philip Wellby, 1904); Edward Carpenter, *The Intermediate Sex: A Study of Some Transitional Types of Men and Women* (London: Swan Sonnenschein, 1908).
70. Aleister Crowley, "Pentecost," lines 11–14, *The Sword of Song, Called by Christians the Book of the Beast* (Benares: Society for the Propagation of Religious Truth, 1904).
71. Aleister Crowley, *The World's Tragedy* (1910; Phoenix, Ariz.: Falcon Press, 1985); Crowley, *The Confessions*, 851.
72. Patricia Anderson, *When Passion Reigned: Sex and the Victorians* (New York: Basic Books, 1995); Georges Bataille, *Death and Sensuality: A Study of Eroticism and the Taboo* (New York: Walker, 1962); Michel Foucault, *The History of Sexuality*, vol. 2, *The Use of Pleasure*, trans. Robert Hurley (New York: Pantheon, 1985); Peter Gay, *Education of the Senses* (New York: Oxford University Press, 1984); Michael Mason, *The Making of Victorian Sexuality* (Oxford: Oxford University Press, 1994); Lisa Z. Sigel, *Governing Pleasures: Pornography and Social Change in England, 1815–1914* (New Brunswick, N.J.: Rutgers University Press, 2002); Jeffrey Weeks, *Sex, Politics and Society: The Regulation of Sexuality since 1800* (London: Longman, 1981).
73. Michel Foucault, *The History of Sexuality*, vol. 1, *An Introduction*, trans. Robert Hurley (New York: Pantheon, 1978), 35.
74. Richard von Krafft-Ebing, *Psychopathia sexualis: Eine klinisch-forensische Studie* (Stuttgart: Enke, 1886).
75. Aleister Crowley [Bishop, George Archibald], *White Stains: The Literary Remains of George Archibald Bishop, a Neuropath of the Second Empire* (Amsterdam: privately printed, 1898).
76. Kaczynski, *Perdurabo*.
77. Frank Edward Manuel, *The Eighteenth Century Confronts the Gods* (Cambridge, Mass.: Harvard University Press, 1959).
78. Verter, "Dark Star Rising," iii.
79. Richard Payne Knight, William Hamilton, and Joseph Banks, *An Account of the Remains of the Worship of Priapus, Lately Existing at Isernia, in the Kingdom of Naples* (London: T. Spilsbury, Snowhill, 1786); Nikolaus Pevsner, "Richard Payne Knight," *Art Bulletin* 31, no. 4 (1949), 293–320; Lionel Cust and Sidney Colvin, *History of the Society of Dilettanti* (London: Macmillan, 1898); Cecil Harcourt-Smith and George A. Macmillan, *The Society of Dilettanti: Its Regalia and Pictures Described by Sir Cecil Harcourt-Smith, C.V.D., D.Litt., Secretary of the Society, Together with an Outline of Its History 1914–1932 and a List of Members Elected*

during that Period Compiled by George A. Macmillan, D.Litt., Secretary of the Society (London: Macmillan, 1932).

80. Richard Payne Knight, William Hamilton, and Joseph Banks, *A Discourse on the Worship of Priapus and Its Connection with the Mystic Theology of the Ancients* (London: J. C. Hotten, 1865); William Hamilton, *The Worship of Priapus: An Account of the Fête of St. Cosmo and Damiano, Celebrated at Isernia in 1780* (London: George Redway, 1883).
81. Godwin, *The Theosophical Enlightenment.*
82. Richard Francis Burton, *The Kama Sutra of Vatsyayana Translated from the Sanscrit. In Seven Parts* (Cosmopoli [London]: printed for the Kama Shastra Society, 1883); *Ananga-Ranga: (Stage of the Bodiless One); or, The Hindoo Art of Love (Ars Amoris Indica)* (Cosmopoli [London]: printed for the Kama Shastra Society, 1885); *The Book of the Thousand Nights and a Night*, 10 vols. (Benares: Kama-Shastra Society, 1885; 7 supplemental vols., 1886–1888); *The Perfumed Garden of the Cheikh Nefzaoui: A Manual of Arabian Erotology* (Cosmopoli [London]: printed for the Kama Shastra Society, 1886).
83. Richard Francis Burton and Leonard Smithers [Anonymous], *Priapeia or the Sporting Epigrams of Divers Poets on Priapus* (Cosmopoli: privately printed, 1890); *The Carmina of Caius Valerius Catullus* (London: privately printed, 1894).
84. Edward Rice, *Captain Sir Richard Francis Burton: The Secret Agent Who Made the Pilgrimage to Mecca, Discovered the Kama Sutra, and brought the Arabian Nights to the West* (New York: Charles Scribner's Sons, 1990), 370.
85. Anthropological Society of London, *Memoirs Read before the Anthropological Society of London, 1865–6*, vol. 2 (London: Trübner, 1866).
86. Edward Sellon, *The Gita Radhica Crisna, a Sanscrit Poem* (London: William Rock, 1850); *Annotations on the Sacred Writings of the Hindus, Being an Epitome of Some of the Most Remarkable and Leading Tenets in the Faith of that People, Illustrating Their Priapic Rites and Phallic Principles* (1865; London: privately printed, 1902); "Some Remarks on Indian Gnosticism, or Sacti Puja, the Worship of the Female Power," in Anthropological Society of London, *Memoirs Read*, 264–76.
87. C. Staniland Wake, "The Influence of the Phallic Idea in the Religions of Antiquity," *Journal of Anthropology* 1, no. 2 (1870), 199–227; "The Origin of Serpent-Worship," *Journal of the Anthropological Institute of Great Britain and Ireland* 2 (1873), 373–90; "The Suastika and Allied Symbols," *American Antiquarian and Oriental Journal* 16, no. 1 (1894), 41–43; *Serpent Worship, and Other Essays, with a Chapter on Totemism* (London: George Redway, 1888); *Sacred Prostitution and Marriage by Capture* (privately printed, 1929).
88. Hodder M. Westropp and C. Staniland Wake, *Ancient Symbol Worship: Influence of the Phallic Idea in the Religions of Antiquity* (New York: J. W. Bouton, 1875). For a biographical study of Westropp, see Paul T. Nicholson, "Hodder Westropp: Nineteenth-Century Archaeologist," *Antiquity* 57 (1983), 205–10.

89. C. Staniland Wake, "*Rivers of Life; or, Sources and Streams of the Faiths of Man in All Lands, Showing the Evolution of Faiths from the Rudest Symbolisms to the Latest Spiritual Developments*" [Review], *Journal of the Anthropological Institute of Great Britain and Ireland* 12 (1883), 568–73; James George Roche Forlong, *Rivers of Life, or, Sources and Streams of the Faiths of Man in All Lands* (London: Bernard Quaritch, 1883).
90. Hodder M. Westropp, *Primitive Symbolism, as Illustrated in Phallic Worship or the Reproductive Principle: With an Introduction by General Forlong* (London: George Redway, 1885), iii.
91. Roger Goodland, *A Bibliography of Sex Rites and Customs: An Annotated Record of Books, Articles and Illustrations in All Languages* (London: George Routledge and Sons, 1931). Although the literature continued to expand after that date, Goodland's comprehensive bibliography, summarizing the literature up to the publication of Crowley's *Magick in Theory and Practice*, is a practical terminus for the present discussion.
92. See *The Equinox* III (1) (1919), 22–25.
93. Crowley, *The Confessions*, 327.
94. Ibid., 255.
95. Aleister Crowley, *Snowdrops from a Curate's Garden* (privately printed, 1904; reprint ed. Martin P. Starr, Chicago: Teitan Press, 1986).
96. Aleister Crowley [The Late Major Lutiy and another], *Bagh-i-Muattar: The Scented Garden of Abdullah the Satirist of Shiraz* (London: privately printed, 1910), 4.
97. Colette Colligan, "'A Race of Born Pederasts': Sir Richard Burton, Homosexuality, and the Arabs," *Nineteenth-Century Contexts* 25, no. 1 (2003), 1–20.
98. Kaczynski, *Panic in Detroit.*
99. Hargrave Jennings, *The Rosicrucians: Their Rites and Mysteries* (London: John Camden Hotten, 1870; rev. and enl. ed., London: Chatto and Windus, 1879).
100. Helena Petrovna Blavatsky, "An Open Letter Such as Few Can Write," *Spiritual Scientist* 3 (September 23, 1875), 25–27.
101. Helena Petrovna Blavatsky, "Buddhism, Christianity and Phallicism," *Lucifer* 18 (July 1896), 361.
102. Theodor Reuss, *Lingam-Yoni oder die Mysterien des Geschlechts-Kultus* (Berlin: Ausgabe, 1906).
103. Crowley, *The Confessions*, 710.
104. Georg von Welling [Gregorius Anglus Sallwigt], *Opus Mago-Cabbalisticum et Theologicum* (Frankfurt: Gedruckt bey A. Heinscheidt, 1719); Arthur Edward Waite [Anonymous], "*The Rosicrucians, Their Rites and Mysteries*" [Review], *Walford's Antiquarian Magazine and Bibliographical Review* 11 (June 1887), 423–25; Arthur Edward Waite, *The Real History of the Rosicrucians* (London: George Redway, 1887); Robert A. Gilbert, "The Masonic Career of A. E. Waite," *Ars Quatuor Coronatorum* 99 (1986), 6–20.
105. See Urban, "The Beast with Two Backs."

106. Aleister Crowley, *Magick without Tears*, ed. Israel Regardie (St. Paul, Minn.: Llewellyn, 1973), 74–75.
107. See Hugh B. Urban, "The Omnipotent Oom: Tantra and Its Impact on Modern Western Esotericism," *Esoterica* 3 (2001), 218–59. Also see K. Taylor, *Sir John Woodroffe, Tantra and Bengal* (London: Routledge Courzon, 2001).
108. Sir John Woodroffe [Arthur Avalon], *Principles of Tantra* (London: Luzac, 1914); *Shakti and Shâkta: Essays and Addresses on the Shâkta Tantrashâstra* (London: Luzac, 1918); *The Serpent Power, Being the Shat-Chakra-Nirupana and Paduka-Panchaka* (London: Luzac, 1919); *The Garland of Letters: (Varnamâlâ) Studies in the Mantra-shâstra* (Madras: Ganesh, 1922).
109. The connection between Crowley and Tantra is explored in Henrik Bogdan, "Challenging the Morals of Western Society: The Use of Ritualized Sex in Contemporary Occultism," *The Pomegranate* 8, no. 2 (2006), 211–46.
110. Laurence Oliphant, *Scientific Religion, or Higher Possibilities of Life and Practice through the Operation of Natural Forces*, 2nd ed. (London: William Blackwood and Sons, 1888).
111. Edward W. Berridge [Respiro], *The Brotherhood of the New Life: An Epitome of the Works and Teachings of Thomas Lake Harris*, 5 vols. (London: E. W. Allen, 1896).
112. Howe, *Magicians of the Golden Dawn*.
113. Richard Kaczynski, "Of Heresy and Secrecy: Evidence of Golden Dawn Teachings on Mystic Sexuality," *Eidolon* 7 (1993), 4–7.
114. Quoted in Richard Kaczynski, *Perdurabo Outtakes*, Blue Equinox Journal 1 (Royal Oak, Mich.: Blue Equinox Oasis, 2005), 73.
115. *The Equinox* I (4) (1910), 327–28.
116. "Unser Orden besitzt den Schlüssel, der alle maurer.·. und hermetischen Geheimnisse erschließt, es ist die Lehre von der Sexual-Magie, und diese Lehre erklärt restlos alle Rätsel der Natur, alle freimaurerische Symbolik, und alle Religions-Systeme." *Oriflamme* (September 1912), 21; translation from Reuben Swinburne Clymer, *The Rosicrucian Fraternity in America: Authentic and Spurious Organizations as Considered and Dealt with in Treatises Originally Published and Issued in Monograph Form* (Quakertown, Pa.: Rosicrucian Foundation, 1935), 2:613–14.
117. Aleister Crowley [Frater Perdurabo], *The Book of Lies* (London: Weiland, 1912).
118. Kaczynski, "Evolution of Magical Practice."
119. Crowley, *The Confessions*, 710.
120. While these three are likely teachers for Kellner's knowledge of Yoga, they are not likely sources for any system of sexual magic preserved in the OTO. See Richard Kaczynski, "Carl Kellner's Esoteric Roots: Sex and Sex Magick in the Victorian Age," *Beauty and Strength: Proceedings of the Sixth Biennial National Ordo Templi Orientis Conference* (Riverside, Calif.: United States Grand Lodge Ordo Templi Orientis, 2009), 77–103.
121. John Patrick Deveney, *Paschal Beverly Randolph: A Nineteenth-Century Black American Spiritualist, Rosicrucian, and Sex Magician* (Albany: State University of New York Press, 1997), 250.

122. Paschal Beverly Randolph, *Eulis: Affectional Alchemy* (1874; Quakertown, Pa.: Confederation of Initiates, 1930), 47.
123. Deveney, *Paschal Beverly Randolph*.
124. Paschal Beverly Randolph, *Seership! The Magnetic Mirror* (Boston: Randolph, 1870), 44.
125. Hargrave Jennings, *The Letters of Hargrave Jennings*, ed. Invictus (Bath: Robert H. Fryar, 1895), 43.
126. Hermes Trismegistus, *Divine Pymander*, 1884.
127. Hargrave Jennings, *Phallicism, Celestial and Terrestrial, Heathen and Christian* (London: George Redway, 1884). The Nature Worship and Mystical Series consisted of the following titles, all privately printed in London: *Sex Mythology* (1898); *Phallism: A Description of the Worship of Lingam-Yoni in Various Parts of the World, and in Different Ages* (1889); *Ophiolatreia: An Account of the Rites and Mysteries Connected with the Origin, Rise, and Development of Serpent Worship in Various Parts of the World* (1889); *Phallic Objects, Monuments and Remains* (1889); *Cultus Arborum: A Descriptive Account of Phallic Tree Worship with Illustrative Legends, Superstitions, Etc.* (1890); *Fishes, Flowers and Fire as Elements and Deities in the Phallic Faiths and Worship of the Ancient Religions of Greece, Babylon, Rome, India, &c.* (1890); *Archaic Rock Inscriptions: An Account of the Cup and Ring-Markings on the Sculptured Stones of the Old and New Worlds* (1891); *Nature-Worship: An Account of Phallic Faiths and Practices, Ancient and Modern* (1891); *Phallic Miscellanies: Facts and Phases of Ancient and Modern Sex Worship* (1891); *Mysteries of the Rosie Cross: Or, The History of That Curious Sect of the Middle Ages, Known as the Rosicrucians* (1891). Godwin disputes that all ten of these anonymous volumes are consistent with Jennings's style and interests. See Joscelyn Godwin, "Hargrave Jennings," *Hermetic Journal* (1991), 66.
128. Joscelyn Godwin, Christian Chanel, and John P. Deveney, *The Hermetic Brotherhood of Luxor* (York Beach, Maine: Samuel Weiser, 1995), 47–48.
129. Deveney, *Paschal Beverly Randolph*; Godwin, *The Theosophical Enlightenment*; Godwin, Chanel, and Deveney, *The Hermetic Brotherhood of Luxor*; Freeman B. Dowd, *The Temple of the Rosy Cross: The Soul, Its Powers, Migrations, and Transmigrations*. 4th ed., rev. (Salem, Mass.: Eulian Publishing, 1901); *Regeneration: Being Part II of the Temple of the Rosy Cross* (Salem, Mass.: Eulian Publishing, 1900).
130. J. Gordon Melton, *Rosicrucianism in America* (New York: Garland, 1990).
131. "Die rosenkreuzerischen, esoterischen Lehren der Hermetic Brotherhood of Light wurden reserviert für die wenigen Eingeweihten des Okkulten Inneren Kreises." *Oriflamme* (September 1912), 15–16.
132. Ida Craddock, *Heavenly Bridegrooms*, ed. Theodore Schroeder (New York: privately printed, 1918).
133. Paschal Beverly Randolph, *The Book of the Triplicate Order: Rosicrucia, Eulis, Pythianæ* (San Francisco: Woman's Publishing, 1875).
134. Both texts appear in Ida Craddock, *Lunar and Sex Worship*, ed. Vere Chappell (York Beach, Maine: Teitan Press, 2010). For biographical details on Ida Craddock,

see Vere Chappell, *Sexual Outlaw, Erotic Mystic: The Essential Ida Craddock* (San Francisco: Red Wheel/Weiser, 2010); and Leigh Eric Schmidt, *Heaven's Bride: The Unprintable Life of Ida C. Craddock, American Mystic, Scholar, Sexologist, Martyr, and Madwoman* (New York: Basic Books, 2010).

135. *The Equinox* III (1) (1919), 280.
136. Letter from Aleister Crowley to Theodore Schroeder, March 24, 1919, Theodore Schroeder Papers, Collection Number 17, Morris Library, Southern Illinois University at Carbondale.
137. Letter from Charles Stansfeld Jones to Theodore Schroeder, January 20, 1919, Theodore Schroeder Papers.
138. Letter from Karl Germer to Theodore Schroeder, April 17, 1946, Theodore Schroeder Papers.
139. Louis T. Culling, *The Complete Magick Curriculum of the Secret Order G∴B∴G∴* (St. Paul, Minn.: Lewellyn, 1971), 72.
140. Louis T. Culling, *A Manual of Sex Magick* (St. Paul, Minn.: Llewellyn, 1971).
141. Marcelo Motta, *Sex and Religion: "The Equinox" v. 5 no. 4* (Nashville: Thelema Publishing, 1981).
142. Aleister Crowley, "Ecclesiae Gnosticae Catholicae Canon Missae," *The International* 12, no. 3 (1918), 70–74; "Ecclesiæ Gnosticæ Catholicæ Canon Missæ," *The Equinox* III (1) (1919), 247–70.
143. Crowley, *Magick without Tears*, 311.
144. Crowley, *Magick in Theory and Practice*, 179–82.
145. Crowley, "The Crisis in Freemasonry," 132–33.
146. Kaczynski, *Panic in Detroit*, 75.
147. Godwin, *The Theosophical Enlightenment*, 342.
148. William Butler Yeats, *The Autobiography of William Butler Yeats* (New York: Doubleday, 1958), 226; *The Equinox* I (3) (1910), 219.
149. *The Egyptian Book of the Dead: The Book of Going Forth by Day; Being the Papyrus of Ani (Royal Scribe of the Divine Offerings),* trans. Raymond O. Faulkner, ed. Eva Von Dassow, conceived by James Wasserman (San Francisco: Chronicle Books, 1994).
150. *The Equinox* I (2) (1909), 261.

7

Aleister Crowley and the Yezidis

Tobias Churton

MANY ASPECTS OF Aleister Crowley's life and work remain unexplained. Not the least of these aspects lies in Crowley's statement that the true author of *Liber AL vel Legis* (believed by Crowley to be his "Holy Guardian Angel," Aiwass) bore the "true most ancient name of the God of the Yezidis." Crowley believed this observation provided a fundamental link between Thelema and "the Sumerian Tradition." Was Crowley suggesting that the God of the Yezidis was the true author of *The Book of the Law*? What in fact did he mean by "the God of the Yezidis"?

This essay will outline the religious ideas associated with the remarkable Yezidi Kurds of northern Iraq, western Iran, and Georgian Armenia. Yezidism, considered by some commentators to be the parent of Middle Eastern religion,[1] will be compared and contrasted with the message contained in *Liber AL vel Legis* and in Crowley's philosophical writings. The essay will, furthermore, assess in general terms whether the being responsible for *Liber AL vel Legis* had anything in common, beyond a possible etymological kinship, with the being respected by the Yezidis.

Cephaloedium Working, Abbey of Thelema (Villa Santa Barbara), Cefalù, Sicily, 1920–1921

File K.1. of the Yorke Collection (held at the Warburg Institute, University of London) contains Crowley's notes for a New Commentary on *The Book of the Law*. A portion of the notes speculates as to the identity of the author of the work, held by Crowley to be his Holy Guardian Angel, Aiwass:

> LXXVIII. The number of Aiwass, the Intelligence who communicated this Book. Having only hearing to guide me, I spelt it AYVAS [איואס; samekh = 60; aleph = 1; vau = 6; yod = 10; aleph = 1], LXXVIII, referring it to Mezla, the Influence from Kether, which adds to the same number. But in An. XIV [1918] there came unto me mysteriously a Brother, [Samuel Aiwaz Jacobs[2]] ignorant of all this Work, who gave me the spelling OYVZ [ציוז; zain = 7; vau = 6; yod = 10; ayin = 70] which is XCIII, 93, the number of Thelema and Agape, which concentrates the Book itself in a symbol. Thus the author secretly identified himself with his message.
>
> But this is not all. Aiwaz is not (as I had supposed) a mere formula, like many angelic names, but is the true most ancient name of the God of the Yezidis, and thus returns to the highest Antiquity. Our work is therefore historically authentic, the rediscovery of the Sumerian Tradition. (Sumer is in lower Mesopotamia, the earliest home of our race).

Several paragraphs later, Crowley begins his commentary on the first verses of *The Book of the Law*, the principal deities of which ("Nuit" and "Hadit") he further relates to the "Sumerian Tradition," the latter supposed to be at the root of Yezidi religion.

1. Had! The manifestation of Nuit.[3]

> The theogony of our Law is entirely scientific. Nuit is Matter, Hadit is Motion, in their full physical sense. They are the Tao and Teh of Chinese philosophy or . . . the Noun and Verb in grammar.
>
> Our central Truth—beyond other philosophies—is that the two infinities cannot exist apart. . . . I must mention that the Brother previously mentioned [Samuel Aiwaz Jacobs] identifies them with ANU and ADAD the supreme Mother and Father deities of the Sumerians. Taken in connexion with the Aiwaz identification, this is very striking indeed.

Crowley further writes that what is being revealed is "cosmographically the conception of the two Ultimate Ideas: Space, and That which occupies Space." Furthermore, "these two ideas may be resolved into one, that of Matter: with Space its 'Condition' or 'form' included therein. This leaves the idea of 'Motion' for Hadit, whose interplay with Nuit makes the Universe. Time should perhaps be considered as a particular kind of dimension of Space."

It should be noted that the god referred to as "Hadit" is a poor contemporary transliteration of the name of the god who appeared on stele 666 at the Egyptian Museum in Cairo, the funerary stele that inspired Crowley so profoundly in his search for a self-authenticating and historically valid spiritual system. Improvements in Egyptological skills allow us to see the winged disk at the top of the stele as Hor-behedet: "The Behedite the great god Lord (of) the sky," as the stele itself expresses the god's identity in hieroglyphics. The French translation, made by Egyptian Museum staff at Crowley's behest, used the words *hudit* and *houdit*, but Crowley very quickly appears to have settled on "Hadit" in his poetic rendering of the stele's contents;[4] why he should have done so is not clear.

Hor-behedet was a form of Horus worshipped in the city of Behdet, a district of ancient Edfu. He is depicted in the form of a winged solar disk; the omnipresence of Ra and Horus is suggested. Crowley saw the god in terms analogous to Nicholas of Cusa's description of the universe as a reflection of God: "an infinite sphere whose centre is everywhere, circumference nowhere."[5] Crowley was thinking of a dynamic, infinitesimally small point that is, paradoxically, both every thing's center and the center of everything. He believed this conception lay behind the image of the winged disk, with its suggestion of perfection, centrality, infinite extension, and dynamism.

The conception also suggests the common description of the alchemist's philosopher's stone as being everywhere found, but nowhere seen. By analogy, we do not see "the light," but objects illuminated thereby. The sun is the manifest image of this principle, and the sun is symbolized in alchemy as a circle with a center point. It was Crowley's supposition that fundamental facts of nature, appropriate to persons capable of abstract reasoning, had been revealed to, or had been formulated by, our distant ancestors, as gods. The civilizations were dead, but the "gods" lived on.

Upon arriving in Cairo, Rose Crowley told her husband that he had offended "Horus" and ought to invoke him. To Crowley's astonishment, a midnight invocation of the god in a rented Cairo apartment in the spring of 1904 led to the aural reception of *The Book of the Law*, with its direct message both to its scribe and those who would hear him. What was the provenance of this message in terms of its relation—or otherwise—to the religion of the Yezidis?

Aiwass

Aiwass, a name, apparently, first heard by Crowley on the lips of his wife Rose,[6] appears in *The Book of the Law* as "the minister of Hoor-par-kraat." This latter figure is the infant Horus, Horpakhrad, or Harpokrates, often shown sitting on his mother Isis's lap, sucking his finger. This manual gesture was mistaken by the Greeks for a sign of initiatory silence, and it was as a god of silence that Harpokrates would be known; Crowley accepted the traditional designation.

The infant Horus (Latin spelling) was often confused with Horus the elder. As Her-nedj-tef-ef (Horus, Avenger of His Father) he avenged his father Osiris's death by defeating and casting out his "evil uncle," Set. Hor then became the divine prototype of the pharaoh. Crowley was as interested in the idea of the avenging child as he was in the background to the denigration of Set.

According to *The Book of the Law*, Aiwass was in some way delivering a message from the angry, divine child: the gods were speaking; Crowley listened. According to an account in Crowley's publication *The Equinox of the Gods*, his encounter with the minister of Harpokrates (April 8, 9, and 10, 1904) was indirect, but colorful:

> The Voice of Aiwass came apparently from over my left shoulder, from the furthest corner of the room [in Crowley and Rose's apartment].... The voice was passionately poured, as if Aiwass were alert about the time limit [between noon and 1:00 P.M.].... I had a strong impression that the speaker was actually in the corner where he seemed to be, in a body of "fine matter" transparent as a veil of gauze, or a cloud of incense-smoke. He seemed to be a tall, dark man in his thirties, well-knit, active and strong, with the face of a savage king, and eyes veiled lest their gaze should destroy what they saw. The dress was not Arab; it suggested Assyria or Persia, but very vaguely. I took little note of it, for to me at that time Aiwass was an "angel" such as I had often seen in visions, a being purely astral.[7]

He put the essence of the experience quite clearly in a commentary on *The Book of the Law* written at the Hotel du Djerid at Nefta in Tunisia in September 1923:

> The Secret was this: the breaking down of my false Will by these dread words of mine Angel freed my True Self from all its bonds, so that I could enjoy at once the rapture of knowing myself to be who I am.[8]

According to Crowley's viewpoint, the visible man known as Aleister Crowley was but an instrument and projection into this world—a limitation in fact—of a greater being whom Crowley found it most intellectually convenient and logical to regard as an independent entity, even of himself. Nevertheless, it is possible to regard this projection as working "both ways," for it is difficult to deny that the image the "scribe Crowley" had in his mind's eye of Aiwass was rather similar to an idealized image of himself, discernible elsewhere in his writings and self-images.

Readers may examine the famous photograph of Crowley dressed as a Persian prince on his arrival in Cairo in 1904 (Crowley was certainly "well-knit, active and strong," if not yet "in his thirties"). See also the famous painting of himself as *To Mega Therion 666*.[9] One may speculate as to whether Aiwass was "coming through" the man Crowley or the image of Aiwass was the work of Crowley's own idealizing imagination. Crowley himself might have said, Cannot both be true? For if Crowley is a projection of Aiwass, surely Crowley's projection of his ideal self would be Aiwass also.

However, Crowley would be the first to admit that to the thoroughgoing skeptic, absolute proof that the whole thing was not the "work of his imagination" would be impossible to furnish. As his sometime friend Charles Cammell exclaimed, "Explain me the riddle of this man!"[10]

What would it mean for Crowley to think that the name of Aiwass was the true, secret name of the God of the Yezidis?

In magick, the true name of a thing encapsulates its essence. One may "become the god" without exclusively monopolizing that being's presence. On the other hand, the relation of Holy Guardian Angel to subject is traditionally intimate and consistent, not occasional and self-willed. Crowley is not necessarily saying that his Holy Guardian Angel is the God of the Yezidis, but that the essential formula (contained perhaps in the kabbalah of the name) partakes of the same magical identity as that being worshipped by Yezidis.

By analogy, I might breathe oxygen through a formula of combined gases in a pressurized canister underwater, or I may breathe oxygen on the peak of Kilimanjaro. It is oxygen, the same physical formula, but it is not an identical incidence of that formula. Furthermore, and most important, one's reception of its qualities will depend on one's receiving apparatus. Vision is dependent upon capacity. As Blake said, "A fool sees not the same tree a wise man sees." Talent recognizes genius, but mediocrity recognizes only itself.

Again, on the other hand, it is to be doubted whether Crowley would, at his most exalted, deny that he *was* a projection of such a being. The exclusive phrase "I and my father are one," to be found on the lips of Christ in John's Gospel, was taken by Crowley to indicate that the speaker was experiencing *Samadhi* or union with his source.[11]

Crowley never lost the enthusiasm, first articulated on reading Karl von Eckartshausen's *The Cloud upon the Sanctuary*,[12] for being in the exalted company of the Secret Chiefs of planetary destiny. As we shall see, this aspiration makes perfect sense within the Yezidi angelic system. The gods of the microcosm were forces of nature discerned in the macrocosm; magick linked the twain. What then could Crowley have meant by the "God of the Yezidis"?

The God of the Yezidis

The word generally employed by Yezidis for "God" is the Kurmanji word *Khudê*, which, according to Lady Drower, was ever on the lips of the pious Yezidi people she encountered in northern Iraq in 1940.[13] As a general term, however, this would not I think qualify as the most ancient and true name of the God of the Yezidis.

There are other possibilities for identifying this name, the first being from the name Yezidi itself. This name first appears in writing in the eleventh century C.E. There are a number of theories as to the origin of this name. Muslim critics have attributed it to the Yezidis' peculiar and, to their opponents, disreputable respect for the Umayyad Caliph Yazid ibn Mu'awiya, despised by Shia Muslims for his part in the death of the Prophet's grandson, Hussein. However, the name "Yezid" itself may be of more antique provenance. It has been suggested that the name stems from *Ized* (angel, God) or *Yazata* (worthy of worship), words found in the *Avesta*, the sacred writings of the Zoroastrians. Other words bear similar meaning. Variants of the Persian *Izd*, or *Ized*, include *Azidi*, *Izidi*, and *Izdi*, or *Yazata* or *Yazd* in Pahlavi, or *Yajata* in Sanskrit. All of these terms generally mean "worthy of worship," usually referring to an angel who intercedes between God and human beings, supervising the affairs of humankind after creation.

Persian roots may be behind some Yezidi words for their holy beings used to this day. *Yazdan* may be behind the Yezidi *Êzdan*, another term for God.[14] Another name for the Yezidis' *Lord of this world* is *Sultan Êzî* or *Êzîd*, deriving apparently from the aforementioned Caliph, and who is also identified with the Sufi Sheykh 'Adi (1073–1161 C.E.), the founder of what would become the vital Yezidi community at Lalish, north of Mosul. *Sheykh 'Adi* and *Êzîd* are also names identified with Tawûsî Melek (Kurmanji), the archangel of the supreme Heptad of angels created by God.

It is a fascinating aspect of Yezidi religion that names and beings are interchangeable in a way that we, with our written traditions, can hardly tolerate.

Figures of Yezidi history may also be divine angels. Having been distinguished in divine service, it is taken that their parenthood was not a result of ordinary human agency—and yet, they may have descendants; Yezidis are joined in some way to the holy beings above and within them. This dynamic in the Yezidi approach to sacred beings resonates with the kabbalistic techniques of *temurah*, *notariqon*, and *gematria* (employed by Crowley); in short, names may change, but values remain. According to Crowley, "'Gods' are the Forces of Nature; their 'Names' are the Laws of Nature. Thus They are eternal, omnipotent, omnipresent and so on; and thus their 'Wills' are immutable and absolute."[15]

Yezidis would have no problem in seeing a "sheykh" like Crowley as being a manifestation of a divine power, once convinced the power was indeed manifested in that person. They might, however, be surprised and perhaps not a little intrigued to hear of Crowley's claim that the ancient name of their "God" shared his "name" with the "minister" of Horus (a sun god). Were they to take the claim seriously, they might discuss how it could be that their supreme Angel could be the minister of Sheykh Shems, their name for the divinity of the sun.[16] But this brings us back to the question of which "God" of the Yezidis Crowley was thinking of when he made his startling identification.

In Yezidi religious discourse, "God" operates in phases of being that may be perceived in people and in nature, in places and in stories, in everyday life and the life hereafter. These phases are given names, but they are neither rigidly clung to nor definitive. Nevertheless, the Yezidis have been reported as possessing a curious acuity of spiritual perception; they may be described as panentheists. Lady Drower visited the Yezidis' holiest sites at Lalish in 1940 and wrote movingly of the experience:

> I am glad, too, that I rose early and saw the shrine at its holiest moment of first dawn. For it was then that I became convinced that some Yezidis, inarticulate and vague as they are about their own dogmas and beliefs, possess to a rare degree a faculty as sensitive as the antennae of an insect, which makes them conscious of things outside the material. They have the instinct to be still and worship, which is the very essence of religion. And of all holy places I have ever visited, during 60 years of life in West and East, the valley of Shaikh 'Adi, the Mecca of the most sorely persecuted and misrepresented people in the world, seems to me the loveliest and holiest. Here one may find the spirit of the Holy Grail, or perhaps rather of the glad piety of the Saint of Assisi. Something

lingers here unpolluted, eternal and beautiful: something as quiet as the soul and as clear eyed as the spirit.[17]

This perceptiveness suggests that in no way does the fluidity of the tradition bring confusion; rather, the deliberate keeping of the tradition to a non-written form, and learned by mind to mind and heart to heart, is a positive benefit to maintaining the living spirit of the faith. The implication seems to be that while the laws of the world that we know derive from the spiritual world, the spiritual world is not subject to them. What this world is subject to, according to the Yezidis, is the governance of the archangel known as "the Peacock Angel" or Melek (Lord or King) Tawus.

In this figure, I think, we may find Crowley's "God of the Yezidis."

Melek Tawus

According to Yezidi tradition, God consigned his creative work to seven angels, created in the "Pearl," his first creative expression. Their names vary according to the source of information. A version of the *Meshef Resh* (Black Book) obtained by Carmelite monk Father Anastasius from a Yezidi ("a tall devil with big black eyes and long hair") in May 1904 gives the following names for the angels. It should be noted that most members of the Heptad are also considered as manifest in beings with a terrestrial role in Yezidi historical traditions.

'Ezra'îl = Melek Tawus
Derda'îl = Sheykh Hesen
Irafîl = Sheykh Shems
Mîka'îl = Sheykh Obekr
Jibra'îl = Sejjad el-Dîn (Sejadîn)
Shemna'îl = Nasir el-Dîn
Tûra'îl = Fekhr el-Dîn[18]

This list is not consistent in Yezidi traditions, but it is nonetheless a fair representation of the tradition.

The most important being to the Yezidis is their special guardian, Melek Tawus, represented in the form of a peacock. His name is also to be found as 'Ezazîl where Ezra'îl is Secad el-Dîn (the Browne-Guest version).[19] There is clearly a link between the tradition of the Yezidis concerning the angel 'Ezazîl and the angel who appears in late antiquity as Azazel. Azazel is singled out for special censure in the famous *Book of Enoch* (IX.6) as one that revealed to men "the eternal secrets which were in heaven which men were striving to learn" and who is condemned for it. Around 180 C.E., Irenaeus rants against the Gnostic Marcus, a follower of Azazel, a "fallen and mighty angel." Marcus is described as

> a perfect adept in magical impostures, and by this means drawing away a great number of men, and not a few women, he has induced them to join themselves to him, as to one who is possessed of the greatest knowledge and perfection, and who has received the highest power from the invisible and ineffable regions above.[20]

He could have been describing an incarnation of the "Aleister Crowley" of popular imagination.

From the Gnostic perspective, Azazel's passing on of eternal knowledge was a boon to humankind, like the serpent of the Gnostic Ophite and Naassene traditions, whose gift of gnosis leads to the demiurge's condemnation of Adam and Eve. The Yezidi perspective on the angel 'Ezazîl bears some resemblance to the Gnostic angel, but one should not hasten to push the comparison too far. In the Yezidi tradition, Melek Tawus is the stern benefactor of humankind, set by God to govern the destiny of the human race. He does not delight in evil or attempt to trip human beings up into immoralities.

Nevertheless, the *Meshef Resh* offers some interesting parallels to Gnostic traditions. In the *Meshef Resh*, Gabriel leads Adam into Paradise, where he is told he may eat of all the fruit but not of wheat. Adam remains in Paradise for one hundred years, after which he is visited by Melek Tawus, who asks Adam how he can expect to have progeny if he does not eat wheat. Melek Tawus teaches Adam the ways of agriculture—that is one way of interpreting the myth. As written, Adam becomes bloated on the grain and Melek Tawus leads him out of Paradise, whereupon he is left to his own devices—and a bloated stomach. God sends a bird that pecks at Adam, creating his anus and simultaneous relief.[21] Human beings will have to learn by experience.

The provenance of the *Meshef Resh* is still unresolved. It is not a dogmatically authoritative source for Yezidi beliefs, but the story offers a picture of the Peacock Angel that is at least suggestive. Melek Tawus has arguments with the absolute God, but he is not cast out; he is not a fallen angel. In fact, God recognizes his exemplary loyalty and lets him manage human affairs. Melek Tawus offers human beings both knowledge and freedom. This is the majestic message of Melek Tawus's self-revelation recorded in the *Jelwe*, the Divine Revelation or

Effulgence, attributed to the Tawus-inspired mind of Sheykh 'Adi. As we shall see, it bears some comparison with the spirit of *Liber AL vel Legis*.

Such a being or conception of a being is not at home in the monotheisms of Christianity, Judaism, and Islam. Not content with dubbing the mighty angel Melek Tawus a devil, persons hostile to the Yezidis have regarded him as Shaitan himself. This conception has been used to justify pogroms against the Yezidi people. In 1940, a Yezidi *qewwal* (sacred musician) complained to Lady Drower: "They say of us wrongly, that we worship one who is evil." Lady Drower's thoughts on concluding her conversation with the *qewwal* bear repeating here:

> It seemed probable to me, after this talk, that the Peacock Angel is, in a manner, a symbol of Man himself, a divine principle of light experiencing an avatar of darkness, which is matter and the material world. The evil comes from man himself, or rather from his errors, stumblings and obstinate turnings down blind alleys upon the steep path of being. In repeated incarnations he sheds his earthliness, his evil, or else, if hopelessly linked with the material, he perishes like the dross and illusion that he is.[22]

Deeply grieved by this hideous caricature of their religion, the Yezidis forbid the saying of the word *Shaitan* or even words that sound like it. The Englishman Austen Henry Layard visited the Sheikhan (territory of the Yezidis in northern Mesopotamia) in the 1840s and left a remarkable description of their life, troubles, and beliefs. He described the horror of the Yezidi people when he accidentally emitted the forbidden word:

> Every place, from which a sight could be obtained of the dancers, was occupied by curious spectators. Even the branches above our heads were bending under the clusters of boys who had discovered that, from them, they could get a full view of what was going on below. The manoeuvres of one of these urchins gave rise to a somewhat amusing incident, which illustrates the singular superstitions of this sect. He had forced himself to the very end of a weak bough, which was immediately above me, and threatened every moment to break under the weight. As I looked up I saw the impending danger, and made an effort, by an appeal to the chief, to avert it. "If that young Sheit"—I exclaimed, about to use an epithet generally given in the East to such adventurous youths: I checked myself immediately; but it was already

> too late; half the dreaded word had escaped. The effect was instantaneous: a look of horror seized those who were near enough to overhear me; it was quickly communicated to those beyond. The pleasant smile, which usually played upon the fine features of the young bey, gave way to a serious and angry expression. I lamented that I had thus unwillingly wounded the feelings of my hosts, and was at a loss to know how I could make atonement for my indiscretion—doubting whether an apology to the Evil principle or to the chief was expected. I endeavored, however, to make them understand, without venturing upon any observations which might have brought me into greater difficulties, that I regretted what had passed; but it was some time ere the group resumed their composure, and indulged in their previous merriment.[23]

Layard was mistaken to consider Melek Tawus the Evil principle—it was a common error, reflected in the treatment of the Yezidis offered by Crowley's admired author, Madame Blavatsky. Blavatsky's libelous treatment bears repetition, as it may have been a source for Crowley's first conception of the Yezidis:

> They are called and known everywhere as devil-worshippers; and most certainly it is not either through ignorance or mental obscuration that they have set up the worship and a regular inter communication with the lowest and the most malicious of both elementals and elementaries. They recognize the present wickedness of the chief of the "black powers"; but at the same time they dread his power, and so try to conciliate to themselves his favours. He is in an open quarrel with Allah, they say, but a reconciliation can take place between the two at any day; and those who have shown marks of their disrespect to the "black one" may suffer for it at some future time, and thus have both God and the Devil against them. This is simply a cunning policy that seeks to propitiate his Satanic Majesty, who is no other than the great Tcherno-Bog (the black god) of the Variagi-Russ, the ancient idolatrous Russians before the days of Vladimir.[24]

Crowley admired Madame Blavatsky but recognized her limitations as a serious commentator of fact. Crowley may rather have derived his first knowledge of the Yezidis from Layard, the kind of daring adventurer who, like Sir Richard Burton, was much to Crowley's taste.

What of the authentic conception of Melek Tawus, that of the Yezidis themselves?

We now have some examples of the Yezidi *qewls*, that is, sacred songs, translated by the leading scholar of Yezidism, Philip Kreyenbroek. They offer a picture of Melek Tawus as "the ancient one," "the eternal one." He was not born and does not give birth; he is the king of the world, lord of men and jinns. Making Adam eat forbidden food, he helped him to live in the world. He has come to earth to help the Yezidis. He is "Angel of the Throne," "Master of firmament, moon and sun," "Judge," "remedy," "healer," "the living one," "the glorious one."

> Oh my Lord, by your eminence, by your rank and by your
> sovereignty,
> Oh my Lord, you are generous, you are merciful,
> Oh my Lord, you are forever God,
> You are forever worthy of praise and homage. (v. 1)
>
> Oh my Lord, you are the angel who is king of the world,
> Oh my Lord, you are the angel who is generous king,
> You are the angel of the awesome Throne.
> Oh my Lord, from pre-eternity you have always been
> the ancient one (v. 2)
>
> You are the eternal one, you dwelt in the source of light,
> You are the eternal one, you are the living one, the glorious.
> You are one, praise is due to you (v. 5)
>
> Oh my Lord, you are the judge of the entire world,
> Oh my Lord, you imposed repentance on man,
> Oh my Lord, you are the judge of intercession. (v. 15)
>
> You are wise, we are aliens,
> Oh my Lord, you always know where our remedy is,
> Oh my Lord you are an intimate friend to strangers. (v. 18)
>
> Oh my Lord, you are the creator, we are creatures,
> You are the desired, we are the desire. (v. 21)[25]

These are extracts from the twenty-one-verse *Hymn of Melek Tawus*. It is clear that Madame Blavatsky had never seen this work—or any other authentic *qewls* of the Yezidis. On the other hand, one can well imagine Crowley adding his asthmatic voice to this potent chant.

Are there etymological reasons to suppose that Melek Tawus was the figure in Crowley's mind when he spoke of the name of Aiwass or Aiwaz as being the name of the ancient God of the Yezidis? Since there is no god of that name in either Yezidi or even ancient Sumerian or Babylonian tradition (Crowley may have had access to some unknown source), it is reasonable to suggest Crowley had heard of the name Melek Tawus or some variant of the name. If we enter the Crowleyan kabbalistic worldview, we can see that once we subtract the honorific "Melek," we have a name with some kabbalistic potential, as well as aural resonance: *Tawus*.

By 1920, when he began his New Commentary, Crowley would have had numerous opportunities to become acquainted with the name of Melek Tawus. By 1900, at least half a dozen manuscripts of the Yezidi sacred books were available for study. In 1895, for example, Oswald Parry's *Six Months in a Syrian Monastery* included Cambridge orientalist E. G. Browne's translation of both the *Jelwe* and *Meshef Resh*. In September 1891, the Bibliothèque Nationale in Paris acquired a manuscript (BN Syr. MS. 306) of the same works, copied by one Abdul Aziz, a member of the Syrian Orthodox Church who lived in the predominantly Yezidi village of Bashiqa. There was, moreover, a particular stir in the world of oriental scholarship after Père Anastase made copies of these works in the Jebel Sinjar in 1904, one month after Crowley received *The Book of the Law*. Anastase declared his disclosure to science of these works significant; it was suspected that Yezidi beliefs antedated the Mosaic revelation. Crowley could hardly have been unaware of the interest.

When looking at the name TAWUS, or TA'US or (in Kurmanji) TAWUSI, Crowley would have noticed a possible variant of the name of his Holy Guardian Angel, nestling close to the letter *T*: T AWUS. *AWUS*. We have seen at the beginning of this essay that Crowley was happy to see "Aiwass" written as AYVAS (in Hebrew) or even as OYVZ, as these transliterations bore meaningful kabbalistic values. It should be borne in mind that Crowley *heard* the name; he was not instructed as to how it should be spelled in English. "Awus" sounds more like "Aiwass" than either "Ayvas" or "Oyvz." One might object that one has "lost" the *T*—not necessarily so. In Crowley's kabbalistic universe, the Hebrew letter teth (ט) has great significance. First, it may signify "flesh."[26] The Hebrew glyph is in the shape of a serpent biting its own tail, reminiscent of the Gnostic *ourobouros*, symbolic of eternity. It is attributed to the eleventh tarot key, called "Lust." Its kabbalistic numerical value is nine, which number is powerfully associated with creation. Its Yetziratic attribution is the Zodiacal sign Leo, the lion, a solar sign and, of course, the Lord of the Zodiac, for Love ("under Will") makes the world go round. The astrological sign for Leo closely resembles a serpent. Crowley frequently calls teth the "Lion-Serpent." He associates it with the divinity of the sexual, the "Lord of this world."

It should be observed, furthermore, that at the Yezidis' most sacred precincts, namely, the shrines of Lalish, the predominant carvings on the shrines depict the sun and the stars. Even more suggestive is the famous door from the stone courtyard (the "market of mystical knowledge") to the Shrine of Sheykh 'Adi. There are depicted a comb (to unravel or plait Fate?), the staff of the religious leader, intertwined triangles (Seal of Solomon?), the stars, the sun, and a lion. Most prominent of all is an immensely striking black serpent, the height of a man, renewed in its coloring by a local dye administered by the shrine's guardians.

Crowley would have loved Lalish. It is sad that he never visited it, for to the sensitive eye it exhibits that very union of matter and spirit that Crowley regarded as central to his system.

In respect of which union, it should not pass unmentioned that the letter teth has a particularly strong symbolic role in Crowley's consonantal glyph for Shaitan, or Set, or Satan. In Hebrew: שטנ, ShTN (shin, teth, nun), where Sh (ש) is the Magic Fire, T (ט) is the Lion-Serpent, and N (נ) is the "Scarlet Woman" or feminine component. According to an editor's note on Crowley's text on the subject:

> Teth is related to the solar symbolism of Capricornus, the sign in which the sun is annually reborn, and Nun with the Scorpio-dragon symbolism of Babalon, the Scarlet Woman. The name ShTN then combines Hadit (the Sun) and Nuit (the Moon) in one glyph. Shaitan, which derives from the ancient Egyptian god Set, the sun in the south, and which blackens everything and was therefore later cursed, had some special attraction for Crowley. In fact, in his capacity as the Great Beast, he identified himself with Shaitan, another name for his Holy Guardian Angel, Aiwass.[27]

Modern etymology regards *Sheitan*, or *Shaitan*, as an Arabic word, possibly based on the Hebrew *Satan*, understood in the canonical book of Job (sixth to fourth century B.C.E.) as "the Adversary" or prosecuting counsel of a man in his judgment before God. Crowley's "Shaitan" is likewise divorced from popular ideas of a satanically evil Devil. It is interesting to note that in reverse of Yezidi practice, Crowley was content to use the word *Shaitan*, though in a peculiar, special sense, since it bore no embarrassment to him, but made no reference in his work whatsoever to Melek Tawus. Perhaps Crowley regarded "Tawus" as a genuinely "secret name" to be treated with propriety.

Whether this be true or not, it now seems likely that Crowley's understanding would recognize "Aiwass" or "Aivaz" or "OYVZ" in the combination of teth and AWUS. For him, I conjecture, the teth would qualify the dignity of the name Tawus.

To conclude this treatment of the identity of Melek Tawus, it is instructive to hear Lady Drower's response to a privileged performance of *qewls*, on the third day of the great Spring Festival at Lalish, the sixth day of Nisan (April 19), 1940:

> But what pagan spirit had usurped the shrine of the Saint? The night's vigil with its turbanned worshippers, its chants, and its prayers might indeed have passed as the devotions of a Sufi sect, mystical and eclectic indeed, but still Moslem in outward appearance. Today the mask was away and I seemed to see a laughing face peering from behind it. It was a glad god, an ancient god, a young god, that would dance in before long, naked and unashamed.[28]

Perhaps Lady Drower had read Crowley's *Hymn to Pan.*[29]

Yezidi Beliefs

This study would not be complete without an outline of the Yezidi religion, in which reverence for Melek Tawus plays such an intrinsic part. Yezidis are mostly Kurds, but probably have Persian, Assyrian, Armenian, and Arab forebears as well. Numbering fewer than a quarter of a million, their population has declined after more than a thousand years of persecution. Persecution, abduction, and murder of Yezidis continue to this day.

Yezidis are found in the Sheikhan, north and east of Mosul, in the Jebel Sinjar, west of Mosul, in southeastern Turkey, and in Georgian Armenia. There is a community of Yezidis in Germany as a result of hostile conditions in Turkey and Iraq. Their religion has been described as a "mystical pantheism" (Lady Drower). They call it "the Tradition"; in their own words, they are "Sunnites." The Tradition is vouchsafed by Melek Tawus, the mighty angel who governs the world with the blessing of *Khudê*, the absolute deity. "His ocean is deep"[30]—such is his perfection and limitlessness.

Until recently, Yezidis learned their religion exclusively through oral tradition; literacy among the *Mirids* (laity) was frowned upon. That has changed. A number of their religious songs have been published, along with the *Jelwe*, a short epiphany of Melek Tawus attributed to Sheykh 'Adi b. Musafir, who flourished among Hakkari Kurds in the twelfth century C.E. A descendant of the Umayyad line, the Sufi Sheykh 'Adi, fellow student with some of the greatest names in Sufism, arrived in the Hakkari Mountains after having left his birthplace in the Bekaa Valley in Syria to study theology in Baghdad. His arrival at Lalish, some fifty miles north of Mosul, transformed the practice of the religion that existed before his arrival. Sufism changed the older religion, but it is clear that the older religion changed Sufism also.

One is born a Yezidi—as with being born a Jew, religion and racial and family identity are one. Yezidis believe they are in the special care of Melek Tawus. The Peacock Angel may communicate his will through the *Kocheks*. The *Kocheks* were traditionally the seers and visionaries of the faith. Above the *Kocheks* are the Sheykhs who come from distinct clans. It has been observed that the Sheykhs appear to be physically different to the laity, being of darker skin. The *Baba Sheykh* is the ruler of the *Kocheks*. Religious guidance is sought from the *Pirs* (every Yezidi should have a *Pir* as guide), the order of *Feqirs*, and the Sheykhs. The head of the Sheykhs is the *Baba* (Father) *Sheykh*, who is always of the Fekhr el-Dîn branch of the Shemsani Sheykhs.[31]

There are three branches of Sheykhs: the Shemsanis, the Qatanis, and the Adanis. The princely house (the Chol family) is thought to be connected to the Qatani branch of Sheykhs. The *Mir*, currently Tehsin Beg, is the ruling prince of the Yezidis, and the royal residence is traditionally the castle at Ba'drê in the Sheykhan. The *Mir*'s person is held to be a manifestation of the divine; he is entitled to money and services.

Far from the Sheykhan, the religion came traditionally to Yezidis through the travels of the *qewwals*. The *qewwals* embody the mystical essence of the faith in their religious songs and playing of *def* and *shebab* (tambour and flute). They also carry the small number of *senjaqs* to the disparate clans of Yezidi people. According to Philip Kreyenbroek, who visited Lalish in 1992, this system is suffering greatly in present times. The *senjaqs* are bronze images of the Peacock Angel that have survived the many attacks on the faith; the *qewwals* receive money for showing the *senjaqs*. Money is also paid to the guardians of the many shrines at Lalish. They collect dust from the shrines, roll it up with water from the sacred Kanîya Sipî spring at Lalish, and give it to the believers as trusted remedies for many ailments. These little balls are called *berat*.

The religion of the Yezidi people consists in honoring God, being truthful, being clean, respecting their prince, giving to the poor, and maintaining the Tradition. This includes regular visits to Lalish for festivals, when possible. Yezidis follow strict rules of marriage (the Sheykhly branches are endogamous). Many Yezidis experience baptism at special cisterns at Lalish, though this is not a salvific necessity. They abstain from some foods (such as lettuce).[32] They should listen to the voices of the *Pirs* (religious assistants to the Sheykhs), *Kocheks*, and Sheykhs. They are taught to respect the religion of others while never forsaking their own. Much knowledge and inspiration consists in participating in the *qewls*.

Yezidis believe in Paradise, but not in hell.[33] They do not believe in a dualistic conflict between God and a dark power. Evil comes from men's hearts, and men are responsible for what they think and do. A bad life will lead to a compensatory reincarnation. In 2004, a newspaper reporter asked a Yezidi what he thought would happen to Saddam Hussein. The Yezidi suggested he would return as a donkey; he would have to bear the load of others in sundry conditions.[34]

Care for graves and shrines (*mezar*) and special respect of the sun as a living symbol of God are important. A Yezidi is to kiss the ground where the sun first strikes. Prayers may also be said at midday and sunset. Wednesday is a holy day for the Yezidi, and the eve before it holy also.

The old life of the Yezidis holds many fascinations for those who are interested in the ancient customs of the Near East. A bull is sacrificed at the Shrine of Sheykh Shems in Lalish. Sheykh Shems is both historical figure and the divinity of the sun. The name "Shems" is reminiscent of the Mesopotamian god "Shamash" (the Sun), known throughout the old East.

Sufic mysticism, or rather gnosis, is important to the Sheykhs, but it has been suffused with a profound vision of the divinity hidden in or expressed by nature. Water is very important; caves, mountains, trees, and valleys have religious significance. Yezidis believe in nature spirits, subject to Melek Tawus; Lalish is "the site of Truth" that descended from heaven. God's will is expressed in the creation; to be close to it is to participate in the proper governance of Melek Tawus. All inspiration comes from God. Only God knows everything; his knowledge utterly transcends human reason. What we know is thanks to him.

Yezidi people are permitted to drink alcohol; this may in part explain why they have a long-standing association with the Caliph Yezîd, criticized in Shia tradition for his tolerance to life's pleasures, as well as his part in the death of Hussein. Yezidis are taught that Jews, Christians, and Muslims are latecomers to religion. Where their beliefs agree with the Yezidis' own, well and good; where not, Yezidis must reject those beliefs. Yezidis date their origins to Adam, the first man, through his third son, Seth (the same name as the ancient Egyptian sun god "Set" or "Seth"). This is significant to those concerned with the survival of Gnostic ideas in contemporary religion (including Crowley's magical system).

According to variant texts of *Meshef Resh*, Adam and Eve had an argument about which of them was capable of bringing forth progeny. Each put the product of his or her fertility in a jar. After a season, Eve's jar was opened, revealing a putrid mass; Adam's jar opened to reveal a boy and a girl. "Now from these two our sect [*sic.*], the Yezidis, are descended. . . . After this Adam knew Eve, and she bore two children, male and female; and from these the Jews, the Christians, the Moslems, and other nations and sects are descended. But our first fathers are Seth, Noah, and Enosh, the righteous ones, who were descended from Adam only."[35]

This genealogy is very similar to the "Priestly" genealogy of Seth given in Genesis 5:1–30: Adam, Seth, Enosh, Kenan, Mahalel, Jared, Enoch, Methuselah, Lamech, Noah. It may be contrasted with the genealogy of Cain given by the "Yahwist" in Genesis 4:17–18: Adam, Cain, Enoch, Irad, Mehujael, Methushael, Lamech.[36]

The role of Seth in offering a new future to the human race after the denigration of Cain has inspired many myths. Josephus wrote in the first century C.E. of how Seth was "a virtuous man" who left children of "excellent character" who "were the inventors of that peculiar sort of wisdom which is concerned with the heavenly bodies, and their order." According to Josephus, Adam predicted the world's destruction by fire and by flood, in response to which Seth's progeny inscribed their discoveries on pillars of brick and stone. "Now this remains in the land of Siriad to this day."[37] This legend was familiar and significant to the first Freemasons, from at least the early seventeenth century.[38] It was also familiar to the authors of the *Three Steles of Seth*, a work found within the codices discovered in the vicinity of Nag Hammadi in 1945 and written before 265 C.E.[39] Sethians appear to have existed prior to contact with Christianity. By the third century, some Sethians identified Christ as an incarnation of Seth, the new man whose line was pure, founder of what they called "the immovable race," guardians of the gnosis, with the implication that come the predicted cataclysms of fire and flood, the Sethians would stand.

Crowley, of course, with his special interest in the Egyptian Set (pronounced "Seth" by the Greeks and whom some scholars identify as the source for the biblical Seth),[40] drew synthetically on such ideas of the Gnostics as were available to him, writing a memorable Gnostic Mass.[41] Sethian ideas are strongly associated with the Gnostic Ophites, worshippers of the Serpent who offers immortal knowledge, healing, and so on. Could the Sethians, Ophites, and the forebears of the Yezidi people share a common ancestry?

The confluence of Sethian mythology, serpent cult, Sufic gnosis, and Zoroastrianism, as well as Egyptian and ancient Mesopotamian mythology, provides rich material for speculation. No direct links have been proved; it is unlikely that they could be. The pool of ideas and experiences that have drawn on these myths and reprojected them is shared by many manifestations of oriental religious consciousness; the formative ideas and images are of very ancient provenance.

Yezidis and the Sumerian Religion

Anthropologist Sami Said Ahmed told an interesting story of how a Yezidi friend gave him two papers on Yezidi beliefs.[42] In them, legendary tales were taken as fact; each paper contradicted the other. Ahmed eventually found the papers contained real facts and genuine articles of Yezidi belief, disguised. When told of this, the Yezidi replied, "The book which I presented to you contains only one (fact) of the thousands (of facts) of Yezidism." The friend declared that "Yezidism is the mother of all Eastern religions."

It is understood that Yezidism in its contemporary form is the product of years of struggle with neighboring faiths, leading to cross-faith but transvalued language use (for example, Jesus is regarded as an angel, or as a manifestation of Sheykh Shems). Furthermore, the impact of Sheykh 'Adi's sojourn in Lalish generated a revolution in the hierarchy of the faith—though it would seem from the evidence that Sheykh 'Adi and members of his family were themselves immensely affected by what they discovered among the Kurds of that region. Nevertheless, after his death, hostile observers believed Sheykh 'Adi's disciples had gone much further than Sheykh 'Adi himself—in particular, indulging in an excessive veneration for the Sheykh. Sheykh 'Adi's Sufi *tariqa* (the "path" of the *'Adawiyya*) was regarded as Islamic, though suspect by a number of medieval Islamic commentators.[43] It spread to Syria and Egypt.[44] Its Lalish manifestation developed quite differently to the "export version."

Manuscripts discovered in the Sinjar attributed to Sheykh 'Adi make it clear that their author regarded himself as having achieved in himself divinity: "How dare ye deny me when I am truly your God and I wipe out and I write down (destiny). . . . How dare you deny me . . . when I, the Ancient of Time, created the world? And ye ask me about my lower abode. I tell you of the dominion which was established on the rock." Furthermore: "I am a unique Sheykh; and it is I, myself, who created things. It is I who received a book, a book of good tidings. It came from my God piercing the mountains. It is to me that all men come. They come in submission and kiss my feet."[45] Little wonder that Yezidis take the Sheykh as a manifestation of God. In Crowley's system, Sheykh 'Adi was *Ipsissimus*. At this level, Crowley and the Sheykh should have been in some kind of exalted, impersonal communion.

Links between Crowley's life and system with the Sufis are legion. On his arrival in Cairo in 1904, he "got a sheikh to teach me Arabic and the practices of ablution, prayer and so on, so that at some future time I might pass for a Moslem among themselves. . . . My sheikh was profoundly versed in the mysticism and magic of Islam, and discovering that I was an initiate, had no hesitation in providing me with books and manuscripts on the Arabic Cabbala."[46] However, links between Crowley's system, Yezidism, and ancient Sumerian religion, as suggested in Crowley's New Commentary on *Liber AL vel Legis*, are far vaguer and perhaps fanciful, relying on issues of interpretation and not a little wishful thinking.

Anu and Adad were not, as allegedly asserted by Crowley's correspondent, Samuel Aiwaz Jacobs, the mother and father gods, respectively, of the Sumerian religion; neither was "female." Anu was the son of Anshar and Kishar; his name signified the sky and he reigned over the heavens. A possible parity with Nuit, perhaps, but Adad was not a sun god; Adad was a god of the storm. As such he might have had some parity with the early conceptions of Set, god of the desert heat, wind, and storm, but not "Hadit." If one were to look for a parallel to the winged sun disk of Hor-behedet ("god of the sky"), the very same image of winged disk may be found in the national god not of the Sumerians but of the Assyrians. Asshur, identified with the Babylonian god Anshar, was the Assyrians' father of all the gods and maker of the sky of Anu and of the underworld.

While there are parallels of meaning among this pantheon, we do not find the two dynamic principles whose union makes the universe that are central to *The Book of the Law*. Thelema was not the system of some ideal, ancient world culture. It is, as Martin P. Starr maintains, a synthesis, supported by a fresh revelation (principally, the Cairo Working).

Seeking Sumerian mythology within the religion and folklore of the Yezidis could keep speculators busy among the matted skeins of comparative folklore for a long time—and the result would be speculative. Given that it is an oral tradition, there is no possibility of proving whether a thing believed three hundred years ago was believed thirteen hundred years ago. Furthermore, it is impossible to place the Yezidi religion with certainty, before it was first referred to in the texts of opponents in the eleventh century. There are nonetheless a number of features that suggest some acquaintance with ancient religions of Mesopotamia, in spite of Kreyenbroek's view that it is to the traditions of Zoroastrian Iran (as well as thirteenth-century Sufism) that one should look in locating common features of Yezidi traditions.[47]

One of the most significant ancient figures that we find venerated in the Yezidi traditions is the divinity of the sun. *Shems* is clearly a form of *Shamash*, a word not exclusive to Mesopotamian religion, though, arguably, derived from it. Customary Babylonian descriptions of Shamash's appearance are reflected in the following paraphrase: "Every morning the scorpion-men who inhabit the Mountain of the East and defend its approaches, open in the mountain's flank a great folding door. From it will spring on its daily journey, Shamash, the sun-god."[48] This conception of the sun god breaking through the mountains may be compared with the quotation attributed to Sheykh 'Adi (above): "It came from my God piercing the mountains." This was Crowley's god also: the sun, called by some (including Crowley) the only rational divinity. Whether the Yezidis had at any time made the explicit Crowleyan link between the sun and "his vice-regent on earth," the phallus, is not known.

I am not aware of any evidence to support the late Kenneth Grant's belief that Shaitan was worshipped by the ancient Sumerians. Melek Tawus also is not to be found there, on the basis of extant evidence. DNA studies may someday reveal whether the civilization of the Sumerians was the "earliest home of our race"—though which race Crowley meant by this, we do not know.

Philosophical Resonance

Anyone who is familiar with *AL-Jilwah* (the Revelation), "which the outsiders may neither read nor behold,"[49] and *Liber AL vel Legis* (the Cairo Revelation) cannot fail to discern a curious mutual resonance of tone and meaning between the two. Similar resonance applies to aspects of Crowley's mature philosophy and that of the beliefs of the Yezidis in general. So much should be clear from what has preceded, but it is worth recapitulating some obvious parallels where one might suppose a kindred state of mind to be present in both.

Obviously, scholarship is in no more a position to assert that the mind-set of Aiwass (spokesman for the dynamic universe) has been shared by the angel Melek Tawus than it might support the article of Yezidi faith that Sheykh 'Adi was inspired to repeat words spoken by the "Peacock Angel." All we can do is examine something of what may have been behind Aleister Crowley's belief that Aiwass was the "true most ancient name of the God of the Yezidis." The following texts from the *Jilwe* and from *The Book of the Law*, for example, exhibit common features such that an uninformed person might consider the passages as issuing from a common source.

I was, and am now, and will continue unto eternity, ruling over all creatures and ordering the affairs and deeds of those who are under my sway.[50]

There is no place in the universe that knows not my presence.[51]

I am alone: there is no God where I am.[52]

In the sphere I am everywhere the centre, as she, the circumference, is nowhere found.[53]

I direct and teach such as will follow my teaching, who find in their accord with me joy and delight greater than any joy wherewith the soul rejoiceth.[54]

I give unimaginable joys on earth: certainty, not faith, while in life, upon death; peace unutterable, rest, ecstasy; nor do I demand aught in sacrifice.[55]

He who is accounted mine, dieth not like other men.[56]

I guide without a scripture; I point the way by unseen means unto my friends and such as observe the precepts of my teaching, which is not grievous, and is adapted to the time and conditions.[57]

I allow everyone to follow the dictates of his own nature, but he that opposes me will regret it sorely.[58]

Thou hast no right but to do thy will.[59]

I remember necessary affairs and execute them in due time. I teach and guide those who follow my instructions. If anyone obey me and conform to my commandments, he shall have joy, delight and goodness.[60]

I requite the descendants of Adam, and reward them with various rewards that I alone know. Moreover, powers and dominions over all that is on earth, both that which is above and that which is beneath, are in my hand.[61]

> Let my servants be few and secret, they shall rule the many and the known. These are fools that men adore; both their gods and their men are fools.[62]

> I will not give my rights to other gods.[63]

> O ye who observe my injunctions, reject such sayings and teachings as are not from me. Mention not my name or my attributes, as strangers do, lest ye be guilty of sin, for ye have no knowledge thereof.[64]

These extracts are not exhaustive. However, one should not push the idea of implicit parallel too far, since one might make a far longer list of critical differences between the texts. On the other hand, one text emerged from the twelfth century and one from the twentieth; they clearly had different purposes and were addressed to different persons. Crowley's revelation was considered to be innovative of a New Aeon; the *Jelwe* asserts a continuity, albeit as a distinct revelation. Nevertheless, it is the *Jelwe* that promotes the idea quite explicitly that Melek Tawus expects new chiefs to be appointed over new "generations" and to preside over new eras. The neo-Rosicrucian idea shared by Crowley of the Secret Chiefs, and of his own peculiar appointment within the angelic scheme, fits perfectly consistently, in principle, within the governance of Melek Tawus declared in the *Jelwe*:

> Every age has a Regent, and this by my counsel. Every generation changes with the Chief of this World, so that each one of the chiefs in his turn and cycle fulfils his charge. . . . The other gods may not interfere in my business and work: whatsoever I determine mine, that is.[65]

> I surrender active control into the hands of those whom I have proved, who are in accordance with my will, friends in some shape or fashion to such as are faithful and abide by my counsel. I take and I give; I make rich and I make poor; I make happy and I make wretched, according to environments and seasons, and there is none who hath the right to interfere, or to withdraw any man from my control.[66]

> The ordering of the worlds, the revolution of ages, the changing of their regents are mine from eternity.[67]

> Moreover, I give counsel to the skilled directors, for I have appointed them for periods that are known to me.[68]

> I appear in divers manners to those who are faithful and under my command . . . but my own shall not die like the sons of Adam that are without. . . . I direct aright my beloved and my chosen ones by unseen means.[69]

Conclusion

Was Aleister Crowley guided by Melek Tawus? Did the Logos of the Peacock Angel enter that of Crowley when he took down the words of *The Book of the Law*? Are Set, Horus, Melek Tawus, and Aiwass members of the same metaphysical "club"? Are Yezidis prototypes, or long-lost cousins, of Thelemites? Do we find Crowley's "Law of Liberty" in the Yezidi religion? Is the Yezidi faith the true *fons* of advanced "Western" esoteric inspiration? Should Christian Rosenkreuz have gone not to Damar but to Lalish? Was Crowley a Yezidi prophet? Fortunately, I did not set out to answer these questions; solutions to them are beyond the bounds of rational scholarship. What this study has been able to show is that while Crowley may not have believed that the "God of the Yezidis" dictated *The Book of the Law*, he did have reason to support his view that Aiwass and the being worshipped by Yezidis had some kinship, and perhaps even identity.

This essay has also gone some way to demonstrate that the "Shaitan" respected by Crowley was not the devotee of cosmic evil and moral rottenness who exists in the world picture of fundamentalist Christians, Jews, and Muslims. The Yezidis have been grievously hurt by the identification; Crowley was persecuted and reviled for it—Crowley and the Yezidis have that much in common at least. Crowley was a very intuitive man. In matters magical, his intuition was unique. I think it was this famous intuition that led him to perceive a link between his own work and the inner life of the Yezidis. This was the same intuition that enabled him to envision the special role of Elias Ashmole, among others, in the passage of the gnosis through time. He did not follow up all his intuitions with extensive scholarship; he did not need to. Like a good master, he gave hints and the simple injunction, *Seek and ye shall find*. Scholarship, to a degree, supports his intuition.

Notes

1. See Sami Said Ahmed, *The Yazidis: Their Life and Beliefs* (Miami, Fla.: Field Research Projects, 1975).
2. Samuel Aiwaz Jacobs (1891–1971), Iranian-born typographer and proprietor of the Golden Eagle Press, was considered by Crowley to have provided key evidence for the origins of *Liber AL*. Crowley–Jacobs letters survive, copied in the 1950s when Philip Kaplan, an American bibliophile, introduced Jacobs to Karl Germer. One of

them is a letter permitting Jacobs to publish Crowley's *The Heart of the Master* "on the usual business terms." I am indebted to Martin P. Starr for this information. Details concerning Jacobs and his peculiar contact with Crowley can be found in chapter 15 of my *Aleister Crowley: The Biography* (London: Watkins, 2011).

3. *Liber AL vel Legis* I:1.
4. See Aleister Crowley, *The Holy Books of Thelema* (New York: Samuel Weiser, 1989), 250–51.
5. Compare: "In the sphere I am everywhere the centre, as she, the circumference, is nowhere found." *Liber AL vel Legis* II:3. Nicholas of Cusa (*De docta ignorantia*, II:2) was quoting from the popular twelfth-century pseudo-Hermetic treatise the *Book of the XXIV Philosophers*, though the conception that "God is an infinite sphere whose centre is everywhere, circumference nowhere" is consistent with the eclectic spirit of the authentic *Corpus Hermeticum* (circa third century C.E.). While Cusanus saw the "God" of the axiom as indicating God's reflection in the universe, Pascal's *Pensées* (1670) substituted the expression "the whole of Nature" for "God": "*C'est une sphère infinie, dont le centre est partout et la circonférence nulle part*" (sec. 2, "The Misery of Man without God," 71–72).
6. "Aiwass is the name given by Ouarda the Seer [Rose Crowley] as that of the Intelligence communicating." Aleister Crowley, *The Commentaries of AL*, ed. Marcelo Motta (London: Routledge & Kegan Paul, 1975), 6.
7. Aleister Crowley, *The Equinox of the Gods* (London: OTO, 1936), 117–18.
8. Aleister Crowley, "*AL*, The Commentary Called D(jeridensis) Provisionally by 666" (1923), folder 16, Yorke Collection, Warburg Institute, University of London.
9. Hymenaeus Beta, ed., *An Old Master: The Art of Aleister Crowley* [exhibition catalog] (London: October Gallery, April 1998), 9.
10. C. R. Cammell, *Aleister Crowley: The Black Magician* (originally *Aleister Crowley: The Man, the Mage, the Poet*, 1951; London: New English Library, 1969), 60.
11. "The Gospel of John too, is full of dithyrambs expressing the results of mystic practice." Aleister Crowley, *Crowley on Christ* [*The Gospel According to St. Bernard Shaw*], ed. Francis King (1953; London: C. W. Daniel, 1974), 112.
12. Karl von Eckartshausen, *Die Wolke über dem Heiligtum* (1802).
13. E. J. Drower, *Peacock Angel, Being Some Account of Votaries of a Secret Cult and Their Sanctuaries* (London: John Murray, 1941).
14. Phillip Kreyenbroek, *Yezidism: Its Background, Observances and Textual Tradition* (Lewiston, N.Y.: Edwin Mellen Press, 1995), 92. Verses reprinted with permission.
15. Aleister Crowley, *Magick*, ed. John Symonds and Kenneth Grant (London: Routledge & Kegan Paul, 1973), 62, footnote.
16. Sheykh Shems is, according to Kreyenbroek, also a member of the Heptad, and holder of such links with God as to suggest that he actually is God, or the deputy (*wezîr*) of Sheykh Adi (who is also Melek Tawus). Yezidis do not define rigidly their religious and mystical terminology. Kreyenbroek, *Yezidism*, 97.
17. Drower, *Peacock Angel*, 171.
18. Kreyenbroek, *Yezidism*, 99.

19. John S. Guest, *The Yezidis: A Study in Survival* (New York: Methuen/Routledge & Kegan Paul, 1987), 202.
20. *Adv. Haer.*, Book I, XIII, in *The Ante-Nicene Fathers*, trans. Alexander Roberts and James Donaldson (Grand Rapids, Mich.: Wm. B. Eerdmans, 1981).
21. Isya Joseph, *Devil Worship: The Sacred Books and Traditions of the Yezidis* (Kila, Mont.: Kessinger, 2005), 38.
22. Drower, *Peacock Angel*, 7.
23. Austen Henry Layard, *Discoveries at Nineveh: A Popular Account of Discoveries at Nineveh* (New York: Derby, 1854), chap. 8. In a footnote, Layard explains, "The term Sheitan (equivalent to Satan) is usually applied in the East to a clever, cunning, or daring fellow."
24. Helena Petrovna Blavatsky, *Isis Unveiled: A Master-Key to the Mysteries of Ancient and Modern Science and Theology* (New York: J. W. Bouton, 1877), 2:197.
25. Kreyenbroek, *Yezidism*, 244–47.
26. See Crowley, *Magick*, 418, footnote.
27. Editor's note in Aleister Crowley, *The Magical Record of the Beast 666*, ed. John Symonds and Kenneth Grant (London: Duckworth, 1972), 192.
28. Drower, *Peacock Angel*, 126.
29. Crowley, *Magick*, 125.
30. Kreyenbroek, *Yezidism*, 92.
31. Ibid., 127.
32. Interestingly, lettuce was the food special to the Egyptian god Set.
33. They may, however, use "hell" as a comparative. For example, when entering the valley of Lalish, the "Paradise" of this "Site of Truth" (as it is called) is contrasted with the "hell" of the ordinary world outside it. Punishments and consequences occur in the world around us.
34. Yezidi teacher Hamed, interviewed by Susan Martin, *St. Petersburg Times*, September 2004. He went on to say: "We respect other religions—everyone who respects God, we respect him. Why can't they respect us?"
35. Joseph, *Devil Worship*, 39.
36. S. H. Hooke, *Middle Eastern Mythology* (Harmondsworth: Pelican, 1978), 127.
37. Josephus, *Antiquities of the Jews: The Works of Flavious Josephus*, trans. William Whiston (Edinburgh: William P. Nimmo, 1865), bk. 1, chap. 2, 3.
38. See Tobias Churton, *The Golden Builders: Alchemists, Rosicrucians, and the First Freemasons* (New York: Weiser, 2005), pt. 3.
39. Note by James M. Robinson and Frederick Wisse in *The Nag Hammadi Library*, ed. James M. Robinson (Leiden: E. J. Brill, 1984), 362.
40. See Eliza Burt Gamble, "The Phoenician and Hebrew God Set or Seth," in *The God-Idea of the Ancients (or Sex in Religion)* (New York: G. P. Putnam's Sons, 1897).
41. According to Martin P. Starr, Crowley "admitted his work was synthetic, he even termed Thelema 'the synthetic religion' in a prospectus for series of courses for which he was seeking paying students in New York in 1915." E-mail to the author, July 15, 2005.

42. Ahmed, *The Yazidis.*
43. Kreyenbroek, *Yezidism*, 29ff., 50ff.
44. John Guest photographed the inscription on the mausoleum of Zein ed-Din Yusuf, in Cairo—a relic of the *'Adawiyya tariqa* in Cairo. Guest, *The Yezidis*, plate 24.
45. Quoted in Anis Frayha, "New Yezidi Texts from Beled Sinjar, 'Iraq," *Journal of the American Oriental Society* 66 (1946): 38–39.
46. Aleister Crowley, *The Confessions of Aleister Crowley*, ed. John Symonds and Kenneth Grant (London: Routledge & Kegan Paul, 1979), 388.
47. Kreyenbroek, *Yezidism*, 57–61. Note especially: "All that can be confidently asserted, therefore, is that the religions of the Yezidis and the Yaresan have sprung from intensive contacts between Islam and a cult of Iranian origin which contained both Zoroastrian elements and traits that cannot be traced back to mainstream Zoroastrianism" (61). Also: "The "cultural environment in which these faiths originated appears to have had a genius for adopting alien elements and integrating these into its traditional system. As a result, isolated elements of various origins abound in the Yezidi and Ahl-e Haqq traditions. These are hardly of major significance, however, for understanding the early development of these systems" (61, n. 130).
48. Felix Guirand et al., eds., *Larousse Mythologie Générale* (Paris: Librairie Larousse, 1959), 57.
49. Joseph, *Devil Worship*, 31.
50. Guest, *The Yezidis*, 200–202.
51. Joseph, *Devil Worship*, 31.
52. *Liber AL vel Legis* II:23.
53. Ibid., II:3.
54. Guest, *The Yezidis*, 200–202.
55. *Liber AL vel Legis* I:58.
56. Joseph, *Devil Worship*, 31ff.
57. Guest, *The Yezidis*, 200–202.
58. Joseph, *Devil Worship*, 31.
59. *Liber AL vel Legis* I:42b.
60. Joseph, *Devil Worship*, 31.
61. Ibid.
62. *Liber AL vel Legis* I:11.
63. Joseph, *Devil Worship*, 31ff.
64. Guest, *The Yezidis*, 200–202.
65. Ibid.
66. Ibid.
67. Ibid.
68. Joseph, *Devil Worship*, 31ff.
69. Ibid.

8

Frenzies of the Beast

THE PHAEDRAN *FURORES* IN THE RITES AND WRITINGS OF ALEISTER CROWLEY

Matthew D. Rogers

ALEISTER CROWLEY WAS certainly the most notorious occultist of the twentieth century, and also one of the most prolific. While he is often addressed simply as a rebel for his anti-Christianity and unconventional mores, or as an innovator with particular respect to his new religion of Thelema, it is clear that Crowley saw an important part of his work as consisting of a certain conservation—or, at least, co-optation—of traditional ideas. Biographers often remark upon his appropriation of symbols, structures, and material from the Hermetic Order of the Golden Dawn, but his writings show his tremendous drive toward systematizing and syncretizing other materials that fall well outside the curricula that he had encountered as a member of that particular initiatory society. Crowley himself was quick to point out his debts to Theosophical Society founder and sibyl H. P. Blavatsky and his legacy from the work of Alphonse Louis Constant, better known among occultists as Eliphas Lévi.[1] Furthermore, he often acknowledged the instruction he had received from Theodor Reuss in the latter's Ordo Templi Orientis (OTO),[2] and he claimed to have incorporated materials from the contemporary manifestations of Asian mystical systems, learned firsthand during his various travels on that continent.[3]

Crowley was the recipient of an extensive formal education, and his zeal for study in the esoteric and occult traditions certainly acquainted him with ideas and works from far earlier periods than the sort of late nineteenth-century mélange that served as a backdrop to his efforts to organize his doctrines and practices. In a paper issued as instruction to his disciples, he makes a pointed allusion to the traditions of Hellenic antiquity as a figure of esoteric knowledge:

> Or as a scholar may learn some secret language of the ancients, his friends shall say: "Look! he pretends to read this book. But it is unintelligible—it is nonsense." Yet he delights in the Odyssey, while they read vain and vulgar things.[4]

At an early point in his public career as an occultist, Crowley wrote that the antique mystagogues "caused to be written in symbols by one of the lesser initiates the whole Mystery of Godliness, so that after the renaissance, those who were fitted to the Work might infallibly discover the first matter of the Work and even many of the processes thereof. Such writings are those of the neo-Platonists."[5] While Blavatsky did reference the Neoplatonists,[6] and the Golden Dawn made extensive use of the *Chaldean Oracles*,[7] those occultist receptions of antique Hellenic materials took forms distinctly different from the ones enjoyed in their unique reception by Crowley.

A vital feature of the Platonist transmission into the Renaissance and later esotericism is the classification of the *furores*, or "frenzies," from Plato's *Phaedrus*.[8] This doctrine, along with its elaborations by later Platonists, was an important concern in the tremendously influential work of Marsilio Ficino.[9] It was carried over into the writings of Henry Cornelius Agrippa von Nettesheim in his *Occulta Philosophia Libri Tres*,[10] and it featured strongly in the work of Giordano Bruno.[11] Crowley was possibly alluding to the chariot as the figure for the human soul in the *Phaedrus*[12] when he wrote in 1912, "Man is only himself when lost to himself in The Charioting,"[13] since it was in that same year that he made a thorough exposition of his own reinterpretation of the Platonist frenzies.[14] The latter exposition was titled "Energized Enthusiasm: A Note on Theurgy," and Crowley first published it in his own occult journal *The Equinox*, with a remark in the table of contents that it had been "Rejected by *The English Review*."[15]

The word *theurgy* in the title of the article is certainly suggestive of the Neoplatonists, particularly Iamblichus, whose *De Mysteriis* was a key reference for Crowley. Among other things, Iamblichus was the source of the term *Augoeides*, which Crowley often used to denote the tutelary genius or Holy Guardian Angel.[16] And *enthusiasms* (*enthusiasmoi*) is Iamblichus's preferred term for the frenzies.[17] But, although "Energized Enthusiasm" claims to provide an examination of "the methods of the Greeks" in antiquity, it includes no references to the names of specific Greek texts or thinkers. Nevertheless, the debt to Plato's *Phaedrus*, although tacit, is unmistakable. Early in the essay, Crowley compares genius and mania, and he describes them as "exactly parallel (nowhere meeting),"[18] which concisely evokes and counters the *manic* = *mantic* equivalence that Plato uses to identify madness with divine inspiration.[19] Crowley distinguishes inspiration, which he calls "organized," from madness, which is "chaotic." If Crowley had preferred to follow Plato, he could have discriminated between what Plato denominates as "two kinds of madness, one resulting from human ailments, the other from a divine disturbance of our conventions of conduct."[20] But "divine disturbance" does not fit into Crowley's theurgy. Instead, his perspective reflects a sentiment that he later summed up with characteristic wit in *The Gospel According to St. Bernard Shaw*:

> The mystic attainment may be defined as the Union of the Soul with God, or as the realization of itself, or—there are fifty phrases for the same experience. The same, for whether you are a Christian or a Buddhist, a Theist or (as I am myself, thank God!) an Atheist, the attainment of this one state is as open to you as is nightmare, or madness, or intoxication.[21]

So according to Crowley, for whom it is "easier . . . to extend my connotation of 'man' than to invent 'God,'"[22] the species of inspiration are not divine *mania*, *furores*, or frenzies, but rather "methods," and the sense of instrumental causality that this term implies is evident throughout his discussion of them.

Aside from this basic divergence of worldview, "Energized Enthusiasm" includes another significant and surprising alteration of the Platonist set of divine inspirations. Crowley acknowledges only *three* "methods of discharging the Lyden Jar of Genius." He itemizes Dionysus, Apollo, and Aphrodite, the gods that inspired the mantic, oracular, and erotic frenzies, but he has discarded the Muses and their poetic frenzy! As will become apparent, the methods attributed to the three gods differ from their traditional frenzies, but it is curious that Crowley should omit the Muses, especially when the opening sections of "Energized Enthusiasm" very specifically use literary production as a gauge of inspiration.[23] There are two likely reasons for the change. On one hand, Crowley was sufficiently preoccupied with poetry (and with literary posterity) for him to have agreed with Ficino that the inspiration of the Muses necessarily accompanies the manifestation of any one of the other three species of inspiration.[24] Crowley categorically understood artists to be the forerunners of adepts,[25] and he claimed for the virtue of the traditions of European religion, "We are the poets!"[26]

On the other hand, Crowley's reduction of four frenzies to three methods appears to be laying the groundwork for a synthesis with other triads, such as the ones referenced in the invocation that forms the brief opening section of "Energized Enthusiasm":

> I A O the supreme One of the Gnostics, the true God, is the Lord of this work. Let us therefore invoke Him by that name which the Companions of the Royal Arch blaspheme to aid us in the essay to declare the means which He has bestowed upon us![27]

The Gnostic I A O is a three-lettered name of god, which Crowley and his Golden Dawn instructors understood to stand for a triad of deities: Isis, Apophis, and Osiris, according to the Rosicrucian-themed ceremony of their Adeptus Minor grade.[28] Similarly, the "name which the Companions of the Royal Arch blaspheme" is a reference to a masonic word that was communicated under the "Rule of Three," requiring that it be spoken only in "a trible [*sic*] voice"—that is, by three initiated Companions together.[29] A. E. Waite indicates further that the Royal Arch name refers to a triune deity.[30] These esoteric trinities also serve to tie Crowley's work in this instance to his ambitions for the transformation of initiatory groups, including masonic rites, to include his doctrines.

Michael J. B. Allen has given worthwhile attention to the manner in which Ficino evaluated and altered the sequence of Plato's frenzies.[31] If we look to the same issue in "Energized Enthusiasm," the original manuscript shows that Crowley had first written them as "Apollo, Dionysus, Aphrodite," which—except for the omission of the Muses—conforms perfectly to Plato.[32] And it is in this sequence that he provides them with more detailed treatments in the subsequent sections of the essay.[33] But a later correction to the manuscript, reflected in the published version, changed the sequence for their introductory mention to "Dionysus, Aphrodite, Apollo," in order to create the rhetorical parallel with "wine, woman, and song."[34] And these latter three are indeed what Crowley intends: he has transformed the prophetic, mantic, and erotic frenzies into the musical, pharmaceutical, and sexual methods.

In his discussion of the musical method, attributed to Apollo, Crowley places the human voice foremost, but he especially praises the violin and the tom-tom.[35] Crowley's interest in these two instruments is in large part attributable to two of his associates: Leila Waddell and G. M. Marston, respectively.

The Australian violinist Waddell was Crowley's lover of some years, whom he honored with such epithets as "Mother of Heaven."[36] She had played violin in his Rites of Eleusis theatrical rituals, and she continued performing later, under Crowley's direction, as the protagonist of a musical play *The Snowstorm*[37] and with a backup ensemble of female fiddlers as the Ragged Ragtime Girls.[38] Crowley claims that Marston's "experiments in the effect of the tom-tom on the married Englishwoman are classical and conclusive" and that Marston, a naval commander, had demonstrated that the tom-tom could reliably create erotic disinhibition in women "usually unacquainted with sexual satisfaction."[39] Waddell and Marston both did their first magical ritual work with Crowley on the same occasion, when they assisted him in a ceremony at Marston's home to evoke the martial spirit Bartzabel.[40]

At about the same time as the Bartzabel operation, Crowley was also involved with innovations in the pharmaceutical method that he classed under Dionysus. His allusion in "Energized Enthusiasm" to "the elixir introduced by me to Europe"[41] is quite certainly to his preparation of the psychoactive American cactus peyote, the source of mescaline, which he routinely referenced by the now-obsolete botanical name *Anhalonium lewinii.*[42] He had been experimenting with this drug intermittently since 1907.[43] Crowley's interest in, and experience with, the use of varied drugs to alter consciousness was by then already of long standing. Early on, he had read William James regarding nitrous oxide experiments, and his Golden Dawn mentor Allan Bennett had also tutored him in pharmacology. Bennett's poor health had led him to experiment with cocaine, opium, and morphine, and he shared both his expertise and his drug supply with Crowley.[44] Crowley had also taken hashish extensively during his travels and had written a detailed essay for *The Equinox*, under the pseudonym Oliver Haddo, filled with quotes from the *Chaldean Oracles* and comparing his hashish experiences to various Yogic trance states.[45] But in "Energized Enthusiasm," at a time when narcotics were still freely purchasable over the counter in England, Crowley chose to narrow his prescriptions to alcohol and tincture of peyote.

Crowley subscribed to phallicist theories of religious origins, but he claimed that "when you have proved that God is merely a name for the sex instinct, it appears to me not far to the perception that the sex instinct is God."[46] Crowley's extreme and unconventional applications of the "method of Aphrodite" are among the most fully established features of his personal career. His bisexuality was a settled fact in practice, although he exercised a certain measure of discretion about it, because homosexual conduct—unlike narcotics possession and use—was a prosecutable offense in the British courts.

Crowley biographer Martin Booth speculates that Crowley bought his house in Scotland in 1899 partly because of a desire to avoid having his homosexual activity investigated by the London police.[47] Just a couple of years before writing "Energized Enthusiasm," Crowley had penned the *Bagh-i-muattar*, a pseudonymous, faux Persian mystical treatise entirely couched in homoerotic imagery.[48] Crowley's sexual activities were well integrated with his magical work and personal mythopoeia. Identifying himself as the Beast 666 of the Apocalypse, he considered his first wife Rose to be the "Scarlet Woman" as his consort and as a clairvoyant medium for messages from the Secret Chiefs, hidden adepts, and higher spiritual powers.[49] Later on, Crowley would assign the office of Scarlet Woman to others in their turn. These were typically distinguished by their ability to receive mysterious communications after intensive bouts of sexual activity with the Beast.[50]

Despite Crowley's protestations that "Energized Enthusiasm" depends more on ancient doctrines than on his own observations,[51] it seems apparent that his articulation of these methods owed much to his experiences in previous magical ceremonies. There are two excellent examples from the few years immediately preceding his 1912 composition of the essay. In the first case, he combined the musical and pharmaceutical methods. This work, which began in Dorset in 1910 with Leila Waddell and Commander Marston, involved Crowley reading poetry while Leila played violin, with all the participants under the influence of Crowley's "elixir." Crowley wrote, "We got such wonderful spiritual results that we tried to reduce all to a rule."[52] The later result of this creative environment was Crowley's Rites of Eleusis, a series of seven linked pieces of experimental theater offered to the paying public under the auspices of Crowley's magical order A.'.A.'.. The Rites were premised on planetary symbolism and included magical ceremonies, recitations of copious poetry written by Crowley and Swinburne, violin playing by Waddell, and ecstatic dancing by Victor Neuburg.[53] In the "Rite of Luna" that concluded the series, each audience member was served a "Cup of Libation" that contained fruit juice infused with a mild dose of opiates and peyote tincture.[54] Raymond Radclyffe, reporting for the *Daily Sketch*, seems to have been affected by these methods: after he had witnessed a good amount of "weird and impressive" ceremony and had drunk three Libations, Waddell's violin solo brought him to the point of believing that "most of us experienced that Ecstasy which Crowley so earnestly seeks."[55] In the manuscript of "Energized Enthusiasm," Crowley had written at one point regarding "the Rites of Eleusis," but he amended it to read "the ancient Rites of Eleusis," lest his readers confuse the classical mystery cult with his modern performances.[56]

A second case that must have influenced Crowley's theorizing was the "Ab-ul-Diz Working," which was, among other things, the inauguration of his second Scarlet Woman, Mary Desti. This magical undertaking was chiefly a hybrid of the sexual and pharmaceutical methods, and it took place in Switzerland in late 1911. Crowley and Desti were pursuing an ongoing sexual relationship, which had started at a London party and progressed through liaisons at her Paris apartment.[57] During their excursion to Switzerland, Desti began to have visions, initially surmised by Crowley to be "a morbid phenomenon due to over-excitement of Bacchus and Eros."[58] Crowley's rather hostile and sensationalistic biographer John Symonds writes that Crowley's attribution of her state to alcohol and sex "might have added with more truth, drugs,"[59] but there is actually no indication anywhere that Desti had consumed drugs other than alcohol at that point. Corroboration would be found in Crowley's own subsequently published private record of the Ab-ul-Diz Working, which is obviously the primary source for Symonds's account.[60] Desti's initial frenzy grew, under Crowley's guidance, into a series of four "operations" intended to exploit Desti's visionary state and permit her to communicate with an entity described as the wizard Ab-ul-Diz. Crowley asked Ab-ul-Diz—through Desti—"What shall I do to Seer? Shall she be 391 (*normal*) or under C_2H_6O or 31 (*Dr 4.*)?"[61] This sort of encryption was a standard procedure with Crowley, who sought to ensure that he would get answers from the adept in the vision, without interference from the conscious mind of the seer. He used "391" as a code for "normal," as he noted in the record, and he referred to alcohol by a chemical formula, trusting that Desti was unversed in chemistry. The third option "31" was a code for his peyote potion, abbreviated to AL (*Anhalonium lewinii*) and transliterated to the Hebrew אל, for which the *gematria*—or isopsephic sum value—was thirty-one. "*Dr 4*" apparently indicated his intention to administer four drops. But Ab-ul-Diz insisted that alcohol would be sufficient for future sessions. Accordingly, the record for the next operation specifies, "Seer being excited by half bottle of Pommery 1904, and by Eros." The major consequence of Desti's visions was to give Crowley the incentive to write something that Ab-ul-Diz called *Book Four*.[62] Produced in four parts issued from 1912 through 1936, this was to become Crowley's great textbook of occultism, in which he first used the word *magick* with a terminal *k* in order to distinguish his system from its competitors.[63]

These "theurgic" origins of Crowley's Rites of Eleusis and *Book Four*, among other experiences, must certainly have contributed to his theories of inspiration in "Energized Enthusiasm." But that essay includes a final section that provides a stylistic contrast to everything that has come before. Crowley's intellectualized discussion of the "classical methods" of enthusiasm is interrupted in what appears to be midstream, and he concludes with a long narrative describing a ritual to which an unnamed "distinguished poet" has fortuitously invited him. The two of them attend a ceremony in a secluded chapel with a couple dozen other initiates of the masonic Rose Croix degree, during which the three methods of Crowley's theories are applied. There is music from an unseen organ, and litanies are sung in Greek by the ritualists. There is a drug, in the form of a mysterious beverage drunk by all the attendees. And the presiding officers of the rite, a High Priest and Priestess, decorously copulate on a platform painted with a large cross while the chapel fills with perfumed purple smoke. At the end of this tale, Crowley gives a catalog of his subjective impressions in the resulting state of ecstasy, as he is alternately "lost to everything" and enraptured by explosions of presence and awareness.[64]

Crowley does not disclose any proper names or places regarding this ceremony, although his autobiography suggests that if the story is true, then the mysterious poet approached him while he was "hovering between London and Paris."[65] Paris might be more likely, in that Crowley remarks that his host "reads English fluently, though speaking but a few words." Crowley could have given the poet "the Word of Rose Croix" as described, since he was indeed an initiated Freemason holding that degree. Despite difficulties regarding the "regularity" of his membership with respect to the United Grand Lodge of England,[66] Crowley had been initiated to the ultimate thirty-third degree (33°) of the Scottish Rite in Mexico, and he was confirmed in his status as a high-grade initiate by masonic organizer and author John Yarker, who was a mason in good standing and the head of several other rites (albeit themselves of marginal legitimacy) in England.[67]

Still, one may certainly wonder whether the fabulous tale of this ceremony is genuine; the inclusion of masonic obligations of secrecy seems to conveniently eliminate any evidentiary data from the world of the profane. In fact, it appears that the portentous announcement of Crowley's introducer, "You are about . . . to compare your ideal with our real,"[68] actually *inverts* the status of the two parts of the essay. The first sections, with their long discussions of the sacramental "moral attitude" to be applied to the musical, pharmaceutical, and sexual methods,[69] owe at least as much to Crowley's own actual experiences and personal history as they do to the ancient theories to which he attributes them, whereas the final section appears to be an account of his imagined ideal, in which he gives literary vent to the frustrated impulse of this reasoned conclusion:

> The obvious practical step to take is to restore the rites of Bacchus, Aphrodite and Apollo to their proper place. They should not be open to every one, and manhood should be the reward of ordeal and initiation. . . . But I am only too well aware that such a picture is not likely to be painted. We can then only work patiently and in secret. We must select suitable material and train it in utmost reverence to these three master-methods, of aiding the soul in its genial orgasm.[70]

It is noteworthy that Crowley chose a masonic Rose Croix chapter for the secret setting of his ideal ceremony of enthusiasm. Such a chapter would have been a constituent body for the eighteenth degree of the Ancient and Accepted ("Scottish") Rite, or one of its high-grade predecessors or imitators. The three Christian theological virtues of Faith, Hope, and Charity were a principal focus for the 18° Rose Croix ritual in the English chapters of Crowley's day.[71] Intriguingly, this could involve a correlation to which Ficino alluded, in which the preeminence of the amatory frenzy was related to the priority of *caritas* in the thirteenth chapter of Paul's epistle to the Corinthians.[72] By situating the exemplar ritual of his essay in a Rose Croix chapter, Crowley may have intended to draw a connection between his triad of methods and the three virtues of the Rose Croix ritual, so that the place of Faith would be taken by Dionysus (formerly the mantic frenzy, and now the pharmaceutical method), Hope would be Apollo (the prophetic frenzy, become the musical method), and Charity would be Aphrodite (the erotic frenzy, now the sexual method). In this fashion, Crowley would conclude his essay with a parallel to his opening invocation, alluding cryptically to his threefold technique through the esoteric correspondences of high-grade Freemasonry and Rosicrucianism.

Having concluded in his essay, "By the use of the three methods in one the whole being of man may thus be stimulated,"[73] Crowley did indeed go on to apply the methods as an integrated technique in his subsequent undertakings. Perhaps the first such project of substance was the "Paris Working," a set of sex-magical rituals with the poet Victor Neuburg commencing on the first day of 1914. Although the ceremonies of the Paris Working were intended to invoke Mercury and Jupiter, the methods of Apollo, Dionysus, and Aphrodite were duly observed. For Apollo's music, there were at first thirty minutes or more of elaborate incantations in rhymed and metered English poetry to prepare the ritualists, under Crowley's rubric of "The Building of the Pyramid."[74] Then there were "The Holy Hymns to the Great Gods of Heaven," a variety of Latin verses composed by Crowley and Walter Duranty,[75] from which to select the one to be chanted repeatedly for the appropriate god during the ceremony. The "Hymn" for a given operation is usually referenced in the record as the "Versicle," and they all contained highly explicit sexual wording. For example, the usual versicle for Jupiter was as follows:

> *Haud secus ac puerum spumanti semini vates*
> *Lustrat; dum gaudens accipit alter aquas;*
> *Sparge, precor, servis, hominum rex atque deorum*
> *Juppiter omnipotens, aurea dona, tuis.*
>
> (And just as when the priest purifies the boy
> With foaming seed, while the other rejoicing accepts the waters,
> Sprinkle, I pray, Jupiter, king of gods and men, all powerful,
> Golden gifts upon thy servants.[76])

The vast majority of the twenty-four operations of the Paris Working involved at least an attempt at sex between the two men, and in many cases the act was brought to a climax. Regarding pharmaceutical considerations, the magicians were instructed to "drink yellow wine" by Hermes in the second operation of the working. Once more, in the eleventh operation, Jupiter directed that "one of the Brethren at least be reduced always to exhaustion by wine, and by the infliction of wounds, and by the ceremony itself."[77] They appear to have followed these instructions as well as they could. Symonds writes that for these rituals, "The brethren arrived in a receptive frame of mind, assisted by a good dinner with brandy or champagne and perhaps the drug proper to Hermes, anhalonium lewinii."[78] But as with the Ab-ul-Diz Working, there is no solid corroboration for the use of the latter drug from Crowley's subsequently published private records. In fact, the transcription of the eighth operation shows Neuburg's speculative remark "*Anhalonium* visions must be very similar to this."[79] There would be scant reason for the record to distort Neuburg's experience of the drug in a personal document that contained the much more damaging information about his sexual congress with Crowley. As Crowley summarized it in his autobiography, the magicians "obtained many astonishing results of many kinds, ranging from spiritual illumination to physical phenomena."[80] In the notes to his private record, the "General Result" shows satisfaction with having improved his own financial position, an assessment that Neuburg had received the qualities of hospitality from Jupiter (but that they were abused by his guests), and a speculation that the Paris Working was somehow related to the beginning of the Great War later that same year.[81] Crowley continued to practice his triple method of "theurgy" for the rest of his life, documenting in detail a wide variety of workings.

In "Energized Enthusiasm," an essay putatively composed for inclusion in the *English Review*, Crowley is at pains to discriminate the *use* of the three methods of enthusiasm from their *abuse*. He itemizes a list of acceptable conditions for sex, since its sacramental status "limits the employment of the organs,"[82] and he insists, "So consonant is this system [of the three methods] with the nature of man that it is exactly parodied and profaned not only in the sailor's tavern, but in the society ball."[83] While Crowley's lifelong position on these methods could be summed up with the biblical expression *παντα καθαρα τοις καθαροις*,[84] later writings reflect a relatively more libertarian or even antinomian standpoint. For example, as regards sexuality, he wrote over a decade later:

> There shall be no property in human flesh. The sex-instinct is one of the most deeply-seated expressions of the will; and it must not be restricted, either negatively by preventing its free function, or positively by insisting on its false function.[85]

When Crowley wrote "Energized Enthusiasm," he still believed that his unusual willpower made him immune to drug addiction.[86] Later, however, while struggling with his own recognized heroin addiction,[87] he still wrote:

> If you are really free, you can take cocaine as simply as salt-water taffy. There is no better rough test of a soul than its attitude towards drugs. If a man is simple, fearless, eager, he is all right; he will not become a slave. If he is afraid, he is already a slave. Let the whole world take opium, hashish and the rest; those who are liable to abuse them were better dead.[88]

In addition to his theories of the three methods, a prominent feature of "Energized Enthusiasm" is vitriol directed against Protestantism, which Crowley castigates as "the excrement of human thought" as well as a "consistently bestial interpretation of all things human and divine," and which he charges with having transformed sexuality into "vilenesses."[89] Having been raised among the ultra-Protestant Plymouth Brethren, for whom his father was a preacher, Crowley spent the remainder of his life in outspoken reaction to Christian moralism and pious superstition.[90] In an early manifesto for his cultural and magical agenda, he allied himself with the Neoplatonism of pagan antiquity in an overt attempt to champion a deep European tradition in opposition to what he saw as the degeneracy of modern Christianity.

> In a word, to-day Christianity is the irreligion of the materialist, or if you like, the sensualist; while in Paganism, we may find the expression of that ever-haunting love—nay, necessity!—of the Beyond which tortures and beautifies those of us who are poets.[91]

It is small wonder that in the generation after his death, Crowley came to figure as a prophet of rebellion for a counterculture that extolled "sex, drugs, and rock and roll" as the means to fulfillment. But it is instructive to see how he cast himself as the perpetuator of the ancient traditions of the Neoplatonists, a role that appealed to him in part for the leverage it afforded him in his taunting of Protestantism. His interpretation of the classical enthusiasms involved their considerable transformation. What had been four divine phenomena became three human practices. Yet if he were to be reproached for presenting a triad that no more resembled Plato's frenzies than it did the Christian Trinity, he might have responded with a mocking insistence that all of these concealed an identical wisdom from the exalted perspective of the adepts.

> Whoso has been crucified with Christ can but laugh when it is proved that Christ was never crucified. The historian understands nothing of what we mean, either by Christ or by crucifixion, and is thus totally incompetent to criticise our position. On the other hand, we are of course equally ill-placed to convert him; but then we do not wish to do so; certainly not *qua* historian. We leave him alone. Whoso hath ears to hear, let him hear! and the first and last ordeals and rewards of the Adept are comprised in the maxim "Keep silence!"[92]

Notes

1. Crowley highlights his relationship to these two figures in the opening sentence of an autobiographical brief: "Some six months after the death of Eliphas Levi Zahed, in the year (1875 E.V.) of the foundation of the Theosophical Society, was born a male child." Aleister Crowley, "The Master Therion: A Biographical Note," in "*The*

Equinox" III (10) (New York: 93 Publishing, 1990), 13. Crowley's itemized evidence for his status as Lévi's reincarnation is in his *Magick: Book 4: Liber ABA*, ed. Hymenaeus Beta (York Beach, Maine: Samuel Weiser 1994), 176–78.

2. Aleister Crowley, *The Confessions of Aleister Crowley: An Autohagiography*, ed. John Symonds and Kenneth Grant (London: Jonathan Cape, 1969), 701, 709–10.
3. On Crowley's Yoga studies in Asia, see ibid., 255–56; and Martin Booth, *A Magick Life* (London: Hodder & Stoughton 2000), 142–44. John Symonds, *The Magic of Aleister Crowley* (London: Frederick Muller, 1958), 97ff., alleges questionably that Crowley learned Tantra on his travels, and this is a topic of cardinal interest to Symonds's sometime collaborator and Crowley's student of that later period, occultist Kenneth Grant. Grant's own interest in Tantra was probably to blame for the fact that Crowley actually got around to mentioning it in his last book-length work, *Aleister Explains Everything* (published posthumously as *Magick without Tears*). Even then, Crowley merely wrote vaguely of having studied "numerous writings on the Tantra," among other sources of Indian lore. Aleister Crowley, *Magick without Tears*, ed. Israel Regardie (Tucson, Ariz.: New Falcon, 1991), 232. Grant's craving for Tantric instruction was finally satisfied by David Curwen, a full OTO initiate who had *not* received his Tantrism through OTO. This relationship is documented in Grant's correspondence memoir *Remembering Aleister Crowley* (London: Skoob 1991)—itself dedicated to Curwen, iii, 47–49.
4. Aleister Crowley, "Liber Porta Lucis sub figura X," in *The Holy Books of Thelema* (York Beach, Maine: Samuel Weiser, 1989), 16:40.
5. Aleister Crowley, "Eleusis (Epilogue and Dedication)," in *The Works of Aleister Crowley* (Foyers, Scotland: Society for the Propagation of Religious Truth 1907), 3:225.
6. Helena Petrovna Blavatsky, *Isis Unveiled*, vol. 2, *Theology* (New York: J. W. Brouton, 1877), praises the late Neoplatonists (40–41), alleges their influence on Christianity (84), distinguishes Neoplatonic theurgy from Spiritualist mediumism (118), and discusses the end of the Alexandrian school (252–54).
7. For example, the Golden Dawn initiation ritual for the Practicus $3^{\circ} = 8^{\square}$ grade included many quotes from the *Chaldean Oracles*, including fragments 32, 35, 133, 163–64, and 146–50. See the ritual in R. G. Torrens, *The Secret Rituals of the Golden Dawn* (New York: Samuel Weiser, 1973), 150–54.
8. Plato, *Phaedrus*, in *The Collected Dialogues, Including the Letters*, ed. Edith Hamilton and Huntington Cairns (Princeton, N.J.: Princeton University Press, 1961), 244–45, 265.
9. See, for example, Marsilio Ficino, "*De divino furore:* On Divine Frenzy," in *The Letters of Marsilio Ficino*, ed. Oskar Kristeller (Corte Madera, Calif.: Gingko Press, 1975).
10. Henry Cornelius Agrippa, *Three Books of Occult Philosophy*, trans. James Freake (London: Cthonios, 1986), bk. 3, chaps. 45–49, 499–508.

11. Bruno's principal exposition on the frenzies is contained in his *De gl' eroici furori*, where it is quite evident as early as the third dialogue of the first part. John Charles Nelson, *Renaissance Theory of Love: The Context of Giordano Bruno's "Eroici furori"* (New York: Columbia University, 1958), 174–80, provides citations and quotes supporting the debt of Bruno's texts to the *Phaedrus*. Similar, though less specific, claims are made in Frances Yates, *Giordano Bruno and the Hermetic Tradition* (1964; Chicago: University of Chicago Press, 1991), 272–73, 280–82.
12. Plato, *Phaedrus* 246a, 491.
13. Aleister Crowley, *The Book of Lies* (York Beach, Maine: Samuel Weiser, 1980), 26.
14. For these dates of authorship, see Crowley, *The Confessions*, 687.
15. *The Equinox* I (9) (1913), xxi.
16. Aleister Crowley and J. F. C. Fuller, "The Temple of Solomon the King," *The Equinox* I (1) (1909), 159–60. See also John Symonds, *The Great Beast*, rev. ed. (Frogmore, England: Mayflower, 1973), 115.
17. Iamblichus, *On the Mysteries of the Egyptians, Chaldeans and Assyrians*, trans. Thomas Taylor (London: Bertram Dobell, 1895), bk. 3, chaps. 4–9, 121–34ff.
18. Aleister Crowley, "Energized Enthusiasm: A Note on Theurgy," *The Equinox* I (9) (1913), 23.
19. Plato, *Phaedrus* 244a–d, 491.
20. Ibid. 265a, 510.
21. Aleister Crowley, *Crowley on Christ* [*The Gospel According to St. Bernard Shaw*], ed. Francis King. (1953; London: C. W. Daniel, 1974), 116.
22. Crowley, "Energized Enthusiasm," 22.
23. Ibid., 17–21.
24. Michael J. B. Allen, *The Platonism of Marsilio Ficino: A Study of His Phaedrus Commentary, Its Sources and Genesis* (Berkeley: University of California Press, 1984), 62.
25. Crowley, "Eleusis," 222.
26. Ibid., 229.
27. Crowley, "Energized Enthusiasm," 19.
28. Darcy Küntz, ed., *The Complete Golden Dawn Cipher Manuscript* (Edmonds, Wash.: Holmes, 1996), 174, gives the original source. Crowley's much more elaborate reception of it is demonstrated in the anonymous essay "Qabalistic Dogma," appended to the first volume of his *The Works of Aleister Crowley*, 1:265–68, and again in his summary of Golden Dawn materials in "The Temple of Solomon the King," *The Equinox* I (3) (1910), 208–12.
29. Douglas Knoop and G. P. Jones, *The Genesis of Freemasonry* (London: Q. C. Correspondence Circle, 1978), 283–84.
30. "The writing on the figurative veil of the HOLY ARCH, for those who have eyes to see, is: '*Sancta Trinitas unus Deus*.'" Arthur Edward Waite, *The Secret Tradition in Freemasonry* (London: Rider, 1937), 153.
31. Allen, *The Platonism of Marsilio Ficino*, 47–48.

32. The seventh recto page of Crowley's bound, unpaginated original manuscript "Energized Enthusiasm: A Note on Theurgy" (1912), Harry Ransom Humanities Research Center, University of Texas at Austin; compared with Plato, *Phaedrus* 265b, 511.
33. Crowley, "Energized Enthusiasm," 35–38.
34. Ibid., 23.
35. Ibid., 35–36.
36. Booth, *A Magick Life*, 325.
37. Crowley, *The Confessions*, 658.
38. Booth, *A Magick Life*, 308.
39. Crowley, "Energized Enthusiasm," 33–34.
40. Booth, *A Magick Life*, 285. For Crowley's detailed account of the full ceremony and its results, see Crowley, "The Bartzabel Working," in *The Vision and the Voice, with Commentary and Other Papers* (York Beach, Maine: Samuel Weiser, 1998).
41. Crowley, "Energized Enthusiasm," 37.
42. Symonds, *The Great Beast*, 151.
43. Ibid., 274; Booth, *A Magick Life*, 286.
44. Israel Regardie, *Roll Away the Stone: An Introduction to Aleister Crowley's Essays on the Psychology of Hashish* (St. Paul, Minn.: Llewellyn, 1968), 16–17; Symonds, *The Great Beast*, 39; Booth, *A Magick Life*, 101–2. For an example of Crowley's cocaine use from a Crowley-Bennett 1899 magical working, see Symonds, *The Magic of Aleister Crowley*, 105–6.
45. Regardie, *Roll Away the Stone*, 4; in the same book, Regardie reproduces Crowley's 1908 essay, 95–151.
46. Quoted in ibid., 54.
47. Booth, *A Magick Life*, 116.
48. Aleister Crowley, *The Scented Garden of Abdullah the Satirist of Shiraz* [*Bagh-i-muattar*], ed. Martin P. Starr (Chicago: Teitan Press, 1991). For additional context, see Symonds, *The Magic of Aleister Crowley*, 92.
49. Revelation 13 and 17, respectively.
50. Booth, *A Magick Life*, 183.
51. Crowley, "Energized Enthusiasm," 22.
52. Quoted in Booth, *A Magick Life*, 286. Compare also Symonds, *The Great Beast*, 151.
53. Crowley, *The Confessions*, 635–38; Symonds, *The Great Beast*, 152–53. The scripts for the Rites themselves were published as a supplement issued with *The Equinox* I (6) (September 1911).
54. Booth, *A Magick Life*, 287.
55. Quoted in ibid., 287–88.
56. Compare the eighth recto page of the original manuscript with the published version in *The Equinox* I (9) (1913), 24.
57. Booth, *A Magick Life*, 297–99.
58. Aleister Crowley, "The Ab-ul-Diz Working," in *The Vision and the Voice*, 300.

59. Symonds, *The Great Beast*, 155.
60. Compare Crowley, "The Ab-ul-Diz Working," with Symonds, *The Magic of Aleister Crowley*, 147–69, and Symonds, *The Great Beast*, 154–74. Crowley, *The Confessions*, 676–78, is, of course, a supplementary source, although much less detailed.
61. Crowley, "The Ab-ul-Diz Working," 323.
62. Ibid., 311–12; Crowley, *The Confessions*, 677; Symonds, *The Magic of Aleister Crowley*, 158.
63. Booth, *A Magick Life*, 301. The four parts of Crowley's *Book Four* (*Liber IV*), also known as *ABA* and most simply as *Magick*, were not issued in a single volume until 1994.
64. Crowley, "Energized Enthusiasm," 38ff.
65. Crowley, *The Confessions*, 687.
66. Booth, *A Magick Life*, 303.
67. Crowley, *The Confessions*, 628–29.
68. Crowley, "Energized Enthusiasm," 38.
69. Ibid., 28–34.
70. Ibid., 32–33.
71. Christopher McIntosh, *The Rosicrucians: The History, Mythology, and Rituals of an Esoteric Order*,3rd rev. ed. (York Beach, Maine: Samuel Weiser, 1997), 143, quotes at length from *The Text-Book of Advanced Freemasonry*, a particularly reliable late nineteenth-century exposure of English high-grade masonic ritual.
72. Marsilio Ficino, "Commentary on the *Phaedrus*," in Michael J. B. Allen, *Marsilio Ficino and the Phaedran Charioteer* (Berkeley: University of California Press, 1981), 84.
73. Crowley, "Energized Enthusiasm," 28.
74. A description with verbatim excerpts is in Symonds, *The Magic of Aleister Crowley*, 102–4.
75. Aleister Crowley, "The Paris Working," in *The Vision and the Voice*, 353.
76. Ibid., 406–7.
77. Ibid., 356, 380.
78. Symonds, *The Magic of Aleister Crowley*, 106.
79. Crowley, "The Paris Working," 374.
80. Crowley, *The Confessions*, 720.
81. Crowley, "The Paris Working," 398.
82. Crowley, "Energized Enthusiasm," 25.
83. Ibid., 28.
84. "To the pure, all things are pure." Crowley, "Eleusis," 220, citing Titus 1:15 without attribution.
85. Aleister Crowley, *The Law Is for All*, ed. Louis Wilkinson and Hymenaeus Beta (Tempe, Ariz.: New Falcon, 1996), 42.
86. Booth, *A Magick Life*, 336

87. Ibid., 379–82, 401–2, 458; Symonds, *The Great Beast*, 313–24.
88. Crowley, *The Law Is for All*, 110.
89. Crowley, "Energized Enthusiasm," 24, 27, 31.
90. Crowley, *The Confessions*, 36–57; Booth, *A Magick Life*, 3–20; Symonds, *The Great Beast*, 23–25.
91. Crowley, "Eleusis," 220–21.
92. Ibid., 221.

9

Aleister Crowley—Freemason?!

Martin P. Starr

IT MAY SURPRISE some and horrify others to learn that Aleister Crowley (1875–1947), the twentieth century's best-known mage, was ever remotely associated with Freemasonry. Although, unbeknownst to him at the time of joining, all his affiliations were with unrecognized and irregular bodies, Crowley's status as a Freemason went largely unquestioned—by non-masons—throughout his life. Events show that the distinctions of Regularity meant much to his masonic contemporaries and little to the rest, where Crowley's reputation as a Freemason preceded him, as when the Nazi Geheime Staatspolizei arrested Crowley's German disciple Karl Germer in February 1935 for the "crime" of being a friend of the "Hochgradfreimaurer Crowley." This essay examines Crowley's masonic contacts, Regular and otherwise, with the express purpose of separating the myths from the masonic realities, a task never previously attempted, and thereby elucidating the life of an influential figure in esoteric studies whose writings attract growing critical attention.

From Nesta Webster and the British fascist movement down to Lyndon LaRouche, Crowley's name and association with Freemasonry, much like that of Albert Pike, has been dragged in as a red herring in the "orgy of cant" that typifies the anti-masonic outpouring of right-wing conspiracy theorists. In a masonic context, Crowley is perhaps best remembered, like his nemesis A. E. Waite, as a literate early twentieth-century enthusiast of the esoteric school of masonic interpretation. Yet despite his interest in founding (if not running) organizations, Crowley was a social revolutionary and had little use for existing structures; this would prove to be his bane where English Freemasonry was concerned. Crowley's life was significantly affected by a number of masonic brethren whose careers have been the subjects of articles in recent volumes of *Ars Quatuor Coronatorum* (*AQC*), the journal of the Quatuor Coronati Lodge of Research No. 2076, including Dr. William Wynn Westcott (*AQC* 100 [1987], 6–32) and Theodor Reuss (*AQC* 91 [1978], 28–46), and some that could benefit from further scholarly attention, most prominent among them being John Yarker, whose Antient and Primitive Rite of Freemasonry devolved to the Ordo Templi Orientis (OTO), a non-masonic esoteric society now largely identified with Crowley's work. The present essay does not attempt to delineate the history of either organization, but refers to each in its place when Crowley attempted to obtain the recognition or involvement of the Regular masonic authorities.

Beginnings

Crowley was born Edward Alexander Crowley on October 12, 1875, in Leamington, Warwickshire, the son of prosperous Plymouth Brethren parents. He was educated privately, at schools run by the Plymouth Brethren, and finally at Tonbridge, to matriculate at Trinity College, Cambridge, in the fall term of 1895. There he was first able to step free of his family and their narrow intellectual atmosphere, which forbade virtually all literature. After reflecting on the limits of mortality and human endeavor, in a search for a method to explore the spiritual world, Crowley took up the study of medieval magic, starting with A. E. Waite's *The Book of Black Magic and of Pacts*. Crowley, intrigued by Waite's hinting that "he knew of a Hidden Church withdrawn from the world in whose sanctuaries were preserved the mysteries of initiation," wrote the author in the spring of 1898, asking for an introduction; Waite (who was not yet a mason) replied with the suggestion that Crowley read *The Cloud upon the Sanctuary* by Karl von Eckartshausen, an early nineteenth-century devotional text of "Rosicrucian" mysticism, and Crowley studied the work assiduously over the Easter vacation of 1898. A chance meeting in Switzerland later that year brought Crowley into contact with the Hermetic Order of the Golden Dawn, the fin de siècle's most influential English esoteric society.

Crowley's initiation into the grade of Neophyte of the Golden Dawn took place in the (second) Mark Mason's Hall, Great Queen Street, on November 26, 1898. In a real sense, this is Crowley's first distant brush with Freemasonry, as the Golden Dawn was created and led by an interlocking directorate of esoterically inclined Freemasons, with ritual and organizational structure closely modeled on the Craft and certain Appendant Bodies. The parallels and blatant borrowings (e.g., the scepters of the First and Third Principals in the masonic order of the Holy Royal Arch are used in the Golden Dawn rituals by the "Hierophant" and "Hegemon"), which seem so obvious to a contemporary masonic student, provoked little comment by Crowley, who took his initiation with deadly seriousness as his entry into the "Hidden Church of the Holy Grail."

By the time Crowley joined the Golden Dawn in 1898, Westcott had "withdrawn his labours" from both the First and Second Order the year prior owing to official pressure from the Home Office. Westcott also tired of the increasingly dictatorial methods of his colleague Samuel Liddell Mathers, fellow member of the Societas Rosicruciana in Anglia, Westcott's right hand in the creation of the Golden Dawn, and the sole author of its magically inclined "Rosicrucian" Second Order, Ordo Rosae Rubeae et Aureae Crucis. Crowley met Westcott in person only once, on April 17, 1900,[1] but he saw Mathers frequently and had a high regard for the latter's abilities as a magician and a scholar.

It is hardly surprising that when the London "adepti" began openly to turn against Mathers in early 1900, Crowley immediately pledged himself to Mathers's defense. Mathers, setting a fine example of masonic amity, proceeded to denounce Westcott privately for having forged the alleged correspondence with the German adepts upon whose foundation the warrant for the Golden Dawn was established. Crowley was sent to London as Mathers's envoy, and the whole fabric of the order began to unravel in the face of the accusations of fraud leveled against Westcott. As far as Crowley was concerned, the matter ended in April 1900 with the "Battle of Blythe Road," which reduced the Golden Dawn to a fight in a police court over regalia. Little did Crowley know, his part in the breakup of the Golden Dawn and his subsequent efforts to force Westcott to "come clean" publicly as to its origins made certain he would be shunned by Westcott's friends and colleagues when he was endeavoring to regularize his position in England as a mason.

Mexico City

On the advice of two unnamed members of the Golden Dawn whom he met in Mathers's company in Paris, Crowley set sail for Mexico in late June 1900. They are likely to have furnished Crowley with his introduction to

> Don Jesus Medina, a descendant of the great duke of Armada fame, and one of the highest chiefs of Scottish Rite free-masonry. My cabbalistic knowledge being already profound by current standards, he

> thought me worthy of the highest initiation in his power to confer; special powers were obtained in view of my limited sojourn, and I was pushed rapidly through and admitted to the thirty-third and last degree before I left the country.[2]

The "Supreme Grand Council, thirty-third, etc., etc., also for the world at large, founded by the Duke of Medina and Sidonia, Commander of the Spanish Armada"[3] was, in the words of masonic scholar John Hamill, "a minuscule irregular body," and the conferral of the 33° in Mexico City by Medina-Sidonia granted Crowley no regular masonic standing. Whatever documentation Medina-Sidonia furnished Crowley, no trace of it survives among Crowley's voluminous papers; my attempts to trace Medina-Sidonia's archives in Mexico have not met with success. The Golden Dawn connection to Medina-Sidonia seems likely, as the latter shared Crowley's interest in ritual magic; they worked together to establish a new order, the Lamp of Invisible Light, with Medina-Sidonia as its first high priest. Clearly the candidate was not impressed; Crowley comments on the conferral of the 33° that "it did not add much of importance to my knowledge of the mysteries; but I had heard that freemasonry was a universal brotherhood and expected to be welcomed all over the world by brethren."[4] Crowley was in for his first in a series of rude shocks where masonic recognition was concerned.

Paris

Shortly after his Mexican initiation, Crowley began to discuss Freemasonry with "some broken-down gambler or sporting-house tout," and he was refused recognition based on a difference in the grip. Crowley reacted with a "measureless contempt for the whole mummery." However, Crowley, who was a skilled amateur of chess and had planned a career in diplomacy, persisted and tried another gambit while he was resident in Paris in 1904 in his bid for masonic regularity. He petitioned Anglo-Saxon Lodge No. 343, a lodge chartered in 1899 by the Grande Loge de France, a body unrecognized by the United Grand Lodge of England and thus the majority of the regular masonic world, on June 29, 1904.

The petition gives his name as Aleister St. Edward Crowley, occupation poet. His petition was signed by the lodge's Secretary, the Reverend James Lyon Bowley, who was, according to Crowley, chaplain to the British embassy in Paris. Bowley had begun his masonic life as a regular mason; he was initiated in the Apollo University Lodge No. 357 in Oxford in October 1889 and resigned in 1899. He served as Provincial Grand Organist in the Provincial Grand Lodge of Oxfordshire for the year 1892.[5] One could see how Bowley's presence in the lodge could have led Crowley to believe it was Regular. There is no record of Bowley having any connection with English Freemasonry after 1899; the presumption is that Bowley resigned his connection with English Freemasonry when he joined Anglo-Saxon Lodge No. 343, in which he was the thirtieth member on its roll. Crowley's petition was countersigned by the Worshipful Master of Anglo-Saxon Lodge No. 343, Edward-Philip Denny, the seventh member on its roll.

Crowley was initiated on October 8, 1904, presumably passed the following month, and raised on December 17, 1904; he is listed in the "Tableau annuel" dated December 31, 1904, with the Grand Lodge number 41210, Lodge number 54. Crowley was "warmly welcomed by numerous English and American visitors to our Lodge," thus reinforcing his belief that all was masonically well. He wrote enthusiastically about his experience to his brother-in-law, Gerald Kelly, later president of the Royal Academy of Art:

> If you are not yet a Mason, it is worth your while to become one in a French lodge. Ask Bowley, who likes *Tannhäuser* [a long poem by Crowley], or says he does, and all sorts of sweet things.[6]

From the records made available for this essay, Crowley last appears as a member of Anglo-Saxon Lodge No. 343 in 1908. His name does not appear in the 1934 published list of members of the Grande Loge de France.

London and The Equinox

After Crowley returned to England in 1908, he began work on a serial publication titled *The Equinox*, in which he would at last carry out his plan to reveal the true history of the Golden Dawn and its founders. He wrote to W. Wynn Westcott on July 25, 1908 (letter in Private Collection "C"), demanding that Westcott deposit with the British Museum the "cipher manuscripts" upon which the Golden Dawn was founded or otherwise account for their reception and disposition if they were no longer within his care; without setting forth these facts publicly, Crowley averred that Westcott was party to an ongoing fraud. Crowley followed up this letter on October 24, 1908, with a call upon Westcott's associate in the Societas Rosicruciana in Anglia, Arthur Cadbury-Jones, with whom he had previously corresponded, and repeated his demands.[7] None of this could have endeared him to Westcott, who had both an official and a masonic reputation to uphold.

Crowley announced in *The Equinox* the publication of the Second Order ritual, which appeared in the March 1910 issue. Mathers sued Crowley to restrain publication, claiming to be the chief of the Rosicrucian Order. On his own initiative, Cadbury-Jones sent to all the daily newspapers an open letter under Westcott's signature, written from the Societas Rosicruciana in Anglia office, distancing it from the orders and parties in *Mathers v. Crowley*:

> I shall be glad if you will allow me space in your columns to state that the "Societas Rosicruciana in Anglia" is not connected with the "Rosicrucian Order" mentioned in a recent appeal in the High Courts, and that Mr. A. Crowley, neither is, nor ever was a member of this Society.[8]

Crowley in turn attempted to deflect some of the criticisms of his "brother masons" that he was an oath breaker in publishing the Golden Dawn ritual by claiming he did so in a good cause, and handed a laurel to Westcott in the process:

> I wish expressly to disassociate from my strictures on Mathers Brother Wynn Westcott his colleague; for I have heard and believe nothing which would lead me to doubt his uprightness and integrity. But I warn him in public, as I have (vainly) warned him in private, that by retaining the cipher MSS. of the Order, and preserving silence on the subject, he makes himself an accomplice in, or at least an accessory to, the frauds of his colleague.[9]

One can be certain this mollified Westcott not at all. Westcott was not one to be bullied by Crowley, and we will see that his influence could be far-reaching, at least in the *minutum mundum* of English Freemasonry.

Enter Reuss and Yarker

Mathers's defeat by Crowley and the attendant publicity resulted in the latter's being deluged by innumerable "sole authentic Chiefs of the Rosicrucian Order." One of the more persistent of these was Theodor Reuss, Frater Superior and Outer Head *in mundo* of the Ordo Templi Orientis.

The primary basis of Reuss's various fraternal enterprises, including the OTO, was a charter for a German Sovereign Sanctuary of the Antient and Primitive Rite issued September 24, 1902, by its Grand Hierophant 97°, John Yarker, to Reuss and two colleagues. When Reuss first came to call on Crowley in the spring of 1910,[10] he at once offered Crowley the VII° of the OTO, which was considered to be the equivalent of the 33°. By this time Crowley's interest in Freemasonry had cooled considerably, as he thought it "either vain pretense, tomfoolery, an excuse for drunken rowdiness, or a sinister association for political intrigues and commercial pirates."[11] Reuss attempted to convince Crowley that there were a few men who took Freemasonry seriously and, more important, that the rites concealed profound magical secrets.

No doubt Reuss spread the good word about Crowley to John Yarker, who sent his *Arcane Schools* to Crowley for review. The review, which appeared in the September 1910 issue of *The Equinox*, was written with the usual Crowleyan flourish toward those he wished to praise. It contains these sentiments, pregnant with the assumptions of the Esoteric School of Freemasonry and a precursor of what was to come:

> He [Yarker] has abundantly proved his main point, the true antiquity of some Masonic system. It is a parallel to Frazer's tracing the history of the Slain God.
>
> But why is there no life in any of our Slain God rituals? It is for us to restore them by the Word and the Grip.
>
> For use, who have the inner knowledge, inherited or won, it remains to restore the true rites of Attis, Adonis, Osiris, of Set, Serapis, Mithras and Abel.[12]

Yarker, old and with few allies left alive, welcomed Crowley with open arms, gladly recognizing his Mexican 33° and granting him an honorary membership patent dated November 13, 1910[13] in the Antient and Primitive Rite of the irregular "Cerneau" Scottish Rite, the legitimacy of whose claims Yarker had argued in print for decades. In addition, Yarker granted the equivalent degrees in the other "fringe" rites he controlled, the 95° of the Rite of Memphis and the 90° of the Rite of Misraim. Between Yarker and Reuss, there must have been enough links to cover the world of irregular masonry, so much so that Crowley found:

> From this time on I lived in a perfect shower of diplomas, from Bucharest to Salt Lake City.[14] I possess more exalted titles than I have ever been able to count. I am supposed to know more secret signs, tokens,

> passwords, grand-words, grips, and so on, than I could actually learn in a dozen lives. An elephant would break down under the insignia I am entitled to wear. The natural consequence of this was that, like Alice when she found the kings and queens and the rest showering upon her as a pack of cards, I woke up.[15]

Reuss again visited Crowley in the spring of 1912, claiming that Crowley had clearly published the central secret of the IX° of the OTO and must be obligated to secrecy. After some persuasion, Crowley took him seriously, and Reuss immediately proceeded to issue a charter dated April 21, 1912,[16] in the name of "Aleister St. Edward Crowley, 33°, 90°, 95°, X°," styling him National Grand Master General for Great Britain and Ireland, with the British section to be denominated Mysteria Mystica Maxima.

Yarker, perhaps anticipating his demise, gave Crowley a further "Dispensation" dated August 7, 1912, "to take precedence of all previously constituted Authorities with special power to revive the dormant Mount Sinai and Rose of Sharon,"[17] two London chapters of the Antient and Primitive Rite. It was perhaps at Yarker's insistence, considering that a mason of the Antient and Primitive Rite was supposed to be "a member of a Lodge in good standing, working under a Grand Lodge of Free and Accepted Masons,"[18] that Crowley once again tried to establish a connection with regular masonry.

Crowley at Great Queen Street

Crowley came to call on August 19, 1912, on W. J. Songhurst, Secretary of the Quatuor Coronati Lodge; it is not clear from his letter, typed on stationery with the return address of 52, Great Queen Street, if their meeting was at the Quatuor Coronati office or elsewhere. It is significant that Songhurst felt it prudent to give "due and timely notice" to Westcott:

> You will be interested to know that I had a call yesterday from Aleister McArthur [*sic*] Crowley. He produced a Certificate, showing that he is a member of the Anglo-Saxon Lodge, warranted in Paris by the Grand Lodge of France. He is desirous of joining an English Lodge, but I told him plainly that as far as I am concerned, I should refuse his admission to any English Lodge with which I am connected. I recommended that he should see the Grand Secretary in order to get official information, and he promised to do so. But when I called there later in the day I

> found that he had already made enquiries early last week, and that the information there given exactly coincided with mine.[19]

It is not certain if these incidents are the same ones Crowley refers to in his *English Review* article "The Crisis in Freemasonry," written under the pseudonym of "a Past Grand Master," where the story has rather a different ending:

> I returned to England some time later, after "passing the chair" in my Lodge [Anglo-Saxon Lodge No. 343], and, wishing to join the Royal Arch, called on its venerable secretary.
>
> I presented my credentials. "O Thou Grand Architect of the Universe!" the old man sobbed out in rage, "why dost Thou not wither this impudent impostor with Thy fire from heaven? Sir, begone! You are not a Mason at all! As all the world knows, the people in Z— [Paris] are atheists and live with other men's wives."
>
> I thought this a little hard on my Reverend Father in God my proposer [Rev. J. L. Bowley]; and I noted that, of course, every single English or American visitor to our Lodge in Z— stood in peril of instant and irrevocable expulsion on detection. So I said nothing, but walked to another room in Freemasons' Hall over his head, and took my seat as a Past Master in one of the oldest and most eminent Lodges in London![20]

It is surely not the first time an unauthorized visitor crossed the threshold of a lodge in Great Queen Street, but it is difficult to imagine what Crowley thought he gained by this maneuver, as the recognition he sought still eluded him. One wonders if Crowley ever connected his being shut out of English Freemasonry to his behavior toward Westcott, who undoubtedly had many defenders. But Crowley did not take his Golden Dawn motto of *Perdurabo* (I shall endure) lightly, and he was destined to try one more time to obtain masonic recognition in his native country.

Exit Yarker, Enter Mrs. Besant?

The death of John Yarker on March 20, 1913, pitted Crowley against the Co-Masonic Theosophists for the corpse of the Antient and Primitive Rite. The stage was set for the conflict when the 1912 "Jubilee" edition of *Oriflamme*, the official organ of the OTO and the German Sovereign Sanctuary of the Antient and Primitive Rite, announced that at Yarker's request "Brother J. J.

[*sic*] Wedgwood" was made "an honorary Master Mason and attached him to the Lodge 'Holy Grail' in Munich as an honorary member." James Ingall Wedgwood was many things, among them the Very Illustrious Supreme Secretary to the British Federation of the Co-Masonic Order, led by its Very Illustrious Most Puissant Grand Commander, Mrs. Annie Besant. Word had come to Crowley that the Co-Masons had claimed to have "bought" the Antient and Primitive Rite and were going to turn it into a vehicle for the worship of the "Coming Christ" or Alcyone, better known as Krishnamurti.

Richard Higham, a longtime member of the Antient and Primitive Rite, convoked a meeting of its Sovereign Sanctuary in his home city of Manchester on June 28, 1913. Crowley protested the presence of Wedgwood, whom he challenged to prove himself a mason; Wedgwood replied with the mildness of a clergyman that if Crowley was right in his contention that Wedgwood was no mason, that Wedgwood was equally entitled to object to Crowley's presence, "it being the first condition of membership that a candidate should be a freemason in good standing under the jurisdiction of the Grand Lodge of England."[21] After a diatribe by Crowley, attacking Besant, "the nominal mistress" of the Theosophical Society, and her occult partner C. W. Leadbeater, "a senile sex-maniac" who is "the hand which moves the wooden-headed pawn Wedgwood, hardly a man, certainly no Mason,"[22] the meeting disbanded, to regroup at Crowley's London studio on June 30, 1913, without Wedgwood and without incident, electing Henry Meyer to replace Yarker as Sovereign Grand Master General of the Rite. This convocation marks the effective terminus for the Antient and Primitive Rite, for it was Crowley's intent to consolidate all the "bodies of initiates" into the system of the OTO, and he quickly lost all interest in Yarker's rite. But there remained that nagging matter of masonic recognition, so Crowley strove for the last time to obtain the approval of the United Grand Lodge of England.

Great Queen Street, Round 2

In the midst of his conflict with the Co-Masons, Crowley attempted to strengthen his own hand while raising another against his Theosophical opponents by calling upon Sir Edward Letchworth, Grand Secretary of the United Grand Lodge of England, in these terms:

> I wish to appeal to the fraternal Brothers of the Lodge of England in the following circumstances. I was made a Master Mason December 17,

> 1904 in Lodge 343 Anglo-Saxon in Paris, working under the Grand Lodge of France. My proposer was the Rev J. L. Bowley, who I understand has been the Provincial Grand Officer in the Oxford Province, and I fully understood from him that the Anglo-Saxon Lodge was duly recognized by the Grand Lodge of England, and in fact numbers of admitted English Masons have attended the Lodge while on the other hand I have always been received with the greatest fraternal welcome in many lodges both in England and India, and no question has been raised as to my status except in the Grand Chapter of the Royal Arch at Freemasons' Hall. I must admit that at that time I was annoyed by what seemed to me a narrow-minded view of masonry. As the Ritual of my initiation was that in use all over England, and no such alteration of landmarks had taken place as that which has caused the breach between the G[rand] Lodge of England and the G[rand] Orient. And I shall consequently prepare to support the G[rand] L[odge] of France in its claim to the validity of its initiations. I am now, however, credibly informed that recently the Grand Lodge of France has tolerated and even recognized so-called co-masonry, and in these circumstances I see no course open to me but to resign from that Lodge, not only on masonic grounds, but because co-masonry is merely a mask for the cult of "Alcyone," which I have no hesitation in describing as the most impudent blasphemy and filthy fraud that has ever been attempted in the history of the world.
>
> I write to assure you of my thorough loyalty and allegiance to the principles of the Grand Lodge of England and I ask your fraternal kindness to make it as easy as possible for me to regularize my position.[23]

The reply to this letter is no longer in the archives of the United Grand Lodge of England, but it could not have been helpful. Crowley's later writings show no awareness of the establishment on November 5, 1913, of the Grande Loge Nationale Indépendente et Réguliere pour la France et les Colonies Françaises, now known as Grande Loge Nationale Française. This Regular body was recognized with alacrity by the United Grand Lodge of England on December 3, 1913. Crowley's approach could not have come at a less politically opportune time.

The question remains, what could Crowley have expected to gain from his sudden partial capitulation to established authority? The United Grand Lodge of England at that time had a growing concern about Co-Masonry, but it surely did not need or want Crowley as an ally. Some may see in this letter more than a measure of hypocrisy used to Machiavellian purposes. Crowley insisted that the OTO in no way infringed on "the just privileges of duly authorized Masonic Bodies"—the words chosen to allow plenty of room for future hairsplitting if needed.[24] In truth, although the OTO admitted men and women on an equal basis, unlike Co-Masonry, its rituals and teachings were not those of any regular masonic body, and on this basis it could have been cleared of the charges of being a clandestine masonic organization.

On the same date of his letter to Sir Edward, Crowley wrote to Edward-Philip Denny of Anglo-Saxon Lodge No. 343, asking if the lodge might secede from the Grande Loge de France in the face of its toleration of Co-Masonry and seek the recognition of the United Grand Lodge of England; Denny's answer, if he made one, does not survive in Crowley's papers.[25]

"Sole and Supreme Authority"

Having failed to establish himself masonically, and being incapable of obtaining any masonic recognition in England for the Antient and Primitive Rite, which had been opposed with vigor since its inception in 1872 by the Supreme Council 33° for England and Wales, Crowley abandoned the unequal contest of authority by retreating to a high ground he could fashion after his own lights, namely, the OTO. It could well be argued that Crowley absent Yarker was not greatly interested in Freemasonry per se, but found its forms and methods useful for his own purposes, as has been true for many other organizers of esoteric societies. But in the OTO he had an authority unimaginable in Regular Freemasonry, even though Reuss was its nominal head, and he continued to develop the work of this order without let or hindrance during his American period (1914–1919). Crowley had its candidates swear to acknowledge him as "the sole and supreme authority in Freemasonry"[26] without fear of contradiction, though it is only with difficulty that one could imagine Reuss, who constitutionally was the autocrat of the OTO, consenting to the wording.

During World War I, Crowley and his few North American disciples tried to establish the OTO first in Vancouver, British Columbia, and later in Detroit, Michigan, where his faithful follower Charles Stansfeld Jones lectured to groups on occult subjects and succeeded in interesting a few local masons.[27] On the invitation of the latter, Crowley visited Detroit in April 1919 and again in the fall of that year. His reminiscence of the work in Detroit casts light on Crowley's final view of the relationship between the OTO and Freemasonry:

> The accounts of the new Rite made a great impression; and in particular, attracted the attention of the Supreme Grand Council, Sovereign Grand Inspectors General of the 33rd and Last Degree of the Scottish Rite in the Valley of Detroit, Mich. . . . I was therefore invited to Detroit, and a series of conferences was held. A Supreme Grand Council of the 7th Degree of the O.T.O. was formally initiated.
>
> However, when it came to the considerations of the practical details of the rituals to be worked, the general Council of the Scottish Rite could not see its way to tolerate them, on the ground that the symbolism in some places touched too nearly that of the orthodox Masonry of the Lodges. . . .
>
> In order to meet these views, it was suggested that I should re-write the rituals in an entirely new symbolism, which would in no way be considered as in competition with the accepted ritual of the Craft.[28]

Crowley had completed only a revision of the first four rituals of the OTO when the "Great Lakes Council VII°" fell apart in a swirl of divorces and bankruptcies, ending with Crowley's departure for England in December 1919. It was the last attempt Crowley made to align his order to Regular Freemasonry in any manner. From 1920 to the end of his life in 1947, Crowley did not involve himself personally in Freemasonry or seek the support of any regular masonic authority for the OTO. He deigned to let the masonic trappings of the Antient and Primitive Rite—with its numerous degrees tedious in the extreme to his mind—fade into a dim historical past. Crowley would agree to confer the degrees of the Antient and Primitive Rite, if pressed, only upon Regular masons, and there was little demand for them.[29]

Conclusion

It should not be surprising that a person of radical stripe such as Crowley would not have found a home in English Freemasonry. From John Yarker to Theodor Reuss to Aleister Crowley—he is the last in a line of transmission of what the English masonic scholar Ellic Howe termed "Fringe Masonry," a phenomenon we are unlikely to witness again in Britain or the United States, given the close relations between the recognized Grand Lodges and appendant masonic bodies. From Yarker, Crowley received an alternative narrative of the sources of masonic legitimation along with an abiding distrust in the accepted authorities and a willingness to set himself up in their place. Crowley's ringing endorsements of the "Cerneau" Scottish Rite and his denunciations of the legitimate Supreme Councils derived from the Southern Jurisdiction of the United States of America, which he derisively terms the "Pike Rite," are a distinct echo of Yarker. From Reuss, he received the sanction to mix sex, religion, and social experimentation with the irregular masonic rites they claimed to control. Reuss's involvement with the Ascona Community in Switzerland during World War I forms an interesting parallel to Crowley's "Abbey of Thelema" in Sicily (1920–1923). Out of his combined inheritances from Yarker and Reuss, Crowley distilled his own esoteric, non-masonic organization, which retains a respectful attitude toward Freemasonry and even includes Regular masons among its members, although no longer affiliating them directly to the corresponding degree.

In conclusion, it may be illuminating to consider the following passage. In it do we find a reflection of what utility Crowley the mage and revolutionary saw in Freemasonry?

> When a man becomes a magician he looks about him for a magical weapon; and being probably endowed with that human frailty called laziness, he hopes to find a weapon ready made....
>
> Wagner illustrates this point very clearly in *Siegfried*. The Great Sword Nothung has been broken, and it is the only weapon that can destroy the gods. The dwarf Mime uselessly tries to mend it. When Siegfried comes he makes no such error. He melts its fragments and forges a new sword. In spite of the intense labour which this costs, it is the best plan to adopt.[30]

Notes

An earlier form of this paper was published in *Ars Quatuor Coronatorum* 108 (1995).

1. An undated note by Westcott in Private Collection "C," described by R. A. Gilbert in *The Golden Dawn Companion* (Wellingborough, England: Aquarian Press, 1986), 176, reads: "1900. April 17 Crowley called on me as Mathers friend."
2. Aleister Crowley, *The Confessions of Aleister Crowley*, ed. John Symonds and Kenneth Grant (London: Jonathan Cape, 1969), 202–3.
3. "At Daggers' Point," *New York Sunday Mercury*, July 29, 1883; quoted in *The Kneph* 3, no. 9 (September 1883), 69.
4. Crowley, *The Confessions*, 695.

5. John Hamill of the United Grand Lodge of England graciously supplied the details of Bowley's involvement in English Freemasonry (private communication, October 20, 1986).
6. Letter from Aleister Crowley to Gerald Kelly, undated but c. 1904, G. J. Yorke Collection, Warburg Institute, University of London.
7. Cadbury-Jones details their meeting in a note dated October 24, 1908, Private Collection "C"; it is clear from this note that neither Westcott nor Cadbury-Jones was amused or frightened by Crowley's increasing pressure.
8. Letter, March 24, 1910, Private Collection "C."
9. *The Equinox* I (4) (September 1910), 5–6.
10. There is possible evidence of Reuss being aware of Crowley's work prior to 1910. *Allgemeine Satzungen des Ordens der Orientalischen Templer O.T.O.* (dated January 1906) has on its cover a simplified version of the lamen designed by Crowley around March 1907 and used on the case of Captain J. F. C. Fuller's book on "Crowleyanity," *The Star in the West* (1907); of course, the Reuss publication may well be backdated.
11. Crowley, *The Confessions*, 628.
12. *The Equinox* I (4) (September 1910), 240.
13. Reproduced in Crowley, *The Confessions*, facing page 481.
14. Crowley had some contact with the notorious fraud and degree-monger Mathew Mc Blain Thomson and his "American Masonic Federation," headquartered in Salt Lake City, Utah.
15. Crowley, *The Confessions*, 629.
16. Reproduced in Lady Queensborough [Edith Starr Miller], *Occult Theocrasy* (Abbeville: privately printed, 1934), vol. 2, app. 4, ill. 11.
17. The "Dispensation" itself does not appear to survive; what we have are Crowley's abstracts from it in various letters and a parallel document issued in 1942 to Crowley's successor as Outer Head of the Ordo Templi Orientis, Karl Germer.
18. [John Yarker], *Constitutions, General Statutes and Ordinances of the Sovereign Sanctuary of the Antient and Primitive Rite of Masonry in and for the United Kingdom of Great Britain and Ireland . . .* (1875), 15.
19. Letter from W. J. Songhurst to W. Wynn Westcott, August 20, 1912, Private Collection "C."
20. Aleister Crowley [A Past Grand Master], "The Crisis in Freemasonry," *English Review* 35 (August 1922), 127–34. The corrected page proofs are in the Yorke Collection, where the title appears as "Are You a Mason?," perhaps inspired by the contemporary silent film of the same name. The article is extensively quoted and paraphrased in Crowley, *The Confessions*, 695–710.
21. Crowley, *The Confessions*, 711.
22. [Aleister Crowley], "Report of the Proceedings at Manchester, with a Note on the Circumstances which led up to them," *The Equinox* I (10) (September 1913), xxix.

23. Letter from Aleister Crowley to Sir Edward Letchworth, transcribed from a shorthand draft dated June 27, 1913, Yorke Collection.
24. "As a lawyer you will appreciate the words 'Just' and 'duly authorized'; for that leaves us a loophole if at any time we become strong enough to tell the Grand Lodge of England to do what the old man of Newcastle did when he was so requested. But at the present moment it would simply be silly to make ourselves enemies in influential, however imbecile, quarters. I was extremely annoyed with Yarker when, in senile decay, he visited a Co-Masonic Lodge." Letter from Aleister Crowley to Hugh George de Willmott Newman, August 15, 1944, Yorke Collection.
25. Crowley's proffered cure for irregularity was ahead of its time; in 1964, a portion of the membership of Anglo-Saxon Lodge No. 343 left the Grande Loge de France and reconstituted as Anglo-Saxon Lodge No. 103 under the Grande Loge Nationale Française.
26. See the "Preliminary Pledge-Form of M.·.M.·.M.·." (n.d. but c. 1913); copies are preserved in the Yorke Collection.
27. Jones was raised in Detroit Lodge No. 2, Free and Accepted Masons of the State of Michigan, on April 27, 1920, after Crowley's return to England.
28. Letter from Aleister Crowley to Arnold Krumm-Heller, June 22, 1930, private collection.
29. A notable example is the case of George H. Brook, William Bernard Crow, and Hugh George de Willmott Newman, all "episcopi vagantes," who unsuccessfully attempted in 1944–1945 to have Crowley charter them to confer the combined degrees of the Rites of Memphis and Misraim.
30. Aleister Crowley, introduction to his translation of *The Key of the Mysteries (La Clef des Grands Mystères)* by Eliphas Lévi, *The Equinox* I (10) (September 1913), supplement, viii–ix.

10

"*The One Thought That Was Not Untrue*"

ALEISTER CROWLEY AND A. E. WAITE

Robert A. Gilbert

1898 WAS A good year for armchair magicians, who were spoiled for choice between two textbooks of magic, both of them impressive quartos, appropriately bound in black cloth and aimed deliberately at a self-perceived elite among occultists. The first to appear, in February, was S. L. Mathers's *The Book of the Sacred Magic of Abra-Melin the Mage*, a singular ritual text for the truly dedicated magus—provided he could get past the stilted prose of the prospectus, which suggested, inter alia, that "little doubt need be felt that the present volume will be well received by those earnest Students of Occultism who form a large and ever-increasing factor in the ranks of the reading public."[1]

Hard on the heels of this uninspiring prospectus came another, printed in red and black, with Gothic type for the titles of the grimoires in the book that it offered: a book more dramatic and more decadent than *Abra-Melin*, nothing less than *The Book of Black Magic and of Pacts*. The author was A. E. Waite, already far better known than was Mathers, and there was the added lure of a special subscription price.[2]

It seems unlikely that Crowley, who was yet to launch himself onto the sea of occultism, would have come upon a prospectus for either book by chance, but it is highly probable that George Redway, the astute publisher of Waite's book, sent his prospectus to the principal booksellers in the university towns and major cities of Great Britain. If Crowley was, as he claims, already actively seeking for works on black magic, then Deighton, Bell and Co., at that time the foremost Cambridge booksellers, would have known just what to offer him. We know from Crowley's *Confessions* that they did, that he bought the book, and that he read it. What happened next is less clear.

Crowley later recalled writing to Waite about a passage in the book that was "an oracular obscurity which hinted that he knew of a Hidden Church withdrawn from the world in whose sanctuaries were preserved the true mysteries of initiation."[3] He professed, however, to being unable and unwilling to recall or identify the specific passage that led him to seek this information: "I cannot," he wrote, "dig over the dreary deserts of his drivel in search of the passage which made me write to him."[4] This suggests that in 1929 Crowley no longer owned or had access to a copy of *The Book of Black Magic*, for the seductive paragraph comes very early in the book, on page 11:

> All students of occultism are perfectly well aware of the existence in modern times of more than one Mystical Fraternity, deriving, or believed to derive, from other associations of the past. There are, of course, many unaffiliated occultists, but the secret Fraternities exist, and the keys of mystic symbolism are said to be in their possession.[5]

At the time Waite replied to his then unknown correspondent, "kindly and intelligibly, suggesting that I should read *The Cloud upon the Sanctuary* by Councillor von Eckartshausen. With this book I retired to Wastdale Head for the Easter vacation of 1898."[6] What he found in *The Cloud upon the Sanctuary* was a series of enticing accounts of a hidden Mystery School within Christianity, described variously by the author as "the interior Church," "the invisible celestial Church," and "that illuminated Community of God." And more than this, Crowley would also have read the comments of the translator, Madame Isabelle de Steiger, and of J. W. Brodie-Innes, who wrote the preface. Madame de Steiger associated it with the kabbalah and with the Rosicrucians, while Brodie-Innes suggested that the "Interior Church" was quite compatible with occultism and with Eastern doctrines. This was a far cry from both orthodox Christianity and the ideas of von Eckartshausen, but by 1896—when the book was published—both de Steiger and Brodie-Innes were senior members of the Hermetic Order of the Golden Dawn, and their views did reflect the ideas and ethos of that order.

Twelve years later, in his review of the third edition of *The Cloud upon the Sanctuary* for *The Equinox*, Crowley announced, "It was this book which first made your reviewer aware of the existence of a secret mystical assembly of saints, and determined him to devote his whole life, without keeping back the least imaginable thing, to the purpose of making himself worthy to enter that circle."[7] How he did so is well recorded, but it involved no return to the works of A. E. Waite. In the summer of 1898 Crowley met a mountaineering chemist, Julian Baker, who discussed alchemy with him and introduced him to George Cecil Jones, another chemist and fellow member of the Golden Dawn. Jones recommended that Crowley read and follow the process of *The Book of the Sacred Magic of Abra-Melin the Mage*, which he set about to do. Impressed by his dedication, the two chemists then introduced Crowley to the Golden Dawn, which he entered as a Neophyte at 2:00 P.M. on November 26, 1898,[8] thus beginning his career within "occult fraternities."

Waite had been a member of the Golden Dawn since January 1891, but had left the order temporarily in 1893 to be "Re-admitted by ballot" on February 17, 1896. He did not attain the grade of Adeptus Minor until March 3,1899, and as he seems to have attended meetings only infrequently, it is probable that he was not present for Crowley's admission. There is, indeed, no evidence that he ever knowingly met Crowley, either within or without the Golden Dawn, or that he read any of Crowley's works.[9] But Crowley freely and fully, albeit reluctantly, acknowledged his debt to Waite. In a letter to Louis Wilkinson (December 30, 1944), he wrote:

> Waite certainly did start a revival of interest in Alchemy, Magic, Mysticism, and all the rest. That his scholarship was so contemptible, his style so over-loaded, and his egomania so outrageous does not kill to the point of extinction, the worth of his contribution. If it had not been for Waite, I doubt if, humanly speaking, I should ever have got in touch with the Great Order. . . . Waite occupies a position not unlike that of Samuel Johnson. There is an omnivalence about him, which did just what was necessary at the time.

Despite this grudging respect, Waite subsequently became a bête noir for Crowley. His frequent attacks on Waite's writing, scholarship, and character that are scattered throughout the first volume of *The Equinox* are hysterical and almost paranoid in their intensity. As satire they fail, because they are inordinately long and obsessional in their textual analysis, and they simply puzzle the unbiased reader. Why Crowley indulged in these seemingly pointless attacks is a matter of conjecture.[10]

Waite's literary style is an easy target—and, to some extent, a legitimate one, given Waite's predilection for using ten words where one would be enough—but attacks on his scholarship are less easy to maintain. There are certainly mistakes in some of Waite's translations of the works of Eliphas Lévi, but these are found largely in his first essay in translating Lévi, *The Mysteries of Magic* (1886), not in the more important works, *Transcendental Magic* and *The History of Magic*. Waite also translated complete texts, unlike Crowley, who gives no indication in *The Key of the Mysteries*, his English version of *La clef des grands mystères*, in which he points out Waite's errors with great glee, that he has omitted more than one-third of the book, while giving over his "Translator's Note" to deriding Waite's understanding of French.[11]

Waite was far better informed than Crowley as a historian and analyst of Freemasonry, of alchemy, of the kabbalah, and of the Holy Grail, although his lack of a formal education led to the peculiar literary style that has made an appreciation of his insights into "rejected knowledge" difficult for some scholars.[12] He also had a far better grasp than Crowley did of the ethos of Freemasonry, perhaps because he never went outside the confines of masonic regularity. This enabled him to interact with other masonic scholars and to eschew the unhistorical reveries of such men as John Yarker while following his own path with regard to masonic spirituality. Crowley, however, had no concern for the niceties of masonic behavior (although he happily garnered a large number of irregular masonic and quasi-masonic affiliations that were of minimal masonic worth, and largely meaningless to both members and outsiders of the bodies in question) and, lacking a knowledge of masonic history, chose to laud Yarker's misguided speculations while vilifying Waite.[13] Not that Waite was alone in being derided, for Crowley also dismissed English Freemasonry as a whole: "I have yet to meet an English freemason who knows what the word freemason means, or how it should be spelt."[14]

Crowley was also scornful about Waite as a Rosicrucian. In "Dead Weight," his mocking pseudo-obituary of Waite, he pointed out that although Waite had been initiated in the Hermetic Order of the Golden Dawn, he had not been invited to enter the inner order, and so wrote *The Real History of the Rosicrucians*, in which he had

> proved conclusively that there were no Rosicrucians and never had been, and that if any moderns claimed to be Rosicrucians there was "that difference between their assertion and the facts of the case in which the essence of a lie consists." No sooner had he published these remarks (amid general applause) than it was gently broken to the future saint that the liars he had been denouncing were his own occult chiefs, of whom he had been writing (elsewhere) in language which out-Mahatmaed the most eloquent-mysterious Theosophists.[15]

This was, to say the least, disingenuous. The passage containing these remarks on the Rosicrucians is preceded by a scurrilous account of another of Waite's books, *Devil Worship in France*, which appeared in 1896, with the explicit claim that the Rosicrucian work was a later publication. It was not. As Crowley well knew, *The Real History of the Rosicrucians* had been published in 1887: nine years before *Devil Worship in France* and four years before Waite entered the Golden Dawn.

Despite the frequent distortion of facts and the steady stream of invective directed at Waite, Crowley did openly praise Waite for his achievements in one field. "I have always held Arthur Edward Waite for a good poet," he wrote, "I am not sure that he is not a great poet; but that he is a great mystic there can be no manner of doubt."[16] In a review of one of Waite's earlier volumes of poetry he noted: "Mr. Waite is a really excellent poet withal. All the poems show fine and deep thought, with facility and felicity of expression. 'The Lost Word' is extraordinarily fine, both dramatically and lyrically."[17] Many years later, in "Campaign against Waite," an unpublished part of his *Confessions*, Crowley also stated that "as a poet his [Waite's] genius was undeniable."

Waite does not seem to have reciprocated with either praise or blame for Crowley's poems, although he was certainly aware of them, for the only occasion on which the work of both men was published together was in an anthology of poetry—edited by two former members of Waite's Independent and Rectified Rite of the Golden Dawn. *The Oxford Book of English Mystical Verse*, chosen by D. H. S. Nicholson and A. H. E. Lee,[18] appeared at the end of 1916 and received a very favorable reception. Among esoteric journals that noticed the book were *The Occult Review*, in which the anonymous reviewer noted that "readers of *The Occult Review* will be familiar with such names as A. E. Waite, Nora Chesson, Aleister Crowley, G. M. Hort and Eva Gore-Booth";[19] and *The Co-Mason*, whose reviewer, Miss L. J. Dickinson, mentioned no contemporary poets by name and confined herself to noting that "on every page something lovely and uplifting is revealed."[20]

Only *The Quest* struck a sour note. In his unsigned review of the anthology, G. R. S. Mead mentioned no names, but simply stated that "among the [modern poets] we note the names of some of the contributors to The Quest." To this he added a hostile reference to the poems by Crowley (unnamed but easily identifiable), describing them as "the pretentious kabalistic extravagance of a writer of evil reputation on pp. 520, 521."[21]

The poems of both writers appear to be surprisingly similar. This is, to some extent, inevitable, given that the editors justified their selection not because "any particular poet is of sufficient importance to demand representation as such," but on the basis "that a poet of no matter what general rank has written one or more poems which testify to the greater things and at the same time reach a certain level of expression." Differences of style are clear, but there is an overall concurrence of feeling between Waite's "A Ladder of Life" and Crowley's "The Quest," the ascent of the one being mirrored by the descent of the other. Parallels can also be drawn between Crowley's "The Rose and the Cross" and Waite's "Of Consummation." Perhaps when immersed in poetry Crowley was able to stand aside from his habitual and petty jeering and admire a poet whose verse, in terms of poetic quality, certainly equaled his own.[22]

At least one of Crowley's friends and followers, Ethel Archer, shared his enthusiasm for Waite's poetry. In an article titled "The Poetry of Arthur Edward Waite," contributed to *The London Forum*—a new title temporarily assumed by *The Occult Review*—in 1935, she argued that he was

> the author of the most beautiful mystical verse of this or the preceding century. . . . It is not unusual for a poet to be some twenty or thirty years ahead of his time, in regard to spiritual thought, but Arthur Edward Waite has been half a century in advance, even for the most enlightened of us; and it may well be another fifty years before the majority catch up.[23]

She was not the only member of Crowley's circle to praise Waite. In the course of a review of Waite's autobiography, *Shadows of Life and Thought*, Israel Regardie admitted that

> many have been the occasions when in my heart I have felt a warm glow of gratitude for Arthur Edward Waite for his untiring research and scholarship. This indebtedness to him I have frequently expressed both in speech and in writing. And it is considerably increased by this new book of his.[24]

But he could not refrain from emulating his former master by damning Waite as well as praising him. He claimed that two "advanced Adept members of his own Rosicrucian organisation"—presumably Alvin Langdon Coburn and his wife—had told him that "Mr. Waite has expanded the original Golden Dawn rituals into pompous, heavy parades of impossible turgidity . . . the awful Waite style at its worst."[25] Against this it should be noted that the Coburns had never seen the original Golden Dawn rituals, and had happily worked the rituals of Waite's Fellowship of the Rosy Cross for several years before they "borrowed" them for the benefit of another body, the Universal Order.[26]

Regardie was, admittedly, out of sympathy with Waite's negative attitude toward the Golden Dawn, but this ambivalence, so redolent of Crowley, brings us back to the question, why did Crowley maintain such a bitter literary hostility to Waite? It continued long after *The Equinox* had foundered, surfacing in *The Confessions* of 1929 and in his novel *Moonchild*, also published in 1929 but written in 1917. But these two commercial ventures were no more successful than *The Equinox* had been, so that none of Crowley's critical writing on Waite had other than a minuscule circulation during his lifetime. Was Crowley pouring out his vitriol just for self-satisfaction, or was there another, deeper reason?

There are five possibilities. First, Crowley may have been piqued at Waite's presumed hostility toward him within the Golden Dawn, but this assumes that Waite *was* hostile, whereas he seems to have been merely indifferent to Crowley, who did not figure at all in his own plans for the Golden Dawn, which matured three years after Crowley was ejected from the order. Waite played no part in the events of 1900 and had no contact with Crowley either before or after that time.

Related to this is a second possibility. Was Crowley motivated by hostility to Waite's beliefs and practices? This is unlikely, because Crowley was indifferent to the opinions and behavior of others. Nor were the tenets or rituals of Waite's orders, the Independent and Rectified Rite of the Golden Dawn and the Fellowship of the Rosy Cross, known to Crowley, so he would have been ignorant of the object of his presumed hostility. That he knew even less of Waite's spiritual goals is clear from his ignorance of the meaning of *The House of the Hidden Light*. This curious book, a collection of letters between Waite and Arthur Machen, existed in only three copies printed in 1904. One of these copies once belonged to Gerald Yorke, and Crowley refers to it in his diary entry for May 19, 1939: "Yorke very friendly: bought Waite-Machen book." Subsequently he encouraged Crowley to read it in the hope of making sense of the text; neither of them could do so, but Crowley thought it had a connection with sex magic. It did not; it concerns Waite and Machen's inner spiritual quest.[27]

A third possibility is that Crowley was envious of Waite's literary success, slight though it was, and the mere fact that he continued to find commercial publishers up to the time of his death—a feat that consistently eluded Crowley. He may, perhaps, have been also envious of Waite's literary skill, which was, for all his stylistic awkwardness, considerable; and Waite *was* widely admired by contemporary literati, including John Masefield, Katherine Tynan, and Evelyn Underhill. But Crowley cared nothing for the views of critics, and his literary output was the equal of Waite's in quantity, while even Waite's most fervent supporters could not claim that he is easier to read than is Crowley.

What, then, remains? Was Crowley's literary rage fueled by a lack of response? It is true that Waite consistently ignored Crowley's attacks, of which he was almost certainly aware, as review copies of *The Equinox* would have come into his hands via *The Occult Review*, which happily carried advertising for it. But Waite's monthly "Periodical Reviews" feature in that journal does not contain a single reference to *The Equinox*, and he never once refers to Crowley in his periodical contributions or in his books. Nor is there any mention of Crowley in Waite's private diaries or in any of his known letters. It is as if, for Waite, Crowley simply did not exist.

Perhaps it was not the simple lack of response but the reasons for that diffidence, dignified silence, disinterest, or whatever one chooses to call Waite's nonengagement with Crowley. It is true that privately Crowley showed little or no concern for Waite—apart from the brief reference to *The House of the Hidden Light*, Crowley's diaries for the 1930s and 1940s contain only a single relevant line: on Wednesday, May 20, 1942, Crowley wrote, "A. E. Waite dead: æt 84." Even this, however, is suggestive, for Waite had died late at night on May 19, and Crowley must have received the news as soon as anyone. How, why, and from whom remain unanswered questions, but a letter from Crowley to W. Dawson Sadler, dated December 21, 1944, does indicate a degree of respect for Waite.[28]

In the letter, Crowley gives his account of finding glorious grist for his anti-Waite mill, which was intended to appear as "Arthur Returns from Avalon." He tells Sadler about

> one of the most providential occurrences in my life. No sooner had I landed in New York in 1914, than I found the papers teeming with headlines about Arthur Waite, "Burn the brute, cries Mother-in-Law" "Waite confesses giving poison that killed millionaire Peek." "Dr. Waite's wicked man from Egypt." "Waite confesses to two murders," and so on. I cut out all these headlines, and had them stuck on a page and photographed, and so was able to announce his resurrection to damnation in March 1919. I naturally called the article in No. 10 the Obituary, because the Equinox had to stop for five years, and I thought I had better finish him off.* In actual practice he only died in, I think it was the summer of 1943.

What is intriguing is the footnote: "*If he had died, I shouldn't have made fun of him."

But were Crowley's persistent attacks simply posturing for public consumption? There is, I believe, something more to them. For the limited circle of readers of *The Equinox*, who may well have enjoyed these assaults on a presumed symbol of the staid "establishment" school of occultism, this explanation may suffice, but it does not explain Crowley's continuing need to pillory Waite for at least another twenty years. That need may indeed stem from the most probable reason for Waite's sublime indifference to Crowley's literary virulence. Both men had suffered from an early loss of faith, but unlike Crowley, Waite had become reconciled with the religion of his youth: he could eschew Catholic dogma while retaining its ritual, its atmosphere, and his own interpretation of the doctrines of the mystics of the Church. This, coupled with a stable community of fellow believers who engaged in the "practical mysticism" of his Rosicrucian Order, set Waite in the environment he needed to travel on the road toward union with the Divine. He was content with his lot.

Waite was not, of course, alone in believing that he had attained the summit of mystical experience. Crowley was convinced that he had achieved communion with the Divine, but his reaction was utterly different from that of Waite. He had no desire to follow Waite's contemplative path and preferred the road of self-indulgence and an unsettled life. Whether or not this brought him true fulfillment we cannot know, but he never received the public recognition that he sought and believed that he deserved, and his own belief that he had attained the Great Work was not matched by public perceptions of his life and achievements. Waite, however, was respected and admired in the circles that mattered to him, and in the wider literary world. He also achieved peace of mind and died fulfilled: on his deathbed he traced what he said was a Latin word upon the counterpane . . . and then said: "That's the end."[29] For Waite the end was Unity with God, and it is probable that the word he traced was Unitas, for the end that he had truly attained.

Did Crowley see in Waite an attainment of something that he himself had failed to achieve, or failed to understand—the Interior Church to which Waite had originally directed him—and did that recognition, and the dissatisfaction that went with it, engender a bitterness and envy that found expression in what amounted to literary hysteria? It would explain much that otherwise makes no sense in Crowley's writing, but it remains conjecture. What is certain is that Waite left behind him the means for others to travel on his own way of attainment that leads to union with the Divine.

The same cannot be said for Crowley, the essence of whose systematic body of thinking is encapsulated in the current manifestations of the Ordo Templi Orientis. This order has effectively devolved into a constellation of warring factions with a penchant for litigation. It, or rather they, appear to be at a perpetual distance from the "Interior Church" that Crowley had sought at the beginning of his pursuit of magic.

Perhaps that is what Crowley's followers wanted and what he wanted for them. If such is the case, then the gulf between Crowley and Waite is truly unbridgeable and must be seen as an embodiment of Sidney Smith's famous bon mot. Walking one day with a friend down a narrow "wynd" in Edinburgh, Smith saw two washerwomen screaming at each other from the gables of two houses facing each other across the street. "Those women will never agree," said Smith, "they are arguing from different premises."

Notes

1. Page 2 of the 1897 prospectus for Samuel Liddell MacGregor Mathers, *The Book of the Sacred Magic of Abra-Melin the Mage, as Delivered by Abraham the Jew unto His Son Lamech, A.D. 1458* (London: J. M. Watkins, 1898). This prospectus provides details of the printing of the book, including a note that it was limited to three hundred copies.
2. Arthur Edward Waite, *The Book of Black Magic and of Pacts: Including the Rites and Mysteries of Goëtic Theurgy, Sorcery, and Infernal Necromancy* . . . (London: George Redway, 1898). The prospectus states that the book is to be issued at £2.2s net, but advance subscribers who reply to the prospectus before the unstated date of issue (April 1898) can obtain it for "31s 6d including postage."
3. Aleister Crowley, *The Confessions of Aleister Crowley*, ed. John Symonds and Kenneth Grant (London: Jonathan Cape, 1969), 126.
4. Ibid.
5. Waite, *The Book of Black Magic*, 11.
6. Crowley, *The Confessions*, 126. Easter in 1898 fell early in April, so that Crowley must have read *The Book of Black Magic* in March. This supports the probability of his obtaining the book as an early, albeit indirect, subscriber, as it was not published until April.
7. *The Equinox* I (3) (March 1910), 304.
8. Crowley always gave his date of initiation as November 18, but there was no meeting of Isis Urania Temple on that date. A summons for the meeting of November 26, issued by Baker as Cancellarius (i.e., secretary), includes a note advising the unnamed recipient that meetings were not held as frequently as in the past. They had usually been held once a month.

9. Crowley, however, states that he did meet Waite on one occasion: "In all these years I have met him but once, and then within a certain veil." *The Equinox* I (3) (March 1910), 310. This suggests that they were both present at one meeting of the Golden Dawn, probably in 1899. He also claimed, in an annotation to a copy of Lévi's *History of Magic*, which he had acquired at some time after 1930—when Peter Warlock, the previous owner, had died—that "Waite was expelled from the G.D. by me in 1900." This book was offered for sale by Weiser Antiquarian Books in their catalog no. 13.
10. See, for example, the following contributions to volume I of *The Equinox*: "Wisdom While You Waite" [a review of *The Book of Ceremonial Magic*], no. 5 (March 1911), 133–41; "Waite's Wet or the Backslider's Return," no. 8 (September 1912), 232–42; "Dead Weight," no. 10 (September 1913), 211–33.
11. Crowley's translation was first published as a supplement to *The Equinox* I (10) (September 1913). Thomas Williams, in his critical study *Eliphas Lévi: Master of Occultism* (Tuscaloosa: University of Alabama Press, 1975), takes a sympathetic view of Waite's shortcomings in his interpretation of Lévi because of the lack of source materials at the time. Williams also praises Crowley's "readable and very lively translation" of *The Key of the Mysteries*, but he does not comment on Crowley's omission of the supplement.
12. For example, Gershom Scholem, in *Major Trends in Jewish Mysticism*, rev. ed. (New York: Schocken, 1946), praised Waite for his grasp of the kabbalah, stating, "His work is distinguished by real insight into the world of Kabbalism," although he regretted Waite's uncritical attitude toward "facts of history and philology" (212).
13. See Crowley's review of Yarker's *The Arcane Schools* (1909) in *The Equinox* I (4) (September 1910), 240.
14. Crowley, "Dead Weight," 215.
15. Ibid., 213.
16. Aleister Crowley, review of A. E. Waite, *Strange Houses of Sleep, The Equinox* I (3) (March 1910), 310.
17. Aleister Crowley, review of A. E. Waite, *A Book of Mystery and Vision*, *The Equinox* I (3) (March 1910), 113.
18. Daniel Howard Sinclair Nicholson joined the order in 1910, taking the motto of Per deos ad Deum. The Reverend Arthur Hugh Evelyn Lee had entered earlier, in 1908, and took the motto of Hilarion. He was later a member of the Amoun Temple of the Stella Matutina. Neither man is known to have been associated with Crowley.
19. *The Occult Review* 26, no. 5 (November 1917), 303–4. The review is signed "E. M. M."
20. *The Co-Mason* 9, no. 2 (April 1917), 74–75.
21. *The Quest* 8, no. 4 (July 1917), 711–12. Mead was referring in particular to the poem "The Quest."

22. The third poem by Crowley to be included in *The Oxford Book of English Mystical Verse* is interesting for reasons other than Mead's dislike. A footnote to "The Neophyte," presumably also by Crowley, states, "This poem describes the Initiation of the *true* 'Hermetic Order of the Golden Dawn' in its spiritual aspect." It also suggests that Crowley gained rather more from his initiation than he afterward pretended.
23. *The London Forum* 61, no. 6 (June 1935), 407.
24. Israel Regardie, "A Prophet—So Waite!," *Journal* of the Brotherhood of the Path (1938), 47–50.
25. Ibid.
26. The Universal Order was an English esoteric society dedicated to the propagation of "Universal Wisdom": a body of knowledge based on the traditional metaphysics of the major world religions and philosophical systems. The order was founded in 1911 as The Shrine of Wisdom, but the name was changed to The Universal Order in 1923, the earlier title being retained for its publications.
27. I provide a full account of the background to *The House of the Hidden Light* in the annotated edition published by the Tartarus Press in 2003.
28. At the time of writing, this letter is in the possession of Weiser Antiquarian Books of York Beach, Maine.
29. Letter from Thomas Wild to Joscelyn Forestier-Walker, June 8, 1942; quoted in R. A. Gilbert, *A. E. Waite: Magician of Many Parts* (Wellingborough, England: Aquarian Press, 1987), 160.

11

The Beast and the Prophet

ALEISTER CROWLEY'S FASCINATION WITH JOSEPH SMITH[1]

Massimo Introvigne

Between Religion and Magic

A POPULAR WAY of criticizing new religious movements is to argue that they are perhaps new but not really religious, since the experience they propose is not religious but magic. This is a frequent charge brought against both sects with Christian backgrounds and "new" new religious movements born in the twentieth century. The issue is of greatest importance for any discussion of new religions and deserves further study. The purpose of this essay is to consider the problem of an alleged magic or occult connection in respect of Mormonism. The case study of Mormonism may, however, be relevant for broader issues concerning the relationship between magic and the new religious movements.

Magic and Religion in the New Revelations

In our secular age, the "rumor of angels" written about by Peter Berger[2] is heard more often then one would expect, even if Frithjof Schuon—a disciple of the esoteric teacher René Guénon—wrote in a book about Islam that no genuine new revelation is possible, because of a cyclical theology of history, after the Middle Ages.[3] Perhaps, but any scholar familiar with the so-called new religions of the last two centuries knows that there have been more new revelations in the last two hundred years than in the whole of the Middle Ages, which lasted—according to conventional chronology—for one thousand years. Any scholar who pays serious attention to the "new religions" should also be prepared to consider the new revelations.[4] Not all new revelations—and, indeed, not all angels—are equal. Although the Angel Moroni's visitations to Joseph Smith and the Angel Aiwass's revelation to Aleister Crowley may both be classified as new revelations, it is hard to imagine two revelations more different. In fact, there are a number of different categories of new revelations. For example, special categories may be found among literally thousands of new religions born in Africa, among groups born in the Islamic world, such as the Ahmadis, and among a growing number of large new religions, with millions of followers, in Japan. (The two latter categories, by the way, have been encountered by Mormon missionaries, and it is interesting to note that some similarities in the revelatory structure have been noticed with the Ahmadis,[5] while the Japanese new revelations have only looked "strange" to their Mormon observers.[6])

To many observers of new revelations, one principal difference that has emerged is the difference between *religious* and *magical* new revelations. The very possibility of this distinction implies a theoretical framework within which it is possible to establish a distinction between religion and magic. The great evolutionary model of Keith Thomas—in which religion gradually evolved from primitive magic or mixed forms[7]—is perhaps less useful here than the categories introduced by Mircea Eliade and Julien Ries.[8] Eliade, followed by Ries, does not deny that the categories may merge at some point in a gray area, but insists that magical and religious experiences are fundamentally different. He describes the religious experience as a "hierophany," a manifestation of the divine, and the magical experience as a "cratophany," a manifestation of power. True, both religion and magic have something to do with the Sacred; however, the religious man or woman is in the attitude of listening to the Sacred with reverence, whereas the magician wants to manipulate the Sacred in order to acquire some kind of power (from the "noble" power of reaching a higher state of consciousness to more "mundane" powers such as becoming rich or overcoming enemies).

If a distinction is possible within the elusive area of "new religions," one should also be able to distinguish the "new" or "alternative" movements that are religious from those that are "new magical movements."[9] And what about new revelations? Here again, gray areas abound, but a distinction may also be drawn. One of the best available definitions of the "magical" revelation was proposed by William Butler Yeats (1865–1939) in his essay "Magic," which first appeared in the *Monthly Review* in September 1901. At that time, Yeats was not only a celebrated poet but also had been, for a number of years, one of the leaders of an important magical order, the Hermetic Order of the

Golden Dawn. In fact, he was intimately involved in the Golden Dawn during the period of its most famous divisions and schism, when Yeats sided against young Aleister Crowley.[10] According to Yeats, the main features of the magical "vision" or revelation are as follows:

1. That the borders of our mind are ever shifting, and that many minds can flow into one another, as it were, and create or reveal a single mind, a single energy.
2. That the borders of our memories are as shifting, and that our memories are a part of one great memory, the memory of Nature herself.
3. That this great Mind and great Memory can be evoked by symbols.[11]

Not all magical and occult teachers would agree with this definition, but its advantage is that one immediately sees as the starting point the human mind, which, through a symbolic technique, reaches for the great Mind of the Universe. This is not what happened with Abraham, Muhammad—or Joseph Smith. They were not first in taking the initiative; they did not use any technique in order to reach for the Sacred. They did not claim to have invented a special or magical technique to get in touch with the Sacred. God took the initiative; the Sacred spoke. Their only claim was that they were ready to listen and willing to pass what they had heard to others. From a theoretical standpoint, the distinction between the magus and the prophet is clear enough. In the religious revelation, God starts and leads; in magic, the magus starts and tries to lead the Sacred to where he can eventually manipulate it.

Early Mormonism: Religion and/or Magic?

A case in point that demonstrates that the distinction between religious and magical new revelations is not as clear as one would like is early Mormonism. For the historian of religion there is no doubt that Joseph Smith's revelatory enterprise has all the features of the religious experience and almost no features of the magical experience. On the other hand, magic connections between Joseph Smith, his family, and his revelations have been noted, particularly, but not exclusively, in anti-Mormon literature. Three main areas have been discussed:

1. The presence of folk magic in the early experiences of Joseph Smith and his family
2. The relations of Joseph Smith and other early Mormon leaders with Freemasonry and the masonic element in Temple ceremonies

3. A consistent fascination of a number of magical and occult leaders and teachers for Joseph Smith

It is not my purpose here to review the serious scholarly literature that now exists on the first two points. As far as the folk magic connection is concerned, any comment would consist largely of a review and discussion of D. Michael Quinn's *Early Mormonism and the Magic World View*.[12] I would observe, however, that the sometimes heated discussion this book has generated would perhaps be less emotional if the issue were placed in a comparative context. The incident involving Mark Hofmann—a con man who, before ending up in jail in 1986, persuaded several senior historians that documents forged by himself were genuine, including a letter in which Joseph Smith allegedly reported an apparition involving a magical salamander—called attention to a number of studies that had already demonstrated that a connection exists between the Smith family and folk magic. So what? It is one thing to distinguish between religious and magic experience; it is another to claim that religious experience could exist in a vacuum, entirely free of any folk or magical elements. Magic-free religion exists only in the programs of the churches and in the books of theologians; it has never existed at the level of the rank and file. The Catholic Church has quietly accepted for centuries a folk religion more or less close to magic; recent attempts to fight folk religion in the name of a "pure" and magic-free theology have largely been abandoned where they resulted in the loss of members by the thousands, particularly in Latin America. True, there is a Protestant literature that claims that Protestantism has liberated Christianity from magic and superstitions tolerated by the Roman Church, but this literature is largely propaganda. One has only to read the study by Robin Bruce Barnes on apocalypticism in the wake of the Lutheran Reformation[13]—and there is a large and growing body of research in this field—to be convinced that, not only at a popular level, early Protestants shared with Roman Catholics hidden (and sometimes not so hidden) beliefs in astrology, exorcisms, talismans, amulets, and the like. Even the very liberal Protestantism of the age of the Enlightenment was certainly not entirely magic-free: recent research has concentrated on the "other side" of the Enlightenment, where we find scholars contributing to the *Encyclopedie* in favor of astral influences (although trying to avoid the word "astrology") and Italian rationalist philosophers—followed on this point by Marat, soon to become one of the leaders of the French Revolution—claiming that, in order to dispose of the Catholic idea of the Devil, one had to insist still more vigorously on a "natural" theory of the evil eye.[14] After all, in French, the word *illuminisme* could mean both the Enlightenment of the philosophers *and* the occultism of the "Illuminati."

The same analysis applies to Freemasonry. Masonic history is an enormously complicated blend of rationalism and esotericism, liberal Protestantism and magic—not only in one lodge but often in the head of one individual. A rationalist and deist such as John Toland was, at the same time, the first leader of the magical Ancient Druid Order, which met in the same Apple Tree Tavern where one of the founding lodges of the Grand Lodge of London met in 1717.[15] And Toland's case is far from an isolated example in the masonic world. If an esoteric wing and a rationalist wing have always coexisted in Freemasonry—so that many symbols could be read in two ways—all the intricacies of Joseph Smith's relations with Freemasonry become inconclusive. We know that Smith was first attracted by anti-masonic ideas following the Morgan incident; according to Smith's controversial biographer Fawn Brodie, Lucinda Pendleton Harris, wife of the famous anti-masonic martyr, eventually became a plural wife of Joseph Smith (and it is sure that she moved to Nauvoo).[16] Subsequently, in Nauvoo, Smith became reconciled with Freemasonry, and lodges were granted dispensations in the City of the Saints. Later these lodges were declared irregular by mainline Freemasonry, mostly because they had too many members and were becoming too powerful. This incident—and the influence, alleged or otherwise, of masonic rituals in Mormon Temple ceremonies—have been and are being studied in detail.[17] But if Freemasonry—contrary to the claims of many evangelical Protestants and anti-Mormon authors—is not a "pure" esoteric or magic organization but a mixture of various elements, all this, again, is no evidence that early Mormonism offered a magic rather than a religious experience.

We are, as a consequence, left with the third clue—that is, the fascination of a number of magical and occult leaders for Joseph Smith.

Magical and Occult Leaders Fascinated by Joseph Smith: The Case of Aleister Crowley

One of the most curious incidents in the history of anti-Mormonism began in 1984, when William Schnoebelen and his wife, who had become Mormons in 1980, were converted to evangelical Christianity. Eventually, Schnoebelen was introduced to Ed Decker, a well-known evangelical anti-Mormon, and to the latter's organization Saints Alive. Decker had argued, well before meeting Schnoebelen, not only that Mormonism has a magic connection but also that the God of the Mormon Temple is in reality Lucifer. Beginning in 1986,

Schnoebelen became Decker's spokesman for the alleged magic and satanic character of Mormonism and went so far as to claim "that the Mormon Apostle James E. Faust admitted [to Schnoebelen] in a private interview in 1981 that the Mormon Temple ceremony was a witchcraft ritual and that Lucifer was, in fact, the God of the Temple."[18] Apart from this extreme claim, one wonders why Schnoebelen was taken seriously by (some) anti-Mormons. He seemed, indeed, uniquely qualified to confirm the magic (and even satanic) connection in Mormonism. First of all, Schnoebelen claimed to have been a Roman Catholic priest before converting to Mormonism; the history of his career "from clergy to convert" had been included in a book compiled by Stephen W. Gibson and published by Bookcraft in 1981.[19] Second, Schnoebelen claimed to be an expert in magic and Satanism because he had been initiated a witch in 1968, changed his name in 1973 to Christopher Pendragon Syn (to honor, in his own words, *sin*), and was officially licensed a "Warlock" in 1978 by the Californian Church of Satan, headed by the flamboyant Anton Szandor LaVey. What a prize convert to Mormonism in 1980! But—also—what a prize convert to evangelical Christianity in 1984!

In 1987, Schnoebelen and Decker published a coauthored a book on the alleged Mormon doctrine of Lucifer-God,[20] and the former became a regular speaker at anti-Mormon conferences. He later entered the flourishing market of anti-occult Christian fundamentalist publications with a 1990 book against Wicca and the contemporary witchcraft revival.[21] He continues as a leader of militant anti-Mormonism.

Not all anti-Mormons were enthusiastic about Schnoebelen's claims, particularly the late Jerald Tanner and his wife Sandra, the well-known Salt Lake "career apostates."[22] In 1988, the Tanners interviewed Schnoebelen for three and a half hours, found him wanting, and eventually decided that he would become a nuisance to the anti-Mormon community and should be exposed. The Tanners were well-known to be persistent investigators. They quickly found out that Schnoebelen had never been a Roman Catholic priest. In order to discover this, they had to become acquainted with the little-known phenomenon of the "wandering bishops," that is, people claiming to have been consecrated as bishops along an "independent" line whose orders are recognized as valid, even if not legitimate or regular, by the Roman Catholic Church. In fact, the Roman Catholic Church believes—a theological opinion not shared by the Eastern Orthodox Churches—that a bishop, although separated by the Church or excommunicated, maintains until his death the power to ordain and consecrate people who will become valid (although irregular, and automatically excommunicated) priests and valid bishops.

Anyone consecrated in this way as a bishop (although outside the Roman Catholic Church) may, in turn, create other "valid" (although, once again, irregular) bishops, and so on. Sometimes the matter becomes enormously complicated, because there are no official records of all irregular consecrations. There are, however, in the world today more than one thousand "independent" or "wandering" bishops who make claims to validity, as shown by a directory published by the Institute for the Study of American Religion and by other sources.[23] Some of these "wandering bishops" are dreamers who want to establish a new church around a new theology; "quite a large number" of them—according to the very words of one of their own fold—"are simply people one would not wish to invite to dinner;"[24] some have actually ended up in jail. Many are occultists who wish to acquire the "powers" they believe to be magically connected with being a bishop. The clergy consecrated by these bishops is, by any standard, not a "Roman Catholic" clergy and is rejected as such by the Roman Catholic Church.

Schnoebelen was ordained a priest by two typical "wandering bishops," Julius E. Massey (1901–1978) and Michael Edward Stehlik (consecrated by Massey in 1978 and converted to the Roman Catholic Church—this time the mainline one—in 1981). Both wandering bishops were also connected with the alleged apparitions of the Virgin Mary in Necedah, Wisconsin, to Mary Ann Van Hoof (1909–1984), rejected by the Roman Catholic Church. Not all "priests" consecrated by Stehlik and Massey remained immune from the scandals that often plague such groups: two of them, David Javore and Glen Goergen—both close associates of Schnoebelen, by his own admission—had legal problems arising from the finances of their church and homosexuality; apparently Goergen "even admitted that he had taken nude photographs of three Milwaukee area teenage girls" at a time when he was "involved in a lot of drugs."[25]

The winter 1986 issue of the anti-Mormon *Saints Alive Journal* informed readers "that Schnoebelen was more than an ordinary priest; he had been made a 'gnostic Catholic Bishop'" in 1978.[26] Later—when questioned by the Tanners—Schnoebelen explained that he had "Vallatte [*sic*] succession." The Tanners themselves introduced the misspelling "Vallatte," which refers to Joseph René Vilatte (1854–1929), a key figure in the history of the wandering bishops who obtained an episcopal consecration in 1892 in the Malankara Syrian Church in Ceylon, an Eastern church whose orders are recognized as valid by the Roman Catholic Church. Vilatte is the grandfather of hundreds of wandering bishops—and it is here that Aleister Crowley enters the Schnoebelen saga. Schnoebelen explained to the Tanners that "Vallatte [*sic*] when he travelled through Europe ordained several rather bizarre people . . . who were into the occult, and some of them, in turn, ordained people who, for instance, ordained Aleister Crowley, who was, believe it or not, ordained by an Old Catholic bishop . . . and this whole lineage then made it to America by way of Haiti, and . . . the official title of the Church is the Ecclesia Gnostica Spiritualis, but I just keep the Latin out of it; I just said Gnostic Bishop."[27]

This is, to say the least, only part of the story. A Gnostic Church was founded in France in 1890 by Jules Doinel (1842–1902) without claims to any apostolic succession. Like many similar organizations, the Gnostic Church suffered a number of schisms and splits. In 1913 the leader of one of its branches, Jean Bricaud (1881–1934), finally acquired a line of apostolic succession after being consecrated a bishop by Louis-François Giraud (1876–1950), whose line of succession originated from Vilatte. From this time, the various Gnostic Churches were strongly interested in occultism; prominent occult teachers such as René Guénon (although he later renounced any involvement) and prominent European Freemasons were consecrated as bishops in one or another of these churches in the twentieth century.[28] Bricaud was in contact with all the European occult underground of his time, and he consecrated Theodor Reuss (1855–1923), a prominent occultist, as a Gnostic bishop for Germany. Among the many occult orders controlled by Reuss was the Ordo Templi Orientis (OTO), which allegedly was founded by the Austrian industrialist Carl Kellner (1850–1905), a close associate of Reuss. In 1911 Reuss first met Edward Alexander ("Aleister") Crowley (1875–1947), a young Englishman who was spending the money left by his wealthy Christian father, whom he hated, to explore a number of occult orders and groups that were oriented toward sex magic and/or homosexuality. Crowley was a magical genius, although a bizarre and depraved one. While people such as Bricaud and Reuss did not make any lasting contribution to the large body of already existing magical literature, Crowley's magical system claims thousands of followers even today.[29] There is no serious doubt that Reuss gave Crowley the highest degrees and authority in the OTO; probably he also made Crowley his successor (although the succession was disputed). What is less clear is whether Crowley was also consecrated a Gnostic bishop by Reuss; some assume this consecration to have taken place "without doubts,"[30] but apparently there is no record of it, and if it happened *before* the Vilatte line entered the Gnostic Church via Giraud, no claim of apostolic succession may be made. What is certain is that Crowley rewrote the Gnostic Mass of Doinel and Bricaud in 1913, while he was in Russia, having a good time (and making some money) as manager of a troupe of female musicians and dancers called the

Ragged Ragtime Girls.[31] It is a bizarre ritual, with continuous allusions to sex magic (it is said that some versions of the Mass involve actual, and not mere symbolic, intercourse between a "priest" and a "priestess") and a strange number of "Saints" mentioned in its canon, including Francis Bacon, Richard Wagner, Friedrich Nietzsche, Sir Richard Burton, and Aleister Crowley himself.[32]

Whereas in the main branch of the OTO in the United States most claims to an apostolic succession in the episcopate of the order's leaders—as leaders of Crowley's Gnostic Church—rest on the dubious consecration of Crowley himself, things are indeed different in the "Haitian" branch mentioned by Schnoebelen. One name Schnoebelen strangely failed to mention in his discussion with the Tanners is Michael Bertiaux. Bertiaux, a native of Seattle, attended an Episcopalian seminary, was sent to Haiti as missionary, fell in love with voodoo, and was himself converted to this Haitian form of syncretism rather than converting Haitians to Anglican Christianity. He also met a father and son named Jean-Maine—father Lucien-François (1869–1960) and son Hector-François—who passed on to him another branch of the OTO (combining Crowley and voodoo) and an episcopal succession that probably came from Bricaud without passing through Crowley. Bertiaux eventually settled in Chicago, where he first worked at the US headquarters of the Theosophical Society in Wheaton, Illinois, and then found a job as a social worker for the city of Chicago. For many years Bertiaux was the head of a branch of the OTO; he later became less enthusiastic about Crowley and passed his OTO responsibilities on to other people, but he continues to be a Gnostic bishop and combines the tradition of the Gnostic Churches with what he prefers to spell "Voudon."[33]

Bertiaux, when I first interviewed him in 1990, had only a vague recollection of Schnoebelen, and he was not entirely sure that he had consecrated him. However, I was quite convinced that in the US occult world any reference to both a Haitian connection and a Gnostic Church, taken together, could normally only mean Bertiaux. I interviewed Bertiaux again in 1991, and he had in the meantime found the certificate of consecration of Schnoebelen (whom he knew only as Christopher P. Syn). The certificate, made in duplicate by Bertiaux in French, states that on July 23, 1977, Bertiaux consecrated Syn as a Bishop in the "Ecclesia Gnostica Spiritualis," at the same time appointing him as Grand Master of the "Ordre du Temple" (i.e., the Bertiaux branch of the OTO) and elevating him to the high degrees of the esoteric masonic rite of "Memphis-Misraim."[34] Bertiaux, who studied philosophy, has a rather good background in European philosophy and in some Eastern religions; on the other hand, he does not seem to be particularly interested in Mormonism.[35] Schnoebelen claims to have found some similarities between Mormonism and Crowley's brand of occultism through common implied references to kabbalism (which he prefers to spell, as do some occultists, "Qabalism").[36] Schnoebelen writes that he studied Crowley very seriously: "We got seriously into Crowley, who was certainly the wittiest, classiest and most honest writer on magic in this century"[37]—although he was, Schnoebelen now realizes, "demonic," "satanic," and "diabolical."[38]

It is indeed surprising that—having "seriously" studied Crowley—Schnoebelen failed to find what would, no doubt, have added fuel to the fire of Saints Alive. It was not necessary to find vague kabbalistic similarities between Crowleyan and Mormon symbols if Schnoebelen had read Crowley's biography and works carefully. He would have discovered that the great magus—who hated organized religion and had little respect for Jesus Christ—was fascinated throughout his life by Joseph Smith. Schnoebelen's unique background allowed him to suggest, although in vague terms, a connection between Crowley and Mormonism. I am aware of one precedent only: the *Revue internationale des sociétés secrètes*, founded in France in 1912 by Monsignor Ernest Jouin (1844–1932) as a journal for anti-masonic studies by Roman Catholics, took notice of Aleister Crowley in the late 1920s and quickly discovered the sex magic involved in his system. The articles—anonymous or signed by the anti-masonic Catholic journalist Olivier de Fremond—suggested a possible Mormon connection. However, the idea—taken from anti-Mormon literature of the nineteenth century that had circulated in France—was that the Mormons may have had a "secret sex cult" connected with polygamy and, since Crowley was favorable toward polygamy, he may have had some relationship with the Mormons.[39] Jouin's journal, although published in French only, had readers in the United States, and it was a group of American "friends of Monsignor Jouin" who tried, after his death, to have him canonized as a saint by the Roman Catholic Church.[40] There is no evidence, however, that these references had any impact on American anti-Mormonism.

There are two main passages in which Aleister Crowley clearly states his feelings about Joseph Smith. The first passage is included in Crowley's autobiography, where he explains that "we should found society upon a caste of 'men of the earth,' sons of the soil, sturdy, sensual, stubborn and stupid, not emasculated by ethical or intellectual education, but guided in their evolution by the intelligent governing classes towards an ideal of pure animal perfection." This idea, Crowley claims, is not racist, since "in such a substratum variation will produce sporadic individuals of higher type," and in fact "history affords innumerable examples of the lofty intelligence and the noblest characters shooting up from the grossest stock": "innumerable . . . men of the highest genius came of peasant parentage," and "few indeed of the first class have been born of intellectually developed families." Among these "men of the highest genius" Crowley mentions the French sculptor Rodin, whom he personally knew, Keats, Lincoln, Carlyle, Whitman, the German philosopher and mystic Boehme, and Joseph Smith. It is somewhat surprising that some Americans are included because Crowley, at this point in his autobiography, had just explained that "an adult American is a *rara avis*." However, Crowley explains, on the other hand, that genius is "always constitutionally robust" and physical strength is not a bar to being a genius, as Joseph Smith among others had proved.[41]

The second passage is included in chapter 16 of Crowley's novel *Moonchild*, written in 1917 and first published in 1929. There are, in this novel, two autobiographical backgrounds. The first is the quarrel between various wings of the Order of the Golden Dawn: Crowley sided with one of the founders of the order, Samuel Liddell MacGregor Mathers (1854–1918), in his 1900 fight against other leaders of the order (including Yeats and the celebrated masonic author Arthur Edward Waite [1857–1942]), but later became disillusioned with all these people and founded a Golden Dawn branch of his own, the Astrum Argentinum or Argenteum Astrum. All the leaders of the Golden Dawn are part of a "Black Lodge" in *Moonchild*, and they are ferociously lampooned throughout the novel. The second autobiographical element is the short but intense affair Crowley had in 1911 with Mary d'Esté Sturges, one of the companions traveling with the famous dancer Isadora Duncan. Crowley was introduced to Sturges on October 11, 1911, at the Savoy Hotel in London. The two fell in love, and Crowley quickly discovered that Mary—when excited by sex, alcohol, and drugs—was able to channel higher beings as a medium. The magus took Mary to Zurich and St. Moritz, where the young woman channeled a Turk or Egyptian spirit called Ab-ul-Diz. The spirit gave Crowley important revelations concerning the Golden Dawn, his work, and his persuasion to be the Great Beast foreseen in the book of Revelation. Ab-ul-Diz informed Crowley that he was to write a work on magic called *Book Four*, and in order to do so, he and Mary had to go to Naples where they would find a certain villa that Mary had seen in her visions and had been able to describe. According to Crowley, after a number of adventures, he and Mary eventually found a building called Villa Caldarazzo in Posillipo, Naples, which corresponded exactly to Mary's vision. It was there that Crowley wrote

Book Four, and where, after a few weeks, Mary lost interest in Crowley and returned to Isadora Duncan.[42]

In *Moonchild* Mary d'Esté Sturges—or Sister Virakam, as Crowley magically called her—becomes Lisa la Giuffria. She is contacted by a benevolent order, led by Simon Iff, and engaged in a great work: she has to pass through various initiations and go to Italy, where, near Naples, she could finally give birth to a magical child (a possibility hinted at by Crowley in his secret rituals of the OTO).[43] Simon Iff is an anti–Sherlock Holmes created by Crowley for his detective stories; he solves mysteries through occult insight and Eastern wisdom rather than through Holmesian rationalism.[44] Unfortunately, at the end of the novel, Lisa la Giuffria prefers to follow a human love rather than the Great Work, and the experiment fails. In chapter 16 of the novel, Lisa la Giuffria is in Posillipo (in the villa where Crowley actually stayed with Mary d'Esté Sturges and wrote *Book Four*) with Cyril Grey, the man who should be the father of her magical child. She watches the stars and has a vision of a number of great souls: Maximilian, once emperor of Mexico, General Boulanger, Ludwig II of Bavaria, Chopin, Byron, Tolstoy, Blake, Tchaikovsky, Kipling, Huxley, Strauss, Swinburne, and some "tragic figures" including—possibly—Electra and Salome. At a certain stage of the vision,

> all gave way to a most enigmatic figure. It was an insignificant face and form; but the attributions of him filled all heaven. In his sphere was primarily a mist which Iliel [Lisa la Giuffria] instinctively recognized as malarious; and she got an impression, rather than a vision, of an immense muddy river rushing through swamps. And then she saw that from this man's brain issued phantoms like pigeons. They were neither Red Indians nor Israelites, yet they had something of each in their being. And these poured like smoke from the head of the little man. In his hand was a book, and he held it over his head. And the book itself was guarded by an angelic figure whose face was extraordinarily stern and unbeautiful but who scattered with wide hands the wealth of life, children, and corn, and gold. And behind all these things was a great multitude; and about them were the symbolic forms of exile and death an every persecution, and the hideous laughter of triumphant enemies. All this seemed to weigh heavily upon the little man that had created it; Iliel thought that it was seeking incarnation for the sake of its forgetfulness. Yet the light in his eyes was so pure and noble and magnetic that it might have been that he saw in a new birth the chance to repair his error.[45]

Lest some readers should not recognize the people who "were neither Red Indians nor Israelites, yet they had something of each in their bearing" as Nephites, and "the book" as the Book of Mormon, a footnote by Crowley informs us that the "enigmatic figure" seen by Lisa is, indeed, Joseph Smith.

We have so far no evidence of any significant direct contact Crowley may have had with Mormon missionaries, although it must be noted that Crowley's papers are partially in private collections and not readily available (many, however, are collected at the Warburg Institute in London). Information on his interest in Joseph Smith may come from these sources.

The first and most important known source regarding Crowley's interest in Joseph Smith is Sir Richard Francis Burton (1821–1890). Burton, one of the most famous British explorers and professional travelers of the nineteenth century, visited Utah in 1861 and published his famous *The City of the Saints, and Across the Rocky Mountains to California*, in which he gave a balanced, if colorful, account of Utah and the Mormons.[46] His book became a classic reference on Utah Mormonism—and the reason Fawn M. Brodie became particularly interested in Burton and eventually wrote his biography in 1967.[47] Burton was one of Crowley's favorite heroes; it is not an exaggeration to say that Crowley worshipped Burton, given that he included Burton—as mentioned earlier—among the saints to be invoked in the canon of his version of the Gnostic Mass. Thanks to Crowley, hundreds of people who participate in the Gnostic Masses of the OTO today still invoke Richard Francis Burton as a saint, no doubt without knowing anything about him—and perhaps confusing him with Richard Burton the movie actor of more recent fame. The new version of the Gnostic Mass was written by Crowley in 1913, between his Italian adventure with Mary d'Esté Sturges in 1911 and the first draft of *Moonchild* that he completed in 1917. At that time his cult of Burton was at its height. No doubt Crowley regarded himself as a still greater saint than Burton, and he subtitled his autobiography—originally called *The Spirit of Solitude—An Autohagiography* in 1929. Due to problems at Mandrake Press, Crowley's publisher, the autobiography was not published until 1969. From the beginning, Crowley dedicated the "autohagiography" "to Three Immortal Memories: Richard Francis Burton, the perfect pioneer of spiritual and physical adventure; Oscar Eckenstein, who trained me to follow the trail; Allan Bennett, who did what he could."[48]

Crowley was, in the first part of his life, an accomplished and skilled mountaineer, and Eckenstein was his revered teacher in the mountains; Bennett was his first and most respected occult teacher. Burton, however, is mentioned first as "the perfect pioneer of spiritual and physical adventure," a model Crowley attempted to portray himself. Crowley avidly collected and read almost all of Burton's literary production; accordingly, his first and most important exposure to Mormonism probably came from *The City of the Saints*.

Another possible—and admittedly more tenuous—connection between Crowley and Mormonism is a negative one. If the enemies of my enemy are my friends, Crowley may have taken notice that Sir Arthur Conan Doyle's first Sherlock Holmes novel, *A Study in Scarlet*, was basically an anti-Mormon work.[49] Crowley intensely disliked Conan Doyle for a number of reasons. First, Conan Doyle was a prominent Spiritualist, and occultists such as Crowley despised Spiritualists as adepts of a "lower"—if not intrinsically stupid—form of magic. Crowley regarded the efforts of the novelist to promote Spiritualism as evidence of "Conan Doyle's senile dementia."[50] Second, Conan Doyle considered (and finally rejected) the idea of joining the Golden Dawn in 1898, through a contact with Dr. Henry Pullen Burry and Dr. Robert W. Felkin, both prominent in the anti-Mathers (and anti-Crowley) faction in the struggle of 1900.[51] Third—and perhaps most important—Crowley did not like the rationalism of Sherlock Holmes (the more so because he was aware of the Spiritualism of Conan Doyle). Even in one passage where he approves of a feature of Sherlock Holmes—the "selective study," ignoring all that falls outside his work—Crowley is far from being complementary toward the detective or his creator:

> One of the few gleams of intelligence shown in the works of Conan Doyle is where Sherlock Holmes is ignorant that the earth goes round the sun, and on being told, says that he will at once try to forget it. The case chosen exhibits the chooser as imbecile, for elemental astronomy is certainly important to the detective. But the general idea is sound.[52]

Crowley was familiar with detective stories and created his own detective with the character of Simon Iff. Whereas the British writer G. K. Chesterton, who converted to Roman Catholicism, created with his Father Brown a Catholic anti–Sherlock Holmes, Simon Iff is an occult anti–Sherlock Holmes of a different character. There is a common aim, however, between the Catholic Chesterton and the anti-Catholic Crowley: to show that the methods of Sherlock Holmes could not really work because they ignore substantial portions of the real human mind. Accordingly, the fact that Sherlock Holmes introduces himself as an anti-Mormon in his first story did much, in itself, to recommend to Crowley a fairer general attitude toward the Mormons and Joseph Smith.

The third possible link between Crowley and the Mormons has to do with the former's relationship with Freemasonry. Since the eighteenth century, "regular" Freemasonry governed by the Grand Lodge of England and by its counterparts outside England has coexisted, side by side, with other bodies alternatively labeled as "irregular" or "clandestine." Since the question of regularity within Freemasonry is less clear than many Freemasons prefer to believe, Ellic Howe—writing in a rather official masonic publication—suggested that certain dubious rites and groups be called "fringe Masonry" rather than "irregular."[53] Some "fringe" groups are also "irregular," by any standard, while the label "clandestine" has normally been used by masonic writers in a derogatory way to identify pseudo-masonic aberrations that confer (or sell) spurious "Masonic" degrees to people who would not have been eligible to become "regular" Freemasons.

There exists in Utah a body of anti-Mormon masonic literature that claims that Joseph Smith operated a "clandestine" lodge in Nauvoo, although it was originally chartered by proper masonic authorities. In time, bitter feelings developed between Mormons and masons, and while Freemasonry takes pride in admitting members of whatever creed or religion, Mormons, although only in Utah, were the only members of a religious group to be excluded officially by "regular" Freemasonry. This prohibition was removed from the Code of the Grand Lodge of Utah only on January 31, 1984; it had been in place officially since 1925 and unofficially since at least 1867.[54]

Crowley was in turn admitted—through Reuss, himself a very active "fringe" or "irregular" mason,[55] and other sources—to an incredible variety of para-masonic, pseudo-masonic, and perhaps (but the fact is disputed) genuine masonic bodies. At any rate, Crowley became convinced that his magical system "satisfied all possible requirements of true Freemasonry" and claimed to be "in a position to do for the contending sects of freemasonry what the Alexandrians did for those of paganism."[56] Understandably, the Freemasons rejected his generous offer and where horrified when he claimed that all the secrets of true Freemasonry were connected with an anti-Christian system of sex magic. Crowley, in turn, was incensed because the Masonic establishment rejected his idea and claims to authority. There is no evidence that Crowley knew about the problems Joseph Smith had with masonic authorities in Illinois, which he may have found similar to his own. However, there was one Mormon—admittedly less important in Mormon history than Joseph Smith—who was deeply involved in masonic controversies and had some association with Crowley. Mathew Mc Blain Thomson (1854–1932) was born in Scotland and eventually converted to Mormonism, emigrated to

Idaho in 1881, and finally settled in Salt Lake City. He became notorious as the perpetrator of "the Great Thomson Masonic Fraud," for which he was sentenced by a US district court in 1922 and spent two years in federal prison in Leavenworth, Kansas.[57] Thomson, in fact, made some money by selling "clandestine" masonic degrees to shopkeepers, workers, and other people in the United States. Since Mormons were not eligible to become "regular" Freemasons in Utah, he found the state to be particularly fertile ground. Notwithstanding Thomson's legal problems, his creation, the American Masonic Federation, was remarkably persistent and apparently was still in existence in the 1970s. In Europe Thomson was welcomed by the main "fringe" and "irregular" (but not necessarily "clandestine") Freemasons of his time, including Jean Bricaud—whom we have met in the Gnostic Church—and Theodor Reuss, the man who initiated Crowley into the OTO (and possibly consecrated him as a Gnostic bishop). In 1920 Thomson managed to organize in Zurich, Switzerland, a Universal World Masonic Congress, which was attended by the Swiss Dr. E. Pargaetzi as representative of Bricaud and by Theodor Reuss. A number of "fringe" Masonic bodies were represented, and a Universal Masonic World Federation was founded, presided over by Thomson, with Bricaud as treasurer. The federation had some ambitious projects—including the creation of an international masonic school in Klosters, Switzerland—that were never realized, but it remained in existence for some years. Introducing the congress, which took place in July 1920, the journal *Les annales initiatiques*, organ of Bricaud's Gnostic Church and of other occult organizations, announced in its issue of April–June 1920 that Reuss would be appointed secretary of the new federation. At the end of the congress, however, the Swiss Freemason Hans-Rudolph Hilfiker-Dunn, not Reuss, was appointed secretary; Reuss was not even a member of the board of directors. Apparently, at the beginning of the congress Reuss quarreled with Thomson; it has also been suggested that Thomson paid Reuss to keep the main lights of the stage on himself.[58] But Reuss and Thomson had been friends for some time.

Crowley did not attend the Zurich congress. He was busy in Cefalù, Sicily, managing his Abbey of Thelema, which he wanted to become the world center of the new religion of Crowleyanity. He also became entangled in a number of love affairs. He lived at the Abbey with both Leah Hirsig (who was said to be the only true love of his life—perhaps with his first wife, Rose Kelly) and Ninette Fraux Shumway. Hirsig was the first among a collection of "Scarlet Women" who, in Crowley's apocalyptic imagery, were magically called to complete his role of the "Great Beast"; he called Shumway his "second concubine."

In June 1920 he had just completed a homosexual affair with an Arab named Mohamed Tsaida; the affair had occurred during a trip to Tunis (although Tsaida was apparently not in love with Crowley and asked "a small fee" for his services).[59] When the Zurich congress convened, he was anxiously waiting at the Abbey for Hollywood actress Jane Wolfe, who finally arrived in Palermo on July 23. Interestingly enough, people in Cefalù called Crowley "the Mormon" and the Abbey's group "the Mormon community," apparently because Crowley, having more than one "wife," was easily confused with portrayals of Mormons as polygamists in old popular literature. According to one source, Crowley did not dislike the appellative, and he did not explain to the good citizens of Cefalù that he was, in fact, not a Mormon.[60]

Despite all this activity, Crowley managed to keep in touch with Reuss, and other people associated with the OTO continued to visit the Abbey. He also continued his efforts to advance in Freemasonry. In his Confessions he mentions, for example, "a shower of diplomas from Salt Lake City,"[61] an obvious reference to Thomson. Although Crowley was capable of treating these things in a jocular mode—"an elephant," he wrote, "would break down under the insignia I am entitled to wear"[62]—he was, after all, playing the same game as Reuss and Thomson. Since Thomson liked to claim that he was persecuted as a Mormon by an anti-Mormon Utah Masonry—although this was denied by the prosecutor in his case[63]—this modern "persecution" in which he was somewhat involved may have made Crowley more sympathetic toward the persecuted Mormons of old. And, at that time, it was certainly true that Mormons in Utah were excluded from "regular" Freemasonry, just as Crowley felt excluded despite his claims.

But what kind of sympathy did Crowley actually manifest toward Mormonism and Joseph Smith? Surely it was not the usual respect one would expect to be shown for religious leaders: Crowley knew nothing of such respect, as shown by his treatment of Jesus Christ, the Virgin Mary, and the saints. Crowley's play *The World's Tragedy* has been described by his one-time secretary as "one of the most bitter and vicious diatribes against Christianity that I have ever read."[64] If he had lampooned his own occult alma mater, the Golden Dawn, in *Moonchild*, he was equally ready to lampoon Jesus Christ, the Gospels, and Christianity as a whole.[65] That which the Angel Aiwass, in *The Book of the Law*, revealed to Crowley in 1904 was even more serious:

> Curse them! Curse them! Cue them!
>
> With my hawk's head I peck at the eyes of Jesus as he hangs upon the Cross.

> I flap my wings in the face of Mohamed & blind him. With my claws I tear out the flesh of the Indian and the Buddhist, Mongol and Din.[66]

If neither Jesus, Muhammad, nor even Buddha was respected by Crowley, why was Joseph Smith? For Crowley, the Book of Mormon was surely a vision of Joseph Smith: the Nephites were—as described in Lisa's vision in *Moonchild*—"phantoms like pigeons" coming "from the head" of Joseph Smith. Joseph's angel, however, though "extraordinarily stern and unbeautiful," had been able to create "the wealth of life, children, and corn, and gold" for "a great multitude." Joseph Smith was "noble" where his persecutors' "laughter" was "hideous." Crowley was, above all, an egomaniac. In all of the heroes and saints he worshipped he saw something of himself. Joseph Smith received a book by an angel, as Crowley himself had received *The Book of the Law* from Aiwass in Cairo in 1904. Smith founded a new religion; Crowley made no secret of his conviction that his new religion, Thelema, would eventually also succeed in gathering "a great multitude." Smith and his "multitude" were persecuted by "triumphant enemies" with a "hideous laughter"; Crowley felt persecuted throughout his life.

All of these similarities are *extrinsic* similarities. There are no *intrinsic* similarities. Crowley was not completely certain about the "real" source of *The Book of the Law*, but surely he would not have called it "an error." Joseph Smith's creation was, on the other hand, an "error" that "seemed to weigh heavily upon the little man that had created it." The final vision of Smith seeking a new incarnation "for the sake of its forgetfulness," seeing "in a new birth the chance to repair his error"—based on the karmic law of reincarnation—is entirely foreign to the Mormon worldview. Crowley was fascinated by Joseph Smith as a romantic character, a persecuted hero, but he was not prepared to accept—or even to discuss—the heart of Smith's message. Accordingly, the fact that Crowley—to some extent—admired Smith does not support the anti-Mormon argument that Mormonism is a "magical" rather than a "religious" experience. Crowley recognized the external features common to all new revelations, either religious or magical, and perceived in Smith's revelation an element of greatness he would have liked to claim for himself. But he did not enter the world of Smith's revelation, which was religious and not magical—and a mere "error" in the eyes of Crowley. Thus, it is not enough to observe that Crowley was fascinated by Joseph Smith. When the roots and peculiar features of this fascination are studied, one is forced to conclude that Crowley was fascinated by Smith's revelatory experience rather than by the specific religious features of his revelation. Crowley's attitude, thus, when carefully examined, confirms the differences between a religious new revelation such as Joseph Smith's and a magical new revelation such as Crowley's *The Book of the Law*.

The Aftermath of Crowley's Fascination: Joseph Smith in the New Magical Movements

The results of our investigation are confirmed by the attitude of contemporary new magical movements toward Joseph Smith. Most, if not all, magical movements that have flourished since World War II have been influenced by Crowley, even if they do not like to admit it, and many magical movements have shown a peculiar interest in Joseph Smith. We find some examples today in the new Spiritualist groups that participate in "channeling," in some occult movements and orders, and in the UFO cults. The last of these—a phenomenon with thousands of followers that is now receiving appropriate scholarly attention—have often been founded by people with occult or magical backgrounds who have translated their "mystic antecedents" into a space language acceptable to UFO devotees.[67]

Mormonism has a long history of relations with Spiritualism. While Spiritualists such as Arthur Conan Doyle were convinced that Joseph Smith had been a medium without knowing it,[68] Mormon leaders of the caliber of Parley P. Pratt, Orson Pratt, George Q. Cannon, and, later, James E. Talmage crossed swords with contemporary Spiritualists to argue that their revelations were only a counterfeit of God's true revelations to the Mormon prophets.[69] While many of their arguments merely distinguished between "true" and "false," divine or satanic revelations, Joseph West—writing in the *Improvement Era* in 1920—came closer to the more crucial distinction between magical and religious revelation by observing that real religious revelation is received but not sought and received directly, and never through a third person such as a medium:

> The Lord permits loved ones who have gone before to bring comforting messages to the living . . . in all such cases, the communication is directly with the person for whom is intended, and not through a third, irresponsible person.[70]

Only splinter groups in Mormonism, such as the short-lived Godbeite schism, were really attracted by Spiritualism.[71] Nor did Spiritualism fare much better in the RLDS Church, the nonpolygamist Missouri group now known as the

Community of Christ: its first leader, the Mormon prophet's son Joseph Smith III, first "studied the theory and practice of Spiritualism with enthusiasm" and took part in séances for some time, but some experiences finally convinced him "that Spiritualism was a bankrupt system, not worthy of further investigation." By 1852 "he had completely abandoned the cult" and later, as leader of the RLDS Church, he condemned Spiritualism "mercilessly."[72]

"Channeling" is a present-day form of Spiritualism in which contact is sought with "entities" that may be different (and more complicated) from the usual disincarnate spirits of the dead.[73] One thing modern channeling has in common with "classic" Spiritualism is the habit of claiming Joseph Smith as an early medium (or channel). Professor Jon Klimo, in what is probably the most popular book about channeling, claims that Smith was part of "channeling as a historical phenomenon."[74] Strangely enough, in 1985 this idea found its way into the columns of the liberal Mormon journal *Sunstone*, where the Book of Mormon was compared to such channeled revelations as *A Course in Miracles*.[75] The latter, in fact, is a book apparently received and not sought, since the channel—New York psychologist Helen Schucman—was initially embarrassed by the material she was receiving and tried to reject it. However, if one looks at the content of the respective revelations, they could hardly be more different. Most channeled "new Gospels"—including *A Course in Miracles*—fall within the category of magical revelations we have seen defined by William Butler Yeats. There is a great Universal Mind—seen in Gnostic and pantheistic terms—and we all have fallen from this Divine Unity (in *A Course in Miracles* we are all part of a dream or nightmare of the Son of God). What the channeled Gospels offer us is a way to return to this Unity and reach, at the same time, our Inner Self.[76] In Joseph Smith's revelation, pantheism is conspicuous only for its absence, and God the Father himself is a personage of flesh and bones. Nothing could be more foreign to Mormon theology than a Gnostic universe where anything bodily or material is bad or the result of a fall. Again, if one actually opens the bottle and does not merely stop at labels, there is very little in common between the Sacred Scriptures, such as the Book of Mormon and other Mormon revelations, and the channeled Gospels in the category of *A Course in Miracles*.

Turning now to the occult groups—as opposed to the Spiritualists—a case of interest to Mormons is the Mental Science Institute, which was organized in the late 1960s by Barney C. "Eli" Taylor and has followers around the United States who are attracted by a peculiar brand of herbal magic. Eli borrowed a number of Mormon ideas in his *The First Book of Wisdom* and *The Second Book of Wisdom*, including the idea of the three degrees of glory (celestial, terrestrial, and telestial), the concept of a Mother in Heaven, and the theory that God the Father was once a man. Other ideas in Eli's literature come from Crowley through Gerald B. Gardner (1884–1964), the main figure in the British Wicca revival, or modern witchcraft, who had been a close associate of Crowley (it was even rumored that Crowley wrote some of Gardner's allegedly "ancient" rituals, although Gardner's followers usually deny such rumors).[77] In the Mental Science Institute we have a unique mixture of Mormon and occult-Crowleyan ideas.[78] The matter was the subject of a heated debate between Schnoebelen and the Tanners, where Schnoebelen exaggerated the role of Eli as "the highest ranking Witch in the USA" and argued that both Eli and Mormonism had borrowed from the same ancient tradition. The Tanners correctly replied that the only evidence available indicated that Eli had borrowed his ideas from Mormonism. Schnoebelen admitted that he regarded Dr. J. Gordon Melton, the director of the authoritative Institute for the Study of American Religion, as an authority on the subject. On January 13, 1988, Melton wrote to the Tanners that "Taylor (Eli) does not represent any 19th-century witchcraft tradition which can serve as a common source for both its teachings and those of the Church of Jesus Christ of Latter-Day Saints." "Any similarity between Mental Science Institute and Mormonism on matters of teaching—Melton concluded—is due to Taylor's having taken Mormon ideas and incorporating them in MSI."[79] Not only is this historically accurate, but it is also obvious that Eli's doctrine is basically an occult structure, with some Mormon ideas borrowed and fitting more or less well in a different context (including, for example, reincarnation and a number of magical techniques). Eli Taylor confirms that occultists may be fascinated by some Mormon ideas, but no more.

The same type of extrinsic similarities may be found in the strange world of flying-saucer, or UFO, cults. In 1956, Professor Leon Festinger and his associates published a study titled *When Prophecy Fails* about a UFO cult that waited for a flood that was supposed to destroy North America in December 1954. When the prophecy failed, some members of the group were not shaken, but instead were reinforced in their commitment toward the group. While studying this group, the American sociologists discovered a phenomenon, now known as the Festinger syndrome, that explains why prophetic failure is normally not fatal to religious groups (a tool useful for understanding the history of Jehovah's Witnesses and other groups).[80] This is one of the rare cases in which the scholar became more famous than the object of his scholarship. In their study, Festinger and his colleagues referred to the leader of the cult by the pseudonym Madame Keech. Although the Festinger syndrome is still well-known, few people know what happened to Madame Keech. Madame Keech was alive until 1992. Dorothy Mar (her real name), or Sister Thedra (her magical name), traveled to Peru, where she became a pupil of George Hunt Williamson (1914–1986), a wandering bishop who had also been in touch with George Adamski (1891–1965), perhaps the most famous UFO contactee in the United States. Sister Thedra eventually developed her own theories after she came into contact with various other spatial masters, including the Angel Moroni—yes, the same Moroni of the Book of Mormon. In 1961 Sister Thedra returned from Peru to the United States, and in 1965 she founded the Association of Sananda and Sanat Kumara, headquartered in Mount Shasta, California. At that time, she announced that Moroni would reincarnate in a child and would begin to manifest his powers in August 1975. Although Moroni did not manifest in 1975, the Festinger syndrome struck again, and Thedra was able to maintain a viable occult organization gathered around a variety of materials she continued to channel.[81] Without the precedents discussed above, the sudden appearance of Moroni in the context of occult masters, flying saucers, and wandering bishops would be inexplicable. On the other hand, Moroni was no more than a name or vague reference for Sister Thedra, whose doctrines remain in the UFO-occult tradition and do not include significant Mormon elements.

The same is true for the channeled messages of Moroni received by the Reverend Keith Milton Rhinehart, a Spiritualist minister who is known mostly because of his claim to have spiritually manifested the stigmata (the five wounds suffered by Jesus during the Crucifixion), the same phenomenon experienced by Saint Francis of Assisi and other Catholic saints and mystics. In 1955 Rhinehart founded the Aquarian Foundation, headquartered in Seattle; the foundation's doctrines bear no resemblance to Mormonism.

Finally, if Sister Thedra met Moroni, the French journalist and UFO contactee Claude Vorilhon, known as Raël, met Joseph Smith himself. Raël was taught an "atheist religion" by extraterrestrial beings; the religion is grounded in the belief that the "space brothers"—and not God—created humanity. These extraterrestrials were in turn created by other extraterrestrials, and so on—without end, without God. Men and women—created by extraterrestrial scientists endowed with advanced technology—are not immortal, but something similar to immortality exists, since the space brothers, or Elohim, have decided to re-create certain humans, using special technology on their planets, but only those who deserve it. Raël was taken to the planet of the Elohim in 1975 and discovered that it is indeed a very pleasant place, where the "re-created" humans have learned to "manufacture," through marvelous machines, special "biological robots" in the shape of beautiful men and women who are ready to comply with any possible sexual wish (homosexuality is admitted by Raëlian ethics). Raël himself also profited from the machines, without moderation, and for one night he had no fewer than six beautiful female companions.[82] Raël is of interest for this discussion not because of his erotic space adventures, but because he met the "prophets of old" who have been "re-created" on the Elohim's planet and who now enjoy the good life there. Raël has stated that Jesus and Muhammad are there, and also that Joseph Smith is among them.[83] Since his first book, Raël has declared Mormonism to be a valid religion—valid, of course, in the sense that it disguised a revelation from the Elohim.[84] Since the Raëlian "religion" is basically atheist, it can have no common ground with Mormonism: the reference to Joseph Smith is only one more example to illustrate that all the prophets were really sent by the Elohim.

All these examples—and others that could be added—confirm the conclusion noted above with respect to Aleister Crowley, that all references to Joseph Smith and Mormonism in contemporary magical movements are either very broad and general or extrinsic:

Some notice that both their own sacred books and Joseph Smith's Sacred Scriptures are new revelations (a claim common in channeling), but they fail to distinguish between magical and religious revelations.

Different things may coexist or appear at the same time in the history of religion; other groups show sympathy for Joseph Smith because he was persecuted and they also feel persecuted—this is, obviously, something Joseph Smith may have in common with hundreds of historical figures in the world of religion, magic, politics, or the arts.

Some magical groups are interested in angels and in Moroni as an angel; angels, however, appear in both magical and religious experiences, but the contexts are different.

In some groups, notably in Eli's Mental Science Institute, elements of Mormon theology are used, but—even in the case of Eli's group—they are isolated from their normal Mormon context and used as "bricks" on which to build new structures whose orientation is wholly magical.

Finally, movements and leaders promoting the greatest possible sexual freedom, such as Crowley and Raël, may remember something they have read about Mormon polygamy; however, if such is the case, they ignore almost everything about Mormon polygamy as practiced by nineteenth-century Mormons and as assessed by modern scholarship,

> and very superficially feel that—because their groups, like the early Mormons, conflict with the established culture and religion about their concept of family relations—they have something in common.

All these elements remain extrinsic and do not support a different conclusion from the one I have suggested: Mormon revelation is a typical religious revelation, while magical revelations—and "scriptures" such as Crowley's *The Book of the Law*—come from entirely different experiences. A persistent anti-Mormon may insist that it is strange that, among so many religious leaders, occultists and modern magicians have been especially fascinated by Joseph Smith. But at least one founder of religion has been quoted by new magical movements more often than Joseph Smith. With the exception of Crowley, a fair number of magical movements have reserved a role for Jesus Christ. This is not necessarily a Christian role—on the contrary, "the 'Aquarian Christ' can indeed, be found playing some very unusual roles."[85] But this is hardly the fault of the Christians, and this does not make Christianity a magical experience. The fault of Mormons, if any, was probably to have been kind to the romantic British traveler Sir Richard Francis Burton, whose book on the saints excited the fantasy of a young man named Aleister Crowley, who was to become the leading figure in twentieth-century magic.

Notes

1. This essay originally appeared as "The Beast and the Prophet: Aleister Crowley's Fascination with Joseph Smith," *SYZYGY: Journal of Alternative Religion and Culture*, Volume 3: Issues 1–4 (Winter-Fall 1994). It has been reprinted with permission.
2. See Peter Berger, *A Rumor of Angels* (Garden City, N.Y.: Anchor Books, 1970).
3. Frithjof Schuon, *Comprendre l'Islam* (Paris: Éditions du Seuil, 1974), 54.
4. See an overview in Massimo Introvigne, ed., *Le nuove rivelazioni* (Turin: Elle Di Ci, 1991).
5. See Garth N. Jones, "The Ahmadis of Islam: A Mormon Encounter and Perspective," *Dialogue: A Journal of Mormon Thought* 19:2 (Summer 1986), 39–54.
6. See Spencer J. Palmer, "Did Christ Visit Japan?," *Brigham Young University Studies* 10:2 (Winter 1970), 135–58.
7. Keith Thomas, *Religion and the Decline of Magic: Studies in Popular Beliefs in Sixteenth- and Seventeenth-Century England* (London: Weidenfeld & Nicolson, 1971).

8. For an overview with a bibliography of Eliade's works on this point, see Julien Ries, "Histoire des religions, phénoménologie, herméneutique: Un régard sur l'oeuvre de Mircea Eliade," *L'Herne* 33 (1978), 81–88.
9. The category of "new magical movements" was originally suggested in a conference on Spiritualism organized by the Center for Studies on New Religions (CESNUR) in Foggia, Italy, in 1988; it is more fully expounded in my *Il cappello del mago: I nuovi movimenti magici dallo spiritismo al satanismo* (Milan: SugarCo, 1990). At the consistory of Roman Catholic cardinals held in April 1991, which was devoted, in part, to new religious movements, the introductory report of Francis Cardinal Arinze suggested that most current definitions of "new religious movements" are not comprehensive and that the suggestion to establish a separate category for "new magical movements" should perhaps be accepted. See a summary of Cardinal Arinze's report, "La sfida delle Sette o nuovi movimenti religiosi: Un approccio pastorale," *L'Osservatore Romano*, April 6, 1991.
10. See Ellic Howe, *The Magicians of the Golden Dawn: A Documentary History of a Magical Order, 1887–1923* (London: Routledge & Kegan Paul, 1972); George Mills Harper, *Yeats's Golden Dawn: The Influence of the Hermetic Order of the Golden Dawn on the Life and Art of W. B. Yeats* (London: Macmillan, 1974).
11. William Butler Yeats, "Magic," *Monthly Review* (September, 1901), reprinted in *Essays and Introductions* (London Macmillan, 1961), 28.
12. D. Michael Quinn, *Early Mormonism and the Magic World View* (Salt Lake City: Signature Books, 1987).
13. Robin Bruce Barnes, *Prophecy and Gnosis: Apocalypticism in the Wake of the Lutheran Reformation* (Stanford, Calif.: Stanford University Press, 1988).
14. See Vincenzo Ferrone, *I profeti dell'Illuminismo: La metamorfosi della ragione nel tanrdo settecento italiano* (Rome: Laterzer, 1989); and Introvigne, *Il cappello del mago*.
15. See Michel Raoult, *Les druides: Les sociétés initiatiques celtiques contemporaines* (Monaco: Éditions du Rocher, 1983).
16. Fawn M. Brodie, *No Man Knows My History: The Life of Joseph Smith, the Mormon Prophet*, 2nd ed., rev. (New York: Alfred A. Knopf, 1985), 459–60.
17. On the masonic influence on Temple ceremonies, see David John Buerger, "The Development of the Mormon Temple Endowment Ceremony," *Dialogue: A Journal of Mormon Thought* 20 (Winter 1987), 33–76; Massimo Introvigne, *Les Mormons* (Turnhout, Belgium: Brepols, 1991). For the typical anti-Mormon treatment of the issue, see Jerald Tanner and Sandra Tanner, *The Changing World of Mormonism*, rev. ed. (Chicago: Moody Press, 1981), 534–47; Jerald Tanner and Sandra Tanner, *Mormonism, Magic and Masonry* (Salt Lake City: Utah Lighthouse Ministry, 1983). The relationship between early Mormonism and Freemasonry in Nauvoo and its consequences in Utah have been discussed mostly by Freemasons. See S. H. Goodwin, *Mormonism and Masonry: A Utah Point of View*, 2nd ed. (1921; Salt Lake City: Grand Lodge F. & A.M. of Utah, 1938); and the many works of Mervin B. Hogan, professor

emeritus at the College of Engineering, University of Utah, and former secretary of the Masonic Research Lodge of Utah: *Mormonism and Freemasonry: The Illinois Episode* (Richmond, Va.: Macoy Publishing & Masonic Supply, 1977) (perhaps Hogan's main work); *The Dedication of the Nauvoo Masonic Temple and the Strange Question of Dr. Goforth* (Salt Lake City: privately printed, 1983); *Joseph Smith: Man and Mason* (Salt Lake City: privately printed, 1983); *Dr. Meredith Helm: Illinois' Second Grand Master* (Salt Lake City: privately printed, 1983); *Mormon Involvement with Freemasonry on the Illinois and Iowa Frontier between 1840 and 1846* (Salt Lake City: privately printed, 1983); *The Historicity of the Alleged Masonic Influence on Mormonism* (Salt Lake City: privately printed, 1984); *Mormon Masonry in Illinois Reviewed by a "Grand Master"* (Salt Lake City: privately printed, 1984); *The Temple Mormon and the Masonic Lodge* (Salt Lake City: privately printed, 1986). See also Michal W. Homer, "'Similarity of Priesthood in Masonry': The Relationship between Freemasonry and Mormonism," *Dialogue: A Journal of Mormon Thought* 27 (Fall 1994): 2–113.

18. Jerry Urban, tape-recorded interview with William Schnoebelen, quoted in Jerald Tanner and Sandra Tanner, "Covering Up Syn: Ex-Satanist Brings Confusion to Mormons and Their Critics," *Salt Lake City Messenger* 67 (April 1988), 13. This article is the main source for information on the Schnoebelen incident, along with Schnoebelen's own publications; it is to the Tanners' credit that they never shared the enthusiasm of other anti-Mormons for Schnoebelen's claims.
19. William Schnoebelen and Alexandria Schnoebelen, "We Waited for Six Years," in *From Clergy to Convert*, comp. Stephen W. Gibson (Salt Lake City: Bookcraft, 1981), 67–73.
20. Ed Decker and Bill Schnoebelen, *The Lucifer-God Doctrine: Shadow or Reality?* (n.p.: Saints Alive in Jesus, 1987).
21. William Schnoebelen, *Wicca: Satan's Little White Lie* (Chino, Calif.: Chick, 1990). It is noteworthy that comic books published by Chick Publications have suggested that both Mormonism and the occult revival originally came from anti-Protestant maneuvers masterminded by the Roman Catholic Church and the Jesuits: see *The Force*, issue 15 of Chick's comics series titled The Crusaders. My comment is set forth in "Smash! Superheroes Fight the Pope," *30 Days* (U.S. edition) (January 1991), 24–28. Eventually, anti-Catholicism finds its way into Schnoebelen's books as well: "The Roman Church," he writes, "is *far closer* to Paganism than it is to Christianity. Even many Pagans have noticed the resemblance. Many witches have sought out the Roman priesthood as part of their magical development." *Wicca*, 85. *Magick* and *magickal* are spellings preferred by the modern occult movement, both to distinguish itself from stage magic and for certain hidden meanings of the letter *k*. In 1960, David Brion Davis had noticed similarities in anti-Mormon, anti-Catholic, and anti-masonic literature; see his "Some Themes of Counter-subversion: An Analysis of Anti-Masonic, Anti-Catholic, and Anti-Mormon Literature," *Mississippi Valley Historical Review* 47 (September 1960), 205–24. Davis did not suspect that these "themes" were apparently still alive and well in certain circles.

22. See Lawrence Foster, "Career Apostates: Reflections on the Work of Jerald and Sandra Tanner," *Dialogue: A Journal of Mormon Thought* 17:2 (Summer 1984), 35–60.
23. Gary L. Ward, comp., *Independent Bishops: An International Directory* (Santa Barbara, Calif.: Apogee Books, 1990).
24. Stephan A. Hoeller, "Wandering Bishops," *Gnosis: A Journal of Western Inner Traditions* 12 (Summer 1989), 25.
25. *Capital Times* (Madison, Wis.), February 5, 1980.
26. Introductory notes to William Schnoebelen, "Joseph Smith and the Temple of Doom," *Saints Alive Journal* (Winter 1986).
27. Quoted in Tanner and Tanner, "Covering Up Syn," 8.
28. For an overview of the Gnostic Churches, see Introvigne, *Il cappello del mago*, 233–56.
29. The standard biography of Crowley is John Symonds, *The Beast 666: The Life of Aleister Crowley* (London: Pindar Press, 1997), which supersedes Symonds's earlier works. Symonds is not among Crowley's admirers. A much more sympathetic account is found in Christian Bouchet, *Aleister Crowley (1875–1947): Approche historique d'un magicien contemporain* (Nantes: Ars, 1988), which was originally a dissertation by a member of a French branch of the Ordo Templi Orientis. Other valuable works include Francis X. King, *The Magical World of Aleister Crowley*, 2nd ed. (London: Arrow Books, 1987); Israel Regardie, *The Eye in the Triangle: An Interpretation of Aleister Crowley*, 3rd ed. (Phoenix, Ariz.: Falcon Press, 1986); Israel Regardie and P. R. Stephensen, *The Legend of Aleister Crowley*, 2nd ed. (Phoenix, Ariz.: Falcon Press, 1983); Gerald Suster, *The Legacy of the Beast: The Life, Work, and Influence of Aleister Crowley* (London: W. H. Allen, 1988); Charles Richard Cammell, *Aleister Crowley: The Man: The Mage: The Poet* (London: Richards Press, 1951); PierLuigi Zoccatelli, ed., *Aleister Crowley: Un mago a Cefalù* (Rome: Mediterranee, 1998); Marco Pasi, *Aleister Crowley e la tentazione della politica* (Milan: Franco Angeli, 1999). On Reuss the main reference is Helmut Möller and Ellic Howe, *Merlin Peregrinus: Vom Untergrund des Abendlandes* (Würzburg: Königshausen & Neumann, 1986).
30. Bouchet, *Aleister Crowley*, 10.
31. John Symonds, *The King of the Shadow Realm: Aleister Crowley, His Life and Magic* (London: Duckworth, 1989), 152–54.
32. See the most recent edition of the rituals used by the main US branch of the OTO: Aleister Crowley, *Liber XV Ecclesiae Gnosticae Catholicae Canon Missae* (San Francisco: Stellar Visions, 1986).
33. See his main work: Michael Bertiaux, *The Voudon Gnostic Workbook* (New York: Magickal Childe, 1988).
34. Michael Bertiaux, interviews with the author, Chicago, August 1990 and June 1991; Eccıesia Gnostica Spiritualis, certificate of consecration of Christophe (*sic*) P. Syn of July 23, 1977 (collection of the author).

35. Bertiaux, interviews with the author.
36. Schnoebelen, *Wicca*, 198, 224.
37. Ibid., 40.
38. Ibid., 194.
39. The various articles of the *Revue internationale des sociétés secrètes* on Crowley and the OTO were republished in the French Crowleyan magazine *Thelema*, from vol. 1, no. 1 (1983) to vol. 3, no. 10 (1985).
40. See Ch. Sauvetre, *Un bon serviteur de l'Eglise: Monseigneur Jouin (1844–1932)* (Paris: Casterman—Ligue Franc-Catholique, 1936); Marie-France James, "Jouin, Ernest," in *Ésotérisme, occultisme, franc-maçonnerie et Christianisme aux XIXe et XXe siècles: Explorations bio-bibliographiques* (Paris: Nouvelles Éditions Latines, 1981), 156–58.
41. Aleister Crowley, *The Confessions of Aleister Crowley. An Autohagiography*, 2nd ed., ed. John Symonds and Kenneth Grant (London: Routledge & Kegan Paul, 1979), 730–31.
42. See Symonds, *The King of the Shadow Realm*, 135–52.
43. See Francis King, ed., *The Secret Rituals of the O.T.O.* (New York: Samuel Weiser, 1973), 233–39. Later, a Californian disciple of Crowley, Jack Parsons (1914–1952), with his partner Marjorie Cameron, conducted an experiment similar to those described in *Moonchild*, without the approval of Crowley. It is interesting that the experiment was witnessed and recorded by L. Ron Hubbard, the future founder of Scientology, who quickly broke with Parsons and later claimed to have infiltrated Parsons's OTO lodge on behalf of US Navy Intelligence. Marjorie Cameron continued her career as an occult artist and poet and portrayed Kali and Babalon in Kenneth Anger's 1954 underground movie *Inauguration of the Pleasure Dome*. See John Whiteside Parsons, *Freedom Is a Two-Edged Sword: Essays*, ed. Marjorie Cameron and Hymenaeus Beta (New York: Ordo Templi Orientis, 1989).
44. See a collection of these detective stories: Aleister Crowley, *The Scrutinies of Simon Iff* (Chicago: Teitan Press, 1987).
45. Aleister Crowley, *Moonchild* (London: Mandrake Press, 1929), 226.
46. Sir Richard Francis Burton, *The City of the Saints, and Across the Rocky Mountains to California* (London: Longman, Green, Longman and Roberts, 1861).
47. Fawn M. Brodie, *The Devil Drives: A Life of Sir Richard Burton* (New York: W. W. Norton, 1967).
48. Crowley, *The Confessions*, 27.
49. Arthur Conan Doyle, *A Study in Scarlet* (London: Ward Lock & Bowden, 1894). The best discussion of Conan Doyle's relations with Mormonism is Michael W. Homer, "Sir Arthur Conan Doyle: Spiritualism and 'New Religions,'" *Dialogue: A Journal of Mormon Thought* 23:4 (Winter 1990): 97–121.
50. Crowley, *The Confessions*, 895.
51. Howe, *The Magicians of the Golden Dawn*, 199–200.
52. Crowley, *The Confessions*, 567.

53. Ellic Howe, "Fringe Masonry in England, 1870–85," *Ars Quatuor Coronatorum* 85 (1972): 242–95. *Ars Quatuor Coronatorum* is the journal of the research lodge connected with the United Grand Lodge of England.
54. See Homer, "'Similarity of Priesthood in Masonry,'" 100–13.
55. See Ellic Howe and Helmut Möller, "Theodor Reuss: Irregular Freemasonry in Germany, 1900–23," *Ars Quatuor Coronatorum* 91 (1978), 28–46.
56. Crowley, *The Confessions*, 704, 707.
57. Thomson's story has been told, from the point of view of "regular" Freemasonry and of the prosecution in his court case, by the prosecutor himself in that process: Isaac Blair Evans, *The Thomson Masonic Fraud: A Study in Clandestine Masonry* (Salt Lake City: privately printed, 1922).
58. On the Zurich congress see Serge Caillet, *La Franc-Maçonnerie Egyptienne de Memphis-Misraim: I. Histoire* (Paris: Cariscript, 1988), 62–66. I am grateful to Serge Caillet and the late Robert Amadou for further information on the congress and the rumor that Reuss was actually paid by Thomson.
59. Symonds, *The King of the Shadow Realm*, 260.
60. Ibid., 264. On Crowley as "the Mormon" in Cefalù, see Pietro Saja, "Aleister Crowley e il suo soggiorno a Cefalù," *Il Corriere delle Madonie* (November–December 1985 and January 1986).
61. Crowley, *The Confessions*, 629.
62. Ibid., 621.
63. See Evans, *The Thomson Masonic Fraud*.
64. Israel Regardie, Introduction to Aleister Crowley, *The World's Tragedy* (Phoenix, Ariz.: Falcon Press, 1985), vi.
65. See Aleister Crowley, *Crowley on Christ*, ed. Francis King (London: C. W. Daniel, 1974).
66. *Liber AL vel Legis* III:51–53; Ordo Templi Orientis, *Editio princeps* (London: OTO, 1938), 47.
67. See Jean-Bruno Renard, *Les extraterrestres: Une nouvelle croyance religieuse?* (Paris: Cerf, 1988), 103.
68. See Michael W. Homer, "Recent Psychic Evidence: The Visit of Sir Arthur Conan Doyle to Utah in 1923," *Utah Historical Quarterly* 52 (Summer 1984), 264–74; and Homer, "Sir Arthur Conan Doyle."
69. See references to the *Journal of Discourses*; and James E. Talmage, *The Articles of Faith* (Salt Lake City: Deseret News, 1899), 236.
70. Joseph A. West, "Sir Arthur Conan Doyle's 'New Revelation' and 'Vital Message,'" *Improvement Era* 24 (November 1920), 6–13.
71. See the works on Godbeites by Ronald W. Walker: "The Commencement of Godbeite Protest: Another View," *Utah Historical Quarterly* 42 (1974), 215ff.; "The Liberal Institute: A Case Study in National Assimilation," *Dialogue: A Journal of Mormon Thought* 10 (Autumn 1977), 74ff.; "When the Spirits Did Abound: Nineteenth-Century Utah Encounter with Free-Thought Radicalism," *Utah Historical Quarterly* 50 (1982), 304ff.

72. Roger D. Launius, *Joseph Smith III: Pragmatic Prophet* (Urbana: University of Illinois Press, 1988), 62–64.
73. On channeling and its differences from "classic" Spiritualism, see Massimo Introvigne, "Il 'channeling': Uno spiritismo moderno?," in *Lo spiritismo*, ed. Massimo Introvigne (Turin: Elle Di Ci, 1989), 35–94.
74. Jon Klimo, *Channeling: Investigations on Receiving Information from Paranormal Sources* (Los Angeles: Jeremy P. Tarcher, 1987), 94.
75. Scott C. Dunn, "Spirit Writing: Another Look at the Book of Mormon," *Sunstone* 10:6 (June 1985), 17–26.
76. See *A Course in Miracles: Text, Workbook for Students, Manual for Teachers* (Tiburn, Calif.: Foundation for Inner Peace, 1986). The three parts were published separately in 1975 by the same publisher.
77. On this discussion see Margot Adler, *Drawing Down the Moon: Witches, Druids, Goddess-Worshippers, and Other Pagans in America Today*, 2nd ed. (Boston: Beacon Press, 1986); Doreen Valiente, *The Rebirth of Witchcraft* (London: Robert Hale, 1989). See also chapter 12 in this volume.
78. See Eli, *The First Book of Wisdom* (n.p.: Author, 1973); Eli, *The Second Book of Wisdom* (n.p.: Author, n.d.); and the entry "Mental Science Institute" in *The Encyclopedia of American Religions*, 3rd ed., ed. J. Gordon Melton (Detroit: Gale Research, 1989), 791.
79. See Tanner and Tanner, "Cover Up Syn," 21. Melton has personally confirmed these ideas; J. Gordon Melton, personal interviews, May 1990.
80. See Leon Festinger, Henry W. Riecken, and Stanley Schachter, *When Prophecy Fails* (New York: Harper & Row, 1956).
81. See Melton, *Encyclopedia of American Religions*, 677.
82. See (in English translation) Raël, *The Message Given to Me by Extra-terrestrials: They Took Me to Their Planet* (Tokyo: ADM Corporation, 1986).
83. Raël, personal interview, January 1989. Raël has since confirmed in public speeches that Joseph Smith was among the "re-created" prophets he met.
84. Raël, *Le livre qui dit la vérité: Le message donné par les extra-terrestres* (Clermont-Ferrand, France: Editions du Message, 1974), 91.
85. Eileen Barker, *New Religious Movements: A Practical Introduction* (London: HMSO 1989), 192.

12

Crowley and Wicca

Ronald Hutton

THE SPIRITUAL TRADITION with which Aleister Crowley is most closely associated is that of Thelema, as propounded in *The Book of the Law*. The latter represents a classic religious revelation, being allegedly a body of teachings delivered by three deities to Crowley, as evangelist, using a disembodied entity as mouthpiece. Whether Thelema can be regarded primarily as a religion is, however, controversial, as many of the few thousand people who currently make it their central spiritual system seem to do so as a means to individual self-empowerment and view it as a means to enable humans to deal with apparently supernatural forces from a position of strength. As such, it has more in common with magic, according to definitions employed in Europe since ancient times, than with religion, which has traditionally been regarded as concerned primarily with honoring divine beings and enabling humans to engage in respectful communication with them. This would, of course, accord with Crowley's own enduring reputation, which has always been that of a magician and occultist rather than a religious teacher.[1] He has also, however, long been associated with the appearance of a different tradition, which, although full of magical elements, is also very clearly a religion and has currently many more adherents than Thelema: modern pagan witchcraft, or Wicca.

Both the origins of Wicca and the precise part that Crowley played in them remain uncertain and deeply controversial, and the space given to these matters by all his most recent biographers is both scant and underresearched.[2] Nonetheless, they are important because of the size of Wicca's following (amounting at the least to tens of thousands), its considerable influence on other forms of modern Paganism, and its arguable status as the only fully formed religion that England has ever given the world. As there is no doubt that Crowley had an important influence upon Wicca, his true place in religious history, as opposed to that in the history of magic(k), may be as the godfather of Wicca rather than as the father of Thelema. It is also fairly clear that Crowley's own interest in pagan witchcraft was minimal—if indeed he ever knew of its existence—in comparison with the interest taken in him by the first known Wiccans; thus the true relationship was that of Wicca with Crowley, rather than vice versa. What is also probably beyond dispute is that the key figure in that relationship was Gerald Gardner, the person who was certainly the great evangelist, and possibly the creator, of the Wiccan religion.

The outline of Gardner's dealings with Crowley is now both certain and fairly well-known. Crowley's diary proves that they met for the first time on May Day 1947, when Gardner visited the older man in his boardinghouse (effectively his retirement home) at Hastings.[3] He was accompanied by a friend, a stage magician by profession, named Arnold Crowther, and it seems to have been Arnold who was the moving force behind the visit. During World War II he had been given Crowley's book *Magick in Theory and Practice* and had become interested in his work. He was subsequently given Crowley's address by a woman who had engaged Crowther to provide a performance. Arnold immediately wrote to Crowley and so arranged the May Day visit.[4] Both men were impressed by the old magus, but it was Gardner who returned, alone, for three more visits, on May 7, 14, and 27.[5] Surviving letters show that in the course of these visits Crowley initiated Gardner up to the fourth degree of his organization, the Ordo Templi Orientis (OTO), with the name of "Scire" (Latin for "to know"), which remained Gardner's "magical" pseudonym ever after. This level of advancement would have empowered him to found his own division, or "encampment," of the OTO, and that is exactly what Gardner set out enthusiastically to do. He bought Crowley's entire stock of the latter's work *The Equinox of the Gods*, which consists of an extended commentary on *The Book of the Law*, and attempted to acquire further copies; presumably these texts were to be used to educate new recruits in the doctrine of Thelema. Crowley also provided his new disciple with a list of people whom Gardner needed to contact in order to launch his own group, and Gardner sought advice in return regarding the fees that he should charge trainees for initiation to the first degree.[6] As the OTO was moribund in Britain by that date, Gardner was effectively offering to revive it there, and so automatically making himself into its leading figure in the nation under Crowley himself. The old magus did his best to support his new initiate in this work, inviting the prominent London occultist W. B. Crow to direct "all his following" to Gardner for initiation into the order, with a view to founding more new camps.[7]

The revival, and the relationship between the two men, soon ended. At the time of their meeting, Crowley himself was probably already a dying man, and he did not last out the year. At some time in the second half of 1947 Gardner's own health collapsed, and his doctors advised him to recover in a warmer climate, so that he departed to spend the winter with his brother's family in Memphis, Tennessee.[8] He was there when Crowley passed away in December, and on hearing the news wrote immediately to the dead man's landlord, Vernon Symonds, to inform him that Crowley had chartered Gardner as leader of the OTO in Europe. Gardner used this claim in an attempt to get his hands on any manuscripts of rituals of the order, and any ceremonial equipment, that had been in Crowley's possession when he died, offering to buy them from his executors.[9] Clearly his ambitions had now expanded from an attempt to revive the order in Britain, starting by initiating new members to the lower grades, to becoming its head in an entire continent. To Crowley's closest remaining friends in England, there indeed seemed nobody better equipped or willing to take on the job, and Frieda Harris wrote to Karl Germer, leader of the OTO in the United States, in an attempt to locate Gardner and offer it to him. In January Gardner and Germer came into contact, and the former asked the latter to meet him in New York on March 19, as he was preparing to sail for England.[10] Gardner subsequently claimed that the meeting had taken place, and Germer had indeed recognized him as head of the order in Europe; there seems to be little reason to doubt this.[11]

Gerald Gardner had thus become Aleister Crowley's "magical" heir on his side of the Atlantic, but he rapidly lost his enthusiasm for the role. As he explained in a letter written a couple of years later to Crowley's literary executor, John Symonds, he found himself unable to gather enough people interested in continuing the OTO under his direction: of those who had seemed most promising, some had proved to be abroad and others to live too far away to work with him.[12] It may be added that, although Gardner showed considerable and sustained enthusiasm for ceremonial magic, he never exhibited much interest in Crowley's particular doctrines concerning it, including the Law of Thelema. Throughout the correspondence mentioned above, his chief concern lay in obtaining rituals rather than in understanding and articulating a theoretical structure to accompany them. In the letter to Symonds he admitted that he had never come into possession of scripts for any of the order's ceremonies above the fourth, and these lower-degree workings contained very little material of direct relevance to magic. In 1949 he published a novel, *High Magic's Aid*, which served as his swan song to the order. On its title page he proudly identified himself as a member of the OTO, giving his magical name and his degree.[13] The contents, however, had nothing to do with the OTO or any of Crowley's teachings. They dealt, instead, with a mixture of high ceremonial magic of the traditional kind, especially taken from Samuel Liddell Mathers's Victorian edition of the *Greater Key of Solomon*, and beliefs and rites of the witch religion that he was soon to promote.[14] From the moment that this book appeared, Gardner devoted himself wholly to Wicca, and he never behaved again as a member of Crowley's order, let alone as its European head.

In all the contemporary documents that chronicle the relationship between the two men, there is no mention of witchcraft of any kind. By 1950, however, in his letter to Symonds, Gardner told a story of their meeting that was to be repeated regularly, in different forms, over the next three decades. By this date he was beginning to promote his witch religion, and he claimed that Crowley "was very interested in the witch cult, and had some idea of combining it with the Order, but nothing came of it." Ten years later, in his ghosted autobiography, Gardner had made a significant addition to the story, that the older man had declared that he would not himself enter the witch religion because "he refused to be bossed around by any damn woman" (Wicca is centered upon a high priestess) and could not understand the lack of financial profit in it.[15] This account was later repeated by Arnold Crowther, though it is not clear from the published evidence that Crowley made the alleged comment on the first, May Day, meeting when Arnold was present as a witness or during the later visits that Gardner paid to him alone.[16]

The story, however, takes a different form as well, one that also appeared very early and from a "Gardnerian" source. In December 1953, Crowley's former friend and pupil Gerald Yorke expressed an interest in Wicca, which was by now being nationally publicized through interviews given to the mass media by Gardner and his fellow witches, as well as through private channels such as Gardner's earlier letter to Symonds. Gardner, whose public pose at this time was as the scholarly discoverer of the witch religion, mediating between its practitioners and the world, put Yorke in touch with a Wiccan high priestess of the highest degree. From her magical name, she was clearly Doreen Valiente, who was in the decades to come to make a great reputation as a Wiccan author and speaker, but who at this time had actually been introduced to the religion, by Gardner himself, only six months before, having read of it in a magazine report.[17] She told Yorke that she had been brought up in the religion by her parents, a fiction that seems designed to bear out Gardner's account (published in his subsequent books) of how Wicca had survived by being carried on secretly in families. She also told him that Crowley had himself been initiated into the religion and left it because he did not like the dominance of women in it. She added that this explained why Wiccan rituals now contained some of Crowley's work—a fact that will be discussed below, and that Yorke himself would certainly have noted and commented upon, as soon as he was able to hear or read any.[18] The following year, in the book in which he announced the existence of Wicca to the world, Gardner himself claimed that Crowley had told him that he "had been inside when he was very young," and that this could be related to the fact that the Wiccan liturgy included material that sounded like his work.[19] The belief that Crowley had himself encountered Wicca in his youth, and had either refused to join it or done so and left it or been expelled from it, now disappeared from view for ten years, to reappear in published sources in the 1970s. In these it was either represented as a rumor passed on to the author by other sources or as a fact known to the writer by privileged means conveyed through a secret tradition.[20]

There seem to be three different ways of accounting for these stories, in their different forms. One is that they are all true: that Crowley indeed encountered Wicca as a young man and discussed his reactions to it with Gardner. I personally think this to be the least likely, for two reasons. The less important is that there is no absolutely impeccable and unequivocal evidence for the existence of Wicca itself before the 1940s. The more significant is that Crowley had one of the best recorded of modern lives, reflected in his own detailed memoirs and large numbers of diaries, poems, letters, and accounts of magic(k)al workings, as well as abundant testimony by others. There is no reference in any of this material to anything that sounds like Wicca; the closest is an account of a secret society at Cambridge in his undergraduate years, run by a clergyman and known to outsiders as the Belly-banders. It was reputed to have seven degrees of initiation, and it got its nickname from the rumor that in the taking of the highest degree the candidate was flogged. Crowley took the first degree and found that the rite consisted of being blindfolded and waiting in vain for something else to happen.[21] From his account, this group had nothing in common with Wicca except the blindfolding (common to initiations into most Victorian secret societies) and the reputed flogging (a ritual actually found in Wicca from the first initiation onward). This lack of testimony is compounded by traits in Crowley's own nature: his acquisitiveness, vindictiveness, and egotism. Had he known Wicca and enjoyed it, it is hard to imagine that he would not have incorporated parts of its workings into his own systems. Had he rejected it, or been rejected by it, as most versions of the story insist, then it is hard to believe that he would not have made his contempt or anger clear in later private or unpublished writings.[22] Instead he has left no recorded reference to any witch religion, or to any personal contact with witchcraft itself.

The second explanation is that Wicca was not in fact mentioned during any of Crowley's meetings with Gerald Gardner, and that the latter made up the stories that it was as part of his subsequent promotion of it. This would mean that all the subsequent versions of them were based on Gerald's original one, which was itself fallacious. It is not an attractive exercise to accuse him of outright dishonesty in this fashion, but various people who knew him have expressed the opinion that Gardner was (according to their individual viewpoints) either a mischievous or a devious man, with a large element of the prankster in his makeup. There are several surviving accounts of how he was caught out in attempted deceptions by friends and colleagues,[23] and his surviving correspondence with Cecil Williamson shows him quite ready to fake museum exhibits and rituals in order to deceive the public—though not, it may be noted, in a Wiccan context.[24] In that context, however, he was certainly prepared to allow, or to encourage, priestesses initiated into his tradition to pass themselves off to outsiders as members of the long-surviving witch families that he claimed had brought Wicca down into the twentieth century, thereby appearing to substantiate this claim. This has been seen, as noted above, in the case of Doreen Valiente, and there is another on record.[25] On the other hand, there are some who knew him who have been equally insistent upon his honesty and reliability.[26]

The third explanation for the stories was first suggested by Doreen Valiente herself later in life: that, on being told of Gardner's involvement in Wicca, Crowley pretended to know about it already, as a piece of one-upmanship.[27] This view has recently been repeated by Philip Heselton.[28] It has the effect both of getting around the problem of the lack of reference to Wicca in Crowley's records and of clearing Gardner's name in this context. If it shifts the onus of falsehood to Crowley instead, then it would certainly be in character for the man to wish to compete in a show of knowledge and to invent aspects of his own past.[29] The single problem with it, which still seems a significant one, is in Crowley's diary entries of his meetings with Gardner. They record the aspects of his guest that he found most significant: his possession of a PhD from the University of Singapore and of the Royal Arch degree of Freemasonry. Both were, in fact, to some extent fraudulent: Gardner never received any degrees from that university and never more than the first three degrees in at least orthodox Freemasonry.[30] Clearly Gardner was determined to impress the old magus as a person of some social and scholarly standing. There is, by contrast, no mention of Wicca, even though the revelation that his new initiate was a practitioner of a surviving, and hitherto generally unsuspected, pagan witch religion should have made an impression on Crowley. On the other hand, it is possible that for some reason it did not, and the entries themselves are generally very sparse by that point of the old man's decline. With these observations the puzzle must rest in these pages.

The direct relationship between Crowley and Wicca, therefore, would appear to merit hardly more than a historical footnote. In the span of Crowley's career, his encounter with Gardner features as a minor affair toward the very end of his life, which proved almost entirely inconsequential because of the other man's failure to maintain a commitment to the OTO. In Gardner's career, his love affair with the latter appears as a brief episode that functioned most obviously as a distraction from his life's work of promoting Wicca. Such a view, however, ignores the most important theme in Crowley's relations with the witch religion: the apparent influence of his writings upon its nature and upon the ritual practices that form the core of its tradition. This theme has already been noted above, in the remarks of Gardner and Valiente, and must now take up the remainder of the present essay.

One allegation concerning Crowley's influence upon Wicca can be dismissed immediately: that Gardner paid him directly to write the liturgy for the religion as part of a process of inventing it. It has appeared in print repeatedly since 1970 and fails two tests of evidence. The first is that Crowley's diary is against it, recording neither work for Gardner nor payments for this, and the second is that none of the material in Crowley's style that appears in Wiccan contexts consists of apparent original work; it is, rather, taken from his published output.[31] This said, it seems that the relationship between that published work and the Wiccan liturgy falls into three distinct phases, corresponding to different periods in the development of the rituals concerned.

Of these, the first is by far the most important, complex, and baffling. It centers on a single manuscript: Aidan Kelly's great archival discovery, "Ye Bok of ye Art Magical," which he recognized in the 1970s as containing the earliest known recension of Wiccan rituals.[32] A number of points need to be made at once about this text, relevant to the present discussion. First, it is a collection of materials assembled from different sources and designed to resemble a medieval or early modern grimoire, written in ornate calligraphy and colored inks. As such, it was presumably intended for an actual group working ceremonial magic. At some point, however, it was retired from "active" service and had an afterlife as a notebook in which new texts were scribbled before being written up carefully elsewhere. Second, there is no absolute means of dating the entering of any of the contents in "Ye Bok." Some of the Wiccan rites that appear in it are fairly obviously earlier drafts of ceremonies that were then published in Gardner's novel *High Magic's Aid*, which means that they were written into the manuscript by 1948 at the latest. This does not, however, do much to identify the period at which they themselves were put into "Ye Bok," let alone when they were composed, and the grimoire as a whole may have been the result of a long and intermittent period of compilation or a brief and intense one. Third, "Ye Bok" is fairly certainly the work of Gerald Gardner himself, as the scribbled entries correspond to his handwriting in letters to friends, while most of the ornamented work has flourishes characteristic of Gardner when engaged in more careful penmanship. Fourth, its method of composition involved the inscription of material at regular intervals, leaving blank pages between that could be filled up with further passages at a later date. Many of the blank pages were never filled, but many others were, especially in the first half of the volume. This process gives a very rough guide to the sequence in which entries were made, in that those made in the primary sequence are likely to be earlier than those used to fill up pages initially left blank, and those in the primary sequence in the first half of the book are probably earlier than those in the second half. The lack of precision in such a system is, however, deeply worrying, and it combines with the lack of either any proper dating for the composition of the work or any knowledge of the context in which it was carried out to render analysis a highly speculative business.

What is more certain is the provenance of most of the entries, which were taken from clearly identifiable published sources. In terms of the simple number of pages covered, works written, edited, or directly influenced by Crowley represent the single largest body of matter on which the manuscript drew: they feature on 139 of the 250 pages on which entries were eventually made. This is, however, a figure distorted by a single book, the *Goetia* transcribed by Samuel Liddell Mathers and edited and published by Crowley in 1904, from which passages appear on 60 pages. The introduction to the work, and the invocations and seals for all seventy-two of the demons whom it is designed to invoke, are copied with great care, indicating that Gardner was, at this stage of his career, very interested in invoking infernal spirits—or appearing to be invoking them—in the classic "underground" medieval tradition.

All appear on "primary" pages of entry, but in the latter half of the book.[33] Next after this text in order of importance among the works by Crowley is *Magick in Theory and Practice*, published in 1929. Although not among the first passages in the book, the extracts and paraphrases from this work begin relatively soon, as a "primary" entry well within the first third of the completed pages. More were added, both as primary entries in the later part of the volume and as a "fill-up" addition in the very first section, suggesting that it was one of a number of books that Gardner was using simultaneously—or from which he was using notes—to compile "Ye Bok." This technique would, perhaps, indicate a rapid and intense period of composition rather than a slow and episodic one. Four passages were copied in all. The two that are apparently earliest concern the excellence of barbarous names in making conjurations and the efficacy of sacrifice (and especially of blood sacrifice) in magical operations. The "fill-up" one is a close paraphrase of a section on the importance and nature of ritual circumambulation. All these, then, are preoccupied with the theory and practice of a magic based on the attraction and control of spirits, such as that in the *Goetia*.[34] The fourth is of a different quality, and will be discussed below.

One further work by Crowley was incorporated into what appear to be the earlier parts of the manuscript: a passage from *Book 4, Part Two*, coauthored by him (as "Frater Perdurabo") with "Soror Virakam" (Mary d'Esté Sturges) and published in 1913. It is upon the alchemical correspondences of the scourge, dagger, and chain.[35] All these quotations were entered in the large, careful script of the "working" grimoire, and it magnifies their importance that the sections of the latter concerned with ceremonial magic drew on only three other identifiable specific sources. Next in importance is the edition of the *Key of Solomon the King* issued by Samuel Mathers in 1888. This supplied most of the directions in "Ye Bok" for the actual performance of rites, and material from it appears on thirty-nine pages. Quotations from the Bible—consisting of references to sorcerers and magicians, and to ritual nudity—feature on ten, and there are a few lines from Virgil. There are also, however, forty-six pages of apparent extracts, mostly from a work or works on kabbalah, which I have not yet been able to identify. What this all means is that, when the *Goetia* is included, passages taken from works associated with Crowley outnumber all others put together in the sections of "Ye Bok" devoted to ritual magic of the traditional sort. Furthermore, as the attention paid to the conjurations of demons would indicate, it was magic of a traditionally very risqué variety, going far beyond anything associated with the leading societies of British magicians that had operated between 1890 and 1940. Part of Crowley's appeal to Gardner when he was compiling this grimoire seems to have been Crowley's willingness to contemplate, or enact, more "disreputable" forms of magic than the norm—although it needs to be noted that the Wicca that Gardner was later to publicize did not itself contain these forms.

This daring on Gardner's part was, of course, much enhanced by his adoption of a form of magical practice that was explicitly associated with the figure of the witch, and it is time now to consider the rites entered in "Ye Bok" that were later to become integral parts of the Wiccan liturgy. The fact that these appear either as entries that were inserted into blank pages early in the manuscript or as "primary" entries from the ninety-fourth page onward makes it natural to suggest that they were included after many of the passages of ritual magic from familiar sources. As we have no knowledge of the speed at which the manuscript was assembled, however, this may be deceptive, and there is in any case no ideological separation between the ceremonial magic and the earliest Wiccan ceremonies to be entered; rather, they seem like components of the same system, and an alteration in focus seems to occur later, in the development of the Wiccan rites themselves. What can be said is that Crowley was built into the Wiccan texts from the start, just as his influence was integral to the passages of ceremonial magic.

The first- and second-degree initiation rituals may be considered among the earliest Wiccan entries in the "Ye Bok," both from their position in it (including "primary" entries only about a third of the way through) and because of the logic that it is difficult to have a distinctive initiatory tradition—as Wicca is—without initiations.

Both are indeed unlike those of any other order, denomination, or religion, including the OTO, combining elements of masonic initiation with the distinctive emphasis on binding and scourging as a means of ordeal and purification that was certainly a central part of Gardner's own practice. The sacred space is prepared for the initiation with rites that include a double use of a form of the Banishing Ritual of the Pentagram that was developed by Crowley but in this particular case taken from a book by his pupil, Israel Regardie, published in 1932, where Crowley's usage has undergone further slight mutation.[36] At the end of the ritual purification for the first degree, the candidate was expected to swear absolute secrecy on "a knife in my hair," a portion of the rite that was omitted from the version published in *High Magic's Aid*, and from Wiccan liturgy ever after. The exchange of words in which this phrase was set was taken directly from an article by Crowley, titled "Two Fragments of Ritual," that had been published in his periodical *The Equinox* in 1913.[37] It is even possible that it was struck out of the initiation rite in the novel for fear that somebody would recognize that part of what was supposed in the story to be a medieval witch religion had been composed by a twentieth-century magician.

If that was indeed the case, then it may in turn possibly be linked to the fact that the highest-degree initiation, the third, is mentioned in *High Magic's Aid* but—unlike the other two—is not portrayed, and its text is not given. Gardner explained afterward to Symonds that he had removed it because the witches who had taught it to him "went up in steam" at the idea of publishing it.[38] This is easy enough to believe, as the rite centers on an act of—literal or symbolic—sexual intercourse, but it is also notable that it includes a major element of phrases drawn from that master of sex magic, Crowley himself.[39] They all concern the sacred union of female and male and are taken from the Gnostic Mass, though with slight changes of words that make them depart from any known version of Crowley's text; the closest, however, is that (once again) in *Magick in Theory and Practice*. In addition, the texts of both the first- and the third-degree initiation rites in the book employ the device of a row of several "V" signs as a cipher, which is also found in several works by Crowley, and hitherto unique to them, although the precise usage of it in the initiations is different.[40] Whereas the Crowley-derived material vanished from later versions of the first two initiations, that in the third-degree one remained central.

Crowley's work was also of crucial assistance in the development of another essential component of later Wiccan practice, the delivery of a set speech by a high priestess, representing a loving goddess, who incites her devotees to rapture; in later parlance this is known (after masonic precedent) as "the Charge." The first version appears near the opening of the final third of the manuscript and consists of a close paraphrase of words spoken by the priestess in the Gnostic Mass: again, the nearest match is in *Magick in Theory and Practice*.[41] Near the very end of the volume—the penultimate entry—is a much more complex and extended text that fulfills the same function. It is labeled "Leviter Veslis," misspelled Latin for "The Raising of the Veil," and it is easy to be reminded instantly of the title of the section of the Gnostic Mass that contains the speech by the priestess already entered earlier: "Of the Opening of the Veil." The declaration that follows was crafted together by somebody using two books, interpolating lines from parts of each to produce an effective composite whole. One of these books was the *Aradia* of Charles Godfrey Leland, which purported to be the "gospel" of a surviving religion of Italian witches, and the section paraphrased was that in which the goddess of the religion declared its creed. The other was Crowley's own third volume of *The Equinox*, published in 1919 and commonly known as *The Blue Equinox*: quotations and paraphrases were taken from three different works within that collection: "The Law of Liberty," "Liber XV: Cordis Cincte Serpente," and

"Khabs am Pekht."[42] The composer was obviously either working at some speed or content to create liturgy with an economy of effort and originality. This is certainly how Gardner himself worked at times: sections of his later books on Wicca craft together data in a similar way. There is also, however, a parallel with how he treated his initiates or colleagues in Wicca: Doreen Valiente later told how, "probably" at Yule 1953, he had given her after lunch the task of composing a liturgy for the seasonal ceremony to be held that very evening. She used ideas taken from a carol in Alexander Carmichael's collection of Hebridean folklore, *Carmina Gadelica*, to produce an invocation that has remained a standard part of the Wiccan seasonal rite ever since.[43]

The very last entry in the sequence of those intended for ceremonial use, after "Leviter Veslis," consisted of a set of seasonal rituals designed to honor the four great festivals of the early Wiccan year. These completed the basic liturgical equipment needed for a mystery religion, and (for the first time) assumed the existence of a group of members with recognized leaders, a high priestess and high priest. Again, they were composed with considerable economy, being very scant in set liturgy and making heavy use of the same material: a verse from the same poem by Rudyard Kipling, in his children's novel *Puck of Pook's Hill*, being recited at both the May Eve and August Eve celebrations. In this context, it is not surprising to find lines of Crowley used in preceding Wiccan rites in "Ye Bok" recycled for recitation at the February Eve and May Eve meetings.[44] It is possible that his work was used to influence other points in the Wiccan rites: for example, the ceremony by which cakes and wine are consecrated bears some resemblance to the blessing of both in the Gnostic Mass.[45] It is also true that these rites drew on other identifiable sources: Freemasonry, Leland, and Kipling have already been noted. Even when the possible points of influence are disregarded, however, and the other sources are taken into account, Crowley remains the single greatest source of liturgy consistently used for these first known Wiccan rites, just as he was the single greatest source for the ceremonial magic in "Ye Bok of ye Art Magical." He remained of use as the manuscript was retired from active service as a grimoire and turned into a notebook. One of the scribbled additions was an invocation designed to be employed to rid a person of misfortune or illness. It was set in the classic Gardnerian context of purification by binding and scourging, but the text to be recited consisted of Crowley's poem "La Fortune," from a volume of his collected works, with the name of the goddess removed to substitute another more commonly associated with Wicca.[46]

The vital importance of Crowley in the compilation of Gardner's grimoire must therefore be obvious, both in the provision of actual texts and in a more general influence: in breaking free from the Judeo-Christian framework still employed by the majority of British ritual magicians of the early twentieth century, in placing consecrated sexuality at the heart of ritual symbolism, and in providing the precedent of a rapturous goddess, represented by a human priestess, inspiring worshippers to acts of love and liberty. It should also be noted, however, that Crowley's work and ideas were being appropriated for and adapted to a framework quite different from his own: the complete absence in Gardner's grimoire of the magus's characteristic recitations of the Law of Thelema, or indeed his usage of the term *magick*, is an immediate signal of the fundamental distinction between the two systems.

This now begs the question of how the personal relationship between the two men can be plotted onto the literary relationship between Crowley and Wicca, and here there is a choice to be made. Either Gardner compiled "Ye Bok of ye Art Magical" before he met Crowley on May Day 1947, and sought his acquaintance because he was already making use of his work, or else he began to compose the grimoire after meeting the other man, galvanized by the consequences of his initiation into the Ordo Templi Orientis. Both views have arguments in their favor, which to a great extent balance each other out.

One such argument centers on the significance of the passages from the *Key of Solomon* that feature so prominently in "Ye Bok"; Gardner subsequently used other quotations from the same work in his novel *High Magic's Aid*. On his own copy of the novel, Gerald Yorke scribbled that he had himself lent Gardner the copy of the *Key* from which he had taken the extracts.[47] As the two Geralds were introduced by Crowley in May 1947,[48] this could mean that the entire grimoire was composed after that date and before the completion of the novel in (at the latest) the second half of 1948. It would in that case have been compiled to satisfy Gardner's need for rituals that could be enacted by an initiatory group dedicated to ceremonial magic, apparently expressed in his letter to Vernon Symonds. On the other hand, the passages from the *Key* used in the grimoire are not the same as those employed for the novel. There is no reason Gardner should not have borrowed a copy of the work at a much earlier stage, or selections from it made by somebody else, and inserted those into "Ye Bok"—in which case he would have needed to borrow another, in 1947, to get more material from it for the novel.[49] Conversely, however, there is no absolute proof that Gardner did not use Yorke's copy of the *Key* for both grimoire and novel, choosing different passages for each.

Then there is the matter of the "witch's cottage." This was a genuine early modern half-timbered building that had been acquired by Gardner's friend John Sebastian Marlow Ward and transported to be an exhibit in the Abbey

Folk Park, an open-air museum of old buildings that Ward had opened near Barnet, Hertfordshire, in 1934. Ward had decorated and furnished it to represent the cottage of a sixteenth-century witch, and, after the park finally closed in 1945, Gardner bought the building and transported it, in turn, to land that he shortly afterward purchased with a friend. This was in a wood adjoining a naturist club, Five Acres, of which Gardner was himself a director. He had thus put into place a perfect building for the working of ritual magic, in a secluded and private spot next to a club that could provide a recruiting ground for initiates and a cover for the ritual nudity that was to be a hallmark of Wiccan practices.[50] This is exactly what happened there by the early 1950s. It is very easy to imagine that "Ye Bok of ye Art Magical" was either composed or utilized to serve this group, at the time when the cottage was acquired, and that Gardner went on to meet Crowley, in the following year, to enhance his knowledge of magic and perhaps to gain some authority in the wider world of ceremonial magicians.

Against this may perhaps be set the subsequent testimony of Gardner's niece Miriam, daughter of the brother with whom he stayed in Tennessee, to whom he had showed the cottage when she visited him in late 1946. He gave her the impression that Gerald's intention at that time was to purchase the entire club and to redevelop it in part as a museum or folklore center, of which the cottage was the first component. In her memory, the cottage itself had not been associated at that time with Wicca, or even ritual magic, but with Ward's own branch of heterodox Christianity, the Old Catholic Movement.[51] This would fit with the fact that Gardner was himself ordained a priest in one division of that movement, the Ancient British Church, on August 29, 1946. In that case, the cottage was not at first intended to function as the setting for a Wiccan coven but as an esoteric Christian chapel.[52] It may, of course, be the case that Gardner chose to conceal altogether from his niece his involvement with Wicca at this time. If that was so, he apparently continued to do so during the months of winter 1947–1948 when he was living with her family in Memphis.[53] Once again, he may have been observing discretion—although he made no secret of the fact that he made a side trip from Memphis to New Orleans to study voodoo—or he may not yet have committed himself to Wicca.

The Ancient British Church formed only a part of Gardner's complex and ever-developing spiritual allegiances at this period. In his own representation of his past, published in 1960,[54] he was initiated into Wicca in 1939, and from that moment onward it formed the center of his religious life. In this perspective his meeting with Crowley was a side issue, of no consequence to his overall intellectual development. Recent research, preeminently that of Philip Heselton, has revealed a different story, in which Gardner joined a succession of different spiritually motivated groups in 1946 and 1947.[55] They were, in apparent order of date, the Ancient British Church (in August 1946), the Ancient Druid Order (by December 1946), and then the Ordo Templi Orientis (in May 1947). He cannot be found quite certainly to have identified himself with Wicca until July 1950. Each act of membership represented a move to a more daring, radical, and countercultural form of tradition, in which his study of voodoo in the winter of 1947–1948 may also have formed a step. Each, also, represented a greater point of elevation in the tradition concerned: priest in the Ancient British Church, member of the council of the Ancient Druid Order, European head of the OTO, and finally the effective leader of Wicca itself. Heselton's own reading of this pattern is that Gardner was already, as he claimed to be, a committed Wiccan, but that his curiosity and energy led him to experiment with other forms of spirituality alongside, and to reject each in turn as wanting. In a review of Heselton's work, Chas Clifton has suggested that it could be better read as the story of a man who took membership in one group after another, searching for a tradition that suited him best and gaining confidence and knowledge as he went, until he and certain friends developed Wicca itself as the finest expression of his needs.[56] In the present state of the evidence, both views are sustainable.

The place of Crowley's own work in this cross fire of argument is, almost inevitably, equivocal. There is no reason whatever why Gardner should not have drawn on it to compile "Ye Bok of ye Art Magical" before meeting the man himself; and Arnold Crowther's possession of *Magick in Theory and Practice* would certainly have given him easy access to one of the key works used in the compilation. On the other hand, it is also possible that Gardner's meeting with Crowley fired his interest in the great magician's work and—indeed—in the practice of ceremonial magic. *The Equinox of the Gods*, which he was given as part of his training by the magus, would have done little to satisfy this, and (as said) he was left lacking in actual rituals. It may well be that he went on to develop the latter himself, drawing in part on other works by Crowley and combining them with a range of further sources. Once again, either suggestion is credible.

The remaining two phases of Crowley's relationship with the witch religion may be swiftly summarized. The second consists of Gardner's continued use of Crowley's work as source material after the completion of "Ye Bok of ye Art Magical." The latter still seems to have been in use as a working grimoire during 1949, because it contains an addition to the first-degree initiation rite apparently copied from an article published in a magazine, edited in London by Gardner's friend Ross Nichols, in the course of that year.[57] If so, by that date (at the latest) it was one of two different manuscripts that Gardner was using for ritual. The other also survives and was dubbed "Text A" by Janet and Stewart Farrar in the 1980s, as the oldest recension of the Wiccan liturgy known by them to exist at that time.[58] Since it contains rites in the final form into which they were put during the amendments in "Ye Bok of ye Art Magical," it was commenced later than that work; also, like "Ye Bok," it had a career as a ceremonial text before being turned into one of hasty notes. It was assembled, likewise, by the technique of interspersing entries through most of its length with blank pages between, which were later filled up. The later, scribbled, passages include extracts from Robert Graves's book *The White Goddess*, published in 1948, while a page from a magazine dated February 1950 is pasted over the contents page (an action that presumably marked a stage in the work's "decommissioning" as an active grimoire). These pointers provide some rough indication of the span of years within which its composition may be located.

Philip Heselton's patient work has identified many of the sources on which it drew, and which were both much more numerous and more heterogeneous in kind than those used for "Ye Bok of ye Art Magical." They include the work of several famous poets and novelists, and various books on the history and nature of religion and magic; in addition, there remains a significant quantity of unattributed material.[59] What is very clear is that the work of Crowley continued to feature in each layer of additions. The boldly and carefully inscribed ritual texts carried over from "Ye Bok" retained most of the elements of it that they already embodied. To these were added many further passages, written in a large and clear enough hand to be read aloud easily, and these included poetry of Crowley's (such as the verses to the goddess Nuit here labeled "Ah! Ah!") and further quotation from the Gnostic Mass and *Book 4*. The hastily jotted notes that were added last contained more information from *The Equinox*. Clearly the dead magician remained an important source of inspiration to Gardner, although now one among many, and it may also be significant that the scribbled information includes a disproportionate amount on the alleged occult activities of the medieval Knights Templar. This may well reflect Gardner's lingering sense of his position as a leader of the Ordo Templi Orientis, which, as its name ("Order of the Eastern Templars") suggests, looked back to the Knights Templar as spiritual ancestors.

The final phase of the relationship between Wicca and Crowley's work consisted of Gardner's progressive attempts to diminish, and to deny, the extent of his association with, and debt to, the dead magician. It was a feature of the period from the mid-1950s onward, and apparently occurred for three interdependent reasons. The first was that Wicca was now completely up and running as an independent tradition for which Gardner claimed an unbroken continuity from ancient times, and it was this, rather than its borrowings from twentieth-century sources, that he needed to emphasize. The second was that Crowley himself had become bigger news than ever in the wake of John Symonds's celebrated biography of him, *The Great Beast*, which appeared in 1951. While it established him posthumously, in the eyes of the public, as the most important of modern ritual magicians, it was by no means admiring of its subject, and in large part played up his reputation as a man of extraordinary follies and vices, as well as of talents. As a result, it contributed mightily to Crowley's enduring notoriety, as well as his fame, and made him a figure whom one could represent as a mentor and teacher only with some risk to one's own tradition. Gardner's consciousness of this problem would certainly have been accentuated by the advice of the most important and influential of his early initiates, Doreen Valiente.

According to her recollections published many years later, when Gardner first initiated her he tried to pass off the Wiccan liturgy that he used by that date as having been handed on to him by the coven that had, originally, initiated him. She immediately recognized that it contained passages of Crowley (and Leland and Kipling) and thought that he was "none too pleased at my recognition of its sources."[60] He explained this to her with his now famous declaration that "the rituals he had received from the old coven were very fragmentary, and that in order to make them workable he had been compelled to supplement them with other material." He claimed to have used Crowley's writings in particular for two reasons: first, because as a high-ranking initiate of Crowley himself, he felt entitled to do so, and, second, because they "breathed the very spirit of paganism and were expressed in splendid poetry."[61] This seems to be as close to a personal statement of Gerald Gardner's ways of working, of his attitude toward Crowley, and of what he was actually doing between 1947 and 1950 as we are ever going to get. It may be noted in particular that he took full personal responsibility for the insertion of the extracts from Crowley (and others) into the rites, and also that he felt able to undertake this process only after his initiation by the old magician himself; but perhaps too much cannot be laid on words reported at second hand and recalled many years later.

Both of them recognized that the element of Crowley in the ceremonies was at once unusually large and particularly glaring, and their initial strategy to cope with this problem was (as shown above) inclusive: to suggest that Crowley had himself been involved with Wicca at some stage. Valiente's attitude, however, subsequently hardened after the publication in 1954 of Gardner's book on their religion, *Witchcraft Today*, which attracted inquiries from many prospective initiates. In her own (subsequently recalled) words, she told Gardner that Wicca would never take off "so long as the influence of the later Aleister Crowley was so prevalent and obvious" within it. She thought that "Crowley's name stank," and that "as a person, he was simply a nasty piece of work"; it is significant that she twice mentioned John Symonds's autobiography in connection with these opinions. Gardner's reaction was to give her full permission to rewrite the rituals, "cutting out the Crowleyanity as much as I could and trying to bring it back to what I felt was, if not so elaborate as Crowley's phraseology, at least our own and in our own words."[62] Like many exercises in ostensible religious "restoration," this was actually a brilliant one of creation, and Valiente's compositions contributed powerfully to the individual character of Wicca as a tradition, and to its subsequent success.

Gardner himself cooperated fully with her wishes, both in accepting the alteration of the liturgy and in distancing himself from Crowley. In his public version of his own life story, released in 1960, he placed most emphasis on his relationship with Wicca itself, as an encounter with a surviving pagan religion, from his initiation into it in 1939 to his emergence as its leading publicist in the 1950s. The chapter devoted to Crowley was an exercise in belittlement. He dismissed the man himself as merely a charming charlatan and showman, who exploited others and could understand neither the female-centered nature of Wicca nor the lack of financial profit in it for its leaders (both remarks implicit condemnations of Crowley himself). Gardner admitted that he had joined the Ordo Templi Orientis and that many people had regarded him as Crowley's successor, but claimed—in direct contravention of the facts—that he had never wanted the role of leader within the order and had never even the slightest inclination to make anything of his power to establish a division of it.[63] The clear intention of these words was to amplify the stature of Gardner himself, and Wicca, at the expense of Crowley and the latter's own teachings, and their effect was to encourage a hostility between Wicca and Thelema that persists in some quarters to the present time.

In summary, therefore, all that can confidently be suggested about the relationship between Aleister Crowley and Wicca is that it must have lain somewhere on a spectrum defined by two extreme positions. The "minimalist" position is that Gerald Gardner's account of his own past was broadly correct, and that his central loyalty was given to the witch religion ever since he discovered and entered it in 1939, but that the old magician's writings fulfilled a temporary important function in filling gaps in the original Wiccan rituals and so enabling Gardner to present new initiates with a more impressive and coherent body of liturgy. Even this position, therefore, would credit Crowley with a significant, if limited and transitory, role in the success of Wicca as a modern religion, both in terms of the quantity of his work employed for this purpose and for its contribution to, or compatibility with, the ideology of Wiccan practice. The "maximalist" position holds that without Crowley there would have been no Wicca, because Gardner's encounter with the man and his writings, in 1947, provided the vital influence, and impetus, for Gardner to develop a new religion in partnership with his own collaborators and initiates. Where the truth lies within this spread of possible interpretations is a question that may possibly never be answered, but it seems that all interpretations acknowledge two things as verified. The first is that, although Wicca at first drew heavily on Crowley's writings, it was in essence a tradition of a very different kind to any that he described or sought to establish himself. The second is that, nonetheless, as Wicca was presented to the world at the opening of the 1950s, Aleister Crowley was the most important single identifiable influence upon it next to Gerald Gardner himself.

Notes

1. Crowley's relationship with religion is analyzed in Ronald Hutton, *The Triumph of the Moon: A History of Modern Pagan Witchcraft* (Oxford: Oxford University Press, 1999), 171–80.
2. Martin Booth, *A Magick Life* (London: Coronet, 2001), does not deal with the issue. Short discussions appear in Lawrence Sutin, *Do What Thou Wilt* (New York: St. Martin's Griffin, 2002), 409–10; and Richard Kaczynski, *Perdurabo* (Tempe, Ariz.: New Falcon, 2002), 447–48.
3. MS 23, Gerald Yorke Collection, Warburg Institute, University of London.
4. This is the story as told later by Arnold's wife, Patricia: Patricia Crowther, *Witch Blood! The Diary of a Witch High Priestess* (New York: House of Collectibles, 1974), 72–78. I am very grateful to Philip Heselton for the loan of this work.
5. MS 23.
6. MS D5, Crowley to Yorke, May 9, 1947, Gerald Yorke Collection; and MS E21, Gardner to Crowley, June 14, 1947, Gerald Yorke Collection. I am basing my discussion on these letters rather than on the famous charter that Gardner later exhibited as giving him authority from Crowley to found an encampment, which is now in the Greenfield Collection of the OTO archive in the United States. This seems to be in essence a genuine document, but one drawn up by Gardner rather than

Crowley himself and containing various anomalies that make it a dangerous source for what was actually transacted between the two men. A full discussion of the charter is in Philip Heselton, *Gerald Gardner and the Cauldron of Inspiration* (Milverton, Somerset: Capall Bann, 2003), 197–203.

7. Clive Harper, "Gerald Gardner and the O.T.O. Part 1," *Nuit-Isis* 10 (1991), 9.
8. The information on Gardner's health is from Scrapbook EE2, fo. 340, Gerald Yorke Institute; and Gardner to Symonds, December 24, 1947, posted on http://www.geraldgardner.com/index/gardner.shtml. That on his family is from Morgan Davis, "From Man to Witch—Gerald Gardner 1946–1949," posted on http://www.geraldgardner.com in 2002, 30, 40.
9. Gardner to Symonds, December 24, 1947.
10. These letters, now in the OTO archive, were published in the Thelema Lodge OTO newsletter in November 1992. I am very grateful to Melissa Montgomery for giving me a copy of this work.
11. Scrapbook EE2, fo. 340.
12. Ibid.
13. Both, however, as has often been noticed, were wrong: there was an extra *r* in the name, and the degree was a Golden Dawn one rather than one of the OTO. It is possible that Gardner did this deliberately, to conceal the real equivalents from noninitiates, or that it was the result of mere confusion, carelessness, and the malady that always inflicted his spelling. The fact that the name is given correctly on the title page indicates that some of these latter factors are at the least relevant.
14. Gerald Gardner, *High Magic's Aid* (London: Michael Houghton, 1949).
15. J. L. Bracelin, *Gerald Gardner: Witch* (London: Octagon, 1960), chap. 14.
16. Patricia Crowther, "The Day I Met Aleister Crowley," *Prediction* (November 1970), 14. This represents Arnold's "ghosted" recollection of the visit; see *Pagan Dawn* 145 (Samhain 2002), 23.
17. Doreen Valiente, *The Rebirth of Witchcraft* (Custer, Wash.: Phoenix, 1989), 35–40.
18. Scrapbook EE2, (Valiente) to Yorke, Gerald Yorke Collection. A letter from Gardner himself to Yorke, dated October 24, 1952, and also in the scrapbook, is concerned mainly with telling Yorke about Wicca and arousing his interest in it. I am very grateful to Brad Verter for drawing my attention to this source.
19. Gerald Gardner, *Witchcraft Today* (London: Rider, 1954), 47.
20. These tales are considered in detail in Hutton, *Triumph of the Moon*, 218–21.
21. Aleister Crowley, *The Confessions of Aleister Crowley*, ed. John Symonds and Kenneth Grant (London: Jonathan Cape, 1969), 109.
22. This argument is taken further in Hutton, *Triumph of the Moon*, 220–21.
23. See ibid., 239, and sources given there.
24. Gardner to Williamson, n.d. but 1951, June 1951, and November 6, 1951, Williamson Papers, Museum of Witchcraft, Boscastle. I am very grateful to the owner, Graham King, for allowing me to read these sources.

25. Doreen Valiente noted acidly that a high priestess called Dayonis did so in a newspaper interview in 1957; Valiente, *The Rebirth of Witchcraft*, 74. Valiente had apparently—and, in view of the lapse of time, understandably—forgotten that she had earlier done exactly the same thing. The interview was printed in *The People* (November 3, 1957), 9, and the claim was indeed made there by Dayonis. Frederic Lamond, who was in Dayonis's coven at the time, has confirmed both that the claim was false and that it was Gardner himself who first made it on her behalf; personal communication, August 16, 1996. Likewise, it is hard to believe that Valiente would have told Yorke what she did without the approval and encouragement of her initiator and mentor, especially as she repudiated it all in print many years later, and in view of the famous probity of her character as revealed in later years.
26. See James Laver's foreword to Bracelin, *Gerald Gardner*. Although, while declaring that Gardner was a splendid fellow in general (which few have ever denied), Laver says nothing specific about the reliability of his statements on the history of Wicca. Wholly unequivocal, however, is Patricia Crowther, who, among five Wiccans still alive who knew Gardner personally and worked with him ritually, is the one who remains completely convinced of his probity.
27. Doreen Valiente, *Witchcraft for Tomorrow* (London: Hale, 1978), 15.
28. Heselton, *Gerald Gardner*, 191.
29. These traits are shown up particularly well in Sutin's recent biography, *Do What Thou Wilt*.
30. Valiente, *The Rebirth of Witchcraft*, 41–42; Heselton, *Gerald Gardner*, 187–88; and personal communication, June 29, 2005.
31. This issue is considered in detail in Hutton, *Triumph of the Moon*, 217–18.
32. Information on its nature and location are given in ibid., 227–36 and 448.
33. On 157–61, 165–88, 205–24, and 229–41.
34. On 12–13, 60–63, and 132–38 of "Ye Bok." Compare the passages in Aleister Crowley, *Magick in Theory and Practice* (Paris: Lecram, 1929), 68–71, 80–81, and 92–99.
35. On 114–17 of "Ye Bok" and 27–30 of Aleister Crowley, *Book Four, Part II* (London: Weiland, 1913).
36. Israel Regardie, *The Tree of Life* (London: Rider, 1932), 150. It is transcribed into "Ye Bok" on pages 44–45.
37. This was first noted by an American scholar, Roger Dearnaley (personal communication, July 17, 2000), and later independently discovered by another, David Fickett-Wilbar (who also writes as Ceisiwr Serith) (personal communication, May 15, 2005). The passage is on pages 83–90 of the periodical concerned, and on 95–96 of "Ye Bok." David Fickett-Wilbar's Web site is http://www.ceisiwrserith.com.
38. Scrapbook EE2, fo. 340.
39. Found on 110–11 and 224–25 of "Ye Bok." The last two pages seem to have now disappeared from the original manuscript, but they survive in various different transcriptions of it.

40. This was first noticed by Robert Matheisen and is credited to him by Aidan Kelly in the latter's unpublished, computer-disk, commentary on "Ye Bok," 15.
41. On 191–93 of "Ye Bok."
42. This was first realized by Roger Dearnaley, and then independently by David Fickett-Wilbar (see note 37, above). Both men are excellent scholars, and it is hoped that their citation in the present essay will encourage and enable them to publish in a more open forum. "Leviter Veslis" is on 263–68 of "Ye Bok."
43. Janet Farrar and Stewart Farrar, *Eight Sabbats for Witches* (London: Hale, 1981), 148.
44. On 278–88 of "Ye Bok."
45. On 28 of "Ye Bok."
46. This was first noticed by Carl Watson, credited by Aidan Kelly on page 3 of the "1953" section of his computer-disk study of the Wiccan liturgy. The text is on page 29 of "Ye Bok" and on page 120 of volume 3 of the Foyers edition of *The Works of Aleister Crowley* (Foyers, Scotland: Society for the Propagation of Religious Truth, 1907).
47. This book is now held as part of the Yorke Collection in the Warburg Institute.
48. MS D5, Crowley to York, May 9, 1947.
49. A point apparently first made by Roger Dearnaley (personal communication, July 17, 2000) and repeated by Philip Heselton in *Gerald Gardner*, 295.
50. On this subject see Hutton, *Triumph of the Moon*, 213–14; and Heselton, *Gerald Gardner*, 135–67.
51. Davis, "From Man to Witch," 8–12.
52. Heselton, *Gerald Gardner*, 135–67.
53. Davis, "From Man to Witch," 14–28.
54. Bracelin, *Gerald Gardner*.
55. Hutton, *Triumph of the Moon*, 212–23; Heselton, *Gerald Gardner*, 79–214.
56. Chas Clifton, review of Heselton, *Gerald Gardner*, in *The Pomegranate* 6.2 (November 2004), 267–71.
57. This is discussed in Hutton, *Triumph of the Moon*, 233.
58. Janet Farrar and Stewart Farrar, *The Witches' Way* (London: Hale, 1984), 3. I am very grateful to Philip Heselton for presenting me with a full photocopy of this work, and to its present owner, John Belham-Payne, for access to the original.
59. Heselton, *Gerald Gardner*, 281–87.
60. Valiente, *Rebirth of Witchcraft*, 47. This comment needs to be read in the light of the letter on the subject that Doreen allegedly sent to Aidan Kelly; see Kelly, *Crafting the Art of Magic* (St. Paul, Minn.: Llewellyn, 1991), 97.
61. Valiente, *Rebirth of Witchcraft*, 57. An earlier and briefer account of the same statement is found in Doreen Valiente, *An ABC of Witchcraft Past and Present* (London: Hale, 1973), 154.
62. Valiente, *Rebirth of Witchcraft*, 60–61.
63. Bracelin, *Gerald Gardner*, chap. 14. This book was officially written by Jack Bracelin, actually (in the main) written by Idries Shah, and inevitably based on Gardner's own memories for its whole substance up until the mid-1950s. See Hutton, *Triumph of the Moon*, 205, 445.

13

Through the Witch's Looking Glass

THE MAGICK OF ALEISTER CROWLEY AND THE WITCHCRAFT OF ROSALEEN NORTON

Keith Richmond

Speak Not of the Beast

ALEISTER CROWLEY IS widely recognized as being among the most influential, and the most vilified, of the many occultists to have achieved fame or notoriety during the twentieth century. Somewhat ironically, the attacks on Crowley focused largely on his personality and lifestyle, rather than on the specific aspects of the occult and religious studies and practices around which his life revolved. On the occasions that his detractors did make mention of his magick or creed of Thelema, these were usually dismissed with banal generalizations about "Satanism" and "black magic," and without any attempt at offering a serious critique or analysis.

This silence—or at least absence of considered comment or criticism—was not limited to those outside the esoteric milieu, and indeed seems particularly noteworthy when it came to Crowley's occultist contemporaries. The majority of these—friend and foe alike—seem to have chosen either to ignore Crowley or to dismiss him and his works in just a few short sentences. The obvious exceptions to this rule were followers and former followers such as Charles Stansfeld Jones and Kenneth Grant, who have both written extensively on Crowley and his works. Generally, however, there seems to have been an unspoken rule that one should "speak not of the Beast."

The reasons for this silence are perhaps not too difficult to discern. Crowley's reputation was decidedly unsavory, and some occultists might have been concerned that even to criticize him could result in their being tarred by association. Others would have been afraid of being drawn into an unseemly spat or even fearful of lawsuits, for Crowley had shown himself to have a litigious streak, albeit one that in its greatest test failed utterly to deliver the required results. Then there was what might be termed "professional envy"—individuals or groups who were engaged in establishing their own occult credentials were probably not especially keen to draw attention to a rival, particularly one whose work had quite possibly been a strong influence on their own.[1]

Whatever its causes, the silence has been profound, and very few of Crowley's contemporaries—or near contemporaries—have chosen to record how they saw the writings of the Beast in relation to their own work.

The Remarkable Miss Norton

One of the few who did make serious comment on Crowley was Rosaleen Norton (1917–1979), the Australian artist who gained widespread notoriety as "the witch of Kings Cross." Norton was an outspoken nonconformist whose confronting and unabashed art, bohemian lifestyle, and willingness to proclaim her occult beliefs publicly—while at the same time being loudly critical of contemporary Christianity and middle-class values—made her an easy target for social conservatives. Even more than Crowley, she suffered from a torrent of hostility unleashed at her by officialdom and the popular press.

As a consequence, she came to occupy a unique position in Australian history, that of the country's most persecuted—and prosecuted—female artist. Accusations of "indecency" leveled at some of the paintings displayed in her 1949 Melbourne exhibition resulted in her being the only woman artist ever to be charged with "having exhibited obscene articles" in the state of Victoria. Similar charges against her book *The Art of Rosaleen Norton*, published in Sydney in 1952, gave her the doubtful honor of being the only Australian artist ever to have had a book of her works prosecuted for "obscenity" and also resulted in the work being banned in the United States.[2] Worst of all, she also became the only Australian artist (male or female) ever to have had works destroyed by judicial sanction, when, having expired all avenues for appeal, several of her pictures that had been seized by police from an exhibition in the Kashmir Café in Sydney in 1955 were finally consigned to the censor's fires in 1960.[3]

When not attacking Norton for her moral failings and "improper" artworks, the popular press delighted in creating mildly salacious pieces about her that portrayed her as a colorful and eccentric local character. Many hundreds, if not thousands, of newspaper and magazine articles were written about her, and she was also the subject of a smaller number of radio and television accounts.[4] As a consequence she became Australia's best-known occultist, occupying a position in the nation's popular imagination that was in many ways analogous to that held by Crowley in the United Kingdom.

The woman who attracted so much attention was born in New Zealand in 1917 and had moved with her family to Sydney, Australia, in the mid-1920s. A willfully independent child, she possessed a keen intelligence that was largely unconstrained by the fetters of convention. To the alarm of parents and teachers alike, she developed a fascination with what would now be termed horror fiction. Although there can be no certainty about it, it was arguably her reading of this macabre literature, which often teemed with ghosts, witches, vampires, demons, and other supernatural elements, that first sparked her interest in the occult.

In her autobiographical writings Norton recounted a number of unusual childhood experiences to which she ascribed occult meanings. In the more sensational of these accounts she implied, and sometimes even stated, that she had been aware of their occult nature even as they took place. That is—to borrow the title given to one of her more popular autobiographical narratives—she had been "born a witch" and had known it all along.[5] However, in her more sober reflections Norton generally allowed that her understanding of the esoteric quality of these occurrences had come with the benefit of hindsight, and that at the time they actually took place the experiences "were not then thought of in the terms in which I have been describing them."[6]

According to the most reliable of Norton's accounts of her esoteric autobiography—that which she gave in the course of an interview with Dr. L. J. Murphy of Melbourne University in 1949—she did not begin to involve herself seriously in the study of the occult until 1940, and it was then that she had her first "mystical experiences."[7] Interestingly, however, in a short note headed "The Crowley Pattern and Connections," in which Norton briefly itemized some of the links between herself and the Beast, she indicated that there had been some form of connection as early as 1939.[8] Unfortunately she did not elucidate, but presumably this involved either her meeting someone who introduced her to Crowley's work or her discovering one of his books. Given the timing, it is tempting to speculate that this might have been the catalyst, or at very least a significant part of the process, that moved Norton to immerse herself in the study of the occult.

Whatever the cause, once her interest had been fired, Norton dove deeply into the study of all things esoteric. As would be the case throughout her life, her occult activities were largely intuitive and experiential rather than theory based, although she did read a variety of books on the occult, psychology, and symbolism. In particular the literature of the Theosophical Society and the writings of Carl Gustav Jung—specifically the latter's work on symbols, archetypes, and the "collective unconscious"—played an important part in her early investigations, providing a theoretical framework upon which she could order and interpret her practical experiences.

In her early experiments Norton sought to tap into a part of the unconscious that she believed housed "the accumulated knowledge of mankind," a stratum referred to by the Theosophists and others as "the Akashic record."[9] To do this she would enter a trance or meditative state, using the type of preparatory practices that would be familiar to practitioners of ritual magic or certain types of meditation: she first sought to still or suppress her conscious mind while at the same time surrounding herself with various symbols, objects, colors, and scents that she felt were in some way in harmony with the "other" with which she sought to make contact.

Norton also experimented briefly with "automatic drawing," whereby she would still her conscious mind and allow drawings to flow from deep within, but she soon abandoned this, choosing instead simply to record in her art the entities and vistas she encountered during her explorations. For five months she continued her experiments, experiencing what she described as a state of "exalted consciousness," in which she found herself brimming with creative, intellectual, and intuitive energy. Then, for some two years, she abandoned her investigations.

When she returned to them, Norton focused her attention on "automatic writing." She would later record that during the nine or ten months in which she engaged in this practice she received the "rough outlines of a philosophical and metaphysical conception of the Universe and life beyond death which by no stretch of the imagination could I attribute to my normal self."[10] Much of the information was "fragmentary and incomplete," and it was only later, through further experimentation or the study of esoteric literature, that Norton was able to "correlate and supply the missing factors."[11]

An Introduction to Witchcraft

Unfortunately, details of Norton's occult explorations at this time, particularly their chronology, are scant, although we do know that her interpretation of what took place was heavily influenced by her reading of Margaret Murray's *The Witch Cult in Western Europe* (1921) and *The God of the Witches* (1933). In these works Murray hypothesized that "witchcraft," in its medieval European context, was actually a survival of an ancient, possibly neolithic, pagan religion that worshipped a masculine horned deity. One of the forms in which the

Horned God was recognized was Pan, a deity for whom Norton had felt a special affinity since she first encountered him in her childhood reading. In her now-forming cosmology Norton recognized Pan as the "Great God" of the planet, who both encompassed and presided over all living things, human and nonhuman, on all the planes of existence.

Elements of the vocabulary of "traditional witchcraft"—as postulated by Margaret Murray—were sometimes used by Norton to describe and define her experiences; most notably, she chose to refer to herself as a "witch" rather than a "magician" or any of the many other available synonyms. Still, above all she was eclectic, and the letters and notes in which she mentions her esoteric activities contain references to many other systems. Thus when looking back on this period some dozen years later she defined some of her experiences in purely kabbalistic terms, observing that "in 1942–43 I was a fully conscious initiate of the Supernals—Chokmah and Binah—with 'understanding' of Kether in Atziluth."[12] In contemporary letters she wrote of séances and experiments with clairvoyance in terms that would not have been unfamiliar to the Spiritualists of an earlier generation.

Throughout this period of experimentation Norton was married to Beresford Conroy, her lover of several years, whom she had wed on Christmas Eve of 1940. Drafts of her letters to him show that he shared her occult interests, but equally there is no doubt that she was the driving force in that aspect of their lives. Their marriage was every bit as unconventional as their esoteric beliefs, and Norton at times enjoyed an exuberant sex life involving a number of other partners, presumably with her husband's approval.

An acquaintance of the time, who would go on to become a lover and one of her most significant magical partners, was a young poet named Gavin Greenlees. Norton and Greenlees first met in mid-1944. World War II then raged, and the two seem to have met not long after Beresford Conroy had joined the army and been shipped north for training, prior to going on active service in the Pacific. Greenlees was only fourteen years old; he still lived at home with his parents in Melbourne but was visiting Sydney, where he was introduced to Norton at the launch party for one of the issues of *Pertinent*, a little magazine to which all three had contributed. Although a huge difference in age and experience separated Norton and Greenlees, they nonetheless developed a strong rapport.

Greenlees was certainly no ordinary fourteen-year-old, and to say that he had a quick and precocious mind is to indulge in understatement. A voracious reader of modern literature, he had amassed a personal library of some two hundred volumes and exhausted the collections of four local libraries by the age of twelve, at which point he applied himself to the colossal holdings of the Melbourne Public Library (now the State Library of Victoria).[13]

Following the launch of *Pertinent*, Greenlees grudgingly returned to Melbourne, overflowing with a newfound fascination for both Rosaleen Norton and the occult. He threw himself into the study of magic, in particular the works of Crowley, which he found in generous supply at his beloved Public Library.[14] *Magick in Theory and Practice* was a constant companion; indeed, he became so familiar with it that he was said to be able to recite lengthy passages of it from memory.[15] Using Crowley's reading lists as a starting point, he then broadened his studies to encompass all aspects of occult, mystical, religious, and philosophical theory.

Curiously, at the very time that Greenlees began to apply himself to the study of Crowley's works, Norton was in the process of forming a friendship with the writer Dulcie Deamer, one of the few people in Australia who could claim an association, albeit indirect, with the Beast. Like Norton, Deamer had been born in New Zealand and had ended up making her home in Kings Cross, although, as she was born a generation before Norton, her heyday had been in the early 1920s, when Norton was still a child. The two women had been acquainted through Bohemian circles for some time, but they actually got to know one another and become friends early in 1945.[16]

Deamer too had more than a passing interest in the occult—as evidenced in both her fiction and her verse—although she seems to have had little time for Crowley, whom she once described as an "unsavory person."[17] Despite this rather offhand dismissal of the Beast, Deamer had had far more opportunity to find out about Crowley than most, for she had been a close friend of his Sydney-based disciple Frank Bennett. Indeed, Deamer had been such a close friend of Bennett's that he had extended an invitation to her to partake in an alfresco Crowleyan sex-magick ritual, an offer she apparently declined. Bennett had of course studied with Crowley at his Abbey of Thelema in Cefalù and also served as his emissary in Australia. Norton's letters to Conroy reveal that she and Deamer engaged in a variety of occult activities, including scrying and tarot reading. Given Deamer's history and the occult interests that she shared with Norton, it seems all but unthinkable that they would not have discussed Crowley, but neither appears to have left any record of it if they did so.

Not long after Deamer and Norton had become friends, the young Gavin Greenlees appeared unexpectedly on the scene, having fled his parents' home and run away to Sydney. There he sought out Norton, renewed their acquaintance, and soon became her lover.[18] Norton discovered that the theoretical knowledge of comparative religion, occultism, and philosophy that Greenlees had acquired by studying the works detailed in Crowley's reading lists provided a valuable adjunct to her own largely intuitive approach to the subject. As she would later write, "Gav has enabled me to tabulate my earlier Occult experiences, through his knowledge of Comparative Philosophy."[19] In a presumably related comment, she recorded 1946 as being one of the years that was important in the developing "Crowley Pattern and Connections," in her life.[20]

The span between 1946 and 1949 is one of the least-chronicled periods of Norton's adult years. In mundane terms we know that it was a time of considerable hardship: Conroy returned from military service after the war's end, and the two parted company permanently. Norton found herself in extreme financial difficulty and barely managed to sustain herself with a series of odd jobs, moving from one form of temporary accommodation to another. She apparently continued her relationship with Greenlees, who himself existed in similar if not more parlous circumstances. She kept at her art, even managing one or two exhibitions, and continued her occult studies, but little has survived regarding them.

Fortune at last seemed to smile on Norton in 1949, when she was given the opportunity to exhibit her art at the Rowden-White Library of the University of Melbourne. The event was well publicized and attracted considerable attention, including that of the local vice squad, which spirited away several of her pictures on account of their alleged obscenity. The charges went to court, and eventually Norton won the case, although it was a somewhat hollow victory, as the talk of obscenity largely overshadowed the exhibition and helped neither her artistic career nor sales of her pictures.

The exhibition and ensuing fracas had numerous unintended consequences. One was that Norton and Greenlees had more time in Melbourne than they had initially anticipated, which gave them the opportunity to visit another person with Crowley links, the bookseller Norman Robb. Robb had lived in Sydney during the 1920s and, like Deamer, had been introduced to Crowley's works by Frank Bennett. Bennett had encouraged Robb to start a correspondence with Crowley and had also assisted him in collecting the magician's works, presumably in the hope of eventually "converting" him to Crowley's creed of Thelema. Robb did manage to pen what was probably the first positive essay on Crowley to be published in Australia, but their correspondence faltered after a few letters, and Robb's interest in the Beast failed to extend beyond an appreciation of his poetry, and even that soon waned.

Something—perhaps news of Crowley's death in December 1947—reawakened Robb's interest, and he began collecting the Beast's works with renewed vigor. Publicly Robb tended to understate his enthusiasm for

Crowley, but the zest with which he sought out his works, and his correspondence with many of Crowley's former associates—including Gerald Yorke, Karl Germer, P. R. Stephensen, Edward Noel FitzGerald, and others—suggests a more than casual interest.

As it happened, Robb also hosted a poetry program on one of the major local radio stations, and by odd coincidence he had met the then-schoolboy Gavin Greenlees and broadcast a few of his poems some seven years earlier. That aside, there seems little doubt that when Greenlees and Norton made their way to Robb's shop, it was Crowley and magick, not literature and poetry, that was at the forefront of their minds. Nothing is known of what took place at their meetings, other than that on one ill-fated visit the couple arrived so heavily under the influence of some drug that they were incapable of coherent speech. On that occasion Robb refused to let them into the shop and instead spoke briefly and sharply with them outside, before leaving them perched in the gutter in a state of stupor.[21]

Fortunately, Norton was in much better shape when, a few weeks later, she took part in a psychological evaluation of herself. The evaluation had originally been suggested by her legal counsel as part of a defense strategy, but that had been rendered unnecessary by the unexpectedly swift conclusion of the obscenity trial. However, Norton and those in the Psychology Department at Melbourne University who were to conduct it were greatly excited by the prospect of the project and decided to proceed anyway.

For present purposes, by far the most interesting aspect of the examination was the lengthy statement about the nature and origin of her occult beliefs that Norton made as a part of it.[22] One aspect of this that immediately strikes the reader is its saturation with the language and concepts of Theosophy, kabbalah, and ritual magic and the terminology of Jungian psychology. Indeed, it is so replete with the jargon of these different schools of thought that it would make difficult reading for anyone not familiar with such literature. That said, while the cosmology outlined clearly owes much to these same schools, it also contains elements that are uniquely Norton's own.

In her statement Norton postulated the existence of a variety of different, yet overlapping, "realms of Existence," some of which were the domain of different "classes of beings from Man; highly evolved unhuman intelligences." These worlds and their denizens—we would know them as Gods and angels, devils and demons, fairies, sprites, elementals, and all between—had first been observed by Norton in visions or while exploring in her "plasmic" ("astral") body.

As her abilities grew, Norton found it easier to cross into these realms and to connect with the entities that inhabit them, some of whom became her near-constant companions. She would probably have pointed out that a number of these entities, who she would later refer to as "the familiars," had been her companions all along, but that she had simply been unaware of their presence until her own consciousness had been suitably attuned to it. Now that she was aware of them, their participation became crucial to the magical practice that was fast becoming a major facet of her life.

At the core of this magic lay the assumption that while it might be difficult for humans to make contact with other realms, the reverse was not the case, and the "unhuman intelligences" often played a part in the direction of events in "the plane of dense matter" (the "physical" world). It was an idea that Norton would sometimes express in her pictures, with images of an "otherworldly" puppeteer manipulating oblivious humanity. These "unhuman intelligences" existed in seemingly infinite array, from "gods" down to humble (yet still powerful in human terms) sprites and "elementals." Depending on their position within the hierarchy, they could, in the right circumstances, be persuaded, cajoled, or even—though Norton herself would not have dreamed of doing such a thing—coerced into doing the occultist's bidding.

In many respects Norton's core ontology was similar to that of the "Ceremonial" school of magic, the teachings of which Crowley had learned in the Hermetic Order of the Golden Dawn. There were, however, also significant differences. Norton elaborated on some of these in a letter that she wrote comparing some aspects of of her own system with that of Crowley's some half a dozen or so years later:

> My affiliations are mainly with what is called the Elemental Kingdom and the realm of non-human intelligences. These in themselves are neither good nor evil. Unlike the other type of magician referred to I would no more enslave or entrap such beings into working for me, than I would do so to my other friends. [My] invocations and conjurations of these entities do not force them against their will. Consequently I find the elaborate pentacles and guards against them required by the "Faustian" school are rendered unnecessary.[23]

Norton continued on to observe, "Yet another point wherein Crowley and I differ very definitely concerns sacrifices." Although Crowley certainly did not engage in this practice as often as his detractors in the popular press suggested, there is no doubt that he did sometimes use it, as when he slit the throat of a pigeon during a ritual to summon the demon Choronzon or crucified a frog as part of a ritual aimed at banishing the "dying God" of the old religion and ushering in the New Aeon.[24] Regardless of motive or precedent, Norton was vehemently opposed to animal sacrifice. To her, animals—with whom she by all accounts exhibited a remarkable rapport—had just as much right to their lives as any humans; in fact she clearly felt a kinship with animals that she did not feel with most of humanity. When, some years later, a reporter quizzed her on the matter, she furiously denied having anything to do with animal sacrifice, although she did add, perhaps not entirely in jest, "But I wouldn't mind sacrificing a few human beings."[25]

Norton was opposed to animal sacrifice not only on sentimental or ethical grounds, but also because she clearly felt there were strong magical reasons:

> I do not believe animal sacrifice to be advisable under any circumstances whatever, and consider that such a practise would be inefficient magic for reasons which I need not elaborate in this letter.[26]

Despite their differences on the methods of interaction with "non-human intelligences" and the matter of sacrifice, Norton did share Crowley's view of magic as being an essentially neutral tool. When recording her ideas on the subject for Dr. Murphy, she therefore described magic as "the science and art of causing supernormal change to occur," a slight misquote or paraphrase of the now-famous definition formulated by Crowley: "Magick is the Science and Art of causing Change to occur in conformity with Will."[27] By this interpretation it is the magician's will that determines what is good or bad ("black" or "white"), not the act of magic itself. Magic is therefore basically a tool that can be used for a variety of different purposes, depending on the intention of the handler.

With the psychological report completed and the exhibition and resultant court case now behind them, Norton and Greenlees returned to Sydney, where late in 1951 they were arrested on charges of vagrancy—that is, the crime of being indigent. A small article about the arrest in a newspaper led to a meeting between Norton and publisher Walter Glover, who was so taken with Norton's work that he decided to produce a book of her pictures.

From the outset the Fates seemed to smile on the project, and when, unexpectedly, Glover acquired much-needed office space, Norton celebrated their good fortune by decorating a wall of the newly acquired office with a giant mural of Baphomet. This shadowy divinity was said to have been the God of the Knights Templar but had remained in relative obscurity until Eliphas Lévi published a drawing of the deity as a winged, goat-headed figure with a pentagram on its forehead in his *Dogme et rituel de la haute magie* (1854). As

Norton was well aware, Crowley had taken Baphomet as his magical name when he received the Ordo Templi Orientis (OTO) X° title of "Supreme and Holy King of Ireland, Ionia, and all the Britains within the Sanctuary of the Gnosis," thus becoming a Grand Master of the OTO. However, when quizzed by Glover as to the significance of the mural, Norton blithely described Baphomet as "the God of Energy."[28]

Aside from the name's Knights Templar associations, Crowley identified Baphomet with Harpocrates, a child form of the deity Horus, the self-decreed (in *Liber AL vel Legis*) ruler of the New Aeon. In his *Magick in Theory and Practice*, Crowley further identified his Holy Guardian Angel, Aiwass, with Satan, and went on to observe that Satan "is not the enemy of Man, but He who made Gods of our race, knowing Good and Evil; He bade 'Know Thyself!' and taught Initiation. He is 'The Devil' of the Book of Thoth, and His emblem is BAPHOMET, the Androgyne who is the hieroglyph of arcane perfection."[29]

To Rosaleen Norton, Baphomet had a somewhat, but not totally, different significance:

> The God of the Templars is an aspect of the God of the Witches—or rather two aspects thereof. When represented as a skull, as "Death—and What comes after" or the Lord of the Afterlife: whereas a horned idol, as an aspect of Pan—which can be represented by almost any animal, but which is usually represented as a horned being, since the horns have special significance.[30]

Norton did agree with Crowley, and for that matter Eliphas Lévi,[31] that Baphomet/Pan was a fundamentally androgynous figure:

> The concept that Pan represents Man or men or the exclusively male factor in things is erroneous. . . . Pan is the God of This World—meaning the ruler of the Nature Spirits of the Kingdoms of Terra.—So it is a more accurate pronoun, although it includes both the male and female, masculine and feminine aspects.[32]

The book whose production the mural of Baphomet was to oversee at last came off the presses late in August of 1952. It was titled simply *The Art of Rosaleen Norton* and comprised black-and-white reproductions of thirty-three drawings by Norton, some introductory texts, and a number of poems by Gavin Greenlees. Of particular interest to the present discussion is its bibliography.[33]

This was ostensibly included to provide resources for "further reading on the various aspects of symbolism found in this book" but could also be taken as indicative of the works that Norton personally felt to be of most importance.

The bibliography was divided into five sections: "Psychology," "Esotericism," "Folklore and Comparative Religion," "Witchcraft and Demonology," and "Fiction." Of these, "Esotericism" was by far the largest section, containing twelve works: *Isis Unveiled* and *The Stanzas of Dyzan*, by H. P. Blavatsky; *A Treatise on White Magic*, by Alice A. Bailey; *Esoteric Buddhism*, by A. P. Sinnett; *The Tarot of the Bohemians*, by Papus; *Sepher Yetzirah* (the Papus translation, published in his work *The Qabalah*); *The Mystical Qabalah*, by Dion Fortune; *With Mystics and Magicians in Tibet*, by Alexandra David-Neel; *The Bardo Thodol* (*The Tibetan Book of the Dead*; presumably the Evans-Wentz translation); *A Treatise on Magic*, by Eliphas Lévi (probably his *Transcendental Magic, Its Doctrine and Ritual*); and Crowley's *Magick in Theory and Practice*. The "Psychology" section listed seven works, five by of which were by Carl Jung. "Folklore and Comparative Religion" listed only one work: Sir James Frazer's *The Golden Bough*. "Witchcraft and Demonology" listed five works,[34] and "Fiction" six works.[35]

Although not mentioned in the list, a book that utterly fascinated Norton at the time was John Symonds's biography of Crowley, *The Great Beast*. The work had been published the previous November and had sold out almost at once, going through further printings in December 1951 and January 1952. There was of course a considerable time delay before copies eventually made their way to Australian booksellers, and when at last copies did appear on shelves in mid-1952 Norton was desperate to get a copy before they vanished. Impecunious as ever, she practically pleaded with Walter Glover to get her a copy, suggesting it was vital to the progress of her work.[36] Despite being little better-off than Norton himself, and facing rapidly growing debts incurred as a result of the production of *The Art of Rosaleen Norton*, Glover did so.

The publication of *The Art of Rosaleen Norton* brought Norton firmly back into the spotlight of public attention and, as is widely known, resulted in another series of accusations of obscenity, which eventually saw the book effectively banned. It also led to her being befriended by the celebrated English conductor and composer Eugene (later Sir Eugene) Goossens (1893–1962), who held the distinguished positions of chief conductor of the Sydney Symphony Orchestra and director of the New South Wales State Conservatorium. According to both Goossens's family biographer and the account later given by Goossens to the police, the musician had purchased a copy of *The Art of Rosaleen Norton* shortly after its publication and was so impressed with it that he at once wrote to Norton to arrange a meeting.[37]

Norton, Greenlees, and Goossens discovered that they shared a passion for music and art, but what really drew them together was a shared enthusiasm for the occult. This was not a new interest for Goossens: books on the occult and witchcraft rated among his favorite reading material, and his predilection for them was known to trouble his wife, Marjorie. His fascination dated back to his youth and may have come about as a consequence of his friendship with Philip Heseltine, the normally retiring and introverted composer and critic, who would transform himself into the self-created persona of Peter Warlock, an extroverted, drunken, rowdy womanizer who scandalized and delighted Edwardian Britain. Heseltine/Warlock is said to have been deeply involved in the study and practice of magic, and later in his too-short life was acquainted with Aleister Crowley.

Goossens probably never had any direct communication with Crowley. Certainly no letters are known to survive, and Crowley left England for the United States (and later Europe) when Goossens was still in his teens and, aside from brief visits, did not return until the late 1920s, by which time Goossens had himself moved to the United States. From there, in 1946 Goossens moved to Australia, where he was residing when Crowley died in 1947. Despite the absence of any direct connection, there have been persistent rumors within Australian occult circles that Goossens had access to some of Crowley's unpublished writings on sex magic. Given that Goossens is known to have had a passion for erotica as well as the occult, and had both the money and connections to acquire such rarities quietly, such rumors may not be without foundation.[38]

Certainly Goossens became a central figure in Rosaleen Norton's small occult group and an active participant with her, and sometimes Greenlees, in sex-magick rituals. In Goossens, Norton felt that she had found a magical partner who not only matched but also complimented her own occult abilities. In an unpublished note, she observed:

> Just as Gav [Greenlees] has enabled me to tabulate my earlier Occult experiences, through his knowledge of Comparative Philosophy, so Goossens, with his exact esotericism is giving me just what is needed with regard to further practise. For several years the emphasis (in the esoteric sphere) has been, for me, the making conscious of that which was previously done or known unconsciously, and on general precision in *all* activities inner and outer. "Magick in Theory and Practise" in very truth. (If Greenlees represents the theoretical and Goossens the practical aspects, what do I represent?)[39]

It was almost certainly no coincidence that Norton referred to Crowley's magical magnum opus in the above statement, as she saw Goossens as a key part of the link with Crowley, identifying him (by his "magical name") as such in the previously mentioned document in which she outlined her connection with the Beast. In this document Norton further described how, at some time in the preceding years, she had forged an esoteric connection with Crowley. Norton recorded that the reality of this connection had been "shown previously" to Greenlees, but with the passing of time she had been able to confirm it herself as well. She had also been able to fine-tune the "'how' of working and contact" and to renew the connection "in a Time outside 'time' but manifest in [the] latter."

It should perhaps be noted that although this connection took place in another realm, it was no less "real" to Norton than anything that took place in the "here and now." In fact, Norton believed that, when approached properly, some of these other realms harbored less confusion and illusion than was found in that realm in which normal mortals dwelled.

That Norton chose—or was impelled—to make the "connection" with Crowley also indicates that he was of some particular importance to her. It is telling that there is no record of her seeking to engage in contact with other deceased esotericists with whose work she was familiar, such as H. P. Blavatsky, Eliphas Lévi, Alice A. Bailey, Dion Fortune, or George Ivanovich Gurdjieff (like Crowley, the latter three had all died in the mid- to late 1940s). In fact, Norton was generally disinterested in dealing with humans in this realm or any other and found them to be of increasingly less interest or importance—at least from the point of view of occult knowledge.[40]

As she had matured, Norton had become clearer in her own beliefs and cosmology. She now saw the Universe or Existence (in broadest terms) as composed of two main "types or orders," the "Abstract (or Archetypal) and the Actual," each of which contained the other, and comprising "four great planes of Being," three of which were actual and the fourth purely Abstract. Within these were the "three Major Dimensions—Time, Plane and Space." In the case of our world, there were two Great Orders of Being, "Human" and "Non-Human" (Natural/Elemental), each of which had its own Astral, Mental, and Spiritual planes. Pan was at once "Not-Human" and also, as the Planetary Entity, the embodiment of all that makes up the world and it multitudinous realms.[41]

As noted earlier, almost from the outset of her occult explorations Norton had felt an enormous pull toward the realm of the "Not-Human," and now she increasingly identified herself with it. She believed that, although now born in human form, she had in fact had previous incarnations in both realms, and as a consequence had a particular affinity with the denizens of the other-than-human realms: the elementals, daemons, and so on, a number of whom acted, voluntarily, as her "familiars." With a small number of exceptions, whatever kinship or loyalty Norton felt was with these "non-humans," not her fellow human beings.

Reflections on Crowley

Rosaleen Norton felt that her strong attachment to the "non-humans" was yet another clear point of difference between herself and Crowley, who she believed identified almost exclusively with "Man."

> I have no desire whatever to help humanity as such—nor to harm it for that matter. In this I disagree utterly with Crowley over a very fundamental point, which although expressed strangely was a motivating principle of his inner self i.e. The identification of the Beast with Man (and of both with himself) and the will to proclaim the "rule" of Man, as a "superior" being to the gods and other entities. (NB The "Beast" 666 according to both Blavatsky and the Rosicrucians is Primal Matter, and the principle of Manifestation.)
>
> I recognise as teacher any being from whom I can discover or learn some particular technique or specialised knowledge, but no being as master (human or animal) except the superior orders of Devas and Nature Spirits. However with these latter (D. and N. S.) of most types greater and lesser, as with animals, there is a sense of spiritual kinship and identification that arouses a spontaneous loyalty and goodwill in me: towards them, similar to that aroused by human affinities.[42]

From Norton's perspective, Crowley's strong affinity with humanity had limited his active exploration, and hence knowledge, of other realms. Whereas to Norton the beings who inhabited these nonhuman realms were every bit as real as the humans among whom she lived, it seemed that Crowley, on occasion at least, viewed them simply as archetypes to be tabulated in some kabbalistic ledger rather than as individual entities. Not surprisingly, this could lead to confusion and misidentification. In her written musings, Norton made note of an example where she believed Crowley to be in error:

> Aleister Crowley was mistaken when he identified Set Satan Saturn Adonai Abbadon Abraxas with one another. They are totally different beings.[43]

The earlier, lengthier, quote from Norton given above also touched on another important difference between Norton and Crowley: their respective viewpoints on themselves as teachers of the occult arts. At some stage—probably in the late 1950s—the occurrence of some "upsetting inner manifestations" prompted Norton to make some notes toward a personal "manifesto" of her esoteric thought in which she addressed this issue. In the page that served as a sort of preamble to these notes, she made it clear that she had no desire to "found any school or order such as those founded by G[urdjieff] and C[rowley]," although she acknowledged that she "would like personal recognition as an occultist, since (as with art) I have much to express in that field."[44]

In the same document she also declared that while she differed with both Crowley and his contemporary (and, to some extent, rival) George Ivanovich Gurdjieff on various "fundamental points," she also felt a "certain affinity" with the two. She went on: "While respecting them as beings and finding certain elements in their respective teachings interesting and useful to me, I am definitely not a disciple or follower of either."[45]

She expanded further on the nature of one of these "fundamental points" of difference in a letter of complaint that she wrote to an as-yet unidentified journal. The journal had apparently had the temerity to run an article in which it dismissed Norton's occult practices as "a form of Crowleyism."[46] To a committed individualist such as Norton, this was truly a case of "waving a red flag at a bull," and although there was undeniably a certain amount of overblown and probably mock-offended rhetoric in her response, equally there is no doubt that many of the objections she raised were her sincerely held opinions:

> Crowley's aim was to found a new religion, with a continually increasing number of followers. Mine is to practice the Magical Arts in peace and in privacy . . . with the exception of a few friends and colleagues. Far from wanting "converts" I avoid them, as in my opinion blind imitation of any other person's ideas and methods is at best a passing stage, and at worst could result in tiresome fixations.[47]

Norton also wrote emphatically that "I am not a disciple of any person living or dead, and my own attitude is basically quite different from Aleister Crowley's," and she ventured that perceived similarities between their systems were "more apparent than real, as the use of masks, robes, etc are common to practitioners of ceremonial magic the world over, whatever their race may be."

In a more specific assessment she also offered the observation that Crowley's system was rooted in the dualism of what is commonly termed "the old aeon," something that she firmly rejected:

> Crowley's doctrine is in effect based on the concept of "good" and "evil" peculiar to a social and cultural pattern which began some 2000 years ago with Christianity. Mine is distinct from his dualism [and] is fundamentally monist, although not monotheist.[48]

Interestingly, Norton believed that the foundations of her own occultism, although obviously of contemporary relevance, considerably predated the Christian era:

> My ideas and practices have far more in common with the pre-Christian Witch Cults of Ancient Britain and Europe, than later forms of mediaeval (and modern) Ceremonial Magic, exemplified by Dr Faustus, and in Modern Times Aleister Crowley.[49]

In more measured circumstances, Norton was, however, quite happy to acknowledge that she did have a number of points of agreement with Crowley. In another document she set out to itemize these, although sadly only the first four of her points of agreement survive:

1. I agree with his revival of the Dionysiac and positive aspect of life, also with his stressing the importance of Sex as a magical agent.
2. With his ideas about drugs.
3. With his ability to plunge with zest into each fresh adventure or phase of life.
4. With his respect for the I Ching as an oracle.[50]

By the time Norton wrote these words, probably the mid-1950s, her personal occultism had reached its mature expression—that is, she had adopted or perhaps better synthesized an esoteric system that in its basics would remain largely unaltered until her death some twenty years later.

As mentioned earlier, Norton had long felt an affinity with "traditional witchcraft," which she conceived in terms similar to those outlined in the works of Margaret Murray. At some stage, probably in the late 1940s or early 1950s, she had come into contact with an individual or group who claimed to practice a form of traditional Welsh witchcraft called "the Goat Fold" that had reputedly traveled to Australia with the earliest white settlers. By her own account Norton had undergone initiation into "the Goat Fold" and had gone on to found her own group, or coven.

According to that tradition, each coven was presided over by both a male and a female deity, usually Pan and Hecate, and as these were the principal deities of Norton's own coven, she named her group Pan-Hecate in their honor. The exact nature of the initiatory rites has not been publicly revealed, but of course like all such rites they were aimed at inducing an altered state of consciousness in which the individual would be open to forms of understanding and experience not possible on the mundane level. As such, the precise details are of little consequence other than to members of the group themselves, however in broad terms they are similar to those used in groups practicing ceremonial magic from the late nineteenth century onward, as well as in contemporary witchcraft groups.

The aspirant was required to undertake a period of probation, during which he or she was to acquire the basic knowledge and skills necessary for initiation. At the appointed time, the aspirant, termed a "neophyte," was asked a series of questions and, assuming that he or she answered them satisfactorily, the initiation proper began. The neophyte was then instructed to assume a ceremonial position: one hand on the crown of the head and the other on the sole of a foot, and swear an oath of allegiance to the ruling deities of the coven. On being accepted into the coven the neophyte underwent a form of baptism, was given a new name, and was presented with three ritual items: a cord, a candle, and a magically charged talisman.[51]

Although Norton sometimes toyed with the press by making grandiose statements about the membership figures of her coven, the actual number in the inner circle was usually less than a handful; in a candid observation Norton wrote, "I work better alone—or with one or at most two other practitioners."[52] She stated that when not physically in one another's presence, she and the other coven members would communicate telepathically. In cases where she was highly attuned to a particular individual, as with Goossens, this was usually accompanied by "an astral appearance," and although Norton could not always tell "what is being said or thought with my conscious mind," she said that she was able to "sense the general feeling."[53] With others the communication usually took the form of the projection of images rather than words or vocalized thoughts. This was also her preferred method of communication with other covens, as well as with most of the "non-human entities" with whom she communicated.

It was these "non-human entities" that Norton felt were the higher force behind human witchcraft activities. They hosted the "sabbats" or "great meetings" to which witches traveled in astral form, and they, along with other "non-human" entities of a different order who served voluntarily as "familiars," gave guidance and knowledge to those witches who were advanced enough to have connected with them.

The same "non-human entities," rather than books, had also been the source of the most valuable occult instruction that Norton had received. When answering questions as to where she had acquired her information about the "witchcraft rituals" that were at the heart of her occult practices, she wrote that she had "learned a few from fellow Witches, two or three more from books, but I gained my main body of knowledge on the inner planes of Being."[54] Where possible and permissible Norton was happy to work with and share this information with others in her coven, but, as noted earlier, she had no aspirations to take on the role of "teacher" or propagate any movement:

> My basic life-will in relation to this sphere: I do not wish to propagate any cult (even the Witch-Cult), change society, establish a "better world" for others etc. These things leave me entirely indifferent. They are not my job. If my own activities have any effect for or agin such movements so much the better, as I personally enjoy producing dynamic effects—or being instrumental in doing so—for their own sake: not for the sake of results, unless they personally concern me. I have what I prefer to describe as a function rather than a "message" or a "mission" (which words I detest). The function is that of focus and catalyst in relation to certain forces, situations, and people—and this function is best served by my performing my own personal will, and not caring a damn about effects good or bad on other people.[55]

Gerald Gardner and His Witch Cult

Not surprisingly when Gerald Gardner, Britain's self-proclaimed "head witch," came to public notice with the publication of *Witchcraft Today* in 1954, he also attracted the attention of Rosaleen Norton. She wrote to Gardner, several friendly letters went back and forth, and they exchanged gifts: Gardner sent her a copy of his novel *High Magic's Aid* (1949), and Norton sent him and Doreen Valiente—then high priestess of Gardner's coven—some drawings and a copy of her own book.[56]

Norton and Gardner clearly held one another in some esteem, although, reading between the lines of their correspondence, it is apparent that if anything it was Norton rather than Gardner who was the "true believer" in the reality of much that was traditionally associated with witchcraft. Thus in one letter she expressed surprise that Gardner had written in *Witchcraft Today* that he had not come across any of the traditional "Witch-Marks," citing several people within her coven who had them, including herself and Greenlees.[57] In another letter, she responded to Gardner's misgivings about the negative effects that distance might have on the efficacy of a ritual that his group had performed on her behalf:

> Incidentally, I didn't think the distance would make much difference, as other dimensions of being are involved. Entities who are thousands of miles away in Space A can be adjacent in Space B, as has been proved to me on numerous occasions.[58]

The ritual that Norton referred to had taken place on December 13, 1955, and had been aimed at helping Norton with one of her court cases. Apparently in one of their first exchanges of letters Norton had asked Gardner to assist with this, and he had responded affirmatively, and the ritual had been undertaken.[59] Unfortunately, it is unclear exactly which of her court cases the ritual was aimed at winning, as Norton then had a number in progress. One was the consequence of a police raid on an exhibition that she had held at the Kashmir Café, which had seen a number of her pictures seized and Norton charged with "being the owner of an obscene publication" (the paintings). The others, for "making an indecent photograph" and committing an "unnatural offence," had their origins in a series of photographs of Norton and Greenlees engaged in sex-magic rituals that had been stolen by an acquaintance and ultimately turned over to the police. Whichever case it was, Norton was grateful for the support at a time that she would later sometimes refer to as "the persecution."

Grateful though she was, Norton remained somewhat ambivalent in her feelings toward Gardner and his group. Writing at some time in the 1960s, she explored her thoughts on the matter. In large part her difficulty was that, despite his protestations to the contrary, Norton felt that Gardner and his "Wicca" were not really the same as the traditional "Witch Cult" of which she was an adherent. Curiously, one of the chief difficulties that Norton had with Gardner's Wicca was the restrictive nature of the so-called Laws of the Craft he had sought to promulgate in 1957, the introduction of which had also been one of the major causes of the schism with Doreen Valiente:[60]

> Probably by the same token I can't feel a genuine sense of "we-ness" or identity with any group of human beings including the Witch Cult,

> unless they are being attacked as in 1955. Yet I feel an identification and natural unity with the traditional Folk-lore witch that I don't feel with the "Wiccan," some of whose ways and ideas don't appeal to me, if what I have read and heard is correct. For if I am not the Lawgiving and administrative Type, still less am I the accepter of any laws other than that of my own Being.[61]

On what she herself termed an "irrational" level, she noted that she was unable to "feel a true sense of identity with any Human group." To her understanding, Gardner and his group functioned on a very human level, and their connection with the great "unhuman entities" that were the linchpin of her occultism seemed at best to be negligible:

> To me there seems far too much emphasis on the historical and group aspect of the Wiccan, and not nearly enough on other aspects and allied beings. Gardner for instance, refers several times to the "united battery of human wills" as being in his opinion the be-all and end-all of Witchcraft, with which I emphatically disagree. I would rather have the assistance of one powerful Abhuman Familiar than any number of united human wills, although I certainly don't disparage the latter.
>
> Then again, the Wiccan Gods—as presented by Gardner and to a lesser extent Murray, they seem to be mainly a kind of summing up of, respectively, All Men (The God) and All Women (The Goddess) instead of Beings in themselves having correspondences.

Given that it is now widely acknowledged that Gardner "borrowed" much of his material from well-known sources, including Crowley, it is perhaps not surprising that there is a certain similarity in Norton's objections to the teachings of both. Whether Norton was aware of Gardner's borrowings or not is a moot point, although Doreen Valiente, with whom she remained in contact, and who was one of the first to question Gardner about the similarity between his allegedly "traditional" texts and those of Crowley, may well have discussed it with her. Valiente herself had no qualms about utilizing material from other sources and acknowledging it, as when she sent Norton an "Invocation of Pan" that had been written by a friend of hers, with the observation: "It is based, as you will see, upon Crowley's 'Hymn to Pan,' but has been adapted for the Craft."[62]

Such adaptation—as long as it was genuinely creative—is hardly likely to have bothered Norton. Although she was clearly one of the most original and individualistic of twentieth-century occultists, and in broad terms she saw herself as working within a tradition of pre-twentieth-century witchcraft, she had always been happy to learn and adapt what she could from others. To this effect she had indeed once written "My 'Word' could be called 'Synthesis.'"[63]

The Beast—in Balance

It is clear from the many references to Crowley in Norton's writings, which far outnumber those to any other individual occultist, as well as from her "connection" with him, that she felt a special affinity with the Beast. One of her most cherished possessions was in fact a copy of the first edition of Crowley's *Konx om Pax*, a book that was coincidentally one of the Beast's personal favorites.[64] Although Norton was always short of money, and, being a limited edition, the book was never inexpensive, she had somehow acquired a copy in the late 1940s or early 1950s. On one occasion when it looked as if one of her court appearances might lead to her being held in custody for a few days, *Konx om Pax* was the book that she selected to take with her. Later, she even wrote a charming account of the episode, describing her decision to take the book and her lawyer's reaction on seeing it.[65] Despite numerous vicissitudes and periods of great poverty, Norton clung on to her copy of *Konx om Pax*, and it was one of the few possessions of any monetary value that she managed to retain right up until her death.[66]

The details of the rest of Norton's biography are too well-known to need more than broad brushstrokes here.[67] The decade between 1949 and 1959 was both a difficult and an exhilarating time for her. It had started with her most significant exhibition, had witnessed the publication of the book of her art, and had seen her become almost a household name in Sydney, where her striking art and outspoken declaration of her occult beliefs had seen her dubbed "the witch of Kings Cross."

Most of the publicity, however, had been negative, her art book had effectively been banned, and another exhibition had been closed, some of her paintings confiscated and ultimately—in an almost unprecedented action—destroyed.[68] Norton's friend and magical partner Sir Eugene Goossens had been arrested on obscenity-related charges and had left the country in ignominy, and a preexisting condition, coupled with drug use and the stress of repeated court appearances, had seen Gavin Greenlees institutionalized with mental health problems that dogged him for the rest of his life. Norton, too, had suffered from the stress and strain, and although she by no means became a recluse, she certainly withdrew from the limelight and was generally careful to avoid anything that could trigger renewed legal trouble.

As the 1960s progressed, the "sexual revolution" took hold, and increasing numbers of people experimented with the occult and what are now termed "new religious movements," Rosaleen Norton no longer appeared as threatening to the mainstream as she once had. Although personally she was little changed, in society's eyes she had effectively morphed from "menace" to "eccentric."

Norton remained as committed to her witchcraft as ever. As always, she preferred to limit the extent of her occult activities on the "human plane" and worked by herself or within a very small group or coven. Although, with some exceptions, Norton was largely disinterested in introducing new initiates into her circle, or in taking on the role of teacher, she would usually at least offer some suggestions as to avenues of further study to those who approached her sincerely. Among the books that she recommended were those of Dion Fortune and, of course, Aleister Crowley. Should there be any final doubt of the good-humored respect with which Norton regarded the Beast, it might be dispelled by the aphorism that she put down in one of her scrapbooks:

> The late Aleister Crowley, ex-pretender to the titles of the Master Therion, The Most Holy King of Ireland, and the False Prophet of revelations, Must now officially yield his claims. He wasn't the false prophet of revelations, since most of the prophecies In *Liber Legis* have since proved accurate.[69]

Notes

1. A survey of the "borrowings" from Crowley that appear in the teachings or writings of other individuals and groups would be an interesting undertaking. In particular his kabbalistic writings have often been used with minimal or no attribution, as can be seen in Israel Regardie's *The Garden of Pomegranates* (London: Rider, 1932) and *The Tree of Life* (London: Rider, 1932).
2. Rosaleen Norton and Gavin Greenlees, *The Art of Rosaleen Norton, with Poems by Gavin Greenlees* (Sydney: Walter Glover, 1952).
3. For details of Norton's artistic/legal tribulations, see Keith Richmond, *The Occult Visions of Rosaleen Norton* (Sydney: OTO /Kings Cross Arts Guild, 2000).
4. Television did not become widespread in Australia until the late 1960s, by which time Norton's artwork was seen to be less threatening and Norton herself was increasingly at pains to avoid the limelight.
5. [Rosaleen Norton], "I Was Born a Witch," *Australasian Post*, January 3, 1957, 4.
6. Rosaleen Norton, untitled two-page autobiographical fragment, private collection.
7. The Murphy statement is without doubt one of Norton's most reliable autobiographical accounts, not only because it predates most others but also because of the

context in which it was made: as part of a voluntary psychological assessment. A copy of the original document, untitled (hereafter cited as Norton, "Occult Memoir") and comprising nine typed pages, is in a private collection. The "mystical experiences" quote appears on page 2 of this document. The document has also been published in full in Nevill Drury, *Pan's Daughter* (Sydney: Collins, 1988), 30–37.

8. Rosaleen Norton, typed sheet headed "People as Factor in Patterns," undated but early 1950s, private collection. Given the proximity of the years, it is possible that Norton was simply mistaken in this later account, and the year in which the event occurred was in fact 1940.
9. According to occult theory the Akashic record is another realm or dimension in which everything that has or will ever happen, be thought, or be felt is recorded. Theosophical teachings also suggested that the Akasha contained valuable occult information, and it could be visited on the "astral" level.
10. Norton, "Occult Memoir."
11. Ibid.
12. Rosaleen Norton, untitled autobiographical fragment starting "The sign of Leo," undated but mid-1950s, private collection.
13. Edgar Holt, "Boy Poet, 12, Intrigues Critic," *Sunday Telegraph* (Melbourne), November 15, 1942, 21.
14. When I first checked the index cards at the State Library for Crowley in the late 1970s, they indicated an impressive holding of his books. However, when called for most of these could not be found; they were lost, presumably stolen. When I most recently checked the (now superseded) card index, the cards for the absent volumes had also been removed—presumably disposed of as no longer relevant when the data were transferred to a computer system—and all that remained in both old and new catalogs were listings for four works published during Crowley's lifetime and half a dozen or so posthumous publications.
15. Aleister Crowley, *Magick in Theory and Practice* (Paris: Lecram Press, [1930]). The late Walter Glover Sr., publisher of *The Art of Rosaleen Norton*, recalled Greenlees's ability to quote from the work, sometimes at disconcerting moments: he apparently alarmed staff and other inmates by declaiming passages from it while committed to Callan Park mental hospital for treatment in 1955 (personal communication, 1985).
16. In a letter to Beresford Conroy, Norton described getting to know Deamer, observing that "I like her immensely and find her a thoroughly interesting person." Draft of a letter from Rosaleen Norton to Beresford Conroy, undated but circa May 1945, private collection.
17. Quoted in Keith Richmond, *Progradior and the Beast* (London: Neptune Press, 2004), 248.
18. In most published accounts Greenlees does not appear in Norton's life until 1949, around the time of his nineteenth birthday. That Norton and Greenlees assiduously avoided any public reference to their early years together is hardly surprising, given

the opprobrium that a sexual liaison between a youth in his mid-teens and a women in her late twenties would have attracted, although of course their friends were well aware of the relationship. A detailed account is in my soon-to-be published biography of Norton, *Dark Rosaleen* (forthcoming).

19. Rosaleen Norton, untitled manuscript fragment starting "Below the archetypal plane," undated but mid-1950s–mid-1960s, private collection.
20. Norton. "People as Factor in Patterns."
21. Mrs. Estelle Robb, conversation with the author, 1987.
22. Norton, "Occult Memoir."
23. Rosaleen Norton, draft of an unpublished letter to an unidentified magazine, undated but mid-1950s, private collection.
24. Reliable accounts can be found in Richard Kaczynski, *Perdurabo: The Life of Aleister Crowley* (Tempe, Ariz.: New Falcon Press, 2002), 160 and 244, respectively.
25. "No. 1 Witch Uses Plane," *Advertiser* (Adelaide), April 25, 1964, 7.
26. Norton, draft of an unpublished letter to an unidentified magazine. In another fragment Norton observed, "Animal sacrifice should never occur, because the natural instincts and perceptions of animals are perfectly attuned to Nature and to their environment." Rosaleen Norton, draft fragment headed "(from 'No Man' (418))," undated but mid-1950s, private collection; published in Rosaleen Norton, *Thorn in the Flesh: A Grim-memoire* (York Beach, Maine: Teitan Press, 2009).
27. See Crowley, *Magick in Theory and Practice*, xvi.
28. Walter Glover, interview with the author, 1988.
29. Crowley, *Magick in Theory and Practice*, 193, n. 1. Crowley also gave a very obscure discussion of the word's meaning in Aleister Crowley, *The Confessions of Aleister Crowley*, "corrected ed.," ed. John Symonds and Kenneth Grant (London: Routledge & Kegan Paul, 1979), 832–33.
30. Rosaleen Norton, untitled manuscript fragment starting "The God of the Templars," undated but mid-1950s–mid-1960s, private collection.
31. In Lévi's depiction Baphomet was of generally masculine appearance, but with female breasts.
32. Norton, untitled manuscript fragment starting "The God of the Templars."
33. Norton and Greenlees, *The Art of Rosaleen Norton*, 79. Note that the bibliography to the posthumously published second edition (1982) was revised by the new editor, Nevill Drury, and varies quite significantly from the original.
34. *The Mirror of Magic*, by Kurt Seligman; *The Magic Isle*, by W. B. Seabrook; *A History of Witchcraft and Demonology*, by Montague Summers; *Witchcraft in Western Europe*, by Margaret Murray; and *History of Demonology*, by Daniel Moncure (presumably *Demonology and Devil Lore*, by Daniel Conway Moncure).
35. *The Goat Foot God*, by Dion Fortune; *The Golem*, by Gustav Meyrink; *All Hallows*, by Charles Williams; *Winged Pharaoh*, by Joan Grant; *That Hideous Strength*, by C. S. Lewis; and *The Woman on the Beast*, by Helen Simpson.

36. A note in Norton's hand in which she urgently requests that Glover purchase a copy of the book for her is in a private collection.
37. Carole Rosen, *The Goossens* (London: Andre Deutsch, 1993), 340.
38. According to Detective-Sergeant Trevenar, one of the police officers who arrested Goossens for smuggling pornography in March 1956, at the time of his arrest the musician was carrying a manuscript, titled "Sex Magic," that he himself had laboriously copied out in longhand, although unfortunately no one bothered to record the original author of the work. Susan Borham, "The Dark Secret of Eugene Goossens," *Sun-Herald* (Sydney), January 3, 1993, 19.
39. Norton, untitled manuscript fragment starting "Below the archetypal plane."
40. A sense of the small number of living people she found to be of any interest in the early 1950s can be gleaned from the short list of individuals to whom she had Glover send copies of *The Art of Rosaleen Norton*: Edith Sitwell, T. S. Eliot, C. S. Lewis, Carl Gustav Jung, and Albert Einstein.
41. Rosaleen Norton, two-page fragment titled "An Outline," private collection; published in Norton, *Thorn in the Flesh*. Norton also used the words "Man" and "Not-Man" to describe the "Human" and "Not-Human" realms.
42. Rosaleen Norton, untitled two-page autobiographical fragment starting "Some rather upsetting inner manifestations lately," undated but mid-1950s, private collection; published in Norton, *Thorn in the Flesh*.
43. Rosaleen Norton, untitled two-page autobiographical fragment starting "Pan isn't men nor man nor boys nor girls," undated but mid-1950s, private collection; published in Norton, *Thorn in the Flesh*.
44. Norton, untitled two-page autobiographical fragment starting "Some rather upsetting inner manifestations lately."
45. Ibid.
46. Rosaleen Norton, draft of a letter to an unidentified journal starting "I protest strongly," undated but probably late 1950s, private collection.
47. Ibid.
48. Ibid.
49. Ibid.
50. Norton, untitled two-page autobiographical fragment starting "Some rather upsetting inner manifestations lately." Unfortunately, the list is at the bottom of the second page, and it appears as if it continued over to a now-absent third page.
51. D. L. Thompson, "Devil Worship Here!," *Australasian Post*, October 6, 1955, 37. Despite its sensationalist tone, most of the information in this essay reasonably accurately reflects the beliefs of Norton, who is known to have collaborated extensively with the author in its preparation.
52. Rosaleen Norton, untitled two-page autobiographical fragment starting "Only one thing ever makes me afraid," undated but mid-1950s, private collection; published in Norton, *Thorn in the Flesh*.
53. Ibid.

54. Rosaleen Norton, typed sheet headed "Questions, Second Set," undated but circa 1955, private collection.
55. Norton, untitled two-page autobiographical fragment starting "Only one thing ever makes me afraid."
56. Drafts of several of Norton's letters to Gardner, as well as replies from Gardner, Valiente, and another of their coven members, survive in a private collection.
57. Rosaleen Norton, fragment of a draft of a letter to Gerald Gardner, starting "Scire I was interested," private collection.
58. Rosaleen Norton, fragment of a draft of a letter to Gerald Gardner, undated but probably January 1956, starting "Dear Scire, Many thanks indeed," private collection.
59. A decidedly self-important account of events was given by Gardner to a British journalist, who quoted him in a piece that was subsequently syndicated and published in Australia: Peter Lucas, "Witches in the Nude," *People* (Sydney) 9, no. 1 (March 5, 1958), 54.
60. Doreen Valiente, *The Rebirth of Witchcraft* (London: Robert Hale, 1989), 70–71.
61. Norton, untitled two-page autobiographical fragment starting "Only one thing ever makes me afraid." Oddly, in addition to Norton's obscenity trials in Australia, 1955 had witnessed a lot of attacks on "witchcraft" in the British popular press.
62. Doreen Valiente, letter to Rosaleen Norton, postmarked March 22, 1962, private collection.
63. Norton, untitled two-page autobiographical fragment starting "Some rather upsetting inner manifestations lately."
64. Aleister Crowley, *Konx om Pax* (London: Walter Scott, 1907). Crowley wrote glowingly of the work, in particular describing the final essay, "The Stone of the Philosophers," as being "really beyond praise." See Crowley, *The Confessions*, 537.
65. Rosaleen Norton, autobiographical fragment starting "It was the Morning of the Trial," undated but mid-1950s, private collection; to be published in Richmond, *Dark Rosaleen*.
66. Norton died, impoverished, in a hospice in 1979. She left little of monetary value aside from a number of her own paintings, which at that time would have sold for very little (in fact a number were subsequently discarded as worthless trash). With the exception of her copy of Crowley's *Konx om Pax*, her books at the time consisted of just a few shelves of well-used paperbacks, her own battered copy of *The Art of Rosaleen Norton*, and her personal scrapbooks. Her copy of *Konx om Pax* is now in a private collection.
67. See Drury, *Pan's Daughter*; and Richmond, *Dark Rosaleen*.
68. See further Richmond, *The Occult Visions of Rosaleen Norton*, 8.
69. The scrapbook is now in a private collection. The titles listed include a corruption—probably accidental—of Crowley's official title as head of the British section of the OTO: "Supreme and Holy King of Ireland, Iona, and all the Britains within the Sanctuary of the Gnosis."

14

The Occult Roots of Scientology?

L. RON HUBBARD, ALEISTER CROWLEY, AND THE ORIGINS OF A CONTROVERSIAL NEW RELIGION

Hugh B. Urban

> *The magical cults of the 8th, 9th, 10th, 11th and 12th centuries in the Middle East were fascinating. The only modern work that has anything to do with them is a trifle wild in spots, but is a fascinating work in itself, and that's the work of Aleister Crowley—the late Aleister Crowley—my very good friend.*
>
> —L. RON HUBBARD, *The Philadelphia Doctorate Course* (1952)[1]

> *Apparently Parsons or Hubbard or somebody is trying to produce a Moonchild. I get fairly frantic when I contemplate the idiocy of these goats.*
>
> —ALEISTER CROWLEY, letter to Karl Germer (April 1946)[2]

SURELY FEW NEW religious movements have been the subject of more scandal, controversy, media attention, or misunderstanding than the Church of Scientology. Well-known for its high-profile celebrity patrons such as John Travolta, Kirstie Allie, and Tom Cruise and boasting more than seven hundred centers in sixty-five countries,[3] Scientology has also been attacked by government agencies, anticult groups, and the media as a swindling business and a brainwashing cult. Its founder, L. Ron Hubbard, has been described variously as the man who "solved the riddle of the human mind" (by the Church of Scientology),[4] as "a mental case" (by the FBI),[5] and as "hopelessly insane" (by his former wife).[6] Yet remarkably, despite the tantalizing scandal that surrounds it in popular culture, Scientology remains one of the least studied and most poorly understood new religions today. Apart from Roy

Wallis's early study in 1976, J. Gordon Melton's slim overview, and James R. Lewis's recent edited volume, Scientology has rarely been submitted to a careful, critical study by historians of religion.[7] While there is some important scholarship in German and other European languages,[8] there remains surprisingly little available in English.

One of the most controversial and least understood aspects of Scientology is the alleged role of magical and occult traditions in L. Ron Hubbard's early work. Hubbard clearly had some kind of involvement in a series of rites practiced by John Whiteside (Jack) Parsons, an American disciple of the most infamous of all twentieth-century occultists, the self-proclaimed "Great Beast," Aleister Crowley.[9] Yet the exact nature of his involvement is the subject of much debate. On one side, critics of the church, such as Hubbard's own son, L. Ron Hubbard Jr., have suggested that Hubbard was "deeply involved in the occult" and that he even saw himself as the modern successor to the Great Beast.[10] Other ex-members and critics of the church, such as Jon Atack, have alleged that Crowley's magic lies at the secret core of Scientology.[11]

On the other side, the Church of Scientology itself has adamantly denied any connection between Crowley's magic and Hubbard's religious ideas. While it acknowledges that Hubbard did have some involvement with Parsons's magical group, the church claims that Hubbard was in fact working for military intelligence in order to shut down Parsons's occult operations.[12] Indeed, both John Symonds and the London *Sunday Times* were forced to pay sums in settlement after suggesting that there might be a connection between Crowley's magic and the principles of Scientology.[13] Meanwhile, many scholars of new religions, such as Roy Wallis and J. Gordon Melton, have largely dismissed Hubbard's connection to Crowley, arguing that "there is no evidence that Hubbard's system of Scientology owes any great debt to that of Crowley."[14] Other recent works, such as Lewis's edited volume, mysteriously sidestep the question almost completely.

In this essay, I will critically examine the many alleged connections between Hubbard's early system of Scientology and the rituals of Parsons and Crowley. By a careful analysis of all the available material to date—ranging from Parsons's and Crowley's correspondence to testimonies in numerous court cases to Hubbard's own direct and indirect references to Crowley's writings—I hope to arrive at a more balanced position on this complex debate. My central argument is that Crowley's work *does* indeed represent one important influence in Hubbard's complex system—but *only* one influence, which was both mediated through Hubbard's own creative religious imagination and combined with a vast array of other religious, scientific, and literary influences.

As Robert S. Ellwood and Wade Clark Roof have suggested, the 1950s American landscape in which Hubbard founded his new church is perhaps best described as a thriving and rapidly growing "spiritual marketplace." The postwar boom gave birth to a wide array of new religious options, from new spins on mainstream traditions to newly imported forms of Eastern religions and UFO-based movements, appealing to an eager and affluent consumer audience.[15] Hubbard, I would suggest, was one of the most creative, experimental, and eclectic new vendors in this marketplace. Indeed, Hubbard is perhaps best understood as a *bricoleur* in the sense of the term used by Claude Lévi-Strauss and Wendy Doniger[16]—that is, a creative recycler of cultural wares who "appropriate[s] another range of commodities by placing them in a symbolic ensemble."[17] An eclectic and ingenious religious entrepreneur, Hubbard assembled a wide array of diverse philosophical, occult, spiritual, and science fiction elements, cobbling them together into a unique, new, and surprisingly successful religious synthesis. In Hubbard's religious bricolage, occult elements drawn from Crowley were indeed one important element, but neither more nor less important than the many other elements drawn from pop psychology, Eastern religions, science fiction, and a host of other goods available in the 1950s spiritual marketplace.

To conclude, I will suggest that the links between Hubbard and Crowley shed important light not just on the origins of Scientology but also on the larger role of new religions in the United States of the postwar era. Indeed, they reveal the complex mélange of occultism, magic, science fiction, and the yearning for something radically new that characterizes American spirituality of the 1950s. However, they also give us some important insights into the role of religion in the twenty-first century, where the most "occult" materials are now globally disseminated through the power of new technologies such as the World Wide Web.

The Babalon Working: Hubbard, Parsons, Crowley, and Sexual Magic in 1940s California

Although Ron has no formal training in Magic, he has an extraordinary amount of experience and understanding in the field.

—JACK PARSONS, letter to Aleister Crowley (1946)[18]

Like the movement he founded, L. Ron Hubbard is a character surrounded by tremendous controversy, confusion, and debate regarding virtually every aspect of his biography. According to the official biographies promoted by the church to this day, Hubbard was a unique combination of rugged explorer, world traveler, and engineer, equally accomplished as a "humanitarian, educator administrator, artist and philosopher,"[19] "a daredevil barnstormer, a master mariner, [and] a Far East explorer," as well as the founder of a revolutionary new religious philosophy.[20] Born in Nebraska in 1911, Hubbard claimed to have been initiated by Blackfoot shamans in Montana, then to have traveled widely in Asia and learned the secrets of Eastern sages, holy men in India, as well as "Buddhist priests . . . and the last remaining magician from the line of Kublai Khan's court."[21] Back in the United States, he claimed to have pursued the sciences, studying engineering and atomic physics at George Washington University, before enjoying a decorated naval career during World War II.

Virtually every detail of Hubbard's life narrative, however, has been the subject of debate, and many critics have argued that most if not all of his official biography is a fabrication. Indeed, after reviewing the large body of biographical materials produced in the lawsuit *Church of Scientology of California v. Gerald Armstrong* in 1984, Judge Paul Breckenridge was led to conclude that "the evidence portrays a man who has been virtually a pathological liar when it comes to his history, background, and achievements."[22] But perhaps no aspect of his early biography is more contested or the subject of more intense legal debate than his period of involvement with Jack Parsons and the ritual magic of Aleister Crowley.

Hubbard met Parsons in 1945 after he was discharged from the U.S. Navy and moved into Parsons's rooming house ("the Parsonage") in Pasadena, California. Called by some the "James Dean of the occult," Parsons was a brilliant young engineer who helped develop rockets and explosives for the US government and even had a crater on the moon named after him.[23] In addition to his scientific research, however, Parsons was an avid practitioner of the occult who from 1941 on was deeply involved with Crowley's esoteric group, the Ordo Templi Orientis (OTO). The head of the Agape Lodge of the OTO in Los Angeles, Parsons became the Great Beast's most infamous American disciple. Indeed, Parsons seems to have dedicated himself to putting Crowley's most radical magical ideas into practice—though often in ways that made the Beast himself uncomfortable. Sharing Parsons's interest in science fiction and magic, Hubbard quickly struck up a close friendship and was soon made an intimate partner in these rites, despite his lack of any formal training. As Parsons wrote to Crowley in early 1946, he regarded Hubbard as a sort of natural magus with an innate grasp of Crowley's teachings.

He also noted that Hubbard appeared to have already been in contact with his own Guardian Angel, whom he called "the Empress," and so was already well advanced on the path of magic:

> Although Ron has no formal training in Magic, he has an extraordinary amount of experience and understanding in the field. From some of his experiences I deduce he is in touch with some higher intelligence, possibly his Guardian Angel. He describes his Angel as a beautifully winged woman with red hair whom he calls the Empress, and who has guided him through his life and saved him many times. . . . He is the most thelemic person I have ever met and is in complete accord with our own principles. He is also interested in establishing the New Aeon.[24]

However, in order to understand the complex links among Crowley, Parsons, and Hubbard, we first need to cover at least a few of the basic points about Crowley's life, philosophy, and practice of ritual magic.

Some Major Themes in Crowley's Magick in Theory and Practice

The whole and sole object of all true Magical and mystical training is to become free from every kind of limitation.
—CROWLEY, *Little Essays toward Truth*[25]

Born in 1875, the son of a preacher in the highly puritanical Plymouth Brethren sect, Aleister Crowley was in many ways a striking embodiment of the tensions within the late-Victorian world. Raised in strict Christian morality, he would quickly abandon the Victorian Christian world in which he was born to explore the full range of occult, magical, and esoteric ideas available in the late nineteenth and early twentieth centuries. His first initiation into the practice of magic occurred in 1898, when he was introduced to the Hermetic Order of the Golden Dawn, an affluent and elite group that also attracted other artists, poets, and intellectuals, including W. B. Yeats. However, Crowley soon left the Golden Dawn in order to pursue his own magical philosophy and, indeed, his own vision of a new era in human history.[26] Beginning in 1910, Crowley became involved with the Ordo Templi Orientis and eventually became its most influential but controversial leader. Combining Western occult traditions with

Eastern practices such as Tantra and Yoga, the OTO made the practice of sexual magic the innermost, esoteric core of its ritual operations.[27]

Crowley's writings on magic, ritual, and the occult are vast and wide-ranging. For the sake of this essay, I will focus primarily on Crowley's classic work *Magick in Theory and Practice*. Written under the name of "the Master Therion" (TO ΜΕΓΑ ΘΗΡΙΟΝ, "the Great Beast"), *Magick* is arguably Crowley's most influential text and the one explicitly cited by Hubbard in his lectures. Here I will briefly mention just a few of Crowley's ideas that are most relevant to Hubbard's early Scientology movement.

First and foremost, Crowley repeatedly emphasizes that Magick is in fact a *science*. In order to distinguish his practice from parlor tricks and stage illusions, Crowley spells *Magick* with a *k* and insists that it is an exact science based on specific laws and experimental techniques. Hence his book begins with a "postulate" followed by twenty-eight "theorems" that are presented as "scientifically" as chemistry, mathematics, or physics. And this science is fundamentally about knowledge—that is, the correct knowledge of the individual self and its potential. In short, "Magick is the Science of understanding oneself and one's conditions."[28]

Second, the fundamental law of Crowley's science is Thelema (ΘΕΛΗΜΑ), or "Will," which he adapts in part from Rabelais's *Gargantua and Pantagruel* and probably in part from Nietzsche's will to power. The law of Thelema is "Do what thou wilt," meaning that every individual should pursue his or her own true will, whatever that may be, and reject any social, psychological, or institutional structures that impede that will. For Crowley, "Every man and woman is a star. . . . Every man and every woman has a course, depending partly on the self, and partly on the environment which is natural and necessary for each. . . . A man who is doing his True Will has the inertia of the Universe to assist him."[29]

A key part of realizing one's true nature is attaining the knowledge of and conversation with one's Guardian Angel. Indeed, "the Single Supreme Ritual is the attainment of the Knowledge and Conversation of the Holy Guardian Angel."[30] Crowley himself claimed to have come into contact with his own Guardian Angel, Aiwass, in 1904 while in Egypt, and it was through Aiwass that he received the revelation of his seminal work, *The Book of the Law*.[31] As Crowley suggests, contact with one's Guardian Angel is the most important aim of the magus, for the Guardian is in fact his truest, innermost self, his "'star' or 'inmost light'" and "original, individual, eternal essence."[32] As such, "This is the most important of all magical secrets that ever were or are or can be. To a Magician thus renewed the attainment of the Knowledge and Conversation of the Holy Guardian becomes an inevitable task."[33]

Another central part of the magician's practice, described in great detail in *Magick*, centers on the Body of Light or Magical Being. Crowley's Body of Light closely resembles ideas of astral projection and out-of-body experience, which became popular in the first half of the twentieth century through works such Sylvan Muldoon's widely read books *The Projection of the Astral Body* (1929) and *The Phenomena of Astral Projection* (1951). As Muldoon describes it, the astral or spiritual body can be detached from the physical body and sent on long journeys to "visit scenes far distant," "traveling at a rate of speed only less than that of light waves."[34] Crowley takes this earlier idea of the astral body even further. The magus, he writes, should think of his astral or magical body as a kind of "creative force, seeking manifestation; as a God, seeking incarnation."[35] The magus must thus learn to cultivate his Body of Light, practicing the art of separating it from the physical body and sending it forth to explore the astral plane:

> Develop the Body of Light until it is just as real to you as your other body.... The first thing to do ... is to get the body outside your own... . you begin by imagining a shape resembling yourself standing in front of you.... Try to imagine how your own body would look if you were standing in its place; try to transfer your consciousness to the Body of Light.... keep on looking about you as you rise until you see landscapes of the astral plane.[36]

Once developed by the magus, the Body of Light is capable of "going anywhere and doing everything," traveling through space to every known planet and even to astral realms beyond the physical universe:

> The essential magical work ... is the proper formation of the Magical Being or Body of Light.... it is able to go anywhere and do anything.... he may be able to penetrate the utmost recesses of the heavens, or conduct vigorous combats with the most unpronounceable demons of the pit.[37]

> It must learn to travel on every plane; to break down every obstacle which may confront it. This experience must be as systematic and regular as possible; for it is of no use merely to travel to the spheres of Jupiter or Venus, or even merely to explore the 30 Aethyrs, neglecting unattractive meridians.[38]

Ultimately, the magus who cultivates his true will, who becomes intimate with his Guardian Angel and masters the ability to travel in the Body of Light, is all-powerful. He can subjugate all forces in the universe and bend all things, earthly or spiritual, to his will; indeed, he is "capable of being, and using, anything which he perceives for everything that he perceives is in a certain sense a part of his being. He may thus subjugate the whole Universe of which he is conscious to his individual Will."[39]

> For there is no power either of the firmament or of the ether or of the earth or under the earth, on dry land or in the water, or whirling air or of rushing fire, or any spell or scourge of God which is not obedient to the necessity of the Magician.[40]

The final goal of magic is thus the ultimate realization of the infinite power and potential of each individual self and its true will. Because "every man and woman is a star," each of us is not only part of God but in fact ourselves a God: "Every man and woman is not only a part of God, but the Ultimate God.... Each one of us in the One God"; indeed, "Each simple elemental self is supreme, Very God of Very God."[41]

The Descent of Babalon: Hubbard and Parsons Invoking Babalon

Our Lady Babalon must descend to triumph.
—HUBBARD, quoted in Parsons, *Book of Babalon* (1946)[42]

Crowley's work had a tremendous influence on the development of occultism, ritual magic, and modern witchcraft through the United Kingdom, Europe, and the United States in the second half of the twentieth century. As Jeanne Forman recalled from this period of Parsons magical rites, "They were tinkering with magic spells as they had with rockets."[43]

The most remarkable of Parsons's magical operations was a complex series of rites called the "Babalon Working," begun in early 1946. Babalon is a key figure throughout Crowley's magical writings, described variously as "Earth, the Mother of us all" and as "the Womb wherein all men are begotten and wherein all shall rest"; she is also identified as the Scarlet Woman, the embodiment of female sexuality, lust, and fertility.[44] Building on some of Crowley's ideas about the birth of a "magickal child" or "Moonchild,"

Parsons hoped to create a supernatural offspring that would be the embodiment of ultimate power: "The purpose of Parsons' Babalon Working seems to have been the birth of a child—the Moonchild—into whom Babalon would incarnate. . . . this child would be 'mightier than all the kings of the Earth.'"[45] On February 23, 1946, Parsons wrote excitedly to Crowley, claiming that he had in fact found his elemental, a beautiful redhead named Marjorie Cameron. His elemental, in turn, was to serve as his partner in sexual rituals designed to bring about the birth of the Moonchild, who would incarnate Babalon in human form.[46]

According to Parsons's remarkable personal accounts of these rites, Hubbard was intimately involved in the Babalon Working. Parsons was apparently impressed with Hubbard's natural power of "astral vision" and recorded that, on the night of March 2, 1946, Hubbard had described "a vision he had that evening of a savage and beautiful woman riding naked on a great cat-like beast."[47] Based on his ability to see on the astral plane, Hubbard was asked to serve as Parsons's seer or "Scribe" during the Babalon Working; indeed, Hubbard became nothing less than the "voice" for Babalon herself, who spoke through him and was recorded by Parsons. As Babalon described herself, speaking through the voice of Hubbard, on March 2–3, 1946:

> She is flame of life, power of darkness, she destroys with a glance, she may take they soul. She feeds upon the death of men. Beautiful—Horrible.[48]

> Oh thou who art moral tremble; given it is until thee a feat never before performed in the annals of your histories, never before accomplished unsuccessfully. Many have dared, none succeeded. Our Lady Babalon must descend to triumph.[49]

Apparently, Parsons believed that he and Hubbard's rituals had been successful. Thus, on March 6, he wrote excitedly to Crowley: "I have been in direct touch with One who is most Holy and Beautiful mentioned in the Book of the Law. . . . First, instructions were received direct through Ron, the seer. . . . I am to act as instructor guardian guide for nine months; then it will be loosed on the world."[50] The implication here is that Parsons believed he had successfully "conceived" a supernatural being, who would then "gestate" for nine months before being born into the world. Ironically, however, Crowley himself was by no means approving when he learned of Parsons and Hubbard's ritual activities. On the contrary, he seems to have been quite upset, writing to Karl Germer in April 1946: "Apparently Parsons or Hubbard or somebody is producing a Moonchild. I get fairly frantic when I contemplate the idiocy of these goats."[51]

The magical collaboration between Parsons and Hubbard was short-lived, however, and Parsons himself would not live to see his dream of the Moonchild fulfilled. In 1946, Hubbard, Parsons, and Parsons's former girlfriend and sister-in-law, Betty, formed a partnership called Allied Enterprises. Their scheme was to purchase yachts on the East Coast, sail them to California, and then sell them for a profit. Parsons put up $20,970.80, almost the entirety of his life's savings, while Hubbard put up a mere $1,183.91. Upon hearing of the scheme, Crowley himself suspected that Hubbard was playing Parsons for a fool and was planning to betray him. In a cable to Germer, he wrote: "Suspect Ron playing confidence trick—Jack Parsons weak fool—obvious victim prowling swindlers."[52] Indeed, Parsons soon concluded that Hubbard had stolen not just his girlfriend but all his money and chased him down in Miami. As Hubbard and Betty attempted to flee on one of the yachts, Parsons performed a ritual curse involving the "invocation of Bartzabel," the spirit of Mars. Curiously enough, a sudden squall came up and forced Hubbard's ship back to port.[53]

Perhaps the most remarkable part of this whole story about Hubbard, Parsons, and secret sexual rites is that the Church of Scientology *actually admits that all of this really did happen.* In October 1969, the London *Sunday Times* published an article that documented Hubbard's links to Parsons and Crowley; the church promptly threatened legal action and forced the *Times* to a pay an out-of-court settlement. The Church of Scientology then published a statement in the *Times* in December 1969, asserting that these rites *did* indeed take place but that Hubbard was sent in on a special military mission in order to break up this secret black magic group. This he successfully did, the church claimed, "rescuing" the girl (Betty) and shutting down the whole occult operation:

> Hubbard broke up black magic in America. . . . he was sent in to handle the situation. He went to live at the house and investigated the black magic rites and the general situation and found them very bad. . . . Hubbard's mission was successful far beyond anyone's expectations. . . . Hubbard rescued a girl they were using. The black magic group was dispersed and destroyed.[54]

It is worth noting, however, that neither the Church of Scientology nor any independent researcher has ever produced any evidence to support this claim.

The "Affirmations" of L. Ron Hubbard

> *You will never forget these incantations. They are holy and are now become an integral part of your nature. I can have no doubts of my psychic powers. My magical ability is high and clear.*
>
> —The "Affirmations" of L. Ron Hubbard (circa 1946–1947)[55]

One of the most important documents for making sense of the possible Crowley-Hubbard link and the question of the occult roots of Scientology is a curious text called the "Affirmations" (or "Admissions") of L. Ron Hubbard. Composed sometime around 1946 or 1947, the "Affirmations" are alleged to be Hubbard's own personal writings, apparently meant to have been read into a tape-recording device and then played back to Hubbard himself.[56] Scientology's own legal position on the document seems to indicate that it does indeed consider this church property and does intensely want to keep control of the text. According to a mutual release and settlement agreement between the Church of Scientology of California and Gerald Armstrong in 1986, Armstrong agreed to return a number of confidential documents to the church, including all copies of Hubbard's "Excalibur manuscript" and "all originals and copies of documents commonly known as the 'Affirmations' written by L. Ron Hubbard." Here the church clearly indicates that the text was *written by L. Ron Hubbard*, and it seems difficult to understand why the church would file suit to retain ownership of the text were it not an authentic document.[57] During the Armstrong case, portions of the "Affirmations" were read into the record, despite the protests of Mary Sue Hubbard's attorney, who argued that the document is "far and away the most private and personal document probably that I have ever read by anybody."[58]

Throughout their pages, the "Affirmations" indicate that their author is engaged in some kind of magical ritual and is hoping repeatedly that his "magical work is powerful and effective."[59] In fact, the "Affirmations" describe themselves as "incantations" designed to become an integral part of the listener's nature, impressing upon him the reality of his own psychic power and magical ability. Perhaps more significant, however, is the fact the "Affirmations" also make repeated mention of a female Guardian figure, who is the most important spiritual adviser and aid to the listener. The emphasis on the Guardian here seems to have been directly influenced by Crowley's *Magick in Theory and Practice*, which, as we have seen above, emphasizes that contact with the Guardian Angel is the most important task for the adept.

> Nothing can intervene between you and your Guardian. She cannot be displaced because she is too powerful. She does not control you. She advises you. You may or may not take the advice. You are an adept and have a wonderful and brilliant mind of your own . . .
>
> You are light and you are good. You have the Wisdom of all and never doubt your wisdom. You have magnificent power but you are humble and calm and patient in that power. For you control all forces under you as you wish. The strength of your Guardian aids you always and can never depart or be repelled.[60]

Finally, much like Crowley's *Magick*, the "Affirmations" also assert that one who is in contact with the Guardian is virtually invincible and all-powerful. He is a perfected—indeed divine—being, who is in direct contact with God and is even appointed as the ruler of his own kingdom:

> God and your Guardian and your own power bring destruction on those who would injure you. But you never speak of this for you are kind. A sphere of light, invisible to others, surrounds you as a protecting globe. All forces bounce away from you off this.
>
> You are a child of God. You are perfect.
>
> The most thrilling thing in your life is your love and consciousness of your Guardian. She materializes for you. You have no doubts of her. She is real. She is always with you. You love her very much. You trust her. You see and hear her. . . .
>
> You are eternal. You are satisfied to live within God. . . . You will never die. . . . You recall all your past times on earth. You have and will live forever. You are part of God. You are the crown prince of your small section of the Universe.[61]

Regardless of whether the "Affirmations" really were written by Hubbard, we will see below that most of these themes reappear in Hubbard's later works and lectures on Scientology from the 1950s onward.

In addition to the "Affirmations," however, there is also one other curious item among the documents cited in the Armstrong case that bears the tantalizing title "The Blood Ritual." Apparently this document was "so sensitive that no part of it was read into the record."[62] Although this document has never been publicly released, Armstrong and others who have seen it state that it describes a ceremony dedicated to the Egyptian goddess Hathor and also mentions the deities Nuit, Re, Mammon, and Osiris. According to Atack's description of the document, the ceremony "consisted of Ron and his then wife mingling their blood to become One."[63] Atack also speculates that Hathor may have been identical with Hubbard's Guardian Angel mentioned in the "Affirmations" and in Parsons's letters.

In any case, it is difficult not to see Crowley's influence here. Crowley invokes Egyptian deities such as Nuit and Osiris throughout his magical rites, and his *Magick in Theory and Practice* contains explicit directions for the invocation of Hathor, the Goddess of Love: "Suppose that you are invoking Hathor, Goddess of Love, to descend upon the Altar. Standing on the square of Netzach, you will make your invocation to her, and then dance an inward spiral deosil ending at the foot of the Altar, where you sink on your knees with your arms raised above the Altar as if inviting Her embrace."[64] In sum, if "The Blood Ritual"—like the "Affirmations"—is indeed an authentic work by Hubbard, then it is in perfect continuity with his involvement in Crowley's magic.

The Birth of Dianetics and Scientology: The Science of Total Freedom

The black enchantment is slavery. . . . We've a magic word to break it and a science to be applied.
—L. RON HUBBARD, *Dianetics: The Evolution of a Science* (1950)[65]

Scientology is a religious philosophy in its highest meaning as it brings man to Total Freedom.
—HUBBARD, "Religious Philosophy and Religious Practice" (1960)[66]

Not long after parting ways with Parsons, Hubbard began to turn his attention from science fiction and occultism toward developing a new science of the human mind and ultimately an entire new religion. Hubbard's new science of "Dianetics"—which he first described in an article in the magazine *Astounding Science Fiction* in 1950 that was then released in book form later that year—promised to be a revolutionary breakthrough for humankind, comparable to "the discovery of fire, and superior to the wheel and the arch."[67] In his account of the origin of Dianetics, Hubbard claims that he had in fact explored every known human attempt to understand the mind, including all manner of mysticism, shamanism, hypnosis, faith healing, and drugs. Again, as a kind of *bricoleur* or "rag and bones man," Hubbard himself claims that he had been through the "countless odds and ends" of human spiritual ideas to discover his new science. Thus he traveled the world to meet

> the shamans of North Borneo, Sioux medicine men, . . . a magician whose ancestors served in the court of Kublai Khan and a Hindu who could hypnotize cats. Dabbles had been made in mysticism, data had been studied from mythology to spiritualism. Odds and ends like these, countless odds and ends.[68]

> Attempts were made to discover what school or system was workable. Freud did occasionally. So did Chinese acupuncture. So did magic healing crystals in Australia and miracle shrines in South America. Faith healing, voodoo, narcosynthesis . . .[69]

Hubbard's early practice of Dianetics, it is true, had little in common with Crowley's Magick (although his choice of the term *Dianetics*, ostensibly from the Greek *dia* and *nous*, meaning "through the mind," is worthy of a note here).[70] For the most part, Dianetics was designed to help individuals locate moments of unconscious pain (called "engrams") located in their "reactive mind" (which Hubbard equates with Freud's unconscious).[71] Through a therapeutic process called "auditing," the individual can locate these painful engrams, remove them from the reactive mind, and so achieve a state called "Clear"—a state of optimum psychological and physical well-being.[72]

However, while Dianetics was initially extremely successful, it was relatively short-lived as a pop-psychological fad and had largely fallen into disarray by 1951.[73] Already by the end of 1953 and the beginning of 1954, Hubbard had largely abandoned Dianetics for a new and even more ambitious movement—indeed, a new "church"—called Scientology. While the early Dianetics system had focused primarily on achieving the state of Clear and optimal mental health in this lifetime, Scientology had far more ambitious spiritual aims. Much like Crowley's magical system, Scientology is explicitly defined as a "science," and specifically the science of "knowingness." "Scientology is defined as the science of knowing how to know. . . . Built on organized axioms, the science more closely resembles an 'exact science' such as physics or chemistry or mathematics."[74]

In Scientology, the primary emphasis is on what Hubbard called the "thetan"—the immortal spiritual dimension of the individual—and on the liberation of the thetan from the world of matter, energy, space, and time (MEST).[75] At the same time, Scientology is concerned not only with the events of this lifetime but also with past-life experiences in previous incarnations. For example, in his text *Have You Lived before This Life?* Hubbard records the stories of individuals who had remembered lives from as long as fifty-five billion years ago, often on other planets, recounting such remarkable experiences as seeing a giant manta ray underwater while repairing the atomic engines of a spaceship.[76] The benefits of Scientology are also claimed to be far beyond those of even the optimum state of "Clear." Individuals who have been through Scientology auditing and realized the spiritual potential of the thetan lay claim to a wide variety of superhuman achievements. These include not just optimal psychological and physical health but also more remarkable benefits such as the power to see through walls,[77] telepathic communication,[78] "remote viewing" or seeing events from great distances outside the body,[79] and even the ability to rearrange molecules in order to fix broken appliances such as coffeemakers and air conditioners. "I love it," wrote one enthusiastic member, "like Superman!"[80]

Crowleyan Elements in Early Scientology

> *It's very interesting reading to get a hold of a copy of a book—quite rare, but it can be obtained, The Master Therion, T-h-e-r-i-o-n. . . . He signs himself "The Beast." "The Mark of the Beast, 666." Very, very something or other.*
>
> —HUBBARD, *The Philadelphia Doctorate Course* (1952)[81]

If we acknowledge the fact that Hubbard clearly had some direct involvement in Crowley's OTO rituals just a few years before he founded the Church of Scientology, the more serious question is: Did any of Crowley's ideas or practices actually carry over into the early Scientology movement? Hubbard mentions Crowley by name only twice in any of his known Scientology lectures, calling him his "very good friend"—though it is certain that Hubbard never met the man. These references to Crowley occur in a series of lectures delivered in December 1952 known as the "Philadelphia Doctorate Course," which contain some of the most important early Scientology views of the thetan and its unlimited potential. Hubbard makes it clear in this discussion that he sees a direct continuity between Crowley's magical ritual and the techniques of Scientology. Both are described here as practical techniques involving a specific "cycle of action" intended to produce a desired effect:

> The magical cults of the 8th, 9th, 10th, 11th and 12th centuries in the Middle East were fascinating. The only modern work that has anything

> to do with them is a trifle wild in spots, but is a fascinating work in itself, and that's the work of Aleister Crowley—the late Aleister Crowley—my very good friend. And he did himself a splendid piece of aesthetics built around those magical cults. It's very interesting reading to get a hold of a copy of a book—quite rare, but it can be obtained, *The Master Therion, T-h-e-r-i-o-n*. . . . He signs himself "The Beast." "The Mark of the Beast, 666." Very, very something or other.
>
> . . . Crowley exhumed a lot of the data from these old magic cults. And he, as a matter of fact, handles cause and effect quite a bit. Cause and effect is handled according to a ritual. . . . And that ritual is what you do in order to accomplish this or how you have to go through and how many motions you have to make to come into the ownership of that. . . . each ritual is a cycle of some sort or another.[82]
>
> Now, a magician—getting back to cause and effect and Aleister's work—a magician postulates what his goal will be before he stars to accomplish what he's doing. . . . And the magician was very ritualistic and he would very carefully postulate what effect he was trying to achieve before he would be cause for that effect.[83]

Scientology is then also presented as a "cycle of action" aimed at specific effects and working along similar and equally practical principles. However, whereas Crowley used ritual magic as his cycle of action, Scientology is a "new" cycle of action designed to realize the infinite potential of the human spirit: "Scientology 8–8008 is a design for a new cycle of action. . . . It tells what the cycle of action goes to—an unapplied infinity of potential. And it tells how you get there."[84] In short, Hubbard is saying here that Crowley's ritual magic was effective for realizing the spirit's potential, at least for its time and place, and now Scientology is realizing the same power of the spirit, simply with new, more contemporary, and "scientific" techniques.

As we see in this lecture of Hubbard's, moreover, the thetan or true spiritual identity of the individual is described as having unlimited potential and ability.[85] In Hubbard's early Scientology cosmology, as it developed in the early 1950s, the thetan is ultimately a "godlike" entity that does not now recognize its own powers but can be freed to realize its infinite possibilities. As David Bromley explains Hubbard's view of the thetans:

> In the beginning theta was separate from the physical universe. Theta had no energy or mass, time or location; it was simply energy. Thetans therefore existed before . . . the material universe. At one time thetans were godlike, celestial entities, possessed their own distinctive individuality and created and controlled their own "Home Universes."[86]

The goal of Scientology auditing is, ultimately, to free the thetan from its entrapment in the material universe, to reawaken its unlimited potential, and to restore its original ability to create and control its own universes. As Hubbard defines it, Scientology is simply "knowledge and its application in the conquest of the material universe."[87]

It is difficult not to see parallels here between Hubbard's view of the thetan and Crowley's central teaching that "every man and woman is a star" and that the ultimate goal of magical practice is to realize one's own godlike ability to "subjugate the whole Universe . . . to his individual Will."[88] As more than one observer has pointed out, it seems likely that Hubbard's choice of the term *thetan* (Θ) from the Greek letter theta to refer to the immortal spiritual self had at least some influence from Crowley. Theta is of course the first letter of Crowley's central law of Thelema—which centers on the divine power of the individual will—as well as the first letter of his pseudonym Therion—under which *Magick*, the key text cited by Hubbard—was written. Moreover, the theta is at the very center of one of Crowley's key symbols, the sigil of Babalon, which appears in various works as shown in Figure 14.1.[89] As Crowley explained in his own commentary on this symbol in his *Book of Lies*, the Greek letter theta Θ was first written as ⊙, the

FIGURE 14.1 Sigil of Babalon.
Reprinted with permission of the Ordo Templi Orientis.

astrological symbol for the sun. In his eclectic system, the sun or theta is also the key symbol of the union of the Lingam and Yoni (the Hindu terms for male and female sexual organs, symbolizing the divine creative union): "The centre of all is Theta, which was originally written as a point in a circle, the sublime hieroglyph of the Sun in the Macrocosm, and in the Microcosm of the Lingam in conjunction with the Yoni."[90]

The possibility that Hubbard was borrowing from Crowley's symbolism for his early Scientology teachings might seem a bit tangential at first glance, but it is supported by several other facts. The first is that Hubbard first began to promote his new Church of Scientology as a "religious" organization in 1954 through a newsletter titled *The Golden Dawn*, probably named for the well-known British occult group. As Stephen Kent notes:

> Late in the summer of 1954, Hubbard mailed an advertisement newsletter called *The Golden Dawn* (most likely named after England's famous occult group of which Aleister Crowley had been a member) to about 500 Phoenix, Arizona, homes and initiated a door-to door recruitment in the city.[91]

A second, even more obvious, borrowing from Crowley and from the Golden Dawn, however, was Hubbard's choice of an eight-pointed cross as the key symbol for his new church. As many observers have pointed out, Hubbard's cross seems to be closely modeled on the Golden Dawn cross, which also adorned the back of every card in Crowley's famous tarot deck—the "Thoth" deck—one of the most influential and widely used tarot decks to this day (see Figure 14.2).[92] Even though Hubbard's theological explanation of the image was of course very different,[93] there seems to be little doubt that the image of the eight-pointed Scientology cross—still today the central symbol of the church—is taken from the Golden Dawn/Crowley Rosy Cross.

Finally, one other point to keep in mind here is Scientology's early audience and membership. As various scholars have noted, most of the early followers of Dianetics and Scientology had already been involved in various forms of occult, esoteric, magical, and other alternative traditions long before joining Hubbard's movement. In his sociological study of the early membership of the church, Wallis found that "over half of them had prior involvement in marginal religions, Rosicrucianism, Theosophy, Christian Science, Baha'i . . . hypnosis or Jungian analysis."[94] Thus, a movement that had elements of Golden Dawn/Crowley-style occultism mixed with Eastern

FIGURE 14.2 Rose cross back of Crowley's Thoth tarot deck.
Reprinted with permission of the Ordo Templi Orientis.

religions and depth psychology would not have seemed strange by any means; on the contrary, it would have been extremely attractive to this particular spiritual market.

Exteriorizing the Thetan and the "Grand Tour" of the Universe

The entire technique consists of getting the thetan out of the body immediately . . . and . . . bringing him up to complete self-determinism.

—HUBBARD, *Scientology 8–8008* (1952)[95]

The possible borrowings from Crowley seem even less superficial once we begin to look closely at the content of Hubbard's early Scientology lectures from the 1950s. One of the central themes in Hubbard's lectures from roughly 1952 to 1958 is that the thetan is not only an immortal entity of infinite potential but can also be trained to "exteriorize" or separate itself from the physical body. Hubbard himself, it is true, rejects the use of the specific phrase *astral projection* as a kind of mystical delusion.[96] However, his account of exteriorization—the exact same term used by Muldoon, we might note—is almost identical to Crowley's account of projecting the Body of Light. As in Crowley's magical practice, exteriorization is one of the most important techniques in Hubbard's early Scientology practice and is described in detail in numerous lectures gathered in publications such as *The Philadelphia Doctorate Course* (1952), *Scientology 8–8008* (1952), *The Creation of Human Ability* (1954), and *The Phoenix Lectures* (1954). As Hubbard summarizes the goals of Scientology in 1952: "The entire technique consists of getting the thetan out of the body immediately, unburdening some of the sympathy for the body and . . . bringing him up to complete self-determinism."[97] According to the introduction to his *Philadelphia Doctorate Course*, Hubbard's extensive research had revealed that the thetan could be fairly easily exteriorized from the body through the use of the simple command to "be three feet back of your head":

> Testing revealed that the separation of spirit from the body was a surprisingly simple process. It could be accomplished, in about 50 percent of the cases, with the precise command to "be three feet back of your head." By exteriorizing the thetan from the body, the long-sought goal of religion—spiritual existence independent of the body—had been accomplished, rationally and systematically.[98]

Once the thetan has successfully been taken three feet in back of the head, it could then be directed to go much further, practicing more and more adventurous journeys beyond the MEST body. Indeed, in his lectures collected in *The Creation of Human Ability* and *The Phoenix Lectures*, Hubbard directs the auditor to take the thetan from the earth, to the moon, to the sun, then to venture to other planets: "Be near earth, be near the Moon, be near the Sun. . . . Now find a rock. Be inside of it, be outside of it. . . . Be in the center of the Earth, be outside the earth . . . be near mars. Be at the center of Mars."[99] (Thus an illustration in *The Creation of Human Ability* shows the symbol Θ, for thetan, flying through the solar system.)[100] Then the thetan should be instructed to embark on a "Grand Tour of the Universe," exploring the surfaces of other planets, sliding down plumes on the sun, even going inside of black stars, and so forth:

> The minimum you would do with a Grand Tour would be as follows: teach him to be near certain planetary bodies and teach him to be in things and out of things—in other words, interiorized and exteriorized at will.[101]

> So you say, "Find a plume and slide down on it to the face of the Sun." . . . You could have him find Mars. "Be outside Mars and move down on the surface." But he's immediately going to discover the force field of Mars. I'm sorry this has to be so. It's not science fiction.[102]

> One of the common practices in the Grand Tour is asking him to be inside a black star, outside it, inside it. . . . And oh, boy does that rip him to pieces, because there are black stars up there which are so heavy and dense that electrons can't escape from them.[103]

However, Hubbard states emphatically that this process of exteriorizing the thetan and touring the universe is *not* just an imaginary exercise; the individual really is engaged in an out-of-body planetary tour and should recognize it as such:

> It should be clearly understood by the auditor that the preclear does not simply think about these things or mock them up and view them. The auditor wants the preclear, exteriorized, to go around various places in the actual physical universe and *look* at things and so build his tolerance on the physical universe.[104]

Even if Hubbard eschews the use of the term *astral projection*, his technique of exteriorization is, in his many descriptions, virtually indistinguishable from Crowley's projection of the Body of Light.

Create Your Own Universe: The Esoteric Grades of Scientology and the Infinite Power of the Thetan

> *He would be able to exist without any universe whatsoever or he could create one, but he didn't have to, and he'd have a total knowingness.*
>
> —HUBBARD, *The Phoenix Lectures* (1954)[105]

Much like Crowley, however, Hubbard also claims that the true power of the thetan is not simply its ability to travel outside the body or explore the known universe. Indeed, the power of the thetan is inherently infinite and includes the power to alter, manipulate, or transform the known universe.[106] Much like Crowley's OTO, Scientology eventually came to be organized into a series of increasingly esoteric (and increasingly expensive) levels called Operating Thetan or OT, which begin after one has achieved the Clear state.[107] Hubbard's map of the complete Scientology process is called the Bridge to Total Freedom and lists fifteen OT grades; however, only eight of these seem to have been completed by Hubbard before his death. As a Scientologist rises through the OT grades, he or she learns new secrets about the history of the universe and the true nature of the thetan while at the same time realizing ever more of its awesome powers.

Ultimately, at its highest levels of free operation, the power of the thetan is infinite and unlimited. Indeed, one of the basic definitions of theta or spirit is that it can conquer, manipulate, and organize the physical universe and body: "One of the purposes of theta is postulated as the conquest of, change and ordering of MEST."[108] For example, an exteriorized thetan can heal the physical body, fix broken objects, and manipulate others' bodies from a distance. Indeed, it can even cause the MEST universe itself to appear or disappear at will: "What we're doing is simply taking the MEST universe and we can make it appear or disappear at will for any individual."[109]

Not only can a thetan alter the MEST universe, but also, ultimately, the highest power of a thetan is the ability to "*create its own universe.*"[110] As he developed the "religion" of Scientology in the 1950s, Hubbard described different states of the thetan, such as "Cleared Theta Clear" and then finally "Operating Thetan." Thus, someone who has achieved the state of Cleared Theta Clear is now "a person who is able to create his own universe or, living in the MEST universe, is able to create illusions perceivable by others at will, to handle MEST universe objects without mechanical means and to have and feel no need of bodies or even the MEST universe to keep himself and his friends interested in existence."[111] And any universe the Cleared Thetan chooses to create will be far better and in fact more "real," that is, "sharper and brighter, if anything, than his reality on the MEST universe."[112]

One who achieved the state of Operating Thetan, meanwhile, can essentially "do *anything*" he or she pleases. In contrast to the Hindu or Buddhist goal of *moksha* or final liberation, which Hubbard describes as a mere blissful void, the state of OT is one in which the thetan is not just liberated but also enabled to do anything it desires: the OT is completely free to create anything, to destroy anything, to be anything, to go anywhere her or his will desires:

> He would be able to be anywhere as a finite point or be everywhere as a generalized area. . . . he had shed his dependencies on objects, energies and spaces. . . . he could be *anything* at will.[113]

Indeed, the liberated thetan could freely create her or his own paradise, even populate it with heavenly beings and infinite pleasures, at will:

> "You make forty mock-ups and they dance back and forth; put blue veils on them and put them in a sky with clouds and you have a Mohammedan heaven. You mean, I can do all this?" Well he can not only do all that, but he can fix them up three-dimensionally and he can give them actual separate beingnesses and personalities.[114]

Ultimately, the thetan who truly realizes his own true potential, his power to create and destroy universes, would in effect be "beyond God"—that is, he would be beyond whichever so-called god happened to create this particular MEST universe. In fact, the thetan has been deceived into worshipping such a god by mainstream religion in order to deceive it into forgetting its own godlike power to create and destroy universes: "What passed for God for the MEST universe is not the goddest God there is by an awful long ways. . . . whoever made that MEST universe . . . was a usurper of one's own universe. And this has been sold to the individual and it has sold the individual out of his ability to make a universe."[115]

In sum, even if Hubbard chose to describe his movement with the language of "science" rather than "magic," the goal of Scientology is essentially no different from that of Crowley's system: its aim is to realize the infinite power of the self and to use that power to manipulate, transform, and at last utterly transcend the limits of the physical universe. This, for Hubbard, is the true meaning of the term *self-determinism*—a phrase he uses frequently and defines as the "ability to create space and time in which to create and locate energy and matter. . . . In that state the individual has self-confidence in his control of the material universe."[116] Here, Hubbard's "self-determinism" sounds almost indistinguishable from Crowley's law of Thelema or "do what thou wilt": both rest upon a fundamental belief in the infinite power of the individual will, and both share the ideal of "*total* freedom" of the individual self from all external limitations.

Conclusions: Scientology as Spiritual-Occultist-Sci-Fi Bricolage

"Magic can drive people mad," said the chief.
"Science can make people sane," said Angus
—L. RON HUBBARD, "Battle of Wizards" (1949)[117]

Odds and ends like these, countless odds and ends.
—HUBBARD, *Dianetics: The Evolution of a Science* (1950)[118]

In sum, it seems clear that Hubbard had direct involvement in Parsons's OTO rituals and that there is a significant amount of Crowley's influence in the early Scientology beliefs and practices of the 1950s. Not only did Hubbard and Crowley share a fundamental belief in the unlimited potential of the individual self, but they also used common techniques of exteriorization of the spirit from the physical body, and they ultimately shared a common goal of realizing the infinite, godlike power of the individual self. If we really look closely at the historical connections and the textual evidence, Crowley's ideal of the individual will and the unlimited power of the magus does not seem very different from Hubbard's goal of self-determinism and the realization of the infinite power of the thetan.[119]

Of course, there are also profound differences between Crowley's magical practice and Hubbard's early Scientology movement. As Pendle suggests, Crowley's magic is clearly a product of the late-Victorian era and the tradition of nineteenth-century esotericism, while Scientology is clearly a product of mid-twentieth-century America and fascinations with science and technology. Moreover, Hubbard's religion was also far more successful than the Great Beast could ever have imagined the OTO might be:

> It is hard to ignore certain similarities between Crowley's Thelema and Hubbard's Scientology. Both religions have as leaders charismatic men with logorrheic tendencies. Both preach that man is an immortal spiritual being, that his capabilities are unlimited. . . . While Thelema was born of the Old World, however, Scientology was distinctly a product of the New. The OTO arose out of the Victorian fascination with mysticism, magic, and the secret societies of Europe. Scientology was a product of the twentieth century's childlike trust in scientific knowledge. . . . While Crowley struggled throughout his life to popularize the OTO, the Church of Scientology became hugely successful, and now claims over

> eight million members in some 3,000 churches.... It is, in short, everything Crowley had wanted the OTO to be.[120]

Crowley's magic, I would suggest, is one important element—but by no means the only or most important element—in the rich syncretistic blend that became the Church of Scientology. As an ingenious *bricoleur* or spiritual entrepreneur, Hubbard appropriated elements from a wide range of religious, occult, psychological, and science fiction ideas available in the 1950s "spiritual marketplace," weaving them together into his own unique and surprisingly successful synthesis. Thus, in his early Dianetics practice, we can clearly see the profound influence of Freud, Jung, Adler, Rank, and various other psychological ideas readily available in the mid-twentieth century, as well as the influence of popular self-help works such as Norman Vincent Peale's best-selling *Power of Positive Thinking* (1952).[121] In Hubbard's early Scientology lectures, we can see not only the influence of new scientific ideas and the fascination with new technologies (for example, the use of the E-meter) but also the influence of Eastern religions such as Hinduism and Buddhism (for example, the belief in reincarnation and the supernatural powers of the thetan).[122]

In Hubbard's elaborate speculations about the history of the universe and other planets, we can also see the influence of Hubbard's own prolific science fiction writings (involving, for example, alien races, "superman" powers, and "space opera" narratives, of which the Xenu story ridiculed on *South Park* is only the tip of the iceberg).[123] Finally, as Stephen Kent has shown, Scientology gradually branched out to become more than just a "church"; it is also a vast, transnational network of corporate enterprises. The broader Scientology corporate network includes organizations designed to help businesses, such as WISE (the World Institute of Scientology Enterprises); groups to help fight drug and alcohol abuse, such as Narconon; publishing outlets, such as Bridge and Freedom Publications: audio and video producers, such as Golden Era Productions; and myriad other corporate entities that go far beyond the psychological and spiritual limits of Dianetics or Scientology.[124] In this sense, Scientology is not simply a product of the teeming spiritual marketplace of 1950s America but arguably a kind of microcosm and epitome of the rich, pluralistic foment of the postwar era as a whole.

However, if we really take the time to look closely at the early roots of Scientology, at Hubbard's involvement with Parsons, and at Hubbard's published and unpublished writings from the late 1940s and early 1950s, we can also see the traces of Crowley's Magick in this complex bricolage. For perhaps obvious reasons, these occult elements have been intentionally downplayed, masked and covered over by Hubbard and the church. From the first suggestion of an occult connection in 1969, the Church of Scientology has fiercely denied any such links, continuing to this day to contest them both in print and in court. Unfortunately, the church's intense resistance to any serious research into the origins of Hubbard's work means that the roots of Scientology remain largely obscured, deliberately concealed, obfuscated—in short, "occult."

Of course, the Church of Scientology today exists in the age of the Internet, where it is increasingly difficult to keep much of anything—including the most advanced OT levels or the details of the Babalon Working—very secret. Indeed, beginning with its lawsuit against the Usenet group alt.religion.scientology in 1993, the church has fought a series of major legal battles over confidential Scientology materials posted online and now has an entire office, the Religious Technology Center, dedicated to the protection of its trade secrets in cyberspace.[125] Yet, despite its most intense efforts, the secrets of Scientology continue to circulate freely online. Today, the church faces a host of new enemies in cyberspace, such as the Internet group Anonymous, which has made it its mission to unmask and destroy Scientology. As former Scientologist Robert Vaughan Young put it, "The Internet is going to be Scientology's Waterloo."[126] Perhaps the real challenge facing Scientology today is whether it will continue struggling to maintain control over its esoteric materials, or whether it will adapt to a new age of information technologies in which little if anything remains occult for long. As Hubbard himself remarked in 1954, "You cannot unveil the SECRET and have it ever be quite so secret ever again."[127]

Notes

1. L. Ron Hubbard, *The Philadelphia Doctorate Course* (1952; Los Angeles: Golden Era Productions, 2001), 185.
2. Aleister Crowley, letter to Karl Germer, April 19, 1946, quoted in Lawrence Sutin, *Do What Thou Wilt: A Life of Aleister Crowley* (New York: St. Martin's Press, 2000), 414.
3. Richard Behar, "Scientology: The Thriving Cult of Greed and Power," *Time*, May 6, 1991, http://www.time.com/time/magazine/article/0,9171,972865,00.html.

   Most scholars agree that Scientology's claims about its membership numbers are highly inflated.
4. "L. Ron Hubbard: Founder of Scientology," 2006, http://www.aboutlronhubbard.org/eng/wis3_1.htm.

5. M. A. Jones, office memorandum to Mr. Nichols, from the files of the FBI on L. Ron Hubbard, Dianetics, and Scientology, February 27, 1957.
6. "Mrs. Hubbard Torture Claim," *Los Angeles Examiner*, April 24, 1951, 1.
7. Roy Wallis, *The Road to Total Freedom: A Sociological Analysis of Scientology* (New York: Columbia University Press, 1976); Gordon J. Melton, *The Church of Scientology* (Salt Lake City: Signature Books, 2000); James R. Lewis, ed., *Scientology* (New York: Oxford University Press, 2009). See also Harriet Whitehead, *Renunciation and Reformulation: A Study of Conversion in an American Sect* (Ithaca, N.Y.: Cornell University Press, 1987); Hugh B. Urban, "Fair Game: Secrecy, Security and the Church of Scientology in Cold War America," *Journal of the American Academy of Religion* 4, no. 2 (2006), 356–89. There are also several good articles by Stephen Kent, such as "The Creation of Religious Scientology," *Religious Studies and Theology* 18, no. 2 (1999), 97–126; and "Scientology's Relationship with Eastern Religious Traditions," *Journal of Contemporary Religion* 11, no. 1 (1996), 21–36.
8. Among others, Dorthe Refslund Christensen, *Scientology: Fra terapi tel religion* (Copenhagen: Gyldendal, 1997); Friedrich-Wilhelm Haack, *Scientology—Magie des 20. Jahrhunderts* (Munich: Claudius Verlag, 1991).
9. On the Hubbard-Parsons-Crowley relationship, see John Carter, *Sex and Rockets: The Occult World of Jack Parsons* (Los Angeles: Feral House, 1999); Hugh B. Urban, *Magia Sexualis: Sex, Magic, and Liberation in Modern Western Esotericism* (Berkeley: University of California Press, 2006); George Pendle, *Strange Angel: The Otherworldly Life of John Whiteside Parsons* (Orlando, Fla.: Harcourt, 2005).
10. "Inside the Church of Scientology: An Exclusive Interview with L. Ron Hubbard, Jr.," *Penthouse*, June 1983: "The one super-secret sentence that Scientology is built on is: 'Do as thou wilt.' That is the whole of the law. It also comes from the black magic, from Alistair [*sic*] Crowley. It means that you are a law unto yourself, that you are above the law, that you create your own law." Elsewhere, Hubbard Jr. argued that his father first became involved in magic at the age of sixteen, when he read Crowley's book *The Book of the Law*, and he later decided he would take over the mantle of the Beast. Lecture, June 28, 1984, reproduced at http://www.lermanet.com/scientology-and-occult/tape-by-L-Ron-Hubbard-jr.htm.
11. See Jon Atack, "Hubbard and the Occult," http://www.religio.de/atack/occ1.html; Jon Atack, *A Piece of Blue Sky: Scientology, Dianetics, and L. Ron Hubbard Exposed* (New York: Carol, 1990).
12. Church of Scientology, letter to the London *Sunday Times*, December 29, 1969.
13. Wallis, *The Road*, 111n–112n. See John Symonds, *The Great Beast: The Life and Magick of Aleister Crowley* (St. Albans, England: Mayflower, 1973); Alexander Mitchell, "Scientology: Revealed for the First Time," London *Sunday Times*, October 5, 1969, reproduced at http://www.lermanet.com/scientologynews/crowley-hubbard-666.htm; Atack, *A Piece of Blue Sky*, 89.

14. Wallis, *The Road*, 111. See also Melton, *The Church of Scientology*, 8. The only mention in Lewis's volume is Melton's chapter, which simply repeats what he said previously about the issue in *The Church of Scientology*.
15. Robert S. Ellwood, *The Fifties Spiritual Marketplace: American Religion in a Decade of Conflict* (New Brunswick, N.J.: Rutgers: University Press, 1997); Wade Clark Roof, *Spiritual Marketplace: Baby Boomers and the Remaking of American Religion* (Princeton, N.J.: Princeton University Press, 2001).
16. Claude Lévi-Strauss, *The Savage Mind* (Chicago: University of Chicago Press, 1966), 16–36; Wendy Doniger, *The Implied Spider: Politics and Theology in Myth* (New York: Columbia University Press, 1998): "In the ecology of narratives, recycling is a very old process. Myths, like all things in constant use . . . get broken and fixed again, lost and found, and the one who . . . recycles them is what Lévi-Strauss calls a *bricoleur* . . . and what the British used to call a 'rag and bones man'" (145).
17. Dick Hebdige, *Subculture: The Meaning of Style* (New York: Methuen, 1980), 104.
18. Jack Parsons, letter to Aleister Crowley, early 1946, quoted in Carter, *Sex and Rockets*, 106–7. See John Symonds, *The King of the Shadow Realm: Aleister Crowley, His Life and Magic* (London: Duckworth, 1989), 562–63.
19. Friends of Ron, *L. Ron Hubbard: A Profile* (Los Angeles: Bridge Publications, 1995), 3.
20. Ibid., 102.
21. "L. Ron Hubbard: A Chronicle," 2009, http://www.scientology.org/l-ron-hubbard/chronicle/pg002.html.
22. Decision of Judge Paul G. Breckenridge Jr., *Church of Scientology of California v. Gerald Armstrong*, Superior Court of the State of California, No. C421053, June 22, 1984. See also Stewart Lamont, *Religion Inc.: The Church of Scientology* (London: Harrap, 1986), 19.
23. See Carter, *Sex and Rockets*; Pendle, *Strange Angel*.
24. Parsons, letter to Crowley, early 1946, quoted in Carter, *Sex and Rockets*, 106–7. See also Symonds, *The King of the Shadow Realm*, 562–63.
25. Aleister Crowley, *Little Essays toward Truth* (Scottsdale, Ariz.: New Falcon, 1991), 51.
26. On Crowley's life and writings, see Sutin, *Do What Thou Wilt*; Aleister Crowley, *The Confessions of Aleister Crowley: An Autohagiography* (New York: Hill & Wang, 1969); Kenneth Grant, *The Magical Revival* (New York: Samuel Weiser, 1973); Ronald Hutton, *Triumph of the Moon: A History of Modern Pagan Witchcraft* (New York: Oxford University Press, 2000); Urban, *Magia Sexualis*, chap. 3.
27. See Urban, *Magia Sexualis:* chaps. 2–3; Hugh B. Urban, "The Yoga of Sex: Tantra, Sex Magic and Orientalism in the Ordo Templi Orientis," in *Hidden Intercourse: Eros and Sexuality in the History of Western Esotericism*, ed. Wouter J. Hanegraaff and Jeffrey J. Kripal (Leiden: Brill, 2008), 401–44.
28. Aleister Crowley, *Magick in Theory and Practice*, in *Magick Liber ABA*, ed. Hymenaeus Beta (York Beach, Maine: Samuel Weiser, 1997), 131.
29. Ibid., 127–28.

30. Ibid., 275.
31. "Aiwaz is none other than mine own Holy Guardian Angel, to Whose Knowledge and Conversation I have attained, so that I have exclusive access to him." Ibid., 440. See Sutin, *Do What Thou Wilt*, 124; Symonds, *The King of the Shadow Realm*, 66–67.
32. Aleister Crowley, *The Law Is for All: An Extended Commentary on "The Book of the Law"* (Phoenix, Ariz.: Falcon Press, 1985), 82. "No aspect of the Magick of Thelema is more important than the Knowledge and Conversation of the Holy Guardian Angel. . . . Until attained, no vision, ritual invocation . . . or magical practice can be truly efficacious. . . . the Holy Guardian Angel transfigures the devotee and bestows bliss and an expanded consciousness which is prerequisite to any further spiritual experience." Ibid., 133–34.
33. Crowley, *Magick in Theory and Practice*, 269.
34. Sylvan J. Muldoon, *The Projection of the Astral Body* (1929; New York: Samuel Weiser, 1974), 47. See also Sylvan J. Muldoon, *The Phenomena of Astral Projection* (1951; New York: Samuel Weiser, 1971).
35. Crowley, *Magick in Theory and Practice*, 202.
36. Ibid., 243.
37. Ibid., 201.
38. Ibid., 284.
39. Ibid., 129.
40. Ibid., 184.
41. Crowley, *The Law Is for All*, 76. "The magician becomes filled with God, fed upon God, intoxicated with God. Little by little his body will become purified by the internal lustration of God." Crowley, *Magick in Theory and Practice*, 269.
42. *The Book of Babalon,* March 2, 1946, quoted in Carter, *Sex and Rockets,* 144–45. See Jack Parsons, *The Book of B.A.B.A.L.O.N.* (Berkeley, Calif.: Ordo Templi Orientis, 1982), reproduced at http://www.sacred-texts.com/oto/lib49.htm.
43. Jeanne Forman, quoted in Pendle, *Strange Angel,* 257. On Crowley's broader influence, see Hutton, *Triumph of the Moon*; Urban, *Magia Sexualis.*
44. Crowley, *The Law Is for All,* 229.
45. Carter, *Sex and Rockets,* 150. "He believed he could incarnate an actual goddess on earth, a female messiah named Babalon." Pendle, *Strange Angel,* 264. The idea of the moonchild comes from Crowley's novel *Moonchild* (London: Mandrake Press, 1929).
46. Sutin, *Do What Thou Wilt*, 413. In his introduction to *The Book of Babalon*, Parsons defined the working as "a magical experiment relating to the invocation of an elemental, the thereafter of the Goddess or Force called BABALON, and the results thereof."
47. Parsons, *The Book of Babalon,* March 2, 1946.
48. Ibid. See Carter, *Sex and Rockets*, 136.
49. Parsons, *The Book of Babalon,* March 3, 1946. See Carter, *Sex and Rockets,* 144–45.
50. Parsons, letter to Crowley, March 6, 1946, in Symonds, *The King of the Shadow Realm,* 564.

51. Crowley, letter to Germer, April 19, 1946, quoted in Sutin, *Do What Thou Wilt*, 414
52. Crowley, cable to Karl Germer, May 22, 1946, quoted in Sutin, *Do What Thou Wilt*, 414–15.
53. Mitchell, "Scientology." See Symonds, *The King of the Shadow Realm*, 564.
54. Church of Scientology, letter to the London *Sunday Times*, December 28, 1969. See Atack, *A Piece of Blue Sky*, 89.
55. Gerald Armstrong has posted a copy of the document quoted here on his Web site under the title "The Admissions of L. Ron Hubbard," 2003, http://www.gerryarmstrong.org/50grand/writings/ars/ars-2000-03-11.html. The texts themselves bear no title but were given the names "Affirmations" and later "Admissions" by Armstrong.
56. Gerald Armstrong, telephone interview with the author, February 2009.
57. *Church of Scientology of California v. Gerald Armstrong*, Mutual Release & Settlement Agreement, December 6, 1986, Los Angeles Superior Court, No. C 420153.
58. Quoted in Atack, *A Piece of Blue Sky*, 100.
59. "The Admissions."
60. Ibid.
61. Ibid.
62. Atack, *A Piece of Blue Sky*, 100.
63. Ibid., 101.
64. Crowley, *Magick in Theory and Practice*, 197
65. L. Ron Hubbard, *Dianetics: The Evolution of a Science* (1950; Los Angeles: Bridge Publications, 2007), 110.
66. L. Ron Hubbard, "Religious Philosophy and Religious Practice," *Hubbard Communications Office Bulletin*, June 21, 1960, revised April 18, 1967.
67. Whitehead, *Renunciation and Reformulation*, 52. See L. Ron Hubbard, "Dianetics: The Evolution of a Science," *Astounding Science Fiction* 45, no. 3 (1950), 43–87; *Dianetics: The Modern Science of Mental Health* (Los Angeles: Bridge Publications, 2007).
68. Hubbard, *Dianetics: The Evolution of a Science*, 9.
69. Ibid., 14.
70. Atack, in "Hubbard and the Occult," notes that Hubbard seems to have had a special interest in the name Diana, possibly drawn from the Roman goddess Diana, and speculates that the term *Dianetics* itself might even be a double entendre: "Hubbard was taken with the Roman name of the goddess, Diana, giving it to one of his daughters and also to one of his Scientology Sea Organization boats. Curiously, this boat had been renamed from *The Enchanter* and before Scientology he had owned another called *The Magician*. Hubbard had also used Jack Parsons' money to buy a yacht called *Diane*. 'Dianetics' may also be a reference to Diana. Shortly before its inception, another former US Navy officer and practitioner of the VIIIth degree of the Ordo Templi Orientis had formed a group called Dianism." If we were to pursue Atack's reasoning here—which is admittedly speculative—we might also note that Margaret Murray's widely read but controversial book *Witch Cult in Western Europe: A Study in Anthropology* (Oxford: Clarendon Press, 1921)

identifies Diana as the pan-European goddess worshipped by those who would later be persecuted as witches in the Middle Ages: "Diana is found throughout Western Europe as the name of the female deity or leader of the so-called Witches, and it is for this reason that I have called this ancient religion the Dianic cult" (12). [Editors' note: "Dianism" is the name given to the practice of sexual intercourse without ejaculation, similar to the practice of "Karezza." The term *Dianism* was originated by the American radical and sexual teacher Ida Craddock (1857–1904). The "former US Navy officer" appears to be a reference to Hubbard's contemporary Louis T. Culling, but Culling's exposure to "Dianism" came through his involvement in C. F. Russell's magical order, the Gnostic Body of God (GBG), in which Culling was active in the 1930s prior to his joining the OTO.]

71. See L. Ron Hubbard, "Scientology and the Reactive Mind," *Ability* 75 (May 1958), reproduced in Hubbard, *The Technical Bulletins of Dianetics and Scientology* (Los Angeles: Scientology Publications, 1976), 3:269: "The whole of Freudian Analysis concerns itself with treating the reactive mind. Freud called it the Unconscious."
72. Hubbard, *Dianetics: The Modern Science*, iii: "The Clear has attained a stable state on a very high plane. He is persistent and vigorous and pursues life with enthusiasm and satisfaction. . . . He has attained the full power and use of hitherto hidden abilities."
73. See Wallis, *The Road*, 77–100.
74. L. Ron Hubbard, *Scientology 8–8008* (1952; Los Angeles: Bridge Publications, 2006), 11. See also L. Ron Hubbard, *The Phoenix Lectures: Freeing the Human Spirit* (Los Angeles: Golden Era Productions, 2007), 34.
75. See L. Ron Hubbard, *Dianetics and Scientology Technical Dictionary* (Los Angeles: Publications Organization, 1975), 431–32, 248, 369–70.
76. L. Ron Hubbard, *Have You Lived before This Life? A Scientific Survey* (East Grinstead, England: Church of Scientology, 1968), 53–54.
77. "Success Beyond Man's Wildest Dream!" *Clear News* 6 (December 12, 1969), cited in Wallis, *The Road*, 121.
78. "OT Phenomena Success," *Advance!* 17 (1973), 14.
79. Hubbard, *Dianetics and Scientology Technical Dictionary*, 345. See Harriet Whitehead, "Reasonably Fantastic: Some Perspectives on Scientology, Science Fiction and Occultism," in *Religious Movements in Contemporary America*, ed. I. I. Zaretsky and M. P. Leone (Princeton, N.J.: Princeton University Press, 1974). As one Scientologist recounted: "I have rediscovered what telepathic communication really is. Knowing what someone is 'thinking' before he says it has become part of my everyday communication. I can sit at my desk and *fully* experience the reality of any place, from ocean to snow-capped Sierras." From *Advance Success Stories*, quoted in Whitehead, "Reasonably Fantastic," 584.
80. "OT Phenomena Success," 16–17; see Wallis, *The Road*, 121. Wallis notes that Scientologists claim a variety of supernatural powers that bear a striking resemblance to the spiritual abilities (*siddhis*) claimed by Hindu yogis and Buddhist monks.

Indeed, Scientologists have claimed virtually all of the powers attributed to Buddhas, such as knowledge of previous lives, power of great sight, power to cause events, power to be where one wants, power to be invisible, and power to walk on air. Wallis, *The Road*, 112–13.

81. Hubbard, *The Philadelphia Doctorate Course*, 185.
82. Ibid.
83. Ibid., 188.
84. Ibid., 186.
85. See also Hubbard, *Dianetics and Scientology Technical Dictionary*, 432.
86. David Bromley, "Making Sense of Scientology: Prophetic, Contractual Religion," in *Scientology*, ed. James R. Lewis (New York: Oxford University Press, 2009), 91.
87. Hubbard, *Dianetics and Scientology Technical Dictionary*, 370.
88. Crowley, *Magick in Theory and Practice*, 129.
89. Aleister Crowley, *The Book of Lies, Which Is Also Falsely Called Breaks* (New York: Samuel Weiser, 1972), 108. Figure reprinted with the permission of the Ordo Templi Orientis.
90. Ibid., 109.
91. Kent, "Scientology's Relationship," 31; see also "Out of the West Came the Dawn," *Aberee* (September 1954), 1, 13.
92. Figure reprinted with the permission of the Ordo Templi Orientis.
93. The usual explanation of the Scientology cross is that its eight points represent the eight dynamics or the will to survive on every level of existence, from the individual being up to the Infinite or Supreme Being.
94. Wallis, *The Road*, 57. See also Whitehead, "Reasonably Fantastic."
95. Hubbard, *Scientology 8–8008*, 115.
96. L. Ron Hubbard, *Secrets of the MEST Universe* (Los Angeles: Bridge Publications, 1990), 100.
97. Hubbard, *Scientology 8–8008*, 115.
98. Introduction to Hubbard, *The Philadelphia Doctorate Course*, vii.
99. L. Ron Hubbard, *The Creation of Human Ability* (Los Angeles: Bridge Publications, 2007), 65–66.
100. Ibid., 55.
101. Hubbard, *The Phoenix Lectures*, 465.
102. Ibid., 471.
103. Ibid., 472.
104. Hubbard, *The Creation of Human Ability*, 64.
105. Hubbard, *The Phoenix Lectures*, 382
106. One definition of the goal of Scientology is the individual's "attainment of infinity by the reduction of the apparent infinity of and power of the MEST universe to zero for himself and the increase of apparent zero of one's own universe to an infinity for oneself." Introduction to Hubbard, *The Philadelphia Doctorate Course*, viii–ix.

107. See Urban, "Fair Game."
108. Hubbard, *Dianetics and Scientology Technical Dictionary*, 434.
109. Hubbard, *The Philadelphia Doctorate Course*, 5
110. Ibid., xi.
111. Hubbard, *Scientology 8–8008*, 175.
112. Ibid., 252.
113. Hubbard, *The Phoenix Lectures*, 373; L. Ron Hubbard, *Technique 88: Before Earth* (Los Angeles: Golden Era Productions, 2007), 290.
114. Hubbard, *The Philadelphia Doctorate Course*, 6.
115. Ibid., 14.
116. Hubbard, *Dianetics and Scientology Technical Dictionary*, 381.
117. L. Ron Hubbard, *"Triton" and "Battle of Wizards"* (Los Angeles: Fantasy, 1949), 161–62.
118. Hubbard, *Dianetics: The Evolution of a Science*, 9.
119. "Self-determinism is that state of being wherein the individual can or cannot be controlled by his environment according to his own choice. In that state the individual has self-confidence in his control of the material universe." Hubbard, *Dianetics and Scientology Technical Dictionary*, 381.
120. Pendle, *Strange Angel*, 273.
121. See Norman Vincent Peale, *The Power of Positive Thinking* (1952; Englewood Cliffs, N.J.: Prentice Hall, 1956).
122. See Kent, "Scientology's Relationship," 22; Frank K. Flinn, "Scientology as Technological Buddhism," in *Scientology*, ed. James R. Lewis (New York: Oxford University Press, 2009), 209–24.
123. These "space drama" elements appear throughout Hubbard's lectures of the early 1950s. See, for example, Hubbard, *Technique 88*, 341; Whitehead, "Reasonably Fantastic"; Mikael Rothstein, "His Name Was Xenu: He Used Renegades," in *Scientology*, ed. James R. Lewis (New York: Oxford University Press, 2009), 365–88.
124. Stephen Kent, "Scientology—Is This a Religion?," June 30, 1997, http://www.cs.cmu.edu/~dst/Library/Shelf/kent/religion.html.
125. See Urban, "Fair Game," 380–81; Douglas E. Cowan, "Contested Spaces: Movement, Countermovement, and E-Space Propaganda," in *Religion Online: Finding Faith on the Internet*, ed. Lorne L. Dawson and Douglas E. Cowan (New York: Routledge, 2004), 255–72; Ann Brill and Ashley Packard, "Silencing Scientology's Critics on the Internet: A Mission Impossible?" *Communications and the Law* 19, no. 4 (1997), 1–23.
126. Quoted in John Cook, "Cult Friction," *Radar*, April 2008, http://radaronline.com/from-the-magazine/2008/03/scientology_anonymous_protests_tom_cruise_01.php. See also Chris Landers, "Serious Business: Anonymous Takes on Scientology," *Baltimore City Paper*, April 2, 2008. http://www2.citypaper.com/news/story.asp?id=15543.
127. L. Ron Hubbard, *Dianetics 55* (Los Angeles: Bridge Publications, 2007), 7.

15

Satan and the Beast

THE INFLUENCE OF ALEISTER CROWLEY ON MODERN SATANISM

Asbjørn Dyrendal

DURING AND AFTER his lifetime Aleister Crowley has often been accused of being a Satanist. Partly because of his image and his legacy as inspiration for numerous pop-culture images of black magicians, these accusations have often been transmitted to contemporary Thelemites in general. Perhaps as a corollary to these accusations, modern Satanism is often said to be heavily influenced by Crowley.

Allegations that Thelema is Satanism or that Satanism is a (perverted) form of "Crowleyanity" are mainly presented in passing, as accusations and/or as snide, derogatory remarks. They are rarely founded in any serious understanding of either Thelema or Satanism. Sometimes, however, we find that the latter allegation—that Satanism is but a poor man's Thelema, perhaps combined with inverted Christianity—may be used as a defense of Crowley. An example of this is when Crowley biographer Lawrence Sutin refers to Satanism's founder, Anton LaVey, and his followers in passing as "self-styled Satanists who shave their heads and parrot random phrases from Crowley's writings."[1] I believe Sutin is being not merely unfair but also wrong. This does not, however, mean that there are no similarities, parallels, or direct influences between Thelema and Satanism. There clearly are, but this is a far from simple topic, and few outside the inner circles of Satanist intellectuals seem to have touched on it.[2] The aim of this exploratory essay is to examine some areas in which Satanist philosophy touches on or is influenced by Aleister Crowley's.

Although there are some generally accepted "prototypical" examples of Satanism, no generally accepted academic nomenclature has been established for what should be included in or excluded from the category of Satanism. Jesper Petersen and I have suggested a focus on three *discursive* positions: rational, esoteric, and reactive satanic discourse.[3] These are all characterized, albeit in different manners, by antinomianism, self-religion, the use of certain *S* words (*Satan*, *Satanist*, and so on) as positive identity markers, and a formulated ideological genealogy.

Where does this approach place Crowley? He clearly makes positive use of a tradition of discourse on the satanic that we see in poets from Blake to Baudelaire. He also uses a terminology and understandings of "Satan" borrowed from mainly the esoteric reception of Gnostic scriptures. His discourse as well as his practice makes use of antinomianism, and he made liberal use of a "satanic" image and self-epithets such as "the Beast 666." His discourse makes use of and contributes to a literary tradition of positive discourse on Satan, and it is central to the disembedding of Satan from Christian demonology and reembedding him into an esoteric discourse as something positive. However, Crowley's self-understanding was not as a Satanist, and he had no self-designated satanic ideological lineage to belong to. Thus I would argue that Crowley contributed to bridging the gap between earlier "literary Satanism" and later actualizations of Satanism as organized religion. He should be seen as a central contributor to positive discourse on the satanic, and thus to later formulations of self-identification as Satanist. However, in order to avoid essentializing "Satanism" and involving oneself in anachronism or theological projection, one should probably treat Crowley and other historical figures as influences on the first self-designated Satanist organizations, rather than as examples of Satanism.

In this way, the Church of Satan (CoS) and the Temple of Set (ToS) tend to become the primary examples of early and still existing Satanism, exemplifying rational and esoteric Satanism. I shall focus here on Church of Satan founder Anton LaVey and Michael Aquino, founder of the Temple of Set. These two are central to the history and development of contemporary Satanism (as it is usually understood) and its divergent expressions.[4] How these two may be said to be influenced by Crowley depends in part on what we take *influence* to mean.

Influence

In its loosest sense, *influence* may be taken to mean having some sort of control over—or, at the very least, effect on—the actions, including thoughts, of other people. This opens up the discussion to a wide range of different types and degrees of influence. If we think of influence in relation to *authority*, it may take on the form of power or persuasion.[5] In the latter case, someone has, by way of social standing or otherwise, convinced us that we should listen to his or her ideas and take them seriously. In Bruce Lincoln's schema, *persuasion* exists when we are actually persuaded, *authority* exists when we are willing to act as if we are persuaded, and *power* exists when we are (or feel) forced to change our actions.[6]

All of the above-described types of influence relate to individuals as parts of social networks. Influence is a social phenomenon, whatever form the "social" takes. In social influence theory, peer pressure is often said to be an important source of social influence toward conformity, compliance, and obedience. As with authority and power, however, there is an opposite side of the coin as well. Influence, in the broad sense outlined above, also includes acts of opposition, reluctant agreement, and partial integration occasioned by someone else's ("the authority's") actions.

This, I postulate, is what we see with regard to Aleister Crowley's influence on modern Satanism. There is, in my mind, no question that Crowley has had—and still has—a position as authority among those seeking the left-hand path. His position as a dominating figure in twentieth-century occultism makes him hard to avoid, and both his ideas and his persona make him an interesting figure to engage in the construction of Satanism. His writings have carried consequences, and they still resonate within the vocabularies of modern Satanism. But the phrases used in Satanism are not random, and Crowley is far from being the single most important source of influence. As we shall see, the influence of his ideas and practices ranges from partial acceptance to almost complete rejection.

Satanism and the Church of Satan

Although the point is open to debate,[7] I tend to date the history of Satanism from the founding of the Church of Satan on April 30, 1966. Given this understanding, I do not think Crowley's Thelema a satanic movement, but relate it historically to Satanism as one of its influences.[8] The degree to which this has been the case seems to be both a complicated issue and, internally in the CoS, a *contentious* issue.

Lawrence Sutin was far from the first man to accuse Anton LaVey of being a Crowley rip-off. LaVey himself seems to have answered similar accusations in a letter to *Fate* magazine in 1971.[9] The first priest to be expelled from the CoS, Wayne West, similarly accused LaVey of not merely copying (from

Crowley's *Confessions*) but also forbidding his members to read Crowley.[10] Presumably, the rationale for such a prohibition, which seems both unlikely and unsubstantiated, would have been to prevent members from discovering LaVey's copycat activity.

In his response to *Fate*, LaVey stated that he found some of Crowley's poetry fitting elements in some of the rituals and admired "his literary eloquence." His "drug-befuddled callings-up of Choronzon, et al.,"[11] on the other hand, found little sympathy or interest. Aquino merely notes that the accusations made by West—that *The Satanic Bible* borrowed extensively from *The Confessions*—cannot be true, as the first printing of *The Satanic Bible* took place a month before *The Confessions* was released.[12] Additionally, LaVey seems to have had no trouble owning up to his various other influences, including his extensive borrowing from Ragnar Redbeard's (Arthur Desmond) *Might Is Right*. LaVey praised Arthur Lyons's book *The Second Coming*, in which then CoS member Lyons attributed most of LaVey's ideas on magic to the influence of Crowley. Thus it would seem incongruous that he should borrow extensively further from Crowley while claiming the opposite, laying himself open to just such attacks.[13]

"Biographical" Inspiration and Anton LaVey

We know little with regard to the early influences on LaVey outside his own words. The role of Thelema and Thelemites is one of many interesting and little-researched areas with regard to LaVey's sources of inspiration. From his own recollections, the role would seem to be scant.[14] He may nonetheless have socialized with more Thelemites than is currently known. The esoteric milieu in California during the 1950s and 1960s seems to have been fairly small, and several Thelemites stand out in it.[15] It would be far from surprising to see the same people showing up at many scenes with similar or relevant interests—as has been fairly typical of many esoteric scenes. Although it is unknown to what extent LaVey socialized with the esoterically inclined before instigating his own "Black Circle" and his related lectures, he is known to have frequented the artistic circles in which several Thelemites were involved.[16] In these circles, of course, Kenneth Anger stands out as a well-known Thelemite, but again, we have little knowledge about possible "esoteric" friends of LaVey's outside the Black Circle.

Thus far, then, we have to make do with LaVey's own words. From his own tale, LaVey seems to have first become interested in Crowley because of Crowley's Satanic and carnal, hedonistic image. "The Beast's" satanic image seems to have inspired LaVey to acquire and read a fair amount of Crowley's writings. LaVey himself rarely went into detail, but in several interviews he mentioned salient elements from Crowley's production that made it clear that he was familiar with the texts. However, he seems to have been slightly disappointed with both the convoluted language and the at times sanctimonious tone of the texts. According to his recollections, he concluded after reading Symonds's biography that "the Thelemites' founder was a druggy poseur, whose greatest achievements were as a poet and mountain climber."[17]

Although his judgment could be harsh, it was not all one-sided. LaVey also, as not all have noticed, credited Crowley for both his sense of humor and his business sense. In a 1972 interview with John Fritscher, LaVey stated that, in his opinion, "Aleister Crowley had his tongue jammed firmly in his cheek." He also cast some further doubt on Crowley's satanic image, considering that Crowley was, basically, a pragmatist and "a sweet kind man who was trying to emancipate himself from the throes of a very strict upbringing."[18] Crowley's "greatest wisdom" was, according to LaVey, found in *The Book of Lies*, where he stated, "A sucker is born every minute."[19] This particular gem of wisdom is one that is reflected in many of LaVey's texts. It would, however, be most unfair to attribute it to Crowley's influence, as P. T. Barnum undoubtedly beat them both to it. This is a general problem in assessing the influence of Crowley on LaVey, as they share not only a number of common attitudes but also many common sources of information and influence.[20]

While some of LaVey's critics would have it that he modeled his persona and his attitudes on literature rather than on experience, the character Crowley constructs in his own works was clearly not this model, at least not directly.[21] Given that Crowley inspired a multitude of popular-culture representations of "black magicians," there is, however, a possibility that more than one of these presentations played a role in LaVey's construction of his persona. As the stereotype of black magic villain ("originally" based loosely on Crowley) spread throughout popular culture, it is likely that LaVey had seen the character and considered the element of its usefulness for him.

According to LaVey, his interest in Crowley did, however, suffice to make him approach a lodge of Thelemites during the early 1950s.[22] The experience seems to have left him cold:

> Anton was disappointed to find the Berkeley bunch mystically-minded card readers who emphasized the study of Eastern philosophy, Oriental languages, stars and contemplation to reach the spiritual Nirvana of Oneness. . . . Crowley's followers were rather innocuous—much more ethereal than Anton expected.[23]

The "ethereal" interest in mysticism and the spiritual was something LaVey found unattractive in both texts and practices. This constitutes a vital, albeit *negative*, influence on LaVey, a side of Crowley that constitutes a significant, negative Other: that reputedly "satanic" practitioners, including Crowley and his followers, should be so deeply interested in the spiritual is severely criticized. LaVey's later devastating criticism of "occultism" and "occultniks" was at least partially founded on his experiences with and readings of Crowley and his forebears.

Crowley et al. as Negative Others

LaVey raised his critique of occultism many times, starting out early. The most widely available instances are in *The Satanic Bible* from 1969 and in a 1971 essay titled "On Occultism of the Past." In the former, he keeps mainly to a general critique of spiritual religion; in the latter, he becomes more explicit. Starting out by tearing into Eliphas Lévi, he presents one after the other of esoteric forebears as effectively, although more closeted, Christians, deeply concerned with presenting themselves as holy and righteous. They clothe their marginal insights in arcane language, their texts contain mainly fillers, resulting in works that deserve to be called "prior garbage" and "worthless ravings."[24] Crowley is let off slightly lighter, but he *is* one of the centerpieces of LaVey's critique: Crowley is termed a hypocrite for calling himself by the Devil's terms yet withholding allegiance to Satan, and his occult texts are decried as "millions of words of Kabbalistic mulligatawny" holding some, but little, interest. The *real* value of Crowley's work LaVey finds, is primarily in his art, mainly his poetry, which is

> worthy of inclusion with the likes of James Thompson, Baudelaire, Clark Ashton Smith, and Robert E. Howard. If Crowley was a magician, it was the beauty of his creative art which made him so, not his drug-befuddled callings-up of Choronzon, et al.[25]

From the details of this and other critiques, it would seem that LaVey had some, possibly quite more than passing, familiarity with a selection of Crowley's works, both central and lesser known.[26] West claimed that, as noted above, "On Occultism of the Past" was LaVey's prohibition of reading Crowley. To me it seems more like a generalized criticism of the pretentious style, and the "esoteric" and spiritual focus, of earlier occultisms, Crowley's included.

This does not mean that the Satanist might not find anything of interest or virtue in Crowley's writings, but rather that, according to LaVey, the principles found in the much-praised "forebears" had already been distilled, repeated, and "extended one-hundred fold in *The Satanic Bible* or *The Compleat Witch*."[27] Crowley et al. are treated as ingredients from which one might extract something tasty (useful). Implicitly, then, LaVey seems to state that he has done the job already. What he may have found of interesting principles in Crowley, he has already included in his various works. The rest is dressing, poetry for stimulating the senses and passions in ritual, or it is "Kabbalistic mulligatawny" served up "tongue-in-cheek" to those who crave such meals.

LaVey seems to have used Crowley critically and sparingly, more so than several of his other sources of inspiration. Sometimes Crowley and his followers would become negative points of reference. In addition to passages such as the above, LaVey famously stated, "Those who spell 'magic' with a 'k' aren't."[28] Biographically, LaVey favored "hedonism" balanced with Epicureanism and disapproved of taking drugs,[29] learning perhaps equally from surrounding "hippiedom" and Crowley's example. LaVey showed no interest in kabbalah and displayed only contempt for belief in reincarnation; he thought that a competent satanic magician should be knowledgeable about astrology, but only because he should be able to use this knowledge to manipulate believers.[30]

Where LaVey agreed with Crowley, it may often have been the result of common influences. We may see important similarities between LaVey's philosophy of the strong and Crowley's statements in *Liber Oz*, but it seems doubtful that these were LaVey's primary influence. With regard to their common tendency toward social Darwinist expositions on politics, it seems obvious that LaVey did not borrow his views primarily from Crowley. The influence of a hundred years of similar thoughts, echoed in books explicitly cited and liberally quoted by LaVey, seems to attest to this.

There are, equally, similarities in the thoughts of LaVey and Crowley on being the master of oneself, in their elitism, and in their individualism and opposition to "herd" behavior. Both would have men be gods and take full responsibility for their actions. Both despised Christianity and, in the words of Hugh Urban, "declared all existing religions deceased, bankrupt, hypocritical and irrelevant."[31] Crowley's concept of will seems to have caught LaVey's eye, but as with the similarities mentioned above, LaVey's own notion of will lacks the large, "theological" superstructure of Crowley. While both stress the importance of self-knowledge, LaVey's notion of will is void of, for instance, Crowley's elements of destiny as something other than what one creates. The problem of the conscious will being at odds with True Will does not appear in the same way with LaVey. He is more "simply" Nietzschean—with a liberal dose of Ayn Rand.[32] In LaVey's personal synthesis, Nietzsche and Rand may play a larger role in the many similarities to Crowley than the Beast himself does. Although LaVey certainly borrowed—and, in the case of "Ragnar Redbeard," copied—his product was an original synthesis of many disparate elements. LaVey's personal synthesis seems decidedly his own creation, even though the different ingredients going into it are at times very visible.

Secularizing Magick

My own reading of LaVey is that the principles he found in Crowley are generally reinterpreted in a "secularized" manner, by which I mean that they are stripped of much of their esoteric content and taken out of their esoteric context. In this, LaVey is to some extent following in Crowley's footsteps.[33] Indeed, he at least in one place also legitimates this strategy by quoting Crowley. In the above-mentioned interview with Fritscher, LaVey praised Crowley for his astute playing of the "marks" in producing large amounts of the kind of "gibberish and nonsense" the masses crave, while at the same time communicating that "the real wisdom is about ten lines long."[34]

Secularizing the reception of classical esotericism seems to have been a common trend of the twentieth century.[35] From this perspective, it is not mainly a case of influence; both Crowley and LaVey participated instead in the same venture of applying what they considered to be scientific perspectives to magic. There is, however, a stronger case to be made for influence in the corresponding, *converse*, movement: when both Crowley and LaVey use the term *magick/magic* to describe "everyday" strategies for achieving one's objectives, I believe, with Lyons, that the influence of Crowley is direct.[36] Indeed, there is much to be said for the commonly presented view that LaVey's concept of magic was heavily influenced by Crowley, especially as presented in *Magick in Theory and Practice*.[37] That, however, is not the same as saying they are identical. They clearly are not. In this, as in most other things, LaVey used what he agreed with, left out what he did not, and added things of his own.

Generally, LaVey adopted Crowley's concept of magic as "the Science and Art of causing Change to occur in conformity with Will."[38] Since, however, LaVey divorced himself from Crowley's concept of True Will, "secularizing" it, the understanding differs somewhat from the start.[39] Neither would LaVey necessarily go so far as to agree that every intentional act is a magical act.[40] LaVey stresses that "magic" should exclude "normally accepted methods" for achieving a goal.[41] He does, however, present a similar sort of continuum and differentiates between ceremonial, "higher" magic and more mundane activities that he calls "lower" magic. Both also agree—with most modern occultists—that magic includes "employing hitherto unknown forces in nature."[42] Like Crowley, LaVey also stresses that magic is no substitute for action. One should also apply oneself in the appropriate "mundane" manner in order to achieve one's goals, at least when psychological release is not the only goal of ceremonial magic. (I shall return to this in short order.)

LaVey also follows Crowley to a certain extent in not applying a simple ethical division between "black" and "white" magic. However, LaVey completely disregards the division, stating instead that there "is no difference between 'White' and 'Black' magic, except in the smug hypocrisy and self-deceit of the 'White' magician himself."[43] The alleged altruism of white magic is disallowed by LaVey's anthropology, where the human being is a self-interested animal. This anthropology makes it clear that the real interests behind the most "selfless" magic are still "ego gratification and personal power."[44] As far as I can determine, LaVey would be what Crowley terms a "Brother of the Left-Hand Path," one of those who "refuse blood to the Cup."[45] The concept of "killing"/dissolving the ego in the Abyss seems to be totally alien to LaVey, as is the notion of *unio mystica* embraced by Crowley. The ego is all there is; it is to be cherished and strengthened, and there is nothing with which to unite. Thus LaVey dismisses even Crowley's notion of black magic.

LaVey's notions of practical, lower magic for everyday use may have borrowed something from Crowley's observations, but they seem to be much more influenced by other sources. These include sociologists such as Goffman and Klapp, psychologists such as Reich, Ferenczi, and Freud, and a host of other sources, most of which are explicitly mentioned in the bibliography to his *The Satanic Witch*. Crowley is not mentioned there, and he is not conspicuous by his absence.

However, LaVey seems to make use of Crowley's postulates that "man can only attract and employ the forces for which he is really fitted" and that magic consists in understanding oneself and one's conditions *and* being able to employ that understanding.[46] Although LaVey went easy on the "only," he, like Crowley, stressed the need for knowing oneself as a prerequisite of effective magic. Use of both lower and higher magic demands skill, and knowing one's limitations, abilities, and best strategies is deemed an important aspect of magic. This includes being "able to adjust one's wants to one's capabilities."[47]

Sexuality played an important role for both of them, whether biographically, in their theories of human life and concomitant criticism of Christianity, or in magic. Sexuality is important, both as personal expression and in ritual magic as a tool for achieving one's goals. LaVey considered the release of sexual energy in ritual one of the important strategies for "fueling" the magic work, although primarily in love magic.[48] Again, however, LaVey may have used only some of the basic ideas. Certainly he did not copy Crowley concerning the larger role of sex magick, as it does not fit into LaVey's overall conception of Satanism. His conception of how sexual energy works has multiple sources of influence, but with regard to magic, he shows another important difference from Crowley: sexuality is but one example of the important role of *passion* in effective magic. Much of LaVey's recipe for ritual magic involves stimulating the senses and exhorting the appropriate emotions for the ritual working. This is to concentrate both attention and will, and should work to "isolate the otherwise dissipated adrenal and other emotionally induced energy."[49] This "adrenal energy" is what supposedly fuels the magic. It should also, neatly, serve to release the magician's pent-up energy and passions in a ritual context, relieving the magician from suffering these emotions to excess in everyday life.[50]

This psychodramatic, therapeutic function seems, indeed, to be the *primary* role of the kind of ritual magic LaVey wrote about publicly. While there is ample evidence that he believed, with several later CoS writers, that magic may have efficacy over and above working on and through the psyche of the magician, psychodrama is the central aspect of LaVey's higher magic. This may be one of the reasons his successor as High Priest of the CoS, Peter Gilmore, finds it necessary to stress that although many manage without ritual, the belief in and practice of ritual magic must be accepted as part of what a Satanist *may* choose to do.[51] Since ritual magic neither plays a central role nor is endowed with any claims to special effect, it is up to the individual Satanist to decide whether or not it is something he or she wishes to do.

LaVey let himself be inspired by many different thinkers. Crowley was one of them, but he seems to have been far from the most important. Even where their thinking appears to be alike, LaVey mostly seems to have been influenced more in depth by other sources, sometimes sources (such as Nietzsche) they held in common. The one exception seems to have been LaVey's concept of magic, but when he borrowed from Crowley, he did so critically.[52] The end result shows LaVey as well drawing from several other sources of influence, in addition to his own experiments. However, many other contemporary and later Satanists have drawn more heavily on Crowley.[53] One of those has been Michael Aquino, founder of the Temple of Set.

Michael Aquino and the Temple of Set

If the information on the social influences on Anton LaVey is sparse, it is even more so with regard to Michael Aquino. Here, we are to an even greater extent dependent on Aquino's own words, and they lack most references to his social life. He is, however, liberal with references to his literary influences, and they are amply evidenced in his texts, from H. P. Lovecraft to Plato and Crowley.

Aquino *engages* with Crowley in a more direct way and in greater detail than did LaVey, signaling a much greater interest in Crowley's thoughts. Unlike LaVey, who tended to write texts where his opinions and arguments were presented in brief, Aquino is more expansive. His formal academic training—he holds a PhD in political science—also shows itself in the way he explicitly addresses and argues his way into and around the thinkers he addresses. He goes considerably further into the details of the texts and draws broadly on Western philosophy and science when discussing different topics. There is another important difference in that Aquino and the ToS also *belong* to the esoteric tradition to a much greater degree than LaVey and the CoS. While several Setian writers clearly show that they are still heavily influenced by LaVey, and his kind of philosophy serves as basis for their work, they have added a superstructure onto it that is more esoteric in character.[54]

Crowley is part of that structure, and Aquino both draws on Crowley's biography and engages with and applies his terminology and philosophy. The engagement is both too broad and too complex to be addressed in totality here. I shall only touch lightly on a few of the issues.

Biographical Inspiration: The Second Beast

LaVey mentions Crowley in passing a fairly limited number of times. Aquino engages with Crowley quite frequently. In the sixth draft of his history of the Temple of Set, there are more than three hundred direct references to Crowley and numerous long passages discussing his works, life, and ideas.[55] Aquino has shown a long-standing interest in Crowley as person and magus, starting before his break with the CoS; he wrote several articles showing familiarity with several of Crowley's books during the early 1970s.[56]

With the break, and *in* the break itself, we may see further examples of similarities indicating explicit influence. On a general level, Aquino followed a similar strategy as Crowley did with regard to taking leave of a previous teacher and master. Where Crowley legitimated his self-recognition to a new and higher degree, and thus his independence of Mathers, with and through *Liber AL*, Aquino does something similar in producing *The Book of Coming Forth by Night*. Aquino describes this text as a result of a working of "Greater Black Magic" conducted as a response to the crisis he perceived in the CoS.[57] The resulting text legitimates him as Magus of the Aeon of Set and as heir to the "infernal mandate" of LaVey.[58] Thus he is identified as "a Master who has 'stepped outside' the totality of the existing Æonic formula to alter it in an evolutionary way."[59] Second, in a letter to other, somewhat similarly minded defectors from the CoS ("The Elect," letter dated "June 23, X" [1975]), Aquino legitimates the working with reference to Crowley's concept of Will: "It is the right of a Magister Templi to evoke the Prince of Darkness if it is his Will to do so."[60]

The Book of Coming Forth by Night itself is, moreover, often engaged in a complex intertextual play with Crowley, primarily *Liber AL*, with Aquino setting himself up as heir to Crowley as much as to LaVey.[61] This element is furthered again in his commentary to the book. His claim to the role of heir includes both a deeper ideological engagement with *Liber AL* and a simpler, perhaps slightly tongue-in-cheek, biographical element. In his commentary on *The Book of Coming Forth by Night*, Aquino for a long time included the following passage:

> Collectors of magical happenstance may take note of the following concerning the person of Michael A. Aquino: He was born in 1946, precisely nine months after a Working by Crowley's California disciples to create a homunculus per a secret instruction of Crowley's to the IX degree of his Ordo Templi Orientis. He was also born dead, raising the question of the nature of the force inhabiting his subsequently revived body. On his chest he bears the same whorled swastika of hair borne by Crowley and Buddha.[62]

The last two sentences are clearly a reference to Crowley's self-mythologizing in the first part of *The Confessions*.[63] The reference to the nine months after Parsons's working may similarly be a reference to Crowley's claim to be the reincarnation of Eliphas Lévi, which was formulated in similar terms.[64] In the latest revisions of his comments, this (and the rest of the passage) has been dropped.[65]

With regard to the mode of production, however, he insists that although he felt like something beyond himself was generating it, the book was produced in a state different from the one that produced Crowley's: "There was nothing overtly sensational, supernatural, or melodramatic about *The Book of Coming Forth by Night* working. I simply sat down and wrote it."[66] So whereas "old-time occultists" may see his work as "an imitation of Aleister Crowley's *Book of the Law*," Aquino feels there is "nothing to gain by debating such points of view."[67] Like Crowley, he insists that the text is authentic as far as his own judgment goes, and for Aquino too, his text has been a guiding principle afterward.

Like many others, Aquino distances himself from Crowley's way of life. In *The Book of Coming Forth by Night* and its comments, Aquino connects Crowley's unhappy biography to alleged misunderstandings of the message with which he was entrusted. *The Book of Coming Forth by Night* states:

> The Book of the Law was confusion to all who came upon it, and the creative brilliance of the Magus Aleister Crowley was ever flawed by mindless destructiveness. He himself could never understand this, for he perceived HarWer as a unified Self. And so he was perplexed by a mystery he could not identify.[68]

The central misunderstanding alleged by Aquino is one of Egyptology. The Stele of Revealing, Aquino argues, contains references to other gods and—most important—an older cycle of Egyptian myths than those Crowley thought to identify. In this "original" layer, Horus is not the child of Osiris, but the twin of Set. He is unrelated to the Osirian myth cycle Crowley reads into it. This Horus the Elder—HarWer—is presented by Aquino as "a strange and fitful presence." Since the separation of Set from the duality, into the first form of "isolate intelligence," outside the natural order, HarWer is in one sense a "rest," which "retains some of the self-awareness of the Set-entity, but is equally a part of the objective universe."[69] This duality makes for inconsistency, which is seen as displayed in both Crowley's thought and his actions. Since he does not recognize the true nature of HarWer, he remains "perplexed," a word Aquino relates to what Symonds[70]—most likely mistakenly[71]—alleged to be Crowley's final words.[72]

"Theology" and Aeons

Aquino considers *Liber AL* to be an authentic message with important keys to the Aeon of Set, although they would have to wait until the New Aeon was manifested to be understood. Thus Crowley becomes an important figure for

Aquino to engage, as we can see by the way he adapts important ideas from Crowley. He does so broadly and works out his own understanding (and differences) in some detail.

First of all, we may note that he adopts the word *aeon* from Crowley, but he expresses clear discontent with "the Aeon of Horus." In *The Book of Coming Forth by Night*, Set expresses: "The years of the Aeon of HarWer were confused, and I do not wish to think of them save as curiosities."[73] Aquino instead counts the Setian calendar from the inception of "the Age of Satan," that is, 1966. He also changes the meaning of *aeon* in several ways. Although Aquino accepts that aeons in a certain manner may be seen as consecutive eras, he emphasizes that there are several levels of understanding. In a Lesser Black Magic (LBM) sense, Aquino states, an aeon is more a mind-set one adopts, by condition or choice.[74] Thus many aeons exist side by side: "A Jew, Christian or Moslem exists in the Æon of Osiris, a Wiccan in that of Isis, and a Thelemite in that of Horus."[75] In this sense, aeons cannot be seen as Crowley's periods in catastrophic succession.[76] Indeed, the aeons are presented as a pyramid of "mind-sets" and "it would be very difficult if not impossible to spend all one's time in a 'higher æon.'"[77] Thus we spend different amounts of time in all aeons as "we go about our affairs in the profane world."[78]

I have called Aquino's LBM concept of aeon a "mind-set." Aquino himself explains an aeon as a philosophy related to the Word of a Magus. Where Crowley operates with three aeons and eight magi, Aquino argues: "Each magical Aeon is characterized by a philosophy, which may be summarized by a Formula, which may in turn be summarized by a Word."[79] Although there are clearly more people recognized to the degree of magus than there are aeons—several others in the ToS are recognized to the degree without anyone invoking a new aeon—he seems to argue here that there needs to be more than Crowley's three aeons. He seems mainly, however, to adopt Crowley's divisions. He mentions but Crowley's three preceding aeons, adding only the two necessary further aeons after the Aeon of Horus (1904–1965): the Age of Satan (1966–1975) and the Aeon of Set (1975–).[80]

There is also, explains Aquino, a Greater Black Magic (GBM) understanding of what an aeon constitutes: "a living entity, in which its initiates are 'cells.'" This living entity may be likened to a god, "a creature of the total magical and philosophical energy of material beings who are initiates of that æon."[81] Thus all gods but Set-HarWer are constituted by human activity.[82] In this regard, we find a similar complex interplay between an external and an internal interpretation of "supernatural" beings in Setian thought as one may find in Crowley's. Both Aquino and Crowley seem to insist on an external source behind the expression of their central documents (*Liber AL* and *The Book of Coming Forth by Night*). At the same time, this "externality" is closely related to their psyches, so that there is no dichotomy, but rather continuity between internal and external, at least in the expression of these works.

Crowley famously also states in *Liber Oz*: "There is no god but man." For Aquino, there is also the possibility for men to become as gods, becoming isolate intelligences in emulation of Set. There is no reincarnation—at least not openly expressed—in Aquino's or (to my knowledge) in other Setians' thoughts. But unlike LaVey, Aquino clearly thinks it possible to survive beyond the body. Indeed, Aquino makes it clear that this immortality is something that all conscious beings already have.[83] This is by way of their "godhood," the "Gift of Set": "The core, or true self . . . exists as a *neter* and, when looking outward, sees a universe not of the works of other *neteru*, but of those *neteru* themselves."[84] It is the ability to align one's consciousness with this *neter* that is expressed in Aquino's Word: *Xeper*.[85]

The unique *neter* Set's role as the one who gives humans their intelligence echoes a passage in *Magick in Theory and Practice* where Crowley interprets Satan: "This serpent, SATAN, is not the enemy of Man, but He who made Gods of our race, knowing Good and Evil; He bade 'Know Thyself!' and taught Initiation."[86] This seems to be a fairly good, if partial, description of the role and works of Set according to Aquino. Set makes gods of men by giving them self-awareness and the opportunity to awaken to their godhood. The initiatory system of ToS is said to be for the select few who seek to develop along this path.

Crowley and the Black Brothers

By rejecting, even more explicitly than LaVey, the "annihilation" of the self, Aquino places himself squarely within what Crowley would term "the Black Brothers." Unlike LaVey, however, Aquino discusses the topic explicitly. He relates it to the topic noted above, the separateness, the "divine" unnaturalness of the self that cannot or should not be fused with the natural universe, which is his understanding of Crowley's Nuit. His concept of Will takes this into account, as we may see from his comments on *Liber AL* I:39:

> What is understood by the term "Will" is an expression of mental separateness from Nuit, in that the self is impressing its desire for inertial change upon Nuit. By definition then, the separate Will cannot be harmonious. Harmony with Nuit can occur only when the separate Will is

> destroyed and the mind mechanically fused with the inertia of the Cosmos. This notion has been expressed as "oneness with God," nirvana, etc. From the standpoint of Nuit this is immortalization of the Will; from the standpoint of the individual apart from Nuit it is suicide.[87]

Since Aquino deems that Crowley's Thelema consisted in exactly this fusing of the "individual Will with that of the cosmic whole,"[88] he is in essence inverting the values he finds stated. Crowley's concept of Will is derided as "completely meaningless,"[89] and for the very reasons stated by Crowley to characterize a "Black Brother": Refusal to give up the self.

Crowley's concept is criticized on several grounds. If we look but briefly on another example of Crowley's critique, here from *Liber Aleph*, we may see that Aquino attacks the ground on which the distinction is built:

> Of the Black Brothers, o my Son, will I write these Things following. I have told thee already concerning Change, how it is the Law, because every Change is an Act of Love under Will. So then he that is Adept Exempt, whether in our Holy Order or another, may not remain in the Pillar of Mercy, because it is not balanced, but is unstable. Therefore is the Choice given unto him, whether he will destroy his Temple, and give up his Life, extending it to Universal Life, or whether he will make a Fortress about that Temple, and abide therein, in the false Sphere of Daath, which is in the Abyss.[90]

Daath, "the Abyss," the hidden Sephira, are concepts related to Crowley's reading of kabbalah. But like LaVey, Aquino too rejects kabbalah, stating: "The Cabala . . . is nowhere to be found in *The Book of Coming Forth by Night*, or, for that matter, in the Temple of Set."[91] Thus the concept of crossing the Abyss—and the concomitant processes—becomes largely meaningless. Aquino argues instead that there is no Right-Hand Path to the degree of Magister Templi:

> There is **only** the Left-Hand Path, and it is fraught with danger—not a one-time crossing-the-Abyss test, but a continuous peril that exists from the moment the individual completely realizes him-Self as a Magister.[92]

This topic is developed through consecutive comments to *The Book of Coming Forth by Night*, and Aquino also relates this to Crowley's life.[93] The concepts of a Magister Templi or a magus are, according to Aquino, incompatible with the kind of annihilation of the ego such as he understands Crowley to prescribe. And, he adds, if we look at the way Crowley lived his life, we see no trace of him following the path he seemingly ordains. Instead, his writings attest to his very individual will being present at all times, and his life trajectory follows the tragic one he prescribes for a "Black Brother."[94] Thus Crowley is redefined as a somewhat unwilling, albeit useful, practitioner on the left-hand path.

Magic

To understand Aquino's concept of magic, it is important to note his division between what he calls the subjective and the objective universes. The objective universe is what it sounds like: Nature. The subjective universe belongs to each sentient being, and "may be thought of as one's personal perspective on the objective universe, together with any self-created phenomena one wishes to add to it."[95] The subjective universe is seen as something more than simple imagination. It is also, to use a metaphor, a different realm of "mental essence"[96] with "magical links" to the objective universe. The concept of the "magical link" as a way magic works is borrowed from Crowley, and Aquino's version seems to be a somewhat simplified version of it.[97]

The above-mentioned differences in conceptualizations of will, with a more elaborately defined cosmology than may be addressed here, make for differences in the conceptualization of magic. The influence from Crowley is still clear.[98] As for LaVey, Aquino's concept of magic is linked with change according to will. Describing the process of learning magic as a movement between what Aquino calls the objective and subjective universes, he says that the "trick" is in getting to know them, and "influencing the Magical Links between them and thus **causing change in accordance with will**."[99] Change according to will seems to be conceptualized as change to "the desired state,"[100] again stressing the sovereignty of the individual self.

To take another aspect of Aquino's theory of magic that shows a similar influence from Crowley as with LaVey, Aquino also stresses the importance of doing all the relevant actions in the objective universe. He states for Greater Black Magic that "one must also take advantage of every cooperative force in the objective universe to enhance the working,"[101] and similar attunement to efficacious action is even more important for Lesser Black Magic.[102] Crowley expresses similar thoughts in a more explicit way:

> For instance, is it my will to become a famous physician? I banish all "hostile spirits" such as laziness, alien interests, and conflicting pleasures, from my "circle" the hospital; I consecrate my "weapons" (my various abilities) to the study of medicine; I invoke the "Gods" (medical authorities) by studying and obeying their laws in their books.[103]

Like LaVey and Crowley, Aquino acknowledges and stresses the importance of magic as "mind wrought on mind through matter."[104] This insight should be employed at all levels of magic, but the distinctive nature of magic for Aquino is the use of less obvious means. In this, as in several other areas, he pays closer attention to the thoughts of LaVey than to those of Crowley. This goes especially for the category of Lesser Black Magic, which is almost wholly inspired by LaVey's concept of Lesser Magic.

There is a reason Aquino stresses the "Black" in his description of Setian magic: unlike LaVey, he acknowledges a difference between white and black magic. The rituals of right-hand path religions, including "all conventional religions and occultisms," are considered to be white magic. White magic is, however, considered to be "fraud and/or self-delusion."[105] More precisely, it involves "efforts to deceive the consciousness into believing that it has been accepted into the objective universe."[106] This does not mean that one cannot or should not employ white magic. If it may be used to advantage, it should be used, but in appreciation of the fact that one is temporarily practicing deceit upon one's consciousness in order to achieve a goal. The ToS has a "utilitarian approach to white magic and LBM."[107]

Aquino's concept of white magic does, however, contain a critical stance toward Crowley. This is a critique that runs through much of Aquino's treatment of him: by expressing a wish to align with the natural, "objective" universe, Crowley is deceiving himself with regard to the way the world, the self, the will, and magic works. "True magic" is black magic, driven by a self and a will that stand outside of and seek to influence the inertia of the universe. Crowley seems to be presented as a brother of the left-hand path, but one whose insight is so marred as to be practically problematic. In perhaps the strongest formulation of this criticism, Aquino states:

> The Aeon of HarWer (1904–1965 CE) has left few legacies of practical value to the magician. Those that do exist are heavily tinged with error and inaccuracy. Worthwhile principles may be identified only by those who already possess the sophistication of judgment to formulate those

> principles themselves. This is an important point—and, unfortunately, it is taken only by those who do not need to.[108]

This is a strong formulation of a criticism, which, as we have seen, was similarly raised by LaVey.[109] Aquino's critique is going to a different place, as he, unlike LaVey, does not "secularize" magic further. Instead he engages with Crowley and his philosophy of magick in some detail in order to develop his Setian philosophy further. We may see the confluence of both Crowley and LaVey in Aquino's conceptualization of LBM, whereas GBM is defined more as a further development from Crowley:

> Greater Black Magic (GBM) is the causing of change to occur in the subjective universe in accordance with the will. This change in the subjective universe may cause a similar and proportionate change in the objective universe.[110]

The focus in GBM is on changing the *subjective* universe according to will. That this may also, in time, change things in the *objective* universe is not necessarily the primary goal. "Higher" magic is primarily working on the self, but one should not be deluded that it is work without desire for specific results. On the contrary, the desired results in both subjective and objective universes should be absolutely clear to the magician.

Conclusion

The above discussion of two representatives of Satanism shows that there is indeed a line from Aleister Crowley to contemporary Satanism. But the line is not straight, and the influence Crowley has had should not be misread as Satanists "parroting random phrases" from Crowley. Like most Thelemites, Satanists who read Crowley tend to do it critically. LaVey and Aquino both take from him what fits their own ideas and transform Crowley in reading him. The criticisms they level on the rest are at times severe. This is also a kind of influence, in assisting a direction critical to the towering figure Crowley has become for contemporary occultism.

We see this most clearly in the case of Michael Aquino, who is both the most detailed critic and the one most engrossed in Crowley's thought. The seemingly harsh criticism that Aquino levels against Crowley may be contrasted with the fact that he acknowledges Crowley not only as Magus of the Aeon of HarWer but also as an Ipsissimus.[111] Aquino's cited works refer to a vast number of Crowley's writings, and he seems to know them in some detail. The reading list of the ToS also contains Crowley's complete works, as well as further examples of writings about Crowley and later developments of Thelema. A knowledge of Thelema is considered to be a very important part of a ToS member's studies.

We may contrast this with LaVey's 1971 statement that "you won't learn a damn thing" from Crowley that LaVey has not already "extended one-hundred fold." Still, LaVey not only read Crowley's books in his youth but also later constructed a philosophy of life that has many points of convergence with Crowley's. Whether LaVey adopted it from Crowley or it is "merely" a common vision, both stress a central vision of humans finding their will and performing it. In this, it seems reasonable to see Crowley as one of LaVey's sources of inspiration. LaVey's criticism of Crowley is frank, even harsh, but it is tempered by both sympathy and respect. He would consider Crowley a "de facto" Satanist, "albeit an ultra-romantic one,"[112] marred by his strict upbringing. LaVey also kept a balanced interest for those aspects of Crowley's ideas about magic that he found useful, borrowing important elements of his understanding of magic from Crowley.

More broadly, LaVey shared a similar purpose with Crowley: to create a structure and propagate a vision of freedom from the restrictions of Christianity. The differences in style and content, suggests Carl Abrahamsson, may in many cases be mainly one of two different centuries and two different continents.[113] Two different backgrounds served to shape ideas and personalities differently. Differences in style, and the degree to which the prototypically "religious" is integrated into or overcome by a more secular outlook, seem to reflect the different eras and the "occultures" of their times.[114]

Although both Aquino and LaVey claim to have superseded Crowley, LaVey leaves him more clearly to the side, establishing himself as more independent of his "forebears." Nevertheless, even LaVey pays him some tribute, showing that (some of) Crowley's ideas are interwoven into the fabric of Satanism from the start.

Acknowledgments

Thanks to Carl Abrahamsson for sharing his knowledge and ideas at an early stage, and for his comments on an earlier, partial draft of this essay. This has reduced the number of errors and stupidities. The remaining ones are all mine. Thanks also to Egil Asprem and Jesper Aagaard Petersen for suggestions and corrections.

Notes

1. Lawrence Sutin, *Do What Thou Wilt: A Life of Aleister Crowley* (New York: St. Martin's Griffin, 2000), 5.
2. See, for example, Stephen Flowers, *Lords of the Left-Hand Path* (Smithville, Tex.: Runa-Raven, 1997).
3. See, for example, Jesper Aagaard Petersen and Asbjørn Dyrendal, "Fuelled by Satan: Modern Satanism between Modernity and the Left-Hand Path," in *Cambridge Companion to New Religious Movements*, ed. Olav Hammer and Mikael Rothstein (Cambridge: Cambridge University Press, forthcoming).
4. There are some emic problems with regard to applying the term *Satanism* to both the CoS and the ToS. The CoS reserves the term *Satanism* mainly or exclusively for its own members, whereas members of the ToS prefer to be known as Setians.
5. Bruce Lincoln, *Authority: Construction and Corrosion* (Chicago: University of Chicago Press, 1994).
6. Ibid., 4ff.
7. See Asbjørn Dyrendal, "Satanismens historie," *Humanist: Tidsskrift for livssynsdebatt* 1 (2007), 4–33.
8. There may, of course, be many or few who are inspired by and/or claim dual identities as both Thelemites and Satanists.
9. See Michael A. Aquino, *The Church of Satan*, 5th rev. ed. (2002), 593ff., downloaded from http://www.xeper.org/maquino/index.html.
10. Hiley H. Ward, "Satan Rift Centers in Detroit—Grotto Becomes 'Occultic' Church," *Detroit Free Press*, March 25, 1972, quoted in Aquino, *The Church of Satan*, 562.
11. LaVey, in Aquino *The Church of Satan*, 594.
12. Aquino, *The Church of Satan*, 563. Strictly speaking, the first two parts of Crowley's *Confessions* were of course published in 1929, but a complete, six-part edition was not published until 1969: Aleister Crowley, *The Confessions of Aleister Crowley*, ed. John Symonds and Kenneth Grant (London: Jonathan Cape, 1969). As *The Satanic Bible* (New York: Avon, 1969) was printed in December 1969, I find Aquino's timeline difficult to follow. The point may be moot, as there seems to be nothing in common, either stylistically or content-wise, between *The Satanic Bible* and *The Confessions*.
13. It becomes even less likely when one considers that a well-known Thelemite and Crowley enthusiast, filmmaker Kenneth Anger, was among the central early members of LaVey's circle. Anger, and probably many others, would clearly be in the position to expose "borrowings" from Crowley's lesser-known publications. Instead, critical early members such as Michael Aquino (in *The Church of Satan*) and (especially) Isaac Bonewits downplay the degree to which LaVey was at all familiar with Crowley, or indeed the occult classics *tout court*. See Isaac Bonewits, *My Satanic Adventure: Or I Was a Teenaged Satanist!* version 2.3 (2005), http://www.neopagan.net/SatanicAdventure.html.

14. See, for example, Blanche Barton, *The Secret Life of a Satanist* (Los Angeles: Feral House, 1990).
15. See Martin P. Starr, *The Unknown God: W. T. Smith and the Thelemites* (Bollingbrook, Ill.: Teitan Press, 2003).
16. Information given by Magister Carl Abrahamsson, personal correspondence.
17. Barton, *The Secret Life of a Satanist*, 61.
18. Quoted in John Fritscher, *Popular Witchcraft* (Secaucus, N.J.: Citadel Press, 1973), 187.
19. Ibid.; see Aleister Crowley, *The Book of Lies* (1913; Ilfracombe, England: Haydn Press, 1952), 184.
20. Another statement of Crowley's that seems to be very close to opinions expressed several times by LaVey, but without LaVey's (to my knowledge) ever quoting it, is this: "How easy for the charlatans of oratory to seduce the simple enthusiasm of the soul! What help have we unless we have the wit to know them as ridiculous? There is no limit to the abyss of Idiocy wherein the quacks would plunge us—our only saving reflex is the automatic joke of the Sense of Humour!" Aleister Crowley, *Little Essays toward Truth* (Scottsdale, Ariz.: New Falcon, 1991), 39.
21. See Asbjørn Dyrendal, "Et Satans mannfolk: Den autoriserte Anton LaVey," *Din: Tidsskrift for kultur og religion* 1 (2004), 73–83.
22. According to his recollections (as presented in Barton, *The Secret Life of a Satanist*), this was "a chapter of the Order of Thelema" in Berkeley, in 1951. This "Order of Thelema" in Berkeley is not mentioned in Starr's excellent book on early American Thelema, *The Unknown God*, but it could possibly be the one mentioned as the "still lesser known Order of Thelema" in James A. Eshelman, "The Legacy of Jane Wolfe," *In the Continuum* 5, no. 10 (1996), available at http://www.thelema.org/aa/legacy_of_jane_wolfe.html. If this should happen to refer to the order by the same name in the Motta lineage, the timeline makes it impossible, as Motta was accepted as a probationer in the A∴A∴ only in 1953. Carl Abrahamsson (personal correspondence) instead identifies the Thelemites in question with the known community in Los Angeles.
23. Barton, *The Secret Life of a Satanist*, 61.
24. Anton S. LaVey, "On Occultism of the Past," *Cloven Hoof* 3, no. 9 (1971), quoted from the theory/practice section on http://www.churchofsatan.com.
25. Ibid.
26. This is also attested by some of those who knew him, although Anger seems to think that LaVey treated Crowley lightly and somewhat superficially. See Gavin Baddeley, *Lucifer Rising: Sin, Devil Worship and Rock 'n' Roll* (London: Plexus, 1999), 78.
27. LaVey, "On Occultism of the Past."
28. Anton S. LaVey, *Satan Speaks!* (Portland, Ore.: Feral House, 1998), 166.
29. For example: "Let me state categorically at this point that drugs are antithetical to the practice of magic." Anton S. LaVey, *The Satanic Witch* (1970; Portland, Ore.: Feral House, 1989), 10.

30. Such knowledge could also be useful for obtaining psychological insight into how such systems are made to work by practitioners and believers.
31. Hugh P. Urban, *Magia Sexualis: Sex, Magic, and Liberation in Modern Western Esotericism* (Berkeley: University of California Press, 2006), 203.
32. Urban also writes: "Much of LaVey's writing—such as *The Satanic Bible* and *The Satanic Witch*—bear strong resemblance to the works of Crowley, Friedrich Nietzsche's ideal of the will to power, and existentialism, with a dash of Ayn Rand thrown in for good measure." Ibid., 204. I hesitate to agree fully. First of all, I cannot agree that there is all that much resemblance in either content or style between the books Urban mentions and Crowley's. Second, although I agree with Urban on the sources of inspiration, I would have a little more than "a dash" of Ayn Rand. After all, LaVey himself once stated that what he gave people was "Ayn Rand with trappings." However, I think we should read that critically as well (see James R. Lewis, "Diabolical Authority: Anton LaVey, *The Satanic Bible*, and 'Tradition,'" *Marburg Journal of Religion* 7, no. 1 [2002], 8). There is more to it than that.
33. For example, see Aleister Crowley, *Science and Buddhism* (1903), http://www.geocities.com/nu_isis/sci_budd.pdf; Aleister Crowley, *Magick in Theory and Practice* (1930; Secaucus, N.J.: Castle Books, 1991), xxii.
34. Quoted in Fritscher, *Popular Witchcraft*, 187.
35. See, for example, Wouter J. Hanegraaff, *New Age Religion and Western Culture: Esotericism in the Mirror of Secular Thought* (Leiden: Brill, 1996).
36. Arthur Lyons, *Satan Wants You! The Cult of Devil Worship in America*, 2nd ed. (New York: Mysterious Press, 1988).
37. Indeed, LaVey's introductory chapter on satanic magic in *The Satanic Bible* is titled "Theory and Practice of Satanic Magic."
38. Crowley, *Magick in Theory and Practice*, xii.
39. This issue is too complicated for a full discussion here. In *Magick in Theory and Practice*, Crowley's concept of will is heterogeneous, and, for many purposes, it can be made coextensive with a reading of LaVey.
40. See, for example, ibid., xiii, 107ff.
41. LaVey, *The Satanic Bible*, 110.
42. Crowley, *Magick in Theory and Practice*, xvi; compare LaVey, *The Satanic Bible*, 110.
43. LaVey, *The Satanic Bible*, 110.
44. Ibid.
45. Crowley, *Magick in Theory and Practice*, 192; see also 41ff.
46. Ibid., xviii, xx.
47. LaVey, *The Satanic Bible*, 127.
48. For destruction magic, anger and hatred serve a similar role. LaVey also eschewed ideas about animal sacrifice; if one needed blood, it should be the magician's own. Ibid., 87.
49. Ibid., 111.
50. Ibid., 126.

51. See, for example, Peter Gilmore, *The Satanic Scriptures* (Baltimore: Scapegoat, 2007), 221ff. Many Thelemites equally stress the psychological function of ritual, and that magick is primarily to assist self-development and self-knowledge. Thus the secularization of magick is taking a similar route among a subset of Thelemites, sometimes with LaVey as one of the sources.
52. This is, by the way, also typical of the Thelemites with whom I have discussed this issue over the years, although not to the extent I find with LaVey. It also, of course, shows exactly the (Nietzschean) attitude toward learning that Crowley encouraged in *The Confessions*: "I do not want to father a flock, to be the fetish of fools and fanatics, or the founder of a faith whose followers are content to echo my opinions. I want each man to cut his own way through the jungle" (618).
53. While it may not be very common, there is an overlap between the Thelemic and Satanist ideology and resulting "communities." It seems to have been this way from the early years of organized Satanism, and it continues to be so.
54. See Asbjørn Dyrendal, "Darkness Within: Satanism as Self-Religion," in *Contemporary Religious Satanism*, ed. Jesper Aagaard Petersen (Oxford: Ashgate, 2009).
55. Michael A. Aquino, *The Temple of Set*, 6th draft version (2006), http://www.xeper.org/maquino/index.html.
56. He also authored an "inspired" document, *The Diabolicon*, which may to a limited extent be likened to Crowley's kind of workings.
57. See Aquino, *The Temple of Set*, 8ff.
58. See Michael A. Aquino, *The Book of Coming Forth by Night: Analysis and Commentary* (n.p.: 1985), 20, 11ff.
59. Michael A. Aquino, *Black Magic* (San Francisco: Temple of Set, 2002), 31.
60. Aquino, *The Book of Coming Forth by Night: Analysis and Commentary*, A4–1.
61. As well as to other magi having gone before them.
62. Aquino, *The Book of Coming Forth by Night: Analysis and Commentary*, 20.
63. Crowley, *The Confessions*, 36.
64. See Crowley, *Magick in Theory and Practice*, 51.
65. See Aquino, *The Temple of Set*, 6th draft version, 121; Michael A. Aquino, *The Temple of Set*, 3rd draft version, http://www.xeper.org/maquino/index.html, 107.
66. Aquino, *The Temple of Set*, 6th draft version, 11.
67. Aquino, *Black Magic*, 7.
68. Aquino, *The Book of Coming Forth by Night: Analysis and Commentary*, 17.
69. Flowers, *Lords of the Left-Hand Path*, 232.
70. John Symonds, *The Great Beast* (1951; St. Albans, England: Mayflower, 1973).
71. For a list of different versions of Crowley's final exit, see Sutin, *Do What Thou Wilt*, 417ff. Aquino seems, like LaVey, to be heavily influenced by Symonds's account in his view of Crowley as a person.
72. Aquino, *The Book of Coming Forth by Night: Analysis and Commentary*, 15.
73. Ibid., 24.
74. Aquino, *Black Magic*, 35.

75. Ibid.
76. Formulation from Aleister Crowley, *Magick without Tears* (Scottsdale, Ariz.: New Falcon, 1991), 458.
77. Aquino, *Black Magic*, 35.
78. Ibid.
79. Ibid., 26.
80. We see from this that he considers Satanism to be a successor to Thelema.
81. Aquino, *Black Magic*, 26.
82. Nuit is interpreted in line with Crowley's comment, in *Magick in Theory and Practice*, that "a man who is doing his True Will has the inertia of the Universe to assist him" (xv). The "inertia of the Universe" is Nuit, who is the cosmic whole/objective universe, and whose word is "inertia" (see, e.g., Aquino, *The Temple of Set*, 6th draft version, 141ff.).
83. See, for example, Aquino, *Black Magic*, 55.
84. Ibid., 53.
85. Ibid., 54.
86. Crowley, *Magick in Theory and Practice*, 193n.
87. Aquino, *The Book of Coming Forth by Night: Analysis and Commentary*, A5–9.
88. Ibid., A5–10.
89. Ibid.
90. Aleister Crowley, *Liber Aleph: The Book of Wisdom of Folly* (West Point, Calif.: Thelema Publishing, 1962), 104.
91. Aquino, *The Book of Coming Forth by Night: Analysis and Commentary*, 19.
92. Aquino, *The Temple of Set*, 6th draft version, 119.
93. Aquino does, however, agree with Crowley on the dangers of the process of achieving the insight related to Magister Templi, and the ones insufficiently prepared "do in fact suffer the fate Crowley prescribes." Aquino, *The Temple of Set*, 6th draft version, 119.
94. Ibid. The example used by Aquino here is from "One star in sight." Crowley, *Magick in Theory and Practice*, 237; compare Aquino, *The Temple of Set*, 6th draft version, 118.
95. Aquino, *Black Magic*, 63.
96. Ibid., 68.
97. We can at times see something similar in certain ideas for rituals in the CoS, but the examples I have seen are again "secularized." For example, see Gilmore, *The Satanic Scriptures*, 201ff.
98. There may be a development over time here. In its earliest versions, the instructions on magic Aquino wrote for the introductory package for new members, *The Ruby Tablets of Set*, clearly attested to this influence by its title: *Black Magic in Theory and Practice*. The current version (Aquino, *Black Magic*) drops the last words and is called merely *Black Magic*. This may attest to a lessening of influence by Crowley, but as I have not read the early versions—all the Tablets of Set are said to be developing texts—I cannot really judge this.

99. Aquino, *Black Magic*, 68.
100. Ibid.
101. Ibid.
102. Ibid., 72ff.
103. Crowley, *Magick in Theory and Practice*, 115.
104. Aquino, *Black Magic*, 72ff.
105. Ibid., 86.
106. Ibid., 65.
107. Ibid., 86.
108. Aquino, *The Book of Coming Forth by Night: Analysis and Commentary*, 25.
109. LaVey, "On Occultism of the Past."
110. Aquino, *Black Magic*, 88.
111. Aquino, *The Temple of Set*, 6th draft version, 298.
112. Carl Abrahamsson, personal correspondence. Abrahamsson, a well-known Thelemite as well as a Magister in the CoS, conversed with LaVey on Crowley several times.
113. Abrahamsson, personal correspondence.
114. *Occulture* is a term seemingly coined by Thelemite Genesis P. Orridge and further developed as an analytical term by Christopher Partridge. See Christopher Partridge, *The Re-enchantment of the West*, vol. 1 (London: T&T Clark International, 2004).

Index